THE COMMON GOOD IN
LATE MEDIEVAL
POLITICAL THOUGHT

THE COMMON GOOD
IN LATE MEDIEVAL
POLITICAL THOUGHT

M. S. KEMPSHALL

CLARENDON PRESS · OXFORD

1999

OXFORD
UNIVERSITY PRESS

Great Clarendon Street, Oxford OX2 6DP

Oxford New York

Athens Auckland Bangkok Bogotá Buenos Aires Calcutta
Cape Town Chennai Dar es Salaam Delhi Florence Hong Kong Istanbul
Karachi Kuala Lumpur Madrid Melbourne Mexico City Mumbai
Nairobi Paris São Paulo Singapore Taipei Tokyo Toronto Warsaw

and associated companies in
Berlin Ibadan

Oxford is a registered trade mark of Oxford University Press

Published in the United States
by Oxford University Press Inc., New York

© M. S. Kempshall 1999
The moral rights of the author have been asserted

First published 1999

British Library Cataloguing in Publication Data

Data available

Library of Congress Cataloging in Publication Data
Kempshall, M. S.
The common good in late medieval political thought : moral
goodness and material benefit / M. S. Kempshall.
p. cm.
Includes bibliographical references (p.   ).
1. Common good—History—To 1500. 2. Political science—
History—To 1500. I. Title.
JC330.15.K46 1999
320'.01'1—dc21 98–49502

ISBN 0–19–820716–6

1 3 5 7 9 10 8 6 4 2

Typeset by Jayvee, Trivandrum, India
Printed in Great Britain
on acid-free paper by
Biddles Ltd., Guildford & King's Lynn

For my parents
with love and gratitude

PREFACE

ONE of the greatest attractions in studying medieval scholastic thought is the fluidity of the boundaries between its intellectual disciplines. For the historian, this can also be one of its greatest frustrations since the task of writing about scholasticism requires the skills and knowledge not just of an historian but of a theologian, a philosopher, and a philologist as well. Few scholars can claim expertise in all these fields and, as a consequence, few works on medieval thought are free from lacunae or immune from specialist criticism. This book is no exception as it has proved, in turn, too historical for some theologians, too theological for some philosophers, and too theological and philosophical for some historians. As an historian, I can only enter the plea that, in producing a study of the relationship between the individual and the common good, I have simply tried to contextualize the language of a particular debate in the history of political thought. If this has meant straying into theological, philosophical, and legal territory, then it has only been insofar as this has helped to elucidate the denotations and connotations of the terms in which this debate was conducted. It has certainly meant accepting rather than rejecting the precision with which this language was used. One historian has suggested that the result will not be to everyone's taste. *De gustibus non disputandum.*

Remaining faithful to the linguistic and conceptual exactitude of scholastic argument has meant giving this book a particular structure. One of the aims of this study is to investigate the connection which may, or may not, have existed between metaphysical theory and political thought, between a discussion of how, say, goodness in general can be predicated of individual good things and a discussion of whether, say, the defence of the kingdom makes a particular town liable to pay the taxation demanded by a French king. This juxtaposition of the metaphysical with the political has resulted in the analysis of each scholastic thinker being divided into two separate chapters, the first of which deals with predominantly abstract questions, the second with their practical application. A second aim of this book is to use the notion of the common good as a means of investigating the influence of Aristotle's *Ethics* and *Politics* on scholastic ethical and political ideas. Rather than analyse these ideas theme by theme, I have set them out author by author. There is, of course, always a balance to be struck between, on the one hand, acknowledging the extent to which scholastic theologians were working with the same set of authorities and, on the other, illustrating the extent to which each theologian had their own views on what these authorities might mean. Examining these authors *seriatim* has had the significant advantage of clarifying the particular fusions of Aristotelian philosophy and Christian theology which each individual author was seeking to produce. If the historian is to begin to make sense of the sophistication of scholastic thought, then the monolithic abstractions of 'Aristotelianism' and 'Augustinianism' into which it is frequently resolved must be personalized as well as historicized in all their complexity.

I am very conscious of the debts which have been incurred in the writing of this book, and their acknowledgement here is but a small token of my gratitude. What follows owes its existence, in the first instance, to the knowledge and guidance of Jean Dunbabin and Gervase Rosser, and to the personal and intellectual generosity of György Geréby and David Leopold. Their integrity of scholarship and depth of insight have helped me far more than they may realize. In the second instance, this book owes its existence to the material generosity of the British Academy, the Dean and Students of Christ Church, Oxford, the Warden and Fellows of Merton College, Oxford, and the Trustees of Canon Robert Murray. Without this support, I would not have had the opportunity of refining a D.Phil. thesis into a book nor, together with the Lower Reading Room of the Bodleian Library, would I have been able to profit from environments which were so stimulating and conducive to academic study.

The research which underpins this book has benefited immeasurably from the additional advice and criticism offered by Peter Biller, Ralph Davis, David d'Avray, Robert Dodaro, Mark Edwards, Jane Garnett, George Holmes, Isabel Iribarren, David Luscombe, Alexander Murray, Mark Philpott, Andreas Speer, Rowan Williams, and Joseph Ziegler. It has been sustained by the steadfast encouragement of Joanna Howard, by my colleagues at St Catherine's College, Bill Brewer and Jose Harris, as well as by the kindness and good humour of Katya Andreyev, Martin Conway, Simon Loseby, and Philip Waller. It also owes much to a succession of undergraduates at Oxford whose enthusiasm and intelligence have made tutorials such consistently rewarding exchanges of ideas. Finally, publication in its present form, and by Oxford University Press, would not have been possible without the support of Tony Morris who showed not only an appreciation of what I was trying to do but also patience with the time which it has subsequently taken to do it.

It is my friends and family who have borne the private tribulations of this work, and I am very grateful, therefore, to have been able to rely on their unfailing intellectual, moral, and emotional support, particularly from my sister, Helen Whittingham. My greatest debt, however, as it always will be, is to Sylvia and Kim Kempshall. It is to them that this book is dedicated with love and gratitude.

M.S.K.

Oxford
December 1997

CONTENTS

ABBREVIATIONS

AHDLMA	*Archives d'Histoire Doctrinale et Littéraire du Moyen Âge*
CCCM	*Corpus Christianorum, Continuatio Medievalis*
CCSL	*Corpus Christianorum, Series Latina*
CHLMP	*The Cambridge History of Later Medieval Philosophy: From the Rediscovery of Aristotle to the Disintegration of Scholasticism 1100–1600*, ed. N. Kretzmann, A. Kenny, and J. Pinborg (Cambridge, 1982).
CHMPT	*The Cambridge History of Medieval Political Thought c.350–c.1450*, ed. J. H. Burns (Cambridge, 1988).
CSEL	*Corpus Scriptorum Ecclesiasticorum Latinorum* (Vienna, 1866–)
CUP	*Chartularium Universitatis Parisiensis*, ed. H. Denifle and E. Chatelain (4 vols.; Paris, 1889–97).
Friedberg	*Corpus Iuris Canonici*, ed. E. Friedberg (2 vols.; Leipzig, 1879–81).
MGH	*Monumenta Germaniae Historica* (Hanover, 1826–)
PBA	*Proceedings of the British Academy*
PG	*Patrologia Graeca*, ed. J.-P. Migne
PL	*Patrologia Latina*, ed. J.-P. Migne
RTAM	*Recherches de Théologie Ancienne et Médiévale*
TRHS	*Transactions of the Royal Historical Society*

Introduction

'I don't approve of mixing ideologies,' Ivanov continued. 'There are only two conceptions of human ethics, and they are at opposite poles. One of them is Christian and humane, declares the individual to be sacrosanct and asserts that the rules of arithmetic are not to be applied to human units. The other starts from the basic principle that a collective aim justifies all means and not only allows, but demands, that the individual should in every way be subordinated and sacrificed to the community. . . . Humbugs and dilettantes have always tried to mix the two conceptions; in practice, it is impossible.'[1]

For the historian to approach the relationship between the common good and the individual good in medieval scholastic political thought is to steer a careful course between a methodological Scylla and Charybdis. On the one hand, there is the risk of elevating it into a 'perennial question' in the history of ideas; on the other, there is the danger of a contextual relativism which would reduce the ideas behind such a relationship to little more than an eclectic amalgam of subjective debris. Even after the common good has been separated from modern philosophical debates over the nature of personal identity or communitarian critiques of liberal individualism, and even after its various 'traditions' have been returned to their appropriate theological, philosophical, logical, political, social, literary, and linguistic contexts, any attempt to establish what exactly constituted a *medieval* theory of community, what this 'common unity' meant, and how it related to a notion of the individual, remains highly problematic. Too absolute an antithesis between community and individual presents the common good with too sharp a set of alternatives—either it is the same as the individual good or it is superior. Too smooth a synthesis of community and individual risks obscuring precisely the sort of dialectic which lay at the heart of the scholastic method. If scholastic philosophers and theologians in the late thirteenth and early fourteenth centuries possessed an idea of the individual which might indeed be described as Christian and humane, then they also had a notion of a collective aim for the community, a common good to which the individual was subordinate. They did try to mix the two conceptions, a principle of identity with a principle of superiority, the observation that the individual good is the same as the common good with the statement that the common good is better than the individual good. Whether scholastic political theorists therefore deserve to be called humbugs and dilettantes might not be a subject for historical judgement, but it does raise the question of the precision with which they both defined and employed a notion of the common good.

---

[1] A. Koestler, *Darkness at Noon* (Harmondsworth, 1985), 128.

It lies beyond the scope of this book to attempt a comprehensive account of a concept so fundamental to medieval thought in general, and to scholastic political and ethical thinking in particular. Primarily a critical rather than a speculative study, its intent is accordingly rather more limited—an examination of the meaning of the term 'common good' in the thought of eight influential scholastic theologians during the second half of the thirteenth century and the early years of the fourteenth, namely Albertus Magnus, Thomas Aquinas, Henry of Ghent, Godfrey of Fontaines, Giles of Rome, James of Viterbo, John of Paris, and Remigio dei Girolami. By concentrating on these figures, therefore, the term 'scholastic' is understood in predominantly theological and philosophical terms. Such a choice carries two corollaries. In the first instance, this book does not attempt to examine the use of the common good in canon law, nor does it attempt to reconsider the juristic conceptions of corporation and personality, nor the wider contribution of law to the 'rise of the state' or to the emergence of natural rights.[2] This does not mean that arguments drawn from canon and Roman law were unimportant to scholastic theologians. Henry of Ghent and Godfrey of Fontaines, for example, frequently resorted to legal concepts to support some of their most distinctive political ideas. Nevertheless, the primary focus of this study remains the notion of the common good as it appeared in the faculty of arts and of theology. In the second instance, this book is concerned with the connection between theology and philosophy during this period and, as such, it is concerned with the impact on scholastic thought of Aristotle's metaphysics and Aristotle's natural and moral philosophy.[3] The primary aim of this study is therefore to investigate the effect of the reintroduction of the *Politics* and the *Nicomachean Ethics* on the notion of the common good in terms of two key relationships—between the Christian individual and the political community and between the political individual and the Christian community.

When Georges de Lagarde examined the traditional assumption that the Reformation witnessed the victory of individual autonomy over the hierarchical and corporatist orthodoxy of the Middle Ages, he was led to conclude that the real achievement

---

[2] For these themes, see e.g. S. Chodorow, *Christian Political Theory and Church Politics in the Mid-Twelfth Century: The Ecclesiology of Gratian's Decretum* (Berkeley, 1972); K. Pennington, *Pope and Bishops: The Papal Monarchy in the Twelfth and Thirteenth Centuries* (Philadelphia, 1984); B. Tierney, *Foundations of the Conciliar Theory* (Cambridge, 1955); G. Post, *Studies in Medieval Legal Thought: Public Law and the State, 1100–1322* (Princeton, 1964), esp. ch. 5; B. Tierney, *Religion, Law and the Growth of Constitutional Thought* (Cambridge, 1982); K. Pennington, *The Prince and the Law 1200–1600: Sovereignty and Rights in the Western Legal Tradition* (Berkeley, 1993); J. P. Canning, 'The Corporation in the Political Thought of the Italian Jurists of the Thirteenth and Fourteenth Centuries', *History of Political Thought*, 1 (1980), 9–32; id., 'Ideas of the State of Thirteenth and Fourteenth Century Commentators on the Roman Law', *TRHS* 33 (1983), 1–27; R. Tuck, *Natural Rights Theories: Their Origin and Development* (Cambridge, 1979); A. S. McGrade, 'Ockham and the Birth of Individual Rights', in B. Tierney and P. Linehan (eds.), *Authority and Power: Studies on Medieval Law and Government Presented to Walter Ullmann* (Cambridge, 1980); B. Tierney, 'Tuck on Rights: Some Medieval Problems', *History of Political Thought*, 4 (1983), 429–40; id., 'Origins of Natural Rights Language: Texts and Contexts 1150–1250', *History of Political Thought*, 10 (1989), 615–46.

[3] For the relationship between scholastic theology and philosophy, see E. Gilson, *A History of Christian Philosophy in the Middle Ages* (London, 1955); J. F. Wippel, *Metaphysical Themes in Thomas Aquinas* (Washington, DC, 1984), 1–33.

of the Reformation was, in fact, the substitution of the supreme power of 'the state' for the supreme power of the church. Defining 'secularization' primarily as opposition to the claims and prerogatives of the church, Lagarde located the birth of this 'lay spirit' nearly two centuries earlier, in the secular corporatism of Marsilius of Padua and the anarchic individualism of William of Ockham.[4] Lagarde's interpretation has exercised a significant influence on the way in which late thirteenth- and early fourteenth-century political thinkers have been discussed by twentieth-century commentators. Walter Ullmann, for example, was following Lagarde in spirit if not in substance when he constructed his own version of late medieval 'secularization'. As far as Ullmann was concerned, however, this phenomenon represented not so much a process of institutional differentiation as an incipient theory of secularism for which the catalyst was the rediscovery of Aristotle's *Politics* and *Ethics*. According to Ullmann, the reintroduction of the thesis that political society originated in unfallen human nature served to initiate and systematize a fundamental conceptual dualism between *humanitas* and *fidelitas*. Ullmann thereby saw the reception of Aristotle as a theoretical justification of 'natural man' and of the political community as a purely natural product, a move which enabled the Christian subject, a human being 'divested of his individuality and his will', to become the citizen, possessed of autonomy and of right.[5]

However substantial the reservations which need to be placed on the interpretations put forward by both Lagarde[6] and Ullmann,[7] they still serve as benchmarks for the historiography of medieval scholastic political thought. Their accounts of the scholastic notion of the common good are no exception. According to Lagarde, it was characteristic of scholasticism to view the common good as a corporate whole which was superior to, and distinct from, the aggregate of its individual parts, its individual

---

[4] G. de Lagarde, *La Naissance de l'esprit laïque au déclin du moyen âge,* 3rd edn. (5 vols.; Louvain, 1956–70). Cf. id., 'Individualisme et corporatisme au moyen âge', in *L'Organisation corporative du moyen âge à la fin de l'ancien régime* (Louvain, 1937), 1–59.

[5] W. Ullmann, *Principles of Government and Politics in the Middle Ages* (London, 1961), 231–79; id., *The Individual and Society in the Middle Ages* (London, 1967), 15; id., *A History of Political Thought: The Middle Ages,* 3rd edn. (Harmondsworth, 1975), 179.

[6] J. B. Morrall, 'Some Notes on a Recent Interpretation of William of Ockham's Political Philosophy', *Franciscan Studies,* 9 (1949), 335–69; A. S. McGrade, *The Political Thought of William of Ockham: Personal and Institutional Principles* (Cambridge, 1974).

[7] F. Oakley, 'Celestial Hierarchies Revisited: Walter Ullmann's Vision of Medieval Politics', *Past and Present,* 60 (1973), 3–48. For the natural origin of society, see R. A. Markus, 'Two Conceptions of Political Authority: Augustine's *De Civitate Dei* XIX.14–15 and Some Thirteenth Century Interpretations', *Journal of Theological Studies,* 16 (1965), 68–100. Cf. P. J. Weithman, 'Augustine and Aquinas on Original Sin and the Function of Political Authority', *Journal of the History of Philosophy,* 30 (1992), 353–76. For this naturalism in the Ciceronian tradition, see A. J. Carlyle and R. W. Carlyle, *A History of Medieval Political Thought in the West* (6 vols.; Edinburgh, 1903–36), i. 13–14. Cf. C. J. Nedermann, 'Nature, Sin and the Origins of Society: The Ciceronian Tradition in Medieval Political Thought', *Journal of the History of Ideas,* 49 (1988), 3–26; T. Struve, 'Die Bedeutung der aristotelischen Politik für die natürliche Begründung der staatlichen Gemeinschaft', in J. Miethke and A. Bühler (eds.), *Das Publikum Politischer Theorie im 14. Jahrhundert* (Munich, 1992), 153–71. For the acceptance by hierocratic writers that temporal power was legitimated by its origins in nature, see W. D. McCready, 'Papal *plenitudo potestatis* and the Source of Temporal Authority in Late Medieval Hierocratic Theory', *Speculum,* 48 (1973), 664–5.

goods. It was this corporatism which Lagarde saw culminating in Marsilius of Padua's *universitas civium* and which he saw being destroyed by the refusal of Ockham's nominalist epistemology to acknowledge anything 'real' outside of the individual. For Ullmann too, the superiority of the common good was the quintessential statement of repressive theories of political authority and ecclesiastical hierocracy, a maxim which inspired expropriation by the temporal power and Inquisition by the spiritual. It therefore went hand in hand with a strict application of the corporeal analogy, an organological model of society where the part functions solely for the sake of the whole, the individual solely for the well-being of a community in which it is 'wholly submerged'.[8]

If Lagarde and Ullmann were agreed in seeing the scholastic notion of the common good in firmly corporatist terms, however, then they differed over what influence was exerted upon it by the translation of Aristotle's *Politics* and *Ethics*. According to Lagarde, 'the Philosopher' simply reinforced the principle that the common good was superior to the individual good and, in the process, lent all the weight of his authority to the claims of hierocracy. According to Ullmann, meanwhile, the rediscovery of Aristotle was, in fact, the catalyst for the atomization of this medieval notion of community. Thus, whereas Lagarde believed that Aristotle's naturalism served to strengthen the corporatism and hierocracy already prevalent in medieval thought, Ullmann credited the scholastic interpretation of Aristotle's political philosophy with initiating a process which was to free the individual from both political subjection and the dictates of the church. Viewed from a historiographical perspective, therefore, the first question which needs to be asked of the scholastic notion of the common good is what does it reveal about the secularizing effects of the rediscovery of Aristotle's *Politics* and *Ethics*.

A second point of disagreement between Lagarde and Ullmann concerns the consequences of adopting the hierarchical governance of the universe as a model for the political government of the human community. Their divergence again raises an important issue for an understanding of the scholastic notion of the common good. According to the scholastic conception of the pseudo-Dionysian hierarchy which governs the universe, the notions of unity, being, and goodness were all subject to the same principles of diffusion and participation—emanation of the many from the one and reduction of the many to the one (*omnis multitudo derivatur ab uno et ad unum reducitur*). Such schematization naturally invited discussion of the exact relation which existed between these two elements in the Neoplatonic universe—the emanation of the multiplicity of being from a principle of unity (*proodos* or *exitus*) and the reversion of this multitude to the one (*epistrophe* or *redditus*). In particular, it invited a discussion of whether the difference between emanation and reversion is merely a difference in direction of movement, or whether the hierarchical structure which is created by emanation is separate from the hierarchical dynamic which is produced by reversion? Simply stated, this amounts to asking whether each grade in the hierarchical order of

---

[8] Ullmann, *The Individual and Society*, 36–42.

the universe represents, for the grade immediately below it, the only possible route to attaining its ultimate goal of union with God, or whether the higher grades can, in fact, be bypassed in the ascent of each individual in Creation towards God.

The hierarchical principle of mediation (*infima per media in suprema reducuntur*)[9] certainly posed problems in more than one area of thirteenth-century scholastic thought. One explanation for the appeal of positing an Averroist universal intellect, for example, is that it could be produced by drawing an exact correlation between the structure of the universe and its dynamic. Having insisted that each individual is part of the whole universe, there was a natural temptation to conclude that the soul of an individual human being had to be incorporated into a universal soul in order to be assimilated to God. It is in response to the strictness of this sort of corollary that some modern historians have sought to demonstrate the disparity which existed between the scholastic conception of the metaphysical principles which govern hierarchy in the universe and the scholastic conception of the political principles which govern hierarchy in human society. Controversy over the status of the mendicant orders, for example, clearly prompted several scholastic theologians to discuss whether lower orders might not, in fact, be capable of influencing their superiors and, as a result, brought them to question whether a particular grade in a hierarchy is necessarily proportional to its degree of similitude or proximity to God.

In an ecclesiological context at least, this argument does appear to represent a move away from applying the strict mediation of ends which operates between the orders of the celestial hierarchy to the mediation which should operate between the orders of the church.[10] In a political context, the issue raised is very similar. Some historians have argued, for example, that any modern characterization of the medieval community which completely subordinates the individual to the group as a part to a superior whole has thereby failed to take into account the scholastic distinction between a final and a formal cause, between the teleological dynamic of a hierarchy and its material structure.[11] Once again, the issue can be illustrated by a historiographical comparison between Lagarde and Ullmann. Whereas Ullmann sought to discern a rigid scheme of Neoplatonic procession and reversion in mutually antagonistic 'ascending' and 'descending' structures of authority, Lagarde drew

[9] pseudo-Dionysius, *De Caelestis Hierarchia*, ed. G. Heil, trans. M. de Gandillac (Paris, 1978), IV.3, pp. 98–9; *Dionysiaca: Recueil donnant l'ensemble des traductions latines des ouvrages attribués au Denys de l'Aréopage*, ed. P. Chevallier (2 vols.; Bruges, 1937, 1950), 812–14. Cf. *De Ecclesiastica Hierarchia*, ed. Chevallier, XV, p. 1330.

[10] Y. M. J. Congar, 'Aspects ecclésiologiques de la querelle entre mendiants et séculiers dans la seconde moitié du XIIIe siècle et le début du XIVe', *AHDLMA* 28 (1961), 35–151; D. E. Luscombe, 'The *Lex Divinitatis* in the Bull *Unam sanctam* of Pope Boniface VIII', in C. N. L. Brooke, D. E. Luscombe, G. H. Martin, and D. Owen (eds.), *Church and Government in the Middle Ages* (Cambridge, 1976); id., 'Thomas Aquinas and Conceptions of Hierarchy in the Thirteenth Century', *Miscellanea Mediaevalia*, 19 (1988), 261–77.

[11] M. de Wulf, *Histoire de la philosophie médiévale*, 6th edn. (3 vols.; Louvain–Paris, 1934–47), iii. 254–5. Cf. T. Gilby, *Principality and Polity: Aquinas and the Rise of State Theory in the West* (London, 1958), 109: 'nature was . . . taken in two senses, one was Latin and signified a thing's due position, stage or status in an ordered scheme, the other was Greek and signified rather the immanent purpose springing from within a thing and reaching out to its highest proper goal'.

attention to a more complex 'double ordering' (*duplex ordo*), of material structure and teleological dynamic, of individual humans related towards each other in the common good of society and of individual persons related towards the common good in God.

What made the nature of hierarchy so problematic for scholastic political thought was the introduction of the Aristotelian conception of the human community as a complete or 'perfect' group, as an association whose goal is not just to live, to provide the material means for collective self-sufficiency, but to live well, to live the life of virtue. Nature, it was assumed, would not multiply in many individuals a function which could be sufficiently performed by one individual on its own.[12] If political society was to be an example of such a principle, then the life of virtue should represent a collective rather than an individual achievement. The crux, once again, was the mediation of ends, that is, the principle that the goal of a secondary cause should be secured for the sake of the goal of the first cause, the goal of a tertiary cause for the sake of the goal of the secondary cause, and so on. If the life of perfect virtue, the common good of political society, is the goal of the imperfect individual, and God is the goal of the life of perfect virtue, then it would seem possible to conclude that the individual can secure union with God *only* by means of incorporation into the common good of society. The individual is subordinated to the common good of the political community as a necessary precondition of participation in eternal beatitude. The perfectly virtuous human community is then closer to union with God than the individual human being in that it occupies a higher grade in the hierarchy, because the greater the perfection, the closer the similitude to God. This, at least, is the logic of drawing an *exact* correlation between the position of political society in the structure of the universe and the dynamic of an individual human being's ascent towards God. It is precisely the degree of correlation, however, which is determined by the definition which is given to the goal of the political community, by choosing to describe it as complete or perfect virtue rather than in less elevated terms. The second question which needs to be asked of the scholastic notion of the common good, therefore, is what were the consequences of the moral orientation of Aristotle's 'perfect' political community for the direct communion of the individual human being with God?

The reception of Aristotle's *Politics* and *Ethics* and the application of a pseudo-Dionysian hierarchy were not unconnected issues in medieval scholastic political thought. Indeed, in many respects, it was the combination of a Neoplatonic hierarchy with an Aristotelian life of virtue which lay at the heart of the scholastic understanding of the common good. Both the reception of Aristotle and the operation of hierarchy, however, suffer from a peculiar liability to be misrepresented as soon as they are simplified. As a result, it is essential that any historical analysis of the common good should not only provide a detailed reading of specific texts but should examine the common good in the political, literary, linguistic, intellectual, and historiographical contexts from which it has, perhaps, too frequently been removed.

---

[12] e.g. Bonaventure, I *Sent.* 10.1.1 ad 4, in *Opera Omnia* (10 vols.; Quaracchi, 1882–1902), i. 196.

The 'political context' for the scholastic analysis of the common good is provided by a series of controversies—the debate over poverty and property within the Franciscan order,[13] the dispute between the secular and mendicant masters at the university of Paris,[14] the conflicts between Philip IV of France and Pope Boniface VIII,[15] and the wars between Philip IV and Edward I in Aquitaine and Philip IV and Guy Dampierre in Flanders.[16] Franciscan disagreement over the nature of apostolic poverty seems to have initiated little direct reflection on the nature of the common good with the significant exception of concentrating discussion of ownership (*proprietas*) and lordship (*dominium*) on their connection with the appropriate quantity and employment of material goods ('necessity' and 'reasonable use'). True lordship over property, it was argued, involved its correct use for the sake of what was necessary. The secular–mendicant disputes and the conflicts between Philip IV and Boniface VIII, however, precipitated debates in which a notion of the common good was frequently deployed.

From 1252 until the early 1270s, Guillaume de Saint-Amour, Gérard d'Abbeville, and Nicolas de Lisieux reopened the whole question of the relative merit of the active and the contemplative lives by directly comparing the personal perfection which was secured by the individual monk with the common benefit of the church which was secured by prelates, pastors, and preachers. In the process, they explicitly contrasted the 'individual good' of a life of contemplation with the 'common good' of a life of action. In the 1280s, this dispute flared up again over the implications of the papal privileges which had been granted to the mendicant orders in the bull *Ad fructus uberes*.[17] The common good was now cited as a legitimating criterion for dispensation from the law of the church and, by extension, for disobedience and resistance to any papal decree which failed to fulfil this requirement. As such, the common good came to occupy an increasingly important place in discussions of the pope's possession of an extraordinary power of jurisdiction. It was on this doctrine of plenitude of power (*plenitudo potestatis*), therefore, that much of the most significant political writing of the period came to focus.[18]

---

[13] G. Leff, *Heresy in the Later Middle Ages* (2 vols.; Manchester, 1967), i. 51–166; M. D. Lambert, *Franciscan Poverty* (London, 1961); J. Coleman, 'Property and Poverty', in *CHMPT*, 607–48.

[14] Congar, 'Aspects ecclésiologiques de la querelle entre mendiants et séculiers'; D. L. Douie, *The Conflict between the Seculars and the Mendicants at the University of Paris in the Thirteenth Century* (London, 1954).

[15] T. S. R. Boase, *Boniface VIII* (London, 1933); G. Digard, *Philippe le Bel et le Saint-Siège de 1285 à 1304* (2 vols.; Paris, 1936); C. T. Wood, *Philip the Fair and Boniface VIII* (New York–London, 1967).

[16] M. G. A. Vale, *The Angevin Legacy and the Hundred Years War 1250–1340* (Oxford, 1990), ch. 6.

[17] P. Glorieux, 'Prélats français contre religieux mendiants: Autour de la bulle *Ad fructus uberes* 1281–90', *Revue d'Histoire de l'Église de France*, 11 (1925), 309–31, 471–95; J. Miethke, 'Die Rolle der Bettelorden im Umbruch der politischen Theorie an der Wende zum 14. Jahrhundert', in K. Elm (ed.), *Stellung und Wirksamkeit der Bettelorden in der städtischen Gesellschaft* (Berlin, 1981), 119–53.

[18] G. B. Ladner, 'The Concepts of *ecclesia* and *christianitas* and their Relation to the Idea of Papal *plenitudo potestatis* from Gregory VII to Boniface VIII', in *Sacerdozio e Regno da Gregorio VII a Bonifacio VIII* (Rome, 1954), 49–77; J. A. Watt, *The Theory of Papal Monarchy in the Thirteenth Century: The Contribution of the Canonists* (London, 1965), 105–75; McCready, 'Papal *plenitudo potestatis* and the Source of Temporal Authority'; J. Miethke, 'Geschichtsprozess und zeitgenössisches Bewusstsein: Die Theorie des monarchischen Papats im hohen und späteren Mittelalter', *Historische Zeitschrift*, 226 (1978), 564–99.

The possibility that the common good could be used to sanction resistance to a papal decree, or even the deposition of an errant pope, was carried over into the widely publicized disputes between Philip the Fair and Boniface VIII. Here, however, the common good emerged as a legitimating criterion for action on both sides, royal as well as ecclesiastical, temporal as well as spiritual. As was frequently the case in medieval political thought, arguments in one sphere had a parallel application in the other. This is particularly apparent in the course of the wars fought in Aquitaine and Flanders between 1294 and 1303, wars which are often seen to form a practical political watershed in the development of national taxation. A notion of the common good was central to both conflicts as the kings of France and England repeatedly justified their exactions with an appeal to 'urgent necessity' or the 'defence of the realm'.[19] Less evident, perhaps, but no less significant, is the way in which the common good came to be used as a justification for their exercise of ordinary as well as extraordinary political power—not just for the sake of what was necessary but also in the course of correct or reasonable use.

'Literary context' may conveniently be divided into the methodological questions which are posed by chronological development, textual genre, and argumentative topic. The effects of chronological development on political thought are self-explanatory. Scholastic theologians were responding to changing personal, intellectual, and political contexts, and few historians would now want to make the sort of rigidly systematic claims for a single individual once favoured by, say, the Neo-Thomists. The effects of textual genre are best illustrated in detail. Thus, commentaries on the *Sentences* of Peter Lombard were generally produced at an early stage in a theologian's career and tended to be more reliant on conventional exegesis. The apologetic nature of other academic treatises, on the other hand, resulted in particular emphases being made for particular purposes—Aquinas' *Summa contra Gentiles*, for example, drew heavily on arguments from Aristotle and Avicenna, material which would have been familiar to its intended audience. Commentaries on the texts of Aristotle, meanwhile, were designed primarily to elucidate the *verba et intentio*, not of the scholastic commentator, but of 'the Philosopher' himself. Both Albertus Magnus and Giles of Rome, for example, were at pains to emphasize that their exposition of Aristotle's text did not necessarily represent their own view.[20] A more moot point is what degree of authorial commitment should be attributed to works of polemic, to the publicistic literature which theologians (as well as canonists and

---

[19] J. R. Strayer, 'Defense of the Realm and Royal Power in France', in id., *Medieval Statecraft and the Perspectives of History* (Princeton, 1971), ch. 18. For its more general implications, see F. M. Powicke, 'Reflections on the Medieval State', *TRHS* 19 (1936), 1–18; Strayer, 'The Laicization of French and English Society in the Thirteenth Century', in id., *Medieval Statecraft*, ch. 16; id., 'The Costs and Profits of War: The Anglo-French Conflict of 1294–1303', in H. A. Miskimin, D. Herlihy, and A. L. Udovitch (eds.), *The Medieval City* (New Haven, 1977), 269–91.

[20] Albertus Magnus, *Politicorum Libri Octo*, ed. A. Borgnet, in *Alberti Magni Opera Omnia*, vol. viii (38 vols.; Paris, 1890–9), VIII.6, p. 803; Aegidius Romanus, *Super Libros Rhetoricorum* (Venice, 1542), fo. 1r. Cf. E. A. Synan, 'Albertus Magnus and the Sciences', in J. A. Weisheipl (ed.), *Albertus Magnus and the Sciences: Commemorative Essays 1980* (Toronto, 1980), 6–11.

jurists) contributed to public disputes over mendicancy and papal jurisdiction. These were works, after all, which mixed dialectic with rhetoric, demonstrative proof with the art of persuasion. Such problems do not apply, however, to disputed and quodlibetic questions, the two forms of academic disputation which provide perhaps the most revealing index to issues of contemporary concern but also the most 'authoritative' reflection of the personal opinions of individual masters.[21]

Argumentative topic concerns what might now be called situational ethics. In its most abstract sense, the term 'common good' could be applied to the existence of goodness in the universe and the nature of happiness as the life of virtue. These two elements—the ontological and the moral—were intimately linked through psychology and epistemology. It was the proper function of the human intellect to apprehend the nature of goodness, unity, and being, both in the universe and, ultimately, in God. This goodness, the *ratio boni* (or, to use its homonyms, the universal good, *bonum universale*, and the good in common, *bonum in communi*), was therefore regarded as the natural object of the intellect and the will. If individuals were not acting in accordance with this principle, if they were not correctly directed or ordered towards this common good, then they were, in effect, acting unnaturally. It was in this sense that freedom or liberty could become slavery, a licence to perform evil— the will is free not to act in accordance with goodness.

Such an abstract theory of the common good, however, also has to be set alongside the variety of more concrete questions to which a notion of the common good was applied, questions which included obedience, taxation, punishment, legal dispensation, *pro patria mori*, the toleration of usury, the superiority of marriage over celibacy, and the priority of prelates to members of religious orders. In the process, the degree to which scholastic writers equated one level of thought with another, employing ideas which they derived from philosophical speculation in matters of more direct application, becomes of critical importance.[22] To put it in its simplest form, for the scholastic theologian to conceive of the common good in the universe as a hierarchy of objective goodness in which every rational being must participate in order to be good, clearly invites the possibility that the scholastic theologian will therefore conceive of the common good in human society as a hierarchy of political authority

---

[21] *Les Genres littéraires dans les sources théologiques et philosophiques médiévales* (Louvain, 1982), esp. B. C. Bazan, 'La *quaestio disputata*', 31–49; J. F. Wippel, 'The Quodlibetic Question as a Distinctive Literary Genre', 67–84; J. Miethke, 'Die Traktate "De potestate papae": Ein Typus politiktheoretischer Literatur im späten Mittelalter', 193–211. See also L. Genicot (ed.), *Typologie des sources du moyen âge occidental* (Turnholt, 1972–), fasc. 44–5 (1985) 'Les Questions disputées et les questions quodlibétiques dans les facultés de théologie, de droit et de médecine', parts i–ii.

[22] Cf. M. Grabmann, *Studien über den Einfluss der aristotelischen Philosophie auf die mittelalterlichen Theorien über das Verhältnis von Kirche und Staat* (Sitzungsberichte der Bayerischen Akademie der Wissenschaften, Philosophisch-historische Abteilung; Munich, 1934), esp. 1–75; M. J. Wilks, *The Problem of Sovereignty in the Later Middle Ages* (Cambridge, 1963); A. Gewirth, 'Philosophy and Political Thought in the Fourteenth Century', in F. L. Utley (ed.), *The Forward Movement of the Fourteenth Century* (Columbus, Oh., 1961), 125–64; C. Zuckerman, 'The Relationship of Theories of Universals to Theories of Church Government in the Middle Ages: A Critique of Previous Views', *Journal of the History of Ideas*, 36 (1975), 579–94.

to which every citizen must subordinate all his actions. This will only be a possibility, however, if it is assumed that scholastic theologians picked up a principle of inclusion which applies to the common good in one context and carried it into another context automatically and without qualification. Whether the aim of scholastic theologians was indeed to construct a science on metaphysical foundations and to elevate political thought to the level of abstract theory must remain open to doubt.[23] The third question which needs to be asked of the scholastic notion of the common good, therefore, is what was the connection between metaphysical or moral theory and the theory of political practice?

'Linguistic context' concerns the terminology which was applied to the common good, the language in which it was conceived and discussed. In the absence of the definite article, *bonum commune* or *communis utilitas* could carry either a theoretical or a concrete meaning, the common good or one common good amongst many. To some extent, this was itself implied by the difference between 'good' (*bonum*) and 'benefit' or 'utility' (*utilitas*), since the definition of benefit accommodated the more neutral sense of 'usefulness' as well as the more positive sense of 'effecting good'. These terms were not necessarily mutually exclusive (one phrase could cover both meanings depending on the needs of a given argument) nor were they the only alternatives open to scholastic theologians (compare the equally neutral 'advantageous' or 'congruent', *commodum, conferens, conveniens*). Aquinas provides a good example of the available variety in terminology. Even a cursory list would have to comprise the terms *bonum commune, bonum in communi, bonum communitatis, bona communia, bonum commune totius universi, bonum commune speciei, bonum commune multitudinis, bonum commune iustitiae et pacis, bonum commune civitatis, bonum commune regni, bonum commune domus vel familiae, bonum commune perfectum, bonum commune humanum, bonum commune naturae, bonum commune spirituale*, and *bonum commune morale*. Thus God, although more usually described as the *summum bonum* or *bonum universale*, could also be described as the *bonum commune*, whereas, in its loosest sense, any common good could be termed *quoddam bonum commune, aliquod bonum commune*, or *bonum communiter sumptum*. This range of terminology is, in itself, a point worth making about the scholastic 'notion' of the common good, particularly if the list is extended still further to include its numerous synonyms: *bonum multitudinis, bonum rei publicae, bonum multorum, bonum civitatis, bonum societatis humanae, bonum publicum, utilitas publica, utilitas communis, communis salus, salus totius communitatis*, and *salus rei publicae*.[24]

Linguistic context also concerns the logical categories which were used to describe

---

[23] e.g. Thomas Aquinas, *Selected Political Writings*, ed. A. P. d'Entrèves (Oxford, 1959), p. viii: 'His views on State and government were a deduction from metaphysical premisses.' Cf. C. Flüeler, *Rezeption und Interpretation der Aristotelischen Politica im späten Mittelalter* (2 vols.; Amsterdam, 1992), i. 11–15, 52, where the attempt to move political philosophy beyond the level of merely citing laws and decrees is ascribed to the influence of Avicenna.

[24] For a list of references, see I. Th. Eschmann, 'A Thomistic Glossary on the Principle of the Preeminence of a Common Good', *Mediaeval Studies*, 5 (1943), 142–65; R. Busa, *Index Thomisticus* (Stuttgart–Bad Cannstatt, 1974–80).

the common good, not so much in the sense of what it is to be *good* in common as in the sense of what it is to *be* in common.[25] In logical terms, there were five types of object which could be predicated of a given subject. These predicables were genus (e.g. animal), species (e.g. human, horse), specific difference (e.g. rational, irrational), *proprium* (e.g. Socrates), and accident (e.g. white). Genus, species, and specific difference all have a particular bearing on the relationship between the common good and the individual. A genus was predicated of several subjects which differ in species, a species was predicated of several individual subjects which differ in number, whilst a specific difference denoted the difference between one species and another within the same genus. A genus contains all its species but is not contained by them; a species contains all its individuals and is contained by them. An understanding of genus and species in terms of the categories of whole (*totum*) and part (*pars*) could be further refined by distinguishing between three different types of whole—the universal (which was predicated equally of all its parts in that it is present in its essence and entirety in each of its parts), the integral (which was not predicated of a part in that it is not present in its essence and entirety in each of its parts), and the potential (which is present in each of its parts in its essence but which is present in its entirety only in one pre-eminent part).[26]

Viewed in terms of the common good, the most important distinction here is the distinction drawn between the universal whole and the integral whole. A universal whole is a whole, such as genus or human, which has subjective parts, such as species and Socrates. An integral whole is a whole, such as a house, which has integral parts, such as walls, roof, and foundations. A universal whole exists in each and every one of its subjective parts (human in Socrates) and does not require the collective presence of all of its parts together (Socrates, Plato, Aristotle, Augustine, et al.). An integral whole, by contrast, depends on all its parts being arranged together (a house requires both walls, roof, and foundations). When a subjective part is removed from a universal whole, therefore, the whole can still remain in existence, whereas when an integral part is removed from an integral whole, the whole is automatically destroyed. The exception of a subjective part from its universal whole is accordingly different from the exception of an integral part from its integral whole.

These logical categories were not without their ambiguities. What pertains to a species must always be the same as what pertains to its genus; whatever is predicated of a whole is also predicated of any one of its parts (humankind is rational, every human is rational; the whole house is white, every part of the house is white); in this sense, the whole is the same (*idem*) as the part. A whole, however, could be interpreted collectively or divisively, conjunctively or distributively. A universal whole is distributed by the sign 'all' or 'every' (*omnis*), but this could be applied to the whole collectively (all humankind is saved) or the whole divisively (every human is

---

[25] For what follows, see Aristotle, *Metaphysics* V, *Physics* IV; Boethius, *Liber de divisione* (*PL* 64, cols. 875–92), *Liber de unitate et uno* (*PL* 63, cols. 1075–8); *CHLMP*, parts III–IV. See also M. G. Henninger, *Relations: Medieval Theories 1250–1325* (Oxford, 1989), chs. 1–3.

[26] Aquinas, II *Sent.* 9.1.3 ad 1.

running). An integral whole is distributed by the sign 'whole' (*totus*) and this too could be applied to the whole collectively (the whole house is worth one hundred marks; every individual is hauling a ship but no one individual by himself) or divisively (the whole house is white, every part of it is white). Alternatively expressed, 'whole' could be used 'categorematically' (that is, complete or made up of its parts) or 'syncategorematically' (that is, in accordance with each of its parts). Something could also be part of a whole in an absolute sense or only in one respect. It could also be one of a number of primary or 'principal' parts from whose mutual relation the whole is produced and without which the whole cannot exist (the 'whole' Socrates might be able to lose his finger but he cannot lose his head; the 'whole' hand might be able to lose a fingernail but it cannot lose its finger). Wholes were also not limited to being universal (human, horse) or integral (flock, populace, army). Boethius, for example, had distinguished between a virtual or potential whole (the soul)—which consists of virtues or powers (nutritive parts and sensitive parts)—and a quantitative or continuous whole (such as a body or a line). Definitions of the composition of these wholes could be equally precise. Unity might be by composition (house), aggregation (flock, populace, pile of stones), genus, species, number, and proportion or analogy. 'Plurality', meanwhile, was something potentially divisible into non-continuous parts, whereas 'magnitude' signified something which was potentially divisible into continuous parts. This variety was reflected in the eight distinctions which Aristotle had drawn for the way in which something may be said to be 'in' something else—an integral part 'in' its whole, an integral whole 'in' its parts, a species 'in' its genus, a genus 'in' its species, form 'in' matter, a thing or *res* 'in' its efficient cause, a *res* 'in' its final cause, and a *res* 'in' something which contains it.

That these categories of unity and plurality, whole and part, the one and the many, should be so well developed in scholastic vocabulary was only natural in the faculty of arts, where they were taught in the *trivium* as part of logic, and in the faculty of theology, where they were used to underpin discussions of the Trinity and the immortality of the soul, and where debates over whether matter or form was the principle of individuation threw up a variety of ways in which 'the individual' could be considered (as *quidditas*, for example, or *quantitas, subiectum, suppositum*, and *modus essendi*).[27] From the point of view of political and ethical thought, such sophistication has important implications for the scholastic understanding of the common good in its relation to the individual. Not only were terms such as *singularis, individuum*, and *proprium* primarily logical terms but the 'communities' with which they were compared could be construed in a variety of ways. Thus, a comparison could be drawn either between the relation of common good to individual good and the relation of a genus to its species, or between the relation of common good to individual good and the relation of an integral whole to each of its parts. In the case of the latter, indeed, the comparison carried with it a necessary ambivalence which was of considerable

---

[27] Cf. J. J. E. Garcia, *Introduction to the Problem of Individuation in the Early Middle Ages*, 2nd edn. (Munich, 1988). Cf. id. (ed.), *Individuation in Scholasticism: The Later Middle Ages and the Counter-Reformation 1150–1650* (Albany, NY, 1994).

significance for the common good and its constituent individual goods. For scholastic theologians and philosophers, an integral whole was a whole which is, in one sense, the same as its parts, and, in another sense, different. If the medieval conception of the common good is to be described as 'totalitarian', then it is only in a very literal sense of the word.

Linguistic context also concerns the various senses in which scholastic theologians understood the term 'analogy'. This elastic and often elusive term was used to describe a variety of relations. In essence, analogy referred to the connection which could be posited between different goods in the universe, a connection which stood somewhere between univocity (or synonymy) and equivocity (or homonymy). Univocity involves two things sharing the same name and the same nature, that is, the same definition (*ratio*) of their substance; equivocity involves two things sharing the same name but not the same definition or nature; analogy involves two things sharing the same name but also sharing a relation towards some third object. Within the terms of this distinction, however, analogy could be applied to at least two general types of relation. Analogical predication either implied that different goods derived from a single principle and contributed to a single goal or it implied that different pairs of goods stood in a similar relation towards each other (A:B = C:D). It was in this first sense of the term, therefore, that analogy could be used to describe an individual entity's existence in the universe, its participation in being and goodness. In its second sense, meanwhile, analogy could be used to draw the connection between, say, sight and the intellect (sight is to the body what the intellect is to the soul). In its second sense, therefore, analogical predication provided the logical rationale behind the literary device of simile and metaphor.

Each one of these senses of analogy can be seen to have affected the scholastic understanding of the notion of the common good. The metaphorical application of analogy, for example, produced a close association between the relationship of the whole to its parts and the relationship of the body to its limbs, an association which already had a long tradition in classical and Christian thought.[28] Underpinning this corporeal metaphor, however, lay the logical distinction between analogy, univocity, and equivocity, between being 'like' something and actually being that thing. Aquinas, for example, was quite clear that the similitude of a linguistic analogy was only approximate—if it were not, then the metaphor would actually be the object it was designed only to illustrate.[29] Even with this safeguard, corporeal imagery could still be used with greater or lesser degrees of precision. Take the 'independent' action

[28] T. Struve, *Die Entwicklung der organologischen Staatsauffassung im Mittelalter* (Stuttgart, 1978). Albertus Magnus, for example, attributes the analogy to Plato, Cicero, and Vitruvius (*Pol. Lib. Oct.* II.3, pp. 122–3).

[29] Thomas Aquinas, *Summa Theologiae, Tertia Pars* 8. The *Prima Pars, Prima Secundae, Secunda Secundae*, and *Tertia Pars* are cited henceforth as *Ia, IaIIae, IIaIIae*, and *IIIa*, the commentaries on the *Sentences* as I *Sent.*, II *Sent.* etc. References to Aquinas are to the Leonine edition, *Sancti Thomae de Aquino Opera Omnia iussu Leonis XIII edita* (Rome, 1882–), or, where a text is still in preparation, to *S. Thomae Aquinatis Opera Omnia*, ed. R. Busa (7 vols.; Stuttgart–Bad Cannstatt, 1980).

of the limbs and the observation that the hand does not strike something of its own accord but is simply used by the individual who is doing the striking.[30] Sometimes a strict application of this principle had its advantages—if all humans are derived from Adam as limbs from one body, original sin can be present in all humans whether or not it is in accordance with their will, since the actions of each limb are willed, not by themselves, but by the soul which moves them.[31] At other times, the application had to be made more loosely—the reflex action of the arm to defend the head or the body is used to illustrate an individual's obligation to lay down his life for the community and not the capacity of the ruler to command that the individual should do so.[32] Use of the corporeal analogy, moreover, should not be given undue emphasis. Scholastic theologians were able to draw on a common currency of additional political metaphors which were taken from a wide variety of sources—the harmony of music, the construction and composition of a house, and the motion and guidance of a ship. For Aquinas, at least, the metaphor which was central to his understanding of the common good was not so much the body as the army, a multitude of individuals who were ordered towards one another as individuals but who were also ordered towards their commander and the common goal of victory.[33]

The 'intellectual context' for the scholastic analysis of the common good is the context which presents perhaps the most intractable difficulties. The phrase 'common good' certainly had a much longer pedigree than thirteenth-century discussions of logical categorization and the metaphysics of goodness.[34] The terms *utilitas publica* and *utilitas populi* can be found throughout the texts of Roman law,[35] as can a concise summary of the principle of its superiority to the private good (*utilitas publica praeferendum est privato*).[36] Such usage naturally had repercussions on the law of the church, where notions of *utilitas publica* and *utilitas populi* were not only reiterated but were developed into *utilitas ecclesiae* and *status ecclesiae*, and where an equally firm statement was given of the superiority of the common good to the individual— 'the benefit of several people should be preferred to the benefit or the will of a single person' (*plurimorum utilitas unius utilitati vel voluntati praeferenda est*).[37] Of non-legal

---

[30] Thomas Aquinas, *IaIIae* 58.2; Henry of Ghent, *Quodlibet* XII.13 (below, p. 176); James of Viterbo, *Quodlibet* II.20 (below, p. 216).

[31] Aquinas, *IaIIae* 81.1.

[32] For the tradition, see E. H. Kantorowicz, '*Pro patria mori* in Medieval Political Thought', *American Historical Review*, 56 (1951), 472–92.

[33] e.g. II *Sent.* 1.2.3; III *Sent.* 33.3.1; IV *Sent.* 19.2.2a; *Contra Impugnantes Dei* II.2; *Quaestio Disputata de Veritate* V.3; *ScG* I.42, I.70, I.85, III.64, III.112; *Ia* 15.2, 108.6; *IaIIae* 3.4, 9.1, 111.5; *IIaIIae* 39.2; *Quaestio Disputata de Virtutibus* II.4, II.9; *Sent. Lib. Eth.* I.1; *Sent. super Meta.* VII.2, XII.12; *De Substantiis Separatis* XII. Cf. *Expositio in Iob* VII.

[34] For a useful survey, see P. Hibst, *Utilitas Publica—Gemeiner Nutz—Gemeinwohl* (Frankfurt, 1991).

[35] J. Gaudemet, '*Utilitas Publica*', *Revue Historique de Droit Français et Étranger*, 29 (1951), 465–99; T. Honsell, 'Gemeinwohl und öffentliches Interesse im klassischen römischen Recht', *Zeitschrift der Savigny-Stiftung für Rechtsgeschichte, Romanistische Abteilung*, 95 (1978), 93–137.

[36] Justinian, *Codex*, ed. P. Krüger (Berlin, 1877), VI.51, p. 601; XII.62.3, p. 1101.

[37] Gratian, *Decretum* II 7.1.35 (Friedberg, i, col. 580). Cf. M. H. Hoeflich, 'The Concept of *utilitas populi* in Early Ecclesiastical Law and Government', *Zeitschrift der Savigny-Stiftung für Rechtsgeschichte, Kanonistische Abteilung*, 67 (1981), 36–74; J. Hackett, 'State of the Church: A Concept of the Medieval

medieval political texts, two of the most authoritative—Cicero's *De Officiis* and
Augustine's *De Civitate Dei*—both expressed the view that *communis utilitas* should
be the goal of individual involvement in political society.[38] In the case of Augustine,
moreover, this common good was the result of the biblical injunction that the essence
of *caritas* is not to seek its own benefit: *caritas non quaerit quae sua sunt* (1 Corinthians
13: 5).[39] It was on the strength of these endorsements that Isidore of Seville made the
common good central to his definition of law and contrasted *communis utilitas* with
private advantage.[40] It was in these terms that *utilitas* subsequently became an essential quality of kingship in Merovingian sources and was extended to the kingdom as
utilitas regni.[41] References to the benefit of the kingdom or to the public interest
become even more frequent in Carolingian texts.[42] So too does the lament that it
was being neglected in favour of private interest and personal gain.[43] Both features
appear across the Channel in Asser,[44] and thereafter references are numerous, from
Orderic Vitalis to Matthew Paris.[45] A recognizably Ciceronian notion occurs, not

Canonists', *The Jurist*, 1963, 259–90; Y. M. J. Congar, '*Status ecclesiae*', *Studia Gratiana*, 15 (1972), 3–31,
esp. 4; Eschmann, 'Thomistic Glossary', 136–9; W. Ullmann, *Principles of Government and Politics in the
Middle Ages* (London, 1961), 67–8, 84; T. Reuter and G. Silagi (eds.), *Wortkonkordanz zum Decretum
Gratiani* (5 vols.; Munich, 1990), v. 4715–17. These concepts were picked up by, for example, Anselm and
Gregory VII, see G. R. Evans (eds.), *A Concordance to the Works of St. Anselm* (4 vols.; Millwood, NY,
1984), iv. 1606–7; Gregory VII, *Epistolae*, in *MGH Epistolae Selectae* II.1, IV.23, p. 335. The notion of
status ecclesiae was particularly important in justifying dispensation and defining the office of the pope, see
Congar, '*Status ecclesiae*', 22–8 and, more generally, J. Brys, *De dispensatione in iure canonico, praesertim
apud decretistas et decretalistas usque ad medium saeculum decimum quartum* (Bruges, 1925).

   [38] Cicero, *De Officiis*, ed. M. Winterbottom (Oxford, 1994), I.10.31, p. 13, 19.62, p. 25, 25.85, pp. 34–5,
44.155–6, p. 65; II.18.64, p. 97; III.6.26, p. 119 (*ut eadem sit utilitas uniuscuiusque et universorum*), 6.28–31,
pp. 119–20, 11.46–9, pp. 127–8, 27.100–1, pp. 151–2. Cf. *Rhetorica ad Herennium* II.13; *De Inventione*
I.1, 2, 38; II.48, 53; *De Finibus* III.19.64. Augustine, *De Civitate Dei*, ed. B. Dombart and A. Kalb (*CCSL*
48), XIX, pp. 657–99. Cf. ibid. I.15, p. 16; XV.3, p. 456.
   [39] Augustine, *Praeceptum*, ed. G. Lawless, *Augustine of Hippo and his Monastic Rule* (Oxford, 1987), 94.
Cf. *De Gratia Novi Testamenti* [= *Ep.* 140], ed. A. Goldbacher (*CSEL* 44), XXV.62, p. 207: *unde caritas in
commune magis quam in privatum consulens dicitur non quaerere quae sua sunt.*
   [40] Isidore, *Etymologies*, ed. W. M. Lindsay (Oxford, 1911), II.10, V.21.
   [41] J. M. Wallace-Hadrill, *The Long-Haired Kings* (London, 1962), 216–17, 223; Fredegar, *Chronicle*,
ed. J. M. Wallace-Hadrill (London, 1960), IV.55, p. 46; *MGH Epist.* III, p. 212.
   [42] Einhard, *Vita Karoli Magni Imperatoris*, ed. L. Halphen (Paris, 1947), I, pp. 8, 10; X, p. 32; XI, p. 34
(*vel sibi vel genti utile*); XXX, p. 84. Lupus of Ferrières, *Epistolae*, ed. P. K. Marshall (Leipzig, 1984),
XXXIII, p. 45; LXXXI, p. 80; XCIII, p. 90. *Vita Hludowici*, in *MGH Scriptores* II, pp. 607–48; XVIII,
pp. 615–16. Sedulius Scottus, *Liber de Rectoribus Christianis*, ed. S. Hellmann (Munich, 1906), IV, p. 30.
Nithard, *Historiarum Libri IV*, ed. P. Lauer (Paris, 1926), I.1, p. 4; I.3, pp. 10, 14; I.4, p. 18; II.5, p. 54; II.8,
p. 62; II.10, p. 74; IV.1, p. 118; IV.4, p. 134; IV.6, p. 142; cf. III.5, p. 104; *MGH Leges—Capitularia* I
no. 144, p. 348, no. 160, pp. 376–7.
   [43] Lupus of Ferrières, *Ep.* XCIII, p. 91; Nithard, *De Dissensionibus* I.3, pp. 10, 12; I.4, p. 16; III.2, p. 84;
IV.2, p. 122; IV.6, p. 142; IV.7, pp. 142–3. Cf. *Vita Hludowici* VI, p. 610; Paschasius Radbertus, *De Vita
Walae seu Epitaphium Arsenii* (*PL* 120, cols. 1559–1650), II.19.
   [44] Asser, *De Rebus Gestis Aelfredi*, ed. W. H. Stevenson, rev. D. Whitelock (Oxford, 1959), ch. 91,
pp. 77–8; ch. 105, p. 92.
   [45] Orderic Vitalis, *Historia Ecclesiastica*, ed. M. Chibnall (6 vols.; Oxford, 1969–80), ii. p. 150; iii.
pp. 206, 234, 300; iv. pp. 154, 330; v. pp. 316, 318, 374; vi. pp. 28, 58, 114, 204, 218, 282, 290, 498; Roger
of Wendover, *Flores Historiarum* (London, 1890), i. p. 513; Matthew Paris, *Chronica Maiora*, ed. H. R.
Luard (7 vols.; London, 1872–83), iv. p. 594; v. pp. 7, 144.

unnaturally, in Ambrose,[46] in the *Moralium Dogma Philosophorum*,[47] Peter Abelard,[48] Bernard of Clairvaux,[49] and John of Salisbury,[50] and, largely through the influence of the latter, it continued to be cited by thirteenth-century writers such as Helinand of Froidmont and John of Wales.[51]

Intellectual context is, of course, more than just a question of lexicography and *Quellenforschung*, of tracing the sources and traditions from which various scholastic writers were able to draw their terminology. It is also a question of the interpretation which these writers gave to their sources, of how these legal, Ciceronian, and Augustinian 'traditions' were actually read and used in the Middle Ages. Viewed in these terms, intellectual context must be extended to cover the way in which these different conceptions of the common good were related to one another and, in particular, the way in which they conditioned the impact on thirteenth-century scholastic political thought of a fourth 'tradition', namely Aristotelianism. It has been claimed, for instance, that the principle that the common good should be preferred to the private good embodied a Roman tradition of public spiritedness in Cicero, Seneca, and Justinian which became deeply entrenched in medieval thought. Rather than represent the result of any considered analysis, it is argued, this principle merely expressed a general sense of an individual's duty to humanity which was realized through the exercise of *pietas* and *magnanimitas*. These Stoic virtues were then 'christianized' by Augustine and, in their new guise of *caritas*, incorporated into the law of the church. According to this interpretation, therefore, the introduction of a specifically Aristotelian formulation of the same principle in book I of the *Ethics* amounted to no more than a decorative addition to an already well-worn theme.[52] In a similar vein, it has been argued that a recognizably Ciceronian or 'Stoic' notion of the common good was already a central concern of the thirteenth-century *dictatores*, of pre-humanist writers on civic government, well before the introduction of Aristotle's *Ethics* and *Politics*.[53] According to this interpretation, therefore, it was a Ciceronian or Stoic notion of peace and concord which lay at the heart of the vigorous republican ideology of the northern Italian city-states and which remained largely inde-

---

[46] Ambrose, *De Officiis*, ed. M. Testard (2 vols.; Paris, 1984, 1992), I.28.132, p. 158; III.3.15, p. 86.

[47] *Das Moralium Dogma Philosophorum des Guillaume de Conches, lateinisch, altfranzösisch und mittelniederfränkisch*, ed. J. Holmberg (Uppsala, 1929), pp. 27, 30, 36, 65, 69.

[48] Abelard, *Dialogus inter Philosophum, Iudaeum et Christianum*, ed. R. Thomas (Stuttgart–Bad Cannstatt, 1970), pp. 118–19, 123–4; id., *Theologia Christiana*, ed. E. M. Buytaert (*CCCM* 12) II.48–52, pp. 151–3.

[49] Bernard of Clairvaux, *De Consideratione ad Eugenium Papam*, ed. J. Leclercq and H. Rochais, *S. Bernardi Opera*, vol. iii (Rome, 1963), III.4.18, p. 445. Cf. III.3.13, p. 440.

[50] John of Salisbury, *Policraticus*, ed. C. C. J. Webb (2 vols.; Oxford, 1909), I.4 (i. pp. 26, 34), IV.1 (i. p. 235), IV.2 (i. p. 238), VI.9 (ii. p. 23), VI.19 (ii. pp. 58–9), VII.25 (ii. p. 225).

[51] Helinand of Froidmont, *Flores* (*PL* 212, cols. 721–46), cols. 739, 742; J. Swanson, *John of Wales: A Study of the Works and Ideas of a Thirteenth Century Friar* (Cambridge, 1989), chs. 3–4. Cf. C. Fasolt, *Council and Hierarchy: The Political Thought of William Durant the Younger* (Cambridge, 1991), 149, 218.

[52] Eschmann, 'Thomistic Glossary', 124.

[53] Cf. Brunetto Latini, *Li livres dou tresor*, ed. F. Carmody (Berkeley, 1948); Eschmann, 'Thomistic Glossary', 127.

pendent, even insulated, from the Aristotelian theorizing of the schools of Paris.[54] Judged from the perspective of the common good, it is accordingly at least a possibility that 'the reception of Aristotle' may not have marked the radically new departure in political thought which it is sometimes claimed to represent. Viewed in these terms, 'intellectual context' must extend to its historiography, to the way in which the relations between these legal, Ciceronian, Augustinian, and Aristotelian traditions have been characterized by more recent historical scholarship.

A sense of common identity established and maintained through symbol and ritual was prevalent in social groupings at every level of medieval society—in guilds, confraternities, churches, monasteries, and military orders as well as (or, some historians might argue, rather than) at the level of empire, kingdom, and city-state.[55] To this extent, Otto von Gierke's analysis of the medieval notion of community as an articulated hierarchy of various corporations bears repetition:

Political thought when it is genuinely medieval starts from the whole but ascribes an intrinsic value to every partial whole down to and including the individual. If it holds out one hand o antique thought when it sets the whole before the parts and the other hand to modern theories of natural law when it proclaims the intrinsic and aboriginal rights of the individual, its peculiar characteristic is that it sees the universe as one articulated whole and every being—whether a joint-being (community) or a single being—as both a part and a whole, a part determined by the final cause of the universe and a whole with a final cause of its own.[56]

Gierke's 'organicism', however, has been criticized by historians of scholastic political thought, often on the basis of its perceived challenge to their understanding of the individuality of the Christian soul. It has been argued instead, therefore, that the medieval social group was an association which only possessed a unity of peace, external order, and shared activity and that, as such, it should be seen as a community which supplied the 'insufficiency' of the individual only in terms of material means, intellectual direction, and moral support.[57]

This polarization of organicism and individualism was one reason why twentieth-century Neo-Thomist commentators insisted upon a distinction being drawn between 'individual' (the individual human being as member of the human

---

[54] Q. Skinner, 'Ambrogio Lorenzetti, the Artist as Political Philosopher', *PBA* 72 (1986), 9–11; id., 'Machiavelli's *Discorsi* and the Pre-Humanist Origins of Republican Political Ideas', in G. Bock, Q. Skinner, and M. Viroli (eds.), *Machiavelli and Republicanism* (Cambridge, 1990), esp. 121–34; M. Viroli, *From Politics to Reason of State: The Acquisition and Transformation of the Language of Politics 1250–1600* (Cambridge, 1992), ch. 1.

[55] P. Michaud-Quantin, *Universitas: Expressions du mouvement communautaire dans le moyen âge latin* (Paris, 1970); S. Reynolds, *Kingdoms and Communities in Western Europe 900–1300* (Oxford, 1984).

[56] O. Gierke, *Political Theories of the Middle Age*, trans. F. W. Maitland (Cambridge, 1900), 7.

[57] M. de Wulf, 'L'Individu et le groupe dans la scolastique du XIIIe siècle', *Revue Néoscolastique de Philosophie*, 22 (1920), 341–57, reprinted and expanded in id., *Philosophy and Civilisation in the Middle Ages* (Princeton, 1922), chs. 10–11; E. Lewis, 'Organic Tendencies in Medieval Political Thought', *American Political Science Review*, 32 (1938), 855. See also de Wulf, *Histoire de la philosophie médiévale*, ii. 174–6, iii. 253–5; E. Lewis, *Medieval Political Ideas* (2 vols.; London, 1954), i., ch. 4.

community) and 'person' (the individual human being created in the image of God).[58] Nevertheless, even this Neo-Thomist personalism did not provide an incontravertible solution to the problems posed by the medieval notion of community. Historians were still able to argue, for example, that Aquinas' integration of the individual within the community came dangerously close to 'complete absorption', to a denial of 'the fundamental Christian idea of the supreme value of human personality'.[59] Neo-Thomism, however, did ensure that it was Aquinas upon whom some of the most influential modern expositions of the common good in medieval scholastic political thought came to rest. Thomas Gilby, for example, used the distinction between individual and person to conclude that the respective claims of person and group might not, in fact, be fully reconcilable outside of the kingdom of God. The result was an implicit dualism of theology and justice, the former justifying the supremacy of the person, the latter the supremacy of the community. Aquinas' thought was therefore held up as a representation of the historical dialectic between community and society, between a community in which parts were subservient to an organological whole and a society in which nothing 'personal' was surrendered. 'Between these extremes', Gilby argued, 'was placed a combination, namely the political community which rose from the first and aspired to the second . . . St Thomas's political philosophy can be accordingly presented as a dialectic based on these three abstract types, the pure community, the pure society and the society-community'.[60] Even Gilby, however, found himself forced to concede that Aquinas was inconsistent, even indiscriminate, in his use of terminology. Even Gilby had to accept that the principle of the superiority of the common good was treated differently in Aquinas' commentaries on the *Politics* and *Ethics* than in the more Christian setting of the *Quaestio Disputata de Caritate*. Nevertheless, Gilby still found a unifying principle in a theory of friendship and love. The tension between individual and community, he argued, could be resolved by Aquinas' understanding of Christian *caritas*, of the love which human beings have towards one another and towards God.

Thomas Aquinas is the theologian who is frequently (perhaps too frequently) taken to be representative of scholastic political thought. As such, Gilby's interpretation of Aquinas can conveniently be used to highlight wider issues in the wider scholastic understanding of the relationship between the common good and the individual good. Gilby's defence of Aquinas was based, in the first instance, on giving a central position to *caritas* and to the association or 'communion' (*communicatio*) formed by love and friendship. In the second instance, it was based on drawing a distinction

---

[58]   e.g. E. Gilson, *L'Esprit de la philosophie médiévale* (Paris, 1932), ch. 10. Cf. J. Maritain, *The Person and the Common Good* (London, 1948).

[59]   A. P. d'Entrèves, *The Medieval Contribution to Political Thought* (Oxford, 1939), 26–7. D'Entrèves quotes from the *Summa Theologiae* to prove that Aquinas considered the common good and the individual good to be different in quality (*secundum formalem differentiam*) but from the *De Regno ad Regem Cypri* to prove that he also thought them different only in quantity. The two texts are juxtaposed with a simple 'yet on the other hand'.

[60]   Gilby, *Principality and Polity*, 261. Cf. R. A. Crofts, 'The Common Good in the Political Theory of Thomas Aquinas', *The Thomist*, 37 (1973), 155–73.

between a philosophical and a legal conception of the common good, between a 'Greek' *bonum commune* or *communis utilitas* and a 'Roman' *bonum publicum*, both of which were located beneath a common good in God, the *bonum universale*.[61] In Gilby's eyes, this distinction between Greek and Roman traditions carried significant consequences. 'Which is emphasised', he wrote, 'will depend on whether the community is taken teleologically in a Greek temper as promising the ends and amenities of the good life, or more statically in a Roman frame of mind as a *res publica* or State which establishes a system of rights.'[62] It was within this framework that Gilby sought to explain the 'contrast in tone' within Aquinas' account of the relationship between the common good and the individual good. On both counts—the centrality of *caritas* and the distinction between a functional and a minimalist definition of the common good—Gilby's characterization of Aquinas invites a reassessment of the influence which was exerted on medieval scholastic political thought, not by Aristotle, but by Augustine.

The medieval interpretation of Augustine's political thought is often summarized with the single phrase 'political Augustinianism', shorthand for the sort of hierocracy which was championed by Gregory VII and which was given its quintessential expression by Giles of Rome.[63] Augustine's own political thought, however, and in particular his analysis of Cicero's definition of the political community in book XIX of *De Civitate Dei*, was far from offering so simple a theory. Indeed, modern interpretations of Augustine's political theology have revealed their most significant fault lines over what exactly Augustine was intending to achieve by replacing Cicero's definition of the *res publica* as 'an association of a multitude united by a common sense of what is right and by a community of interest' (*coetus multitudinis iuris consensu et utilitatis communione sociatus*) with his own definition of the *res publica* as 'an association of a multitude of rational beings united by a common agreement on the objects of their love' (*coetus multitudinis rationalis rerum quas diligit concordi communione sociatus*).[64]

Was the removal of what is just or right (*ius*) from the first definition intended to demonstrate that non-Christian political authority (i.e. the pagan Roman Empire) was *necessarily* unjust and illegitimate because it failed to give God and the Christian church their 'due'? If this was its purpose, then Augustine's own, second definition may well have been intended ironically, as a demonstration of just how broad a definition of legitimate political authority would have to be in order to comprehend non-Christian government, so broad, in fact, as to be virtually meaningless since it would also include a society of thieves. On this reading, it is certainly only a short step to the interpretation which is generally associated with the medieval

---

[61] Gilby, *Principality and Polity*, 190.   [62] Ibid. 220–1.

[63] H.-X. Arquillière, *L'Augustinisme politique: Essai sur la formation des theories politiques du moyen âge*, 2nd edn. (Paris, 1955). Cf. U. Mariani, *Chiesa e stato nei teologi agostiniani del secolo XIV* (Rome, 1957); J. N. Hillgarth, 'L'Influence de la Cité de Dieu de saint Augustin au haut moyen âge', *Sacris Erudiri*, 28 (1985), 5–34.

[64] Augustine, *De Civitate Dei* (*CCSL* 48), II.20–1, pp. 51–5; XIX.21, pp. 687–9; XIX.24, pp. 695–6. Cf. Isidore, *Etymologies*, IX.4.5.

understanding of Augustine, namely that political legitimacy is intrinsically connected to 'true' Christian justice, to the righteousness (*iustitia*) which can only be achieved through a correct relation towards God and, more significantly, through a correct relation towards His Church and His vicar on earth.

Alternatively, Augustine's substitution of a second definition can be understood as an attempt to provide a criterion of legitimacy for those 'mixed' communities of just and unjust humans which existed after the New Testament and under the new dispensation. According to Augustine, the *civitas Dei* and *civitas terrena* represent twin communities which are formed, respectively, by love of God and love of self, the former concerning itself with the common good as a means towards the end of heavenly society, the latter replacing it with considerations of personal power and domination.[65] These communities may be conceptually distinct, however, but they are only eschatologically separable. If they are identifiable only on the Day of Judgement, therefore, then the relationship, in this world, between political society and the 'pilgrimage' of the individual Christian must have much looser parameters. On this reading, Augustine's own definition of the *res publica* may constitute his gloss on the sort of peace, concord, and qualified agreement (*pax et concordia*; *quaedam compositio voluntatum*) which represents the only realistic goal for human political authority in such circumstances.[66] If Christians 'use' whatever degree of peace and order is capable of being established on this earth in order to secure their ultimate goal of eternal communion with God, while non-Christians 'use' such peace and order in order to enjoy the vanities of personal glory and material benefit, then the 'common usefulness' (*communis utilitas*) of political society becomes 'an area of indeterminacy' where a modest degree of peace and order can be experienced by both types of community and by both types of individual.[67]

Choosing between these two different interpretations of Augustine's political thought has clear consequences for understanding his view of the role of law (is it an educative means of ensuring personal morality or a limited instrument for providing external peace and stability?) and of the nature of virtue (is it an absolute standard of correctly ordered love towards God or a sliding scale of relative degrees of goodness?). It also affects the extent to which Augustine can be seen to have envisaged political society serving as a *remedium peccati*, as a remedy for the effects of original sin (is it a necessary means to the higher good of salvation or a general barrier to the worse evils of unrestrained self-interest and self-love?). Viewed from the perspective of

---

[65] Augustine, *De Genesi ad Litteram*, ed. J. Zycha (*CSEL* 28.1), XI.15, pp. 347–8.

[66] For a definition of *pax* and *salus communis* as mortal goals which are secured as part of the natural order, see e.g. Augustine, *Contra Faustum*, ed. J. Zycha (*CSEL* 25), XXII.75, p. 673.

[67] For the classic statement of this argument, see R. A. Markus, *Saeculum: History and Society in the Theology of St. Augustine* (Cambridge, 1970), recapitulated in 'The Latin Fathers', in *CHMPT*, 103–16. For critiques, see G. Bonner, '*Quid imperatori cum ecclesia?* St. Augustine on History and Society', *Augustinian Studies*, 2 (1971), 231–51; R. Williams, 'Politics and the Soul: A Reading of the City of God', *Milltown Studies*, 19–20 (1987), 55–72; O. O'Donovan, 'Augustine's City of God XIX and Western Political Thought', *Dionysius*, 11 (1987), 89–110. See also H. Marrou, 'Civitas Dei, civitas terrena—num tertium quid?', *Texte und Untersuchungen zur Geschichte der Altchristliche Literatur*, 64 (1957), Studia Patristica II, pp. 342–50.

medieval political thought, the point is not whether one of these alternatives provides the 'correct' interpretation of *De Civitate Dei* but whether Augustine's account of political society was capable of being read in more than one way. In the late twelfth century, for example, at least one attempt was made to modify Augustine's polarization of the two cities in order to acknowledge the existence of a third community which was made up of good and evil people and which experienced a peace which could be defined simply as the absence of war and private conflict.[68] If it is possible, on this basis, to argue that 'political Augustinianism' provided scholastic theologians with an ambivalent political philosophy, with a political theology which could be characterized *either* by the minimal expectations of a sombre realism *or* by the functional ideal of a hierocratic perfectionism, then this is an important perspective from which to approach late medieval scholastic thought. Its precise significance for the scholastic understanding of the common good lies in the different meanings which each interpretation provides for the goal of human society.

When Augustine substituted his own definition of the political community in place of Cicero's, he removed the stipulation not only of a common sense of justice (*consensus iuris*) but also of a shared benefit or utility (*communio utilitatis*). He did so because of the etymological derivation of utility from using, of *utilitas* from *uti*. According to Augustine, there was a fundamental distinction to be drawn between *uti* and *frui*, *usus* and *fruitio*, between making use of something (or someone) as a means towards an end and 'enjoying' something (or someone) as an end in itself. For Augustine, either every good in Creation could be used as a means by which to achieve the ultimate goal of eternal beatitude or it could be enjoyed as an end in itself. Strictly speaking, *uti*, *usus*, and *utilitas* were terms which, in Augustine's view, could only be applied to the correct use of a created good, to the proper orientation of individual human actions towards God. Anything else was an abuse (*abusus*), since the only correct object of enjoyment or fulfilment (*fruitio*) is God Himself.[69] When it is transferred to the human community, this distinction between *uti* and *frui* is usually discussed in terms of the difficulties which it presents for Augustine's understanding of Christian *caritas*, given that it appears to imply that love of self and love of God extend to love of neighbour only in the sense of 'using' other human beings as a means of securing one's own ultimate goal in God.[70] When it is applied specifically to the political community, however, it also explains why Augustine was unable to countenance a Ciceronian definition of *res publica* for the non-Christian Roman Empire which still included *utilitas* as one of its criteria.

[68] Rufinus, *De Bono Pacis* (*PL* 150, cols. 1593–1638), II.8–18 (cols. 1614–25). Cf. H. Fuchs, *Augustin und der antike Friedensgedanke: Untersuchungen zum neunzehnten Buch der Civitas Dei* (Berlin, 1926), appendix IV, pp. 224–48; Y. M. J. Congar, 'Maître Rufin et son *De Bono Pacis*', *Revue des Sciences Philosophiques et Theologiques*, 41 (1957), 428–44.

[69] Augustine, *De Doctrina Christiana*, ed. R. P. H. Green (Oxford, 1995), I.7–10, pp. 14–16. Cf. O. O'Donovan, '*Usus* and *fruitio* in Augustine *De Doctrina Christiana* I', *Journal of Theological Studies*, 33 (1982), 361–97.

[70] *De Doctrina Christiana*, I.39–40, pp. 28–30. Cf. O. O'Donovan, *The Problem of Self-Love in Augustine* (New Haven, 1980); W. R. O'Connor, 'The uti/frui Distinction in Augustine's Ethics', *Augustinian Studies*, 14 (1983), 45–62.

By insisting on a definition of *utilitas* as correct use, as true benefit, Augustine was himself contributing to a much older debate, originally precipitated by the Sophists, which took the form of discussing whether justice in political society is simply a matter of social convention and calculated self-interest.[71] The resulting interest in the relationship between what is right (*ius*) and what is advantageous (*utile*) had become central to Stoicism and had prompted the series of set-piece discussions staged by Cicero with which Augustine was familiar and through which the debate became well known to medieval writers. In books III and IV of *De Finibus*, for example, Cicero had outlined (and rejected) the Stoic doctrine of 'preferables', namely the classification of virtue or moral worth (*honestum*) as the only good which is to be pursued and the relegation of *utilia* (such as health and prosperity) to being indifferent or morally neutral goods (*adiaphora*) which can be preferred but which do not necessarily contribute to virtue. It was in *De Officiis* that Cicero had given his most comprehensive analysis of this debate, first by drawing a conceptual distinction between these two types of good, between a good of intrinsic moral worth (*honor, dignitas*) and a good which was useful or advantageous (*utilitas*), and then by demonstrating that only what is morally virtuous is truly advantageous.[72] There is a clear affinity here between Cicero's account of *utilitas* and *honor* and Augustine's distinction between *uti* and *frui*. Indeed, Augustine himself makes the connection explicit—*honestum* is what is sought for its own sake and is the subject of enjoyment; *utile* is what is directed towards something else and is the subject of use.[73]

To treat the term *communis utilitas* in the light of Cicero's equation of *honestum* with *utile*, and of Augustine's distinction between *uti* and *frui*, raises a number of important issues for the scholastic understanding of the common good. In the first instance, there is the question of the consistency with which Augustine's strict definition of *utilitas* was, or even could be, maintained in the face of the disparate applications which the same term had been given by other authorities. In the *Ethics*, for example, Aristotle had classified three categories of good—the morally worthy, the useful, and the pleasurable—each of which could form the object of the will and the goal of friendship.[74] In *De Inventione*, Cicero had placed the most immediate form of human association—friendship—alongside glory and power in the category of *utile* rather than *honestum*, as something which is sought for the advantages it will confer rather than for its own sake.[75] In *De Doctrina Christiana*, meanwhile, Augustine had himself defined certain human institutions as advantageous and necessary for life (*commoda et necessaria ad usum vitae*).[76] In each case, *utilitas* was

---

[71] For what follows, see M. Colish, *The Stoic Tradition from Antiquity to the Early Middle Ages* (2 vols.; Leiden, 1990), i. 89–104, 126–58; ii. 142–238. Cf. G. Verbeke, *The Presence of Stoicism in Medieval Thought* (Washington, DC, 1983), esp. ch. 3.

[72] Cf. *Moralium Dogma Philosophorum*, pp. 68–9.

[73] Augustine, *De Diversis Quaestionibus LXXXIII*, ed. A. Mutzenbecher (*CCSL* 44), XXX, p. 38.

[74] Aristotle, *Nicomachean Ethics* II.3 1104^b30–31; VIII.2 1155^b17–21.

[75] Cicero, *De Inventione*, II.53.159–56, 168.

[76] Augustine, *De Doctrina Christiana*, II.96, p. 102. According to O'Donovan ('Augustine's City of God', 97), Augustine manages to restrict *utilitas* to mean use which is ordered towards the true end of

open to a much looser interpretation than the strictures of either *De Officiis* or *De Civitate Dei* might have implied.

In the second instance, there is the question of what effect was produced by the reintroduction of Aristotle. In *De Finibus*, Cicero had described the difference between Aristotelian and Stoic ethics as a difference between two conceptions of the good—measuring individual actions on a sliding scale of goodness up to and including the supreme good, and measuring individual actions on an absolute scale as *either* good *or* evil *or* morally indifferent.[77] When Aristotle's *Ethics* was translated in the thirteenth century, therefore, it became possible for medieval writers to reassess the direct force of this comparison. It also became possible to compare both the Aristotelian and the Stoic schemes with Augustine's insistence that every action was *either* a virtue (when it used a created good as a means towards the attainment of God) *or* a vice (when it abused a created good as an end to be enjoyed in itself). Augustine's refusal to countenance any virtue in the pagan Roman citizen or any justice in the non-Christian political community was necessarily thrown open to review once Aristotle could be cited in support of a position which ascribed degrees of goodness to virtue or degrees of legitimacy to political communities.

In the third instance, there is the question of the relationship between, on the one hand, constructing an ideal political community on the basis of moral virtue and the supreme good and, on the other, putting forward a model of conduct and organization which was actually realizable in practice. This question had already generated a contrast within Aristotle's political philosophy between the ideal community in the *Ethics* and the best practicable community in the *Politics*, between the life of virtue under kingship or an aristocracy and the achievement of stability under a polity. It had also prompted criticism to be levelled against Stoicism for producing a moral and political philosophy which bore little or no relation to how humans actually behaved. This was the criticism which Cicero's *De Republica* and *De Legibus* had, in part, been designed to meet by holding up Rome as the prime example of a political community which was, in practice, founded on *ius* as well as *utilitas*, which had actually succeeded in equating justice with mutual advantage. This particular claim may subsequently have been challenged by Augustine but the general question remained applicable to his own version of the just political community in *De Civitate Dei*. Is a community of love and fellowship attainable on this earth or is the most which can be expected from sinful human beings a limited degree of peace and material security?

Considered within its own political, literary, linguistic, intellectual, and historiographical terms of reference, the scholastic notion of the common good provides the means with which to assess the transformations which have often been taken to characterize late thirteenth- and early fourteenth-century scholastic political philosophy as a result of the reintroduction of Aristotle's *Ethics* and *Politics*. In some respects, an 'Aristotelian' common good served to strengthen and formalize existing

enjoyment in God but is unable to employ *uti* with comparable precision and often writes 'use' when he really means 'abuse'.

[77] Cicero, *De Finibus*, II.12.37–8, 13.43, 21.68.

notions. Viewed in these terms, the *Ethics* and the *Politics* may simply have added to an existing mélange of ideas from which scholastic theologians were free to pick and choose.[78] In other respects, an Aristotelian common good provided an agenda of its own. According to Aristotle, the goal of the political community is not just to live but to live well, not just to attain material self-sufficiency but to achieve the common good of the life of virtue. Viewed in these terms, the *Ethics* and the *Politics* raised questions which went to the heart of scholastic ethical and political thinking. Given that humans live in political society, in what sense is this political society directed towards their ultimate goal of eternal beatitude? Does it actively secure this goal or does it simply make it possible? Does it make people morally virtuous or does it simply provide some of them with an environment within which virtuous activity can take place? How these questions were answered by scholastic theologians would clearly depend on how they tackled two fundamental issues. First, they had to find a means of integrating the Aristotelian account of the life of virtue within a Neoplatonic account of the operation of hierarchy in the universe, accommodating the perfection of Aristotle's moral community but without endangering the direct communion of the individual human being with God. Second, they had to decide between different definitions of the common good which political society could be assumed to secure, between moral goodness and material advantage, between *bonum commune* and *communis utilitas*.

When scholastic theologians tackled the relationship between human society and eternal beatitude, therefore, they read into Aristotle's *Ethics* and *Politics* many of the same questions which were prompted by Augustine's *De Civitate Dei*. In setting up an analysis of the scholastic notion of the common good as a comparison between Aristotelian and Augustinian ideas, the contrast between these intellectual traditions should certainly not be exaggerated. Indeed, if a distinction between what is morally good and what is advantageous can be traced to Aristotle, Cicero, *and* Augustine, then the denominations 'Aristotelian', 'Ciceronian', and 'Augustinian' need to be seen less as a set of monolithic, mutually exclusive alternatives than as a series of overlapping currents. Nevertheless, within the confines of ethical and political thought, 'Aristotelian' and 'Augustinian' remain a serviceable means of distinguishing between two definitions of the common good—on the one hand, as moral goodness and the life of virtue and, on the other, as material advantage and the security of peace. Which of these two definitions was chosen carried significant theoretical consequences. Classifying the goal of political society as *bonum commune* meant analysing the connection between goodness in the human community and goodness in the universe; classifying the goal of political society as *communis utilitas* meant analysing the

---

[78] A. Black, 'The Individual and Society', in *CHMPT*, 589. Cf. id., *Political Thought in Europe 1250–1450* (Cambridge, 1992), intro.; id., 'Society and the Individual from the Middle Ages to Rousseau: Philosophy, Jurisprudence and Constitutional Theory', *History of Political Thought*, 1 (1980), 145–66. For *auctoritas* as a waxen nose which can be turned in various directions, see Alan of Lille, *De Fide Catholica* (*PL* 210, cols. 305–430), I.30, col. 333. Cf. M.-D. Chenu, *Toward Understanding St. Thomas*, trans. A.-M. Landry and D. Hughes (Chicago, 1964), ch. 4.

connection between material advantage and moral goodness, between using peace in the human community and using this peace correctly. When scholastic theologians tackled the relationship between human society and eternal beatitude, their reading of Aristotle and Augustine and their choice between different definitions of the common good carried practical political consequences too. Classifying the goal of political society as moral goodness or as material advantage meant analysing the connection between the authority of the temporal power and the authority of the spiritual power. It is in these terms, therefore, that the scholastic notion of the common good finally raises the question of the relationship which may, or may not, exist between the reintroduction of Aristotle's political ideas in the late thirteenth century and the 'desacralization' of political authority in the early fourteenth century.

I

Albertus Magnus—Aristotle and the Common Good

In book I of the *Nicomachean Ethics*, Aristotle opens his enquiry into happiness by examining the goals of various branches of human knowledge—medicine is directed towards health, shipbuilding towards a ship, military strategy towards victory, economics towards wealth. Since the teleological process of choosing to undertake something for the sake of something else cannot be extended indefinitely, Aristotle suggests that there must be one goal which is secured for its own sake. He identifies this goal as the supreme good, *to agathon kai to ariston*, and defines its science as politics. Politics, he concludes, is the branch of knowledge which orders all other disciplines towards this supreme good, the human good of happiness. Aristotle then closes this part of his discussion with the following observation:

For even if the good is the same [*tauton*] for an individual and for a city-state, that of the city-state appears to be greater [*meizon*] and more perfect [*teleioteron*] both to attain and to preserve. Although it is satisfactory [*agapeton*] to secure the good for one person alone, it is nobler [*kallion*] and more divine [*theioteron*] to secure it for a people or for city-states.[1]

Aristotle's identification of the supreme good of happiness as the goal of political science has at least two important consequences for his ethical and political thought. In the first instance, it establishes a profoundly social conception of human fulfilment—individuals secure the supreme human good by participating in the political community. In the second instance, it explicitly combines what might otherwise have been seen as mutually exclusive alternatives—the principle that the common good is the same as the individual good and the principle that the common good is superior to the individual good.

Aristotle's immediate concern in book I of the *Ethics* is to establish that the supreme good for humankind is happiness. In the process, however, he is also drawn into a more general discussion of what it is to be 'good', of what it means to predicate goodness of different individual things. The result is a highly compressed critique of

[1] Aristotle, *Nicomachean Ethics*, ed. L. Bywater (Oxford, 1894), I.2 1094b7–10, p. 2. For general introductions, see W. F. R. Hardie, *Aristotle's Ethical Theory*, 2nd edn. (Oxford, 1980); J. O. Urmson, *Aristotle's Ethics* (Oxford, 1988); T. H. Irwin, *Aristotle's First Principles* (Oxford, 1988), chs. 16–21. For 'happiness', see J. L. Ackrill, 'Aristotle and *Eudaimonia*', *PBA* 60 (1974), 339–59; A. O. Rorty (ed.), *Essays on Aristotle's Ethics* (Berkeley, 1980), 15–33. For this particular passage, see Irwin, *Aristotle's First Principles*, 352–4; R. A. Gauthier and J. Y. Jolif (eds.), *L'Éthique à Nicomaque*, 2nd edn. (3 vols.; Louvain–Paris, 1958–9), ii. 10–12; J. A. Stewart, *Notes on the Nicomachean Ethics of Aristotle* (Oxford, 1892), 23–4.

the Platonist idea that there is a single Form of the Good which is universally predicable of all good things and which exists as a separate substance in itself. Rather than adopt such a notion, Aristotle maintains that the term 'good' has, in fact, as many senses as the term 'being' in that the predicate goodness, like the predicate existence, can be applied to all the logical categories (substance, quality, relation, etc). In Aristotle's view, because goodness can be predicated of things which are in different categories, the term 'good' must accordingly carry as many meanings as there are differences between these categories. Rather than posit a single Form of the Good, therefore, Aristotle maintains that there are categorically different kinds of goodness—a substantial good, a qualitative good, a relational good, and so on. At the same time, however, Aristotle does not reject the idea of any sort of unity in goodness. To predicate goodness of individual things may not be a matter of synonymy (univocal predication such that two things share the same name and the same definition for their substance or nature) but nor is it simply a matter of homonymy (equivocal predication such that two things accidentally share the same name and have entirely different definitions). According to Aristotle, the predication of goodness requires the adoption of an intermediate position. He closes this part of his discussion, therefore, with the suggestion that individual good things have a relation to one another which is more than accidental, either by deriving from a single principle and contributing towards a single end or by analogy (such that two things share the same relation towards a third object, such as sight in its relation to the body and intellect in its relation to the soul).[2]

Aristotle's critique of a universal Form of the Good has consequences for the common good and its relation to the individual which are just as important as his identification of the supreme human good of happiness. In the first instance, it establishes that a knowledge of what is good for humankind does not require a knowledge of any single Form of goodness existing throughout the universe. In the second instance, it invites a comparison of the way in which goodness in general relates to individual good things with the way in which the good which is common to humankind relates to individual human goods.

Aristotle's treatment of happiness and goodness was available to medieval scholastic theologians and philosophers from the beginning of the thirteenth century in the truncated form of the *Ethica nova*.[3] Even this partial translation raised a number of significant issues, not the least of which was how Aristotle's supreme human good of happiness could be connected to the universal good which exists in God.[4] Other

---

[2] Aristotle, *Ethics* I.6 1096ᵃ11–ᵇ31.

[3] *Ethica nova*, ed. R. A. Gauthier (*Aristoteles Latinus* XXVI.2), pp. 66–7. For the reception of the *Ethics*, see Gauthier and Jolif (eds.), *L'Éthique à Nicomaque*, i. 74–85; *Ethica Nicomachea, Praefatio*, ed. R. A. Gauthier (*Aristoteles Latinus* XXVI.1), pp. 15–16; G. Wieland, 'The Reception and Interpretation of Aristotle's *Ethics*', in *CHLMP*, 657–72; id., *Ethica—Scientia practica: Die Anfänge der philosophischen Ethik im 13 Jahrhundert* (Münster, 1981).

[4] A. J. Celano, 'The *finis hominis* in the Thirteenth Century Commentaries on Aristotle's *Nicomachean Ethics*', *AHDLMA* 53 (1986), 24–35; G. Wieland, 'Happiness: The Perfection of Man', in *CHLMP*, esp. 675–6; Wieland, *Ethica—Scientia Practica*, 140–97.

problems arose from its communal nature. A collection of typical examination questions from the faculty of arts at Paris in the 1230s, for example, asks whether the same happiness can be participated in by all (or, for that matter, by many) individuals and whether this 'most perfect' of goods is capable of being shared by all (or many) things.[5] Nevertheless, it was only in the middle of the thirteenth century that Aristotle's conception of the common good could be given a detailed exposition in the context of the whole of his moral thinking when a complete Latin text of the *Ethics* was made available for the first time. In the early 1240s, Hermannus Alemannus translated Averroes' paraphrase or middle commentary on the *Ethics*,[6] together with the *Summa Alexandrinorum* (an Arabic epitome), and, in 1246–7, Robert Grosseteste translated all ten books, together with the annotations of a number of Greek commentators.[7] It was Grosseteste's translation which rendered the principles of identity and superiority from book I of the *Ethics* in the form which came to be widely disseminated throughout the second half of the century: *si enim et idem est uni et civitati, maiusque et perfectius quod civitatis videtur et suscipere et salvare. amabile quidem enim et uni soli, melius vero et divinius genti et civitatibus.*[8] More importantly, it was Grosseteste's translation which enabled Aristotle's discussion of happiness and goodness to be considered not only within the terms of reference set by book I but also in the light of the discussion of justice in book V, friendship in books VIII and IX, and contemplative happiness in book X.

The first scholastic theologian to take up the challenge of producing a commentary on the complete text of Aristotle's *Ethics* was Albertus Magnus. As the Dominican master at Paris in the 1240s, Albertus embarked upon a systematic exposition of all of Aristotle's works on natural science, a task which was to engage his scholarly

---

[5] M. Grabmann, 'Das Studium der Aristotelischen Ethik an der Artistenfakultät der Universität Paris in der Ersten Hälfte des 13 Jahrhunderts', reprinted in id., *Mittelalterliches Geistesleben III* (Munich, 1956), 138. When it came to discussing civil society—the life of the soul in the good of others (*in bono aliorum*) or in the good of all humans living together according to a common law (*in bono omnium communiter secundum legem communem*)—the Paris *quaestiones* considered it a subject, not for ethics, but for the disciplines of ruling and of politics, citing Cicero's *De Officiis* as the textbook for the first and 'laws and decrees' (namely Justinian's *Codex* and Gratian's *Decretum*) for the second.

[6] Averroes, *Aristotelis Opera cum Averrois Commentariis* (editio Iuntina, 2nd edn., 11 vols.; Venice, 1562–74), iii, esp. fo. 181r; *Summa Alexandrinorum, L'Etica Nicomachea nella tradizione latina medievale*, ed. C. Marchesi (Messina, 1904), appendix, pp. xli–lxxxvi, esp. p. xlii.

[7] *The Greek Commentaries on the Nicomachean Ethics of Aristotle in the Latin Translation of Robert Grosseteste*, ed. H. P. F. Mercken (Corpus Latinum Commentariorum in Aristotelem Graecorum VI.1, 3; Leiden, 1973, 1991). Cf. *Eustratii et Michaelis et Anonyma in Ethica Nicomachea Commentaria*, ed. G. Heylbut (Commentaria in Aristotelem Graeca XX; Berlin, 1892); H. P. F. Mercken, 'The Greek Commentators on Aristotle's Ethics', in R. Sorabji (ed.), *Aristotle Transformed* (London, 1990), 407–43. For Grosseteste's own notes, see S. Harrison Thomson, 'The "Notule" of Grosseteste on the *Nicomachean Ethics*', *PBA* 19 (1933), 195–218; Mercken (ed.), *The Greek Commentaries*, 45*–64*. For the date and content of the translation, see D. A. Callus, 'The Date of Grosseteste's Translations and Commentaries on the Pseudo-Dionysius and the *Nicomachean Ethics*', *RTAM* 14 (1947), 186–210; J. H. Dunbabin, 'Robert Grosseteste as Translator, Transmitter and Commentator on the *Nicomachean Ethics*', *Traditio*, 28 (1972), 460–72; Mercken (ed.), *The Greek Commentaries*, 33*–66*.

[8] *Ethica Nicomachea, Recensio pura*, ed. R. A. Gauthier (*Aristoteles Latinus* XXVI.3), p. 142. Cf. *Ethica Nicomachea, Recensio recognita*, ed. R. A. Gauthier (*Aristoteles Latinus* XXVI.4), p. 376; *Auctoritates Aristotelis*, ed. J. Hamesse (Louvain–Paris, 1974), p. 233: *bonum quanto communius, tanto divinius*.

attention for the next twenty years.[9] It was right at the start of this programme, soon after his return to Cologne in 1248 and before 1252, that he tackled the recently translated text of the *Ethics*, delivering a course of lectures which combined exposi-tory comments with specific questions.[10] Some fifteen years later, towards the end of the 1260s, Albertus Magnus decided to write a second commentary, this time as a series of extended paraphrases incorporating what he had gleaned from the other Aristotelian texts which he had been expounding in the intervening period.[11]

Taken together, these two works effectively set out the terms of reference in which an Aristotelian notion of the common good would have to be discussed by all subsequent scholastic theologians. It is Albertus Magnus, therefore, who provides the most appropriate starting-point for a general analysis of the common good and its relation to the individual in late thirteenth- and early fourteenth-century political thought. Taken separately, however, the chronological separation of Albertus' two commentaries also reveals something more precise, namely the effect on this analy-sis of an increasingly thorough knowledge of other Aristotelian texts. It is Albertus Magnus, therefore, who also gives an insight into a *developing* scholastic understand-ing of the two issues which had been raised by Aristotle's discussion of the common good in book I of the *Ethics*—what is the relation between the principle of superiority and the principle of identity, and what is the relation between the supreme human good of happiness and the good which is analogically predicable of individual good things?

When Albertus Magnus first turned to Aristotle's discussion of the relationship between the individual and the common good in book I of the *Ethics*, his exposition was nothing if not brief. His selectivity, however, is revealing. As a commentator, Albertus' initial reaction to the principles of identity and superiority was to tackle them within what he took to be Aristotle's own terms of reference. According to Albertus, it was in order to justify identifying the goal of political science as the human good that Aristotle had to insist that the good of an individual is the same as the good of a people because, if they were not the same, then Aristotle would have had to identify the goal of political science as some other good. As for the relationship

   [9] J. A. Weisheipl, 'The Life and Works of St. Albert the Great', in id. (ed.), *Albertus Magnus and the Sciences: Commemorative Essays 1980* (Toronto, 1980), 13–51; S. Tugwell, *Albert and Thomas: Selected Writings* (New York, 1988), 3–39; A. de Libera, *Albert le Grand et la philosophie* (Paris, 1990). Prior to Grosseteste's translation of the complete text of the *Ethics*, Albertus had composed the *Tractatus de Natura Boni*, ed. E. Filthaut, in *Alberti Magni Opera Omnia* (Münster, 1951–) vol. xxv.1 and *De Bono*, ed. H. Kühle, C. Feckes, B. Geyer, and W. Kübel, in ibid., vol. xxviii.
   [10] *Super Ethica commentum et quaestiones* [henceforth *Super Ethica*], ed. W. Kübel, in ibid., vol. xiv.1–2. Cf. J. H. Dunbabin, 'The Two Commentaries of Albertus Magnus on the *Nicomachean Ethics*', *RTAM* 30 (1963), 232–50; C. Vansteenkiste, 'Das erste Buch der Nikomachischen Ethik bei Albertus Magnus', in G. Meyer and A. Zimmerman (eds.), *Albertus Magnus, Doctor Universalis 1280–1980* (Mainz, 1980), 373–84; Wieland, *Ethica—Scientia Practica*, 203–7, 272–81, 307–15.
   [11] *Ethicorum Libri Decem* [henceforth *Ethica*], ed. A. Borgnet, in *Alberti Magni Opera Omnia* (38 vols.; Paris, 1890–9) vol. vii. For the dating, see Dunbabin, 'Two Commentaries', 245 (1267–8); Gauthier and Jolif (eds.), *L'Éthique à Nicomaque*, i. 79 (1268–70). Cf. J. A. Weisheipl, 'Albert's Works on Natural Sciences [*libri naturales*] in Probable Chronological Order', in id. (ed.), *Albertus Magnus and the Sciences*, 575 (1262–3).

between common good and individual good, Albertus suggests that these goods differ by virtue of one being larger and the other smaller. From Aristotle's own terminology Albertus accordingly picks out the one term which readily lent itself to such a quantitative comparison—'greater' (*maius*). Ignoring altogether the presence of 'better' (*melius*) and 'more perfect' (*perfectius*), Albertus then confines the remainder of his discussion to explaining what Aristotle might have meant by 'more divine' (*divinius*). The greater divinity of the common good, Albertus suggests, needs to be understood in the context of the passage in *De Anima* in which Aristotle had discussed generation as a final cause of nature:

an animal produces an animal, a plant a plant, in order that they may have a share in the immortal and the divine in the only way they can. For every creature strives for this, and this is the final cause of all natural functions. . . . What persists is not the individual itself but something in its image, not identical as a unit, but identical in form.[12]

It was this statement which had subsequently prompted Avicenna to comment that, if the purpose of generation is for a species to continue in existence, then this is a principle which God has inspired in everything which exists. It is this observation which is now taken up by Albertus—Aristotle's attribution of greater divinity to the common good simply means that it too expresses the conservation of the species.[13] For anything to be termed divine demonstrates either that it comes immediately from God or that it possesses some reflection or similitude (*similitudo*) of divine goodness. In the first sense of the term, political happiness is not divine, but in the second sense (*quasi formaliter*) it is. The continuation in existence of a species is a divine principle because it represents an assimilation of as much of God's eternal nature as Nature is capable of.[14] Although such assimilation is not possible in one individual, it *is* realizable through a succession of individuals into infinity.[15] The good of an individual human, in other words, is necessarily limited by that human's own mortality, but, by participating in the common human good, the same human being can share in a natural immortality. In expounding Aristotle's comparative terminology, therefore, Albertus' initial account of *divinius* maintains the quantitative interpretation which underpinned his account of *maius*. Viewed within a definite period of time, the common good is the aggregate total of individual goods; viewed within an indefinite period of time, it is an unending sequence of individual goods.

---

[12] Aristotle, *De Anima*, trans. W. S. Hett (Loeb, 1957), II 415ᵃ28–ᵇ1, 6–7, p. 87. Cf. *Politics* I.2 1252ᵃ28–30.

[13] *Super Ethica* I.2, p. 11. *Avicenna Latinus: Liber de Anima seu sextus de naturalibus I-II-III*, ed. S. van Riet (Leiden, 1972), II.1, p. 108. Albertus' own commentary on *De Anima* (ed. A. Borgnet, vol. v) was written *c.*1254–7 (Weisheipl, 'Albert's Works', 568–9); for his analysis of this passage, see pp. 215–16. Cf. Albertus Magnus, *Politicorum Libri Octo* [henceforth *Pol. Lib. Oct.*], ed. A. Borgnet, in *Alberti Magni Opera Omnia*, vol. viii, II.9, p. 182.

[14] *Super Ethica* I.10, p. 55. Cf. I.7, p. 33; IV.2, p. 229.

[15] *Super Ethica* I.11, p. 58. Cf. I.12, p. 66; V.3, p. 321 (where Albertus glosses greater divinity in terms of its similarity to God—the common good possesses greater eternity, greater community, and greater simplicity than the individual good).

When Albertus came to compose his second commentary on the *Ethics*, his second bite at the relation between the common good and the individual good reveals a very different and altogether more complex treatment of the principles of identity and superiority. On this occasion, Albertus chooses to open by distinguishing between a universal whole (which is present in essence in any one of its parts) and a potential whole (which is present in any one of its parts only in power or virtue), and attributes the properties of the latter to the good of the political community. By way of illustration, Albertus draws a parallel with a victorious army. The victory of an army, he explains, is composed of individual powers or virtues (such as provisioning, marshalling, and fighting) but it is only when all these individual virtues are gathered together and directed towards a single goal that victory is made complete (*perficitur*). As for the relationship which exists between this common good and its constituent elements, Albertus glosses Aristotle's use of *melius* with the observation that the closer (*propinquius*) something is to victory, the better it is. This proximity is exemplified by the commander of the army—the individual in whom victory exists—and likewise by the ruler of the political community—the individual in whom the common good exists.[16] Albertus then explains how this statement relates to the principle of identity, to the fact that it is not just the good of the army and the good of its commander which are one and the same but the good of the army and the good of each individual soldier. The proximity of every individual to the common good, Albertus suggests, is not determined by quantity—each individual does not possess a fixed amount of the common good—but by analogy—the actions of individuals possess the principle of goodness (*ratio boni*) 'in proportion to' the ultimate good. The good of the individual soldier is thus the same as the good of the whole army, not in number, species, genus, or defining principle (*diffinitiva ratio*), but in proportion or analogy to a single entity. Albertus supports this contention with a mathematical illustration drawn from Grosseteste's translation of Eustratius and from a pseudo-Euclidian treatise (Fig. 1.1).[17] The Greeks, he writes, called this type of proportion *reperim*, this being the name which was given to the arm of a balance (B) in which the heavier of two weights has been placed. This arm, when allowed to move freely (B'), will suddenly move from a position of equilibrium towards the right angle (c) drawn downwards from the centre of the circle described by both arms of the balance. Thereafter, the heaviness of the weight will be proportional to the size of the angle (b) through which the descending arm moves in the bottom right-hand quarter of the circle.

Albertus' argument in his second commentary on the *Ethics* is circular in more than one sense. In order to make his illustration work as a model for the relationship

---

[16] *Ethica* I.3.14, p. 48. Cf. *Super Ethica* IV.5, p. 243; *Pol. Lib. Oct.* VII.3, p. 648.

[17] Mercken (ed.), *The Greek Commentaries*, p. 24; Paris Nat. Lat. 10260 fo. 171r (I owe this reference to the kindness of G. Gereby and A. Classen). Albertus' fondness for such illustrations is a characteristic feature of his commentary. e.g. *Ethica* IX.3.1, p. 584; X.1.1, p. 601. Cf. P. M. J. E. Tummers, 'The Commentary of Albert on Euclid's Elements of Geometry', in Weisheipl (ed.), *Albertus Magnus and the Sciences*, 479–99.

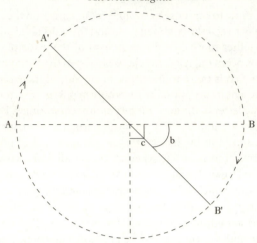

Fig. 1.1. Albertus Magnus, *Ethica* I.3.14, p. 48.

between individual good and common good, Albertus is clearly presupposing that goodness can be identified with heaviness, the size of the angle at the centre with the proximity of an individual to the common good.[18] The right angle at the centre (c) is equivalent to the common good—the larger the angle at the centre (b), the heavier the weight; the nearer the individual, the greater his good. What is equally clear, however, is that Albertus has moved some way from the rather limited exposition of Aristotle's analysis of the common good which he had given in his first course of lectures on the *Ethics*. The common good is now a single entity—individual goods share in it to a greater or lesser extent according to their proximity to a certain standard, to a point of common reference. A similar transformation has occurred in Albertus' explanation of greater divinity. In his second commentary, this attribute is understood, not in terms of the continuity of a species, but in terms of unity, the ordering of all things towards participation in one. It is 'more divine' for the human good to be secured for a people or for a city, Albertus explains, because this accords with the divine principle of directing multiplicity towards unity. For this conclusion Albertus is indebted to another observation which had been made by Eustratius but which he had not used in his first commentary. According to Eustratius, Aristotle's comparative terminology should be understood in the sense that it is better for goodness to be diffused over more things and in the sense that any good action is a divine action. It was this last definition which had prompted Eustratius to make the observation which Albertus now quotes—the ruler of the political community is, in fact, similar to God because he secures what is good for the community and avoids what is bad.[19]

[18] For the analogy between love and weight, see Augustine, *De Civitate Dei*, ed. B. Dombart and A. Kalb (*CCSL* 47–8), XI.28, p. 348; *Confessions*, ed. J. J. O'Donnell (Oxford, 1992), XIII.9, p. 187.

[19] *Ethica* I.3.14, pp. 48–9. Cf. *Ethica* I.8.1, p. 136; Mercken (ed.), *The Greek Commentaries*, p. 29.

A comparison between Albertus' treatment of the common good in his first commentary on the *Ethics* (*c*.1248–52) and the exposition which he gives in his second commentary (*c*.1267–70) reveals differences in content as well as approach. One consideration which seems readily to account for this change is Albertus' acquaintance with Aristotle's *Politics*, a text which was only translated in the early 1260s, some ten years after Albertus' first commentary on the *Ethics* had appeared.[20] Albertus certainly lost no time in producing a commentary on this work between 1263 and 1267,[21] and, when he turned to the *Ethics* for a second time, he appears to have approached the text with these new arguments still fresh in his mind. The common good, therefore, is now seen from the rather different perspective of Aristotle's analysis of the natural growth of the political community. According to book I of the *Politics*, the city-state is a natural association (*communicatio*) which aims to secure the most primary (*principalissimum*) of all goods. The political community may have come into being for the sake of staying alive, for the sake of material self-sufficiency, but it continues in existence for the sake of living well, for the sake of living in accordance with virtue. The city-state is the 'perfect' association because it is completely self-sufficient and, as such, it represents the goal of all other human associations—it is naturally prior (*prius*) to the individual and to the household, just as the whole is prior to the part. Indeed, since a human being cannot be self-sufficient when he is separated from the city-state, the individual stands in the same relation to the political community as a part of the body does to its whole—if the whole body is destroyed, then its parts will not exist except in name (that is, except homonymously or equivocally). This, in Aristotle's view, is what makes the human condition specifically human—an individual who does not need political association must either be an animal or a god.[22]

When Albertus produced his commentary on the *Politics*, his exposition kept closely to this line of argument. Of all the different human associations, he writes, it is the political community which is the most natural, most primary, and most self-sufficient, which is prior in nature, and which is instituted for the sake of the best goods. In order to explain these superlative terms, Albertus refers to the superiority of the common good in book I of the *Ethics* and, in the process, shows none of the reticence which he had shown over *melius* in his first commentary on this text. The

---

[20] *Aristotelis Politicorum Libri Octo cum vetusta translatione Gulielmi de Moerbeka*, ed. F. Susemihl (Leipzig, 1872). For an earlier, incomplete translation, see *Politica I–II, Translatio prior imperfecta*, ed. P. Michaud-Quantin (*Aristoteles Latinus* XXIX.1). For the dating of both works, see F. Bossier, 'Méthode de traduction et problèmes de chronologie', in J. Brams and W. Vanhamel (eds.), *Guillaume de Moerbeke: Recueils d'études à l'occasion du 700e anniversaire de sa mort (1286)* (Leuven, 1989), 288, 292. Cf. C. Flüeler, *Rezeption und Interpretation der Aristotelischen Politica im späten Mittelalter* (2 vols.; Amsterdam, 1992), i. 15–29; id., 'Die Rezeption der Politica des Aristoteles an der Pariser Artistenfakultät im 13. und 14. Jahrhundert', in J. Miethke and A. Bühler (eds.), *Das Publikum Politischer Theorie im 14. Jahrhundert* (Munich, 1992), 127–38.

[21] For its composition, see *S. Thomae de Aquino Opera Omnia*, vol. xlviii, pp. A.8–10; Weisheipl, 'Albert's Works', 575–6; Flüeler, *Rezeption und Interpretation der Aristotelischen Politica*, 22–3.

[22] Aristotle, *Politics* (ed. Susemihl) I.1–2, pp. 1–10. Cf. *Super Ethica* IV.12, p. 272; VI.11, p. 468; *Ethica* III.1.1, p. 196; III.2.1, p. 236; V.1.4, p. 337; V.3.3, p. 367; VI.2.24, p. 442.

good of a city, he writes, is better than the good of an individual and the good of a people is most divine (*divinissimum*).[23] What Albertus then chooses to highlight, however, is Aristotle's correction of those people who labour under the misapprehension that the goods sought by the various human associations differ only in quantity, in the number of individuals which each comprises. It is the refutation of this 'error', the very error which Albertus himself had committed in his first course of lectures on the *Ethics*, which he now takes as his guiding principle. When Aristotle divides the collectivity (*compositum*) of the political association into its several component parts (husband and wife, ruler and subject, master and slave), each one of them performing a different function, Albertus points out that the goods which are secured, and the associations which secure them, differ not just in quantity but in kind (*secundum speciem*). The good which is secured by the household, therefore, differs in kind from the good which is secured by the political association. Thus, the good which is secured by the association of husband and wife—the conservation of the human species—is different in kind from the good which is secured by the association of the political community—the life of virtue.[24]

Once Albertus Magnus had read the *Politics*, his earlier analysis of common good and individual good in the *Ethics* clearly stood in need of substantial revision. This provides one very good reason why Albertus' second commentary on the *Ethics* replaced a difference in quantity with a difference in kind and substituted the conservation of the species with the direction of multiplicity towards unity. In his revised analysis of book I of the *Ethics*, however, Albertus was also drawn into a much closer examination of the discussion of abstract goodness with which Aristotle had originally framed his comments on the common good of happiness. In particular, Albertus now picked up on Aristotle's insistence that the identity which exists between goodness in general and particular good things is not univocal or equivocal but analogical—the identity which characterizes a group of different individual things when they share the same relation towards some other entity or towards each other.

In book I of the *Ethics*, Aristotle had put forward two ways in which individual good things could be connected to each other in a manner which was neither univocal (synonymy) nor equivocal (accidental homonymy) but somewhere in between. Such a connection, he had suggested, could be posited either on the basis that these goods are derived from one principle (*ab uno esse*) and contribute towards one end (*ad unum contendere*) or on the basis of an analogical relation whereby they exhibit the same proportion towards each other in the form $A:B = C:D$ (as sight is to the body so the intellect is to the soul).[25] Aristotle himself appears to have regarded these options as two separate alternatives but he had declined to offer any further elucidation on the

[23] *Pol. Lib. Oct.* I.1, p. 8. Cf. *Super Ethica* VII.2, pp. 634, 640.

[24] *Pol. Lib. Oct.* I.1, pp. 8–10. Cf. *Pol. Lib. Oct.* II.1, p. 93; *Super Ethica* VI.1, pp. 392–3, X.15, p. 769.

[25] Aristotle, *Ethics* I.6 1096^{b}26–9; *Recensio pura*, p. 148. For discussion of this particular passage, see Gauthier and Jolif (eds.), *L'Éthique à Nicomaque*, ii. 45–7; Stewart, *Notes on the Nicomachean Ethics of Aristotle*, 86–8. Cf. *Super Ethica* VII.14, p. 580; R.-A. Gauthier, 'Le Cours sur l'*Ethica nova* d'un maître ès arts de Paris, 1235–40', *AHDLMA* 42 (1975), 120–1.

grounds that it was a subject best discussed in detail elsewhere. Albertus Magnus, however, was swift to pick up the hint, once again in the light of an additional Aristotelian text on which he had also completed a commentary in the mid-1260s. This time, Albertus took his cue, not from the *Politics*, but from the *Metaphysics*.[26]

In arguing that there were as many ways of being 'good' as there were of being 'a being', Aristotle had invited a comparison between the nature of goodness in book I of the *Ethics* and the nature of being in book IV of the *Metaphysics*. In seeking to explain the relation which exists between individual good things, therefore, Albertus was naturally drawn to explore the parallel between, on the one hand, Aristotle's description of how 'good' could be used in a variety of senses whilst also deriving from one principle and contributing towards one end and, on the other, Aristotle's description of how 'being' could be used in a variety of senses whilst also referring to one central principle and one particular nature. Thus, in the *Metaphysics*, Aristotle had illustrated the different ways in which something can be said 'to be' by drawing attention to the different ways in which something can be termed 'healthy'. This is a term, he had argued, which can denote something which is either productive of health or indicative of health or preservative of health.[27] That there is still a connection between these different senses of the same term, that they represent more than just a case of accidental homonymy, is indicated by the fact that all these different uses have a single point of reference, namely 'health' or rather the health of one particular individual. For Aristotle, the same principle should also be applied to the term 'being'. Although being is a term which can be predicated of each of the ten categories, all these different senses of the term have a single point of reference, a single focus, namely substance, the first category, in that all the other nine categories (quality, relation, etc.) depend on the prior existence of one particular subject. For there to be a certain quality, a certain relation, and so on, there must first be some substance to which they can all refer—there must first be something in existence which can possess that particular quality, that particular relation, etc.

As far as Albertus Magnus is concerned, Aristotle's account of goodness should follow the same course as Aristotle's account of being. This, at least, is the inference which he seems to have drawn from Aristotle's otherwise elliptical observation that different individual goods are connected to one another by being derived from one principle and contributing towards one end. Of Aristotle's two proffered alternatives for the relation between individual good things in book I of the *Ethics*—by reference to one principle and by analogy—Albertus is certainly more interested in the first than he is in the second. Indeed, Albertus regards the first alternative to be just as much an example of analogical relation (namely analogy of attribution or proportion) as the second (analogy of proportionality). According to Albertus, in fact, the analogical predication of goodness in individual good things is best understood in terms

---

[26] Aristotle, *Metaphysics*, ed. G. Vuillemin-Diem (*Aristoteles Latinus* XXV.3.2); Albertus Magnus, *Metaphysica*, ed. B. Geyer in *Opera Omnia*, vol. xvi.1–2, a work which was composed *c.*1264–7 (Weisheipl, 'Albert's Works', 576).

[27] Aristotle, *Metaphysics* IV.2 1003ª35–ᵇ1. Cf. *Metaphysics* XI.3 1060ᵇ36–1061ª7.

of their relation to a single principle or goal. This single good, the principle and goal of all others, is an essential or primary good towards which each of them is directed. As an example, Albertus cites the similarity between the relation of the direction of a ship to its captain and the direction of a city to its judge. The direction of a ship is different in kind from the direction of a city, and the captain and the judge follow different rules, but both forms of authority share the same proportion, the same relation to one thing. In the case of goodness, Albertus concludes, something is good, better, or best 'in proportion to' the primary good (*primum bonum*) which perfects everything according to its nature. This primary good is a good in itself but it is also the efficient cause of goodness in every good thing. In its ultimate form, according to Albertus, this supreme or primary good is God. God is the supreme good, not by collection or composition (both of which would imply some sort of deficiency in His simplicity), but by attribution in the sense that all the goodness of every good thing primarily belongs to God as its efficient, formal, and final cause.[28] Although Albertus concedes that God cannot be invoked in an exposition of what a pagan philosopher had written, he still maintains that the underlying principle is exactly the same in the *Ethics*. Aristotle's supreme good, he states, is the principle and cause according to which all things are good; it is the ultimate good 'by analogy' in the sense that other things are good with reference to it.[29]

Albertus' familiarity with the text of the *Metaphysics* exercised as significant an influence on his discussion of the common good in his second commentary on the *Ethics* as his familiarity with the text of the *Politics*. In both instances, he was forced to reassess his earlier understanding of the relationship between the common good and the individual. If the *Politics* prompted him to modify his earlier description of the quantitative superiority of the common good, then the *Metaphysics* prompted him to look much more closely at what it means for something to be described as being good in common. It was by analysing Aristotle's account of the relation between particular good things in the light of the *Metaphysics*, therefore, that Albertus removed much of the force of any opposition between individual good and common good. By concentrating on the literal meaning of analogy as proportion, Albertus was able to use a geometrical model as a means of explaining the degrees of proximity which could exist between individual and common good. Perhaps the most revealing aspect of Albertus' revised analysis of the common good, however, is the effect which his familiarity with the *Politics* and the *Metaphysics* had upon his understanding of the nature of the supreme human good of happiness, the good which is common to all individual humans.

It is a striking feature of Albertus' second commentary on the *Ethics* that, whereas Aristotle himself had simply maintained that happiness is a good composed of all those goods which are subordinate to it, Albertus feels obliged to give much greater precision to the nature of this composition. According to Aristotle, the supreme good of humankind is activity in accordance with the complete or perfect virtue which is

---

[28] *Ethica* I.2.1–4, pp. 17–22.   [29] *Ethica* I.2.7, p. 28.

natural to humans, and, if this happiness is the goal of political science, then the ultimate goal of the political community must be the life of virtue.[30] According to Albertus, happiness is therefore a collection of individual goods in the sense of being a potential or virtual whole.[31] This is, perhaps, the most fundamental sense in which Albertus conceives of the relation between common good and individual good in the political community in his second commentary on the *Ethics*. Happiness is composed of goods, not in the sense of being a collection of discrete individuals, but in the sense of being a potential whole in which all the faculties and activities of particular virtues are 'virtually' present and perfected. In producing many things which are causally dependent on it, Albertus explains, something may itself be simple and one, but it can still have, within itself, the virtues of everything which is subordinate to it. Thus, the composition of the ultimate and supreme good does not preclude this good possessing an essentially simple nature. Component goods are present in it, not according to their diversity, but according to their analogy or proportion to the single entity which constitutes the principal and essential cause of their being (that is, their remaining in existence) and their 'virtue' (that is, their capacity to act as a cause).[32] This is therefore the gloss which Albertus gives to Boethius' definition of happiness as the perfection of all good things when they are collected together (*status omnium bonorum congregatione perfectus*).[33]

The relation between happiness and its constituent virtues is a relation which Albertus chooses to analyse in some depth in his second commentary on the *Ethics*. Discussing how happiness is an activity which is produced by exercising the virtues, for example, Albertus suggests that a parallel can be drawn with victory because victory is present in the commander of an army but is made complete by subordinate individuals exercising all their virtues. For this illustration, Albertus is dependent, once again, on the *Metaphysics*, where Aristotle had used victory, the goal of the army, as an analogy for the universe because of the fact that each of them represents a whole which is divided between the ordering of its parts and the good of its commander.[34] As a model for happiness and its component virtues, Albertus supplements the victory of an army with two other metaphors, this time drawn from the *Physics*. In establishing certain basic rules of mechanics, Aristotle had sought to prove that, if a whole force can move a ship a certain distance, it does not necessarily follow that half the force could move it a lesser distance, nor even the same distance given a longer time. If this were to be the case, he had argued, then a single individual would clearly be able to pull the ship over a distance whose proportion to the entire distance

---

[30] *Super Ethica* III.10, p. 191; *Pol. Lib. Oct.* IV.9, p. 376; VII.2, p. 638; VII.6, p. 670.

[31] *Ethica* VI.4.1, p. 456. Cf. *De Bono* I.2.1, p. 23; II.2.10, p. 112.   [32] *Ethica* I.5.1, p. 58.

[33] *Ethica* I.6.2, p. 87; I.6.4, p. 89; Boethius, *Philosophiae Consolatio*, ed. L. Bieler (*CCSL* 94), III.2, p. 38. Cf. *Super Ethica* I.3, p. 17; *Ethica* VI.4.1, p. 456; IX.3.2, p. 587; X.2.1, p. 622; *De Bono* III.3.14, p. 179.

[34] Aristotle, *Metaphysics* XII.10 1075ª11–15; ed. Vuillemin-Diem, p. 266. For Albertus' analysis of this passage, see *Metaphysica*, ed. B. Geyer, XI.2.36, pp. 527–8. Cf. *Super Ethica* VI.2, p. 406; VI.18, p. 510. For the connection between order in the political community and the divine order of the universe, see Aristotle, *Politics* VII.4 1326ª32–4, p. 260.

is the same as the proportion of his individual force to the force of the whole group. The text continues:

This explains the fallacy of Zeno's contention that if a bushel of millet makes a noise in falling, every grain must make its proportionate noise. For it may well be that in no period of time could the one grain make such a stir in the air as the whole measure does. Nor need it be able, if alone, to effect that portion of the total movement which may be assigned to it in accordance with its proportion to the whole mass; for it cannot be regarded, except potentially, as having any separate action in the total movement effected.[35]

Just as the sound made by a falling bushel of millet cannot be made by any one of the grains on its own, so a ship being hauled by a group of people cannot be moved by any one of these people on their own. The movement of the ship is only perfected when all the individuals are ordered towards pulling the first person in the line.[36] In his own exposition of book VII of the *Physics*, Albertus had concluded that the virtue of one part is ordered to a second, the virtue of this second part is ordered to a third, and so on, until the collectivity comprised by these partial virtues constitutes the virtue of the whole. Each individual part only possesses a potential to produce the action of the whole.[37]

Taken together, these three illustrations (the victory of an army, the sound of falling millet, and the movement of a ship) provided Albertus with a principle which became fundamental to his ethical and political thinking—certain types of community can secure a goal by collective action which it is impossible for their individual members to secure on their own. Albertus wrote his commentary on the *Physics* in *c.*1248–50, the same period in which he was delivering his first course of lectures on the *Ethics*. It is noticeable, however, that those passages in these lectures which allude to the collectivities of ship and millet from the *Physics* do *not* include their metaphorical application to the good of the political community. This absence is, of course, readily explicable if it is accepted that this was a period in which Albertus was still wedded to a quantitative notion of the common good. In his first commentary on the *Ethics*, therefore, the principle that a *collectio* can effect something which its individual constituents cannot, is only cited in contexts such as how a disposition of character is produced in an agent by the sequential accumulation of individual actions (just as a sequence of drops has the potential for breaking a rock but only the final drop will effect the complete action, so a sequence of actions produces a disposition even though it is only the final action which perfects the work of its predecessors and actually instils the disposition in the agent).[38]

When Albertus came to comment on the *Politics* in the mid-1260s, the picture changes dramatically. From the outset, it is clear that his rethinking of the qualitative

---

[35] Aristotle, *Physics*, trans. P. H. Wicksteed and F. M. Cornford (2 vols.; Loeb, 1934), VII.5 249^{b}27–250^{a}24, pp. 257–61.

[36] *Ethica* I.5.3, p. 60.

[37] Albertus Magnus, *Physica*, ed. P. Hossfeld, in *Opera Omnia*, vol. iv.1–2, VII.2.vii, p. 547.

[38] *Super Ethica* II.4, p. 106.

difference between common good and individual good extended to comprise the illustrations which could now be considered applicable to the political community. Summarizing Aristotle's critique of Plato's *Republic* in book I, for example, Albertus was faced with the argument that a political community which is reduced to absolute unity will not be a political community, and that it should, instead, be considered as comprising many elements which have functions which differ in kind. In order to prove the point, Aristotle had drawn a contrast between a political community and a military alliance. Whereas a political community, he had argued, is comprised not only of many individuals but of individuals who differ in kind, a military alliance depends on component elements which are different in number alone. This does not affect the usefulness of a military alliance since, in military terms, the many will prevail over the few.[39] Nevertheless, Albertus takes the preponderance of a greater weight as an invitation to discuss the collectivities which had been described in book VII of the *Physics*.

In order to pull a greater weight, Albertus explains, it is not necessary for there to be several things which differ in kind. The only requirement is that there should be a multitude whose collective strength can move the weight, just as a bushel of millet can make a sound which any one grain cannot make on its own and just as a ship can be moved by a group united in their power of pulling when it cannot be moved by any one person pulling on their own.[40] A military alliance, however, is not the same as an army, nor is pulling the weight of a ship the same as sailing that ship on the sea. Both an army and a ship are comprised of individuals who differ in kind as well as quantity—the well-being (*salus*) of a ship is secured by the different functions of oarsmen, lookouts, sailors, and helmsmen, whilst the victory of an army is secured by cooks, armourers, and grooms.[41] Where Aristotle had proceeded to liken the political community to an army or to a ship, therefore, and the ruler of the political community to a commander or a captain,[42] Albertus is happy to accept the force of both comparisons. The military, he writes, is indeed an association (*quaedam communicatio*) which possesses the order of a political community in the sense that the good of the army consists of victory and its commander.[43] Both a ship and an army are associations which display quintessentially 'political' characteristics, namely justice, friendship, and the ordering of individual actions towards a common good.[44]

Once again, it would seem to have been Albertus' familiarity with the *Politics* which enabled him, in his second commentary on the *Ethics*, to invoke the illustrations of falling millet, a hauled ship, and a victorious army in a way which he had studiously avoided in his first commentary on the text. The supreme human good, Albertus writes, is self-sufficient because it contains everything which pertains to happiness, to the perfect and ultimate good. This would not be possible, however, without the collective presence of four virtues, the first three of which are concerned

[39] Aristotle, *Politics* II.2 1261ª22–30, pp. 60–1.
[40] *Pol. Lib. Oct.* II.1, p. 93. Cf. Giles of Rome, *De Regimine Principum* (Venice, 1502), III.i.8; III.ii.3.
[41] e.g. *Pol. Lib. Oct.* III.2, p. 318; III.4, p. 232; *Ethica* I.3.10, p. 42.
[42] e.g. *Pol. Lib. Oct.* VI.5, pp. 594, 596; *Pol. Lib. Oct.* III.4, pp. 232–3; VI.1, p. 564; *Ethica* III.1.8, p. 223.
[43] *Pol. Lib. Oct.* V.6, p. 496.   [44] *Ethica* VIII.3.1, p. 537.

with the different activities of the individual (namely those which are performed on his own, in the household, and in the political community) and the fourth with the ultimate goal of happiness. It is this final virtue, Albertus states, which is represented by the pulling of a ship, the sound of a falling bushel of millet, and the good which is present in the commander of an army. This is a virtue which derives its capacity to act from its individual constituent elements but which is ultimately present in the whole in such a way that it cannot be attributed to the parts on their own. It must therefore be attributed to the parts in the same way that sound is attributed to the grains of millet and movement of the ship to those pulling it—it is attributed to the parts only when they are united in a whole.[45]

In examining the relation between happiness and its constituent virtues in his second commentary on the *Ethics*, Albertus considers one final context in which Aristotle had suggested that the common good could be the same as, but different from, its constituent goods. On this occasion, Albertus' model comes from within the text of the *Ethics* itself. According to book V of the *Ethics*, when justice is exercised towards other human beings, there is a sense in which it is complete or perfect virtue, not a part of virtue but the whole of virtue. According to Aristotle, therefore, justice and virtue represent the same quality of mind in an individual, and differ only according to their essence—when virtue is a disposition it is virtue but when it is exercised towards others it is justice.[46] When Albertus came to discuss justice in his second commentary on the *Ethics*, therefore, he was faced with a formula for the combination of identity and difference in book V which was very close to his own discussion of the common good in book I.

Following the Greek commentary translated by Grosseteste, Albertus explains that justice is the same as virtue in its substance but different in principle (*idem subiecto . . . differens ratione*);[47] it is general or common to the virtues in terms of its subject-matter but it is different in terms of its form (*quantum ad esse quod dat formam*).[48] In defining what this common nature means, Albertus turns once more to the terms of an analogical relation and to the nature of a potential whole. Even if justice is itself not a single subject (it has as many subjects as there are virtues), it is still a single agent and a single goal to which individual virtues are related in their different ways.[49] Justice is complete virtue in the sense that it is a potential whole which is constituted by the virtues, by everything which is capable of being ordered towards happiness.[50] General justice is 'all virtue' because all the acts of virtue are present in it as a group (*congregatio*). This collective presence, however, does not imply the unity of subject which is present in a human being or a soul (or, for that matter, in the simplicity of God) but a unity of form, a form which is shared by the

    [45] *Ethica* I.6.3, p. 88.

    [46] Aristotle, *Ethics* V.1 1129b25–1130a13; *Recensio pura*, ed. Gauthier, p. 229: *est quidem enim eadem, esse autem non idem.*

    [47] *Ethica* V.1.4, p. 337. Cf. *Eustratii et Michaelis et Anonyma in Ethica Nicomachea Commentaria*, p. 211; *Aristotelis Opera cum Averrois Commentaria*, iii, fos. 234r–235v.

    [48] *Super Ethica* V.3, p. 323.   [49] *Ethica* V.1.4, p. 338.

    [50] *Ethica* V.1.2, p. 334; V.2.2, p. 341.

virtues and which, in a certain sense, makes them all either species or objects subject to those species.[51]

According to Albertus, it is the essence of justice to concern itself *both* with what is common *and* with what is particular or individual. The existence of the human community depends on 'communication', on the exchange of individual possessions which alone makes self-sufficiency possible, and, as such, there must be a principle which concerns itself with what is in common and which determines the fairness of this exchange and distribution. This principle of ordering what is personal towards what is in common is the principle of right (*ius*) or justice. It is a moral order, according to Albertus, in the sense that the good of an individual is ordered towards the good of many which is, in turn, ordered towards the good of the city and towards the 'more divine' good of the people. It is this ordering which constitutes the form or principle which Albertus considers to be peculiar to legal justice. The subject-matter of such justice is general in that it comprises all those goods (whether material possessions or individual virtues) which are ordered towards the community in the sense of being shared or distributed according to geometric or arithmetic proportion.[52] It is general because it comprises all those things which create and preserve happiness and all of its parts, whether they are essential to it or are simply instrumental (by being ordered to the happiness of citizens in the political community).[53]

The successive accounts of the relation between the good of the human community and the good of the individual which Albertus provides in his two commentaries on the *Ethics* reveal the developments in understanding which were brought about by his increasing familiarity with the *Politics* and the *Metaphysics*. Albertus' analysis of an 'Aristotelian' common good came to depend upon his grasp of two fundamental issues—how to describe the analogical predication of goodness in individual goods and how to define the superiority of a common good which was qualitatively distinct from the individual goods of which it was composed but with which it was also identical. If the influence of Aristotle's *Politics* is evident from the way in which the good of the human community comes to be discussed in terms of a difference in kind rather than just quantity, then the influence of the *Metaphysics* (and the *Physics*) is evident from the way in which it comes to be discussed in terms of the nature of a potential whole.

Army, ship, millet, and justice are certainly not the only Aristotelian metaphors with which Albertus analyses the collective nature of happiness in the political community. The more conventional classical and Christian image of a body comprised of limbs or members is also used as a means of illustrating the diversity of function which exists amongst different individuals and the mutual cooperation which is therefore required to complete something which cannot be secured by any one individual on their own.[54] Nevertheless, in Albertus' mind, the collectivities of army, ship, millet, and justice

---

[51] *Ethica* V.1.4, p. 337. Cf. *Super Ethica* VI.6, p. 429; *De Bono* V.3.1–2, pp. 290–7; V.4.1–2, pp. 300–1; V.4.6, p. 304.

[52] *Super Ethica* V.2, pp. 312, 315. Cf. *Ethica* V.3.11, p. 382; *Pol. Lib. Oct.* VII.2, p. 640.

[53] *Ethica* V.1.3, p. 335. Cf. *Super Ethica* V.3, p. 323; V.4, p. 325.

[54] *Pol. Lib. Oct.* I.1, pp. 14–15; VI.5, pp. 594, 596. Cf. *Ethica* V.2.9, p. 357.

clearly served to demonstrate the peculiar quality of the connection between the construction of the political community and the construction of a potential whole.[55]

The success of Albertus' analysis of the relationship between the common good and the individual good clearly turns on the cogency of his use of these four metaphors—the relationship between military victory and the soldiers of an army, the sound of a falling bushel and the movement of its individual grains, the motion of a ship and the actions of the individuals moving it, and the generality of justice and the particularity of its constituent virtues. Each one of these relationships, in their different way, represents a common activity which is only made possible through the collective action of a group of individual parts united in a whole. Each one of these relationships, however, also presented Albertus with difficulties of their own when they were used to describe how the individual good and the common good are the same. These difficulties are best illustrated by charting Albertus' attempts to apply his abstract theory of justice and virtue to the concrete political action of ruling the political community and laying down one's life on its behalf.

In both his first and second commentaries on the *Ethics*, Albertus expounds the principle of identity in the context of Aristotle's need to prove that the human good really is the goal of political science. In his second commentary, however, the issue is raised in the more precise context of identifying the common good with the good, not of any individual in the community, but of its ruler. Aristotle had opened book VII of the *Politics* with the categoric assertion that the life of happiness is the best life for the political community as well as for the individual. There can be no doubt, he insisted, that the happiness of the individual is the same as that of the political community.[56] Viewed from this perspective, for the individual good to be described as one and the same as the common good in book I of the *Ethics* may appear to be a straightforward equation. For Aristotle, however, this was far from being the whole story. Since one of his working assumptions in the *Politics* is that not all the members of a political community will be completely good people, even in the best constitution, he had spent some time considering whether the virtue of the good citizen is the same as the virtue of the good man. In book III of the *Politics*, Aristotle had concluded not only that the good citizen is not *necessarily* the same as the good man (since the excellence of the citizen is relative to the quality of the government to which he is subject) but also that, even in the best constitution, the degree of goodness which is appropriate to each citizen will be dependent on the function which that citizen fulfils within their community. This did not mean that, in the best constitution, the virtue of the good citizen is *never* the same as the virtue of the good man. It did mean, however, that this equation will occur only when the citizen is the ruler, since the freedom which is involved in ruling presupposes the exercise of a certain sort of practical wisdom which is not required in being a subject.[57]

---

[55] e.g. *Ethica* VI.1.3, p. 397.

[56] Aristotle, *Politics* VII.1–2 1323ᵃ14–1324ᵃ23, pp. 238–46. Cf. VII.3 1325ᵇ14–33, pp. 255–6; VII.15 1334ᵃ11–13, p. 311.

[57] Aristotle, *Politics* III.4–5 1276ᵇ16–1278ᵇ6, pp. 161–73.

Having read book VII of the *Politics*, therefore, when Albertus Magnus came to consider the principle of identity between individual and common good, he was well aware that to maintain that the happiness of the individual consists of the activity of virtue meant maintaining that the activity of virtue is also the happiness of the political community. The happiness of humans considered individually (*singulariter*), he concludes, is one and the same (*una et eadem*) as their happiness considered collectively (*in communi*) in the political community.[58] Having read book III of the *Politics*, however, Albertus was also aware that Aristotle's equation of the virtue of the good man with the virtue of the good ruler meant that the common good of the community could also be identified with the individual good of its ruler alone. Once the common good was defined as the life of virtue, in fact, it took only a small step to conclude that the ruler exemplifies the common good whilst his subjects do so only 'in proportion to' their ability and function. According to Aristotle, the difference between the virtue of the ruler and the virtue of the ruled is a difference of quantity but also a difference in kind—whereas the ruler must possess moral virtue in its entirety (*perfecta moralis virtus*), his subjects need only have the degree of virtue which is appropriate for the fulfilment of their specific functions.[59]

Book III of the *Politics* had significant implications for the relationship between the individual and the common good. When Albertus came to discuss Aristotle's argument in his commentary, in fact, he makes an explicit cross-reference to the principles of identity and superiority in book I of the *Ethics*.[60] In his second commentary on the *Ethics*, therefore, it was only natural for him to gloss the principle of identity in terms of the relationship between the virtue of the good citizen and the virtue of the good man qua ruler. Happiness is the perfect activity of the soul in every virtue but this perfection derives from the virtues which are under its command. It is therefore like victory—a good which is present in the commander of an army but which is only effected through other disciplines such as provisioning, marshalling, and armouring.[61] The political good is the activity of happiness in the *res publica*. Although it is present in a single individual—as an activity of the person involved in political life—it is composed of the various virtues and powers which are ordered towards that person, each one of which possesses the principle of goodness by virtue of the relation which it has to him.[62] If the individual good is the same as the common good, then this equation is only fully realized in the person of the ruler; for other members of the political community, the identity is simply proportional or analogous.

Aristotle's insistence in the *Politics* on the identity which exists between common good and individual good in the person of the ruler raised one other important question. Given that the individual good is, in this instance, the same as the common good, which of them has the greater priority in the intention of the ruler? Does the

---

[58] *Pol. Lib. Oct.* VII.2, pp. 632–3. Cf. III.4, p. 231; VII.11, p. 708; VII.13, p. 719; VIII.1, p. 756.
[59] Aristotle, *Politics* I.13 1260ᵃ14–20, pp. 53–4.   [60] *Pol. Lib. Oct.* I.9, p. 79.
[61] *Ethica* I.3.10, p. 42.   [62] *Ethica* VII.2.1, p. 500.

ruler aim to secure the common good in the expectation that his own individual good will result, or does he aim to secure his individual good in the knowledge that it is the same as the common good? Albertus had already followed Aristotle in making the common good central to the classification of the various forms of government to which the human community could be subject. The common good served, in particular, as the point of distinction between three good forms (kingship, aristocracy, timocracy) and three bad (tyranny, oligarchy, democracy). Albertus first came across this argument in a somewhat abbreviated form in book VIII of the *Ethics* but it was in the *Politics* that it had emerged as a clear litmus test for distinguishing correct from perverse forms of government.[63] Albertus' commentary on the *Politics* accordingly sets it out in some detail. Aristocracy, he remarks, is ordered towards the common good of the life of virtue and requires ruling power to be given to each individual in accordance with their moral virtue.[64] Oligarchy, meanwhile, is the rule of the rich few in pursuit of their own self-interest. Democracy, likewise, is the self-interested rule of those in power, in this case of the many individuals who act, not as individuals, but as a single group in pursuit of liberty. As such, democracy is defined by Albertus as the tyranny of the people, a perverse form of government which (as he suggests on more than one occasion) is characteristic of the city-states of Lombardy.[65] Timocracy or polity, on the other hand, represents a mixed constitution, the rule of the many acting as individuals in pursuit of the common interest, some of them exercising the life of virtue themselves, others simply providing the instrumental goods which are necessary for the activity of happiness.[66]

Aristotle's distinction between kingship and tyranny provides Albertus with the sharpest of contrasts between common good and individual self-interest. Whereas a ruler works for the common benefit of his people and a king aims to secure what is beneficial to his subjects,[67] a tyrant has the simple objective of providing what is beneficial to himself, acting and legislating for his own advantage rather than that of his people.[68] The best form of government is therefore kingship, whilst the worst is tyranny. The king lacks nothing. He is self-sufficient in every good, he excels in virtue, and he possesses in abundance all its instrumental accoutrements (wealth, glory, and friends). As a result, the king will extort nothing from his subjects but will use whatever payments or subsidies he does receive for the benefit of the *res publica*,

---

[63] *Pol. Lib. Oct.* III.5, p. 234; III.8, p. 279.   [64] *Pol. Lib. Oct.* III.4, p. 231.

[65] *Pol. Lib. Oct.* II.9, p. 181; IV.4, p. 345; IV.11, p. 397; IV.12, pp. 405, 409; V.7, pp. 510, 519; VI.4, pp. 585, 589–90. Cf. C. Martin, 'The Commentaries on the Politics of Aristotle in the Late Thirteenth and Fourteenth Centuries, with Reference to the Thought and Political Life of the Time', D.Phil. thesis (Oxford, 1949); id., 'Some Medieval Commentaries on Aristotle's Politics', *History*, 36 (1951), 29–54.

[66] *Ethica* VIII.3.2, p. 540. Cf. *Pol. Lib. Oct.* II.3, p. 127.

[67] *Super Ethica* V.9, p. 353; VIII.10, p. 633.

[68] *Super Ethica* IV.3, p. 230; IV.4, p. 240; VIII.10, pp. 632–3; VIII.11, p. 637. Cf. Aristotle, *Politics* IV.10 1295ᵃ19–22, pp. 415–16. Although the association of tyrannical government with self-interest was not without precedent in medieval authorities (e.g. Basil of Caesarea, *Homiliae* V.2, *PG* 31, col. 1763), the prevailing association was with the rule of will (*voluntas*) rather than law (e.g. John of Salisbury, *Politcraticus* IV.1, p. 235). This is a definition which Albertus himself continues to use (e.g. *Pol. Lib. Oct.* IV.4, p. 347).

thereby aiming to secure in every area the common good of his people. The tyrant, by contrast, orders everything for his own benefit, neglecting and thereby harming the whole community in pursuit of his own profit and private advantage.[69]

If the opposition of self-interest and common good is most marked in the person of the tyrant, however, Albertus is still left with the task of harmonizing individual good and common good in the person of the king. In equating the good ruler with the virtuous individual, Albertus argues that the good of the political community is essentially (*per se*) ordered towards the community but is also accidentally (*per accidens*) ordered towards the good of the particular individual who occupies the position of authority in that community. The art of politics, Albertus explains, like other branches of knowledge such as medicine or physical training, is ordered towards a common good and, as such, the authority which is exercised in all three arts, by the ruler, the doctor, and the trainer, is exercised for the good of the ruler/ doctor/ trainer as well as of the subject/patient/athlete. However, whereas the connection of the common good to the latter is essential (*per se*), its connection to the former is accidental (*per accidens*).[70] Aristotle's own example in the *Politics* had been the ship—the captain is a captain but he is also a member of the crew and, as such, although he gives commands to the oarsmen and to the sailors, he steers for the common benefit of the ship and of himself. The difference in the captain's motivation towards his own benefit and towards the benefit of the ship, Albertus explains, lies in the fact that he orders his authority 'essentially' towards the good of those subject to him but only 'accidentally' towards himself insofar as he shares in the same common benefit. Albertus adds an example of his own from rather closer to home. Teaching, he suggests, is a discipline in which the teacher benefits the student *per se*. In doing so, however, the teacher also benefits himself *per accidens*. In both cases, the consequence for the relationship of the ruler to the common good of his subjects is the same—the virtuous individual wills the common good *per se* and his own good *per accidens*.[71]

When Albertus came to comment on the *Ethics* for a second time, therefore, he possessed, in the *Politics*, a clear and straightforward model for the identity of the individual good and the common good and the priority which should be accorded to them by each person—the common good is to be sought *per se*, the individual good *per accidens*. What is so intriguing about his second commentary on the *Ethics*, however, is that this is a model which Albertus found difficult to apply to what Aristotle had actually written in the *Ethics*.

When Aristotle had discussed the four cardinal virtues, he presented them in the sequence fortitude, temperance, justice, and prudence, an arrangement which immediately prompts Albertus to ask whether this order should, in fact, have read justice, prudence, fortitude, and then temperance. Since justice and prudence concern the good of people in general, whilst fortitude and temperance concern the good

---

[69] *Pol. Lib. Oct.* II.3, p. 128; III.4, p. 233; III.5, pp. 234–5, 237; III.8, p. 281; III.9, p. 287; IV.5, p. 353; IV.8, pp. 369–70; IV.9, pp. 375–80; V.7, pp. 512, 520. Cf. *Ethica* V.2.9, p. 355; V.3.1, p. 365; VIII.3.2, pp. 540–1.
[70] Aristotle, *Politics* III.6 1278^{b}37–1279^{a}8, p. 176.   [71] *Pol. Lib. Oct.* III.4, pp. 230–3.

of an individual, Albertus floats the possibility that Aristotle should have considered
justice and prudence *before* considering fortitude and temperance because the good
of a people (*bonum gentis*) is better (*melius*) than the good of an individual. In the
event, Albertus ends up justifying Aristotle's original sequence on the grounds that
to give priority to fortitude and temperance does not indicate their superiority in an
order of merit but their priority in time—no individual can be correctly ordered
towards other people if he is not already correctly ordered towards himself.[72] Much
the same principle is employed when Albertus discusses the relative merits of Aristotle's two types of practical wisdom—prudence and political prudence—virtues
which had been described in book VI of the *Ethics* as identical in quality of mind but
different in essence.[73] Prudence, Albertus explains, directs individuals in their own
private actions but also in those actions which concern other humans and thereby the
rest of society. In order to be fully credited with the virtue of prudence, therefore, an
individual must perform good actions insofar as he is an individual in his own right
but also insofar as he is a member of a household or of a political community.[74] For
Aristotle, it had been Pericles and people like him who best represented this combination, perceiving what was good for themselves but also what was good for others.[75]
When Albertus compares Aristotle's two types of prudence, therefore, political prudence is presented as having the greater primacy (*principalior*), and for the same
reason which had justified the order of the cardinal virtues—the good of the community is more divine than the individual good. Pericles and his ilk, Albertus writes,
order their personal good towards the divine good of the household and the (even
more) divine good of the political community.[76] As with all the moral virtues,
Albertus concludes, the more they secure the good of the community, the greater the
perfection which they possess.[77]

Having used the common good as the criterion with which to rank the moral
virtues, Albertus then queries the status of bravery within this order on the grounds

---

[72] *Super Ethica* III.11, p. 196. A similar line of argument is employed for the virtue of liberality, defined
by Albertus as giving away what is superfluous, what is not necessary to requirements. Humans, he
explains, are ordered both towards themselves and towards other individuals but it is only when they possess sufficient goods for their own individual existence that they should administer any surplus for the
conservation of the species (*Super Ethica* IV.1, p. 224. Cf. *Super Ethica* IV.6, pp. 247–8).

[73] Aristotle, *Ethics* VI.8 1141ᵇ23–4. Cf. R. Lambertini, 'Individuelle und politische Klugheit in den
mittelalterlichen Ethikkommentaren', *Miscellanea Mediaevalia*, 24 (1996), 464–78.

[74] *Super Ethica* VI.11, p. 469; *Ethica* VI.1.24, pp. 441–2.

[75] Aristotle, *Ethics* VI.5 1140ᵇ7–11.

[76] *Super Ethica* VI.11, p. 470; *Ethica* VI.1.10, p. 418.

[77] For the competing claims of justice and prudence to be the most perfect of the virtues, each of them
securing the common good, see *Super Ethica* V.3, p. 321; IX.2, p. 660; *Ethica* I.6.8, p. 95; I.7.15, p. 129;
I.9.1, p. 139; V.1.4, p. 337. For the claims of prudence to comprehend all the other virtues, to be 'common'
to all the virtues, see *Super Ethica* V.6, p. 336. Albertus appeals to the same military analogy—prudence is
like a military commander in the sense that, although the *dux* is self-sufficient in his own activity of ruling,
he still has to order his soldiers towards the other activities and duties undertaken by the army. The one
difference between prudence and military command is the fact that the activity of prudence is itself the
goal of such actions, whereas the activity of the commander is ordered towards a further goal, namely
victory (*Super Ethica* VI.7, pp. 437–9).

that fortitude might be termed a virtue which is concerned, not with the common good, but with its practitioner's own individual good. Albertus' immediate response is to maintain that bravery is, in fact, a virtue whose exercise is, by definition, intimately bound up with the common good. In his view, fortitude amply fulfils both of the qualities which Aristotle had himself listed as essential characteristics of virtue in book II of the *Ethics*—it must concern itself with what is difficult and what is good.[78] Not only is bravery concerned with the most difficult of situations—conflict in battle—but it is also concerned with the most superlative of goods—the good of the human community, a good which is better than the good of a single individual. Indeed, Albertus argues that, in causing the individual to fight for the *res publica* or, more generally, to perform any action by which the 'community' is protected and preserved, the virtue of bravery contributes more to the common good than even the individual virtues of prudence or justice. In fact, it is only through the exercise of fortitude that justice and the *status rei publicae* can be maintained.[79] The preservation and defence of the common good are thus essential to Albertus' definition of bravery.[80] Brave individuals fight for the good of the political community, the well-being of the *res publica*, the freedom of their fellow-citizens, the observance of the laws, and the integrity of virtue.[81]

In justifying the position of bravery in the hierarchy of the virtues, Albertus does not emphasize the role of the common good at the expense of the individual's own good. Indeed, by acknowledging that bravery is ultimately exercised for the sake of the good of virtue,[82] Albertus is drawn into a detailed discussion of what motivates an individual to perform the quintessentially brave action, namely the sacrifice of all one's worldly goods, including one's life, for the sake of the political community. In the process, Albertus reveals just why he found it so difficult to transfer to the *Ethics* the principle which he had found so useful in the *Politics*—the individual aims at the common good *per se* and his own good *per accidens*. The question which Albertus considers is straightforward. When a virtuous individual performs an act of self-sacrifice, is his bravery prompted (i) by the common good, (ii) by his individual good as well as by the good of the community, or (iii) by the individual good more than the good of the community?

In book III of the *Ethics*, Aristotle had distinguished between two types of individual good which could motivate an act of bravery, thereby separating 'true' bravery from what he termed 'political' bravery. True bravery, he had argued, is performed for the sake of virtue. Political bravery, on the other hand, describes an action which is performed for the sake of the personal honour and glory which the individual will then receive from the other members of the political community.[83] Whilst Albertus accepts this restriction on the sort of individual good which should

---

[78] Aristotle, *Ethics* II.3 1105ᵃ8–10.   [79] *Super Ethica* III.8, p. 180.
[80] *Super Ethica* V.4, p. 326; *Ethica* I.4.2, p. 52. Cf. *Pol. Lib. Oct.* II.8, p. 175.
[81] *Super Ethica* V.15, p. 380; *Ethica* III.2.6, p. 243; X.2.4, p. 630.
[82] *Super Ethica* III.10, pp. 190–1; *Ethica* III.2.7–10, pp. 246–9.
[83] Aristotle, *Ethics* III.8 1116ᵃ17–29.

inspire virtuous action, he still proceeds to consider whether even an act of true bravery is a good for the virtuous individual (*bonum sibi*) when, on the face of it, the performance of such an action simply results in his death. In his first commentary on the *Ethics*, Albertus' initial response had been to agree that, insofar as the virtuous individual is considered in his own right, it is true to say that his death is not a good for himself. At the same time, however, he had also insisted that, insofar as the individual is a member of the political community, it does rebound to his own good when human society is enabled to remain secure in its pursuit of virtue.[84] By the time Albertus was commenting on book V of the *Ethics*, he was taking a slightly different tack but his underlying position is the same. If the virtuous individual were to suffer no harm to himself by allowing the community to be damaged, then he would indeed be under a greater obligation to secure his own well-being at the expense of the well-being of his fellow-humans. In Albertus' eyes, however, this can only be a hypothetical scenario. In his opinion, it would simply be impossible for the good of the community to be neglected without the individual thereby incurring damage and dishonour to his own good. As a result, it must be in the virtuous individual's own interest to prefer to die for the sake of such well-being, to lay down his life for the good of the community.[85]

An insistence that bravery is in the interest of the virtuous individual even when it leads to his own death is expressed one more time when Albertus comments on book IX of the *Ethics*. Leaving aside the possibility that the individual will receive a reward in the next life (a belief, incidentally, which Albertus does not restrict to the Christian faith),[86] he suggests that Aristotle's definition of bravery entails two other possibilities for individual reward. The first is the reward of glory, of living on in the memory of one's fellow-humans (a definition which would seem to be indistinguishable from the sort of bravery which Aristotle had already dismissed as 'political' bravery); the second is the reward which the individual derives from preferring to die for the freedom of his community rather than to live with the dishonour of not having done so. It is this second reward which is closest to Aristotle's own argument, that the truly virtuous individual will prefer, in death, a once-and-for-all and supreme act of virtue to a life which would otherwise consist only of many moderately good actions. In sacrificing his own good for his friends and for his community, the individual secures his primary goal, the supreme activity of virtue, on account of which he should be prepared to neglect all other lesser goods.[87] Indeed, in this sense, the virtuous individual should ideally have the greatest love for himself, even if, in other circumstances or within other terms of reference, he should not.[88] This is the solution which Albertus carries forward to his second commentary on the *Ethics*. The virtuous individual should risk his life for the sake of the good of virtue because he should have a higher regard for the good of virtue than for the good of his own temporal existence. To die in such circumstances is, Albertus states, more

[84] *Super Ethica* III.11, p. 196.   [85] *Super Ethica* V.3, p. 322.   [86] *Super Ethica* III.11, p. 196.
[87] *Super Ethica* IX.9, p. 687.   [88] *Super Ethica* IX.9, p. 685.

beneficial to the individual (*utilior sibi*) than to continue living but in the absence of moral worth (*dignitas*).[89]

Albertus' analysis of bravery and self-sacrifice is, in many ways, a test case for his insistence on the principle of identity between the common good and the individual good, not least because of the central position which this debate had occupied in the course of Aristotle's own argument in the *Ethics*. As soon as Aristotle had defined justice as the exercise of complete virtue towards other humans, the relationship between individual humans became central to his understanding of the nature of happiness as the life of virtue. Aristotle had accordingly followed his discussion of justice in book V of the *Ethics* with an extended treatment of friendship in books VIII and IX. For Albertus, this train of thought was bound up, in the first instance, with the fulfilment or perfection of humankind's social and political nature. The human good of happiness, he argues, can only be considered in its entirety as the self-sufficient life which is led in the company of parents, children, wife, friends, and fellow-citizens.[90] The progression from solitary self to family unit, and from family unit to political community, is therefore a hierarchy of increasing perfection—the individual and private good is ordered towards the good of the household, and the good of the household is then ordered towards the good of the political community.[91] Humans can be considered, therefore, either in themselves or as social and political participants.[92] If ethics is concerned with the perfection of a virtuous individual in himself (*in seipso*), then politics is concerned with this perfection insofar as that individual is a natural member of a household and of a political association.[93]

For Albertus, however, the natural sociability of humans is also a question of the intrinsically communicative quality of goodness itself. This was the principle, after all, on which Eustratius had relied in order to explain Aristotle's use of the comparative term *melius* and which was drawn, ultimately, from pseudo-Dionysius. In the second instance, therefore, Aristotle's movement from justice in book V of the *Ethics* to friendship in books VIII and IX was, for Albertus, an expression of a principle which was inherent in all goodness, namely that it should communicate its good just as the sun extends its light to all things.[94] For Albertus, the human good of the political community is no exception to this rule. Since every good is communicative of its own goodness and extends this goodness to others, the 'communion' which defines the political 'community' must be the diffusion of goodness to other people.[95] If

---

[89] *Ethica* IV.2.5, p. 302.   [90] *Ethica* I.6.3, p. 88. Cf. Aristotle, *Ethics* I.7 1097ᵇ8–11.

[91] *Ethica* VI.2.24, p. 442.

[92] Albertus also distinguishes between the individual and the person but this is not in order to contrast the solitary self with the political self. The force of this distinction is, instead, to separate the private individual from the public office-holder (*Super Ethica* IV.1, p. 223; X.16, p. 772; *Ethica* IV.1.11, p. 291; *Pol. Lib. Oct.* II.5, p. 144; V.1, p. 428).

[93] Albertus Magnus, *Pol. Lib. Oct.* I.1, p. 6. For the division between, and the relative ordering of, the respective spheres of ethics, economics, and politics, see *Ethica* I.1.7, p. 16; I.3.1, p. 29; VI.2.24, p. 442.

[94] pseudo-Dionysius, *De Divinis Nominibus* IV.1, ed. Chevallier, in *Dionysiaca*, i. 146–7. Cf. Albertus Magnus, *Ethica* I.2.6, p. 26; IV.1.2, p. 275; IX.3.2, p. 588. More generally, see Tugwell, *Albert and Thomas*, 39–129; H. F. Dondaine, *Le Corpus Dionysien de l'université de Paris au XIIIe siècle* (Rome, 1953).

[95] *Ethica* IV.1.2, p. 675.

humankind is by nature a political animal, therefore, then this should be understood in the sense not only that it is intrinsic to the perfection of human nature to live together in a life of virtue but also that it is intrinsic to the nature of being good for this goodness to be communicated to others. It is this communication in the activity of virtue which, for Albertus, lies at the heart of Aristotle's account of the exercise and operation of friendship.[96]

According to book VIII of the *Ethics*, true friendship is the friendship which exists between those virtuous individuals who will one another's good. Their motive in so doing is not the benefit which each of them thereby acquires for themselves (although Aristotle had not denied that this was a natural consequence of their relationship) but the good of the other person. Thus, although friendship results in reciprocal benefit, it is, in Aristotle's view, more of the essence of friendship to love than to be loved.[97] In any association in which humans communicate with one another (Aristotle's own examples were, once again, a ship and an army), there must be a principle of justice but also a principle of friendship. Individual sailors and individual soldiers, Albertus comments, order their victories towards the common good of the whole. If the presence of a common good presupposes the operation of justice, however, the fact that each individual wills this good for another person must also presuppose the operation of friendship. Friendship must therefore exist *wherever* individuals associate for some common good and order their actions towards it.[98]

Although true friendship, for Aristotle, is ideally a relationship between people who are equal in their virtue, he had accepted that it could also cover relations of inequality—between parents and children, husbands and wives, old people and young people, rulers and subjects. In these cases, the love which is demonstrated by one individual for another will necessarily be in proportion to the other person's virtue and function.[99] Since a human community, by definition, comprises parents and children, husbands and wives, old people and young people, rulers and subjects, a political community will necessarily be characterized by the friendship of unequals as well as equals, but the same principle will apply—individuals will love the good of other individuals in proportion to their virtue, function, and worth. The connection between justice and friendship is therefore particularly close. As Albertus puts it, friendship, like justice, is concerned with a common good, a good in which many individuals are associated in accordance with their individual worth.[100] Just like justice, the goodness which is common to all friendship is not common in genus or species but common in proportion.[101]

It was at this stage in the argument that Aristotle's account of friendship had run up against the principle of identity between individual and common good. If friendship originates in love of self, and if the goal of human life is for each individual to live a life of virtue, how can such reflexivity be squared with the love which the

---

[96] *Ethica* IX.3.2–3, pp. 588–92.

[97] Aristotle, *Ethics* VIII.3–4 1156ᵇ7–1157ᵇ5; VIII.8 1159ᵃ12–1159ᵇ24.　　　[98] *Ethica* VIII.3.1, p. 537.

[99] Aristotle, *Ethics* VIII.7 1158ᵇ11–1159ᵃ12.　　　[100] *Ethica* VIII.3.5, p. 545.

[101] *Super Ethica* IX.8, p. 681.

individual must also have for the common good which is the goal of friendship, the common good which is goodness in itself (*bonum simpliciter*)? In analysing the nature of self-love, Aristotle had certainly been careful to distinguish the self-love which is characteristic of the good person from the self-love which is characteristic of the bad. True self-love is ordered towards the good of the virtuous individual but also towards the good of family, friends, citizens, and fellow-humans. Its supreme expression is the sacrifice which the virtuous individual should be prepared to make of all his worldly goods (be these wealth, power, honour, property, and even life itself) in order to secure the good of others, the common good. In making this sacrifice, however, Aristotle had insisted that what the individual is thereby choosing is the greater good for himself, the greatest of goods, his own greatest good of moral virtue.[102] By using the term *maius bonum* Aristotle effectively presented Albertus with a dilemma—how could the application of these comparative and superlative terms to the individual good in book IX be made consistent with the attribution of superiority to the common good in book I? Which has the greater relative priority in the intention of the virtuous individual who performs an act of self-sacrifice, securing his own greatest good or securing the common good of others? If the human good of virtue is now the good which the individual secures for himself, what is the precise nature of the common good of the political community for which this sacrifice is made?

Albertus' initial solution to this problem is to insist on a more precise definition of 'the individual'. In expounding Aristotle's account of self-love, Albertus maintains that, if an individual continually strives to perform all those good and just actions which are dictated by virtue, he will necessarily acquire for himself absolute good-ness, the good which is good in itself (*bonum quod secundum seipsum bonum est*). Legit-imate self-love, therefore, consists of securing, for oneself and for one's own sake, the greatest goods (*optima et ea quae sunt maxime bona*), the goods which are absolutely good (*bona simpliciter*). Albertus accordingly follows Aristotle in defining 'self' in a strict sense as the principal quality which determines what it is to be an individual human being, namely the intellect of the soul. This is the 'self' which is loved and nurtured by legitimate self-love. The truly good individual will therefore exhibit the greatest love for his intellect, not in order to possess a particular good here and now, but in order to possess absolute truth and absolute goodness. Indeed, if such love were to be exhibited by every human being, Albertus suggests, if every individual were to strive for absolute goodness and to perform the best actions, then all those goods which are necessary for life would be present for everyone collectively. Each individual would thereby secure those goods which are the greatest goods for him in terms of his own nature, namely his intellect. This is the good of each individual in the strictest sense—the virtue which is natural to the human intellect.

Where, then, does this leave the common good? It is at this point that Albertus starts to modify his earlier definition of the common good and introduces a critical

---

[102] Aristotle, *Ethics* IX.8 1169ª11–b2; Mercken (ed.), *The Greek Commentaries*, pp. 274–80; *Aristotelis Opera cum Averrois Commentaria* iii fos. 137v–138v. Cf. Aristotle, *Ethics* VIII.7 1159ª10–12.

distinction between the common good as the supreme good of virtue and the common good as the consequence of individual virtuous behaviour for the rest of the community. To demonstrate true self-love, Albertus argues, is to be essentially good and, by doing what is essentially good, the individual will thereby benefit both himself and others. By choosing what is best, the individual chooses what is best in its own right as well as what is best for himself. Where Aristotle had stated that the virtuous individual should perform many actions for the sake of friends and country, therefore, actions which may include giving up money, property, honours, and even life itself, Albertus states that the virtuous individual should do so in order to procure the good of virtue for himself (*procurans sibi ipsi bonum*), the good which is good for himself in terms of his true self, his intellect. Such a sacrifice will, it is true, also secure a great good for others, be it the general welfare (*salus rei publicae*), the well-being of the political community (*salus patriae*), or the well-being of one's friends (*salus amicorum*). Nevertheless, this common good of 'well-being', although considerable, is small in comparison to the great good which the individual himself secures by being the cause of such well-being to others (*salus omnium*).

The good which the virtuous individual secures for himself, in short, is essential goodness, the good in itself, a good which is the greatest good and greater than any other good (*id . . . quod simpliciter bonum est, maius est et maximum: et hoc superbonus tribuit sibi ipsi*). It is the greatest good for the individual that he should be the cause of preserving everyone else in goodness (*causa salutis omnium in bono*).[103] Albertus understands Aristotle to mean that the individual secures the common human good for himself at the same time as the rest of the political community is enabled to pursue it. He thereby produces an alternative definition for the good of the political community in book IX, a definition which is different from the supreme good of virtue and happiness in book I. It is now well-being (*salus*), the benefit of other individuals, the condition of health and security within which the life of virtue can be pursued.[104] This is not a common good which is greater, better, and more divine than the individual good; it is a common good of material security which results from the individual's pursuit of his own greatest good, the supreme good of virtue and happiness.

Albertus Magnus provides a particularly rich and detailed insight into the initial stages of the scholastic understanding of an Aristotelian conception of the common good. Book I of the *Ethics* presented two fundamental points for discussion—how to reconcile a principle of identity with a principle of superiority and how to apply the analogical predication of goodness in general to the supreme human good, to the goodness which is common to all individual humans. A comparison of Albertus' first commentary on the *Ethics* in *c*.1248–52 with his second commentary in *c*.1267–70 reveals just how much of the increasing sophistication of Albertus' answer to these

[103] *Ethica* IX.3.1, pp. 584–6.
[104] For the definition of *utilitas aliorum* as either *salus animae* or *salus corporis*, see e.g. Augustine, *De Musica* VI.14.45 (*PL* 32, cols. 1186–7).

questions was due to his reading of the *Politics* and the *Metaphysics* in the mid-1260s. By exploring the parallels between goodness and existence, Albertus was able to use analogical predication as a means of explaining that individual goods are related by being derived from one principle and directed towards one goal. By using the metaphors of the victory of an army, the sound of falling millet, the movement of a ship, and the relationship between general justice and its constituent virtues, Albertus was able to describe how human happiness is an activity made possible by the collective action of individuals united in a whole.

At the same time, however, Albertus' investigation of the relation between common good and individual good also exposed significant tensions within an Aristotelian conception of the common good. In book I of the *Ethics*, the common good is described as the same as the individual good because the individual good of virtue is the same as the supreme good of human happiness. It is described as superior to the individual good, meanwhile, because it represents a potential whole which is made up of individual virtues. In book IX of the *Ethics*, the argument moves from an abstract discussion of individual virtue to the practical reality of an individual citizen, from happiness and goodness in general to the good of a political community. In the process, Albertus is forced to consider an alternative model. In analysing bravery and self-sacrifice, he continues to describe the individual good as the same as the supreme good (absolute goodness, good in itself). However, this good is now considered to have a claim on the individual which is prior to the well-being (*salus*) of the political community which will result from his concentration on virtue.

Although there is no necessary inconsistency between these two arguments, it is still striking that, in order to cater for the explicit superiority of good for the individual in book IX of the *Ethics*, Albertus has to make room for a more limited, even material, definition of good for the community than the one which he had provided in book I. The common good is now, not the supreme good of virtue produced by justice and friendship, but the security and the well-being of the political community, the preservation of other human beings in goodness. As a result, Albertus' analysis opens up the possibility of a quite separate line of enquiry for the scholastic understanding of the common good. An Aristotelian common good invited discussion not only of the relation between the principles of identity and superiority but also of the correlation between its more abstract definition as happiness and virtue and its more concrete expression as security and well-being.

2

Albertus Magnus—Common Good and Common Benefit

When Albertus Magnus analyses the principles of identity and superiority in book I of the *Ethics* and the actions of bravery and self-sacrifice in book IX, the coherence of his account hinges on the different shades of meaning which can be given to the terms 'common good' and 'individual good'. On Albertus' reading, the common good can be considered in the sense of human happiness but also in the sense of the security of the human community; the individual good can be considered in the sense of living a life of virtue but also in the sense of possessing material property and temporal existence. Shades of meaning should not, in this instance, be taken as a euphemism for any lack of conceptual clarity. On the contrary, Albertus' sensitivity to these differences in definition takes the form of carefully teasing out the various distinctions between the different types of good which can be found across the entire series of human associations, from the friendship of one individual with another individual to the congregation of all individuals in the political community. It is the precision of this differentiation which enables Albertus to resolve the apparent discrepancy between the superiority of the common good in book I and the superiority of the individual good in book IX— the common good of happiness may be superior to the individual good of virtue but the individual good of virtue is superior to the common good of material security. Albertus' classification of these different types of good, however, does raise one further issue for his understanding of the relationship between individual and common good. If a distinction is being drawn between, on the one hand, the supreme goodness of happiness and virtue (*bonum simpliciter*) and, on the other, the well-being and security of the community (*salus rei publicae*), does this amount to the creation of two separate scales of value by which any human action can be measured and, if so, must these different criteria always be in harmony? To put it another way, Albertus' distinction between different types of good invites an examination of his understanding of the wider relationship between goodness and utility, between *bonum* and *utilitas*.

Albertus' basic definition of goodness is drawn straight from book I of the *Ethics*. According to both Aristotle and the Stoics, Albertus reports, the good is that which all things seek (*bonum quod omnia appetunt*).[1] For Albertus, this means that every action is performed on account of the supreme or divine good in the sense that

---

[1] *Ethica* I.3.7, p. 39. Cf. Augustine, *De Civitate Dei*, ed. B. Dombart and A. Kalb (*CCSL* 47–8), XIV.8, p. 423.

nothing is willed unless it possesses some similitude of this *summum bonum*.[2] Although the actual good which something seeks is not the absolute good in itself but the good which is particular to that thing, this particular good would not have the capacity to move something's will unless it possessed some aspect of the primary good.[3] As far as Albertus is concerned, to maintain that 'the good is that which all things seek' also means drawing a distinction between an intrinsic appetite for what is good and an intrinsic appetite for what is ordered towards a good.[4] Viewed in these terms, he argues, goodness can be defined in two ways. Something can be good in its own right when it is sought for its own sake, or it can be good on account of another good which it enables to be secured. This distinction—between those things which are good in essence (*per se*) and those things which are good on account of something else (*propter aliud*)—is summarized by Albertus as a distinction between what is good (*bonum*) and what is useful (*utile*).[5] Something which is essentially good (*bonum simpliciter*) is permanently and universally good, whereas something which is a useful good (*bonum utile*) is good only at certain times and for certain purposes and people.[6]

Albertus' distinction between what is good and what is useful takes its cue from book II of the *Ethics* where Aristotle had identified three objectives—the honourable, the pleasurable, and the useful—each of which can motivate an individual to choose one course of action rather than another.[7] According to Albertus, the honourable and the pleasurable (or, as he terms them, the absolute good and the sensory good) are both chosen for their own sake; the useful, on the other hand, is chosen on account of something else (*propter aliud*).[8] Later, Albertus classifies the same three objectives as, respectively, the absolute good (*bonum simpliciter*), what is good for oneself here and now (*bonum sibi et nunc*), and the advantageous good (*bonum conferens*).[9] For Albertus, therefore, a good is either ordered towards a goal or it is a goal in itself. If it is ordered towards a goal, then it is useful; if it is attached to a goal, then it is pleasurable; and if it is a goal in itself, then it is honourable. Only the honourable is essentially good; the useful and the pleasurable do not share in this definition of goodness (*ratio boni*) except within certain terms of reference (*secundum quid*).[10] Just what these terms of reference might be are set out when Albertus defines usefulness as serving as an instrument or an aid towards the acquisition of an honourable or a pleasurable good. What is useful, he concludes, is not necessarily good except with reference to the further goal for which it is instrumental. If this goal is the same good towards which the useful would naturally be ordered, then it constitutes a good use (*bonus usus*); if not, then it represents a bad use (*abusus*).[11]

The distinction within goodness between *bonum honestum* and *bonum utile* is deployed by Albertus in a number of different contexts and in a number of different

---

[2] *Super Ethica* IV.3, p. 229.   [3] *Ethica* I.3.6, p. 38.   [4] *Ethica* V.1.2, p. 333.
[5] *Ethica* I.4.16, p. 80. Cf. *Ethica* I.8.1, p. 135.   [6] *Ethica* V.3.9, p. 380.
[7] Aristotle, *Ethics* II.3 1104^{b}30–1. Cf. *Ethics* VIII.2 1155^{b}17–21; *Politics* VII.14 1333^{a}30–^{b}2, (ed. Susemihl), pp. 306–7.
[8] *Super Ethica* II.3, p. 101.   [9] *Ethica* II.1.8, p. 162.   [10] *Super Ethica* VII.12, p. 574.
[11] *Ethica* VIII.1.2, p. 519.

guises. An 'honourable' good, for example, can be expressed as *honestum, dignum, honorabile, nobile,* or *decus,* whilst a 'useful' good can be expressed as *utile, conferens, congruum,* or *expediens.*[12] This distinction is naturally not deployed when it is not needed, particularly when the term *bonum* is sufficiently comprehensive on its own. Utility and pleasure, after all, are understood by Albertus to be the automatic consequences of an honourable good.[13] There are occasions, however, on which Albertus does choose to emphasize particular combinations of the two terms. He can refer, for example, to 'the good and the honourable' (*bonum et honestum*), to 'the good and the useful' (*bonum et utile*), or even to 'the useful order of goodness' (*ratio boni utilis*).[14] This precision is particularly noticeable in political contexts, a subject for which Albertus often relies upon a specific combination of goodness and utility. In his first commentary on the *Ethics,* for example, he defines the primary goal of politics as the honourable good and then defines the result of such activity as the useful and the pleasurable. Both the useful and the pleasurable, Albertus explains, are ordered towards the honourable—the useful represents those material goods which are instrumental to virtue whilst the pleasurable represents those bodily goods which are ordered towards the useful and thereby (at one remove) to the honourable. As examples of the pleasurable, Albertus cites athletic and military exercises, games which keep citizens physically healthy and teach them how to combat their enemies.[15] In Albertus' second commentary on the *Ethics,* the goods of the political community are divided into three categories which correspond to each of the three classes of goodness—the goods of the soul (such as the virtues), the goods of the body (such as health and strength), and those exterior goods which are instrumental to human interaction. Of these three categories, the goods of the soul are termed the greatest and most primary of goods because it is on their account that the other two categories are sought.[16] These primary goods, moreover, also constitute the only one of the three categories which is intrinsically ordered towards the ultimate good of happiness—bodily goods and exterior goods may be good by nature but, unlike the virtues, they can always be put to bad use (*malus usus*) as well as good.[17] Indeed, Albertus points out that it was for this very reason that Eustratius had wondered whether useful goods such as health or war might not, in fact, be excluded from a definition of political life, since they could clearly be used for evil purposes. Eustratius' response had been to distinguish between the existence (*esse*) of happiness and the potential

---

[12] e.g. *Super Ethica* VIII.5, p. 608; *Pol. Lib. Oct.* V.6, p. 499; VI.1, p. 556.

[13] *Super Ethica* III.6, p. 166; X.2, p. 712; *Ethica* VIII.1.2, p. 523.

[14] *Ethica* IX.3.1, p. 583; *Pol. Lib. Oct.* VI.6, p. 614; VII.14, p. 738; *Super Ethica* VII.15, p. 583.

[15] *Super Ethica* VIII.9, p. 629. Like Plato, whose fears he knew via Boethius, *De Musica* I.1 (*PL* 63, col. 1169), Albertus is clearly concerned lest the immoderate use of music should lead to lasciviousness in the citizen body. Music is restricted accordingly to those contexts in which it is useful to some honourable good, such as when it serves as a spur to devotion.

[16] *Ethica* I.6.13, pp. 99–100.

[17] There is also a category of good which is 'useless' in the sense that it is not ordered towards any goal. Albertus gives the example of God who cannot, by definition, be ordered towards anything else (*Super Ethica* VI.10, p. 463).

(*posse*) of happiness, that is, between a definition of the human good as the most perfect and self-sufficient good and a definition of the human good as the arrangement
of all goods, exterior and interior, when they are collected together to make happiness possible. According to Eustratius, Aristotle's inclusion of health as part of happiness was dependent on using the second definition of happiness—it is in terms of
its greatest potential that happiness comprises everything which is instrumental to it
and must therefore include the health which is necessary for conducting political
activity. Albertus' own solution follows suit. Medicine, military strategy, and archi-
tecture can all be put to bad use in political life, but they are themselves naturally
good insofar as they are activities which are instrumental to happiness.[18]

By exploiting the distinction between what is good and what is useful, between
what is honourable and what is beneficial, between an end and the means towards
that end, Albertus establishes two key criteria according to which the various 'goods'
of the political community can be classified—*bonum* and *utilitas*. The consequences
for his understanding of the common good are considerable. At the most general
level, Albertus found this distinction expressed in the political community in the
form of a twofold function. According to Aristotle, the purpose of human association
is not just to live, to live a life of material self-sufficiency, but to live well, to live the
life of virtue. Humankind is therefore a political animal in the sense that association
in a common life enables humans not only to achieve a degree of material sufficiency
which they cannot achieve on their own but also to perfect their disposition to lead a
life of virtue which they cannot realize outside such an environment.[19] Human associations must accordingly exhibit more than just the form of subsistence which they
share with animals, the 'gregariousness' expressed in feeding together as a group.
They must also exhibit communication in the activity of the mind, association in the
specific activity which defines them as human beings rather than as animals.[20]

Aristotle's distinction between these two functions of the human community—
material self-sufficiency and the life of virtue—offered Albertus a political expression of the conceptual distinction between utility and goodness. Defined with
reference to the first function, the goal of political association could be termed
common utility (*communis utilitas*); defined with reference to the second, it could be
termed common good (*bonum commune*). In picking up this parallel, Albertus does
not always choose the terms *communis utilitas* and *bonum commune*.[21] Both the commentaries on the *Ethics* and the commentary on the *Politics* reveal the variety in terminology which can be used to denote 'what is in common' within the political
community—*communitas, universalitas communitatis, civilitas, communicatio, civilis
communicatio, communicatio civitatis, communicatio politica, commune, communio, communiter conferens, conferens civitatis, utilitas civitatis, communes utilitates, civitas et communitas, communitas civilis, communitas civitatis, commune civitatis, res publica, bonum
commune populi, communicatio rei publicae, commune rei publicae, communis res publica,*

---

[18] *Ethica* I.7.7, p. 117. Cf. *Super Ethica* I.10, pp. 51–2; IV *Sent.* 49.6, p. 674.
[19] *Super Ethica* IV.12, p. 272.   [20] *Ethica* IX.3.3, p. 592.
[21] For their use as a single phrase, see e.g. *Pol. Lib. Oct.* III.4, p. 232.

urbanitas, politia, and *politia communis.*[22] Utility, meanwhile, is a term which is applied to numerous other types of human association, from temporary trading ventures to the navy, the army, and the monastic orders, each one of which provides a benefit which is common to all parties to the association.[23] Nevertheless, when Albertus wants to, or (perhaps more accurately) needs to, draw a distinction between moral virtue and material utility in the political community, he is clearly able to do so. When he does, *bonum* is the word which is consistently employed for virtue, whereas *utilitas* or *commodum* is the word which is used to describe food, clothing, walls, or geographical location—anything, in short, which is materially useful or advantageous to the political community but which can itself be used well or used badly.[24] According to Albertus, virtuous activity in the political community requires, if not the superabundance, then at least the presence of many material goods.[25] Without such material provision, without the goods of fishing, for example, or of woolmaking, metalwork, and woodwork, the good of the political community would not be perfect. Individuals cannot live the life of happiness without the mechanical professions, without the 'instrumental utilities' which make that life possible.[26] The perfect political community, therefore, consists of activity in accordance with perfect virtue but it is based, in its turn, on all those things—material wealth, friends, and political authority—which form an instrumental part of such a life.[27] The virtues are the prime example of an essential or honourable good, since they are interior goods which are quintessentially ordered towards happiness; material wealth and power, meanwhile, are simply useful goods, since they are exterior goods which are merely instrumental to happiness.[28]

The distinction between *bonum* and *utilitas*, between what is morally good and what is materially advantageous, is clearly central to Albertus' understanding of Aristotle's account of why individuals associate with one another qua members of a political community. However, if Albertus makes the twin provision of material utility and the pursuit of virtue the defining feature of collective human association as a political community, then he also makes it the defining feature of the form which this association takes between particular individuals *within* this community. The

---

[22] *Pol. Lib. Oct.* III.4, p. 233; VII.6, p. 699; *Ethica* VIII.3.2, p. 540; *Super Ethica* V.3, p. 322; *Pol. Lib. Oct.* II.2, p. 99; III.4, p. 231; VII.6, p. 669; *Pol. Lib. Oct.* II.1, p. 91; III.4, p. 231; *Pol. Lib. Oct.* II.1, p. 90; II.6, p. 153; III.6, p. 247; IV.14, p. 418; *Pol. Lib. Oct.* III.6, p. 247; *Pol. Lib. Oct.* II.6, p. 151; III.6, p. 249; *Pol. Lib. Oct.* III.4, p. 233; V.7, pp. 503, 512; *Ethica* I.3.1, p. 30; *Pol. Lib. Oct.* III.5, pp. 234–5; *Pol. Lib. Oct.* IV.9, p. 375; *Pol. Lib. Oct.* IV.12, p. 405; VII.4, pp. 655, 658; *Pol. Lib. Oct.* VII.8, p. 687; *Pol. Lib. Oct.* V.8, p. 544; *Pol. Lib. Oct.* II.2, p. 99; *Pol. Lib. Oct.* II.8, p. 170; *Pol. Lib. Oct.* VI.6, p. 614; *Ethica* V.1.4, p. 337; *Pol. Lib. Oct.* II.3, p. 128; *Ethica* V.1.4, p. 338; *Ethica* V.2.2, p. 341; *Ethica* VIII.3.13, p. 577; *Ethica* V.2.4, p. 344, VIII.3.2, p. 540; VIII.3.13, p. 577; *Pol. Lib. Oct.* II.1, p. 91; III.4, pp. 230–1; V.6, p. 495; *Pol. Lib. Oct.* V.5, p. 478.

[23] *Pol. Lib. Oct.* I.1, p. 11; *Ethica* VIII.3.1, pp. 537–8.

[24] *Pol. Lib. Oct.* VII.4, pp. 655–9; VII.9, p. 695; *Ethica* VI.2.24, p. 442.

[25] *Super Ethica* X.11, p. 753; X.16, p. 772; *Ethica* I.7.1, p. 106.   [26] *Ethica* I.3.1, p. 30.

[27] *Pol. Lib. Oct.* II.2, p. 116; *Ethica* I.7.7, p. 117.

[28] *Ethica* V.3.11, p. 382. Cf. *Ethica* VI.32, p. 449; VII.2.2, p. 501; *Super Ethica* X.2, p. 712. For the etymological connection of *honestum* with *honor*, and its definition as the goal and reward of virtue, see *Ethica* I.1.5, p. 12; III.2.4, p. 240; *Pol. Lib. Oct.* V.7, p. 511.

distinction between *bonum* and *utilitas*, in other words, also governs Albertus' understanding of Aristotle's account of how individuals associate with one another qua individual human beings. Since goodness is the quality which makes something the object of someone's love, it necessarily follows that any division of goodness into its component categories must be mirrored by a similar division within the love which motivates friendship.[29] This is why Aristotle had accompanied his classification of the honourable, the pleasurable, and the useful with a corresponding classification of friendship. Friendship too, he had argued, can be divided into three types—the honourable, the pleasurable, and the useful. Albertus follows suit. In deploying the distinction between honourable and useful goods as a means of differentiating between different types of friendship, moreover, Albertus is also able to cite the traditional scholastic distinction between benevolent love (*amor benevolentiae*) and concupiscent love (*amor concupiscentiae*). Benevolent love, the love of friendship, is concerned with the good of the individual who is loved, whereas concupiscent love is concerned with the good of the individual doing the loving.[30] On this basis, since the friendship which has utility as its goal and the friendship which has pleasure as its goal are both concerned with the individual doing the loving, Albertus suggests that both useful and pleasurable friendship should be classified under *amor concupiscentiae* and that they should therefore, strictly speaking, be termed only similitudes of friendship.[31] It is only the friendship which has the honourable as its goal, the friendship which is ordered towards the life of virtue, which qualifies as an expression of *amor benevolentiae*. Only this type of friendship will qualify as the true and perfect form of friendship.[32]

Like Aristotle, Albertus regards friendship as the virtue without which the political good, and, by extension, the life of happiness, cannot be perfected amongst humans.[33] As a result, both Aristotle and Albertus analyse friendship and political association as expressions of the same type of relationship and, as such, they both assume that considerations which govern the exercise of one relationship will also govern the exercise of the other. This connection between friendship and political association, therefore, has significant consequences for the course which is taken by Albertus' exposition of the common good. In discussing the good which is produced by friendship, for example, Albertus makes the relationship between friends follow the same formula as the relationship between ruler and subjects. The ruler aims primarily to secure the common good, whereupon his individual good will follow as a consequence; the common good is therefore sought *per se* and the individual good *per accidens*.[34] Friendship reveals the same principle at work. According to Albertus, friendship which is ordered towards an honourable good will also carry useful and pleasurable goods in its wake.[35] An honourable good, after all, can be understood automatically to provide utility (*utilitas*) or advantage (*conferens*) for its participating

---

[29] *Ethica* VIII.1.2–3, pp. 519–23.   [30] *Super Ethica* VIII.3, p. 599; IX.6, p. 675.
[31] *Ethica* VIII.1.3, p. 521.   [32] *Ethica* X.1.5, p. 610; *Super Ethica* prol., p. 1.
[33] *Ethica* IV.3.1, pp. 315–16.   [34] See above, p. 45.
[35] *Ethica* VIII.1.3, pp. 522–3.

individuals.[36] True friendship, therefore, will move an individual to love a friend in his own right. The many benefits and pleasures which result from true friendship, from communication in what is good, remain exactly that—'consequences' which are only 'accidentally' willed by the person doing the loving. The friendship which is founded on utility or pleasure, on the other hand, moves an individual to love this utility or pleasure in its own right and love his friend only 'accidentally'.[37]

In drawing such a firm connection between friendship and political association, however, Albertus also presented his analysis of the common good of the political community with certain difficulties. By insisting, for example, that friendship is a term which should be restricted to those individuals whose relationship is directed towards a life of virtue and moral goodness, it became only reasonable to ask whether, having drawn such a conclusion for the relationship of one individual with another individual, a similar conclusion should also be drawn for the relationship between several individuals qua members of the political community. If a friendship which is based on material benefit can only qualify as a similitude of friendship, what is the status of a political association which is likewise based on utility alone?

The short answer to this question is that Albertus never moves away from his theoretical position that the goal of the political community should be to secure the life of virtue. When he first raises the possibility that the goal of political life might be limited to the provision of a more material utility, he is quick to dismiss the suggestion. This is what happens, for example, when he examines a definition of law which describes legislation as something which not only commands people to live according to every virtue but also prohibits them from living according to every kind of sin.[38] In analysing the positive and negative halves of this definition, Albertus carefully isolates the negative formulation according to which laws would be instituted, not in order to make people good and make them live a life of happiness, but merely to prevent them from suffering injustice and stop them from being unjust towards each other. Two possible arguments are adduced in support of such a proposition—the first is that law is instituted for the sake of evil people in order to prevent them from being wicked; the second is that law is, by its very nature, a coercive power and, as such, cannot itself instil goodness in people because goodness must be the result of a free and voluntary act.[39] Albertus' response to this negative definition of the function of legislation is to argue that law not only commands those actions which contribute directly to the common good but also gives an indication of how members of the political community ought to live in the future. The prudent legislator, he states, not only has the task of framing laws which will make members of the political community live as they should do but he also (and this is a much more primary concern)

---

[36] *Ethica* IV.3.1, p. 316. Cf. *Super Ethica* VIII.3, p. 601 citing Cicero, *De Amicitia*, trans. W. A. Falconer (Loeb, 1923), XIII.44–51, pp. 156–62.

[37] *Super Ethica* IV.4, p. 241; VIII.2, p. 598; VIII.3, p. 601. Cf. above, p. 50.

[38] *Ethica* V.2.2, p. 341.

[39] *Ethica* V.2.8, pp. 353–4. Cf. Aristotle, *Politics* III.9 1280ᵇ3–5, pp. 185–6; Mercken (ed.), *The Greek Commentaries*, pp. 312–13, quoting Plato, *Republic* II 359A.

has the task of training those who will be good in the future such that his laws might ultimately remove all wickedness and dispose every individual to live the best life. The prudent legislator, therefore, primarily intends to make citizens just and to provide them with a training or discipline in everything through which virtue is 'perfected' and benefit brought to the whole community (*commune rei publicae*).[40]

In explicitly distancing himself from the view that law is instituted only to curb the worst aspects of human behaviour, Albertus demonstrates just how positive was his conception of the moral function of law and the political community. Theory, however, was not necessarily the same as practice. The longer answer to how Albertus conceived of the connection between utilitarian friendship and utilitarian political association depends on his analysis, not of justice, but of harmony or *concordia*. Initially, Albertus appears to have drawn a strict parallel between the operation of friendship amongst individual human beings and the operation of concord amongst members of a political community. In his first commentary on the *Ethics*, for example, he defines concord in terms which are very similar to those which he uses for true friendship—each of these relationships is characterized by agreement in a common good. As a result, since friendships which are based on the pleasurable or the useful are always concerned with a private good, there can be no *concordia* in these relationships unless their usefulness or pleasure is ordered, in its turn, towards the common good.[41] In Albertus' first commentary on the *Ethics*, in other words, concord, like friendship, is necessarily restricted to those associations of individuals which pursue the common good of virtue and not just utility or pleasure. Once Albertus had read the *Politics*, however, his view of political communities seems to have become rather more flexible. Summarizing the argument of book VI, for example, Albertus maintains that a constitution or form of government is the ordering of those individuals who associate in a political community. The best form of government, he concludes, will therefore consist of 'good order' between nobles (*insignes*) and the people.[42] Having defined this mutual ordering, however, Albertus does not discuss whether such concord, is, like friendship, *necessarily* the same as the ordering of individuals towards the ultimate human good of virtue and happiness. Indeed, by the time Albertus was writing his second commentary on the *Ethics*, he was clearly prepared to air the possibility that this political concord might not be the same as true or perfect friendship on the grounds that, even though it represents agreement between individuals on what is good, it is still only a similitude of friendship because it can comprise associations which are based on utility and pleasure *without* being ordered towards the life of virtue. Significantly, this suggestion is accompanied by a further reference to the claim that laws are instituted in order to ensure that there will be no injustice rather than to ensure that people will act through reason. On this occasion, Albertus is rather more accommodating to a negative formulation of the function of law. If this suggestion were true, Albertus concedes, then the primary goal of the

---

[40] *Ethica* V.2.2, pp. 341–2.   [41] *Super Ethica* IX.7, p. 679.
[42] *Pol. Lib. Oct.* VI.1, pp. 560, 562; VI.4, p. 585.

exercise of authority in such a community would be concord where concord is defined, not as agreement on the common good of virtue, but simply by its opposite, by the absence of discord and contention.[43]

By describing concord as an ordering of individuals in which their pleasure and benefit are capable of being directed towards the common good of virtue, in which they should theoretically be directed towards the common good, but in which this does not have to happen in order for it to warrant being classified as *concordia*, Albertus sets up a connection with his definition of a useful good as something which is capable of being ordered towards obtaining what is honourable.[44] In his second commentary on the *Ethics*, Albertus accordingly classifies concord, not just as true friendship, but also as 'political' friendship, as the ordering of individuals for the sake of mutual utility. Albertus continues to insist that true friendship will require an association of people to direct their love towards a single common good, namely the good of virtue, and that, in this case, political concord *will* be identical with true friendship. However, Albertus now concedes that this stipulation does not have to be fulfilled before the term concord can be applied to a political community. Indeed, Albertus accepts that true friendship might not, in fact, exist in any human community, either because individuals tend to show their love for one another rather than for a single, common goal, or because individuals tend to associate for the sake of a good which is simply pleasurable or useful, or because they tend to agree only on a good which is advantageous to the political community. In such circumstances, the sort of concord which human communities generally demonstrate is political friendship, a form of friendship which differs in principle from true friendship because it does not have the single common good of virtue as its goal.[45] This type of concord, the concord of political friendship, is the order which unites imperfect political communities. Strictly speaking, concord may be a good which, like friendship, can only be termed truly good when it is ordered towards an honourable good, towards the life of virtue. Like friendship, however, this does not necessarily prevent it from also being applied to associations of individuals which are only ordered towards what is useful rather than towards what is morally good.

By accepting that the political community can be defined by its provision of mutual benefit rather than moral goodness, by the presence of political friendship rather than true friendship, Albertus is making a significant concession. The qualified definition of concord which is produced in his second commentary on the *Ethics* can be read as a Christian concession to the reality of sinful human society. According to Augustine, the pairing of concord with peace, *pax et concordia*, represented a sober assessment of what political authority could practicably achieve in a fallen world. Such realism is certainly present in Albertus' writing. In his first commentary on the *Ethics*, for example, in the course of establishing that virtue constitutes an interior activity, Albertus discusses the case of the doctor who does not always cure

---

[43] *Ethica* VIII.1.1, pp. 517–18.   [44] *Ethica* VII.2.2, p. 501. Cf. above, p. 55.
[45] *Ethica* IX.2.4, p. 577. Cf. *Super Ethica* IX.12, p. 699; Aristotle, *Ethics* IX.6 1167ᵇ2–4.

his patient. Whilst the doctor's exercise of his medical knowledge is always a good, he argues, the practical effect which this exercise may actually have on any given patient is determined by the imperfection of the material with which he is dealing. Albertus suggests that a parallel therefore exists with the peace of the *res publica*, a good which is always sought by the prudent person, but which, as an exterior act of virtue exercised towards other people, may not, in fact, be the result of his actions due to the imperfection of the material on which the virtuous person is working. Nevertheless, Albertus concludes, it is still better to have intended health or peace than not to have exercised medicine or prudence.[46] Albertus' qualified definition of concord in the political community, however, was also firmly rooted in his reading of Aristotle's *Politics*. In this instance at least, Augustine and Aristotle were far from being mutually exclusive authorities. A significant portion of the *Politics*, after all, had assumed that stability (that is, the avoidance of *stasis*) is a far more realistic goal for the majority of human societies than happiness and the life of virtue. Albertus' own references to peace are certainly instructive in this regard. In his commentary on book V of the *Politics*, for example, Albertus uses the couplet 'peace and tranquillity' (*pax et quies*) in the course of describing Aristotle's advice for the stability of all political constitutions, imperfect as well as perfect, tyrannies as well as aristocracies.[47] Although Albertus insists that book II of the *Politics* has already demonstrated that there is nothing so beneficial to members of a political community as to become accustomed to a life of virtue, he is at least prepared to concede that peace or well-being (*salus*) is still beneficial and advantageous to everyone. Peace, like concord, can be defined accordingly as merely the absence, or the opposite of, sedition.[48]

Albertus' use of two definitions of concord—concord as agreement on the common good of virtue and concord as cooperation in mutual benefit—is closely tied to his distinction between two types of friendship—true friendship amongst individuals in pursuit of moral goodness and similitudes of friendship amongst individuals in pursuit of utility and pleasure. In both instances, Albertus is drawing on the distinction within goodness between *bonum honestum* and *bonum utile*. This is a revealing perspective from which to judge his understanding of the common good of the political community. According to Albertus, *concordia* and *pax* are benefits which result from the exercise of moral goodness but they are also goods which are instrumental to the activity of happiness. As such, concord and peace should always be ordered towards the life of virtue. They should not be sought on their own account, as ends in themselves, but as the means which secure a further good, the common human good of happiness. There are clearly times, however, when Albertus is also prepared to recognize that concord and peace can exist in political communities which fall short of fulfilling such an ideal. On these occasions, concord seems to serve as a common denominator for all human communities, a goal of stability which is tailored to imperfection and sin rather than to perfection and virtue.

---

[46] *Super Ethica* II.2, p. 101.   [47] *Pol. Lib. Oct.* V.1, p. 428. Cf. *Pol. Lib. Oct.* VII.2, p. 637.
[48] *Pol. Lib. Oct.* V.6, p. 495. Cf. V.2, p. 443; V.6, p. 449.

Albertus' discussion of concord reveals an acute awareness of the difference between theory and practice. The political community *should* be ordered towards the life of virtue and moral goodness, but it *can* be ordered towards material security and mutual benefit. Expressed in these terms, it is clear just how much Albertus' argument depends on the ability to distinguish, within the order of goodness, between moral good and utility, between *bonum* and *utilitas*. Peace and concord are 'useful' goods, goods which are capable of being abused as well as being used well, and as 'useful' goods they carry a necessary ambivalence. Expressed in these terms, it is also clear just how far the distinction between *bonum* and *utilitas* underpins his analysis of the relationship between the common good and the individual in books I and IX of the *Ethics*. The difference between *bonum honestum* and *bonum utile* enables Albertus to interpret the common good of human society in two senses—as the life of moral virtue and as the peace of political concord. It is this ambivalence which is reflected in Albertus' account of self-sacrifice and his use of the word *salus*, a term which could cover both the spiritual and the physical well-being of the body politic. For Albertus and for Aristotle, health served as an important analogy for human happiness. For Albertus, *salus* can therefore mean true health and true well-being (including the healing of salvation), but it can also simply mean material and physical well-being. In the first sense, *salus* denotes happiness, activity in accordance with perfect virtue— this is the common good to which the individual good of temporal existence is necessarily subordinate. In its second sense, however, *salus* denotes the common good of the political community which results from the self-sacrifice of the individual who lays down his life in pursuit of the good of virtue. This common good is the common utility which will subsequently be used, well or badly, by the surviving members of the political community after the virtuous individual has died.

Albertus uses the distinction between *bonum honestum* and *bonum utile* to provide two glosses on the 'common good' of human society. On the one hand, it can be defined in terms of happiness, moral goodness, the life of virtue, and true friendship; on the other, it can be defined in terms of peace, material security, mutual benefit, and political friendship. As a general rule, Albertus keeps these two definitions separate and appeals to one or the other depending on the particular context of his argument. There are times, however, when Albertus does explore the practical ethical and political consequences of bringing these two sets of criteria into direct conflict. One of the more striking features of his analysis of the common good, in fact, is the way in which it includes a series of specific questions, each one of which is prompted by opposing the demands of individual moral goodness to the requirements of common political utility. Albertus' interest in such conflicts can be traced from very early on in his work. One important consequence of Albertus' initial identification of the common good as the good of the species, for example, is illustrated in his commentary on book IV of the *Sentences* (a work which was completed in 1249 and which accordingly shows every familiarity with the *Ethics*) when he sets out the relative merits of celibacy and marriage. If celibacy secures good for the individual whereas marriage secures good for the species, which of the two goods should take priority?

In discussing this question, Albertus concedes to the advocates of celibacy the point that God's injunction to be fruitful and increase in number (Genesis 1: 28) was designed to supply an immediate deficiency in the human population and that, once this deficiency had been met, this command could no longer be regarded as binding. What Albertus is not prepared to accept, however, is an unqualified elevation of celibacy as an absolutely superior good, a claim which was justified by another Old Testament text (Sirach 26: 20) that no balance can weigh the value of a chaste soul. This principle may be true, Albertus argues, when the scale which is being used to measure these goods is that of the personal, individual good, but it is not true when the scale of measurement is the common good. The common good, he states, and in particular the preservation of the human species, outweighs (*praevalere*) a personal, individual good. In order to prove the point, Albertus appeals to book I of the *Ethics*—the good of the city is a better good (*melius*) and the good of a people is the greatest (*maximum*). However, this does not mean that Albertus believes that marriage is superior to celibacy. If he maintains that the species is more worthy (*dignior*) than the individual, and that it is better that it should be preserved at the expense of the individual, then he is keen to restrict the operation of this principle to those instances (of which Genesis 1: 28 is a prime example) in which it is a case of the survival of *either* the species *or* the individual. Since the purpose behind God's injunction to marry and procreate has now been achieved, he concludes, common good and individual good can no longer be treated as mutually exclusive alternatives. Now that humankind has become plentiful, it is abstinence from marriage which has become meritorious.[49]

A similar conflict between common good and individual good is set up when Albertus considers the question of celibacy from the perspective of canon law—can dispensation be made from an oath in order to permit an individual to marry for the sake of a better good (*propter melius bonum*)?[50] Dispensation from the law had been tackled by Aristotle in book V of the *Ethics* in the course of discussing *epikeia* or equity. Albertus understood Aristotle's argument to mean that, since it is in the nature of law to cover the general rule rather than the particular case, a discretionary power must be given to the judge or political authority in order to remedy those instances in which adherence to the letter of the law will not, in fact, secure the common good, the well-being of the *res publica*.[51] In the case of dispensation from a vow of celibacy, this definition presented Albertus with a clear conflict between adhering to the law of personal perfection and promoting the common good of the species. His initial solution is to argue that, although chastity is a better good in itself, it can be a

---

[49] Albertus Magnus, *Commentarii in IV Sententiarum*, ed. A. Borgnet, in *Opera Omnia*, vols. xxix-xxx, 26.10, p. 112. Cf. IV *Sent.* 31.21, p. 234.

[50] J. Brys, *De dispensatione in iure canonico, praesertim apud decretistas et decretalistas usque ad medium saeculum decimum quartum* (Bruges, 1925), 209-21.

[51] *Super Ethica* V.15, pp. 379-80; *Ethica* V.4.1, pp. 383-4. Cf. *Pol. Lib. Oct.* II.8, p. 172. For the background, see P. G. Caron, 'Aequitas et interpretatio dans la doctrine canonique aux XIIIe et XIVe siècles', in *Proceedings of the Third International Congress of Medieval Canon Law* (1971), 131-41; id., 'Aequitas' romana, 'misericordia' patristica ed 'epicheia' aristotelica nella dottrina dell' 'aequitas' canonica (Milan, 1977).

lesser good when it is considered within a particular genus, in this case, when it affects the common utility of the church (*communis utilitas ecclesiae*). Any individual, he explains, can be viewed in two ways, either in their own right or as a common member of the church, and criteria which apply in one sphere do not necessarily apply in the other.[52] Albertus recognizes that this distinction still leaves open the question of a direct comparison between individual good and common utility. His very next question, therefore, points out that, if marriage brings many people to Christ and to the church, and if the common good of the church is much better (*multo melius*) than the individual good, then surely it is permissible for dispensation to be made for an individual whose marriage will result in so many goods? Albertus' response to this suggestion is to distinguish between the two types of good which are involved in making such a decision. A particular oath, he concludes, can be exchanged for another oath of equal goodness (such as fasting in return for alms-giving) or for an oath which has less intrinsic goodness but greater corresponding benefit (*recompensatio*). It is this second type of exchange which can be used to pro-duce a direct comparison of celibacy to marriage. Albertus draws a parallel with the comparison of contemplation to action. Echoing Aristotle's observation that it is better for a needy person to make money than to engage in philosophy, Albertus maintains that a particular individual can surrender a contemplative life in return for an active life of service to the whole community.[53] Since the common good is better than any particular good, an individual good can sometimes be exchanged in order that the individual can be of benefit to many other people.[54]

Albertus' discussion of celibacy in his commentary on the *Sentences* clearly demonstrates that, when he came to deliver his first course of lectures on the *Ethics*, he already had a firm grasp on the conflict which could be produced by opposing moral goodness to common benefit. In his first commentary on the *Ethics*, this con-flict is set up, once again, as a comparison between the contemplative and the active lives. In discussing whether God has the greatest love for the individual whose life is spent in contemplation, Albertus concludes that there are two scales of measurement on which such an assessment can be carried out—purity (on account of which the greatest love does indeed belong to the contemplative) and utility (on account of which the greater merit and reward belongs to the individual who converts the souls of others to God). Albertus himself points out the parallel with theological debates over the relative merits of the active and contemplative lives and the relative merits of the married and celibate states. In both these pairings, one alternative can be char-acterized by greater purity and dignity, the other by greater utility and merit.[55]

---

[52] IV *Sent.* 38.15, p. 415.

[53] IV *Sent.* 38.16, pp. 416–17. Cf. *Super Ethica* VI.1, p. 396; VI.17, p. 495; X.13, p. 761; *Pol. Lib. Oct.* II.10, p. 190, quoting Aristotle, *Topica* III.2 118ª10–11.

[54] IV *Sent.* 38.18, p. 419.

[55] *Super Ethica* X.16, p. 775. Cf. *Super Ethica* X.13, p. 761. In his *Enarrationes in Evangelium secundum Lucam*, ed. A. Borgnet, in *Opera Omnia*, vol. xxiii, X.41–2, p. 89, Albertus extends these points of com-parison. The contemplative life of Mary is superior in terms of unity, purity, eternity, certainty, and delight; the active life of Martha is superior in terms of benefit, merit, bravery, strength, assistance in the

The consequences of this dual standard for the relationship between the common good and the individual good are spelled out in more strictly Aristotelian terms when Albertus compares the relative merits of political happiness and contemplative happiness. Albertus lists three possible arguments against the proposition that contemplative happiness is better (*melius*) than political happiness. First, there is the statement attributed to Boethius that every good derived in common shines more beautifully (*pulchrius*).[56] Second, there is the principle from book I of the *Ethics* that the good of a city is more divine (*divinius*) than the good of one individual. Third, there is the argument that, in Nature, those things which hold sway over many others are more worthy (*digniora*). Albertus' solution to these arguments is to distinguish between the two meanings of *melius* which are produced by the two meanings of goodness—more honourable (*honorabilius*) and more useful (*utilius*). In the first sense of good, contemplative happiness is 'better', whereas, in the second sense, it is political happiness.[57] Albertus repeats this conclusion right at the end of his commentary on book X. Contemplative happiness and political happiness, he argues, can be considered according to two scales of measurement. Either they are judged in terms of worth and honour (*dignitas et honestas*) or in terms of utility (*utilitas*). Judged by the first standard, contemplative happiness is much more worthy than political happiness because it concerns what is best in humankind and is not ordered towards any other goal. Judged by the second criterion, political happiness is more potent (*potior*) because it provides all the necessities of life. For the good of the people to be described as 'more divine' in book I of the *Ethics*, he concludes, requires a quite specific meaning of the term. Political happiness is 'more divine' in the sense that it has a greater similitude to God in the act of bestowing goodness and delight on His creatures. Contemplative happiness, meanwhile, is 'more divine' in the sense that it has a greater similitude to God in the act of understanding and taking delight in His nature.[58]

In establishing two standards by which the active and the contemplative lives can be judged—intrinsic moral goodness and utility—Albertus does not always treat them in parallel, as separate scales of measurement. When he does consider the relationship between contemplative and political happiness within a single frame of

---

necessities of life, and gracious action. Cf. Cicero, *De Officiis* I.70, pp. 28–9; W. P. Haggarty, 'Augustine, the Mixed Life and Classical Political Philosophy: Reflections on *compositio* in book XIX of the City of God', *Augustinian Studies*, 23 (1992), 149–63. For the polemical context of this debate, see below, pp. 107–9.

[56] Seneca, *Ad Lucilium Epistulae Morales*, ed. L. D. Reynolds (2 vols.; Oxford, 1965) I.6, p. 10. Cf. *Super Ethica* VIII.7, p. 621; *Pol. Lib. Oct.* II.2, p. 109; Albertus Magnus, *Super Dionysium De Caelesti Hierarchia*, ed. P. Simon and W. Kübel, in *Opera Omnia*, vol. xxxvi.1, IV.7, p. 73. Compare Boethius, *Philosophiae Consolatio*, ed. Bieler (*CCSL* 94), III.10, pp. 53–6; Augustine, *De Civitate Dei*, ed. Dombart and Kalb (*CCSL* 47–8), XV.5, p. 458; Bonaventure, I *Sent.* 10.1.1, in *Opera Omnia*, i. 195.

[57] *Super Ethica* I.7, p. 35. Cf. *Pol. Lib. Oct.* VII.2, p. 639. *Divinius*, however, is not even mentioned. Three MSS accordingly change the wording of Albert's second argument from *divinius* to *dignius* (*Super Ethica* I.7, p. 35). Cf. *Pol. Lib. Oct.* VII.13, p. 721.

[58] *Super Ethica* X.13, p. 761. Cf. *Ethica* X.2.2–3, p. 627; Aristotle, *Politics* VII.2 1324ª25–35, pp. 246–7; VII.3 1325ᵇ4–30, pp. 255–6.

reference, he is unequivocal in ranking goodness over utility. Since contemplative happiness is loved on its own account, he states, whereas political happiness is loved for the sake of a further goal, contemplative happiness must be better than political happiness in absolute terms (*simpliciter loquendo*).[59] Although it is not possible for a single nature to have several ultimate goals, a single nature can still have several goods, some of which are ordered towards others. Thus, although the human good is comprised of political as well as contemplative happiness, the political is still ordered towards the contemplative in that it removes impediments to its fulfilment.[60] Contemplative happiness is therefore the ultimate human good and, as such, it is more worthy than political happiness.[61] Contemplative happiness is more worthy than political happiness in that political happiness is ordered towards it, just as a good which is good in its own right is better and more worthy than something which is useful.[62] Any goal is more worthy than that which is chosen on its account.[63]

By applying the distinction between *bonum* and *utilitas* to the relationship between the active and the contemplative lives, Albertus is able to resolve the apparent discrepancy between Aristotle's definition of happiness as activity in accordance with perfect virtue in book I of the *Ethics* and Aristotle's definition of happiness as contemplation of the good in book X. However, the existence of two separate criteria in accordance with which any individual action can be judged presents his exposition of Aristotle with several more practical questions. Perhaps the most striking is the claim that what is honourable and what is advantageous might be mutually exclusive courses of action within the political community.

The possible opposition of two actions, one of which is morally worthy and the other advantageous, had, of course, a very long tradition in classical moral and political philosophy.[64] The details of this tradition were available to medieval theologians primarily in the form in which they had been transmitted by Cicero's *De Officiis*. According to Cicero, any opposition between *honestum* and *utile* was always more apparent than real, since personal advantage was always the necessary consequence of performing a morally virtuous action. The origins of this debate were also reflected in Aristotle's *Ethics*, a fact of which Albertus had been made acutely aware by Grosseteste's translation of the Greek commentaries on the text. The anonymous commentator on book III, for example, had argued for exactly the sort of mutual exclusivity which Cicero had been determined to exclude. According to the commentator, what is useful can be opposed to what is good in the sense that something which is naturally evil can be put to a good use and can thereby become good. Evil actions such as lying and adultery, he had suggested, cease to be evil when their goal is something useful. One such useful goal is the removal of a tyrant. Such was the

---

[59] *Super Ethica* I.7, p. 35. Cf. *Enarr. in Luc.* X.41–2, pp. 89–90.

[60] *Super Ethica* VI.17, p. 496; VI.1, p. 393. Cf. *Super Ethica* VI.10, p. 460; X.9, p. 742; X.13, p. 761; *Ethica* I.6.1, p. 85; I.6.4, pp. 88–9; X.2.1, p. 623.

[61] *Super Ethica* VI.18, p. 513; VII.12, p. 573; *Ethica* X.2.2, p. 626; *Pol. Lib. Oct.* VII.13, p. 721.

[62] *Pol. Lib. Oct.* VII.13, p. 721.

[63] *Super Ethica* VI.1, p. 395; VI.2, p. 411; VI.10, p. 460; VI.18, p. 507.   [64] See above, p. 22.

force of this statement that, when Grosseteste translated these observations along-side the text of Aristotle's *Ethics*, he clearly considered it necessary to append a cat-egoric restatement of the Christian belief that no sin should ever be committed in order to secure some utility or avoid some suffering.[65]

When Albertus came to comment on book III of the *Ethics*, therefore, he was faced with an intriguing question. He was well aware of the theological position which underpinned Grosseteste's reservations—Romans 3: 8 condemned the principle that evil should be committed in order that good may result, whilst Augustine had expli-citly picked out lying, adultery, and theft as crimes which could never become good by virtue of their intended goal, even if this was a greater good.[66] In his first commen-tary on the *Ethics*, therefore, Albertus starts by endorsing this tradition. Lying, he states, is an evil of the first order since it contradicts virtue. Whatever the nature of the danger it is designed to avert, therefore, it is an action which should not be performed. Adultery, likewise, is always associated with an evil goal and, as a result, however great the benefit to the *res publica* which it might produce, this is never sufficient to make such an action either good in itself or good to perform. There is one category of evil, however, for which Albertus *is* prepared to accede to the Greek commentator's pos-ition, namely when an action simply results in the debasement (*vilitas*) of the indi-vidual who performs it. Giving money under duress to a tyrant, he suggests, or doing something dishonourable for him, are evils which *can* be countenanced. Such actions amount to an acceptable use of intrinsically bad activity in that they are to be per-formed in order to avoid the loss of life or some other disadvantageous consequence.[67]

When Albertus came to comment on book IV of the *Ethics*, however, his initial condemnation of lying is subjected to some significant qualifications. Albertus bases his argument on a wide-ranging distinction which he now chooses to draw between the perfection of political virtue and the perfection of theological virtue. Theological virtue, he writes, is ordered towards a goal of infinite goodness and, as a result, there is no corresponding benefit (*recompensatio*) which should sidetrack someone from such an incommutable good. Political virtue, however, can be regarded in a quite dif-ferent manner. Since political virtue is ordered towards a goal of finite goodness, namely the maintenance of the political community, it *is* possible for greater weight to be given to the advantage or disadvantage which the political community will derive from a particular action. It is in this sense that lying can, in fact, be used to avert danger to the political community. Defined in political terms, lying is, in itself, essentially evil but only when there is nothing to justify setting political truth on one side. The utility of the community provides exactly this sort of exception. Lying is not an evil when it serves a political utility.[68] This is, to say the least, a striking

---

[65] Mercken (ed.), *The Greek Commentaries*, pp. 238–9.

[66] *Super Ethica* V.15, p. 380; *Pol. Lib. Oct.* VII.11, p. 705; *De Bono* V.1.4, pp. 276–80. Cf. Augustine, *Contra Mendacium*, ed. J. Zycha (*CSEL* 41), I.1, p. 470; VII.18, pp. 489–90.

[67] *Super Ethica* III.1, p. 142. Cf. II.7, p. 125.

[68] *Super Ethica* IV.14, p. 288. Cf. Cicero, *De Officiis*, I.159–60, pp. 66–7; Gregory the Great, *Regulae Pastoralis Liber* (*PL* 77, cols. 13–128), III.11, col. 64. See also *Super Ethica* V.15, pp. 380–1. Cf. *De Bono* I.2.6, p. 33.

conclusion. Indeed, when Albertus came to comment on book V of the *Ethics*, it is noticeable that he uses it with much greater circumspection than in book IV, particularly when it is a matter of the second of the Greek commentator's examples, namely adultery. If one wants to uphold this claim and argue that an act of adultery which secures the death of a tyrant should not receive its due legal punishment, then Albertus suggests that it is possible to do so by treating such an action in political terms, that is, as an action which is ordered towards the political good. Viewed in these terms, he concludes, the adulterer does not merit the punishment which is prescribed by law because of the corresponding benefit which this action has brought to the political good. However, if the same action is considered in terms of the divine good, namely as an action which is ordered towards the possession of eternal life in God, then, however great the good which might be secured by the adulterous act, there is no corresponding benefit which will sway the judgment passed by God.[69]

In his first commentary on the *Ethics*, it would appear that Albertus hovers between accepting the logic of the Greek commentator's position (that a common benefit can outweigh an individual evil) and simply establishing divergent criteria (political goodness and theological goodness) by which a particular action should be judged. Clearly there are some evils, such as rendering payment or obedience to a tyrant, which Albertus is always prepared to justify on the grounds that they are useful, either because they avoid a greater evil or because they contribute to the common good. Murder, for example, is always an evil when it is defined in terms of killing a person qua human, but it becomes a good when it is an act of retributive justice against a thief whose crime is defined as being contrary to human well-being (*salus hominum*).[70] Usury, on the other hand, is an evil which does not become a good but which can still be permitted on account of its great utility to the political community in that it prevents the multitude from suffering material and moral damage. Although usury is still an evil action for a particular individual to perform, Albertus suggests that this is not a consideration for political law which, by definition, aims to secure the good of the city and the people rather than the good of the individual, the good of many people more than the good of one person. A law which is concerned with the divine good, on the other hand, yields precisely the opposite conclusion, since not only does the divine good constitute the good of an individual *as well as* the good of a multitude but it is also an infinite good which is incapable of being balanced out by any corresponding benefit. The divine law of the New Testament, therefore, because it is itself perfect and aims to secure the perfection of both the multitude and every individual person, cannot permit an evil action such as usury. All it can do is tolerate a lesser good. Albertus admits to seeing no inconsistency in permitting usury from the perspective of the common good but prohibiting it as an evil for an individual person. A different principle, he insists, applies in each case. Beyond recognizing that the political community is dealing with imperfect subject-matter, however,

---

[69] *Super Ethica* V.15, pp. 380–1.   [70] *Super Ethica* II.7, p. 125.

the disparity between the divine good and the good of the political community is left unresolved.[71]

By the time Albertus is tackling the good use of an evil action in his second commentary on the *Ethics*, his position has undergone some revision but the attempt to provide an extenuating justification remains the same. Albertus now distinguishes between three aspects to any evil act—the status of the agent, the offensiveness of the action, and the utility (or lack of it) to the *res publica*. Usefulness to the *res publica*, he argues, can indeed redeem the performance of an evil action. This is what happens, for example, when an individual tells a lie in order to preserve the well-being (*salus*) of others, a scenario which appears to have been prompted by Plato's concession that a doctor can lie about a medicine in order to avoid terrifying a patient.[72] According to Albertus, although the act of lying is evil, and will always remain evil, it is not prosecuted as such by the civil legislator. In fact, since the evil of lying is redeemed by the duty of piety towards the community, such an action can be termed 'dutiful deceit' (*mendacium officiosum*).[73] The same principle governs Albertus' account of the political punishment of an act of adultery where the act in question has been committed with the intention, not of transgressing the bonds of marriage, but of betraying a tyrant who is bent on reducing his subjects to slavery. Albertus cites the case of Judith and Holofernes (Judith 8–14). Betrayal, Albertus concludes, is always an evil; so too is lying and adultery. To speak of them being redeemed, therefore, is not to claim that they cease to be evils, simply that they will not be punished by the legislator. Such an exercise of clemency is justified by the common utility which lying and adultery can, in certain circumstances, produce. Albertus admits that there are offences which it is impossible to redeem because of the degree to which they subvert reason, virtue, nature, and custom. Such actions, in his opinion, should on no account be performed, however great the urge to do so. Indeed, death should be preferred in their stead.[74] Lying, however, does not fall within this category. If telling a lie is associated with a greater political utility than speaking the truth (if telling the truth will damage the political community, for example, or if telling a lie will save someone's life, reputation, or fortune), then an individual should take the more prudent course of action and choose the lesser of two evils. Such action has nothing to do with the perfection or correctness of virtue but is simply dictated by necessity. In this sense, the lie is said to 'occur' rather than be intended in its own right. This type of lie is not to be reckoned as a good but as a politically tolerable, even necessary, evil.

---

[71] *Super Ethica* IV.4, p. 239; V.16, pp. 384–5.

[72] Mercken (ed.), *The Greek Commentaries*, p. 227. Cf. Plato, *Republic* II 382 C, 389 B, V 459 C; C. Page, 'The Truth about Lies in Plato's Republic', *Ancient Philosophy*, 11 (1991), 1–33.

[73] The phrase itself originates with Augustine e.g. *Ep.* 40, ed. Goldbacher (*CSEL* 34), p. 71. Cf. *Les Premières Polémiques thomistes I: Le Correctorium Corruptorii 'Quare'*, ed. P. Glorieux (Paris, 1927), 267–75. More generally, see Augustine, *Contra Mendacium*, *De Mendacio*, ed. Zycha (*CSEL* 41); M. Colish, *The Stoic Tradition from Antiquity to the Early Middle Ages*, 2nd edn. (2 vols.; Leiden 1990), ii. 189–98; T. Feehan, 'Augustine on Lying and Deception', *Augustinian Studies*, 19 (1988), 131–9; id., 'Augustine's Moral Evaluation of Lying', *Augustinian Studies*, 21 (1990), 67–81; id., 'Augustine's Own Examples of Lying', *Augustinian Studies*, 22 (1991), 165–90.

[74] *Ethica* II.2.6, p. 181; III.1.5, pp. 200–1. Cf. *Ethica* V.4.1, p. 384; *Pol. Lib. Oct.* VII.11, p. 705.

Lying is justifiable, Albertus concludes, as an expression of the piety which an individual has towards his neighbour, since, with the exception of the individual who departs from the truth, 'dutiful deceit' is an action which benefits everybody.[75]

Albertus' application of the distinction between the honourable and the useful is a highly significant feature of his commentaries on Aristotle, not least because it demonstrates that later commentators such as Leonardo Bruni were wrong to read so much into Grosseteste's failure to translate *to kalon* as *honestum* rather than simply as *bonum*.[76] Albertus uses the polarity between individual moral worth and common utility in a series of set-piece debates—comparing the contemplative and the active lives, describing the relative merits of celibacy and marriage, separating interior virtue from exterior or bodily goods, distinguishing the individual as an individual in his own right from the individual as part of the church or political community, and contrasting the individual good as the subject of the divine good and divine law with the good of the multitude as the subject of the political good and civil law. Perhaps the most striking result of these discussions is Albertus' suggestion that a good action can be defined *either* in terms of political virtue *or* in terms of theological virtue and his conclusion that goodness in one sphere is not necessarily the same as goodness in the other. The fact that Albertus subsequently emphasizes that lying and adultery, even if they can be politically and judicially tolerated, will always remain evil acts for the individual to perform would seem to indicate that he is not setting up parallel criteria of virtue by which the acts themselves can be judged. He certainly makes no attempt to draw any connection with Aristotle's discussion of whether the virtue of a good man is the same as the virtue of a good citizen. This is a discussion which Albertus consistently interprets as a separation of private and public spheres of activity and not as the creation of any relativist standard of moral judgement. In Albertus' hands, the distinction between the good man and the good citizen is used to highlight the individual who is a good person in his own right but a bad member of the political community, not to justify the individual who is a bad person but a good citizen.[77]

By concentrating on the punishment of an evil action rather than on the nature of the action itself, by asking whether there is a corresponding benefit (*recompensatio*) rather than whether an evil can itself become good, Albertus ends up closer to Augustine's view of tolerable evil and venial sin than his initial reaction to the anonymous Greek commentator might have promised. Nevertheless, even if Albertus is careful to state that lying is an evil which 'occurs' rather than an evil which is

---

[75] *Ethica* IV.3.2, pp. 320–1.

[76] *Leonardo Bruni Aretino, Humanistisch-philosophische Schriften mit einer chronologie seiner Werke und Briefe*, ed. H. Baron (Leipzig, 1928), 79. Compare e.g. *De Bono* I.5.1, pp. 68–72; II.2.4, p. 104; III.5.3, p. 207; IV.1.5, p. 245; V.2.1, p. 282.

[77] *Super Ethica* V.4, pp. 326–7. Cf. *Ethica* V.2.2, p. 342. Compare the comments of G. Post, 'Philosophy and Citizenship in the Thirteenth Century: Laicisation, the Two Laws and Aristotle', in W. C. Jordan, B. McNab, and T. F. Ruiz (eds.), *Order and Innovation in the Middle Ages: Essays in Honour of J. R. Strayer* (Princeton, 1976), 401–8.

intended, he still describes it as a necessity if humans are to live together. Lying is the result of piety towards one's neighbour and duty towards one's community. In the process, the principle that the common good is superior to the individual good appears to have created the possibility that the individual can sacrifice his own good of virtue in order to benefit everybody else in the community. In his commentary on book IX of the *Ethics*, Albertus argues that the individual should be prepared to sacrifice two of the three categories of individual good—exterior goods and bodily good—for the sake of virtue. In his commentary on books III, IV, and V of the *Ethics*, he seems to suggest that there are certain circumstances in which the third category— the good of virtue—can also be sacrificed for the common good of the political community. By putting forward at least the possibility of such a conclusion, in however guarded a fashion, Albertus opened a long line of debate over which evils are so heinous that they should never be performed for, and in no circumstances be outweighed by, a corresponding benefit to the community.

In studying the initial reception of the *Ethics* and the *Politics* by Albertus Magnus, it is important to draw attention to the amount of non-Aristotelian thought which is incorporated into his commentaries on the two texts. The very frequency of Albertus' citation from scriptural, patristic, and Stoic sources clearly demonstrates that integration within a wider frame of reference was an important part of the intention behind his exposition of Aristotle's argument. Albertus' analysis of the *Politics*, for example, is shot through with illustrations of kingship and tyranny from the Bible, whilst his questions on the *Ethics* are frequently cross-referenced to Cicero. In examining the notion of the common good, it is therefore only natural that Albertus should have drawn on existing treatments of the same concept, from Cicero's *De Officiis* for example, Augustine's *Regula*, Boethius' *Consolatio Philosophiae*, or from the *De Caelestis Hierarchia* and *De Divinis Nominibus* of pseudo-Dionysius. These are the texts which provided him with his definition of God as the perfect sum of all goods or as the supreme good (*summum bonum*), with the presupposition that goodness in the universe (*bonum in communi*) communicates its good (*bonum est diffusivum sui*), and with the principle that the function of love is not to seek its own good but to prefer what is in common (*caritas non quaerit quae sua sunt quia communia propriis anteponit*). Albertus was thereby able to combine these authorities with the notion which he found set out in the *Ethics*—the principles of identity and superiority in book I, the equation of justice with complete virtue in book V, and the relation between self-love and friendship in books VIII and IX.

At the same time, however, Aristotle's discussion of bravery and self-sacrifice in book IX of the *Ethics*, together with his description of contemplative happiness in book X, presented Albertus with an agenda of its own. It was Albertus' analysis of these issues which provided the framework for much of the subsequent interpretation of the text by scholastic theologians. Three questions would now be central to any understanding of the role of the common good in political society—the relationship between the common good in book I and the individual good in book IX; the identification of general justice with the individual virtues in book V; and the relative values of the active life in book I and the contemplative life in book X. By deploying ontological and epistemological arguments to describe 'the common good' in political and ethical contexts, moreover, Albertus also raised the more general question of just how applicable metaphysical principles were to the actual reality of political life. His appeal to the nature of analogical predication and to the good which all things seek explicitly envisaged some correlation between the principles which governed goodness in general and the principles which governed the common good of the human community. His reading of Aristotle's *Politics*, however, showed him that, in practice, this correlation might be neither as precise nor as uniform as book I of the *Ethics* had suggested. An 'Aristotelian' conception of the common good presented a particularly complex picture.

Right at the start of his first commentary on the *Ethics*, Albertus records the opinion that there are three branches of knowledge which deal with human conduct. First, there is moral science whose goal is happiness and whose subject-matter is the human good (*bonum humanum*); second, there is economic science whose goal is material good and whose subject-matter is the household; third, there is political, legal, or civil science whose goal is public peace and whose subject-matter is the political community.[78] Any attempt to analyse Albertus' moral and political philosophy naturally invites consideration of the exact relationship which he envisaged existing between these three categories, between the life of virtue, the provision of material goods, and the establishment of peace. Was the goal of political authority, as Aristotle had maintained, to secure the life of virtue, the object of law to make men good? Or was the goal of political authority, as Cicero and Augustine had maintained, to secure the peace and material sufficiency which was instrumental for such a life, the object of law simply to restrain the worst excesses of sinful human behaviour? It is difficult to avoid the conclusion that Albertus' response to these alternatives was deliberately equivocal. On the one hand, he argued that the common good of the human community is an association of true friendship which is ordered towards the pursuit of virtue and happiness. On the other, he argued that the common good of the human community is the concord of political friendship which is ordered towards the utility of peace. Albertus accordingly understood the common good of the political community in two fundamental senses. A distinction between two different types of good—moral worth and utility, *bonum honestum* and *bonum utile*—produced two different scales of measurement—*bonum* and *utilitas*. In practical terms, this distinction forced Albertus to demonstrate some delicate intellectual footwork when discussing the place of celibacy, contemplation, lying, adultery, and usury within the human community. In theoretical terms, this distinction provided Albertus with a twofold definition of the goal towards which the political community can be ordered. Albertus maintained the firmly 'Aristotelian' ideal that the function of the political community is to secure happiness, activity in accordance with perfect virtue—the

[78] *Super Ethica* prol., pp. 2–3.

common good which had been described in the *Ethics*. Depending on the context, however, Albertus could also express the firmly 'Augustinian' recognition that a more realistic achievement of the political community is to produce a limited degree of harmony, peace, and material self-sufficiency, the common good which had been described to some extent in the *Politics* but which had received its fullest treatment in *De Civitate Dei*.

3
Thomas Aquinas—Metaphysics
and Hierarchy

Whilst the influence of Albertus Magnus on scholastic philosophy and theology extends much further than simply serving as a preparatory guide to Aquinas, an examination of the connections between the two theologians can still prove instructive. This is particularly true of his role as a scholastic commentator on Aristotle's ethical and political thought where Albertus provides a natural, and much-needed, point of reference for Aquinas' understanding of the common good.[1] According to Albertus' analysis of the comparative terminology in book I of the *Ethics*, the superiority of the common good to the individual good can be justified from at least three perspectives—Aristotle's account of the analogical predication of goodness in the universe, the pseudo-Dionysian principle that all good is communicative of its own goodness, and the epistemological theory that individual humans are attracted to the good as the natural object of their intellect and their will. When Aquinas came to discuss the common good of the human community, it accordingly took the form of a wide-ranging investigation of each of the three elements which were outlined in Albertus' exposition. In the first instance, Aristotle's account of analogical predication prompted him to analyse the participation of individuals in existence and goodness in the universe. In the second instance, the pseudo-Dionysian schema of communicative goodness made him examine the way in which the operation of hierarchy directs individual goods towards their ultimate perfection in God. In the third instance, the operation of the intellect and the will precipitated a discussion of the naturalness of the relationship between goodness and human volition.

Viewed in the light of Albertus Magnus' exposition of the *Ethics*, the central question which is posed by Aquinas' understanding of the individual and the common good is the extent of the correspondence between each of Albertus' metaphysical elements (analogy and participation, communication and hierarchy, intellectual apprehension and volition) and the model which Aquinas considered appropriate for the good of the political community. Thus, if Aquinas' commitment to the superiority of the moral good of human society is to be read as a justification of the complete absorption of the individual within the community, then the most natural place to find evidence for it would be in his association of the comparative terminology of

---

[1] For the connection between their respective commentaries, see Thomas Aquinas, *Sententiae Noni Libri Ethicorum* (Rome, 1969), 235*–57*, and, more generally, J. Weisheipl, *Thomas d'Aquino and Albert his Teacher* (Toronto, 1980).

book I of the *Ethics* with the operation of an all-inclusive hierarchy of goodness in the universe. By the same token, if Aquinas' commitment to the value of the individual human being is to be read as a safeguard against the claims of the political community, then the most natural place to find evidence for it would be in his recognition of the dissimilarity between these metaphysical principles of goodness and the operation of human society, in his acknowledgement of a distinction between goodness in the universe and the good of the political community.

The main historiographical difficulty in tackling a specifically 'Thomist' notion of the common good has always been its diversity, its capacity to be described in different terms and to be applied simultaneously to speculative theology, metaphysical theory, political thought, and situational ethics. Context has therefore provided the key to the more sensitive analyses of Aquinas' handling of the common good in all its various guises—as the universal good, as the object of love, as the goal of justice, as the life of virtue, and as the continuation in existence of the species.[2] Such respect for context, however, has not prevented the search for a more systematic account, for an interpretation of the relationship between the individual good and the common good in which their respective claims to priority are resolved in perfect harmony *whatever* the nature of the common good under discussion, be it theological, philosophical, political, or ethical. The search for such a grand unified theory was thus one of the principles which informed the Neo-Thomist exegesis of 'personalism', a reading of Aquinas' political and ethical thought which was designed, in part, to defend him against the charge that his adoption of the principle that the common good is superior to the individual good effectively sacrificed human individuality by completely subordinating the citizen to the superior collectivity of society.[3] For Neo-Thomists, the good of the political community was made up merely of the instrumental utilities of peace, security, and mutual assistance. The term 'person', meanwhile, described the rational intellect, the defining characteristic according to which humankind is created in the image of God and is able to attain the beatific vision. By putting these two definitions together, Neo-Thomist personalists produced a clear and straightforward interpretation of the relationship between the individual and the common good. The 'individual' is ordered towards the common good of the political community but this material good is, in turn, ordered towards the eternal happiness of the 'person'.

Even though Aquinas himself never applied a distinction between 'individual' and 'person' in a specifically political context, a Neo-Thomist interpretation of the human community does have its attractions, not least because of its apparent affinity with the account of the individual and the common good which was put forward by Albertus Magnus in his commentary on book IX of the *Ethics*. Aristotle's discussion

---

[2] I. Th. Eschmann, 'A Thomistic Glossary on the Principle of the Preeminence of a Common Good', *Mediaeval Studies*, 5 (1943), 123–65.

[3] See e.g. E. Gilson, *L'Esprit de la philosophie médiévale* (Paris, 1932), 195–213; I. Th. Eschmann, '*Bonum commune melius est quam bonum unius*: Eine Studie über den Wertvorrang des Personalen bei Thomas von Aquin', *Mediaeval Studies*, 6 (1944), 62–120.

of self-sacrifice prompted Albertus to change his definition of the good of the political community from the common good of human happiness in book I to the material security and well-being of human society in book IX. It appears to have prompted a very similar reaction by his pupil. Thus, according to Aquinas' interpretation of self-sacrifice, the virtuous individual secures for himself the good of virtue (*bonum honestum*) in exchange for the bodily goods of material benefit. True self-love secures the greatest goods for the principal constituent of the individual human being, namely intellect or reason. However, as a consequence of seeking for this self what is essentially good (*bonum simpliciter*), the individual will also prove beneficial (*utilis*) both to himself and to others because the result of his virtuous activity will be that everyone else in society will receive what they need through mutual assistance. In sacrificing money, honours, exterior goods, life, and even the opportunity to perform further virtuous actions, the individual will thereby secure what is morally worthy (*honestum*), a good which is greater (*maius*), better (*melius*), and superior (*eminentius*).[4]

If Aristotle's account of the individual and the common good in books I and IX of the *Ethics* elicited two different views of the good of the human community from Aquinas as well as Albertus, then there is an understandable temptation to conclude that a systematic exposition of the rest of Aquinas' political thought will reveal a uniformly clear distinction between these two definitions. On the one hand, there should be human happiness, the moral goodness in the universe to which human reason is naturally subordinate; on the other, there should be material utility, the benefit of political society which is subordinate to the moral worth of each human being. It is on this basis, for example, that Neo-Thomist personalism presents the common good in God, the *bonum in communi*, and the common good of happiness as final causes, as ultimate goals for the individual human being, whereas it reduces the common good of the political community to acting as an efficient cause, to facilitating the means towards these ends, to being the arena in which those goods which are instrumental to the activity of virtue are provided.[5]

Whatever its attractions, however, a Neo-Thomist interpretation of the human community stands in need of substantial qualification.[6] It should go without saying that just because a conceptual distinction between two types of good was available to Aquinas does not mean that it was applied with the sort of systematic rigour that some modern commentators might prefer. The relation between the individual good and the good of the political community provides a case in point. Any commentator who wishes to restrict Aquinas' understanding of the common good of political society to a notion of external order, to the provision of material benefit and instrumental utility, has the awkward task of explaining why Aquinas consistently emphasizes

---

    [4] Aquinas, *Sententiae Noni Libri Ethicorum* [*Sent. Lib. Eth.*] IX.8–9.

    [5] e.g. A. Modde, 'Le Bien commun dans la philosophie de saint Thomas', *Revue Philosophique de Louvain*, 47 (1949), 221–47.

    [6] The best introduction to, and critique of, a personalist reading of Aquinas remains A. P. Verpaalen, *Der Begriff des Gemeinwohls bei Thomas von Aquin: Ein Beitrag zum Problem des Personalismus* (Heidelberg, 1954).

the profoundly *ethical* character of the good of the community. Outside of the immediate terms of reference of book IX of the *Ethics*, in fact, Aquinas appears to have been only too happy to emphasize the subordination of the individual to a superior moral good of the political community. It is the presence of this moral dimension, expressed in explicitly Aristotelian guise as the life of virtue, which establishes such a close connection between the good of the political community and the nature of goodness in the universe. This connection makes the common good of human society more than just an efficient cause. For Aquinas, the common good of the political community is a final cause, it is the life of happiness, of activity in accordance with perfect virtue.

It is the corollary between happiness and goodness in the political community which makes Aquinas' interpretation of the relationship between the individual and the common good so problematic. Modern disagreement over the Thomist notion of the common good is, at root, a disagreement over the strictness with which Aquinas applied metaphysical principle to political thought. Modern disagreement over Aquinas' understanding of the common good, in other words, originates in a debate over the precision with which Aquinas took Albertus Magnus' philosophical and theological exposition of goodness and used it as a framework for his analysis of political society.

At its most abstract, Aquinas' notion of the common good is the universal good, the 'good in common', the order of goodness which is dependent upon God. In order to explain the presence of this universal goodness in individual things, Aquinas, like Albertus Magnus, followed Aristotle's account of analogical predication. By combining the critique of Plato's Form of the Good from book I of the *Ethics* with the discussion of goodness and being from book IV of the *Metaphysics*, Albertus put forward two possible definitions of the analogical relation between individual goods. Either they derive from a single principle (*ab uno esse*) and contribute towards a single goal (*ad unum contendere*) or they share the same relation or proportion towards each other such that there is no relation between the analogates themselves other than the similarity of the relation within each of them (a relation which can be expressed in the ratio A:B = C:D). Albertus himself was far more interested in the first of these definitions (analogy of attribution or proportion) than the second (analogy of proportionality). As a result, by concentrating on the parallels which could be drawn between goodness and being as 'transcendentals' (that is, as predicates which transcend the ten categories), Albertus drew a firm connection between the way in which 'good' could be predicated of several different things and the way in which 'being' could be used in a variety of senses whilst also referring to one central principle and one particular nature. In particular, Albertus explored Aristotle's comparison between being and health. Thus, whilst something can be either productive of health, indicative of health, or preservative of health, all three senses of the term have a single point of reference, namely health itself or the health of one particular individual. In the case of being, Albertus identified this single point of reference as substance in that the other nine categories depend on the prior existence of one particular subject. In the case of goodness, he identified this single point of reference as the primary or supreme good.[7]

Aquinas' own account of the universal good is very close to the analysis of analogy of attribution which he found in Albertus Magnus.[8] According to Aquinas, the analogical predication of goodness in individual good things derives from their relation to a single principle or goal (*omnia bona dependent ab uno primo bonitatis principio vel in quantum ordinantur ad unum finem*).[9] This single principle or goal is the supreme good, the essential or primary good which is both a good in itself and the cause of goodness in every good thing. In expounding the twin components of this definition, Aquinas draws two corollaries from the comparison made with health. First, health is predicated essentially or primarily of its single point of reference (e.g. Socrates), and only secondarily of its accidental manifestations (e.g. Socrates' colour, skin, medicine, and food). Second, this primary analogate (Socrates) is the cause of the secondary analogates (colour, skin, medicine, food) either in the sense that these secondary analogates are ordered towards the primary analogate as their final cause (*ad unum contendere*), or because they are related to the primary analogate as their agent or efficient cause (*ab uno principio*), or because they are related to the primary analogate as their subject or material cause. On Aquinas' reading of analogical predication, therefore, the division between primary and secondary, prior and posterior, creates a close connection between causality and participation. Thus, health is predicated of these secondary analogates (colour, skin, medicine, food) only because of their relation to the primary analogate (Socrates). In just the same way, victory is predicated primarily of the army commander and only secondarily of soldiers, armourers, and grooms because the latter share in victory only by virtue of their relation to the army commander.

For Aquinas, the connection between analogy and participation is a connection between the logical understanding of predication and the ontological reality which underpins it.[10] An effect has a quality which is similar to its cause and, to that extent, can be said to participate in it. Aquinas' interest in this connection stems from the use to which it can be put in emphasizing the dependence of all created beings on God. According to Aquinas, all created beings, as secondary analogates, are imperfect likenesses or similitudes of the primary analogate, namely God. The 'participation' of Creation in the goodness of God, in other words, is a participation by similitude or by likeness. Everything is called good, he argues, by reason of its likeness to divine goodness, a likeness which formally constitutes its own goodness, whereby it is

---

[7] See above, pp. 34–6.   [8] For analogy of proportionality, see *Q. Disp. de Verit.* II.11.

[9] *Sent. Lib. Eth.* I.7.

[10] For what follows, see J. F. Wippel, 'Metaphysics', in N. Kretzmann and E. Stump (eds.), *The Cambridge Companion to Aquinas* (Cambridge, 1993), 85–127, esp. 88–99; id., 'Thomas Aquinas and Participation', in J. F. Wippel (ed.), *Studies in Medieval Philosophy* (Washington, DC, 1987), 117–58. Cf. Gilson, *L'Esprit de la philosophie médiévale*, ch. 14; id., *The Christian Philosophy of St. Thomas Aquinas* (London, 1957), 236–48.

termed good. All created things, therefore, represent one goodness but also many goodnesses.[11] This combination of unity and plurality, the one and the many, is fundamental to Aquinas' account of the universe and its relation to God. In giving being and goodness to creatures, God acts as an efficient cause. This being and goodness, however, remains really distinct from the nature of these creatures in that they will always be composites of existence (*esse*) and essence (*essentia*). Essence and existence are identical in God alone; all other creatures participate by likeness in the self-subsisting existence of God. Thus, every part of Creation participates in existence in general (*esse commune*) but this existence itself participates in the divine existence, namely God, the only being who is in Himself self-subsisting existence (*esse subsistens*). Participation in goodness follows the same principle. Goodness in Creation does not derive from God as from a univocal agent since Creation and God are not in the same species or genus. Goodness is 'in' God as the first or primary cause of all things; it is in Him in a transcendent or excellent way. It is in this sense that God can be termed the highest or supreme good (*summum bonum*).[12]

In discussing the nature of God as the supreme good, Aquinas draws an important distinction between objective beatitude (*beatitudo quantum ad obiectum*) and subjective beatitude (*beatitudo quantum ad actum*), that is, between the supreme good in itself (*summum bonum simpliciter*) and the supreme good in the sense of what is participated in by a creature (*summum bonum in genere bonorum participabilium a creatura*). In the first sense, God can be termed the supreme, transcendent good which exists apart from all other things. In the second sense, God can be described as the happiness which is shared in by all creatures, the *summum bonum* which is common to all good things and from which they derive their goodness by participation.[13] All things can therefore be termed good with reference to this primary good inasmuch as they somehow participate and resemble it (*in quantum participat ipsum per modum cuiusdam assimilationis*). In this sense, all things can be said to be good by means of the divine goodness which is the pattern, source, and goal of all goodness.[14] God can therefore be termed the common good (*bonum commune*) because of the comprehensiveness of His position as the final and efficient cause of all individual goods. God is the universal good which transcends but also sustains all particular goods.[15]

Analogical participation in God by likeness and causality provides the first metaphysical principle of goodness which underpins Aquinas' account of the common good—the participation of all individuals in goodness in the universe (*bonum in communi*). This principle, is, in turn, inextricably bound up with a second—all good is communicative of its goodness (*bonum est diffusivum sui*). It is a tenet fundamental to Aquinas' theology that the nature of God is to be both good *and* communicative of

---

[11] *Ia* 6.4.   [12] *Ia* 6.3.

[13] *Ia* 26.3; *IaIIae* 34.3. For the distinction between the objective end (*finis cuius*) and the subjective end (*finis quo*), see Aristotle, *De Anima* II.4 415^{b}20. God is what is reached, beatitude is that by which He is reached.

[14] *Ia* 4.3, 6.4.   [15] *IaIIae* 90.2.

His goodness.[16] If 'deity' signifies this first attribute (that is, the essence of God), then 'divinity' signifies the second (that is, the existence and the goodness of God in which all things participate).[17] Aquinas infers from this second attribute that goodness can be equated with being (*bonum convertitur cum ente*) and concludes that all things participate in the goodness of God insofar as they have existence. It is in this sense that God is the common good for all being (*bonum commune omni enti*).[18] This principle, however, is more than just a question of individuals participating in goodness and being. Participation necessarily leads to the further diffusion of goodness by the individual participants themselves. If God is both good in Himself and communicative of His goodness, therefore, then Creation too will be both good and communicative of its goodness.[19]

The combination of these two metaphysical principles, participation and communication, gives Aquinas a distinctive understanding of what it means to talk about the common good in the universe. Since God is the common good of all being, the more common a created good is and the more it communicates its goodness, then the more it will resemble its divine exemplar. In other words, it will be both better (*melius*) and more divine (*divinius*).[20] Moreover, since a particular thing's degree of goodness constitutes its degree of perfection, created things can also be said to communicate their goodness to others according to the extent to which they possess perfection. Such perfection is, again, a representation of a divine principle. It is within these terms of reference, therefore, that Aquinas argues that the more common something is, the more perfect it is (*perfectius*).[21] Every creature, to the extent that it possesses any perfection, represents God (*repraesentat*) and is like Him (*est ei similis*) because God, being essentially and universally perfect, has pre-existing in Himself the perfections of all His creatures.[22] At the same time, a creature is not 'like' God in the same way that it is 'like' another member of its species or genus. A creature resembles God in the way that an effect in some way resembles (*aliqualem similitudinem*) a transcendent cause by imperfectly reproducing its form.[23] It is this remoteness and imperfection which prevents Aquinas' theory of participation from being construed as a univocal account of goodness and being, and therefore as a pantheist view of the universe. For Aquinas, the possession of being and goodness by individual creatures is always limited by their own nature. Nevertheless, with this reservation, Aquinas can still conclude that the good of the universe is more representative of divine goodness, the good of many better than the good of one.[24]

---

[16] *Summa contra Gentiles* II.45; *IaIIae* I.4 in/ad 1. Cf. *Compendium Theologiae* I.124, and, more generally, *Expositio in Librum Boethii De Hebdomadibus*.

[17] *Expositio super Romanos* I.6. Cf. IV *Sent.* 49.1.1a ad 3; *ScG* I.40.

[18] *IaIIae* 54.3; *ScG* II.32. Cf. *Ia* 60.5.

[19] *ScG* I.37; *De Substantiis Separatis* XII. Cf. *ScG* III.69; J.-P. Jossua, 'L'axiome "bonum diffusivum sui" chez S. Thomas d'Aquin', *Revue des Sciences Religieuses*, 40 (1966), 127–53; J. G. Bougerol, 'Saint Bonaventure et le pseudo-Denys l'Aréopagite', Actes du Colloque Saint Bonaventure, *Etudes Franciscaines*, 18 (1968), 33–123, esp. 81–104.

[20] *ScG* III.24; II *Sent.* 11.1.2. Cf. IV *Sent.* 49.1.1c in 1.   [21] *ScG* I.38, I.40, III.21; *IIaIIae* 50.1.

[22] *Ia* 4.2.   [23] *Ia* 13.2, 5. Cf. *Ia* 6.2.   [24] *Comp. Theol.* I.124.

Aquinas used Aristotle's account of analogical predication as the basis for his own account of the relationship between goodness in general and individual good things, and he used the nature of participation by likeness and causality in order to explain the relationship between the created universe and God. In both instances, he also drew on pseudo-Dionysius' account of hierarchy. Aquinas conceived of the universe as a Neoplatonic hierarchy, as the emanation (*exitus*) of the multiplicity of being from a single principle, namely God, and the reversion (*redditus*) of all these individual elements in Creation back towards this unity, back towards their Creator. This conception produces a third metaphysical principle of goodness—the hierarchical arrangement of goodness in the universe such that individual goods are ordered towards their ultimate good in God. Thus, if the principle of communicative goodness in the universe is produced by the principle of participating in the likeness of God,[25] then this principle produces, in its turn, a principle of dynamic reversion which brings individual beings back towards God. The perfection that is goodness accordingly entails two elements, being good and bringing others to this goodness. The similitude to God which the universe possesses, therefore, requires not only that everything should 'be' and should be 'good', but also that one thing should be ordered above another in a hierarchy and move lesser goods towards their ultimate end.[26] According to Aquinas, there is accordingly a second sense in which a good may be said to be 'more divine'. It is more divine to be the cause of goodness to oneself and to others (rather than merely to oneself) because it is more divine to act in partnership with God in directing subordinate goods towards Him.[27] As soon as the universe is considered not only as a hierarchy of emanation but also as a hierarchy of reversion, a hierarchy in which individual creatures are ordered towards their ultimate goal by means of their immediate superiors,[28] then the common good has to be considered as a final rather than an efficient cause. Goodness in the universe, in other words, is not just an effusion of goodness (which means that it acts as an efficient cause) but it is a communication of goodness (which means that it acts as a final cause).[29]

The final element in Aquinas' metaphysical conception of the common good is provided by the integration of his account of a hierarchy of goodness and being with his analysis of human psychology and epistemology. Aquinas' treatment of moral virtue centres on a definition of the human good as a life which is lived according to the rule and measure of reason.[30] This good of reason (*bonum rationis*) is tied to the

---

[25] *Q. Disp. de Verit.* XXI.5.   [26] *Comp. Theol.* I.124; *De Sub. Sep.* XII.

[27] IV *Sent.* 49.1.1c; III *Sent.* 35.1.3a ad 2. Cf. *IaIIae* 111.5 in 2, *IIaIIae* 124.3 in 3. Aquinas can also gloss *divinius* as a term relative to Aristotle's own historical context (*IIaIIae* 99.1 ad 1) and to the principle closest to Aristotle's own intention, namely an eternal good of the species (IV *Sent.* 26.1.2 in 3. Cf. IV *Sent.* 31.1.1 in 1). As in Albertus Magnus, *maius* is the term most susceptible to a quantitative interpretation of the common good, either in absolute terms or in terms of proportion (*IaIIae* 113.9). However, Aquinas specifies that, when an object so described is a virtue, it can also sustain a qualitative comparison, and in this sense *maius* is equivalent to *melius* (*IIaIIae* 123.12). Thus, as with *divinius*, he considers it to be of 'greater' virtue to act upon another person than merely to act upon oneself (*IaIIae* 111.5 in 2).

[28] *Comp. Theol.* I.124; *De Sub. Sep.* XII; IV *Sent.* 49.1.1c.

[29] *Q. Disp. de Verit.* XXI.1 ad 4. Cf. *Ia* 5.4 ad 2.   [30] *IaIIae* 64.1 ad 1. Cf. *IaIIae* 55.4.

principle of goodness (*ratio boni*) by means of Aristotle's premiss that the good is that which all things seek (*bonum quod omnia appetunt*). For Aquinas, 'that which all things seek' must be identified as the supreme good since there is nothing good, which is not a similitude of, and a participant in, the supreme goodness in God.[31] This is therefore the principle which governs what humans desire with their rational appetite, namely the will. The proper object of the will, Aquinas argues, is the good in common, the good which all humans have as their common goal. Particular goods can thus become the objects of will only insofar as they participate in the universal principle of goodness.[32] That an object is good, however, is not in itself sufficient to move the human will. It must also be apprehended as such by the intellect. Therefore, if the action of the correctly functioning will is its inclination towards the universal good in common, then this presupposes, in its turn, the action of the intellect.[33] This gives Aquinas a fourth metaphysical principle of goodness—the natural object of both the intellect and the will is the common good. Once again, this is a principle whose origins are divine. God apprehends the good of the whole universe since He is its creator and ruler; hence, whatever He wills, He wills in accordance with the principle of the common good (*sub ratione boni communi*), that is, his own goodness, the good of the whole universe. Since the human will is created in the image of God, it will therefore only be correctly ordered when it follows its divine exemplar and refers a particular good to the good in common. Indeed, in doing so, a formal correspondence is established between the human will and the will of God.[34]

Aquinas' account of the intellect and the will accordingly leaves him with a clear criterion for establishing something's place in the hierarchy of the universe. The more perfect something is in virtue, the higher it is in the order of goodness, the more 'common' is the good it desires, and the more widely does it secure this good in things other than itself. These degrees of perfection are therefore degrees of increasing community in that it is a greater perfection for something to be good in itself and the cause of goodness in others than simply to be good in itself.[35] Imperfect things tend towards their own good, namely the good of an individual; perfect things tend towards the good of a species; more perfect things tend towards the good of a genus; the most perfect, that is God, secures the good of all being, the good of the universe.[36]

This is a brief outline of a complex series of arguments. Put together, the combination of Aquinas' four metaphysical principles of goodness (all individuals participate in existence and goodness in the universe; all good is communicative of its goodness; individual goods are ordered in a hierarchy towards their ultimate good in God; the

---

[31] *Sent. Lib. Eth.* I.1.
[32] *Ia* 59.1, 82.4; *Q. Disp. de Verit.* XXV.1. Cf. *Ia* 103.2, 105.4; *IaIIae* 1.2 ad 3; *IaIIae* 9.1.
[33] *ScG* II.48. Cf. *Q. Disp. de Malo* I.4; *De Sub. Sep.* XX. The will remains free because only in eternal beatitude can man truly apprehend the essence of God and the necessary connection of particular goods with Him, with His goodness, and with His good in common. In this life, there is a discrepancy between human will and its objects, particular goods which are unable to fulfil the desire for the good in common and which therefore do not necessarily compel (*IaIIae* 10.2). For the relative superiority of the will and the intellect, see *Ia* 82.4.
[34] *IaIIae* 19.10.   [35] *Ia* 103.6. Cf. *Ia* 108.3 ad 2.   [36] *ScG* III.24.

natural object of the intellect and the will is the common good) has significant implications for his understanding of the relationship between the individual and the
common good. Viewed in these terms, for example, it becomes clear why, when
Aquinas turned to book I of the *Ethics*, he had little difficulty in glossing the superiority of the common good with the same pseudo-Dionysian principles of goodness
which had been used by Albertus Magnus.[37] Faced with Aristotle's comparative terminology, Aquinas argues that 'greater divinity' is an entirely appropriate term for a
good which reflects the nature of God as the universal cause of all goods. Since a final
cause is more potent (*potius*) the more things to which it extends its influence, and
since the good of the community is the ultimate goal of human life (*bonum humanum*),
then not only is this common good more divine but so too are those humans who are
responsible for the *res publica*.[38] As a result, when Aquinas comes to express the principle of the superiority of the common good over the individual good outside of his
commentary on the *Ethics*, he is happy to recycle various combinations of Aristotle's
comparative vocabulary (*maius*,[39] *maius et divinius*,[40] *divinius*,[41] *melius et divinius*,[42]
melius[43]) as well as a number of alternative terms (*potius, eminentius, nobilius, prius*)[44]
and several different verbs (*praeferre, praepollere, excedere, praeeminere, praepon-
dere*).[45] For all his emphasis on the good of the political community as a final cause,
however, for all his endorsement of the common good as a good which is greater,
better, and more divine than the individual good, Aquinas stops short when he comes
to the fourth and final comparative term from book I of the *Ethics*, namely *perfectius*.
Indeed, Aquinas' apparent reluctance to ascribe greater perfection to the good of the
political community provides a revealing insight into his own understanding of the
nature of the connection between the metaphysical operation of goodness in the universe and the position of the common good in human society.

Perfection can be ascribed to something as a means of describing its degree of
goodness but it is a term which also defines its proximity to the ultimate end in God.

---

[37] See above, pp. 32, 49. Cf. *Summa Theologiae*, trans. T. Gilby et al. (61 vols.; Blackfriars edn.;
London, 1964–80), vol. xiv, appendix 3, pp. 182–93; F. O'Rourke, *Pseudo-Dionysius and the Metaphysics
of Aquinas* (Leiden, 1992).

[38] *Sent. Lib. Eth.* I.2. Cf. *De Sub. Sep.* X; *Super Librum Dionysii De Divinis Nominibus* IV.2; *Super
Librum De Causis* III, X; *IIaIIae* 45.3 ad 1; *Sent. super Meta.* VI.3.

[39] *IaIIae* 113.9; *IIaIIae* 39.2, 42.2; *De Duobus Praeceptis Caritatis* II.

[40] *IIaIIae* 39.2.

[41] II *Sent.* 9.1.3, 29.1.3, 32.2.2; III *Sent.* 1.1.2, 32.1.5d, 35.1.3a, 35.1.4a; IV *Sent.* 2.1.3, 15.2.4a, 24.3.2c,
26.1.2; *Q. Disp. de Verit.* V.3; *ScG* II.42, III.17, III.136; *Ia* 108.6; *IaIIae* 97.4; *IIaIIae* 31.3, 88.11, 141.8;
De Duob. Praec. Carit. II. Cf. *semper divinius* (*ScG* III.69, III.125); *divinissimum* (*Sent. Lib. Eth.* X.11).

[42] IV *Sent.* 31.1.1; *Sent. Lib. Pol.* I.1.

[43] *ScG* I.41, III.146; *IaIIae* 111.5; *Q. Disp. de Virt.* III.2; *Responsio ad Lectorem Venetum de Articulis
XXX* 21; *Responsio ad Lectorem Venetum de Articulis XXXVI* 23; *IIaIIae* 47.10, 124.3, 124.5; *Comp.
Theol.* I.124; *Sent. Lib. Pol.* I.4; *De Duob. Praec. Carit.* II. Cf. IV *Sent.* 38.1.4a (*multo melius*).

[44] IV *Sent.* 49.5.3b; *IIaIIae* 152.4; *De Sub. Sep.* X; *IIIa* 65.3; *Q. Disp. de Verit.* V.3; *ScG* I.70; *Sent. Lib.
Pol.* I.1 (but cf. IV *Sent.* 2.1.3, 23.2.4b). For *prius*, see Aristotle, *Politics* I.2 1253ª18–20 (ed. Susemihl),
p. 9.

[45] *IaIIae* 83.1; *Q. Disp. de Virt.* III.2 ad 7; *Quodlibet* IV.8.1; *IIaIIae* 68.1 (*semper praeferre*); II *Sent.*
32.2.2; II *Sent.* 23.1.2; *IIaIIae* 58.6; II *Sent.* 29.1.3.

According to Aquinas, the more perfect something is, the closer it must be to God.[46] Applied to the good of the political community, however, the combination of perfection, final causality, and hierarchy presented Aquinas with a problem. Neither Albertus nor Aquinas sought to deny the fact that the human community as a whole could secure certain common goods which individuals on their own could not, cooperating in an army in order to defeat an invading enemy, for example, or combining the professions of agriculture and industry in order to provide material self-sufficiency. However, the identification of the human good of happiness as the 'more perfect' good of the political community suggested that the common good of the political community might constitute a superior level of goodness in the universe. If the hierarchy of reversion is characterized by the reduction of multiplicity to unity, the ascent of individuals to the supreme goodness of God, then a 'more perfect' common good would seem to imply a higher degree of unity into which individuals have to be incorporated in order to progress towards their ultimate goal of eternal happiness in God.

The judgement of the goodness of anything depends upon its reference to the whole universe in which every part has its own perfectly ordered place.[47] The principle of goodness in the universe (*ratio boni in communi*) presupposes the participation, the natural subordination, of the individual's intellect and will in a hierarchy of goodness which culminates in God. If a 'more perfect' political community is to be inserted into this scheme, then one possibility would be to regard this community as an all-inclusive common good in which the individual must participate in order to secure his 'most perfect' goal in God. Such a conclusion, however, rests on one important presupposition, namely that what is true of the good in common in the universe is also true of the common good of human society. For this correlation to work, then what is true of the good which all things seek and which is predicated analogically of all things (*bonum in communi*) must also be true of the common good of the political community (*bonum communitatis*). As a result, just as Averroes' universal intellect could be seen to embody a denial of the individuality of the human soul, a 'more perfect' good of the political community appeared to present a similar threat to the individuality of the human being.[48] The question posed for Aquinas' political theology is straightforward. Is the mediation of ends within the hierarchy of goodness so strict that the individual human being cannot attain his ultimate good in God without the good of human society? Or can the operation of the hierarchy of goodness be modified to make exception for the individual such that a human being can attain eternal beatitude directly, without the mediation of the human community?

Aquinas seems to have been well aware of the potential difficulties which were presented by positing the common good of the political community as a more perfect stage in the hierarchy of goodness which culminates in God. This is one reason why *perfectius* should be the comparative term from book I of the *Ethics* which is the least frequently cited in specifically political contexts. Aquinas is quite content to

---

[46] *IIaIIae* 50.1; *ScG* I.38, III.64.   [47] *Ia* 49.3. Cf. *Ia* 47.2 ad 1.   [48] See above, p. 5.

accept that the common good of the human community is something 'greater', 'better', and 'more divine', but he uses 'more perfect' to describe the common good in human society only in the context of explicitly spiritual goods.[49] It might also explain the way in which Aquinas uses the analogy of the army. In his commentary on the *Metaphysics*, he employs two models. In the first, he presents the goal of the army as victory, a common good which is secured through military discipline and the individual victories of individual soldiers.[50] In the second, he follows both Aristotle and Albertus Magnus in dividing the goal of the army (namely victory) into its intrinsic and extrinsic goods (namely the mutual ordering of its parts and the good of its commander). According to this model, the good of the army is greater in the person of the commander than in the order of its parts because a goal is always greater in goodness than those things which are ordered towards it.[51] Of the two illustrations, Aquinas uses the second more frequently than the first and, as an analogy for the universe, the reason for his preference is clear. Just as the good of the commander is the goal of the army, so the goodness in God is the goal of all Creation, the external good on whose account the hierarchical order of the universe depends.[52] Thus, whilst the goal of the universe is the order of the universe itself (that is, a good which exists within it), this is, in turn, ordered towards the ultimate goal of the universe (that is, a good which is extrinsic or external).[53]

As an analogy for the political community, however, the army analogy poses a number of problems. As a rule, Aquinas is careful to state not only that the good of the ruler towards which individuals are ordered is the common good but also that the good of a community consists of more than just the organization of its individuals towards the greater good of its ruler.[54] Nevertheless, difficulties begin to emerge the more closely this analogy is defined. Even when the common good of the army is described as victory, it is open to the inference that an individual soldier will only secure this goal, however well he himself fights, if his fellow-soldiers fight with him and in a similar fashion. For an individual's ultimate goal to be dependent on the success of the group may hold true for an army but is it an aspect of the analogy which is strictly applicable to the political community? Is the individual good of the citizen subordinate to the common good of the community in such a way that the citizen cannot secure his ultimate end in God without it? The same question can be asked of the second Aristotelian metaphor which is used by Albertus Magnus and then adopted by

---

[49] *De Perf. Spir. Vit.* XVII. Cf. *Tabula Libri Ethicorum* (an alphabetical handbook composed by Aquinas' secretaries but drawn from Albertus Magnus' first commentary on the *Ethics*) I.1.a. If Aquinas is reluctant to use *perfectius* of political society, then he is still prepared to use it for the universe. Likewise, although he does not use *dignius* to describe the superiority of the common good over the individual, he does use *nobilius* and *eminentius* (*ScG* I.70, II.45; *Q. Disp. de Verit.* V.3).

[50] *Sent. super Meta.* VII.2.

[51] *Sent. super Meta.* XII.12. Cf. *Metaphysics* XII.10 1075ᵃ11–15, ed. Vuillemin-Diem (*Aristoteles Latinus* XXV.3.2), p. 266.

[52] *Ia* 108.6.   [53] *Ia* 103.2 ad 3.

[54] IV *Sent.* 19.2.2a. Cf. III *Sent.* 33.3.1; *De Regimine Iudaeorum ad Ducissam Brabantiae* VI. This is what distinguishes civil from servile subjection in the *Politics* (*Ia* 92.1 ad 2; *Ia* 96.4). Cf. *C. Imp. Dei* IV.15. In *IaIIae* 9.1 and 111.5, the common good is left simply as the order of the parts.

Aquinas, namely that of the gang hauling a ship. Both the victory of an army and the movement of a ship require the collective power of many individuals in order to secure a result which is unattainable by any one individual on his own.[55] When Aquinas comes to treat these analogies in the context of the political community, it is noticeable that he qualifies both models in order to make specific reservation for the individual. The whole, he writes, is capable of an operation which is not the operation of any one part—the army fights its battle, the gang moves its ship. The individual, although part of this whole, nevertheless retains an operation which is not the operation of the whole, just as the soldier retains an operation which is not the operation of the army.[56]

Where the difficulty arises in the application of the army analogy to the political community is not so much in the 'structure' of hierarchy, as a form of governance or order, but in the 'dynamic' of hierarchy, as the means by which its constituent individuals can secure their ultimate goal. Aquinas, unfortunately, does not choose to explain the precise nature of a soldier's individual mode of operation, nor its relation to the action of the whole. Whether this marks an attempt to avoid the tensions implicit in introducing an Aristotelian definition of a 'more perfect' good of political society into a hierarchy of goodness must therefore remain conjecture. Corroborative support can be gained, however, from the parallels which exist in what Aquinas has to say about the connection between celestial hierarchy and earthly government when he compares the way in which God governs the universe through intermediaries and the way in which a king rules his kingdom through his ministers.[57]

In his commentary on the *Sentences*, Aquinas sets out how the three celestial hierarchies correspond to three royal ministries: those who operate immediately around the person of the king, those whose duties concern the rule of the kingdom as a whole, and those whose duties cover the government of a specific part. Thus, the orders of the first hierarchy (Seraphim, Cherubim, and Thrones) are concerned with God, the orders of the second hierarchy (Powers, Virtues, and Dominions) are concerned with the community of the whole universe, and the orders of the third hierarchy (Principalities, Archangels, and Angels) are concerned with its subsidiary parts. The connection with royal government is then examined in some detail. Aquinas divides the second celestial hierarchy into its three orders according to the three ways in which the government of a community secures the common good of peace. First, a judgement must be made as to what is due to each individual—this corresponds to the order of Powers. Second, this judgement must be efficacious—this corresponds to the order of Virtues. Third, this judgement must be just—this corresponds to the order of Dominions.[58] Likewise, Aquinas divides the third

---

[55] *De Sub. Sep.* XII; above, pp. 37–8.   [56] *Sent. Lib. Eth.* I.1. Cf. Aristotle, *Physics* VI.10 240^{b}13–14.

[57] Cf. *Ia* 112.3. For the use of temporal rule as an illustration for both the celestial hierarchy and the divine hierarchy of the whole universe, see *Ia* 108.2; II *Sent.* 10.1.1; IV *Sent.* 24.2.1, 45.3.2; *ScG* III.76–7; *Ia* 22.3, 103.6, 110.1; *IIaIIae* 184.6; *Quod.* III.6.3; *Q. Disp. de Verit.* XXVII.3. Cf. D. E. Luscombe, 'Thomas Aquinas and Conceptions of Hierarchy in the Thirteenth Century', *Miscellanea Mediaevalia*, 19 (1988), 273–5.

[58] II *Sent.* 9.1.3; *Ia* 108.6. Cf. pseudo-Dionysius, *De Caelestis Hierarchia*, ed. G. Heil, trans. M. de Gandillac (Paris, 1978), VI.2–VII.1, pp. 104–8; VIII.1, pp. 119–22; IX.1–2, pp. 128–30; *Dionysiaca:*

celestial hierarchy into its three orders according to their respective modes of activity. Principalities are concerned with one 'province' within the universe; Archangels are concerned with individual human beings when these individuals secure the good of many other humans (it was thus an Archangel, Gabriel, who announced the births of Christ and John the Baptist); Angels are concerned with individual human beings when they are in isolation.[59]

Aquinas repeats this scheme in the *Summa contra Gentiles* but with some modifications. It is the order of Principalities which is now said to be concerned with the common good but this common good is defined, not as peace, but as the good of the political community or of a people. The ministry which pertains to this order is accordingly defined more precisely as the arrangement of kingdoms, as the transfer of rule from one people to another, and as the instruction of princes. Archangels, meanwhile, also concern themselves with a human good, but this human good is defined, not as the common good, but as a good which pertains to an individual yet which is beneficial (*utile*) to many other individuals as well (the examples given are the observance of divine worship or articles of faith). Gabriel again serves as a representative of the order of Archangels, although the individual with whom he is concerned and who is 'beneficial' to many other individuals is no longer Christ nor John the Baptist, individuals *through* whom goodness will come to many, but Mary, the individual *to* whom the announcement of future benefit to humankind is made.[60]

Aquinas compares the orders of this third celestial hierarchy one final time in the *Summa Theologiae*. Like army commanders, he writes, Principalities initiate, lead, and direct others in actions which are ordered towards an ultimate goal. Angels, on the other hand, simply ensure that these actions are executed. Archangels, meanwhile, lie somewhere between the two—they are Angels with respect to Principalities but Principalities with respect to Angels.[61] Aquinas explains this differentiation by relating it more directly to the humans with whom the activities of each of these orders are concerned. Whilst custody of particular individuals pertains to Angels, he argues, custody in general pertains not to one order but to several because superior orders are more universal in their authority. Aquinas thereby concludes that custody of the whole of humankind pertains to the order of Principalities and, he adds, perhaps (*vel forte*), to Archangels.[62] The hesitation is worth noting. In the *Summa contra Gentiles*, Aquinas drew a distinction between Principalities and Angels on the grounds of their respective responsibilities. Thus, Principalities were concerned with 'the common good of the political community or of a people' whereas Archangels were concerned with 'a good which is beneficial to many'. In the *Summa Theologiae*, the distinction between these two types of good becomes hard to maintain when the

Recueil donnant l'ensemble des traductions latines des ouvrages attribués au Denys de l'Aréopage, ed. P. Chevallier (2 vols.; Bruges, 1937, 1950), ii. 831–42, 869–77, 892–902; Gregory the Great, *XL Homiliae in Evangelia* 34.9–10 (*PL* 76, cols. 1251–2).

[59] II *Sent.* 9.1.3. Cf. Giles of Rome, *De Ecclesiastica Potestate*, ed. R. Scholz (Weimar, 1929), II.13, pp. 123–5.
[60] *ScG* III.80.   [61] *Ia* 108.6.   [62] *Ia* 113.3.

example which is chosen to illustrate 'a good which is beneficial to many' is the salvation of the whole of humankind. To put it another way, activities which belonged to distinct orders when the question was one of governance (the common good of a people, the good of many people brought about by one individual) become fused when the perspective is that of the dynamic (the common good of salvation secured through one individual). Once the celestial hierarchy is viewed in terms of its operation as a final cause rather than as an efficient or a formal cause, Principalities and Archangels have to be regarded as equivalent, their only point of distinction lying, not in the number of individuals for whom they are responsible, but in the number of individuals to whom each order directly communicates.

Whatever the dangers of counter-factual analysis, it is often helpful to understand what Aquinas avoids saying, to examine where he departs from a model rather than maintain it to the letter, and, most significantly, to consider why he might have done so. This is particularly important in the case of his use of hierarchy where his theoretical model is frequently tailored to meet the requirements of a particular application. It is thus a feature of Aquinas' application of hierarchy to earthly government that, in certain circumstances, it stops short of a strict mediation of ends. This can be seen at a very practical level. When Aquinas draws a parallel between the operation of the celestial hierarchy and the government of the earthly church, for example, he is careful to leave room for the *praetermissio ordinis*, that is, the suspension of the normal operation of the hierarchical dynamic such that the mediating action of particular orders can be bypassed. In this case, it is Aquinas' defence of the mendicant orders against bishops and secular clergy which prompts him to argue that a lesser order can sometimes act upon its superior rather than a superior order always acting upon its inferior.[63] It also operates on a more abstract plane. In the *Summa contra Gentiles*, Aquinas draws a distinction between the different ways in which God acts in the universe. In the celestial hierarchy, for example, God always acts on inferior angels through the mediation of their superiors. In the human hierarchy, on the other hand, God will occasionally abrogate the mediation of angels or of Nature and act directly Himself. In this case, it is Aquinas' desire to incorporate a hierarchy of causality without limiting God to the remoteness of a first cause which prompts him to emphasize God's immediate knowledge of, and action upon, all things.[64]

These qualifications can fruitfully be compared with Aquinas' approach to the common good as a mediating end within the hierarchy of goodness in the universe. Just as too rigid a descending structure limits the direct action of God within Creation, so too rigid an ascending structure limits the immediacy of humankind's return to its Creator. In his use of the term *perfectius*, in his description of the army

---

[63] Y. M. J. Congar, 'Aspects ecclésiologiques de la querelle entre mendiants et séculiers dans la seconde moitié du XIIIe siècle et le début du XIVe', *AHDLMA* 28 (1961), 35–151; Luscombe, 'Thomas Aquinas and Conceptions of Hierarchy'. Cf. M. M. Dufeil, 'Ierarchia: Un concept dans la polémique universitaire parisienne du XIIIe siècle', *Miscellanea Mediaevalia* 12 (1980), 56–83; S. H. Beer, 'The Rule of the Wise and the Holy: Hierarchy in the Thomistic System', *Political Theory*, 14 (1986), 391–422.

[64] *ScG* III.76. Cf. *ScG* I.70; *Ia* 5.5, 106.3.

analogy, in his account of the orders of the third celestial hierarchy, and in his discussion of divine knowledge and agency, Aquinas seems to be trying specifically to avoid the conclusion that, by virtue of its higher rank, a community is closer than an individual to God. This intention becomes clearer still in his treatment of the way in which the eternal salvation of individual human beings relates to the largest 'community' of all, namely the created universe.

At the heart of Aquinas' account of God's government of the universe is the principle that the whole is superior to the part. The providential government of Creation, he argues, involves three parameters—a goal (God, that is, goodness as a final cause), an order structured towards that goal (the universe, that is, goodness as an efficient or formal cause), and a rule for that order (divine law).[65] When several things are directed or ordered towards a goal, they can be described both as ends in themselves (*propter se*) and as means towards a still higher end (*propter aliud*). When something in the universe is correctly ordered, therefore, it is governed in both senses. Incorruptible parts of the universe are thus governed by God *propter se* and *propter aliud*. When something departs from this order, it ceases to be an end in itself and it is governed by God only in the sense that it is ordered as a means towards something else. Corruptible parts of the universe are thus governed only *propter aliud*. It is in this second sense that God's providence governs the existence of evil. Evil is not ordered or governed as an end in itself, but only as something which is ordered towards a greater good, namely the good of the universe. God does not approve of evil; He simply allows it to exist.[66]

Aquinas' account of concessionary providence is based on the analogy of a whole being superior to any of its parts. The good of the universe, Aquinas writes, is of greater import than the good or evil of a particular thing, just as the good of a people is more divine than the good of one man.[67] This principle covers a multitude of evils and goods. According to Aquinas, providence allows physical corruption to take place only because it produces the continuation of the species and thus the perfection of the whole universe.[68] God permits humans to be tempted and to sin, therefore, but only because good will ultimately be brought forth.[69] Indeed, in Aquinas' view, if there were no evil, then the good of humankind would be greatly diminished. If there were no illness, for example, good health would not be appreciated; if there were no persecution, there would be no virtue of martyrdom; if there were no corruption of the air, there would be no fire; if there were no iniquity, there would be no praise of justice.[70] In all such instances, the good which is ultimately brought forth is the good of the universe. It is for this reason that God allows the human soul to be infused into a body from which it contracts corruption. The multiplication of humankind is ordered towards the perfection of the universe and should not be abrogated merely

---

[65] IV *Sent.* 49.1.2e.

[66] II *Sent.* 29.1.3 ad 4. Cf. *Q. Disp. de Verit.* V.3–4, discussing John the Damascene, *De Fide Orthodoxa* (*PG* 94), II.29, cols. 963–70.

[67] *Ia* 48.2 ad 3. Cf. *Ia* 47.2.   [68] *Q. Disp. de Verit.* V.3 ad 2. Cf. *Expos. super Romanos* VIII.6; *Ia* 23.7.

[69] II *Sent.* 23.1.2.   [70] *ScG* III.71; *Ia* 22.2; *Ia* 48.2.

to avoid the infection of original sin.[71] This notion of providence also gives Aquinas his explanation for the existence of such imperfections as inequality and women. The perfection of the universe, he states, the good of the whole, is better than the good of an individual part.[72]

God's providential order for the universe, the good of the whole universe, is the 'structure' of the hierarchy in Creation. The perfection of the whole, after all, is the end of *any* form of government, be it divine, royal, or paterfamilial (a principle which Aquinas justifies by appealing to book I of the *Ethics*—a common good is superior to an individual good, just as the good of a people is more divine than the good of a city, a family, or a single person).[73] God's providential goal for the universe, on the other hand, the 'dynamic' of the hierarchy in Creation, is the eternal salvation of humankind. Given this dual aspect (*duplex ordo*), it was clearly incumbent upon Aquinas to decide how this structure and this dynamic, the order of the universe and the salvation of humankind, could be related within a single hierarchy. Aquinas was well aware that his emphasis on the principle that a perfect whole is superior to its parts presented him with a particular difficulty in this regard. In the case of miracles, for example, he raises the possibility that God's suspension of the principles of Nature indicates that the good of a whole can be ordered towards the good of its parts. If this is the case, however, and if the good of the universe is greater than any particular good, then surely it is inappropriate for God to change the order of the universe for the sake of one human being or one people? Aquinas' response is simply to deny that miracles represent a conflict between the good of the whole and the good of the part. It is not the order of the universe which is violated, he argues, but the order of one particular thing towards another.[74] This is Aquinas' solution to the problem posed by miracles. It does not solve the wider problem of how the perfection of the universe can be ordered towards humankind when humankind is considered as a part of this whole.

Aquinas sets this problem out at some length in the *Summa contra Gentiles*. God's relation to the universe is based on the completeness or perfection of the good which the whole of Creation constitutes. God wills this good more than He wills any particular good within it because the universe constitutes a more complete similitude of His goodness.[75] Moreover, since any particular good is ordered towards the good of the whole as an object is ordered towards its goal, as the imperfect to the perfect, then the good of the universe is the reason why God wills each particular good within it.[76] The better the effect of an action, then the greater the priority it has in the intention of its agent. Since the best effect in Creation is the perfection of the universe, the ordering of its separate parts towards its whole should have the greatest priority in the mind of God.[77] Every agent has the intention of inducing its own similitude in its

[71] II *Sent.* 32.2.2. Cf. *IaIIae* 83.1.
[72] *Ia* 92.1 ad 1; *ScG* II.44. Cf. *Ia* 48.2; *De Sub. Sep.* XII; *ScG* I.85.
[73] *Q. Disp. de Verit.* V.3; II *Sent.* 32.2.2.
[74] *Q. Disp. de Potentia* VI.1. Cf. Augustine, *Contra Faustum*, ed. J. Zycha (*CSEL* 25), XXVI, pp. 730–1.
[75] *ScG* I.85. Cf. III *Sent.* 2.1.1c; *Ia* 49.3.   [76] *ScG* I.86.   [77] *ScG* II.44.

effect, at least according to the capacity of that effect to receive it, and the more perfect the agent, the more perfect the result. Since God is the most perfect agent, the
universe must reflect this perfection in the way in which it is capable of doing, namely
as multiplicity reflecting unity. Whilst it is in the nature of the universe that it should
be composed of diverse elements, it is the ordering of all these elements as a unity
which constitutes its perfection, since the perfection of the whole is better than the
individual parts on their own. This is the lesson which Augustine had drawn from
Genesis 1: 31—when God saw the individual parts of Creation they were 'good' but
when He saw all that He had made it was 'very good'. Only when the parts were taken
together were they *very* good, since the order of the universe is the ultimate and 'most
worthy' perfection in Creation.[78] According to Aquinas, this reading of Genesis
could also be supported by Aristotle. The greatest, the most perfect good in Creation
is the good order of the universe, and, as such, the good order of the universe is what
is principally willed and caused by God. Whoever directs something towards an end
naturally has the greatest care for that which is closest to the ultimate end because the
other ends are ordered towards this end. The ultimate end of the divine will is His
divine goodness, the nearest thing to which among created things is the good order
of the whole universe. Of all Creation, therefore, God has the greatest care for the
order of the universe.[79]

Aquinas restates the issue both in his commentary on the *Sentences* and in the
Summa Theologiae. The whole universe is more perfect than its parts, and something
which is more perfect must have a greater similitude to God. Effects are always like
their causes in that for something to act as a cause is to impose its form on something
else. The perfection of its effect will therefore be dependent upon the extent to which
it reflects the form which its cause produces, the form which is 'intended' by its
cause. An effect's perfection and form, in other words, consists in resembling its
cause.[80] A universal effect is therefore closest in likeness to a universal cause and,
since the universe is the universal effect and God is the universal cause, the universe
must have more similitude to God than one particular effect such as human nature.[81]
However, if the good order of the universe constitutes a perfect whole, the level in the
hierarchy of Creation which is closest to God and the most representative of divine
goodness and causality, where does this leave humankind?

The relation between the macrocosmic universe and the microcosmic human
being had been subject to a long intellectual tradition.[82] Whether everything in
Creation is made on account of humankind (*quod omnia sunt propter hominem*) was
accordingly a commonly disputed question. In attempting his own reconciliation of

---

[78] *ScG* II.45. Cf. *Ia* 25.6 in 3; Augustine, *De Civitate Dei*, ed. B. Dombart and A. Kalb (*CCSL* 47–8),
XI.23, p. 342; *Confessions*, ed. J. J. O'Donnell (Oxford, 1992), XIII.28, p. 201; *De Genesi contra Manichaeos*
(*PL* 34, cols. 173–220), I.21.32, cols. 188–9.

[79] *ScG* III.64. Cf. Aristotle, *Metaphysics* XII.10 1075ª11–13. For a discussion, see O. Blanchette, *The
Perfection of the Universe according to Aquinas: A Teleological Cosmology* (University Park, Penn., 1992).

[80] *Ia* 6.1.   [81] III *Sent.* 2.1.1c; *IIIa* 4.1 in/ad 4. Cf. *ScG* IV.53–5; III *Sent.* 1.1.2, 2.1.1.

[82] M.-D. Chenu, *Nature, Man and Society in the Twelfth Century* (Chicago, 1960), 24–37; J. McEvoy,
The Philosophy of Robert Grosseteste (Oxford, 1982), ch. 6.

a universe which reflects divine goodness with a universe which is anthropocentric, Aquinas starts by differentiating three purposes within the divine will. God wills humans to possess reason in order that they may be human; He wills humans to exist in order that they may complete the universe; He wills the good of the universe, however, because it is fitting for His goodness. The shift in terminology between each of these propositions is immediately apparent. Unlike humankind, the good of the universe is assigned no end of its own (*quia* rather than *ad hoc*) and it is described in terms not of causality but of appropriateness or fittingness (*decet*). From the outset, therefore, it would seem that, in this context, Aquinas deliberately avoids applying the terms 'perfection' and 'similitude' to the whole universe.[83]

Aquinas bases his subsequent argument on the centrality of rational creatures to Creation, that is, on the principle that inferior creatures are directed or ordered towards rational creatures but that rational creatures are governed for their own sake. In terms of a hierarchy of ends this means that those creatures which cannot themselves secure the ultimate end in God must be ordered towards those which can. According to Aquinas, this does not contradict the principle that all parts of the universe are ordered towards the perfection of the whole because, just like the human body, individual parts should be considered as helping one another towards the perfection of the whole. Nevertheless, he still argues that different parts can be considered as differing in worth (*nobilitas*) such that the 'principal' parts of a whole are those parts which are required to constitute that whole, whereas the remainder merely act for its conservation or amelioration.[84] This distinction has important consequences for Aquinas' application of the model of part and whole to the relationship between human beings and the universe. All parts of the universe are ordered towards the perfection of the whole because the whole does not exist for the sake of the parts but the parts exist for the sake of the whole. However, creatures which possess an intellect have a greater affinity to the whole universe than other creatures do. Whereas the latter participate in the universe only by constituting a part of all being, each intellectual substance is, in a sense (*quodammodo*), all substance inasmuch as it comprehends all being in its understanding.[85]

Like Aristotle, Aquinas argues that the intellectual soul is potentially all things in that the act of cognition leaves the soul, in a sense, assimilated to the thing which it knows.[86] Out of context, and without the controlling *quodammodo*, this would have been a dangerous conclusion to draw, risking, as it did, the equation of an individual human intellect with a universal intellect. Nevertheless, it served its immediate purpose. Aquinas reconciles God's relationship to the whole universe with God's

---

[83] *ScG* I.86.
[84] *ScG* III.112. Cf. *Expositio in Iob* VII. For the basis of this distinction between integral and contributory parts in the political community, see Aristotle, *Politics* IV.4 1291ᵃ24–28, p. 390, VII.9 1329ᵃ35–9, p. 279.
[85] *Ia* 12.4, 17.3, 75.5, 76.2 ad 4, 84.1, 84.2 ad 2, 85.2. Cf. Aristotle, *Metaphysics* XII.10 1075ᵃ16–25; *De Anima* III.8 431ᵇ21.
[86] *ScG* III.112. Cf. *ScG* I.44.

relationship to humankind by arguing that, whilst all parts are ordered towards a perfect whole, some of these parts can, on their own, constitute the whole themselves. Humankind, therefore, is not just a part of the whole of Creation. Humankind incorporates lesser forms in Creation and, in this sense, is a more complete representation of the divine order. The intellectual soul is closer to God's likeness than lower creatures (*magis ad similitudinem Dei*) because it is able to attain the fullness of goodness, albeit by means of many powers and activities, in which respect it is not as close as higher beings, namely angels.[87] Indeed, in this respect, the image of God is more perfect in angels than it is in humankind because their intellectual nature is more perfect. Nevertheless, although the angels are, in absolute terms, closer to the image of God than humankind is, humankind is more like God within certain terms of reference, namely when the image of God is considered in terms of its accidental qualities.[88] In this respect, humankind is certainly closer to the image of God than the universe. The perfection of the universe is not the perfection of a single subject but the perfection of a single order. The only way in which the whole universe could be said to be in the image of God, therefore, would be if it had a Platonic rational soul, a possibility which, Aquinas states, is clearly contrary to Christian teaching.[89]

Aquinas preserves the position of humankind against the claims of the universe by means of three arguments. First, he specifies the exact nature of the reflection of God's goodness in the universe. Second, he distinguishes between the different types of part which can exist within a whole. Third, he refines a strict hierarchy of ends such that some parts can have a goal of their own as well as being ordered towards the whole. These are the arguments to which Aquinas always returns whenever the perfection of the whole universe is juxtaposed with the special position of humankind. When Aquinas discusses whether the image of God is found only in rational creatures, for example, he carefully defines the divine similitude which is attributed to the universe. Every part of Creation possesses divine similitude to some extent but this is not the same as being in the divine image, an attribute which is restricted to those creatures which possess an intellect. Whilst some creatures therefore participate in divine goodness to a minimal degree, others will do so 'most worthily'. As a result, the similitude of divine goodness, in the sense of the worthiest participation in it (*nobilissima participatio*), cannot be said to occur in the whole universe except by virtue of its worthiest parts, namely its intellectual natures.[90]

It is on the basis of this metonymy,[91] therefore, that Aquinas is able to reconcile the perfection of the whole universe with the ordering of some of its parts for their own sake (*propter ipsas*) within a single hierarchy of ends. He does so by constructing a hierarchy with four characteristics. First, every creature in the universe has its proper action and perfection, just as the eye has its proper power of sight. Second,

---

[87] *Ia* 77.2 ad 1.   [88] *Ia* 93.4.

[89] III *Sent.* 2.1.1c; *IIIa* 4.1 in/ad 4. Cf. *ScG* IV.53–5; III *Sent.* 1.1.2, 2.1.1.

[90] II *Sent.* 16.1.2. Cf. *ScG* I.86; *Expos. super Romanos* VIII.6; *Q. Disp. de Virt.* II.7.

[91] For the identification of whole with principal part in a different context, see *IIaIIae* 25.7. Cf. IV *Sent.* 17.2.3c ad 2; Albertus Magnus, *Super Ethica* VI. 10, p. 461, *Ethica* VI.2.21, pp. 438–9.

less worthy creatures are ordered towards more worthy creatures, sub-human to human, just as the senses are ordered towards the intellect and the lungs to the heart. Third, all individual creatures are ordered towards the perfection of the universe. Fourth, the whole universe is ordered towards its end in God. These final two stages, however, carry important riders. Aquinas is careful to state that, when the universe is ordered towards God, it is the whole universe together with its individual parts (*cum suis partibus*), and that the universe as a whole is ordered towards this end insofar as divine goodness is represented and imitated in its parts (*in eis*). He is also careful to state that rational creatures have their own goal in God which is secured in a special fashion in that they can attain Him through their proper functions of cognition and love. Aquinas thereby puts even more distance between his position and the unity of the potential intellect. Not only do rational creatures have their own special union with God over and above (*supra hoc*) what they secure through the universe, but the universe itself is now ordered towards God as its end only with all of its parts. Divine goodness is represented in the entire universe and its parts (*in eis*) rather than simply in the whole (*in eo*).[92]

This conclusion certainly does not prevent Aquinas from continuing to concede a degree of divine similitude to the universe. Everything imperfect has a certain participation in the perfect, and even inanimate things still have some participation in the image of God inasmuch as they are effects which bear an image of their cause. Nevertheless, Aquinas insists that not every similitude warrants being termed an image.[93] It is thus intrinsic worth (*dignitas naturae*) which is needed in order to fulfil this definition (*ratio imaginis*). Replying to the objection drawn from Genesis 1: 31, therefore, Aquinas is prepared to accept that the universe is more perfect in goodness than its intellectual creatures but only in terms of the extent and diffusion of this goodness (*extensive et diffusive*). Viewed in terms of its concentration (*intensive et collective*), the similitude of divine perfection is found more in an intellectual creature, in a nature which is capable of attaining the supreme good. To say that only an intellectual nature is in the image of God, therefore, is not to preclude the fact that the universe, by virtue of one of its parts, is in the image of God. However, it is not in the image of God by virtue of parts other than its intellectual natures.[94] Aquinas explicitly refutes the suggestion that human beings, as inferior natures, can attain their higher goal only by rising to the level of angels, their immediate superiors, as well as the argument that their ultimate goal is the perfection of the whole universe of which they form an integral part.[95]

In his account of the providential governance of the universe and its anthropocentricity, Aquinas is well aware of the direction his argument would take if he adhered too strictly to the notions of perfection, of part and whole, and of the mediation of ends. As a result, wherever the immediacy of God's relation to humankind is challenged by an intermediary level in the hierarchy of the universe, his response is to

[92] *Ia* 65.2.
[93] Compare *Ia* 13.5 in 2, quoting Genesis 1: 26: *faciamus hominem ad imaginem et similitudinem nostram.*
[94] *Ia* 93.2. Cf. *Ia* 22.4; Bonaventure, II *Sent.* 40.2.1, p. 927.   [95] *IaIIae* 2.8 in/ad 1–2.

modify the logic of the structure, be it by distinguishing between similitude and image, or between instrumental and principal parts, or between order and intrinsic worth, or between extent and concentration. Alternatively, Aquinas simply cuts the Gordian knot and denies that there is a common criterion by which the good of the universe and the good of humankind can be compared. This is what happens, for example, when he tackles the question of whether the justification of sinners is the greatest work of God, greater even than the creation of the universe. If the good of the universe is greater than the good of one human being, and if justification is ordered towards the particular good of one sinner, then the creation of heaven and earth should presumably be classified as a greater work than the justification of sinners. Aquinas' response to such a suggestion is to distinguish between several possible points of comparison. According to the mode of action (*ex parte modi agendi*), for example, Creation must be the greater work because God created the universe *ex nihilo*; according to the nature of the work itself (*propter magnitudinem operis*), however, justification is the greater work because, unlike Creation, it secures the eternal good of divine participation and not the mutable good of Nature. Aquinas' conclusion is that the good of the universe is greater than the good of a particular individual only if it is accepted that they are in the same genus, that is, only when they are both considered in terms of Nature. If they are considered according to different criteria, therefore, if the good of the universe is considered in terms of Nature but the good of a particular individual is considered in terms of grace (that is, justification), then the good of a particular part can, in fact, be greater than the good of its whole.[96]

The consistency of Aquinas' approach to the relation between the perfection of the universe and the justification of humankind is, in itself, an instructive pointer to how carefully Aquinas could incorporate Aristotelian teleology into a Neoplatonic hierarchy. It also provides an instructive perspective from which to assess how Aquinas saw the operation of goodness in general and, more precisely, how he saw the connection between 'goodness' as a final cause and 'order' as a formal cause. According to Aquinas, the common good of the universe can be defined *either* as the universal good which all things seek and in which all things participate and communicate *or* as the ordering of the parts of the universe towards one another. Aquinas' earliest response to whether all things were made on account of humankind is based accordingly on the twofold principle with which he was familiar from the *Metaphysics*—parts of the universe are ordered towards each other in an intrinsic good but they are also ordered towards the ultimate good as an extrinsic good. Aquinas' expansion of the second part of this equation, however, prompts him to add a third principle of his own. Individuals are ordered towards each other and towards the ultimate good but the act of being ordered towards the ultimate good also results in a mutual benefit (*utilitas*). Every part of the universe benefits another part, Aquinas writes, by helping it secure the ultimate end of divine similitude.

---

[96] *IaIIae* 113.9. Cf. IV *Sent.* 17.1.5a, 46.2.1c; *Super Ioannem* 14.3; *IaIIae* 2.8 ad 3; *IIIa* 43.4; Augustine, *In Ioannis Evangelium Tractatus* (*CCSL* 36), LXXII.3, pp. 508–9.

Aquinas' introduction of a third term, benefit (*utilitas*), into his discussion of the dual operation of goodness in the universe has significant consequences for his understanding of hierarchy. This notion of benefit takes one of two forms. Either something participates in divine goodness only by being ordered towards the benefit of something else, or it participates in divine goodness directly and, in the process, produces benefit for other things. It is the latter definition which Aquinas uses in his commentary on the *Sentences* in order to explain how elements at a higher level in the hierarchy of the universe can, in fact, be ordered by God for the sake of their inferiors. It is this sense of benefit, for example, which accounts for the way in which God not only made humankind in order to make reparation for the fall of angels but also made angels for the sake of humankind. Humankind is not the ultimate goal of Creation, it is merely its beneficiary. Angels are more worthy (*nobiliores*) than humans according to their nature, and they do not have humans as their goal in the same way that corporeal creatures do (by being ordered towards their benefit as a means of participating in divine goodness). Nevertheless, angels can still be said to be ordered towards humans in the sense that humans derive benefit from them, just as a king can be said to be ordered towards a peasant because the peasant derives benefit from the king's peace.[97] Aquinas uses a similar model to explain how the motion of the heavens can be dependent upon the number of the elect. How can the heavens, incorruptible and therefore more worthy (*nobiliores*) than anything which is susceptible to generation and corruption, have as their goal the generation of the elect? His answer is to distinguish between an end or goal (*finis*) and the object in which an activity terminates (*terminus*). An end, he argues, certainly ought to be more worthy (*nobilius*) than those things which are ordered towards it. An end is not the same as an object, however, and an object of a more worthy action can, in itself, be more lowly (*vilius*). Again it is the peasant who serves as an illustration. The security of the peasant represents the object of the action of the king's governance but it does not represent its goal; the goal of the king's governance is the common good.[98]

In his commentary on the *Sentences* and his *Quaestio Disputata de Potentia*, Aquinas' response to the problem of how to retain an anthropocentric universe and an ascending hierarchy from humans to angels to God is to appeal to a particular notion of benefit (*utilitas*) as the good which is done to others in the course of securing one's own good. On this reckoning, whilst inferior parts of Creation only participate in divine goodness by being ordered towards the benefit of superior parts, superior parts will produce benefits for others as a result of their own participation in divine goodness. Aquinas defines this *utilitas* as the good which is done to others.[99] As a result, this notion of benefit is closely connected to his analysis of the operation of

---

[97] II *Sent.* 1.2.3.

[98] *Q. Disp. de Potentia* V.5. Cf. Moses Maimonides, *Guide of the Perplexed*, trans. S. Pines (Chicago, 1963), III.13, p. 454. Compare Albertus Magnus, *Super Ethica* VIII.9, p. 269, where a distinction is drawn between the primary goal of intent (*finis principalis qui est finis intentionis*) and the goal which is the result of the action (*finis qui est terminus operis*).

[99] III *Sent.* 35.1.4.1c.

grace. According to Aquinas, grace orders some of its goods towards the perfection of the individual upon whom they are conferred and some of its goods towards the benefit of others, a division which follows the principles set down in 1 Corinthians 12: 7 (the manifestation of the Holy Spirit is given to each individual *ad utilitatem*), 1 Peter 4: 10, and 2 Corinthians 1: 2. Just as God gave light to the sun in order to illuminate not just itself but the whole world, so He wills that all individual goods should lead to some common benefit.[100] It is on the basis of this division that Aquinas distinguishes between saving or sanctifying grace (*gratia gratum faciens*) and grace freely given (*gratia gratis data*). Whereas sanctifying grace enables individual humans to secure union with God themselves, grace freely given enables them to secure this union for other individuals as well.[101]

The distinction between, on the one hand, sanctifying grace and the individual good of union with God, and, on the other, grace freely given and benefit to others, has striking implications for the relationship between the individual and common good. Had Aquinas developed them, he might then have made a case for the effects of grace freely given being beneficial to other humans simply as a result, as a consequence, of the communication of goodness, and thus for the common good of the human community to be simply the mutual benefit of individuals which is produced by the gifts of grace. Whatever its attractions to modern commentators, however, this is not a line pursued by Aquinas himself. Throughout the main body of his work, the common good of the human community is consistently defined as the external goal towards which individuals are ordered and not as the benefit which results when they are ordered towards the goal of salvation in God. Thus, when Aquinas does compare the respective goods secured by grace freely given and sanctifying grace in the *Summa Theologiae*, he takes a rather different definition of *utilitas* to the one put forward in his commentary on the *Sentences*. Sanctifying grace, he argues, orders humans towards the achievement of their ultimate end, whilst grace freely given orders them only towards the preparatory elements of the ultimate end. Rather than turn to the benefit of peace which is produced for the peasant by the king's pursuit of the common good, Aquinas turns to the analogy of the army and its *duplex ordo*, the good of its order and the good of its commander. Grace freely given orders humans towards the common good of the church, the *bonum commune ecclesiae* which comprises the mutual ordering of humans amongst themselves. Sanctifying grace, meanwhile, orders humans towards a better good, a common good which is separate from this mutual ordering, the *bonum commune separatum* which is God.[102]

One of the many difficulties in assuming that metaphysical principles in scholastic theology are applicable to scholastic political thought is being sure which metaphysical principles are being applied at any one time. In Aquinas' case, the capacity to choose from several different principles for his analysis of the political community is

---

[100] II *Sent.* 29.1.3; *Expositio super II ad Corinthianos* I.2.
[101] *IaIIae* 111.1, 4.   [102] *IaIIae* 111.5. Cf. *IIaIIae* 26.4.

reflected in the range of different models with which the good in human society can be described. At the most basic level, for example, Aquinas conceives of the common good of political society as a unity which is distinct from a simple aggregate of individuals. At its most comprehensive, this unity is derived from Adam,[103] but it is also present in political communities[104] where it derives from the ordering of different individuals towards the goal which they have in common.[105] That the political community constitutes a unity of order was the argument which Aristotle had used to distance himself from Plato in the *Politics*, and Aquinas reiterates the point in some detail.[106] Alternatively, Aquinas can conceive of the common good of political society simply as the result of individual virtuous activity, as the common benefit which necessarily follows from individuals seeking their ultimate good of happiness and virtue. This common good is not so much the good of order as the good which is done to others, the consequence of the operation of grace freely given. In general, however, Aquinas does appear to have been more inclined to adopt one model for the common good in preference to all the others. For Aquinas, the common good of political society was best understood in terms of the double ordering (*duplex ordo*) which he found in Aristotle's *Metaphysics*.

According to book XII of the *Metaphysics*, individual parts of a whole are ordered towards other parts in an intrinsic good of order but they are also ordered towards the extrinsic good of the whole. Both halves of this operation, the formal cause and the final cause, can be described as a common good. The common good is an ordered structure but it is also a shared goal. It was this distinction which enabled Aquinas to separate the structure of the universe from its dynamic, the common good of Creation from the common good of union with God. When this model was applied to the political community, therefore, Aquinas could speak of both the common benefit and the common good, a life of peace and security as well as a life of activity in accordance with perfect virtue. Expressed in these terms, it is clear just how much Aquinas' understanding of the good of political society also owed to the *Ethics*. The differing accounts of the relation between the individual good and the good of the community which Aristotle had provided in book I and book IX of the *Ethics* appear to have clarified a distinction between defining the common good as moral goodness and defining the common good as material benefit. The individual good of virtue is superior to the common benefit of peace and self-sufficiency in which it results, but this individual good of virtue is, in turn, subordinate to the common good of virtue, the human good of the life of happiness.

On the strength of Aquinas' interpretation of the *Metaphysics* and the *Ethics*, at least three possible definitions of the common good of the human community can be identified—the provision of peace and security, the effect of virtuous actions on other people, and the happiness of the life of virtue—depending on whether the

---

[103] *Resp. ad Lect. Venetum de Art. XXX* 21. Cf. *Resp. ad Lect. Venetum de Art. XXXVI* 23; III *Sent.* 1.1.2 ad 6.
[104] *IaIIae* 81.1.   [105] *IaIIae* 93.1 ad 1.   [106] *Sent. Lib. Eth.* I.1.

good of the community is being defined as the instrument, the result, or the goal of the individual's virtuous action. For Aquinas, therefore, there are at least three possible models—order, grace, and goodness—each one of which has differing consequences for the relationship between the individual and the common good in human society. The principle of goodness in the universe (*ratio boni*), for example, necessarily entails the subordination of the individual good to a superior common good in which it participates and on which it depends for its existence. A quite different degree of subordination is produced, however, if the model invoked is the mutual ordering of goods within the universe or the dual nature of grace. If the second definition became progressively less important to Aquinas than the first and the third, then this might not be surprising given that the first and the third together represent the twofold function of the Aristotelian community in both the *Ethics* and the *Politics*—the purpose of political life is not just to live but to live well. Nevertheless, the fact that, at different times and in different contexts, Aquinas can draw on all three of these principles as patterns for the functioning of the political community has not helped the subsequent exposition of his political and ethical thinking.

It may, of course, be unreasonable to expect an entirely systematic analysis of the common good from the vast range of texts which Aquinas composed. Nevertheless, one feature to emerge, even from a picture which is recognized to be so complex, is that Aquinas himself was well aware of the difficulties which too strict a notion of hierarchy could cause when it is combined with the notion of the universe as a perfect whole. Indeed, if Aquinas' approach to this issue reveals one consistent aim, then it is to maintain the position of a 'more worthy' (*nobilior, dignior*) part against the claims of a superior whole. The common good of the universe may be superior to its parts but this does not make it closer to God. If this concern is evident in Aquinas' account of the 'community' of the universe, then it can also be used to clarify the way in which he considers the 'community' of human society. Given that Aquinas is so frequently prepared to apply to human society the metaphysical principles which govern a hierarchical universe, it is vital to bear in mind that these principles were not so inflexible that their application had to mean that individual humans are completely subordinate to a superior community. Far from it, Aquinas' account of the hierarchical universe demonstrates that he is always prepared to modify the language of whole and part in order to allow for the possibility that an inferior level in the hierarchy (humankind) can secure its ultimate goal (God) without being mediated by its immediate superior (the universe). By the same token, the common good of political society may be greater, better, and more divine than the good of the individual human being, but it is not closer to God. It is not, in other words, 'more perfect'.

4
Thomas Aquinas—Love, Justice, and the Life of Virtue

Aquinas' theoretical analysis of the common good offers a series of metaphysical models with which to explain the relationship between the individual and the common good—the analogical participation of individual goods in universal goodness and in God, the communication of goodness to other individuals as a necessary aspect of being good (*bonum est diffusivum sui*), and the benefit which is done to others as the effect of an individual's receipt of grace. It was within these terms of reference, therefore, that Aquinas interpreted the comparative terminology from book I of Aristotle's *Ethics*. The common good is 'greater', 'better', and 'more divine' than the individual good because it represents a closer approximation to the likeness of God. Aquinas appears rather more reluctant to use the term 'more perfect', at least in the context of the political community. Otherwise, his metaphysical account of goodness in the universe left him firmly committed to the general principle that the common good is superior to the individual good. Aquinas' commitment to the principle of superiority, however, was also accompanied by an endorsement of the principle of identity both in his account of the predication of goodness in individual things and in his analysis of the natural inclination of all individuals to will the good. Thus, the individual good shares an analogical identity with the universal good, whilst the individual wills what is good for himself in willing what is good in general. At a human level, this principle of identity also underpins Aquinas' account of the goal of happiness. The common good is the same as the individual good because the individual's good of virtue is the same as the supreme good of human happiness. This too was a principle which could readily be tied to book I of the *Ethics*, where Aristotle's insistence that good for the community is greater and more perfect than good for the individual had been prefaced by the phrase 'even if the good is the same' (*si enim et idem*).

Aquinas' theoretical analysis of the common good, however, is not limited to the terms which he found in book I of the *Ethics*. Aristotle's principle that it is better and more divine to secure the good for a people and for city-states, for example, had been preceded by the observation that it is worthy (*kalon*) to secure it for one person. Aquinas accordingly picks up on this last term (translated by Grosseteste as *amabile*) and uses it to put forward the more general argument that the individual should show greater love for the common good.[1] For Aquinas, the relationship between the

---

[1] *IIaIIae* 26.4.

individual and the common good accordingly becomes a relationship not only between individual goods and goodness in general but also between love for the individual good and love for the common good. As a result, Aquinas, like Albertus Magnus, adds to the account of the common good which he took over from book I of the *Ethics* the account of self-love and self-sacrifice which he found in books VIII and IX of the *Ethics*. Nor was Aquinas' theoretical analysis of the notion of the common good limited to the *Ethics*. Equally formative in his understanding of its role in the universe and in the human community was the concept of the dual order (*duplex ordo*) which he found in book XII of the *Metaphysics*. Individual goods are ordered towards one another in an intrinsic good of order but they are also ordered towards an extrinsic principle of goodness. Viewed in these terms, the common good could be construed as both a formal cause, that is, as the structured arrangement of individual goods, and as a final cause, that is, as the goal towards which this arrangement is directed.

Aquinas' application of the principles of superiority and identity to the human community presents a particularly complex combination of metaphysics and political thought. His translation of a metaphysical analysis of the common good into political theory marked an attempt to accommodate the subordination of the individual good to the common good without making this subordination absolute and all-inclusive. Moreover, defined as the object of love and as the goal of virtue and justice in the human community, Aquinas' theory of the common good had significant implications for some very concrete political questions. Subjects such as correction, punishment, legislation, dispensation, taxation, obedience, resistance, and the exercise of political authority, all presupposed some kind of judgement being made on the relative weight which should be attached to the individual and the common good. Aquinas accordingly provides a detailed examination of the role of the common good in each case. Indeed, it is in the course of discussing each of these issues that Aquinas reveals how far, and how strictly, he was prepared to apply his theoretical ideal of the common good to the actual reality of life in the human community.

According to Aquinas, if the order of goodness in the universe is defined as a hierarchy of perfection in which rank is dependent on degree of commonality, then so is the order of love (*ordo caritatis*). As a result, love is ordered towards the good of the community, towards the good of the species, and, indeed, towards the good of any whole of which a human being might form a part, be it an army, a city, or the community of saints. The more inclusive this common good is, the greater the love which it should inspire. The perfect form of the good towards which this love is ordered is therefore the perfectly inclusive common good in God.[2] If God is the general good which includes angels, humankind, and all Creation, Aquinas argues, then angels, humankind, and all Creation should have a natural love for God which outweighs the love which they have for themselves. This love is a natural love, he explains, because

---

[2] *Q. Disp. de Virt.* II.4 ad 2; *ScG* III.117; *Ia* 60.5 ad 1. Cf. III *Sent.* 30.1.1 ad 4.

when one thing constitutes the principle of being and goodness in something else, the latter always loves the former more than it loves itself. Everything in Creation, therefore, has a greater natural love for God than it does for itself because God is the source of their existence and goodness. Moreover, as far as humankind is concerned, an additional argument pertains which derives from the identity of the essence and the existence (or goodness) of God. In heaven, humans will love God in both senses, perceiving His essence and also loving His goodness, willing the common good in Him. On earth, however, the intellect cannot comprehend the essence of God and humans can know Him only through particular effects. Although this gives the human will the capacity to oppose God, every human being still has a natural inclination to love Him more than their own selves insofar as the existence or goodness of God is the common good for all humankind.[3] If individuals do not will this common good, therefore, they are performing an unnatural act.[4]

In arguing that individuals have a greater love for God than they have for themselves, Aquinas does not deny the existence of a legitimate love of self. There is a good appropriate to every human being and a corresponding love which should be directed towards it.[5] However, in Aquinas' view, the good of any individual is greater when it is more perfect and, since any part is imperfect in itself and is perfected only in its whole, the good of humankind must be made perfect through union with a God who is the primary, perfect, and universal cause of goodness. Humans therefore have a natural inclination to love the goodness in God more than the goodness which they find in themselves.[6] The natural love which human beings have for the common good in God is thus analogous to a part securing perfection in its whole. Just as the good of a part has the good of its whole as its final cause, so every part of Creation loves its own good on account of the common good of the whole universe, the common good in God.[7] A part loves the good of its whole because this good is suitable or congruent (*conveniens*), but it does so, not in order to direct the good of the whole towards itself, but in order to direct itself towards the good of the whole.[8]

If love for the common good in God was to provide Aquinas with a precise parallel for love for the common good of the political community, it should have been a simple case of arguing that individuals love their own good as a result of loving the good of the community as the good on which their own good depends for its existence. Aquinas draws this sort of direct comparison between love for God and love for the political community by means of two illustrations—the natural inclination of the arm to defend the head, and the willingness of the citizen to risk danger and (if necessary) death for the preservation of the community.[9] The demands of love for

    [3] *Ia* 60.5. Cf. Augustine, *De Doctrina Christiana*, ed. R. P. H. Green (Oxford, 1995), I.57, p. 36; Bernard of Clairvaux, *De Diligendo Deo*, ed. J. Leclercq and H. Rochais, *S. Bernardi Opera*, vol. iii (Rome, 1963), VIII–X, pp. 138–44.
    [4] *IaIIae* 109.3.   [5] *Q. Disp. de Virt.* II.4 ad 2.   [6] III *Sent.* 29.1.3.   [7] *IaIIae* 109.3.
    [8] *IIaIIae* 26.3 ad 2. Cf. *Quod.* I.4.3 ad 3.
    [9] *Quod.* I.4.3. For the corporeal analogy, see e.g. John of Salisbury, *Policraticus*, ed. C. C. J. Webb (Oxford, 1909), IV.4, p. 240; T. Struve, *Die Entwicklung der organologischen Staatsauffassung im Mittelalter* (Stuttgart, 1978).

the good of the political community which this comparison produces are certainly comprehensive. Citizens must be prepared to sacrifice their individual goods, their property, even their own lives, in order to preserve, defend, and increase this common good.[10] Aquinas makes the same connection when he argues that greater love must be shown to an individual who in some sense personifies the common good. Just as the saints in heaven love both God and the common good in God, he argues, so members of an earthly community love the person in whom their common good principally consists. As a result, an individual should be prepared to sacrifice his own well-being (*salus*) in order to preserve this person, just as the arm exposes itself to danger in order to preserve the head.[11] Such personification is also not limited to the ruler of a community or the commander of an army. When Aquinas argues that a soldier should give assistance to a stranger who is a comrade, rather than to a relative who is an enemy, it is love for the common good which is taking precedence. He assists his fellow-soldier not as a private person but as if he actually were the whole community.[12] This requirement overrides all other expressions of natural love, even towards one's own parents. Whilst no one person bestows the same good that parents do, an individual must always acknowledge the prior claim of the common good.[13]

In using love for the common good in God as a model for love for the common good of the political community, however, Aquinas is also noticeably careful to specify what this good actually means. Like Albertus Magnus, Aquinas argues that the final cause of self-sacrifice is the good of virtue, a good which the individual should aim to secure for himself by means of an action which is also beneficial (*utilis*) to others.[14] Aquinas uses this account of book IX of the *Ethics* in order to define the love which an individual should have for the good of his neighbour. The good of any individual, he argues, exists in God as a final cause, in himself as a particular effect, but in his neighbour only as a likeness or similitude (*similitudo*). As a result, the individual should love his own good more than he loves the good of his neighbour. He must still be prepared to sacrifice external goods, including the life of his own body, on behalf of his neighbour, but only inasmuch as he thereby secures his own greatest good, namely the good of virtue. An individual should always will a spiritual good primarily for himself and he should never endanger his own soul in order to secure that of his neighbour. The obligation to lay down his life, therefore, an obligation which extends to 'civil death' or slavery, is particularly binding when it secures another person's spiritual life, when, for example, it prevents an individual from being lured away by pagans. Nevertheless, the primary goal of the individual remains the good of virtue, since the individual is choosing his own interior, spiritual good in preference to his own external, corporeal good.[15]

[10] *Q. Disp. de Virt.* II.2. Cf. *IIaIIae* 26.3.
[11] *Q. Disp. de Virt.* II.4 ad 2. Cf. *IIaIIae* 26.2.   [12] *IIaIIae* 31.3 ad 2.
[13] *Q. Disp. de Virt.* II.9 ad 15; *IIaIIae* 31.3 ad 3. Cf. *IIaIIae* 101.3 ad 3, 102.3; Cicero, *De Officiis*, ed. M. Winterbottom (Oxford, 1994), III.90, p. 147.
[14] *Sent. Lib. Eth.* IX.8–9. Cf. above, pp. 51–2.
[15] III *Sent.* 29.1.5; *De Perf. Spir. Vitae* XVI; *IIaIIae* 26.4, 26.5. For the connection of self-sacrifice to martyrdom, see IV *Sent.* 49.5.3b ad 11. Cf. *IIaIIae* 124.3 in 3 (where martyrdom is contrasted with teaching and governance as actions which contribute to the common good); *IIaIIae* 124.5 in/ad 3.

Aquinas may sometimes have been rather less explicit in granting such priority to an individual's moral good, suggesting, on one occasion, that an individual should love his own good 'as much as' he loves the good of his neighbour.[16] His emphasis on the good of virtue, however, remains consistent. Expounding 1 Corinthians 13: 5, for example, Aquinas argues that the principle 'love is not self-seeking' does not imply that the individual should love his neighbour more than himself but that the individual should love what he and his neighbour have in common more than he loves himself and his neighbour as two individuals.[17] What they have in common is the good of virtue. It was thus Aristotle's definition of the common good of the human community as the life of virtue which enabled Aquinas to apply to the political community the same terms which he used for the common good in God. When Aquinas appeals to a string of 'corporatist' images—the whole of which the individual forms a subordinate part, the body of which the individual constitutes an integral member, and the community for which the individual sacrifices his material well-being and even his life—the common good in question is always moral goodness. This good is not the external, corporeal good of one's neighbour, the material utility of peace and security. Whilst these goods may be produced by an individual's actions, the good towards which these actions are ordered, their final cause, is happiness, the common good of virtuous activity, the good which is common to all humans and which is the same as the individual good.

A moral definition of the good of the political community as the life of virtue enables Aquinas to insist on the presence of a principle of identity in the act of laying down one's life for one's neighbour. Self-sacrifice is an act of love for one's own good *as well as* an act of love for a common good. This identification of the individual and the common good, however, is not always so clear-cut. The relative merits of the active and the contemplative lives, for example, present Aquinas with the possibility that the individual and the common good might be mutually exclusive goods in that the active life aims to secure the common good of the whole church, whereas the contemplative aims to secure the individual good of one human.[18] In general, Aquinas seeks to solve this dilemma by distinguishing the different criteria by which each life can be judged. Like Albertus Magnus, he argues that the active and the contemplative lives can be compared either according to their intrinsic worth (*dignitas*) or according to their benefit (*utilitas*). Thus, the contemplative life is better because it more closely approaches the ultimate end of humankind. It is more worthy (*dignius*) because worth signifies the goodness of something on its own account (*propter se*) and the contemplative life is not ordered towards anything other than itself, not even towards eternal beatitude. It is, strictly speaking, a foretaste of heaven. On the other hand, something may be termed good when it is chosen on account of something else (*propter aliud*). It is in this sense that the active life is superior to the contemplative. It is more beneficial (*utilius*) because it seeks the well-being (*salus*) of one's

---

[16] *ScG* III.117; *De Perf. Spir. Vitae* XV–XVI.   [17] *IIaIIae* 26.4 ad 3. Cf. *IIaIIae* 47.10.
[18] *IaIIae* 111.5 in 1. Cf. III *Sent.* 35.1.3a, 35.1.4a in 2.

neighbours.[19] Like Albertus, therefore, Aquinas generally concludes by appealing to a distinction between something which is true without qualification (*simpliciter*) and something which is true within certain terms of reference (*secundum quid*). In absolute terms, the contemplative life is essentially superior to the active. Just as the divine good is greater than the human good, the love of God better than the love of one's neighbour, so the good of the soul is to be preferred to the good of the body. On the other hand, within certain terms of reference, when the point of comparison is benefit, it is the active life which is superior to the contemplative—the good of the multitude should be preferred to the good of one human being.[20]

Aquinas' interest in the question of the relationship between the active and the contemplative lives was more than theoretical. The issue acquired a sharp polemical edge in the 1250s and 1260s as a result of the controversies which arose between secular and mendicant masters at the university of Paris,[21] when the possibilities provided by making an appeal to the 'superior' common good were not lost on the advocates of the secular clergy. The public good, they argued, should be preferred to the individual good. Archdeacons aim to secure the common benefit of the multitude in that they secure, through their active life, the salvation (*salus*) of many souls. Archdeacons should therefore be placed above those who, through their contemplative life, secure the salvation only of their own souls.[22] Gérard d'Abbeville, a leading opponent of the mendicants, accordingly delivered a quodlibet in support of archdeacons and parish priests which argued that the active life is more perfect (*magis perfecta*) than the contemplative because it is more beneficial (*utilis*) and fruitful (*fructifera*), and because the benefit of many individuals is superior to the will of one.[23]

Given that the superiority of the good of many to the good of a single individual is a principle which Aquinas is normally prepared to concede, he naturally takes great care to refute Gérard of Abbeville's attempt to use the same principle against his fellow-mendicants.[24] Thus, although Aquinas insists that the contemplative life is

---

[19] III *Sent.* 35.1.4a. For Aristotle's three types of good (*honestum*, *utile*, and *delectabile*) see e.g. *ScG* III.17; *Ia* 5.6 ad 3; *IaIIae* 34.2 ad 1, 99.5; *IIaIIae* 145.3.

[20] *IIaIIae* 152.4, 185.2 ad 1. Cf. IV *Sent.* 49.1.1c in/ad 1–2.

[21] P. Glorieux, 'Le Conflit de 1252–1257 à la lumière du Mémoire de Guillaume de Saint-Amour', *RTAM* 24 (1957), 364–72; E. Faral, 'Les *Responsiones* de Guillaume de Saint-Amour', *AHDLMA* 18 (1950–1), 337–94; M. M. Dufeil, *Guillaume de Saint-Amour et la polémique universitaire parisienne* (Paris, 1972); id., 'Gulielmus de Sancto Amore: Opera Omnia 1252–1270', *Miscellanea Mediaevalia*, 10 (1976), 213–19; J. D. Dawson, 'William of Saint-Amour and the Apostolic Tradition', *Medieval Studies*, 40 (1978), 223–38; P. Glorieux, 'Les Polémiques *contra Geraldinos*, les pièces du dossier', *RTAM* 6 (1934), 5–41; id., '*Contra Geraldinos*, l'enchaînement des polémiques', *RTAM* 7 (1935), 129–55; id., 'Pour une édition de Gérard d'Abbeville', *RTAM* 9 (1937), 56–84.

[22] *Quod.* III.6.3 in 4. Cf. *Quod.* III.5.2. in 5, where this conclusion is given a more extreme form—it is better not to enter a religious order because to do so actually harms the common good.

[23] Gérard d'Abbeville, *Quodlibet* XIV.1, ed. Leonine, *S. Thomae Aquinatis Opera Omnia*, vol. xli, pp. B.61–2, quoting *Nisi cum pridem* and *Scias*. Cf. *Decr. Greg. IX* I.9.10 (Friedberg, ii. 107–12); *Decretum* II.7.1.34 (Friedberg, i. 579); *Decretum* II.7.1.35 (Friedberg, i. 579–80): *nam et plurimorum utilitas unius utilitati vel voluntati praeferenda est*.

[24] *De Perf. Spir. Vitae* XXIV, XXVI.

essentially better than the active life, he does concede that there is greater merit in suffering some interruption to a life of contemplation when it benefits the well-being (*salus*) of one's neighbour. Indeed, he quotes Paul's dilemma in Philippians 1: 23–4 ('I desire to depart and be with Christ, which is better by far; but it is more necessary for you that I remain in the body') as proof that such sacrifice is indicative of greater perfection in love. Nevertheless, in Aquinas' view, the oath under which a member of a religious order conducts his life still makes his condition more perfect than that of the secular clergy, given that otherwise they both exercise the functions of preaching, pastoral care, and hearing confession which so benefit the multitude.[25] Certain acts of the secular clergy may, in themselves, be superior to certain acts of the religious orders—the salvation of souls, for example, does represent a greater action than fasting or silence. However, if these acts are compared in terms of the goals towards which they are ordered, then the acts of religious orders are superior, since they originate in a life which is devoted exclusively to God. All things considered, Aquinas concludes, the actions of religious orders are much greater than those of the secular clergy.

Unlike Albertus Magnus, who found it easier in this context to elevate the contemplative above the active life by restricting the meaning of *utilitas* to the material necessities of life,[26] Aquinas cannot appeal to a difference in genus in order to elevate the individual good over a common benefit. In his case, the common good secured by the clergy, namely the salvation of others, is definitely spiritual. What Aquinas does, therefore, is to concentrate on drawing a comparison in intention. If an individual aims completely and perfectly to secure his own salvation, he argues, then this is a much greater action than if an individual performs many separate acts to secure the salvation of others whilst sufficiently but not perfectly acting to secure his own.[27] Clearly Aquinas believes that only the mendicant orders succeed in combining the active and contemplative lives so perfectly. He thereby retains a notion of the superiority of the common good but only after he has ensured that it is defined as an active life which complements, rather than conflicts with, the superiority of the individual good served by the contemplative. Teaching, pastoral concern, and manual work serve a common benefit which is superior to the private benefit served by silence, contemplation, and rest from labour, but only when this common benefit is the salvation of souls.[28] If this active life is to be superior to a contemplative life, moreover, then the *salus multitudinis* must be pursued at the same time as perfectly securing one's own salvation. The common spiritual good cannot be pursued at the expense of the individual spiritual good; the individual good must be perfectly achieved in the process.

It is on this basis that Aquinas makes the common good a powerful justification for public support of the work of mendicant friars in the church. Since judicial

---

[25] *De Perf. Spir. Vitae* XXVII. Cf. ibid. XXIX, quoting *Decretum* II.16.1.3 (Friedberg, i. 762) against *Decretum* II.16.1.29 (Friedberg, i. 768–9).

[26] See above, p. 68.   [27] *Quod.* III.6.3 ad 4.

[28] *IIaIIae* 188.6 in/ad 1; *Decr. Greg. IX* III.31.18 (Friedberg, ii. 575–6): *sicut maius bonum minori bono praeponitur, ita communis utilitas speciali utilitati praefertur.*

government of the church, preaching, prayer, and the exposition of scripture all contribute to the spiritual common good, they all have a right to a support which is analogous to what is received by soldiers when they serve the temporal common good by fighting for the peace of the *res publica*.[29] The same argument can be applied to those people who assume voluntary poverty in order to serve the common good. If soldiers and rulers are supported by the community because they dismiss their own concerns in order to serve the common good, then so should those people who give up everything in order to follow Christ and bring benefit to the people by their wisdom, learning, and example, or by their prayer and intercession.[30] Like Albertus Magnus, Aquinas regards teaching as a particularly apposite example of the communicative principle inherent in the order of goodness (the more perfectly someone can communicate a gift, the higher the grade of perfection they occupy).[31] As a result, he vigorously defends the right of religious orders to teach. A monk who follows his order in a cloister is pursuing the private good of his own salvation, whereas the activity of enabling many other individuals to become learned rebounds to the common good of the church. It is therefore not inappropriate for a monk to live outside the cloister and assume the office of teaching. Lesser goods, he writes, can be interrupted for the sake of greater goods, and the common good is to be preferred to the private good. Aquinas will have none of the argument that monks can only assume the function of teaching at times of necessity. The common benefit, he argues, must not be secured in any way but in the best way possible, and the more teachers there are, the more the common benefit will increase.[32]

Aquinas was drawn into a further practical examination of the identity of the individual and the common good in human society when he came to consider the question of fraternal correction in the religious community and to discuss the relationship between love and justice which it entailed. According to Aquinas, since a sinner causes two distinct injuries, to justice and to himself, the role of correction must devolve upon two people. First, there is the sinner's superior, the judicial authority who is responsible for the common good of the community. Second, there is the sinner's neighbour, the individual who is obliged to love his brother's individual good. At the heart of this distinction lies the *duplex ordo* from book XII of the *Metaphysics*. Just as a multitude of soldiers is ordered collectively towards their commander and individually towards each other, so members of a religious community are ordered collectively towards their prelate and separately towards their brothers. The common good and the individual good are the respective goals of each of these orders. Whilst the prelate must direct his flock in pursuit of the common good, individuals must help one another secure their individual goods.[33] It is on the basis of this twofold organization, therefore, that Aquinas sets up fraternal correction as an issue which is governed by two considerations—the punishment which is imposed by justice for the public good and the reproof which is offered by love for the private

---

[29] *Quod.* VII.7.　　[30] *ScG* III.135.　　[31] *Ia* 108.2 ad 2. Cf. above, p. 45.
[32] *C. Imp. Dei* II.3.　　[33] IV *Sent.* 19.2.1–2. Cf. *IIaIIae* 33.1, 33.3.

good of the sinner. Aquinas structures his discussion accordingly, distinguishing between the two acts which are involved in fraternal correction, namely accusation and denunciation. Accusation seeks the punishment of the sinner and secures the common good, whereas denunciation seeks the reform of the sinner and secures the individual good.[34] Following Matthew 18, Aquinas acknowledges that private denunciation should always precede public accusation. Following 1 Timothy 5, however, he also argues that private denunciation is dependent upon the improvement which can be expected in the character of the sinner and the repercussions which his sin has on the community. If no improvement can be hoped for, then Aquinas suggests that consideration should be given to whether the sin infects others (as with heresy or fornication) or whether it harms only one other individual (as with theft or murder). If the sin infects others, then, for the sake of the whole community and at the expense of the reputation (*fama*) of the sinner, the sin must be laid before those in authority.

Not only does Aquinas make the categoric assertion in this context that the good of many should *always* be preferred to the good of one person,[35] but he also gives it a more general application than the sins of heresy and fornication. Public accusation is necessary *wherever* the common good, spiritual or corporeal, is directly endangered.[36] In these cases, it is simply inappropriate to demonstrate the consideration which would otherwise be shown in admonishing the sinner.[37] Preachers and teachers should follow Christ's example and put the salvation (*salus*) of the multitude above the peace (*pax*) of certain individuals.[38] Naturally, it is much better if *both* the individual good *and* the common good can be secured by private admonition offered in love. Extreme remedies, after all, are not necessarily preferable, at least to start with, and a limb should only be amputated when it is incurable.[39] Nevertheless, if the sin in question is a public sin, then Aquinas firmly believes that it should be subject to public correction at the expense of the individual. In Aquinas' view, this demonstration of justice is entirely in accordance with an expression of love, since the *ordo caritatis* prescribes that the common good is to be preferred to the individual good of one's neighbour.[40] The requirements of love and the requirements of justice, in other words, produce one and the same conclusion.

---

[34] *IaIIae* 68.1. Cf. IV *Sent.* 35.1.3 ad 6, where the sinner is not an errant brother but an adulterous wife. For the distinction between accusation and denunciation, see *Decr. Greg. IX* V.1.16 (Freidberg, ii. 737–8). Cf. *Decretum* II.2.7 (Friedberg, i. 483–504).

[35] IV *Sent.* 19.2.3a ad 2. Cf. below p. 169 n. 34.

[36] *Q. Disp. de Virt.* III.2 ad 7. Cf. *Decretum* I.45.17 (Friedberg, i. 166–7), II.24.3.16, 37 (ibid., i. 995, 1000); *Decr. Greg. IX* V.7.9 (ibid., ii. 780–2). For the readoption of heretics into the church, see *IaIIae* 11.4.

[37] *IaIIae* 33.6. Some sins are, of course, of lesser magnitude than others, and, for these, public accusation might be permissible without any preceding admonition since no damage would be caused to the reputation of the sinner. However, if such accusation has a deleterious rather than a corrective effect, or if the community will not thereby derive any benefit, the action loses its justification and the accuser becomes guilty of the grave sin of infamy (IV *Sent.* 19.2.3a).

[38] *IIIa* 42.2.   [39] *Q. Disp. de Virt.* III.2 ad 11–12.

[40] *Quod.* XI.10.1. Cf. *Expos. super ad I Tim.* 5.3.

Aquinas sees love and justice operating in the political community in exactly the same way. As long as some hope of improvement in the character of a malefactor remains, Aquinas argues that the love of friendship should not be withdrawn. Only when a sin is extreme and incurable should this step be taken. In this case, if the harm which will be caused to others outweighs the possibility of reform, then both human and divine law require that the sinner should be killed. Like Albertus Magnus, therefore, Aquinas argues that the common good can justify the death penalty for the most socially damaging of crimes.[41] For Albertus, punishment should always be ordered towards the benefit of the community.[42] For him, this is the negative corollary of defining justice as giving each person their due in accordance with their moral worth and therefore giving more to those whose virtuous actions make a greater contribution to the common good.[43] It is thus the good of the community which justifies the implementation of the death penalty. If a crime has threatened to destroy the political community or its good moral standing, then the perpetrator should be prevented from corrupting the whole community any further, in the same way that an irremediably diseased limb should be amputated in order to save the life of the whole body.[44] According to Aquinas, the implementation of the death penalty still stems from a desire to benefit the sinner in that it provides him with the means of expiating his crime and stopping himself from sinning again. Nevertheless, it is love for the common good which takes precedence. The judge exacts the death penalty, not from hatred, but from love for the public good in preference to the life of the individual.[45]

Every individual considered as an individual human being must love human nature even when it is present in a criminal and, as a result, every individual must shrink from destroying what God has created. The individual considered as one individual human being in relation to many, however, has a duty to the common good. It is this common good which has been destroyed by the criminal and which provides the justification for his execution.[46] Every individual is ordered towards their community as a part is ordered towards its whole and, if an individual poses a threat to this community, then he should be removed so that the common good may be preserved.[47] Not everyone may see it that way of course. The wife of a thief, for example, will put the private good of her family first and seek remission for her husband. The judge, however, must prefer the common good of justice.[48] As a result, the actual process of removing the sinner from the human community is a public, not a private, function. Just as amputation is the preserve of a qualified doctor, so punishment is the preserve of a public authority which is qualified to act for the common good.[49] Just as

[41] *ScG* III.146; *IIaIIae* 25.6 ad 2.   [42] Albertus Magnus, *Super Ethica* V.12, p. 362.
[43] Albertus Magnus, *Ethica* V.2.6, p. 348.
[44] Albertus Magnus, *Super Ethica* X.17, p. 781. Cf. *Ethica* V.2.6, p. 351, where examples of such crimes against the public good are listed as intending to harm a ruler, striking a ruler, adultery with a ruler's wife, and sacrilegious violence.
[45] *ScG* III.146; *IIaIIae* 25.6 ad 2.   [46] *IIaIIae* 64.6.
[47] *IIaIIae* 64.2. Cf. *IIaIIae* 65.1, where amputation is both an analogy and a punishment.
[48] *IaIIae* 19.10. Cf. *Decretum* II.23.4.33 (Friedberg, i. 915).
[49] *IIaIIae* 64.7. Cf. *IIaIIae* 64.3; *Decretum* II.23.5.8 (Friedberg, i. 932–3), 23.8.33 (ibid., i. 965). A similar

the doctor who performs this operation seeks to preserve the harmony and well-being of the whole body, so the ruler of the city seeks the harmony and peace of his citizens.[50]

The equation of love and justice provides Aquinas with a framework for a more general analysis of the role of law in the human community than simply a discussion of the death penalty. Once again, Albertus Magnus had already sketched out the form which such a discussion should take. As the rule and measure by which justice is applied in practice, law is necessarily defined by the same goal, namely the common good, the good of the community, the well-being of the *res publica*.[51] According to Albertus, law is the principle of order in a political community.[52] It is the standard by which justice is correctly applied to particular cases according to the principle that the good of one person should be ordered towards the more divine good of the political community and the people.[53] Albertus accordingly introduces the common good into his definition of both justice and law, in each case citing the authority of Cicero as well as Aristotle. Just law, he states, has its origins in the principle of common benefit in the sense that whoever is governing the human community will make judgments which are congruent with the benefit of the *res publica* or which promote the common good.[54] In his own definition of law, Aquinas follows suit and makes a notion of the common benefit and common good central to his own working definition.[55] Law is an ordinance of reason directed to the common good and promulgated by an authority.[56] Whether this authority is the whole multitude, or a group or an individual acting on its behalf, the appropriate goal of its legislation is the common good.[57] It is the presence of this goal which distinguishes law from mere command.[58] It is a definition which applies to all forms of law. Aquinas interprets the difference between the Old Testament and the New, for example, as a difference between their common goods—the Old Testament was ordered towards a sensible and earthly good, the New Testament towards an intelligible and heavenly good.[59]

Aquinas' introduction of the common good into his definition of law rests on the authority of Cicero, Isidore, and Ulpian.[60] It relies just as heavily on Aristotle. His

---

line of argument supports a just war, waged for the common good of the community but also for the common good of those against whom it is fought. The public authority charged with securing this common good is the soldier, not the judge, but they exercise parallel functions (*IaIIae* 40.1 ad 2; *IIaIIae* 64.7). Cf. *Decretum* II.23.1.2, 23.1.6 (Friedberg, i. 891–3), and, more generally, F. H. Russell, *The Just War in the Middle Ages* (Cambridge, 1975), esp. ch. 7.

[50] *ScG* III.146. Such a sinner is not just a diseased limb. Aquinas quotes Aristotle's opinion that such a person is worse even than an animal and can be killed with much less hesitation than if he were fully human (*IIaIIae* 64.2 ad 3. Cf. Aristotle, *Ethics* VI.6 1150ᵃ7–8; *Politics* I.2 1253ᵃ32–3).

[51] Albertus Magnus, *Super Ethica* V.15, pp. 379–80; V.16, p. 384; VII.4, p. 547.
[52] Albertus Magnus, *Pol. Lib. Oct.* VII.3, pp. 644, 648.
[53] Albertus Magnus, *Super Ethica* V.2, p. 315 (above, p. 41).
[54] Albertus Magnus, *Ethica* V.3.3, p. 367. Cf. *Super Ethica* V.5, pp. 330, 335; *Ethica* V.2.4, p. 344; V.2.11, p. 362.
[55] *IaIIae* 95.3; *IaIIae* 90.2. Cf. *IaIIae* 96.1, 97.4 in 1, 100.2 in 3; *Principium Biblicum* II.
[56] *IaIIae* 90.4.   [57] *IaIIae* 90.3. Cf. *IaIIae* 95.4; *IIaIIae* 122.1 ad 3.
[58] *IaIIae* 90.2. Cf. *IaIIae* 96.1 ad 1.   [59] *IaIIae* 91.5.
[60] J. M. Aubert, *Le Droit romain dans l'oeuvre de saint Thomas* (Paris, 1955), esp. 79–82. Cf. A. Harding,

account of dispensation and equity, for example, draws extensively from book V of the *Ethics*. According to Aquinas, diversity occurs in human law because of the inherent fallibility of human judgement, because of the contingent nature of the common good which it has as its goal, and because of the differences between the people to whom it is applied, the subject-matter with which it is concerned, and the historical period in which it is instituted. Law can therefore cover only a majority of cases with certainty. It is in order to cope with the exceptions that dispensation from the law fulfils its proper function.[61] Such dispensation, however, must always secure the common good, since this is to preserve the fundamental definition of law and the original intention of the legislator.[62] In Aquinas' opinion, therefore, dispensation from the Ten Commandments would be a contradiction in terms, since all these laws necessarily secure the common good. The first four commandments order humans towards the ultimate common good which exists in God, the last six towards the common good which exists amongst themselves, namely the common good of justice.[63] Dispensation is possible, on the other hand, from lesser precepts of law, whether these take the form of fasting, punishment, or even vows of chastity and religious observance.[64] Dispensation from the letter of the law must, in each instance, be justified by the common good. It is this goal which justifies opening the gates of a city under siege,[65] for example, or making changes to customary legislation.[66] It is on similar grounds that the common good can be cited as a reason for tolerating usury,[67] the common benefit as a justification for levying extraordinary taxation in order to meet a threatened invasion.[68] Indeed, in the case of the latter, Aquinas is prepared to argue that, if rulers exact what is justly owed to them for the sake of preserving the common good, then they are not guilty of pillage (*rapina*) even when this exaction is accompanied with violence. Only if rulers exact something with violence when it is not their due, Aquinas insists, when it is not needed for the common good, are they guilty of robbery and depradation; only then are they obliged to make restitution.[69]

Viewed from the perspective of the relationship between the individual good and the common good, perhaps the most instructive example of dispensation occurs when Aquinas discusses the good of the species. This definition of the common good derived ultimately from Aristotle's account of natural generation as a process which counteracts corruption by enabling something which cannot secure eternal being in its individual manifestation to do so in its species.[70] In the human species, this principle serves, in the first instance, to distinguish the political community and the

'The Reflection of Thirteenth Century Legal Growth in Saint Thomas's Writings', in G. Verbeke and D. Verhelst (eds.), *Aquinas and the Problems of his Time* (Louvain, 1976), 18–37.

[61] *IaIIae* 91.4; *IaIIae* 96.1; IV *Sent.* 15.3.2a; *IaIIae* 97.4. Cf. *IaIIae* 96.6; *IIaIIae* 88.10.

[62] *IaIIae* 97.4 ad 1. Cf. IV *Sent.* 38.1.4a; IV *Sent.* 20.1.3b (*utilitas ecclesiae in generali*); *ScG* III.125; *IIaIIae* 88.12, 120.1.

[63] *IaIIae* 100.8. Cf. *IaIIae* 97.4 ad 3, 99.3.   [64] IV *Sent.* 15.3.2a, 20.1.3b, 38.1.4a.

[65] *IaIIae* 96.6. Cf. *IaIIae* 100.8; Cicero, *De Inventione* (Loeb, 1949) II.42.123, p. 292.

[66] *IaIIae* 97.1. For *evidens utilitas*, see below, p. 184.   [67] *Q. Disp. de Malo* XIII.4. Cf. above, p. 70.

[68] *De Reg. Iud. ad Duc. Brab.* VI.   [69] *IIaIIae* 66.8 ad 3. Cf. below, p. 252.

[70] II *Sent.* 20.1.1 in 3. Cf. *Q. Disp. de Verit.* V.3; *ScG* II.93; *Ia* 98.1.

household from more transitory associations.[71] However, it also serves as a point of comparison for the goods which are secured, respectively, by marriage and by celibacy. If the common good of the species is the good which is secured by marriage, and if this common good is superior to the good of the individual, then surely the married state is superior to celibacy since celibacy can secure only an individual good? Aquinas' solution to this proposition is straightforward. Natural inclinations are of two kinds. There are those, such as nutrition, which concern the perfection of the individual, and there are those, such as marriage, which concern the perfection of the multitude. The former, Aquinas argues, carry an obligation for every individual, whereas the latter do not. Marriage, like farming, building, and other such public 'offices', is necessary to the community only as one function among many.[72] In order to be perfect, the human community requires both the married and the celibate, just as the universe requires both spiritual and corporeal substances, and the body requires both eyes and feet. At the same time, whilst the presence of all of these parts may be necessary for the whole, one part may still be intrinsically better than another.[73] Aquinas thereby appeals to the same solution which Albertus Magnus had used in exactly this context. For the common good to be better than the individual good, both goods must belong to the same genus. If they are different, if an individual spiritual good is compared to a common corporeal good, then the individual good is preferable to the common good. Celibacy is therefore preferable to marriage.[74]

   The question of marriage and celibacy provides Aquinas with an opportunity to draw a theoretical distinction between two types of good, the corporeal and the spiritual, and to make a comparative judgement on their relative merits. It also affects his broader analysis of dispensation. As the inclination to secure the common good of the species, the desire to reproduce is a natural instinct which human beings share with animals, although in humans it is subject to the rule of reason.[75] Indeed, it is precisely because it is so necessary for the common good of humankind that the process of generation must be controlled by human reason.[76] However, if the desire to reproduce is guided by reason and ordered towards the common good, it must also, by definition, fall within the purview of justice and law.[77] As a result, reproduction is different from other natural instincts, such as nutrition, which are only ordered towards the good of

---

[71] *C. Imp. Dei* III.4.

[72] IV *Sent.* 26.1.2. The goodness of the species is superior to the goodness in an individual as form is superior to matter (*ScG* II.45). Cf. *ScG* II.93; *Quod.* I.4.3 ad 3; II *Sent.* 32.2.2 (where the principle of generation is set against the transmission of original sin); IV *Sent.* 31.1 in 1; *ScG* III.136; *IIaIIae* 152.4 in 3. Aquinas does not always define the common good secured by marriage as the *bonum speciei*. It can also be the offspring itself, *bonum prolis* (IV *Sent.* 33.2.1 ad 4. Cf. Aristotle, *Ethics* VIII.12 1162ᵃ27–9). Article 210 (169) of the 219 propositions condemned in 1277, reads 'perfect abstinence from carnal acts destroys virtue and the species' (*Siger de Brabant et l'averroïsme latin au XIIIe siècle*, ed. P. Mandonnet, Louvain, 1908, p. 190).

[73] *ScG* III.136.

[74] *IIaIIae* 152.4 ad 3. The same principle accounts for the superiority of the eucharist to the sacrament of marriage (*IIIa* 65.3 ad 1). For Albertus Magnus, see above, pp. 64–6.

[75] *IaIIae* 91.6 ad 3.   [76] *IIaIIae* 153.3. Cf. *IIaIIae* 142.1.

[77] *IIaIIae* 154.2. Cf. *IIaIIae* 154.9; *ScG* III.123.

an individual, towards his own preservation, and which therefore fall within the purview of an individual's own discretion.[78] If the common good of the species and the act of generation are legitimate concerns for the legislator, however, then there should be instances in which dispensation can be granted from a vow of celibacy in order to secure the common good. It is always possible, after all, that the individual good secured by celibacy may impede the greater good of the multitude. For example, a vow of celibacy may stand in the way of a marriage which would bring peace to the entire country. Would this be a sufficient reason, then, for an act of dispensation to take place since, by definition, dispensation must always secure the common good? Faced with this sort of opposition between common good and individual good, Aquinas relies on a straightforward citation of authority in order to provide his solution. Other people, Aquinas writes, (a group which may well have included Albertus Magnus) may think it possible for dispensation from a vow of celibacy to be made for the sake of a common benefit or necessity, but, as far as he is concerned, canon law and Leviticus dictate otherwise.[79] This argument provides a revealing contrast with Aquinas' solution to the relative merits of the individual and the common good as the goals of the contemplative and active lives. In this context, the common good is defined as *communis utilitas*, the material and corporeal good of peace. This good is clearly not in the same genus as the individual spiritual good which is secured by celibacy. It therefore cannot be used to override it in an act of dispensation.

When Aquinas is drawn to consider an apparent conflict between the individual and the common good, he demonstrates some deft readjustments to his normal interpretation of their relationship. When he discusses the act of self-sacrifice in book IX of the *Ethics*, for example, or when he compares the relative merits of celibacy and marriage, he is quite prepared to introduce a much more limited definition of the common good than the one which he recycled from book I of the *Ethics*. In these instances, he elevates the individual good above the common good by restricting his definition of the common good to mean common benefit. Thus, the act of self-sacrifice results in benefit to the community but it is ordered towards the common good of virtue, a common good which is the same as the individual's own good. Likewise, marriage is ordered towards the physical continuity of the species and towards the peace and benefit of the political community, whereas celibacy is ordered towards the spiritual good of the individual, the common good in God. The fact that Aquinas continues to treat the common good of the political community in terms of the inclusive imagery of whole and part, body and member, therefore, should not obscure the fact that, when necessary, he can change his definition of the common good from the

---

[78] *Q. Disp. de Malo* XV.2.

[79] *IIaIIae* 88.11; *Decr. Greg. IX* III.35.6 (Friedberg, ii. 599–600). Cf. J. Brys, *De dispensatione in iure canonico, praesertim apud decretistas et decretalistas usque ad medium saeculum decimum quartum* (Bruges, 1925), 162, 214, 216–18, and, for Aquinas' general theory of dispensation, 261–9. Cf. P. G. Caron, 'Aequitas et interpretatio dans la doctrine canonique aux XIIIe et XIVe siècles', in *Proceedings of the Third International Congress of Medieval Canon Law* (Rome, 1971), 131–41; id., '*Aequitas*' romana, '*misericordia*' patristica ed '*epicheia*' aristotelica nella dottrina dell' '*aequitas*' canonica (Milan, 1977).

life of moral virtue to the common utility of material benefit. The distinction which enables him to make such a switch is the conceptual distinction between *bonum* and *utilitas*.

Aquinas' indebtedness to book V of the *Ethics* continues with his account of 'legal' (or 'general')[80] justice and its differentiation from particular justice. Once again, he draws a connection with the *duplex ordo* from book XII of the *Metaphysics*. Since individuals are ordered both towards the common good and towards one another, he argues, different categories of justice must pertain to each condition. Legal justice, therefore, is the justice which orders the actions of individuals towards the common good, whilst particular justice is the justice which orders them towards their neighbours.[81] This categorization presupposes at least one common factor, namely the ordering of an individual's exterior actions towards another person.[82] Legal justice can therefore also be defined as the justice which orders these exterior actions directly towards the common good but indirectly towards the good of another individual, whereas particular justice can be defined as the justice which orders these actions towards the good of another individual directly.[83] An act of virtue can therefore fall within either category of justice depending on the goal towards which it is directed. An act of bravery, for example, can be exercised either for the preservation of a political community or for the preservation of a friend.[84]

Like Albertus Magnus, Aquinas cites the common good as a criterion with which the moral virtues can be classified into a hierarchy on the basis that the more a virtue pertains to the good of the multitude, the better it is.[85] According to Aquinas, legal justice must therefore occupy the highest rank because it is directed towards the goal of the common good. It is on this basis, for example, that Aquinas reconciles the relative priority which Aristotle and Cicero had given to the virtues of justice and prudence by pointing out that Cicero made justice, not prudence, the most noble of the virtues because he was comparing them in terms of the common good.[86] In associating justice so closely with the common good, however, Aquinas does not deny that prudence too can be directed towards the common good. Indeed,

---

[80] *IIaIIae* 58.5.

[81] *IaIIae* 113.1. Particular justice is further divisible into distributive and rectificatory justice according to whether individual and neighbour are viewed as two distinct parts or as two parts of one whole (*IIaIIae* 61.1).

[82] *IIaIIae* 58.2; Aristotle, *Ethics* V.2 1129ᵇ31–33.

[83] *IIaIIae* 58.7 ad 1. Cf. *IIaIIae* 61.1 ad 4.   [84] *IaIIae* 96.3.

[85] *IIaIIae* 141.8. Cf. IV *Sent.* 2.1.3, 23.2.4b; *IIIa* 65.3 in/ad 1. Cf. *IIaIIae* 142.3 ad 1; IV *Sent.* 15.2.4a; IV *Sent.* 32.4c; *IIaIIae* 32.6; III *Sent.* 33.3.3d; *IIaIIae* 134.1; *Sent. Lib. Eth.* IV.7. For a general discussion, see O. Lottin, *Psychologie et morale aux XIIe et XIIIe siècles* (6 vols.; Louvain–Gembloux, 1942–60), iii. 271–80, and, for Aquinas' treatment of the common good as a criterion for the classification of the virtues and the sacraments, I. Th. Eschmann, '*Bonum commune melius est quam bonum unius*: Eine Studie über den Wertvorrang des Personalen bei Thomas von Aquin', *Mediaeval Studies*, 6 (1944), 62–120.

[86] III *Sent.* 33.2.5 ad 4; *IIaIIae* 58.12. Cf. above, pp. 45–6. Justice can also be bracketed with bravery, the former virtue defending the common good, the latter preserving it (*Expositio super ad Hebraeos* XI.7). Cf. *IIaIIae* 2.5; *IIaIIae* 123.5 (where the equivalence of judicial punishment and the just war is such that the bravery which is exercised for the sake of the common good is not limited to a soldier in battle but extends to a judge and even to a private person); *IIaIIae* 123.12 ad 3; *Sent. Lib. Eth.* III.14.

it is in discussing the respective relations of both justice and prudence to the common good that Aquinas produces one of his most significant models for the relationship between the individual and the common good.

As an exercise of right reason, prudence enables an individual to judge and direct those actions through which he will secure his goal and, as a result, prudence concerns both the individual good and the common good. Like justice, therefore, prudence appears in two forms. When prudence orders an action towards the individual good it is simply termed prudence, but when it orders an action towards the common good it is called *political* prudence. The identity of these two forms of prudence derives from the identity of their respective goals in that the individual good is the same as the common good. Aquinas explains this principle with the observation that whoever seeks the common good of the multitude also seeks their own good as a consequence (*ex consequenti*). He gives two reasons, both of them familiar from his metaphysical account of the common good in God—the individual good cannot exist without the common good, and the good of the part is dependent upon the good of the whole.[87] Having established the grounds on which prudence and political prudence can be regarded as the same, Aquinas then examines the grounds on which they are different. Virtuous dispositions differ according to their object, according to the end towards which they are ordered, and this represents a difference in formal principle (*ratio formalis*). Thus, insofar as the individual good and the common good are formally different ends, the prudence with which each is aimed at is accompanied by a different disposition (*habitus*). The relationship between prudence and political prudence is thus characterized by principles of both identity and difference. Prudence is the same as political prudence insofar as it is an act of right reason applied to human action; it is different insofar as it directs this action towards a different end, namely the individual good rather than the common good. That one of these ends is ordered towards the other, the individual good towards the good of the multitude, means, not that this difference in species disappears, but that the disposition to exercise one type of virtue is 'more primary' than the disposition to exercise the other.[88]

Having established that the relationship between prudence and political prudence is analogous to the relationship between the individual and the common good, Aquinas is left with the question of the connection between political prudence and legal justice. Aristotle, after all, had described the relationship between justice as a virtue in its own right and justice as inclusive of all virtue in very similar terms to those which he applied to the relationship between prudence and political prudence. In both instances, Aristotle had used the phrase 'identical in quality of mind but different in essence'.[89] Aquinas makes the parallel explicit. Prudence, he states,

---

[87] *IIaIIae* 47.10. Cf. *IIaIIae* 50.2 ad 3; above, pp. 80–1.

[88] *IIaIIae* 47.11. Cf. *IIaIIae* 50.1. Nor is this difference in species limited to these two types of prudence. It also covers the prudence which concerns the common good of the household (*IIaIIae* 47.11) and of the army (*IIaIIae* 50.4).

[89] Aristotle, *Ethics* V.1 1129ᵇ26–1130ᵃ14; VI.8 1141ᵇ23–4; *Recensio pura*, ed. R. A. Gauthier (*Aristoteles Latinus* XXVI.3), pp. 229 (*est quidem enim eadem, esse autem non idem*), 261 (*est autem . . . idem quidem habitus; esse quidem, non idem ipsis*).

stands in the same relation to political prudence as virtue does to legal justice.[90] Following the anonymous Greek commentator translated by Grosseteste, therefore, Aquinas states that general or legal justice is identical to all the virtues in subject but different from them in defining principle (*idem subiecto . . . differens ratione*).[91] General or legal justice is virtue insofar as it directs an individual's action but it is justice insofar as it harmonizes with the law and results in the common good.[92] Following Albertus Magnus, Aquinas concludes that legal justice is the same as all the virtues but it differs from them in terms of its defining principle in that it orders an act of virtue towards the common good.[93] Legal justice orders the actions of all virtues towards the common good, just as love orders the actions of all virtues towards the divine good, the good in God. However, legal justice remains distinct from what it orders. Just as love remains a particular virtue according to its essence because it has the divine good as its own, proper object, so legal justice is a particular virtue according to its essence because it has the common good as its own, proper object. A difference in end is a formal difference, a difference in species, and a difference in defining principle (*secundum rationem*). Legal justice is thus the same as all virtue in essence but it is different according to its defining principle (*est idem in essentiam . . . differt autem ratione*).[94]

The terms in which Aquinas describes the relationship between legal justice and all virtue are clearly very close to the terms with which he defines the relationship between political prudence and prudence. Both legal justice and political prudence are distinct in their own right but they are also identical with the individual virtues which they direct. This parallel between legal justice and political prudence has significant consequences for Aquinas' political thought. In the first instance, it provides him with a description of the way in which the common good of a political community is qualitatively different from a mere aggregate of individual goods. The common good of the city and the individual good of one person differ according to a formal difference (*formalis differentia*), that is, a difference in defining principle which is comparable to the difference between whole and part and which is more than just a difference in number.[95] In the second instance, the point of distinction between political prudence and legal justice (legal justice orders every virtue whilst prudence orders every *action* of every virtue)[96] provides Aquinas with the basis for arguing that the individual human being is not completely subsumed within the political community.

Albertus Magnus had already identified the possible practical consequences for the political community of Aristotle's definition of general justice in book V of the

---

[90] *IIaIIae* 47.10 ad 1.

[91] *Eustratii et Michaelis et Anonyma in Ethica Nicomachea Commentaria*, ed. G. Heylbut (Commentaria in Aristotelem Graeca XX; Berlin, 1892), p. 211. Cf. Averroes, *Aristotelis Opera cum Averrois Commentaria* (editio Iuntina, 2nd edn., 11 vols.; Venice, 1560–2), iii fo. 65r–v.

[92] *II Sent.* 35.1.2 ad 4.

[93] *III Sent.* 33.1.1c ad 3. Cf. *Expositio super ad Philippenses* III.2; *IV Sent.* 17.1.1a; *Q. Disp. de Verit.* XXVIII.1; *IaIIae* 60.3. For its connection to sanctity, see *II Sent.* 33.3.4f ad 3. Cf. *IIaIIae* 81.8 ad 1.

[94] *IIaIIae* 58.6.   [95] *IIaIIae* 58.7 ad 2.   [96] *IIaIIae* 50.1 ad 1. Cf. *IIaIIae* 58.6.

Ethics and, once again, his account provides a critical point of reference for the argument of his pupil. As soon as Albertus combined Aristotle's definition of the common good of human society as happiness and the life of virtue with Aristotle's identification of legal justice with all the virtues, it took only a short step to conclude that the object of positive law is the common good and the goal of the legislator is to make the members of the political community lead a virtuous life. This definition of the moral objective of law and the moral orientation of political authority accordingly occurs throughout Albertus' exposition of the *Ethics*.[97] It is the intention of legislation and political authority, he writes, to make members of the political community good people by making them accustomed to perform good actions and thereby to effect a life of virtue.[98] From the outset, however, Albertus is also well aware of the possible consequences which such a goal can have for the scope of human legislation. If justice is composed of all the virtues, is the ruler obliged to ensure that every individual within the community is exercising *every* individual virtue? If justice is the same as all the virtues, can law command *everything* by which any individual might become virtuous?

Albertus' response to such an all-inclusive definition of law is to insist on a number of important qualifications. Every virtue, he writes, can, indeed, fall within the purview of the legislator but it does so to the extent that, when a virtue is put into practice, it has an effect on the community and therefore falls within the competence of political authority. However private and personal some virtues may be in their subject-matter, they become the concern of the community, and therefore of the law, if and when they are the cause of exterior effects.[99] This is not to say, however, that all private virtues *necessarily* have public consequences. Albertus clarifies this point when he interprets Aristotle's distinction between being a good man and being a good citizen as a distinction between performing private and public actions. To be a good individual, Albertus states, concerns private action and as such it is quite possible to be a good individual without knowing how to be good in one's public actions, without knowing how to be a good citizen. Thus, to insist that human beings are essentially political animals because they cannot live the life of virtue outside of an association with their fellow-humans is not to insist that they are obliged to live a life of perpetual (*semper*) public activity without any private activity of their own.[100] Moreover, if general justice concerns all those actions which produce and preserve happiness and its constituent elements, then it only consists of those actions which are *capable* of being ordered (*referibilis*) to the *res publica*.[101] This definition does not cover the passions since, by dint of not being 'actions', passions (fear in the face of danger, for example, or desire in the face of pleasure) cannot be included in a definition of justice as the virtue which comprehends those actions which are capable of

[97] Albertus Magnus, *Super Ethica* III.10, p. 190; IV.4, p. 239; IV.16, p. 299; V.2, p. 315; V.9, p. 351; VI.11, p. 468; X.18, p. 786.
[98] Albertus Magnus, *Ethica* I.9.1, pp. 139–40; II.1.3, p. 153. Cf. Aristotle, *Ethics* II.2 1103^{b}2–5.
[99] Albertus Magnus, *Super Ethica* V.2, pp. 315–16. Cf. ibid., VIII.1, p. 591.
[100] Albertus Magnus, *Super Ethica* V.4, p. 327.   [101] Albertus Magnus, *Ethica* V.1.2–3, p. 335.

being ordered to the whole community. Likewise, because passions only concern the individual who experiences them, they cannot be included in a definition of justice as the virtue which considers the relation of one individual to another individual with respect to their common goods.[102] Although the passions still constitute the physical location of moral virtue (fortitude in fear, temperance in pleasure), they cannot themselves be ordered towards the human community and, as such, they cannot be the subject of legislation. There are some things, Albertus observes, which, by their very nature, cannot be made common.[103]

Albertus' clearest statement of the limitations on the scope of justice in the human community occurs in the course of his discussion of suicide. In assessing whether the person who kills himself does an injustice to ('injures') the political community of which he is a member, Albertus distinguishes two ways in which the good of a community can be considered. This common good is either a good which is distributed amongst its individual parts (in which case injury can only be done to the community if injustice is done to an individual member of that community) or it is a certain form of action which can only be perfomed by the community. As an example of the latter, Albertus suggests defeating the army of an invading tyrant, an act in defence of the *res publica* which cannot be performed by any one person on their own. In such circumstances, he argues, the individual who weakens the virtue of the whole community (by fleeing from the tyrant's army or by committing suicide) necessarily commits an injury to the community since his actions will remove an integral part of the virtue of the community. Suicide may not be an act of injustice against the individual himself (since it is not performed against his own will) but it is an act of injustice against the community (since the community is forced to suffer it against its will).[104] Even though a person who commits suicide may be a wicked person, he might still have become a good citizen by faithfully serving the community. It is the loss of this potential virtue which constitutes the harm caused to the community when he kills himself. He is unjust to his community since he is depriving the community of someone who might otherwise have contributed to that community in the capacity of an army commander, a soldier, or a craftsman.[105] This conclusion leaves one question outstanding. If it is the case that a suicide injures the community, will *any* sin committed by an individual constitute an act against the good of the community? Albertus' response is clear. Some (unspecified) sins are performed as private actions but have no relation to the community. In such cases, Albertus is quite prepared to concede that there is no possibility of any injury being done to the community.[106] Although Albertus does not believe that suicide falls into this category, he clearly leaves scope for the human community to comprise a private sphere of individual activity.

---

[102] Albertus Magnus, *Super Ethica* V.6, pp. 337–8.
[103] Albertus Magnus, *Ethica* V.1.3, pp. 335–6.   [104] Albertus Magnus, *Super Ethica* V.16, p. 385.
[105] Albertus Magnus, *Ethica* V.4.2, p. 387. Cf. Aristotle, *Ethics* V.11 1138ª4–14; *Auctoritates Aristotelis*, ed. J. Hamesse (Louvain–Paris, 1974), p. 240; Augustine, *De Civitate Dei*, ed. B. Dombart and A. Kalb (*CCSL* 47), I.17–27, pp. 18–28.
[106] Albertus Magnus, *Super Ethica* V.16, p. 385.

When Albertus Magnus followed Aristotle and identified justice with all the virtues, he was clearly prepared to combine a reading of the common good of happiness as carte-blanche for legislation on every aspect of the life of virtue with a practical recognition that there are some actions (and passions) which do not fall within the purview of political life. This balance was also struck by Aquinas. He stages a very similar discussion to Albertus when, for example, he appeals to a definition of law as an ordinance of reason which is imposed on individuals as a rule and as a measure of their conduct.[107] Aquinas points out that for someone like Isidore this sort of definition could only mean that law orders everything which is in accordance with reason and that, as a result, law must concern itself not just with the common good but with the individual good as well.[108] Aquinas also observes that Aristotle had gone even further when he had specified that it should always be the intention of the legislator to make people virtuous according to every virtue and that, as a result, law must concern itself with every action of every virtue.[109]

Aquinas' own view goes a long way towards giving law a similarly comprehensive scope. Law, he argues, pertains to reason, the basic principle of all human actions. The goal of reason is happiness, that is, activity in accordance with perfect virtue. Since law is a dictate of reason, it is the purpose of law to make humans virtuous, to turn them into good people. This is one reason why it possesses its coercive power. Law orders the individual towards the community as an imperfect part towards its perfect whole. It can therefore order individual actions towards the common good as their final cause.[110] In order to be good, individuals must be in correct relation to the common good. Since every human being is part of a community, and since the goodness of a part is always considered in relation to its whole, it is impossible for individuals to be good unless they are correctly 'proportioned' to the common good. Conversely, it is impossible for the common good of the community to exist correctly unless its citizens are themselves virtuous.[111] This is why Aristotle had argued that it is only if all individuals strive to perform the most virtuous actions that the common good will be fully realized. Aquinas therefore concludes that, although legal justice may be principally concerned with the exterior actions of virtue, it can also extend to their interior motivation, to the internal dispositions of their individual human agents.[112] Legal justice comprises every virtuous action which relates to the common good. There is no virtue, in other words, whose actions are not capable of being ordered, directly or indirectly, towards the common good.[113]

Likewise, although Aquinas defines justice as a virtue which concerns only the

---

[107] *IaIIae* 90.4.   [108] *IaIIae* 90.2 in 3.   [109] *IIaIIae* 122.1 in 1.
[110] *IaIIae* 90.2, 90.3 ad 2, 92.1. Cf. *IaIIae* 90.3 ad 3.   [111] *IaIIae* 92.1.
[112] *IIaIIae* 58.9 ad 3. Cf. Aristotle, *Ethics* IX.8 1169a8–11.
[113] *IaIIae* 61.5 ad 4, 96.3 ad 3. This is true even of temperance, an action which would seem to concern a purely individual good but which Aquinas includes within the purview of legal justice by distinguishing between different types of common good, 'moral' and 'natural' (*IaIIae* 94.3). Aquinas makes the same point in negative terms. Illegal injustice, he argues, has a special object in that it contradicts the common good, and a general object in that by acting against the common good man can commit every possible sin (*IIaIIae* 59.1).

exterior actions of one individual towards another individual, he points out that exterior actions performed by one individual upon another individual are actions which are performed to all those whom that community comprises. By the same token, therefore, the identification of one individual with all individuals in the community can be extended to cover the agent himself. Actions which are performed by one individual upon himself are actions which are performed to all those whom that community comprises. Thus, if the community is inherent in each individual, then the legal justice which pertains to the whole and which is concerned with the common good can also pertain to the individual actions of each part, of each person towards himself.[114] Once again, it is the issue of suicide which causes this particular line of argument to be put forward. An individual may amputate his own diseased limb in order to save his whole body, undergoing a lesser peril in order to avoid the greater. If this aspect of the corporeal analogy can be applied to the community, then what is to prevent an individual killing himself in order to avoid a greater evil, a wretched life, for example, or the commission of some sin? What if this 'greater evil' were to be construed as the danger which his remaining alive would pose to the common good of the body politic? Aquinas' response is to refute firmly any legitimation of taking one's own life. Suicide is contrary to love and to natural inclination and it usurps the judgement of God. It is in expanding this argument that Aquinas reveals just how inclusive the judicial application of the analogy of part and whole could be. Whatever a part is, he writes, is due to the fact that it is part of a whole. Since human beings are parts of a community, whatever they are, they must be 'of' the community. Thus, when an individual commits suicide, he is committing an injury not just to himself but to the whole community.[115] An individual who kills himself may be viewed in two ways. If he is considered as an individual, then the injury which he has caused to himself makes him guilty of intemperance and imprudence but not of injustice since justice requires an action to be performed towards another person. If he is considered as belonging to something else, however, either as a part of a community or as the creation and image of God, then the individual has injured, not himself, but the community and God and, as such, the suicide can be punished by both human and divine law.[116]

Viewed in these terms, as a part within a whole, it is difficult to conceive of any wrong for which an individual human being might not be punished, since whatever an individual does can be considered to affect the whole of which he forms a part. This, at least, is the implication of Aquinas' argument within the immediate context of his discussion of suicide. What is so striking about Aquinas' argument outside this frame of reference, however, is his introduction of significant qualifications. When Aquinas translates an inclusive theory of legal justice into an inclusive theory of law, he is as careful as Albertus Magnus to say that actions are 'capable of being ordered' (*ordinabile, referibile, referri possunt*) towards the common good rather than 'should be ordered' (*ordinandum, referendum*), and to state explicitly that the phrase 'every

---

[114] *IIaIIae* 58.5.   [115] *IIaIIae* 64.5.   [116] *IIaIIae* 59.3 ad 2. Cf. *IIaIIae* 65.1.

virtue can be ordered to the common good' does not mean every *action* of every virtue.[117] According to Aquinas, divine law is the only law which necessarily covers every action of every virtue. Divine law concerns the relation of individuals towards God in this life and in the next, and, as such, it prescribes everything which is necessary for this relation, intellectual virtues as well as moral virtues, interior dispositions as well as exterior actions.[118] Human law, by contrast, concerns the civil community, the relations of individuals towards one another, and as such deals only with exterior actions. If it deals with interior motives, then it does so only insofar as they have some exterior repercussion. Aquinas firmly separates divine law and human law along the lines laid down by these parameters. Human beings are simply unable to judge the interior disposition of someone's virtuous action. All humans can do is consider the exterior operation of such an act. As a result, since the perfection of virtue requires both disposition and operation, human law cannot be sufficient to ensure true virtue; only divine law can do this.[119] It is from this specifically Christian perspective that Aquinas proceeds to restrict the practical scope of human legislation. When he glosses Augustine's argument that human law cannot punish or prohibit all evil actions, for example, Aquinas argues that to maintain the opposite, with whatever good intentions, would effectively remove the opportunity for many good actions and thereby impede the benefits of the common good which are necessary for human life.[120] Humans themselves are inherently imperfect and they should not be treated as if they were perfectly virtuous. Law should therefore confine itself only to the more serious sins, to those which harm others to an extent which threatens the continuation of human society. Law should still seek to make humans good, but it must do so gradually lest it make them worse.[121]

Aquinas approached the role of justice in the human community, it would appear, from two broad perspectives. On the one hand, he draws from Aristotle an ideal notion of human perfectibility and an all-inclusive model of legal justice; on the other, he accommodates from Augustine the reality of human imperfection in both judgement and action. In theory, therefore, Aquinas argues that general justice comprises all the virtues, that law is instituted to make individuals virtuous, and that the actions which an individual does towards himself are actions which are done towards the whole community. In practice, however, he concedes that human law does not comprise every action of every virtue, that law is instituted to correct only those sins which threaten the continuation of human society, and that there is a sphere of private activity for each individual human being. This division between theory and practice has profound consequences for Aquinas' understanding of the relationship between the individual and the common good. In theory, for example, the common good depends upon the presence of all the virtues amongst its individual citizens. In

---

[117] *IaIIae* 96.3. Cf. *IaIIae* 21.4 ad 3.   [118] *IaIIae* 100.2. Cf. *IIaIIae* 59.1 ad 1.

[119] *IaIIae* 91.4. Cf. *IaIIae* 100.9; *IIaIIae* 104.5. The freedom guaranteed to each individual by the Holy Spirit is based on the same reservation (*IaIIae* 96.5). Cf. below, p. 259 n. 91.

[120] *IaIIae* 91.4. Cf. Augustine, *De Libero Arbitrio*, ed. W. M. Green (*CCSL* 29), I.5.13, pp. 218–19.

[121] *IaIIae* 96.2. Cf. *IaIIae* 107.1.

practice, the good of the community depends upon the presence of these virtues in the ruler alone whilst expectations of virtue on the part of individual citizens are limited to the virtue of obedience.[122] Perhaps the most revealing instance of this disparity between the ideal of moral goodness and the reality of the political community, however, occurs in Aquinas' analysis of obedience and resistance.

Aquinas' classification of correction and punishment as the expression of love and justice has strong parallels with his discussion of the obedience which every individual owes to those who exercise authority in both religious and political communities. In religious communities, for example, it is love for the common good which determines whether an individual should obey his prelate if he is commanded to reveal a sin which one of his brothers is suspected of committing. If it is a matter of general suspicion, Aquinas argues, then the common good of the multitude is involved, and, if the common good is involved, then an individual is obliged to obey his prelate when he is ordered to reveal what he knows of his brother's crime.[123] Once again, Aquinas uses the presence of the common good to reassure his audience that obeying the prelate's command is compatible with the bonds established by the love of friendship. To demonstrate such obedience, he argues, is entirely in accordance with the principle that the common good must always be preferred to the individual good. Indeed, he concludes, no one ought to keep anything secret if it runs counter to the common good.[124]

That obedience should be conditional upon securing the common good, however, is a principle which cuts both ways. The common good can require obedience from a subject but it can also justify disobedience and resistance. According to Aquinas, the obedience owed to all human authority is based on the divine and the natural order,[125] and, as such, it is necessarily limited by the correspondence of that human authority to the precepts of divine and natural law. Human authority may fail this test on two grounds, either in the way in which it has been acquired (by usurpation, violence, or simony) or in the way in which it is abused (by issuing commands which are contrary to virtue, faith, or *ultra vires*). Rulers who are guilty of wrongful acquisition are not true rulers but they can subsequently be legitimated by the consent of their subjects or by the ratification of a superior authority. Rulers who are unable to secure such *post facto* legitimacy, however, or who are guilty of an abuse of power, are legitimate objects of resistance and even tyrannicide.[126] Human authority can also fail to correspond to divine and natural law according to the terms set down by Aquinas' fourfold definition of law. If law is an ordinance of reason which is ordered towards the common good, issued by the authority in charge of the political community, and pro-

---

[122] *IaIIae* 92.1. This is a rare example of Aquinas drawing a distinction between the *bonum commune civitatis* and the *bonum communitatis*.

[123] *Quod.* IV.8.1. Cf. IV *Sent.* 21.3.2 in/ad 2; *Les Premières Polémiques thomistes I: Le Correctorium Corruptorii 'Quare'*, ed. P. Glorieux (Paris, 1927), pp. 399–403.

[124] *IIaIIae* 68.1 ad 3.

[125] *IIaIIae* 104.1. Cf. *Q. Disp. de Verit.* XVII.5; *Les premières polémiques thomistes*, ed. Glorieux, pp. 259–64.

[126] II *Sent.* 44.2.2 ad 5.

mulgated to its subjects,[127] then there are four corresponding criteria which must be fulfilled in order for any human law to be binding. It must be derived from the eternal law, it must be ordered towards the common good, it must emanate from an appropriate authority, and it must be applied equitably to all individuals. Unjust laws are defined by the absence of any one of these criteria, and all of them are simultaneously applicable. Anything which is ordered towards the common good but which is inequitably imposed is still an unjust law, or rather it is not even a law, as Aquinas follows Augustine in denying this status to what amounts to an act of violence.[128]

Aquinas could have argued that obedience to evil rulers is obligatory on the grounds that all power is divinely ordained (Romans 13).[129] This is certainly the line which he takes when he discusses whether more honour should be shown to a good subject than to an evil ruler. Carefully distinguishing between the office of authority and its incumbent, Aquinas argues that, although the good subject should be given priority in absolute terms (*simpliciter*), the reverse is true when the principle of authority is taken into consideration. First, the ruler is the viceregent of God and therefore honour shown to him is honour shown to God. Secondly, the ruler is a public person and therefore what is honoured in him is the good of the church or *res publica*, a good which is greater than the personal merits of the ruler himself.[130] Honour, however, appears to be a different matter from obedience. In the case of tyranny, indeed, Aquinas' conclusion is blunt. Just as God 'wills' evil in order that good may result, so does Creation. In desiring evil to befall a tyrant who is destroying the church, an individual desires the good of the church through the destruction of the tyrant. Nor is it just a question of desire. It is not sinful, Aquinas states, to act in hanging the wicked, provided it is just. Rulers may be ministers of God (following Romans 13) but punishing them can still meet with God's approval on the grounds that it can result in their own castigation and in the common good of the city, a good which is better, more divine, and greater than the life of one individual.[131]

One of Aquinas' most significant justifications of resistance to tyrannical rule takes the form of a detailed analysis of sedition. Opposition to the common good of the *res publica*, he argues, is, strictly speaking, *seditio*, a form of conflict which is distinct from both strife (*rixa*) and war (*bellum*) and which can be defined as a conflict between parts of the same whole. The good with which sedition is in conflict is thus the unity and peace of the multitude.[132] As such, it is the equivalent of schism, both forms of disobedience attempting to place a partial good above the good of a whole.[133] Moreover, if the unity of a multitude (be it a people, a city, or a kingdom) is analysed in

---

[127] *IaIIae* 90.4. [128] *IaIIae* 96.4. Cf. *IIaIIae* 69.4, *IIaIIae* 104.5. Contrast *IaIIae* 93 ad 2.

[129] e.g. Bernard of Clairvaux, *De Praecepto et Dispensatione*, ed. J. Leclercq and H. Rochais, *S. Bernardi Opera*, vol. iii (Rome, 1963), XIII, pp. 275–6.

[130] III *Sent*. 9.2.3 in/ad 3.

[131] *De Duob. Praec. Carit*. II. Cf. *IIaIIae* 40.1 ad 2–3, for similar arguments in support of just wars.

[132] *IIaIIae* 42.1. Cf. Albertus Magnus, *Pol. Lib. Oct*. IV.11, p. 396.

[133] *Expositio super I ad Cor*. I.2. Cf. *IIaIIae* 39.2 in 2.

accordance with the Augustinian and Ciceronian definition of the *res publica* (that is, as an association united by a common sense of what is just and by common benefit), then sedition must be defined with reference to both of its constituent elements, namely the common good as well as justice. For this reason, sedition must be regarded not only as a mortal sin but as a sin which is more grievous than strife in that the common good is greater than the private good. Viewed in these terms, however, resistance to a tyrannical ruler presents a problem. Since it is generally impossible to remove a tyrant without precipitating dissension (because that part of the multitude which supports a tyrant will naturally oppose the part which is trying to remove him), does this not mean that sedition is sometimes not a mortal sin? Aquinas responds to this suggestion by turning the argument on its head. It is the tyrant, not the rebel, who is technically more guilty of sedition because the tyrant is a ruler who is defined by the fact that he secures his own private good at the expense of the common good. The tyrant is therefore the one who is harming the good of the multitude. The sin of sedition primarily concerns those people who instigate it, namely those who rule tyrannically for the sake of a partial, private good. The sin of sedition is only indirectly applicable to those who are then prompted by this tyrannical rule to disturb the common good themselves. Since tyrannical rule is unjust because it is ordered, not towards the common good, but towards the private good of the ruler, resistance to tyrannical rule cannot, by definition, be sedition because it is ultimately ordered towards the common good.

Aquinas uses the notion of the common good to put forward a comprehensive justification of disobedience and resistance to tyranny. At the same time, however, he tempers his theoretical analysis with some significant practical reservations. These include considerations such as whether there is the possibility of appeal to a higher authority, whether there is the physical capacity to resist (*cum facultas adest*),[134] whether scandal or disturbance will result, and whether resistance will, in fact, cause greater harm (*maius detrimentum*) than the original cause of disobedience.[135] This hesitation is, again, reminiscent of the reluctance shown by Albertus Magnus in the same context. When Albertus discussed resistance to the unjust action of political authority, he was unequivocal in his belief that such opposition would, in fact, do more harm to the common good which that authority was designed to safeguard.[136] Aquinas is not so categorical but he is clearly aware of the desirability of insisting on such a qualification. In justifying resistance to a 'seditious' tyrant, therefore, Aquinas sanctions disobedience *provided* that resistance does not cause the multitude greater harm than continuing obedience (*ne maius detrimentum*). Whereas Albertus Magnus invoked loss of life as one possible illustration, Aquinas does not go into details. Even as a general statement, however, it amounts to a significant restraint on his theory of resistance being carried out in practice.[137]

[134] II *Sent.* 44.2.2.   [135] *IaIIae* 96.4. Cf. *IIaIIae* 104.6 ad 3.
[136] Albertus Magnus, *Ethica* V.2.8, p. 354.
[137] *IIaIIae* 42.2; Augustine, *De Civitate Dei* II.21, pp. 53–4.

Placed in the context of Aquinas' metaphysical ideal of goodness, the issue of disobedience and resistance provides one further instance of the potential conflict between the structure of a hierarchy and its dynamic. Indeed, set alongside Aquinas' account of the relationship between the salvation of humankind and the perfection of the universe, or of the relationship between the miraculous intervention of God in Nature and the action of a first cause by means of intermediate causes, the issue is very similar. What happens when an earthly hierarchy does *not* act as a means of securing the goal of its subordinate individuals? What happens, in other words, when the political community does not secure the superior level of goodness in the universe, the common good of virtue? If the perfection of each individual depends on belonging to a society in which the good of human happiness is secured, then any exercise of political authority which prevents this life of virtue from being realized must be construed as a threat to the goal of each individual human being. Viewed in this light, Aquinas' justification of disobedience can be seen as one more example of his readiness to depart from the structure of a hierarchy in order to preserve the dynamic of the individual's ultimate goal. Indeed, in this respect, it is surely no coincidence that Aquinas' handling of sedition and schism is so close to the solution which he offered for miracles. An individual's disobedience to tyrannical rule for the sake of the common good, he states, represents the conflict, not of a part against its whole, but of a part against another part.[138] On the other hand, placed in the context of the application of metaphysical principle to political thought, the issue of disobedience and resistance provides one further instance of the potential conflict between ideal and reality. Aquinas' reservations over the desirability of translating legitimate resistance into actual resistance, in other words, indicate one further example of his acknowledgement of the difference between political theory and political practice.

Following the model of the *duplex ordo* set out in book XII of the *Metaphysics*, Aquinas understood the common good of human society in two different senses. On the one hand, there is the intrinsic or internal common good, the unity of order whereby the mutual relation of individuals in peace and harmony gives them the means of securing their ultimate goal. On the other hand, there is the extrinsic or external common good, the unity of goodness whereby the happiness of the life of virtue is the goal of every individual's activity. Each of these unities represents a different type of good. Order is an instrumental utility, a formal cause, a means towards a further goal (*propter aliud*); goodness is the life of virtue, a final cause, a goal in its own right (*propter se*).

Aquinas' ability to choose between these two definitions of common unity naturally had an important bearing on his analysis of the relationship between the individual good and the common good in human society. Which of the two definitions is deployed necessarily produces a different account of the individual's participation in the political community. The mutual ordering of individuals in peace and harmony,

---

[138] See above, p. 92.

for example, makes justice a matter of disciplining the exterior actions of individuals towards other members of the community. The hierarchy of the *ratio boni*, on the other hand, presupposes increasing degrees of goodness, perfection, and commonality, and, as a consequence, the comprehensive inclusion of the individual good within the common good of virtue. The distinction between *utilitas* and *bonum* accordingly produced two different scales of measurement by which the individual and the common good could be compared. Whilst Aquinas could draw from book I of the *Ethics* for the principle that the common good is superior to the individual good, he could also insist that such a comparison only operates when both goods are within the same genus.[139] As a result, Aquinas was also able to draw from book IX of the *Ethics* the principle that the individual good of virtue has greater priority in the intention of a virtuous individual than the benefit to the community which his virtuous action will produce.

It remains the case, however, that one of these alternatives is more characteristic of Aquinas' political thought than the other. Despite his ability to choose from these two definitions, Aquinas repeatedly emphasizes that the common good of the political community is the moral good of the life of virtue. It is in this context that the principle that the part is the same as the whole (*quodammodo sunt idem*) is used to justify the corollary that the individual good 'results from' the common good (*ex consequenti*).[140] It is on this basis too that Aquinas correlates the common good with general justice. The common good of the political community is identical to, but different from, the good of the individual; justice comprises all individual virtues but is a virtue in its own right. Aquinas' preference for a moral definition of the good of the political community necessarily affects the way in which his political thought has been interpreted. The more moral goodness is stressed, the more the common good of the political community is said to include the individual human being and the more the reservation of a private sphere of activity for the individual effectively disappears.[141] For Aquinas, any virtuous action, even if it ostensibly affects only the person who performs it, still affects 'another person' in the sense of the whole community of which that individual constitutes a part.

Nevertheless, it also remains the case that, when Aquinas needs to insist on certain reservations to the individual's participation in the political community, he does so. Thus, when he discusses membership of the perfect heavenly community, he uses the phrase 'since (*cum*) man is everything he is in virtue of being part of a multitude', whereas, when he discusses membership of the human community, this becomes 'inasmuch as (*inquantum*) man is able to participate in the good of some city of which he is a member'.[142] Likewise, when Aquinas analyses the naturalness of participation in the human community in the context of self-sacrifice, he makes this naturalness explicitly conditional. Where Aristotle had insisted that 'humankind is naturally a social and political animal', Aquinas points out that for an individual to die for his

[139] *IaIIae* 113.9 ad 2. Cf. *IIaIIae* 152.4 ad 3.   [140] *IIaIIae* 61.1 ad 2, 47.10 ad 2.
[141] *IIaIIae* 58.2, 58.12. Cf. *IIaIIae* 58.7 in 2.   [142] *IaIIae* 96.4; *Q. Disp. de Virt.* II.2.

community *would* be a natural inclination *if* he were a natural part of the city.[143] For all his emphasis on the inclusive moral common good of the human community, therefore, Aquinas is very attentive to the potential practical consequences for the individual human being. Where necessary, he is always careful to draw back from making each human being completely subordinate to the whole community.

[143] *Ia* 60.5.

5

The Life of Virtue: Giles of Rome's
De Regimine Principum

During Aquinas' second spell as regent master (1269–72), the university of Paris was stung by a series of disputes over the teaching of Aristotle in the faculty of arts. These controversies culminated in March 1277 when a list of some 219 propositions was condemned by Stephen Tempier, the bishop of Paris.[1] One immediate casualty was a bachelor in theology from the Augustinian Order, Giles of Rome, who was denied the *licentia docendi* after his commentary on the first book of the *Sentences* was deemed to contain 51 censurable propositions. Giles's refusal to recant, and in particular his refusal to withdraw his opposition to the condemnation of the unicity of substantial form in material creatures, forced him to leave the university for Bayeux. In the event, Giles's departure was to prove only a temporary setback to his academic career. By June 1285, he had been rehabilitated, returning to Paris to become the first Augustinian master in theology. Thereafter, he proved a prolific writer and an influential disputant whose writings were swiftly made the official teaching of the Augustinian Order.[2]

The condemnations of 1277 were designed to counter 'errors' in philosophy and theology, and the direct consequences for specifically political ideas were limited. The indirect consequences, however, were considerable, for it was Giles of Rome's

[1] *CUP* no. 473 (i. pp. 543–55); ed. P. Mandonnet, *Siger de Brabant et l'averroïsme latin au XIIIe siècle* (Louvain, 1908), pp. 175–91; trans. E. L. Fortin and P. D. O'Neill, in ed. R. Lerner and M. Mahdi, *Medieval Political Philosophy: A Sourcebook* (Toronto, 1963), 337–54. For the extent to which these propositions reflect the actual teaching of 'radical Aristotelians' such as Siger of Brabant, and for the effects of their condemnation on the faculty of theology, see J. F. Wippel, 'The Condemnations of 1270 and 1277 at Paris', *Journal of Medieval and Renaissance Studies*, 7 (1977), 169–201; R. Hissette, *Enquête sur les 219 articles condamnés à Paris le 7 mars 1277* (Louvain–Paris, 1977); id., 'Etienne Tempier et ses condemnations', *RTAM* 47 (1980), 231–70; F. van Steenberghen, *La Philosophie au XIIIe siècle*, 2nd edn. (Louvain, 1991); id., *Maître Siger de Brabant* (Louvain–Paris, 1977).

[2] *CUP* nos. 522 (i. 633), 542 (ii. 12). A critical edition is in progress under the direction of F. Del Punta and G. Fioravanti (*Aegidii Romani Opera Omnia*, Unione Accademica Nazionale, Corpus Philosophorum Medii Aevi, Florence 1985–). For Giles's career, see P. Mandonnet, 'La Carrière scolaire de Gilles de Rome, 1276–1291', *Revue des Sciences Philosophiques et Théologiques*, 4 (1910), 480–99; P. W. Nash, 'Giles of Rome', in *New Catholic Encyclopaedia*, vi. 484–5; F. Del Punta, S. Donati, and C. Luna, 'Egidio Romano', in *Dizionario Biografico degli Italiani*, xlii. 319–41; D. Gutierrez, *The Augustinians in the Middle Ages 1256–1356* (History of the Order of St. Augustine, i; Villanova, 1984), ch. 6; E. Hocedez, 'La Condamnation de Gilles de Rome', *RTAM* 4 (1932), 34–58; Giles of Rome, *Apologia*, ed. R. Wielockz (*Aegidii Romani Opera Omnia*, III.1; Florence, 1985). For a recent survey of many aspects of his thought see *Medioevo*, 14 (1988).

retirement to Bayeux which gave scholastic political thought one of its most influential treatises, the *Liber de Eruditione Principum sive de Regimine Regum*.[3] Written in *c.*1277–80, apparently in response to a request from Philip III of France, *De Regimine Principum* belonged to the tradition of 'mirror for princes' literature which had recently been flourishing at the Capetian court in the hands of the mendicant orders.[4] What made Giles's work so significant was the circulation which it gave to the idea that a king's rule over the political community must be based on natural principles of government.[5] It was this belief which resulted in *De Regimine Principum* concentrating on Cicero, Vegetius, Isidore, and, above all, on the *Politics* and *Ethics* of Aristotle. Giles's treatise enjoyed immediate popularity, and not just in Latin—it was translated into French in the early 1280s and into Italian in 1288.[6] More than any other *speculum principis*, therefore, *De Regimine Principum* helped diffuse Aristotelian political principles to a broader audience than that of the university schools.[7]

As an Aristotelian *speculum principis*, Giles of Rome's work raises two major issues. In the first instance, its particular distillation of the *Politics* and the *Ethics* was the result of Giles's familiarity with a third Aristotelian treatise, *On Rhetoric*.[8] Although an anonymous Latin version of the *Rhetorica* already existed, it was the translation made in *c.*1269 by William of Moerbeke which had opened the text to detailed scrutiny and which, together with Hermanus Alemannus's translation of Averroes' paraphrase and a gloss by Al-Farabi, had formed the basis of a commentary by Giles in the early 1270s.[9] Produced alongside similar works on the *Physics*, *Metaphysics*, and *De Anima*, apparently as part of a wider exegetical programme, Giles's commentary took the form of a painstakingly literal exposition of Aristotle's text, a fact to which Giles himself drew attention, insisting that his primary responsibility was to expound what Aristotle had meant and suggesting that the commentary should therefore not be taken to represent his own opinion on the subject.[10] Nevertheless,

---

[3] Aegidius Romanus, *De Regimine Principum* (Venice, 1502). For the dating, see S. Donati, *Studi per una cronologia delle opere di Egidio Romano: Le opere prima del 1285. I commenti aristotelici*, in *Documenti e Studi sulla Tradizione Filosofica Medievale*, I.1 (1990), 1–111; I.2 (1991), 1–74.

[4] W. Berges, *Die Fürstenspiegel des hohen und späten Mittelalters* (Leipzig, 1938).

[5] *De Regimine Principum* [henceforth *DRP*], I.i *praefatio*.

[6] *CUP* no. 642 (ii. p. 111); Berges, *Die Fürstenspiegel*, 320–8; Giles of Rome, *Li Livres du gouvernement des rois. A XIIIth Century French Version of Egidio Colonna's Treatise De Regimine Principum*, ed. S. P. Molenaer (New York, 1899). Cf. B. Smalley, *English Friars and Antiquity in the Early 14th Century* (Oxford, 1960), 353. An English version was produced by John Trevisa at the end of the fourteenth century.

[7] For *De Regimine Principum*'s contribution to this genre, and its distinctively 'Aristotelian' emphasis on prudence as the quintessential characteristic of kingship, see R. Lambertini, 'Tra etica e politica: La prudentia del principe nel *De regimine principum* di Egidio Romano', *Documenti e Studi sulla Tradizione Filosofica Medievale*, III.1 (1992), 77–144. Cf. id., 'Philosophus videtur tangere tres rationes. Egidio Romano lettore ed interprete della *Politica* nel terzo libro del *De regimine principum*', *Documenti e Studi sulla Tradizione Filosofica Medievale*, I.1 (1990), 277–325.

[8] Aristotle, *Ars Rhetorica*, ed. W. D. Ross (Oxford, 1959). Cf. D. J. Furley and A. Nehamas (eds.), *Aristotle's Rhetoric: Philosophical Essays* (Princeton, 1994).

[9] Aristotle, *Rhetorica, Translatio Anonyma sive Vetus et Guillelmi de Moerbeka*, ed. B. Schneider (*Aristoteles Latinus* XXXI.1–2); Giles of Rome, *Super Libros Rhetoricorum* (Venice, 1542).

[10] Giles of Rome, *Super Libros Rhetoricorum* [henceforth *Sup. Lib. Rhet.*] fo. 1r. Naturally this makes those passages which Giles chooses for extended comment, and those asides which he still feels moved to

written, as it was, in the years immediately preceding the composition of *De Regimine Principum*,[11] its influence on Giles's own views was not as limited as this disclaimer might imply. In effect, Aristotle's *Rhetorica* demonstrated to Giles just how he should set about combining rhetoric and political thought as a means of putting forward political counsel. Given that these guidelines also included a wealth of material on the individual and common good, therefore, Giles's commentary introduces a new perspective from which to approach both the scholastic reception of Aristotle's political thought and the scholastic understanding of the notion of the common good—the influence of the *Rhetorica*.

The second issue which is raised by *De Regimine Principum* as an Aristotelian *speculum principis* concerns the implications of its handling of the *Politics* and *Ethics* for the relationship between the political authority of the temporal ruler and the spiritual authority of the church. Giles of Rome was influenced by, but also critical of, much of Aquinas' work and he was clearly familiar with both the *Summa Theologiae* and the commentaries on the *Politics* and the *Ethics*.[12] *De Regimine Principum*, however, is a self-consciously political treatise in a sense which sets it apart from Aquinas' abstract political theology and exposition of Aristotle. In this respect, its most instructive point of reference is *De Regno ad Regem Cypri*, a *speculum principis* which was being circulated posthumously under Aquinas' name during the period when Giles was writing his own.[13] A comparison of the two texts is certainly very

include, all the more significant. See J. R. O'Donnell, 'The Commentary of Giles of Rome on the Rhetoric of Aristotle', in T. A. Sandquist and M. Powicke (eds.), *Essays in Medieval History Presented to Bertie Wilkinson* (Toronto, 1969), 139–56.

[11] P. Glorieux, 'Les Premiers Écrits de Gilles de Rome', *RTAM* 41 (1974), 204–8.

[12] Lambertini, 'Philosophus videtur tangere', 279–97; id., 'Il filosofo, il principe e la virtù. Note sulla ricezione e l'uso dell' Etica Nicomachea nel *De regimine principum* di Egidio Romano', *Documenti e Studi sulla Tradizione Filosofica Medievale*, II.1 (1991), 239–79. More generally, see P. W. Nash, 'Giles of Rome: Auditor and Critic of St. Thomas', *Modern Schoolman*, 28 (1950), 1–20. Cf. Wielockz, *Apologia*, ch. 7, who demonstrates that Giles provided a convenient target for those who wished to condemn certain Thomist positions without invoking Aquinas by name.

[13] Some time after Aquinas' death in 1274 an anonymous editor, perhaps Reginald of Piperno, gathered together fragments of an incomplete treatise on royal power and included them in an edition of Aquinas' lesser works. Its purpose and content have been subject to much speculation, particularly in terms of its consistency with the rest of Aquinas' work and the treatise into which it was subsequently assimilated, *De Regimine Principum* by Ptolemy of Lucca. Although manuscript evidence would indicate that book I and the first four chapters of book II are free from any substantial interference by Ptolemy, doubt still remains over the degree of editorial initiative involved in arranging a work which Aquinas himself neither finished nor completed for publication. This is a caveat which needs to be stressed for a text which is frequently treated as central to Aquinas' political thought and as his considered position on the relation between the spiritual and the temporal power. For the MSS, see A. O'Rahilly, 'Notes on St. Thomas IV: *De Regimine Principum*', *Irish Ecclesiastical Record*, 31 (1928), 396–410; id., 'Notes on St. Thomas V: Tholomeo of Lucca, the Continuator of the *De Regimine Principum*', ibid. 606–14. For its composition between 1271 and 1273, see C. Flüeler, *Rezeption und Interpretation der Aristotelischen Politica im späten Mittelalter* (2 vols.; Amsterdam, 1992), i. 28. For the debate on its authenticity, see I. Th. Eschmann's introduction to *St. Thomas Aquinas—On Kingship to the King of Cyprus*, trans. G. B. Phelan (Toronto, 1949). For Eschmann's subsequent reservations, even over the chapters up to II.4, see his 'St. Thomas Aquinas on the Two Powers', *Mediaeval Studies*, 20 (1958), 177–205 and the discussion in J. A. Weisheipl, *Friar Thomas d'Aquino* (Oxford, 1975), 189–95. Contrast L. E. Boyle, 'The *De Regno* and the Two Powers', in

suggestive. Both *De Regno ad Regem Cypri* and *De Regimine Principum* adopt Aristotle's identification of the common good of virtue as the goal of all good government. *De Regno* proceeds to use the subordination of the life of virtue to eternal beatitude as a means of subordinating the authority of the temporal ruler to the authority of the church. *De Regimine Principum*, on the other hand, draws no such corollary. This disparity between the two treatises has important implications for the way in which the *Politics* and the *Ethics* can be understood to have influenced scholastic discussion of the relationship between the temporal and the spiritual power. Was Giles's reticence on this subject indicative of an 'Aristotelian', even 'secular', outlook on the authority of the French king, or did it mark the prudent omission of a highly sensitive topic by an individual who was otherwise convinced of the superior jurisdiction of the church?

Aristotle's treatise on rhetoric presented scholastic philosophers and theologians with a wealth of material on political and ethical subjects, summarizing, duplicating, and sometimes expanding upon, the teaching with which they were already familiar from the *Politics* and the *Ethics*. One consequence of this overlap was that the three texts were frequently circulated in the same manuscript.[14] Another was that it invited consideration of the relationship which existed between the approach which each of them took to the same material. Giles of Rome chose to open his commentary on the *Rhetorica*, therefore, by examining the ways in which rhetoric is related to dialectic and to politics. Giles's discussion was ostensibly prompted by two separate observations. The first is that rhetoric is the counterpart of dialectic, a statement which Aristotle had defended on the grounds that both rhetoric and dialectic are general methods (that is, disciplines which use reason in order to produce a probable conclusion but which do not have any specific subject-matter of their own). The second is that rhetoric is a discipline which is usually applied to human behaviour (that is, to the subject-matter which is specific to politics and to ethics) and that, as such, it has the form (*figura*) of politics.[15]

Faced with the choice of making rhetoric closer to dialectic or to politics, Giles attempts a delicate balancing act. Thus, in giving a faithful rendition of the similarities which exist between rhetoric and dialectic, he also establishes the points on which they differ. Rhetoric, he argues, is primarily concerned with moral issues and the practical intellect, whereas dialectic is primarily concerned with the speculative intellect; rhetoric is concerned with arousing the emotions as a means of persuading the will, dialectic is not; rhetoric has a general audience of the unlearned (*simplex et*

J. R. O'Donnell (ed.), *Essays in Honour of Anton Charles Pegis* (Toronto, 1974), 237–47. Cf. L. Genicot, 'Le *De Regno*: Spéculation ou réalisme?', in G. Verbeke and D. Verhelst (eds.), *Aquinas and the Problems of his Time* (Louvain, 1976), 4–17; L. P. Fitzgerald, 'St. Thomas Aquinas and the Two Powers', *Angelicum*, 36 (1979), 515–56. For Giles's knowledge of *De Regno*, see Lambertini, 'Il filosofo', 270 n. 116.

[14] J. J. Murphy, 'Aristotle's Rhetoric in the Middle Ages', *Quarterly Journal of Speech*, 52 (1966), 109–15.

[15] Aristotle, *Rhetorica*, ed. Schneider, I.2 1356ª25–28, p. 164.

grossus), dialectic an audience of the refined and intelligent (*subtilis et ingeniosus*); rhetoric persuades by means of enthymemes and examples, dialectic demonstrates probability by means of syllogisms and inductive logic; rhetoric is concerned with the particular, dialectic with the universal; rhetoric seeks to secure belief that something is good, dialectic to secure opinion on what is true.[16] Likewise, in accepting that rhetoric is generally concerned with human behaviour in the political community, Giles also establishes the grounds for keeping it separate. Rhetoric is not a part of politics, he argues, because it is not directly concerned with the subject-matter of moral behaviour; the orator discusses particular political propositions insofar as they can be reduced to common principles of persuasion and not insofar as they are particular issues of debate which are applicable only to particular circumstances; the particular is infinite, after all, and cannot form the basis of any science.[17]

Giles clearly considered it important to start his commentary on the *Rhetorica* with a general discussion of the relationship between rhetoric, dialectic, and politics before he embarked upon a detailed exposition of the text itself. The significance of this discussion is underlined by a letter which he wrote soon after the completion of his commentary to a certain Oliverius, a Dominican lector from Anjou who had requested further elucidation on the relationship between rhetoric, dialectic, ethics, and politics.[18] In a rather brusque response, Giles states that rhetoric displays certain characteristics in common with both dialectic and politics but that it is still closer to dialectic than it is to politics. Rhetoric is unlike ethics and politics in that it does not deal with its own special subject-matter in the way that ethics and politics deal with human action. Strictly speaking, therefore, rhetoric should be classified under dialectic, as Aristotle had argued, and not under politics, as Cicero had suggested, since rhetoric conveys knowledge only of general principles about human behaviour and, as a result, deals only indirectly with particular moral activity. Giles then proceeds to draw a series of additional distinctions between the disciplines of ethics and politics. Although politics shares with ethics a concern with human action, it has a different method of approach—whereas ethics is more concerned with a single individual, politics is more concerned with the whole community; whereas ethics simply states that goodness and justice consist of finding the mean, politics demonstrates what is just and unjust by applying laws to particular cases. This final observation enables Giles to conclude his letter with a rather tart observation on Oliverius's own

---

[16] *Sup. Lib. Rhet.* fos. 1r–6r. Cf. S. Robert, 'Rhetoric and Dialectic according to the First Latin Commentary on the Rhetoric of Aristotle', *New Scholasticism*, 31 (1957), 484–98; J. J. Murphy, 'The Scholastic Condemnation of Rhetoric in the Commentary of Giles of Rome on the Rhetoric of Aristotle', in *Arts Libéraux et Philosophie au Moyen Age* (Actes du Quatrième Congrès International de Philosophie Médiévale; Montreal–Paris, 1969), 833–41. Cf. U. Staico, 'Retorica e politica in Egidio Romano', *Documenti e Studi sulla Tradizione Filosofica Medievale*, III.1 (1992), 32–48, 66–7; J. B. Korolec, 'Jean Buridan et Jean de Jandun et la relation entre la rhétorique et la dialectique', *Miscellanea Mediaevalia*, 13 (1981), 622–7.

[17] *Sup. Lib. Rhet.* fo. 17r; Aristotle, *Rhetorica* I.2 1356^b28–1357^a1, pp. 165–6; I.4 1359^b2–18, p. 172.

[18] ed. G. Bruni, 'The *De Differentia Rhetoricae, Ethicae et Politicae* of Aegidius Romanus', *New Scholasticism*, 6 (1932), 5–12. Giles returns to the question in *De Regimine Principum* II.ii.8 and also in his fifth quodlibet of 1290 (*Quodlibeta* Venice, 1504, V.7 fo. 64r).

field of expertise. The science of politics, he argues, may consist of instituting and maintaining laws but it differs from the study of law because it considers legislation to be a subordinate part of moral philosophy. The study of law, in contrast, is conducted, not in a scientific fashion, but as a narrative; in their use of moral philosophy, in fact, students of law are to students of politics what the uneducated masses are to dialecticians trained in logic.

Giles's letter to Oliverius makes it clear that, in this instance at least, he was fully prepared to endorse Aristotle's argument outside of the formal constraints of an academic commentary. For Giles, rhetoric *does* have a greater affinity to dialectic than to politics because it deals with common principles rather than specific cases. Indeed, Giles actually issues Oliverius with a warning against descending from general principles to particular eventualities—to do so is to practise exactly the sort of unreflective political expertise which characterizes sophistry.[19] Giles's use of the phrase *sophisticus politicus* ties this retort to the passage in book X of the *Ethics* where Aristotle had bluntly dismissed the claims of sophists to teach political science. Teachers of rhetoric, Aristotle had insisted, are completely ignorant of both the nature and the contents of the branch of knowledge which underpins the act of legislation; they assume that politics is the same as, or subordinate to, rhetoric, and that legislation is therefore simply a matter of collecting examples of good laws. Instead, they should realize that both the acquisition of political knowledge and the capacity to discern which laws are good require systematic reflection on the underlying assumptions of politics.[20] Aristotle's statement had already provided grist to the mill of those scholastic commentators who wished to distinguish political philosophy from the study of Roman Law. Albertus Magnus, for example, had not only repeated the accusation of sophistry but had identified these self-styled teachers of politics as people who merely collect the judgments of emperors and praetors. He had thereby made the charge of ignorance specific, not to sophists or rhetoricians, but to lawyers and, in particular, to lawyers who relied on Justinian's *Institutes* and *Digest*. Without an understanding of the principles of politics, Albertus argues, without an understanding of the goal of life in the political community or of the different types of constitution, knowledge of political science is impossible.[21]

---

[19] *De Differentia Rhetoricae*, 8.

[20] Aristotle, *Ethics* X.9 1181ᵃ12–19. Cf. Dante, *Monarchia*, ed. P. Shaw (Cambridge, 1995), II.9, p. 90.

[21] Albertus Magnus, *Ethica* X.3.3, pp. 639–40. In his first commentary, Albertus reworks Aristotle's text in the form of a question—is politics the same as rhetoric?—and runs through a series of arguments and counter-arguments, including Cicero's classification of politics or legislation as one of the three types of rhetoric. Albertus concludes that rhetoric and politics are not the same branch of knowledge, nor is one part of the other, because politics is a science which is concerned with action whereas rhetoric is simply concerned with speech (*Super Ethica* X.19, pp. 791–2). Cf. Aquinas, *Sent. Lib. Eth.* X.16. See also *IaIIae* 7.2 ad 3, where Aquinas argues that politics and rhetoric are similar in that they establish what is worthy of praise or blame in specific circumstances, but different in that rhetoric is an act of persuasion and politics an act of judgement. According to Aquinas, physics, dialectic, and rhetoric are all parts of prudence—physics proceeds by demonstration from what is necessary in order to cause knowledge, dialectic proceeds from what is provable in order to create opinion, whilst rhetoric proceeds from conjecture in order to induce supposition or in order to persuade (*IIaIIae* 48.1; cf. *IaIIae* 105.2 ad 8; *IIaIIae* 49.4 ad 3). For the

Giles of Rome's contempt for the 'narrative' study of law is clearly prompted by concerns similar to those which had been aired by Albertus Magnus.[22] Giles's remark about the value of political observation by rhetoricians, however, may also possess an element of self-reference. Coming, as it did, from the pen of an individual who was writing, or about to write, a *speculum principis* for the future king of France, it provides an insight into how he saw his own task in writing *De Regimine Principum*.[23] Giles does not deny that the orator is entitled to discuss the particular details of political action; he simply insists that these should be reduced to the common principles of moral behaviour. When he came to compose his own political treatise, therefore, this is precisely the form which he gives to the counsel which it puts forward and precisely the criterion by which he insists that it should be judged.

De Regimine Principum opens with a lengthy justification of the way in which it has been written. To teach the way in which rulers should govern, Giles explains, is to teach human action. According to Aristotle, however, moral activity does not lend itself to refined investigation (*perscrutatio subtilis*) because of the indeterminacy which is inherent in the diversity and particularity of its subject-matter. In this sense, moral activity stands in complete contrast to sciences such as mathematics, since mathematical demonstration produces certainty of the first order whereas moral issues produce principles only in general outline. Whilst the function of the geometrician may be to demonstrate, the function of the orator is to persuade. Giles accordingly endorses Aristotle's observation that to ignore this categorization, to accept persuasive argument from a mathematician and demand demonstrative proof from an orator or rhetorician, is to make a grave error of judgement.[24] Nor is it only the subject-matter which justifies such a general approach. A similar case can be made on the basis of the goal which Giles's treatise was intended to secure. Again the authority cited is Aristotle—the purpose of undertaking a work on moral issues is not to contemplate knowledge but to become good, not to know the subject but to put it into practice, not to prove what is true but to persuade people of what is good.[25] Since the objective in dealing with moral issues is to become good through the correctness of the will, and since the will is principally motivated by the emotions and by arguments in general outline, it is only appropriate for Giles to use persuasive and typical arguments. He will not use refined argumentation and demonstrative proof, since these are principally designed to illuminate the intellect.[26] The final justification which Giles puts forward for a generalizing approach stems from the character of his audience. Although his treatise is concerned with teaching rulers how to behave and how

---

subordination of rhetoric to dialectic, see R. McKeon, 'Rhetoric in the Middle Ages', in R. S. Crane (ed.), *Critics and Criticism: Ancient and Modern* (Chicago, 1952), 260–96. Cf. P. O. Lewry, 'Rhetoric at Paris and Oxford in the mid-Thirteenth Century', *Rhetorica*, 1 (1983), 45–63.

[22] Cf. Staico, 'Retorica e politica', 71–5. For Albertus' influence on *DRP*, see Lambertini, 'Il filosofo', 252–6.

[23] Staico, 'Retorica e politica', 12–28.

[24] *DRP* I.i.1; Aristotle, *Ethics* I.3 1094[b]11–14, I.7 1098[a]26–29. Cf. Albertus Magnus, *Super Ethica* prol., pp. 1–2; Aquinas, *Sent. Lib. Eth.* I.3.

[25] *DRP* I.i.1; Aristotle, *Ethics* II.2 1103[b]26–30. Cf. *Ethics* X.9 1179[a]33–[b]4.   [26] *DRP* I.i.2.

to command their subjects, Giles insists that it is intended to educate more than just the rich and the powerful.[27] Even though not everyone can be a king or a ruler, he states, everyone should still strive to become worthy of being ruled by knowing how they should obey. Since the whole populace is thus, in a sense (*quodammodo*), the audience of his work, Giles adopts the simple rule of thumb which had been set out in the *Rhetorica*—understanding in an audience is inversely proportional to the number of people it comprises. Since the populace is unable to understand refined argumentation (because so few of them have a sufficiently developed sharpness of mind), *De Regimine Principum* will limit itself to using typical and general arguments in order to establish the moral behaviour which is appropriate for rulers and their subjects.[28]

The remarks with which Giles of Rome prefaces *De Regimine Principum* reveal much about the way in which he viewed his own text. His was a work of moral exhortation which would confine itself to the general and the typical in an attempt to persuade both ruler and subject of the benefits of leading a life of virtue. Such a view has important consequences for how *De Regimine Principum* should be interpreted as 'scholastic political thought'. Rather than be considered as a systematic treatise on ethics and politics, the product of a specialized branch of knowledge which deploys probable arguments in order to convince a trained intellect of a true opinion, *De Regimine Principum* should be seen as a work of rhetoric, the product of a loose dialectical method which is applied to a particular form of human behaviour in order to persuade a wider audience of the general principles of good conduct. There is a clear connection here with Giles's explicit intention in writing his commentary on the *Rhetorica*. Whilst it was certainly intended to provide a detailed guide to Aristotle's account of the art of persuasion, it was also intended to stimulate its audience to acquire a knowledge of *bona mores* and thereby of a life lived according to virtue. This is the motive which is imputed by Giles to the anonymous individual (*vestra discretio*) who had originally commissioned it. The great benefit of Aristotle's treatise on rhetoric, he remarks, is that it provides not only the means of praising or censuring other individuals but also the opportunity of showing oneself and others to be virtuous individuals.[29]

If Aristotle's *Rhetorica* prompted Giles to consider the way in which rhetoric could, and should, be used to inculcate general principles of virtuous behaviour in a non-specialist audience, then it also provided him with guidelines for the ethical and political content of the principles which would thereby be instilled. Aristotle had opened book I, for example, by considering rhetoric from the standpoint that all human beings have a single goal of happiness. According to Aristotle, since humans deliberate over the means to an end rather than over the end itself, the goal of deliberative oratory (that is, counsel offered for or against a particular course of political

---

[27] *DRP* I.iv.5–7; II.ii.7–8.
[28] *DRP* I.i.3; Aristotle, *Rhetorica* III.12 1414ª9–10, p. 306; I.2 1357ª3–4, 11–12, p. 166.
[29] *Sup. Lib. Rhet.* fo. 1r, fo. 31r.

action) is to secure what contributes to happiness, what it is advantageous (*conferens*) for humans to do in order to attain this end. Although deliberative oratory does not discuss what actually constitutes the nature of happiness, it still requires an understanding of what is essentially good and advantageous, namely the good which everything seeks, the good which is sought on its own account or for the sake of which something else is chosen.[30] Having defined happiness as the ultimate goal of humankind and having established the means to this end as the proper subject of deliberative rhetoric, Aristotle had proceeded to identify five political topics as quintessential to deliberative oratory—material resources, war and peace, the import and export of goods, the security (*custodia*) of the community, and the framing of laws. Legislation he regards as particularly important for the security (*securitas*) and well-being (*salus*) of the political community. In order to understand the nature of law, moreover, the orator must first understand the various forms of government which a community can experience and the different courses of action which are appropriate to them.[31] According to Aristotle, therefore, knowledge of the various forms of government provides the greatest and most significant means of persuasion and good counsel in deliberative rhetoric. Four constitutions are set out—democracy, oligarchy, aristocracy, and monarchy—each one of them distinguished by its goal and by the way in which its authority is distributed. Democracy, for example, is ordered towards liberty and distributes its authority by lot; oligarchy is ordered towards wealth and distributes its authority according to honours; aristocracy is ordered towards the knowledge of what is laid down by law and distributes its authority on the same basis. Monarchy, meanwhile, is divided between kingship, where government follows a certain order (*ordo*), and tyranny, where it is unrestrained in its pursuit of security (*custodia*).[32]

Aristotle's discussion of deliberative oratory in the *Rhetorica* presented Giles with a set agenda for any work of political counsel—presuppose that the life of virtue is the goal of human association, discuss legislation as the means by which it is secured, and then analyse the various forms of government to which the political community can be subject and the various actions which will preserve them in existence. The content of *De Regimine Principum* suggests that this advice was taken to heart. The influence of the *Rhetorica* certainly extends much further than Giles's choice of a typical and general style of argument. Take the first two elements which it lays down for a work of political counsel—identifying virtue as the goal of good government and discussing legislation as the means by which it can be secured. According to Giles's commentary on the *Rhetorica*, every good form of government is ordered towards the same goal, namely the goodness of its citizens (*bonitas civium*) and the life of virtue.[33] According to *De Regimine Principum*, the function of the political community is not simply to live but to live well, and to live well is to live according to virtue (*bene enim*

[30] Aristotle, *Rhetorica* I.5–6 1360ᵇ3–1363ᵇ4, pp. 174–82.
[31] Aristotle, *Rhetorica* I.4 1359ᵇ19–1360ᵇ2, pp. 172–4. Cf. *DRP* III.ii.19.
[32] Aristotle, *Rhetorica* I.8 1365ᵇ21–1366ᵃ22, pp. 188–9.   [33] *Sup. Lib. Rhet.* fos. 18v, 30v.

vivere est vivere virtuose).[34] In Giles's opinion, rulers should certainly not ignore the more material constituents of a self-sufficient life, but ideally they should secure a sufficiency of material goods *and* the goods of a life of virtue.[35] Of the two, indeed, it is the life of virtue which forms their primary goal. The political community is thus an association of individuals which has been designed to secure a perfect and self-sufficient life. Its primary purpose is to live well, to live virtuously, to live the life of happiness.[36]

If the life of virtue is identified as the goal of government in *De Regimine Principum*, then legislation provides the means to secure it. The common good is thus the goal of natural law, positive law, and justice in general.[37] The common good is the principal object of the legislator (be it the king or the whole community) and, if a law does not aim to secure the common good, then it is perverse and tyrannical.[38] Since this common good is the life of virtue, the legislator must aim at every good through which citizens can become better and more virtuous people. Laws which aim to secure the common good can therefore command every kind of goodness. In Giles's eyes, to be just according to the law, to live according to legal justice, means aiming at every good, fleeing every vice, and thereby possessing, in a sense, every virtue.[39] Beyond the qualifying *quodammodo*, Giles's account of law has none of the reservations which had been characteristic of Albertus and Aquinas. Goodness and justice are, for him, synonymous.[40]

De Regimine Principum's debt to Aristotle's *Rhetorica* continues with its analysis of the various forms of government to which the political community can be subject. However, although Giles makes a point of emphasizing that the common good is the criterion which separates good from bad forms of government (kingship from tyranny, aristocracy from oligarchy, polity from democracy),[41] it is monarchy with which he is primarily concerned. Not only is kingship the best form of government,[42] but it is also the constitution for which he had himself been asked to offer counsel on the actions which would preserve it in existence.[43] Nevertheless, within these parameters, the life of virtue continues to occupy centre stage. It is pivotal, for example, to Giles's working definition of kingship.[44] The king must be virtuous because he will secure the common good by serving as the exemplar of all the virtues to his subjects.[45] The king must be virtuous so that he can direct others towards the same goal, just as a teacher possesses knowledge in order to pass it on to his pupils.[46] Prudence, in all its

---

[34] *DRP* II.iii.8.   [35] *DRP* II.i.2, III.i.8. Cf. III.ii.8.   [36] *DRP* III.ii.32. Cf. III.i.5.

[37] *DRP* I.ii.10; II.iii.14; III.ii.24; III.ii.26. Cf. III.ii.31.

[38] *DRP* I.iii.5; III.ii.26–7. For the question of whether the political community is ruled better by a good man or by good laws, see *DRP* III.ii.20, III.ii.29, Aristotle, *Politics* III.15–17 1286ª7–1288ª29, and the discussion in T. J. Renna, 'Aristotle and the French Monarchy, 1260–1303', *Viator*, 9 (1978), 312–14. The debate was also touched upon in book I of the *Rhetorica* (I.1 1354ª31–ᵇ4, p. 160; cf. *Sup. Lib. Rhet.* fo. 3v) and underpins Giles's discussion of equity (*Sup. Lib. Rhet.* fos. 43r–44r; cf. Aristotle, *Rhetorica* I.13 1374ª26–1374ᵇ23, pp. 210–11). Cf. Albertus Magnus, *Pol. Lib. Oct.* II.3, p. 129; III.10, pp. 305–9.

[39] *DRP* I.ii.10; I.iii.5; II.iii.18. Cf. *Quod.* IV.18 fo. 56r.   [40] *DRP* I.iv.7. Cf. III.ii.2; III.i.5.

[41] *DRP* III.ii.2. Cf. II.i.3; III.ii.6; III.ii.12.   [42] *DRP* III.ii.3; *Sup. Lib. Rhet.* fo. 18r–v.

[43] *DRP* I.i *praef.*   [44] *DRP* I.i.7; III.ii.6. Cf. I.ii.18; III.i.2; III.ii.7–8.

[45] *DRP* III.ii.6. Cf. I.iv.7; I.ii.31–3.   [46] *DRP* I.ii.3. Cf. I.ii.12; II.i.1.

forms, is therefore the virtue most appropriate to the king's character because it directly facilitates the common good.[47] The same goal also governs his justice, magnanimity, magnificence, bravery, temperance,[48] and even his choice of spouse.[49] A love for the common good, in fact, leads to every virtue.[50] Not unnaturally, although not without reservation, Giles picks up on Aristotle's suggestion in the *Politics* that the truly good ruler possesses an almost divine perfection.[51] Thus, although the common good should also be the primary objective of the king's counsellors,[52] it is particularly incumbent upon the king to love the common good, and to prefer the common good to the private good, because of the peculiarly public, 'common', nature of kingship.[53] Indeed, in Giles's opinion, the king will be rewarded for his actions only when the common good is the true object of his intention. Simply being in a position where he can act like a tyrant but chooses not to do so is a necessary but insufficient cause of merit. Even if, in practical terms, his actions will have the same net effect on his subjects, they remain of little value to the king himself unless they are informed by a disposition to act for the common good.[54]

Aristotle's discussion of deliberative rhetoric clearly exercised considerable influence on the content of *De Regimine Principum* but it was not the only category of rhetoric in the *Rhetorica* on which Giles came to draw for his political ideas. Justice, for example, had also been at the heart of Aristotle's discussion of the other two forms of oratory—forensic (the rhetoric of the law courts) and epideictic (praise or censure of a particular individual).[55] The function of deliberative oratory is thus to recommend the exercise of justice as a good which is advantageous to the community in that it enables humans to live a good moral life together (*bene convivendum moraliter*).[56] However, it is also the function of forensic oratory to secure the goal of justice in accordance with the law, where the law is defined either with reference to a crime which has been committed against a member of the community (*ad unum communicantium*), such as adultery or assault, or with reference to a crime which has been committed against the community itself (*ad commune*), such as refusal to serve in the army.[57] The function of epideictic oratory, meanwhile, is to praise what is noble and good and to herald the benefit which the exercise of justice brings to other individuals. According to Aristotle, the virtue which is praised in an individual is the capacity not only to secure and preserve what is good but also to ensure that this good is

---

[47] *DRP* I.i.3; II.iii.17; III.iii.1. Cf. I.i.2; I.i.12; I.ii.6–9; II.ii.2; III.iii.1.

[48] *DRP* I.iii.3. Cf. I.ii.10–25; II.iii.19.

[49] *DRP* II.i.13, although Giles does not neglect other criteria. Cf. *Sup. Lib. Rhet.* fo. 20v.

[50] *DRP* I.iii.3.

[51] *DRP* III.ii.11; III.ii.30 (*quasi semidei*). Cf. I.i.3; I.i.13; I.ii.4 (*semidei*); I.ii.32 (*homines divini*); II.ii.8 (*quasi semidei*); *Sup. Lib. Rhet.* fo. 21v (*ac si essent dii*); Aristotle, *Politics* III.13 1284ª3–17, 1284ᵇ25–34, III.17 1288ª15–29.

[52] *DRP* III.ii.17, counsel or deliberation (*consilium*) being the subject-matter of deliberative rhetoric (*consiliabilia*). Cf. III.ii.15–20.

[53] *DRP* I.iii.3. Cf. III.ii.27.   [54] *DRP* I.ii.13.

[55] Aristotle, *Rhetorica* I.3 1358ª36–1359ª5, pp. 169–71; *Sup. Lib. Rhet.* fo. 73v.

[56] Aristotle, *Rhetorica* I.6 1362ᵇ27–8, p. 180; *Sup. Lib. Rhet.* fo. 24v.

[57] Aristotle, *Rhetorica* I.13 1373ᵇ18–27, pp. 208–9; *Sup. Lib. Rhet.* fo. 42v.

of great benefit to other individuals. The height of virtue is thus to bring benefit to all people (*excessus enim virtutis omnes beneficiare*). When individual virtues are ranked according to this standard, justice and fortitude are awarded pride of place because they are beneficial (*utilis*) to other people. Whilst both of these virtues benefit others in times of war, justice does so in times of peace as well.[58]

Moreover, for all his emphasis on the centrality of virtue and justice, Giles was also well aware of the difficulties which the implementation of these ideals would meet in practice. In Giles's view, the link between kingship and the common good had a sharper edge than simply demonstrating that the character of the king will determine the character of his people (*qualis est princeps talis est populus*).[59] If royal justice has a positive function, to secure the life of virtue, then it also has a negative one, to restrain the effect of evil. The political community may have originated in the natural human instinct to live well and to live peaceably, but it is also prompted by the desire to resist those individuals who wish to disturb that peace.[60] Thus, even if Giles follows Cicero in arguing that rulers should always prefer to be loved by their subjects rather than feared,[61] he does not discount the need to inspire both. Not every individual is so good and so perfect that all it takes to prevent him from doing evil is a love for what is honourable, a love for the common good and for the legislator. Many people will also require the fear of punishment.[62] This is Giles's main justification for the coercive power of law, just as it had been one of his major reasons for distinguishing between ethics and politics—whereas ethics ensures that humans become good people through love of what is noble, politics ensures that they become good through fear of the coercive power of law to punish.[63] It is coercive power, therefore, which forms the third element in Giles's definition of law. Laws, he states, regulate actions and direct them to the common good but they also have coercive power (*leges . . . sunt quaedam regulae agibilium ordinantes nos in commune bonum habentes coactivam potentiam*).[64] Punishment, up to and including the death penalty,[65] must always be justified by the common good but so too must the exercise of clemency and mercy.[66] When punishment is applied to groups of individuals, it assumes the character of a just war, even if the malefactors are within the community. According to Giles, a just war can be fought in defence of the common good against external foes but it can also be fought against assailants from within, against those deficient individuals whose sedition and oppression have endangered the peace and common good of the whole citizen body.[67] If Giles's political community was supposed to follow the natural principles of government set down by Aristotle, then it also had to be prepared to counter the effects of sin.[68]

---

[58] Aristotle, *Rhetorica* I.9 1366ᵃ23–1367ᵃ33, pp. 189–92; *Sup. Lib. Rhet.* fo. 31r–v. Cf. *DRP* I.ii.4; I.ii.15.
[59] *DRP* I.i.11. [60] *DRP* III.i.6. Cf. III.i.18.
[61] Cicero, *De Officiis*, ed. Winterbottom, II.7.23–4, pp. 77–8. [62] *DRP* III.ii.32; III.ii.36.
[63] *DRP* III.i.5; *De Differentia Rhetoricae*, pp. 8–9. [64] *DRP* III.ii.27. Cf. Aquinas, *IaIIae* 90.4.
[65] *DRP* I.ii.3; III.ii.9; III.ii.24. Cf. I.iv.2. [66] *DRP* III.ii.23.
[67] *DRP* II.ii.18; III.iii.1. Cf. I.ii.14, III.iii.23.
[68] *DRP* I.i.4; II.i.1–3; III.i.1–5. Note, however, the reservations which are expressed in III.i.3 and in II.i.7 (*homo enim natura magis est coniugale animal quam politicum*) quoting Aristotle, *Ethics* VIII.14

Even when allowance is made for Aristotle's account of forensic and epideictic rhetoric, and for Giles's own realization of the reality behind the ideal of justice, it would seem hard to overestimate the particular influence which was exerted by the description of deliberative rhetoric in the *Rhetorica*. Deliberative rhetoric was defined as the act of giving counsel over a course of political action and this is exactly what Giles of Rome set out to do in *De Regimine Principum*. Nor did the influence of the *Rhetorica* stop there. Aristotle's text provided Giles with a detailed framework for his analysis of the life of virtue, the goal of law, and the actions which are appropriate to kingship. It also provided him with instructions on how to set about examining the relationship between the common good and the individual good.

Book I of the *Rhetorica* observes that humans frequently agree on several things which are advantageous. As a result, Aristotle had argued that it is imperative for the deliberative orator to understand how to make a decision between them. An important part of deliberative rhetoric is thus the capacity to distinguish which of two goods is the greater (*maius bonum*) and more advantageous (*magis conferens*) and Aristotle had obligingly produced an exhaustive catalogue of the various ways in which such comparative judgements can be made. Viewed from the perspective of the common good and its relation to the individual, two elements in this catalogue immediately stand out—the principle of inclusion and the principle of sequence. One good is superior to another, Aristotle writes, when it is greater, larger, and more numerous, and when what is exceeded is included within the superior good. Since the good which all things seek is the goal for which everything is done, then a greater number of good things is a greater good than one good or a smaller number of goods. Aristotle makes it clear, however, that this single good or smaller number of goods is still part of the greater number (*connumeratum*) with which it is being compared—the greater number exceeds what is 'included' (*inexistit*) within it. A good which is greatest in one genus, meanwhile, is superior to a good which is greatest in another genus when the first genus is superior to the second. When one good follows (*sequitur*) another good, moreover, the good which it follows is a greater good, since the former is included (*inexistit*) in the latter. Three examples of such a sequence are set out— 'simultaneous' (*simul*), in the way that life follows health; 'potential' (*potentia*), in the way that suffering loss follows sacrilege; and 'consequential' (*consequenter*), in the way that knowledge follows learning.

Aristotle had continued his classification of the criteria which make one good superior to another with methodical precision. Additional examples include a good which is produced by a greater good; a good which is sought for its own sake; a good which is more self-sufficient; a good which is able to exist, or come into existence, without needing anything else; a first principle or a cause; and a good which results from a greater first principle. Other categories comprise degrees of scarcity, abundance,

---

1162a17–18. Cf. *Sup. Lib. Rhet.* fo. 18r (*cum civitas sit aliquid naturale aliquo modo*), fo. 20r.; *Quod.* I.16 fo. 9v. Compare Albertus Magnus, *Super Ethica* VIII.12, p. 644. Cf. Giles of Rome, *In II Librum Sententiarum* (Venice, 1581) 20.1.1, p. 147: *ordo rei publicae in cuiusdam pacis terrenae vinculum coercens etiam peccatores.*

difficulty, ease, deprivation, nobility, desirability, dignity, safety, durability, partici-pation, praise, honour, division, combination (*compositio*), feasibility, and pleasure. Three of these criteria possess a particular relevance for the notion of the scholastic understanding of the superiority of the good of the political community. First, a greater good is a good which is, or has been, judged to be a greater good by many prudent individuals, by more prudent individuals, or by the best prudent individ-uals. Second, a good which is chosen by everyone, or by a majority, is a greater good than a good which is not chosen, or chosen only by a minority. Third, a greater good is a good which is both good for the individual and good in itself (*ipsi et simpliciter*).[69]

Like Albertus Magnus and Thomas Aquinas, Giles of Rome gives considerable prominence to Aristotle's distinction between various categories of goodness, between the good which is morally worthy or honourable (*honestum sive honorabile*), the good which is useful or beneficial (*utile*), and the good which is a source of pleas-ure (*delectabile*).[70] In Giles's case, he was able to draw on the guidelines which had been laid down for comparing these goods as part of deliberative rhetoric. When Giles discusses the goods which can be the subject of political counsel, for example, he distinguishes between external and internal goods. External goods, he suggests, are in turn divided into *utilia* or beneficial goods (such as material resources) and goods which are superior to these (such as honours, liberties, and powers). Internal goods, meanwhile, are divided into goods of the body (such as food) and goods of the soul (such as virtue).[71] The influence of this classification on *De Regimine Principum* is marked. When Giles discusses the benefit (*utilitas*) which his treatise will produce and the supreme goods (*maxima bona*) which will result from putting its teaching into practice, he suggests that there are lesser goods (external goods), median goods (internal goods, such as intelligence, which are common to virtuous and wicked indi-viduals alike), and supreme goods (internal goods, such as the virtues, in which wicked individuals cannot participate). Since the goal of *De Regimine Principum* is the life of virtue, he concludes, this must constitute a supreme good because honourable goods include great pleasure and the benefit of useful goods.[72]

Like Albertus and Aquinas, Giles is also drawn to consider the possibility that what is morally good and what is useful might sometimes be mutually exclusive. Once again, the *Rhetorica* provided Giles with guidelines for making such a compari-son. Prominent in Aristotle's analysis of noble goods had been those actions which are intrinsically good and which are performed, not for one's own sake, but for the sake of others. Aristotle had cited, as examples, those actions which are performed for the sake of one's country (*pro patria*) and which take place at the expense of one's own benefit (*negligens quod suum*).[73] The opposition of the noble to the beneficial on which this statement relies, and which is typified by Achilles' action on the death of Patroclus,[74] had then been turned into a more general principle. According to

[69] Aristotle, *Rhetorica* I.7 1363b5–1365b20, pp. 182–7; *Sup. Lib. Rhet.* fos. 26v–29v.
[70] *DRP* II.ii.12. Cf. II.i.12.   [71] *Sup. Lib. Rhet.* fo. 17r–v.   [72] *DRP* I.i.3.
[73] Aristotle, *Rhetorica* I.9 1366b36–1367a1, p. 191.
[74] Aristotle, *Rhetorica* I.3 1358b38–1359a5, pp. 170–1.

Aristotle, the noble (*honestum*) constitutes what is intrinsically good (*bonum sim-pliciter*), whilst the beneficial (*conferens*) constitutes what is good for the individual (*bonum ipsi*). Thus, the noble is the goal of virtue and the characteristic motivation of young people, whilst the beneficial is the goal of calculation (*ratiocinatio*) and the characteristic motivation of the elderly. It is the peculiar glory of middle age, he concludes, to be guided simultaneously by both the noble and the beneficial.[75]

When Giles comes to comment on Aristotle's paean to middle age, he repeats it verbatim, pausing only to gloss nobility as *honestum et honorabile* and benefit as *conferens et utilis*.[76] When he considers the example of Achilles and Patroclus, however, Giles clearly feels obliged to point out that, even if Achilles' death was not advantageous, it was still a more noble good for Achilles himself. Even if continuing to live would have been to Achilles' advantage and profit (*ei conferens et proficuum*), it was still more noble for him (*ipsi . . . pulchrius*) to die for his friend.[77] Giles's concern to demonstrate the presence of good for the individual is evident one more time in his commentary on the *Rhetorica* when he tackles Aristotle's contention that virtuous and noble actions are not performed for the sake of the individual who performs them (*sui gratia*). Selfless actions, Giles explains, are more praiseworthy than actions performed for one's own sake because they are more honourable. Those actions which are more praiseworthy, he continues, are those which are intrinsically good and which are performed *pro patria* and at the expense of one's own advantage (*commodum proprium*). Not only do such actions possess greater honour but they are also intrinsically good by nature. Goods which are intrinsically good (*bona simpliciter*) are greater goods than those which are good within certain terms of reference (*bona secundum quid*), that is, than goods which are good for one particular individual (*bona isti vel illi*) or which are simply selfish (*bona quae sunt sui gratia*).[78] Giles does not raise the possibility that these two categories might be mutually exclusive until he comes to Aristotle's observation that it is possible to argue that nobody chooses what is intrinsically good but only what is good for themselves.[79] When he does so, however, his opinion is clear. Giles's response is to point out that Aristotle's observation is a hypothetical argument which can be refuted by looking at natural and positive law. Natural law, he argues, is concerned with absolute good (*bonum absolute*), whilst positive law is concerned with what is good for particular individuals (*bonum huius vel illius*). However, although something can be intrinsically good which is not good for a particular individual (*bonum huic*), a positive law will have no force unless it rests upon (*initatur*) natural law.[80] At some level, therefore, there is always a fundamental harmony between the absolute good and what is good for a particular individual.

Throughout his discussion of the relationship between what is absolutely good and what is good for a particular individual, Giles appears determined to interpret

---

[75] Aristotle, *Rhetorica* II.12–14 1388ᵇ31–1390ᵇ13, pp. 247–50.
[76] *Sup. Lib. Rhet.* fos. 68r–69v. Cf. *Sup. Lib. Rhet.* fo. 114r: *prudentis quidem est prosequi proficuum, boni autem honestum*. For a similar characterization of young and old, see *DRP* I.iv.1–4.
[77] *Sup. Lib. Rhet.* fo. 14r.   [78] *Sup. Lib. Rhet.* fo. 32r–v.
[79] Aristotle, *Rhetorica* I.15 1375ᵇ19, p. 214.   [80] *Sup. Lib. Rhet.* fo. 45v.

Aristotle's text in a sense that supports the principle of inclusion which he had already established as a guiding principle of deliberative rhetoric—the individual good is 'included' in the greater good. Thus, when Giles considers the argument that a greater good is the good which is both an intrinsic good and a good for the individual, he makes it clear that this is also an intrinsic good for the individual (*simpliciter et ipsi homini*).[81] Although Giles could accept the possibility that goodness and benefit might sometimes be in opposition, he took care to point out that this conflict could always be reconciled by means of the principle that the greater good is inclusive of the lesser.

Giles's commitment to the principle of inclusion is a marked feature of his commentary on the *Rhetorica*. In *De Regimine Principum*, it is equally dominant. In *De Regimine Principum*, however, it is firmly tied to Giles's understanding of the place of the common good within the *ordo caritatis*. Love for the common good is given its supreme expression by an individual's willingness to sacrifice his own good for the benefit of the whole. Giles accordingly follows Albertus and Aquinas in justifying the sacrifice of property and life by means of the corporeal analogy of part and whole.[82] For Giles, *pro patria mori* is an obligation which is particularly incumbent upon rulers, but it is equally applicable to his subjects.[83] Love for the common good also enables Giles to put the best possible construction on the community of wives which had been prescribed in Plato's *Republic*. Such a community, he argues, should be interpreted in a spiritual, not a material, sense. Any individual should love his fellow-citizens as he loves himself, and he should love their wives, children, and possessions as he loves his own. Only with property may this common love extend to physical sharing.[84] Love for his own wife, meanwhile, is tied to love for the common good when the latter is defined as the good of the species. The function of the marital household is to secure material necessities for each individual and, through procreation, a continuation in existence for the community.[85] This common good is also realized in children. Indeed, it is these particular 'goods in common' which generally hold the community of husband and wife together.[86] What connects the community of marriage and the community of the city is that each represents an object which is loved in common and, according to pseudo-Dionysius, every love is a unitary force (*omnis enim amor est quaedam vis unitiva*).[87] Giles draws a direct parallel between these two types of community. Just as the city unites and contains its citizens because it is their common good, so children unite and contain their parents because they are

---

[81] *Sup. Lib. Rhet.* fo. 29v.   [82] *DRP* I.i.13; I.iii.3; III.i.14.
[83] *DRP* I.i.13; I.ii.23; III.i.14; III.iii.4. Cf. III.ii.36.
[84] *DRP* III.i.15; *Quod.* III.7 fo. 33v. For Henry of Ghent's *Quodlibet* IV.20 (delivered in 1279), see below, pp. 163–4.
[85] *DRP* II.i.7. Cf. I.i.11.
[86] *DRP* II.i.5; II.i.8. Cf. *Sup. Lib. Rhet.* fo. 20v; Albertus Magnus, *Ethica* VIII.3.8, p. 551.
[87] *DRP* III.iii.14. Cf. Augustine, *De Trinitate*, ed. W. J. Mountain (*CCSL* 50), VIII.10.14, pp. 290–1; pseudo-Dionysius, *De Divinis Nominibus*, ed. P. Chevallier, in *Dionysiaca: Recueil donnant l'ensemble des traductions latines des ouvrages attribués au Denys de l'Aréopage* (2 vols.; Bruges, 1937, 1950), IV (i. 167, 214).

their common good.[88] The fruits of marriage, moreover, are peace, friendship, and concord, and to secure these is also the function of the ruler.[89] In both cases, to effect this common good is the function of love.[90]

When Giles turns to analyse the exact nature of the relationship between the individual good and the common good within the *ordo caritatis*, he models his argument on Aquinas' account of the hierarchy of love. According to Giles, the object of love is always the good; the more goodness, the more something participates in the *ratio boni*, then the more superior and intense this love will be; since the order of goodness is found in divine and 'general' goods more than in individual goods, the former will demand a correspondingly greater love. In order to demonstrate the applicability of this principle to the divine good, Giles follows the line of reasoning which had already been put forward by Aquinas—an individual's goodness exists more in the divine good than it does in itself; humankind is totally dependent on the goodness of God in that, without it, no individual can make himself good or preserve his goodness once he has it; humans therefore love God naturally more than they love themselves because the good of each individual comes primarily from God and is preserved in Him better than it is preserved in the individual.[91] When Giles turns to an individual's love for the 'general' good, however, his line of reasoning becomes a little more elusive. The common good, he writes, should always be preferred to the individual good because, according to Aristotle, it is more divine than the individual, and because, in his own view, it includes it.[92] Given a conflict between the two, between the common good and the individual good, the common good should be preferred (*praeponere*) because it is more divine.[93] Some clarification of *divinius* may be gleaned from Giles's use of the statement (attributed to Boethius) that the more

---

[88] *DRP* II.i.8. Cf. II.i.14; II.ii.4 (where Giles refers to children as forming a 'part' of their parents but does not draw any parallel with citizens as 'parts' of the community).

[89] *DRP* II.i.10; III.i.13. Cf. III.ii.10; III.ii.19.

[90] *DRP* III.i.15.

[91] *DRP* I.ii.3. Cf. above, pp. 103–4. Giles puts forward the same argument at greater length in his fourth quodlibet of 1289. Humans, he suggests, should love God more than they love themselves. Because God creates all that is good and preserves it in existence, He is closer (*magis intimus*) to an individual thing than the thing is to itself and contributes more to its continuation in existence. The divine good, moreover, is a total good (*bonum totale*), containing within it everything that is good, and the individual part of Creation should therefore love the whole more than it loves itself. An individual good, finally, is not good except insofar as it participates in the essential good which is God. It should therefore not be loved except on account of the divine good (*Quod.* IV.14 fos. 53v–54r). Note the absence of any mention of love for the common good of the political community—the only analogy used is the natural instinct of the arm to defend the head and the whole body.

[92] *DRP* I.ii.3.

[93] *DRP* I.iii.3; II.iii.14; III.i.14 (*semper bonum commune praeponendum est bono privato*). Cf. III.iii.1 (*excedere*). Although Giles also uses the phrases 'more worthy' (*dignius*) and 'more complete and more perfect' (*totalius et perfectius*), 'more divine' remains his favoured term from Aristotle's *Ethics: si ergo, ut pluries dictum est, bonum commune divinius est quam proprium . . .* (*DRP* III.ii.27; cf. *DRP* I.ii.15; *Sup. Lib. Rhet.* fo. 24v). Cf. I.i praef. (*divinius et communius*); I.i.10; I.i.13; I.i.15; I.iii.3; III.ii.6; III.ii.7; III.ii.26; *De Differentia Rhetoricae*, p. 8 (*semper bonum gentis divinius est quam bonum unius ut dicitur primo ethicorum*). The common good is also more advantageous, *magis expediens et divinius* (I.i.5). Cf. *DRP* III.ii.7, where Giles observes that government is not correct unless it has a certain divinity (*nisi sit quodammodo quid divinum*).

common a good, the more divine it is, because a good derived in common shines more beautifully.[94] Nevertheless, the exact nature of inclusion remains dependent on the strength of the original analogy with the divine good—the common good 'includes' the individual good in the same way that the divine good 'preserves' the individual human good.

Giles's demonstration of the inclusion of the individual good within the common good may rely on the analogy which he draws with the divine good but his choice of terminology reveals an additional source of inspiration. His use of the term 'preserves', for example, has a clear parallel in his commentary on the *Rhetorica* where he glosses the inclusion of a lesser good in a greater good as the 'inclusion or preservation' of this good (*inexistit sive reservatur*).[95] Still more informative is the parallel which is set up when Giles concludes his analysis of the love owed to the divine and common good by referring to the principle of sequence—a lesser good can follow a superior good *consequenter*. All individuals, he states, rulers and subjects alike, will love the divine and common good *primo et principaliter*, and their individual and private goods *ex consequenti*.[96] If the king orders his rule towards the common good, therefore, he will be rewarded in proportion to his responsibility for the good of his nation, a good which is more divine than that of an individual.[97] Giles does not deny that the king who secures the common good will also secure his own individual good, nor, for that matter, does he exclude the possibility that the tyrant who secures his own private good may also secure the common good of his subjects. Where this occurs, however, he insists that it is simply as a consequence (*ex consequenti*) of the primary goals of their respective regimes.[98] It is in this sense that the individual good of the king is equated with the common good of his people. Enlightened self-interest remains the preserve of the tyrant. If the tyrant aims to secure the common good, then it is only as an accidental consequence (*ex consequenti et quasi per accidens*) of pursuing his individual good.[99] Giles's commitment to the inclusion of the individual good in the common good was rooted in his understanding of the *ordo caritatis*, but his explanation of how this principle worked was indebted to the terms with which he had become familiar in commenting on the *Rhetorica*.

In his commentary on the *Rhetorica*, Giles had followed Aristotle in distinguishing between the good which was pursued by individuals on their own and the good which was general to all individuals as citizens. Just as each part of the human body

---

[94] *DRP* II.iii.6; Seneca, *Ad Lucilium Epistulae Morales*, ed. L. D. Reynolds (Oxford, 1965), I.6, p. 10 (see above, p. 67 n. 56). Cf. *DRP* I.ii.19. In his commentary on the *Sentences*, Giles clearly considered this quotation to be an appropriate partner for the principle of superiority from book I of the *Ethics* (II *Sent.* 20.1.1, p. 147). For the question of holding goods in common, see *DRP* II.ii.5–8; III.i.11; III.i.17.

[95] *Sup. Lib. Rhet.* fo. 26v.   [96] *DRP* I.iii.3; see above, p. 142.

[97] *DRP* I.i.13. Cf. *De Regno ad Regem Cypri* I.9.   [98] *DRP* I.i.7.

[99] *DRP* I.i.3. Cf. III.ii.10, where the equation clearly has its tangible advantages. The distinction is sometimes a fine one—compare Giles's remarks on the value of hereditary rule in its effects on the motivation of a king, a consideration which prompts a rare recognition of what is realistic rather than ideal (III.ii.5). Cf. Aristotle, *Politics* V.10 1311^{a}2–4, pp. 555–6; Albertus Magnus, *Pol. Lib. Oct.* III.4, pp. 230–4, who argues that although the good of a polity is essentially (*per se*) ordered towards the community, it is also accidentally (*per accidens*) ordered towards the good of the ruler.

has its own goal, he had argued, so each part of the political community has its own goal insofar as one citizen is different from another. However, in addition to (*praeter*) these individual goals pursued by each part of the political community, there is also a common goal for the whole political community which is sought by all of its citizens.[100] In *De Regimine Principum*, therefore, the common good is the goal not just of the king but of all the inhabitants of his kingdom.[101] Every individual, subject as well as king, secures his individual good as a consequence of securing the common good; the common good should always be preferred to an individual good, but to an individual good which it includes. It is therefore no coincidence that Giles repeatedly emphasizes that the common good is the good of all the people, a principle which is reflected in his phraseology: *bonum commune et bonum omnium; bonum commune et omnium civium secundum suum statum; bonum commune et subditorum; bonum commune egenorum, mediarum personarum et divitum et omnium secundum suum statum.*[102] Giles was familiar with the argument in the *Rhetorica* that the good which is chosen by all individuals, or by a majority, is a greater good than a good which is chosen only by a minority because the good is what everyone seeks.[103] In *De Regimine Principum*, he uses a similar argument to explain why there is only a fine line between polity and democracy. Even a democracy, he states, where the multitude aims to secure its own good, is not wholly removed from aiming at the common good because the good of many individuals is a sort of common good (*quasi bonum commune*).[104] Oligarchy and democracy are, in this sense, better forms of government than tyranny—at least they secure the good of a greater number of people than that of one individual.[105] Thus, if *De Regimine Principum* is concerned with royal virtue, then it is equally concerned with the interests of the governed, the common good of the king's subjects. The common good 'results from' the good of the citizens, 'depends on' the goodness, not just of those people in authority, but of those whom they govern.[106] The goodness of a citizen necessarily results in the common good of the city in a way that it does not necessarily result in the individual good of his neighbour.[107] From the outset, therefore, Giles binds himself to ruled as well as ruler. He is writing, according to the preface, with divine assistance and at the request of the king but also with the support of the good of the nation (*bonum gentis*), a good which is more divine and more common than the good of any one individual such as the author.[108] It is this common good which provides his objective in writing such a manual of instruction—the

---

[100] *Sup. Lib. Rhet.* fo. 19r. Cf. J. Eichinger, 'Individuum und Gemeinschaft bei Ägidius Romanus', *Divus Thomas*, 13 (1935), 160–6, who detects in Giles an unqualified use of the imagery of part and whole and therefore an apparent denial of the worth of individual personality against the community. Compare P. Hibst, *Utilitas Publica—Gemeiner Nutz—Gemeinwohl* (Frankfurt, 1991), 193–7.

[101] *DRP* II.i.3.

[102] *DRP* III.ii.2; III.ii.10 (*bonum subditorum; bonorum ipsorum civium et subditorum*); II.ii.3 (*bonum subditorum*); III.i.15. Cf. III.ii.7 (*bonum multorum*); III.iii.1 (*tranquillitas civium et commune bonum*); III.iii.23 (*commune bonum et pax civium; commune bonum et pax civium et eorum qui sunt in regno*).

[103] See above p. 143.

[104] *DRP* III.ii.4. Cf. Albertus Magnus, *Pol. Lib. Oct.* II.3, p. 129; *De Regno ad Regem Cypri* I.3.

[105] *DRP* III.ii.7.   [106] *DRP* I.ii.10; II.ii.2.   [107] *DRP* I.ii.10.   [108] *DRP* I.i *praef.*

establishment of just government and right rule.[109] The same goal is evident in the coda with which Giles closes. It is through securing the common good and peace of their subjects that rulers will earn their own, eternal, peace in God.[110]

In defining the common good as the life of virtue, as the goal of royal government, as the goal of justice, as the object of love, as the divine good, and as the good of the species, Giles is able to produce a comprehensive notion of the *bonum commune*. On occasion, he can elide several of these elements into a single definition. Taken together, for example, the common good of the kingdom, the divine good, the actions produced by virtue, the peace and tranquillity produced by love, and the maintenance of justice, are said to represent the essential components of the *bonus status regni*.[111] As a general rule, however, Giles refers simply to the *bonum commune*, or to one of its many synonyms, particularly the good of the kingdom: *bonum gentis, bonum regni, bonus status regni, salus regni, bonitas regni, utilitas regni, bonum rei publicae, bonum publicum*.[112] Sometimes he runs the two terms together: *bonum gentis et commune, bonum regni et commune, bonum civile et commune, bonum commune et bonus status regni, bonum commune et salus regni, salus regni et civitatis, salus regni et principatus, bonum regni et principatus, bonum civitatis et regni, bonum civile et bonum regni, bonum patriae vel regni, utilitas et commune bonum hominum, commune profectus et regni profectus*.[113] He can also specify the particular element which is demanded by a particular context: *bonum divinum et commune*,[114] *bonum commune et iustitia*,[115] *pax et commune bonum*,[116] *commune bonum et defensio patriae*,[117] *conservatio speciei et bonum commune*,[118] *bonum honorificum et commune*,[119] *bonum maxime intelligibile et maxime universale et commune*.[120]

Despite the clarity with which he defines these different aspects of the term, however, Giles's use of the common good still leaves a number of questions unanswered. Its implications for resistance, for example, are not developed, naturally enough in a work which was intended for a ruling monarch. In *De Regimine Principum*, the common good provides a pressing argument only for subjects to obey their ruler. The victors in a just war, Giles writes, having fought in their own defence and for the common good, are entitled to the obedience of the vanquished because they are entitled to the

---

[109] *DRP* III.ii.13.   [110] *DRP* III.iii.23.   [111] *DRP* I.ii.4.

[112] *DRP* I.i. *praef.*; I.i.7; I.i.10; I.i.13; I.ii.18; I.iii.3–4; I.iii.6; I.iii.9; II.i.3; II.i.9; II.i.11; II.ii.2; II.ii.8; III.ii.5–6; III.ii.10; III.ii.15.

[113] *DRP* I.i.5; I.ii.4; I.iii.4; II.iii.19; III.ii.6; III.ii.15; III.iii.1; III.ii.9 (*bonum commune regni*); I.i.7 (*bonum regni et bonum commune*); III.ii.5 (*bonum commune et totius regni*); III.ii.9 (*bona communia et regni*); III.ii.9 (*bonum commune vel bonum regni*); II.i.3 (*bonum commune ut . . . bonum regni et civitatis*); I.ii.14; I.iii.4; II.i.3; II.i.13; III.ii.3; III.ii.10; III.ii.17; III.ii.27; III.ii.34; III.iii.1. Cf. *DRP* II.i.8 (*quoddam commune bonum*); III.ii.7 (*quodammodo bonum commune*); III.ii.4 (*quasi bonum commune*).

[114] *DRP* I.ii.23; I.iii.3; I.iii.4.   [115] *DRP* I.iv.2; III.ii.9; III.iii.4.

[116] *DRP* III.iii.23; III.ii.23 (*pax et quies et commune bonum, commune bonum et pax civium*). Cf. III.i.13; III.ii.10 (*pax et concordia*).

[117] *DRP* II.iii.14; III.ii.36; III.iii.1 (*defensio communis boni ut civitatis aut regni*); III.ii.19 (*bonum commune ut defensio regni et bonus status eius*); I.ii.15 (*bonum commune ut tuitio regni et defensio patriae*).

[118] *DRP* II.i.7.   [119] *DRP* III.ii.6.

[120] *DRP* I.i.12, applied by Giles to God (*bonum omnis boni*) as the fount of the order of goodness (*bonum universale et intelligentiae*).

obedience of all those virtuous, wise, and good individuals who will recognize that the common good should be preferred to their own private goods.[121] The rule of good kings is analogous inasmuch as the obedience of good men is unquestioned— because the intention of legislators is to educate their citizens in virtue, the virtue of the good man will be the virtue of the good citizen.[122] The difficulty with this line of argument naturally arises with tyranny, a form of government which, by definition, does not secure the life of virtue, the common good. This might make it a bad government with bad laws, but does it also absolve individuals from their duty of obedience? Like *De Regno ad Regem Cypri*, *De Regimine Principum* uses tyranny as a cautionary tale rather than as a justification for resistance. Despite recognizing, therefore, that, in practical terms, failure to secure the common good will constitute the main threat to the continued existence of a tyranny,[123] Giles avoids discussing whether the tyrant's subjects are, in theoretical terms, justified in rebelling. Instead, he is content to reject the possibility with Aquinas' characteristic reservation 'lest worse evil result'. A tyrannical ruler, he remarks, is more bearable than the evils which would arise from disobedience and transgression.[124]

The most problematic lacuna in *De Regimine Principum*, however, remains the singular absence of any observation on the role of the church. For all Giles's emphasis on 'natural' principles of government, he explicitly envisages the Christian rule of a Christian ruler and takes pains to emphasize the magnitude of the good which will result from instruction in the Christian faith.[125] His treatise is, after all, a work which was intended for a king of France, and it refers to the king accordingly—as a minister of God.[126] However, when it comes to discussing the practical effects which such a foundation will have upon the king's rule, Giles limits himself to generalizations. If the king secures happiness by loving God, then he also secures happiness by doing God's will. Giles does find some textual support for this principle in Aristotle—kings ought to be in good standing with regard to divine matters, since the people will be more obedient if they think their king to be a worshipper and a friend of God and therefore always liable to act justly and avoid evil. It is an explanation, however, on which Giles feels able to improve. If a king possesses friendship with God, then, through the omniscience and omnipotence of divine providence and insofar as it furthers the king's own well-being (*salus*), he will always prosper in his actions. In any case, Giles observes (perhaps with Louis IX in mind), the sanctity of a king has frequently conferred many goods upon his people. 'Standing well with regard to divine matters', he concludes, is a function of the king which ought to be the object and complement of all his other virtues.[127] Nevertheless, the question which he leaves unanswered is the connection which such a relationship implies between

---

[121] *DRP* II.iii.14.　　[122] *DRP* III.ii.21; III.ii.34. Cf. Aristotle, *Politics* III.4 1276^{b}16–1277^{b}32.
[123] *DRP* III.ii.13.
[124] *DRP* III.ii.34. Cf. Giles of Rome, *De Ecclesiastica Potestate*, ed. R. Scholz (Weimar, 1929), I.iii.3, p. 10.
[125] *DRP* II.ii.5.　　[126] *DRP* I.i.12; I.iii.3.
[127] *DRP* I.i.12; III.ii.9. Cf. I.i.5; II.ii.5; III.ii.30; Aristotle, *Politics* V.11 1314^{b}38–1315^{a}4.

the authority of the king and the authority of the visible church. It is on this point that Giles remains resolutely silent. He does introduce the concept of royal counsel but couches it in sufficiently broad terms of 'wise and good men' to defy a more specific conclusion being drawn.[128] The only role which is explicitly commanded by the church is religious education.[129]

Giles's silence on this score might be explained by the limitations which he has imposed upon himself by concentrating on 'natural' principles of government. In his commentary on the *Rhetorica*, for example, he had stopped to point out the restricted nature of the *felicitas* which Aristotle had been discussing and which a commentator was therefore bound to accept. Happiness, Giles states, is twofold—political and contemplative—and only political happiness can be the goal of those contingent actions which form the subject of human deliberation and therefore of deliberative rhetoric. The investigation of contemplative happiness, therefore, is not the topic under consideration in his commentary. Likewise, when Aristotle defines happiness as a self-sufficient good, as the goal towards which the soul is directed by a lifetime's activity of perfect virtue, it is made quite clear that the happiness in question is political happiness. The nature of contemplative happiness, Giles repeats, is not the topic which is currently under consideration.[130] Whether there is a supernatural goal, therefore, and, more importantly, how humans are to be directed towards its attainment, do not, in Giles's view, form part of his present investigation.[131]

Whereas Giles had clearly been concerned to demonstrate that the happiness under discussion in the *Rhetorica* was restricted to political happiness, no such reservation is forthcoming in *De Regimine Principum*. Indeed, rather than repeatedly point out that contemplative happiness falls outside his terms of reference, Giles observes that it is only the *truth* of Aristotle's treatment of political and contemplative happiness which is not part of his present study.[132] Thus, when he does introduce the distinction between political and contemplative happiness,[133] he suggests that the king should aim at both. A ruler's happiness lies in the love of God, he states, and not just in the exercise of prudence. Prudence, indeed, must itself be informed by Christian *caritas*.[134] Giles admits that it is upon political happiness that his own treatise will focus, but not before he has proved that it must first be founded upon the *amor dei*. The king, he states, is tripartite—man, minister of God, and ruler of a multitude. In virtue of his humanity, namely his intellect, the king secures the common good of reason; in virtue of his kingship, he is an instrument of God (*divinum organum*); in virtue of his governing power, he secures the common good of the multitude. The connection with God which is established by the second of these

---

[128] *DRP* III.ii.4.   [129] *DRP* II.ii.5.   [130] *Sup. Lib. Rhet.* fo. 19r–v.

[131] *Sup. Lib. Rhet.* fo. 23r. Giles's repeated assurances were, no doubt, well-advised. Article 172 (176) of the propositions condemned in 1277 reads 'happiness is attainable in this life rather than the next', whilst article 171 (157) reads 'the individual whose intellect and will are perfected in intellectual and moral virtues put forward in the *Ethics* is sufficiently disposed for eternal happiness' (*Siger de Brabant et l'averroïsme latin*, ed. Mandonnet, p. 188). Cf. Lambertini, 'Il filosofo', 268–71. For 'philosophical' happiness, see e.g. A. J. Celano, 'Boethius of Dacia, On the Highest Good', *Traditio*, 43 (1987), 199–214.

[132] *DRP* I.i.12.   [133] *DRP* I.i.4.   [134] *DRP* I.ii.1.

characteristics is self-explanatory but so too, Giles argues, is the connection established by the first and the third. What is God if not the most universal principle of
goodness intelligible by any intellect and the most universal common good of any
multitude? It is in virtue of all three functions, therefore, that Giles counsels the king
to locate his happiness in God.[135] Right at the start of *De Regimine Principum*, Giles
accordingly sets out the benefits which will result from the instruction of rulers in the
principles of good government—the ruler will secure the greatest goods for himself
and for others but he will also possess eternal happiness in the Lord. Giles then
remarks that, since it will be impossible to put the stipulations of *De Regimine Principum* into practice without the assistance of divine grace, it is incumbent upon every
individual, and upon the king in particular, to pray for this assistance. The higher his
authority, Giles explains, the more an individual will require divine grace, and not
just to perform virtuous actions himself but to lead his subjects to a life of virtue as
well.[136] Human law and natural law are, in themselves, insufficient to enable individuals to secure the supernatual good. For this, the divine law and the law of the New
Testament are necessary.[137]

By emphasizing the ruler's need to be aided by divine grace and to be perfected by
Christian *caritas*, Giles produces far more than just an 'Aristotelian' treatise. *De
Regimine Principum* needs to be considered accordingly as a work which is just as concerned with the duties of a *minister Dei* as it is about the exercise of Aristotelian prudence.[138] Nevertheless, this recognition only serves to highlight the problem which
is posed by its Aristotelian emphasis on the life of virtue. As Giles himself admits, in
De Regimine Principum as well as in his commentary on the *Rhetorica*, virtue is a spiritual good, it is a good of the soul.[139] Is such a good the preserve, the sole preserve
even, of the government of kings, or does it involve the supervision of the church? If
virtuous actions require the presence of divine grace, how is that assistance to be
sought or given other than by an individual's prayer? The political implications
of the common good of the life of virtue cry out for a discussion of the relation of
ecclesiastical and secular power but this is a discussion which Giles steadfastly
refuses to stage. It is on this point that a comparison with *De Regno ad Regem Cypri*
becomes highly suggestive.

Like *De Regimine Principum*, *De Regno* establishes the attainment of the common
good as the defining characteristic of kingship. If it is natural for humankind to live
in political society, then it is necessary for this multitude to be ruled, just as the body
has a ruling force which keeps it together and secures the common good of all its
limbs. Indeed, unless there is someone in human society who is responsible for what
concerns the good of the multitude, the community will disintegrate under the pressure of each individual aiming to secure what is congruent with their own good. What
is individual and what is common are, in practice, not identical—humans differ in

---

[135] *DRP* I.i.12.   [136] *DRP* I.i.3.   [137] *DRP* III.ii.30. Cf. *Quod.* II.29 fo. 28r.
[138] Lambertini, 'Il filosofo', 279.
[139] *DRP* III.ii.31. Cf. II.i.12; II.ii.6; III.i.5; *Sup. Lib. Rhet.* fos. 17v, 18r, 19v.

the former and are united in the latter. Besides the principle which moves each individual towards his own good, therefore, there ought to be something which moves that individual towards the common good. This is the function of the ruler.[140] Like *De Regimine Principum*, *De Regno* also follows Aristotle's basic categorization of good and bad forms of government. If a multitude of free people is ordered by its ruler towards the common good of the multitude, then it will constitute a correct and just form of government, but if it is ordered towards the private good of the ruler, then it will be unjust and perverse.[141] The real interest in *De Regno*'s treatment of the common good, however, arises when it comes to defining what the term actually means.

Although the *bonum commune* remains, in one form or another,[142] the goal of good government throughout the course of *De Regno*, a major organizing principle of book I is to separate the life of virtue from the life of peace and material self-sufficiency. In the account of government and monarchy which is given in the first six chapters, for example, the one Aristotelian tenet which is notable by its absence is the insistence that the function of the political community is not just to live but to live well, to live the life of virtue. Initially, the role of the king is limited to providing for the material welfare of his subjects—in chapter 1, it is the necessities of life (*necessaria vitae*); in chapter 5, it is the good of peace (*bonum pacis*). In chapter 2, meanwhile, the good of the multitude is the *unitas pacis*—the more unity and peace, the greater the benefit (*utilitas*)—but the goal which is thereby facilitated is left unspecified.[143] A notion of virtue is introduced for the first time in chapter 7, at the start of a lengthy excursus on the rewards of good kingship. Since the king acts as a minister of God, he should aim to secure the reward, not of wealth, honour, or glory, but of eternal beatitude. Even here, however, the common good is introduced only to highlight the merit of a king who secures the good of the multitude—the greater the good, the greater the virtue, and the common good is greater and more divine than the good of an individual.[144] It is only in chapters 14 and 15, *after* a discussion of eternal beatitude and the way in which it perfects and completes any earthly good, that a notion of *bene vivere*, of living according to virtue, finally makes its appearance as the goal of the human community, as the common good.

This pattern is mirrored in other parts of the argument. Chapter 14, for example, opens by appealing to the analogy of the king as helmsman, keeping his people safe but also guiding them towards a further goal, like a ship towards its harbour. In chapter 2, this harbour is the unity and peace of the multitude. By chapter 14, it has become heavenly beatitude, the harbour of eternal salvation, the goal towards which all Christians are guided by ministers of the church. By chapter 14, moreover, the dissimilarity between what is individual and what is common has been replaced by

---

[140] *De Regno ad Regem Cypri* I.1. Cf. Boethius, *Philosophiae Consolatio*, ed. L. Bieler (*CCSL* 94), III.12, pp. 60–1.

[141] *De Regno* I.1. Cf. I.4, I.10.

[142] *bonum commune* (I.1, 3, 4, 5, 10); *bonum multitudinis* (I.1, 9, 15); *bonum commune multitudinis* (I.1, 14); *bonum commune multorum* (I.1); *bonum et salus multitudinis* (I.2); *bonum publicum* (I.15).

[143] *De Regno* I.2.   [144] *De Regno* I.9.

the more familiar principle of identity—the same judgement must apply to the goal of the whole multitude and the goal of one individual. If this goal were simply bodily well-being, the argument runs, then the duty of ruling would belong to the doctor; if it were the acquisition of wealth, then it would belong to the economist; if it were the understanding of truth, then it would belong to the teacher. The goal of the multitude is, instead, to live according to virtue, to live well, a goal which individuals cannot attain by living on their own. It is immediately pointed out, however, that, in living according to virtue, humankind is ordered towards a further goal, namely eternal beatitude. The goal of the multitude ought to be the same as the goal of each individual and thus the ultimate goal of the community is not just to live a virtuous life but, through this life of virtue, to secure eternal beatitude in God. If this ultimate goal could be secured by natural human virtue alone, then it would certainly be the function of the king to direct individuals towards it. Since it can be attained only by divine virtue, however, this role must fall to divine, not human, government. This divine government is the government of Jesus Christ, His ministers, and His vicar on earth.

The conclusion to *De Regno* is unequivocal. Those who are responsible for subordinate goals must be subject to those responsible for the ultimate goal and they must be directed by their command. The pagan priesthood, for example, was designed to secure temporal goods, goods which were ordered towards the common good of the multitude. Since the latter was, by definition, the primary concern of the king, it was entirely appropriate for pagan priests to be subject to kings. So too in the case of the priests of Israel in the Old Testament where God promised to provide His people with earthly goods. Under the new dispensation, however, humankind is led to heavenly, not to earthly, goods. Kings should therefore now be subject to priests.[145] Those functions which have been ascribed to kings earlier in *De Regno* are not denied, but when chapter 15 returns to the duty of such rulers, it explicitly amalgamates their role as guarantors of material welfare with the nature of the common good as the life of virtue. The temporal ruler, however, is now explicitly described as having been 'instructed in divine law'. By the end of book I, therefore, a sufficiency of material goods has become instrumental to the primary constituent of a good life, the performance of virtuous actions, whilst the task of the ruler has become providing what is necessary for this end. The earlier stipulation that the duty of the ruler is to secure the unity and peace of the multitude is now extended to include the function which he exercises once that unity has been secured—to direct the multitude towards a life of virtue. The ruler must concern himself with staffing government, with providing the legislation which induces people to do good and avoid evil, and with protecting the community from its external foes. In general, the ruler must secure whatever can contribute to the community's continuation in existence. In doing all this, however, the king's role is primarily instrumental. It is to the church that the ruler is ultimately subject.[146] As soon as *De Regno* introduces the notion that

---

[145] *De Regno* I.14.   [146] *De Regno* I.15.

the goal of the temporal ruler is the life of virtue, in other words, it is made abundantly clear that it must be ordered towards a higher goal and under the direction of a higher power—the authority of the church.

Any interpretation of *De Regno* which is based on a particular ordering of its argument poses its own problems for a text whose apparent lack of argumentative and structural coherence has been put down to the possibility that its original folios were lost, mixed up, or rehandled.[147] The logic of arguing that there *is* a structure to the argument, and one which has a significant effect on its meaning, makes the identity of any editor responsible for the (re)arrangement of book I even more of a critical question. Viewed from the perspective of the common good, the issue is more straightforward. If securing the life of virtue is a characteristically Aristotelian definition of the common good, then, in the context of the relationship between the temporal and the spiritual powers, it is a definition which had been successfully tuned to a hierocratic note. *De Regno ad Regem Cypri* clearly recognized its implications and was unqualified in its subordination of the temporal to the spiritual power, of the life of virtue to the ultimate goal of eternal beatitude. Giles of Rome's *De Regimine Principum*, on the other hand, gives the life of virtue and eternal beatitude similar prominence but leaves a similar correlation hanging in the air. It is a discussion which Giles may have deemed prudent to avoid. At the very least, it leaves his initial observation—that his treatise is sufficiently exhaustive to make further discussion superfluous—a rather disingenuous claim.[148]

To discuss *De Regimine Principum* as a work of rhetoric is not to regard the author's beliefs as somehow distanced from the views which the text itself sets out. Rhetoric had a specific meaning for Giles of Rome. It showed him how to handle common principles of human behaviour in society in order to persuade a non-specialist audience to will what is good and advantageous. Deliberative rhetoric, moreover, provided Giles with the ground rules for putting political science into practice. It showed him how to describe general principles rather than specific actions. Deliberative rhetoric also provided Giles with the substance of the counsel which should be put forward—political happiness and what is advantageous to the individual who aims to secure this good; the life of virtue as the goal of kingship and as the objective of justice and law; the goodness of virtuous citizens as the goal of every good form of government; the securing of material resources; the provision of food; the waging of war and the maintenance of internal peace; the protection and defence of the community; the establishment of laws on which the *salus civitatis* depends. In terms of both method and content, Aristotle's *Rhetorica* was just as influential on Giles's political thought as Aristotle's *Politics* and *Ethics*.

---

[147] Thomas Aquinas, *On Kingship to the King of Cyprus*, trans. G. B. Phelan, rev. I. Th. Eschmann (Toronto, 1949), p. xxiv. Cf. M. Brown, '*An sit authenticum opusculum S. Thomae De Regimine Principum*', *Angelicum*, 3 (1926), 300–3.

[148] *DRP* I.i.

De Regimine Principum was a work of political counsel in that it dealt with general moral subjects which were open to deliberation (*consiliabilia*), namely the means by which its audience could secure the undisputed goal of human existence—political and contemplative happiness. By describing the moral actions which are appropriate for a virtuous ruler and his subjects in times of peace and war, Giles produced a treatise on the general theory and practice of kingship. In doing so, however, Giles's intention was not to demonstrate what was true so much as to persuade his audience of the actions and *mores* which would be good and beneficial. This moral purpose underpins Giles's treatise from beginning to end. It is evident from the definition which he gives to political happiness, the goal towards which his own deliberative rhetoric is directed. The good towards which Giles wishes to move both ruler and subject is the common good, the virtuous life which distinguishes good forms of government from bad, which represents the objective of justice and legislation, and which constitutes the goodness of every individual member of the political community.

Having commented on Aristotle's *Rhetorica*, Giles was able to examine the various ways in which such a common good could be compared to the lesser goods which it included and preserved. This was how he was able to accommodate the principle of the superiority of the common good to the individual good with the principle of their identity. One subject, however, remained beyond the scope of either the *Rhetorica*, the *Ethics*, or the *Politics*. In his commentary on the *Rhetorica*, Giles had been able to sidestep the relation between political happiness and contemplative happiness, between the common good and eternal beatitude, by insisting that this subject simply did not form part of his present study. In *De Regimine Principum*, however, the contemplative happiness of eternal beatitude is not only introduced but firmly established as the ultimate goal which should be secured by means of divine grace and through the common good of the life of virtue. Rather than conclude that the temporal power is subordinate to the spiritual power, however, Giles of Rome simply refused to elaborate further. Unlike the author of *De Regno*, Giles was reluctant either to construct this corollary or, more probably, to make this corollary explicit. For the moment at least, the role of the spiritual power in relation to the temporal was a subject on which Giles preferred to keep his own counsel.

6

Henry of Ghent—Self-Love and Inclusion

Despite his prominence in the faculty of theology at Paris between 1276 and 1293, Henry of Ghent cuts a curious figure in the historiography of scholastic thought. What has made him so problematic is his capacity to draw on several different intellectual traditions without producing an entirely convincing synthesis. Fundamental tensions have been detected, for example, in his combination of a Neoplatonic and Augustinian metaphysics with an epistemology based on Aristotle and Averroes.[1] This apparent lack of harmony stems, in part, from Henry's own attitude to using philosophical authorities—if he is prepared to quote Aristotle and Averroes in the course of theological arguments, then he insists that the content of such citation could still be both flawed and insufficient.[2] Even when modern commentators have sought to identify development rather than systematization, it remains debatable whether Henry's writings reveal a departure from certain Aristotelian tenets or a desire to see them accommodated.[3] Small wonder, perhaps, that Henry should be characterized as 'un penseur éclectique et personnel', a theologian whose complexity and subtlety of thought is matched only by an exhaustive, even prolix, style of writing.[4]

Moral and political philosophy may not have commanded as much of Henry's attention as metaphysics and epistemology but his handling of ethical and political subjects reveals a similarly complex juxtaposition of 'Augustinian' and 'Aristotelian'

---

[1] J. Paulus, *Henri de Gand: Essai sur les tendances de sa métaphysique* (Paris, 1938); A. Maurer, 'Henry of Ghent and the Unity of Man', *Mediaeval Studies*, 10 (1948), 1–20.

[2] P. de Vooght, 'La Méthode théologique d'apres Henri de Gand et Gérard de Bologne', *RTAM* 23 (1956), 61–87.

[3] A critical edition is in progress (*Henrici de Gandavo Opera Omnia*, ed. R. Macken et al., Leuven–Leiden, 1979–). References are to this edition for those quodlibets which have been published (I, II, VI, VII, IX, X, XII, XIII); otherwise the edition used is by V. Zuccolius (2 vols.; Venice, 1613) correlated, where necessary, with Oxford, Merton College MS 107. For Henry's relation to Aristotle, see R. Macken, *Opera Omnia*, vol. v, p. xiv; id., 'La Théorie de l'illumination divine dans la philosophie d'Henri de Gand', *RTAM* 39 (1972), 82–112. Cf. S. P. Marrone, *Truth and Scientific Knowledge in the Thought of Henry of Ghent* (Cambridge, Mass., 1985), 43, who dates Henry's re-evaluation of Aristotle to 1279/80, i.e to the period immediately after his involvement in Tempier's commission of inquiry into the arts faculty. For Henry's opposition to Giles of Rome's commentary on the *Sentences*, and for his role in Giles's censure, see *Apologia*, ed. R. Wielockx (*Aegidii Romani Opera Omnia* III.1), ch. 6. Cf. Henry of Ghent, *Quodlibet* II.9, pp. 58–72.

[4] M. de Wulf, *Histoire de la philosophie médiévale*, 6th edn. (3 vols.; Louvain–Paris, 1934–47), ii. 303. Cf. R. Macken, 'Les Sources d'Henri de Gand', *Revue Philosophique de Louvain*, 76 (1978), 5–28; *Opera Omnia*, vol. v, p. xv; Marrone, *Truth and Scientific Knowledge*, 3; F. van Steenberghen, *La Philosophie au XIIIe siècle*, 2nd edn. (Louvain, 1991), 437–9.

elements. Not surprisingly, it too has been criticized on grounds of clarity: 'il s'engage dans les distinctions tellement subtiles et multipliées que ses conclusions se trouvent le plus souvent conditionelles et incertaines'.[5] Indeed, if anything, Henry's moral and political philosophy has proved to be even more elusive than his metaphysics because his *Summa* never received the comprehensive treatment of Creation which had originally been planned.[6] To discuss Henry of Ghent's 'political thought', therefore, is to discuss a series of observations on particular issues which are scattered throughout his quodlibets. Although a degree of consistency can still be posited (both the *Summa* and the *Quaestiones Quodlibetales* were subsequently revised by Henry himself), any analysis has to respect the fragmentary nature of his discussions.[7]

If Henry of Ghent's theology is to be characterized as an uneasy fusion of metaphysical principle with natural philosophy, then this will clearly have significant repercussions for his political thought. It is on these grounds that Henry has sometimes been used to illustrate a more general tension between scholastic metaphysics and political philosophy. By translating the principles of an objective and transcendent goodness into the political sphere, it is argued, Henry only succeeded in producing an uneasy synthesis of Aristotelian social morality and Christian individualism, an absorption of the individual within the community which went much further than Aristotle's 'natural' participation and which was only partially mitigated by his insistence that the individual good must always be included within the common good.[8] By not drawing a distinction between principles which apply to goodness in the universe and principles which apply to the good of the community, it is suggested, Henry serves to demonstrate the dangers of mixing metaphysics with politics.

Henry's understanding of the common good is clearly central to such a characterization. Rather than reveal a heady mixture of metaphysics and politics, however, Henry's references to a metaphysical common good, either as the *ratio boni* or as the object of the will, are notable for their absence from his analysis of explicitly political subjects.[9] Unlike Aquinas, in fact, Henry of Ghent appears to have kept discussion of the good in common largely separate from his account of the good of the human community. Some of the abstract references which he does make are certainly suggestive—when he distinguishes between a natural and an artificial integral whole, for

[5] F. Huet, *Recherches historiques et critiques sur la vie, les ouvrages et la doctrine de Henri de Gand* (Ghent, 1838), 178. Cf. G. de Lagarde, 'La Philosophie sociale d'Henri de Gand et Godefroid de Fontaines', *AHDLMA* 14 (1943–5), 73–142; id., *La Naissance de l'esprit laïque au déclin du moyen âge*, 3rd edn. (5 vols.; Louvain, 1956–70), vol. ii, ch. 8.

[6] Henry of Ghent, *Summa [Quaestiones Ordinariae]* (2 vols.; Paris, 1520), XXI.1 fo. 123r.

[7] R. Macken, 'Les Corrections d'Henri de Gand à ses quodlibets', *RTAM* 40 (1973), 5–51. For the chronology of the quodlibets, see P. Glorieux, *La Littérature quodlibétique* (2 vols.; Paris, 1925, 1935), i. 177–99; J. Gómez Caffarena, 'Cronología de la "Suma" de Enrique de Gante por relación a sus "Quodlibetos"', *Gregorianum*, 38 (1957), 133; *Opera Omnia*, vol. v, p. xvii.

[8] Lagarde, *La Naissance*, ii. 185, 212–13.

[9] e.g. *Summa* IV.2 fo. 31r–v; XXIV.6 fo. 142v. Cf. XL.1 fos. 256v–257r; XLIX.4 fo. 34r–v; XLIX.5 fos. 34v–40r.

example, or when he distinguishes between an absolute good (*bonum simpliciter*) and a congruent good (*bonum conveniens*) in order to separate the primary object of the human will (*bonum simpliciter sub ratione boni*) from the object which it shares with the rest of Creation (*bonum conveniens commune* or *bonum conveniens in generali*).[10] Likewise, when Henry distinguishes between what is common by predication and what is common by participation,[11] or when he distinguishes between two senses (composition and order) in which a number of individual goods can be both many and one (as a means of reconciling the doctrine of the simplicity of God with Boethius' definition of beatitude as 'the perfect condition of all good things collected together').[12] Nevertheless, the implications of these distinctions for how Henry may subsequently have viewed the common good of human society remain just that. In none of these instances is any *direct* connection made with a specifically political community. There remains, therefore, very little textual support for the suggestion that Henry himself was drawing a connection between metaphysical and political goods. This does not mean that Henry's account of the relationship between the good of the individual and the good of the community is entirely lacking in a theoretical dimension. However, when Henry does consider the common good of human society in abstract terms, it is in the context, not of metaphysics, but of love.

Love was a principle which both Aristotle and Augustine had made central to the operation of a political community. As a result, in their discussions of the common good, scholastic theologians were quick to examine the relationship between love for one's own good and love for the good of the community. Albertus Magnus, Thomas Aquinas, and Giles of Rome had all concluded that the supreme expression of such a relationship was the act of self-sacrifice, laying down one's property and even one's life for the sake of the common good. Within this broad consensus, however, there were significant differences of approach. For Aquinas and Giles, the identification of the good of the community as the life of virtue meant that self-sacrifice was the product of a straightforward equation—just as the individual loves the common good in God as the good on which his individual good depends for its goodness and existence, so the individual loves the common good of the human community as the good in which his individual good is included and from which his own good follows as a consequence. For Albertus Magnus, on the other hand, the performance of self-sacrifice was dependent on first clarifying the exact nature of the common good to

---

[10] *Summa* XXV.2 fo. 149v; *Quod.* XIII.9, pp. 56–64. For Henry's account of the will, see R. Macken, 'La Volonté humaine, faculté plus élévée que l'intelligence selon Henri de Gand', *RTAM* 42 (1975), 5–51.

[11] *Summa* XXI.4 ad 1 fo. 128v. Cf. LXXII.1 fo. 255v; LXXV.2 fos. 291v–299r. For the philosophical implications of this distinction, see Marrone, *Truth and Scientific Knowledge*, 64–5; C. Knudsen, 'Intentions and Impositions', in *CHLMP*, 482–3. For individuation, see S. F. Brown, 'Henry of Ghent', in J. J. E. Garcia (ed.), *Individuation in Scholasticism: The Later Middle Ages and the Counter-Reformation 1150–1650* (Albany, NY, 1994), 195–219; *Apologia*, ed. Wielockx (*Aegidii Romani Opera Omnia* III.1), 156–7.

[12] *Summa* XLIX.1 fos. 32v–33r; Boethius, *Philosophiae Consolatio*, ed. L. Bieler (*CCSL* 94), III.2, p. 38. Cf. above, p. 37 n. 33. Henry concludes that, since composition cannot exist in God, it is the unity of order which underpins Boethius' observation—goods are gathered together in God's supreme simplicity in the same way that lines proceeding from the circumference of a circle are 'collected' in its centre.

which such an action was being directed—was it virtue or peace? The individual who lays down his life, he concluded, thereby secures his own greatest good of virtue, the good which is common to the whole community, but this good, in its turn, is superior to the material security which his act of self-sacrifice will subsequently produce for the community.

When Henry of Ghent came to consider the relationship between the individual good and the common good in the context of love, therefore, he was faced not only by the need to clarify his own approach to the motivation behind self-sacrifice but also by a choice of definitions which could be given to the good of human society—was it the goal or the result of virtuous action? The consequences of Henry's decision are of considerable significance, both for an assessment of the scholastic understanding of the common good and for an evaluation of his own reputation as a thinker. Whether Henry of Ghent is to continue being characterized as a theologian who produced an unsatisfactory mixture of metaphysical principle and political reality, or whether he should, in fact, be credited with drawing a distinction between a transcendent common good and the good of the human community, depends to a large extent on a detailed examination of his account of the operation of love.

According to Aquinas, the relationship between the individual good and the common good needed to be placed within a clearly articulated order of love whereby increasing degrees of love should be shown to increasing degrees of community. Viewed from this perspective, what is so striking about Henry of Ghent's analysis is that it repeatedly restricts the *ordo caritatis* to the three categories of love originally established by Augustine—love of self, love of neighbour, and love of God—leaving little or no room for any intermediate good of the community. As far as Henry is concerned, the principle of love for a 'good in common' seems to operate only when this *bonum in communi* exists in God.[13] This is immediately apparent from Henry's reaction to Aristotle's account of natural love and his response to the standard scholastic question which it had prompted—whether a creature with an intellect is capable of loving God more than all other things when it is exercising a purely natural love.[14] Henry opens his discussion by distinguishing the two ways in which an essential good can be loved—either it is loved because it is good in itself or it is loved because it is good for the individual who loves it. Henry uses the first category to answer the original question in the affirmative. An intellectual creature does have a natural love for God above all other things because God is an absolute good, the reason why every other good is loved, and the universal good of which every other good simply forms a part. As far as everything other than God is concerned, however, Henry suggests that an intellectual creature has a greater natural love for itself. In human society,

---

[13] e.g. *Summa* XLVI.3–4 fos. 23r–24v. Cf. Matthew 22: 37–40; Augustine, *De Doctrina Christiana*, ed. R. P. H. Green (Oxford, 1995), I.22–26, pp. 28–36; Augustine, *De Trinitate*, ed. W. J. Mountain (*CCSL* 50), XIV.14.18, pp. 445–6; Aquinas, *IaIIae* 100.3 ad 1.

[14] *Quod.* IV.11 fos. 158v–160v. Cf. Aristotle, *Politics* II.5 1263ᵃ41–ᵇ1; *Auctoritates Aristotelis*, ed. J. Hamesse (Louvain–Paris, 1974), p. 254: *unusquisque naturaliter amat se ipsum.*

therefore, an individual loves himself in the first instance and his neighbour only by extension in that he wills good for himself before he wills good for someone else. Henry cites book IX of the *Ethics* in support of this conclusion—a human being will do and suffer many things for his friends; he will lose money, honour, and even his own life, but, in the process, he will secure good for himself (*procurans sibi ipsi bonum*).[15]

Self-love, of course, is not the same as selfish love, and Henry is quick to acknowledge that both Aristotle's *Ethics* and Cicero's *De Amicitia* had described the beneficial effects which legitimate self-love should have on others. Discussing Aristotle's definition of political happiness, for example, Henry sets up as universally applicable the principle that all parts of Creation are ordered in such a way that they help and sustain one another. This principle applies to the particular virtues which make up political happiness, to the individuals who are exercising these virtues in the political community, and to rulers who are ruling in good and peaceful governments.[16] The same principle also covers the exercise of friendship between individuals in society.[17] Friendship may originate in desiring goodness for oneself[18] but, if an individual loves the good of virtue for its own sake and loves himself on that account, then he will also love his own good of virtue in his neighbour and will love his neighbour on that account. To love oneself more than one loves another individual does not, in Henry's view, represent the perfection of love. For this observation, Henry turns to Richard of St Victor—an individual wills the good of virtue to be loved jointly, by himself and by his neighbour, and it is only in this trinity that love can be made perfect.[19] Friendship may originate in willing good for oneself and others (*benevolentia*), it may be developed by actually doing good to others (*beneficentia*), but it is only consummated by the presence of mutual faith (*confidentia*). It is the exercise of all three types of love which makes individuals 'one' according to Aristotle's definition of a friend as 'another self'.[20] It is for this reason, Henry concludes, that friendship is directed towards the common exercise of all the virtues. Whilst other virtuous actions are performed for their own sake, the actions of friendship are performed for the common benefit of those who love each other (*ut in communem utilitatem sese interamantium producuntur*).[21]

Henry's understanding of friendship clearly represents more than just a polarization between a disinterested love of God and a legitimate love of self which then extends towards one's neighbour. Friendship comprises not only love for one's own good and the good of one's neighbour but also for the good of virtue in which self and neighbour can communicate. Nevertheless, Henry only refers to a 'common benefit' on one occasion and, when he does so, it is not the common good itself which is loved (as Aquinas argued) but the individuals themselves. It is love for other individuals which inspires the actions of virtue which then 'result' in common benefit.

[15] *Quod.* IV.11 fo. 160r; Aristotle, *Ethics* IX.8 1169ᵃ20.   [16] *Quod.* V.17 fos. 282r–287r.
[17] *Quod.* X.12, pp. 274–85.   [18] Aristotle, *Ethics* VIII.5 1157ᵇ33.
[19] Richard of St Victor, *De Trinitate*, ed. J. Ribaillier (Paris, 1958), III.11, pp. 146–7. Cf. Aquinas, *Ia* 32.1.
[20] Aristotle, *Ethics* IX.4 1166ᵃ31–2.   [21] *Quod.* X.12, pp. 281–2.

The extent to which Henry's analysis of the *ordo caritatis* differs from the account put forward by Aquinas is underlined by his treatment of an issue which both Aquinas and Albertus had considered to be an exemplary manifestation of love for a common good—the correction and punishment of sins which damage the community.[22] In his very first quodlibet in 1276, Henry was asked whether an individual in a religious community should publicly reveal a secret sin if his superior has commanded him to do so on oath. Comparing the love which is owed to one's neighbour with the love which is owed to oneself, Henry sets out two conclusions. The greatest act of *caritas* towards one's neighbour, he argues, is to exhort him to correct his sin in private, since there is no circumstance in which one's neighbour should be betrayed and his private sin made public. The same principle applies if the sin in question is one's own. In fact, in this instance, Henry regards the obligation to perform an act of *caritas* towards oneself to be all the greater, since an individual's love for himself should be greater than the love which he has for his neighbour.[23] The correction of a private sin, however, is a different matter from the punishment of a public crime. Like Albertus and Aquinas, therefore, Henry goes on to argue that the punishment of a sinner should be public when the sin in question (theft, for example, or murder) disturbs the peace of the *res publica*.[24] Whilst the biblical injunction to love one's neighbour as oneself still carries the obligation to secure the good of one's neighbour, Henry points out that this duty represents only one side of an equation. Correction has two functions—admonition and punishment—each one of which is motivated by a different intention. Whilst admonition is an act of *caritas* performed for the betterment of the sinner, punishment is an act of authority performed to instil terror into those who witness it.[25]

It is at this point in the argument that Henry begins to part company with Albertus and Aquinas. Unlike Aquinas, who promptly established the relative priority of admonition and punishment by appealing to the superiority of the common good of the community over the private good of the sinner, Henry makes no attempt to bring these functions within a single scale of reference. Indeed, Henry actually quotes 'certain people' (unnamed but who must have included Aquinas) according to whom, if an individual's sin has not been corrected by private admonition and if it continues to have a detrimental effect upon his neighbour and the *res publica*, then it should be denounced to a superior authority. Although Henry does consider this to be a permissible line of argument, he insists that such an act of delation should not be allowed to qualify as fraternal correction because denunciation is primarily ordered towards the goal of securing the public good and not the good of the sinner. Fraternal correction pertains to *caritas*, he states, whereas denunciation pertains to public justice.[26] Significantly, Henry goes no further than simply making this distinction.

----

[22] Aquinas, IV *Sent.* 19.2.3a; *Quod.* IV.8.1; *IIaIIae* 68.1. Cf. Albertus Magnus, *Super Ethica* X.17; *Ethica* V.2.6. For the controversy, see *Les Premières Polémiques thomistes I: Le Correctorium Corruptorii 'Quare'*, ed. P. Glorieux (Paris, 1927), 399–403.

[23] *Quod.* I.33, pp. 191–3.   [24] *Quod.* II.17, pp. 134–5.   [25] *Quod.* V.29 fo. 311v.

[26] *Quod.* IX.28, pp. 313–21. Cf. *Decretum* II.2.1.19 (Friedberg, i. 447–8).

Once again, he compares neither the demands of the individual good of the sinner and the common good of the damaged *res publica*, nor the public good of justice with the *ordo caritatis*. All he does do is appeal to the authority of Augustine.[27] A similar silence occurs when Henry discusses the death penalty for the crime of theft and draws a distinction between the capacity of the criminal to be corrected and the harm which his crime has caused.[28] Although Henry describes theft as an action which is contrary to natural law and to Cicero's *pactum humanae societatis*, and although he appeals to the same corporeal analogy as Aquinas (the amputation of diseased limbs), Henry makes no mention of the common good. 'Harm caused' is considered only in terms of God and one's neighbour.

The impression that Henry of Ghent is determined to avoid positing any principle of love for a common good is strengthened by his reply to the question which Giles of Rome regarded as a prime example of this principle in action—should everything in the political community be held in common? Henry's approach is to reconcile the positions put forward by Plato and Aristotle, and to incorporate them both within a Christian framework, by distinguishing between three conditions of humankind—prelapsarian ideal (exemplified by Plato's *Republic*), postlapsarian practice (exemplified in Aristotle and Cicero), and restoration by grace (exemplified by the heavenly Jerusalem). The basis for each of these conditions, Henry argues, is a different notion of love. Thus, Plato's citizens were united primarily by the object of their love in the sense that each individual loved the possessions of others 'as if they were his own' (*sicut circa propria*) and secured the good of another citizen 'as if it were his own' (*sicut et proprium*). As a paradigm for this principle of identity, Henry appeals to the corporeal imagery of 1 Corinthians 12—individuals are 'members' of one another—and suggests that this is the sense in which Socrates' notorious 'community' of wives and children should be understood. According to Henry, therefore, when Aristotle attacked the community of goods in book II of the *Politics*, he had simply misconstrued the type of unity which was being put forward in the *Republic*. On Henry's reading, Plato's injunctions were entirely in accordance with natural law and did not exclude private use according to the demands of time, place, and right reason. A community of goods may be based on a common affection but this common affection is based, in turn, on an individual's love of self. The greatest peace, concord, and friendship, Henry argues, are secured by the fact that those material goods which belong to another person as his property, and which are shared by everyone as their common possession, are nevertheless one's own insofar as they are the object of one's love. Henry is determined to stress the point. The ideal community, he writes, is connected by the greatest friendship, through which everyone is regarded as another self (*alter ipse*), by the greatest love, through which everyone loves one another as he loves himself (*sicut seipsum*), and by the greatest benevolence, through which everyone wishes for another what he wishes for himself (*vellet alteri quod sibi*).

---

[27] Augustine, *Sermo* LXXXII (*PL* 38, cols. 506–14) 7–8 cols. 510–11.
[28] *Quod.* XI.18 fos. 221v–222r.

Love for what is in common is ultimately defined by the love which an individual has for himself.

Henry is careful, once again, to distinguish self-love from selfish love. The one point which he does concede to Aristotle, therefore, is the recognition that it is impossible for humankind in its natural capacity to possess the degree of friendship which is necessary to secure Plato's ideal community of goods. According to Henry, if natural love will always tend to love what is its own more than it loves what belongs to another, and to love what is good for itself more than what is good for others, then it will do so to an extent which exceeds the legitimate level prescribed by *caritas*. Even Aristotle, for all his recognition of human weaknesses, did not advocate the purely private possession of material goods. To have done this, Henry argues, would have been to advocate the *civitas terrena*, the community founded on selfish love which had been set up by Augustine as one of his two paradigms for human society. By the same token, however, Henry also accepts that the community founded on love of God—Augustine's *civitas Dei*—can only be realized in heaven. Until this perfection is reached, he concludes, human beings must live with the consequences of their own sinful nature. Henry's own prescription for such a condition is a Christian community in which the necessarily imperfect exercise of *caritas* is moderated by the operation of divine grace—the more grace an individual enjoys, the more common his affection will be and the less possessive his attitude to individual goods. Henry's model is the New Testament church, recorded in Acts 4: 32 as having one heart and one soul, and put forward, as such, as Augustine's ideal type for the Christian community. It is a model, however, which Henry recognizes to have limited application. Those 'more perfect' individuals who live in religious communities are able to observe a measure of common possession which is unattainable in political communities, since their perfection is the product, not of natural love, but of grace. Henry's reading of Augustine, therefore, acknowledges the conceptual value of distinguishing between the two cities, between a *civitas terrena* founded on selfish love and a *civitas Dei* founded on the love of God. Henry's reading of Augustine, however, also accepts that the city of God is an ideal which is unattainable on this earth. Some religious communities can certainly achieve an approximation but a more realistic assessment of the limitations on fallen human nature should govern the prospects of a political community doing the same. The capacity of a given human community to secure such an ideal will therefore depend upon the degree to which natural self-love is controlled by the operation of divine grace. Even in a perfect community, however, love for what is in common will still be defined by the love which each individual has for himself.[29]

Henry's account of the operation of love within the human community provides an instructive perspective on his approach to the common good. In precisely those

---

[29] *Quod.* IV.20 fos. 197v–199v. Cf. Aristotle, *Politics* II.1–6; Albertus Magnus, *Pol. Lib. Oct.* II.2, pp. 108–16; VII.8, p. 685; Giles of Rome, *De Regimine Principum* III.i.15 (see above, p. 145); Lagarde, 'La Philosophie sociale', 83–6; id., *La Naissance*, ii. 176–9.

contexts in which Albertus and Aquinas found it appropriate to appeal to an individual's love for a superior common good—friendship, correction, punishment, and personal property—Henry refuses to go further than the categories of love which he found in Augustine. Love of self, love of neighbour, and love of God remain the central components of Henry's political theology. When he does introduce a notion of the common good, it is defined only as the general benefit which will result from human beings loving one another, the product of a mutual affection which originates in the individual's love of self. The implications of this analysis for Henry's understanding of the relationship between the individual and the common good are considerable. They are spelled out in Henry's ninth quodlibet (Easter 1286) when he tackles the question head on—should the individual good be secured in preference to the common good?[30]

Henry's detailed response to this question turns on two fundamental distinctions—between a spiritual good and a temporal good (the former primarily concerning the soul, the latter primarily the body),[31] and between an individual good which is included in a common good and an individual good which is not. By shuffling these different goods in their various permutations, Henry comes up with nine separate conclusions (Fig. 6.1). Henry's first conclusion, for example, depends upon the premiss that the individual good is included in the common good. It is the most straightforward of the nine and, when set alongside the views of Aquinas and Giles of Rome, the most familiar. When a common good (spiritual or temporal) includes an individual good, Henry argues, then, all things being equal, the common good should be secured in preference to the individual good. The remaining eight conclusions, however, depend upon a premiss which both Aquinas and Giles of Rome had resolutely refused to countenance—what happens when the individual good is *not* included in the common good?

Henry's second and third conclusions, where common good and individual good are mutually exclusive temporal goods, follow simple quantitative rules. If an individual is greatly lacking in his individual good (if, for example, he has not eaten for three days whereas his neighbour has not eaten for one), then the individual good should be secured in preference. Reverse the quantities and it is the common good of the neighbour which should be secured. Henry's fourth conclusion, again for mutually exclusive temporal goods, envisages both individual and neighbour to be in moderate need (when, say, neither has eaten for two days) in which case the common good should again be preferred. The justification put forward for this conclusion, however, is more complex than for the first three. According to Henry, although the common temporal good does not include the individual temporal good (if it did, then the former should be preferred automatically), it does include an individual *spiritual* good, since the sacrifice performed by the individual is a meritorious act. Since an

[30] *Quod.* IX.19, pp. 293–5. Cf. Lagarde, 'La Philosophie sociale', 86–9; id., *La Naissance*, ii. 179–80.
[31] *principaliter* is a significant qualification. One category which straddles both corporeal and spiritual is moral virtue, a subject which, for the moment, Henry does not discuss. Cf. below, p. 170.

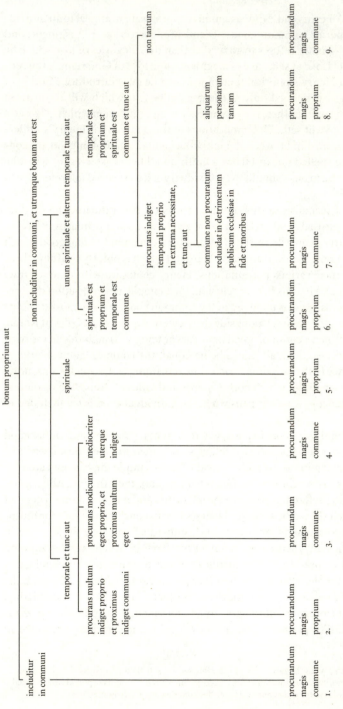

Fig. 6.1. *Quodlibeta aurea* (Venice, 1613), fo. 119r.

individual spiritual good must always be preferred, all things being equal, to an individual temporal good, it is by virtue of this additional consideration that the common temporal good should be secured rather than the individual temporal good. If, in other words, A includes C, then A is to be preferred to C; if A does not include C, then it may still be preferred to C *provided* that it includes B, where B is always preferred to C. The common temporal good 'includes' an individual spiritual good but this inclusion depends upon an act of preference, the choice of the common temporal good at the expense of the individual temporal good. The common temporal good is preferred because it includes the individual good and it includes the individual good because it has been preferred.

In Henry's fifth conclusion, common good and individual good, whilst still mutually exclusive, are spiritual goods. In this instance, it is the individual good which should be secured. Once the goods are spiritual, in other words, the quantitative analysis of temporal goods which has guided the second and third conclusions is reversed. A small quantity of spiritual good must now be secured by the individual, even if this is at the expense of a great quantity for one's neighbour, and even if one's neighbour is in extreme need. An individual should will a small amount of grace and eternal glory for himself rather than a large amount for his neighbour, even if this means willing that he alone will be saved and the rest of humanity damned. Even though some sort of qualification to this statement is implied by Henry's next, and sixth, conclusion (when the individual good is spiritual and the common good temporal, then the individual good should be secured *and much more so than if the common good is spiritual*), Henry offers no further comment. Indeed, his final three conclusions, in which the common good is spiritual, the individual good temporal, and both goods mutually exclusive, beg almost as many questions as they answer. In a sense, Henry's problem is unavoidable, since he has put himself in a position where he needs to bring together two scales of value which have hitherto been kept separate—quantitative measurement for temporal goods and qualitative measurement for spiritual goods. Henry starts, therefore, by making two further distinctions—between an individual temporal good which is in extreme need and an individual temporal good which is not, and between harm which is caused to the faith and customs of the church and harm which is caused only to a few individuals. In his seventh conclusion, he suggests accordingly that, if the individual temporal good is lacking to an extent that the individual is in extreme need (if, and this is Henry's own example, he must eat bread in order to avoid imminent death), but if a competing common spiritual good, when not secured, will cause harm to the faith and customs of the church, then it is the common spiritual good which should be secured even if it results in the death of the starving man. If the neglect of the common spiritual good harms only a few individuals, however, then (and this is Henry's eighth conclusion) it is the individual temporal good which should be secured. If, on the other hand, the individual temporal good has not reached such extreme necessity, if the starving man is not going to die, then (and this is his ninth conclusion) it is the common spiritual good which should be preferred.

It is difficult to give an entirely satisfactory account of what is, in many respects, a highly problematic quodlibetic question, not least because the arguments which Henry puts forward in support of his nine conclusions are so brief.[32] The form which his discussion takes appears to have been prompted partly by Augustine's *De Mendacio*, a text which had explicitly compared the relative value of the temporal or spiritual good of one individual with the temporal or spiritual good of another. Augustine too considers the specific example of an individual stealing bread or committing an evil act in order to secure the eternal salvation of his neighbour, although here Henry may also have owed something to canon law discussions of whether poverty could justify an act of theft if it was necessary in order to stay alive.[33] Several questions arise from Henry's discussion, however, which cry out for further discussion, particularly in his seventh and eighth conclusions where it is difficult to envisage the precise situation which Henry has in mind. In his eighth conclusion, extreme individual temporal necessity might be glossed as a situation in which an ecclesiastical community can give sacramental bread to a starving man. In his seventh conclusion, when the common spiritual good is defined as the faith of the church, the sacrifice of an individual temporal good might be glossed as the death of a martyr or an heretic. When it is defined as the 'customs and conduct' of the church, however, it is much harder to see what Henry is describing—should an individual sacrifice his life simply for the sake of *mores*? It remains a moot point, moreover, whether Henry is entirely consistent in distinguishing between the common spiritual good of the whole church and the common spiritual good of some of its members. Such a distinction sits rather uneasily alongside his second, third, and fourth conclusions, all of which assume that the common good can be personified by one's neighbour. It is only in the seventh and eighth conclusions that a common spiritual good is described as possessing greater or smaller quantities, and even then it is questionable whether the common spiritual good of a few individuals can be neglected without specifying the precise nature of this good. What is at stake is not, at least, the salvation of these individuals—this much is clear from the fifth conclusion. The assumption must therefore be that the spiritual good of which these individuals will be deprived is a lesser spiritual good, a sacrament for example. This might explain the harm done to the *mores* of the church but what does Henry envisage as causing harm to the *faith* of these individuals? In the event, the opposition of a common spiritual good to an individual temporal good provides the most interesting of Henry's permutations and yields, perhaps, his least satisfactory conclusions.

Henry closes his quodlibet by considering two arguments which neatly summarize the conflicting principles which he is attempting to resolve—the justification of

[32] Zuccolius comments (fo. 119r): *harum autem conclusionum solum quartam et quintam videtur auctor probare, cum coeterae notae videantur, nec mediis difficilibus probat eas, ut videre est. idcirco haec volumus satisfecisse.* Cf. Lagarde, 'La Philosophie sociale', 88: 'nous n'avons trouvé chez aucun des maîtres contemporains une analyse aussi précise et aussi fouillée'.

[33] Augustine, *De Mendacio*, ed. J. Zycha (*CSEL* 41), VI.9, pp. 425–7; XII.19, pp. 438–9. Cf. Cicero, *De Officiis*, ed. M. Winterbottom (Oxford, 1994), III.30–1, p. 120; Aquinas, *IIaIIae* 66.7; B. Tierney, *Medieval Poor Law* (Berkeley, 1959), ch. 2.

the superiority of the common good provided by book I of the *Ethics* (the common good should be preferred to the individual good because the common good is more divine) and the justification of the priority of good for the individual provided by book IX of the *Ethics* and by the *ordo caritatis* (the individual good should be preferred to the common good because an individual should love himself before his neighbour). Henry's response to the first of these arguments is to take issue with those theologians such as Albertus and Aquinas who had turned Aristotle's statement into a principle of universal applicability. It is, he insists, not *always* the case that the common good is more divine. In those instances, for example, where he has himself just argued that the individual good should be preferred to the common good (conclusions 2, 5, 6, and 8), the common good cannot be more divine, either in absolute terms (*divinius simpliciter*) or relative to the individual concerned (*divinius procuranti*). Likewise, in those instances where he has just argued that a more divine common good should be preferred (conclusions 1, 3, 4, 7, and 9), such preference should be shown only because the common good includes a 'more divine' individual good (in the sense that, through the act of preference, the common good 'includes' an individual spiritual good, a good which is itself 'more divine' than an individual temporal good). Henry is clearly set on removing the word 'always' from the way in which the comparative terminology of book I of the *Ethics* was being applied to the common good by his scholastic colleagues.[34] If there is anything which is *always* to be secured in preference, he maintains, then it is a more divine individual good which is not included in the common good. As was the case in his fifth conclusion, an individual's spiritual good should always be preferred to a common spiritual good in which it is not included.

Henry is determined to conclude that it is only when the common good includes the individual good that the common good is more divine than the individual good and should therefore be preferred to it; otherwise, it is the individual good which should be secured. Henry's concern is reflected in the fact that four of the eight conclusions which start from the precondition of non-inclusion end up by ceding preference to the individual good. Of the remainder, only one (conclusion 4) justifies the superiority of the common good by explicitly appealing to a principle of inclusion and arguing that, when an individual sacrifices his temporal good, the act of preferring the common temporal good of his neighbour amounts to securing his own individual spiritual good. If Henry is intending this to serve as a paradigm for his other three expressions of preference for a non-inclusive common good (conclusions 3, 7, and 9), then some extrapolation is required. Nevertheless, this does seem to be a reasonable step to take. All three cases can obey the general principle that the individual should always prefer the common good when it includes the individual good, and always prefer the individual good when it does not, with the exception of those

---

[34] The addition of *semper* to Aristotle's comparative terminology derives from Justinian, *Digest*, ed. T. Mommsen and P. Krüger, trans. A. Watson, *Codex Iustinianus* (4 vols.; Philadelphia, 1985), XVII.2.65.5, p. 509.

instances where the act of preferring a non-inclusive common good effectively changes it into an inclusive common good. Such an extrapolation is given added justification by the summary of the *ordo caritatis* with which Henry closes the whole argument. In those cases, he writes, where the common good is to be secured in preference to the individual good, the act of securing what is in common does not abrogate the principle that love originates with the self. Why? Because the common good would not be preferred unless it included the individual good. Henry's attachment to the principle of inclusion and to the primacy of the individual good is based, once again, on the priority of self-love within the *ordo caritatis*.

In 1288, two years after he made this theoretical examination of the relationship between the individual good and the common good, Henry was asked to consider the most important of its practical manifestations—should an individual who does not live in the hope of eternal life still choose, according to right reason, to sacrifice his life?[35] The evident precision with which this question was phrased demonstrates exactly where its target lay since, by inviting discussion of a rational justification for self-sacrifice once that of Christian *caritas* has been removed, it invited discussion of the cogency of the justification for self-sacrifice which Aristotle had offered in book IX of the *Ethics*. With this question, moreover, Henry also came up against the issue which his polarization of spiritual and temporal goods in his ninth quodlibet (together with his deft use of *principaliter*) enabled him to sidestep—what is the position of moral virtue?

Henry had originally dealt with the question of self-sacrifice in his very first quodlibet (1276) when he discussed whether an individual should choose to die rather than to live in suffering.[36] His response was to harmonize book IX of Aristotle's *Ethics* with book III of Augustine's *De Libero Arbitrio* by means of Augustine's distinction between natural and moral evil, between the suffering which occurs through experiencing evil (*miseria poenae*) and the suffering which occurs through doing evil (*miseria culpae*).[37] According to Henry, whereas a desire to avoid the evil of punishment is not a sufficient reason for preferring death to suffering, a desire to avoid the evil of sin certainly is. Making extensive use of Grosseteste's Greek commentators,[38] Henry accordingly argued that book IX of the *Ethics* should be taken to mean not only that the virtuous individual ought to prefer one final act of great virtue to continuing acts of lesser virtue (as Aristotle had maintained) but that, in so doing, such an individual is choosing, not death over life, but death over a life of sin and *miseria culpae*. What continued to trouble Henry, however, was that the statement in

---

[35] *Quod.* XII.13, pp. 67–79. Cf. Lagarde, 'La Philosophie sociale', 91–6; id., *La Naissance*, ii. 180–3.

[36] *Quod.* I.20, pp. 164–70.

[37] Augustine, *De Libero Arbitrio*, ed. W. M. Green (*CCSL* 29), III.6–8, pp. 285–9. Cf. Albertus Magnus, *Ethica* III.2.2, p. 237; Aquinas, *Ia* 48.5.

[38] H. P. F. Mercken (ed.), *The Greek Commentaries on the Nicomachean Ethics of Aristotle in the Latin Translation of Robert Grosseteste* (Corpus Latinum Commentariorum in Aristotelem Graecorum VI.1, 3; Leiden, 1973, 1991), i. pp. 291–3, ii. pp. 272–80. Cf. W. Stinissen (ed.), *Aristoteles over der vriendschap. Boeken VIII en IX van de Nicomachische Ethiek met de commentaren van Aspasius en Michaël in de Latijnse vertaling van Grosseteste* (Brussels, 1963), pp. 147–53.

book IX of the *Ethics* that 'the man who sacrifices his life chooses a greater good for himself' had been written by someone who did not believe in a future life. If this 'greater good' was to be understood as the considerable pleasure which the individual would immediately (and briefly) derive at the moment of his death (as Michael of Ephesus seemed to infer), then Henry professed himself baffled: *sed quomodo hoc, mirabile est dictu*. All Henry could suggest as a solution was that this 'greater good' consisted simply of choosing the lesser of two evils. To this end, Henry quoted the negative formulation of the principle of self-sacrifice which he found in book III of the *Ethics*—the brave man submits to death for the sake of some good *or for the sake of avoiding evil*.[39]

In 1288, some twelve years after delivering this response, Henry took another look at the difficulty presented by the individual who does not believe in a future life. *Quodlibet* XII.13 opens with a summary of the argument familiar from Aquinas. It is a principle of right reason that the common good should be preferred to the private good, the well-being of the *res publica* to the temporal life of the individual. Individuals in the community are like limbs of the body and, just as a limb ought to expose itself to danger for the sake of the body, so the individual ought to risk his life for the *res publica*. Quite clearly, this was a line of reasoning which Henry could not take at face value. His own concern to emphasize the principles of self-love and inclusion called, at the very least, for rather more weight to be given to the role of good for the individual.

Henry starts his examination of self-sacrifice by clarifying the implications of the phrase 'according to right reason'. If a solution is to be correct *secundum rectam rationem*, then it must be applicable to Christian and pagan alike. There can be no 'double truth'. What is true must be true for both theologians and philosophers. Henry establishes this common ground with a summary of the position which he had already put forward in his first quodlibet. A Christian ought to choose to sacrifice himself, not so much because he hopes to be rewarded with future life, but because he realizes that not to do so would be a sin and an offence against God. By the same token, although the virtuous pagan is not afraid to offend God or to risk an eternal punishment in which he does not believe, he does share the Christian's concern not to commit a sin. According to right reason, therefore, both pagan and Christian must always choose virtue and shun vice. Henry proceeds to clarify two other basic points. If an individual lays down his life for the community, he does so only when it is necessary and only when the well-being of the *res publica* cannot be secured by any other means; otherwise he will be guilty of rashness. Even when these conditions are met, however, even when the individual dies for the maintenance of the *salus rei publicae* and for the defence of justice and peace, he should not do so for the sake of his own honour and glory; otherwise, he will be guilty of greed and conceit. To be motivated by glory is only an approximation of bravery, the 'political' bravery which had been described in book III of the *Ethics*.[40] Henry carefully adds a Christian to a pagan authority in order

---

[39] Aristotle, *Ethics* III.7 1116ª11–12; III.8 1116ª28–9.   [40] Aristotle, *Ethics* III.8 1116ª17–29.

to prove the point. According to Augustine, the evils of death and suffering ought to be avoided, but, should they arise, they must be faced with equanimity when avoidance will be the cause of something worse.[41] The avoidance of sin, in short, not the pursuit of honour, is the intention which, in Henry's view, motivates an act of self-sacrifice. The brave man is able to shun the fear of death when he is surrounded by the greatest and most noble dangers—in battle according to Aristotle; for the sake of law, liberty, friends, and the well-being of his country according to the anonymous Greek commentator;[42] for the sake of the good, the goal of virtue, according to Henry.

Once Henry has ruled out the desire for personal glory and the fear of divine punishment, he is free to introduce the argument which had been set out in book IX of the *Ethics*. According to Aristotle, self-love benefits both the virtuous individual and his fellow-humans. For an individual to sacrifice wealth, power, honour, property, and even life itself, benefits others but also secures great nobility for the individual. Indeed, by preferring such moral worth to worldly goods, the individual effectively chooses the greater good, the greatest good, for himself.[43] Henry appends to his summary of this text another passage from book I—since the perfect and self-sufficient good is a matter, not for an individual living by himself, but for an individual living in the company of parents, children, wife, and fellow-citizens, it must be a principle of right reason to be prepared to die for one's friends and for one's country.[44] According to Aristotle, this perfect and self-sufficient good consists of exercising prudence in order to perform acts of moral virtue. For the sake of this good, therefore, it is better and more blessed to lay down one's life, to perform one great act of virtue in a brief moment, than to live a long life performing actions of lesser virtue. Henry's next questions go right to the heart of the issue which so engaged Albertus and Aquinas. Does an individual lay down his life because he secures a good for himself or a good for the community? If the individual secures both, is the good which he secures for himself greater than the good which he secures for the community?

In order to compare the individual good with the common good, Henry introduces a distinction between what is absolutely good or better in itself (*melius simpliciter*) and what is good or better for the individual (*melius ipsi*). His initial solution to the problem posed by book IX of the *Ethics* is therefore straightforward—to die for the community is better in itself, but it is also better for the individual. That an act of self-sacrifice should be *melius simpliciter* is not developed beyond the observation that it is good for many people (*quia pluribus*). That it should be *melius ipsi*, however, is justified (in a similar vein to Albertus) with an appeal to Aristotle's statement that 'every intellect chooses what is best for itself'.[45] Individuals who choose to sacrifice

[41] Augustine, *De Trinitate*, ed. Mountain (*CCSL* 50), XIII.7, p. 395.

[42] Mercken (ed.), *The Greek Commentaries*, ii. p. 278.

[43] Aristotle, *Ethics* IX.8 1169^{a}11–1169^{b}2 (above, pp. 50–1).

[44] Aristotle, *Ethics* I.7 1097^{b}8–11. It is worth noting that Henry chooses to omit the last phrase of this sentence: 'since humankind is, by nature, a social being'.

[45] See above, p. 51. Cf. Mercken (ed.), *The Greek Commentaries*, ii. p. 277; Stinissen (ed.), *Aristoteles over der vriendschap*, p. 151.

their lives, therefore, must be securing a great good (*magnum bonum*) for themselves. Nor is it just a great good. Henry is also content to echo Aristotle's belief that an individual ought to choose to die for the community because he thereby chooses a greater good (*magis bonum*).

Having concluded that it is right for an individual to sacrifice himself for the sake of the community because he will thereby secure the greater good of virtue, Henry spends the remainder of the quodlibet considering whether this applies only when it is a question of political happiness or whether it can be extended to cover contemplative happiness as well. Although Henry concedes that Aristotle himself never applied the distinction between these two types of *felicitas* to the question of self-sacrifice, he clearly considers it important to speculate what Aristotle might have concluded had he done so. Henry's reasoning is revealing. If the obligation to sacrifice one's life is also incumbent upon the individual who is engaged in contemplation, is this because such an action is good for him (*bonum ipsi*) or because it is good in itself (*bonum simpliciter*)? If the contemplative individual lays down his life because it is good in itself, will he still do so even when it is not good for himself, when the two goods are mutually exclusive? In response, Henry immediately rules out the possibility that the contemplative will sacrifice himself knowing that it is not a good for himself except in the sense of being a political good. This cannot be correct, Henry argues, because it would be wrong for anyone to prefer an inferior good to a superior good. The happiness of contemplative virtue is superior to the happiness of political virtue and, as such, should not be sacrificed on behalf of the latter, however great it is. If the contemplative is to sacrifice himself, therefore, it cannot be out of consideration for his own good. Henry is accordingly left with two alternatives. Either Aristotle must have thought that the contemplative is not, in fact, obliged to sacrifice himself because his own good consists in remaining alive, or he must have thought that the contemplative is under this obligation because it is both good in itself and good for himself but good for himself in a different sense than it is for an individual who is actively involved in a political community.

Henry professes a disarming ignorance as to which of these two alternatives represents Aristotle's own opinion. Of one thing, however, he is certain. Aristotle's notion of contemplative happiness is suspect. For the moment, he tries not to rest his argument on such a blunt observation. Of more pressing concern is the argument that, if the contemplative does lay down his life, he will not secure good for himself. If this argument were to be accepted, then it would clearly contradict the principle which Henry himself laid down in his ninth quodlibet, namely that the common good should be preferred only when it includes the individual good. Henry accordingly picks up on the suggestion which was made in the second of his alternative solutions—self-sacrifice is a good for the contemplative but in a different sense than it is good for the political individual. The contemplative ought to sacrifice himself, therefore, not because he acquires good (in this respect he suffers loss), but because he avoids evil. Self-sacrifice is thus good for the contemplative, not in a positive, but in a negative sense. Henry then returns to the point which he has taken such pains to clarify at the beginning of the quodlibet—virtue should be defined as the avoidance of sin—and proceeds to apply it to the political individual as well as the contemplative. The citizen, he writes, should lay down his life because it is an absolute good and because it is a good for himself; it is a good for himself, however, not in the sense of acquiring a good, but in the sense of avoiding doing wrong.

Henry is clearly trying to establish the principle that the act of self-sacrifice secures good for both the contemplative and the political individual. Having just proved that it cannot be good to sacrifice contemplative virtue for the sake of political virtue, even when the latter is as great a good as moral worth, Henry has to find some way of avoiding the suggestion that the contemplative should still lay down his life even though it is not a good for himself. As a result, he is forced to conclude that the good which the contemplative does secure, if not a positive good, is at least a negative good, namely the avoidance of evil. Because Henry is seeking a solution for both the political and the contemplative life, he is also forced to conclude that the same principle must then apply to the political individual—he too must sacrifice himself even when he acquires no positive good, no political virtue. This is a statement, however, which he finds hard to reconcile with the text of book IX of the *Ethics* and with his own exposition of the 'greater good' of virtue.

In book IX of the *Ethics*, the political individual who lays down his life secures the good of a noble and virtuous action. In order for there to be a precise correspondence with the contemplative individual, however, Henry has to suggest that this good can be absent provided that a more significant benefit is present, namely the avoidance of evil. Henry still seeks support for this position from Aristotle but he has to take it from book III of the *Ethics* rather than book IX: 'The more a man possesses all virtue and the more happy he is, the more pain death will cause him. For such a man, life is worth most, and he stands to lose the greatest goods, and knows that this is so, and this must be painful. But he is nonetheless courageous on that account; perhaps, indeed, he is more so because he prefers what is noble in war to all of these.'[46] When Henry quotes this text, however, he slips in his own comment that this would still be the case even if nothing good were to befall the brave man. He admits that this is only hinted at by Aristotle (*quod innuit*), but he does find one sentence which supports this negative conception of the good: 'the mark of the brave man . . . was to endure things that are terrible to a human being . . . because it is noble to do so *and base not to do so*'.[47] Henry has noticeably fewer difficulties in this regard when he turns for support from Cicero. Indeed, strengthened by a string of Ciceronian quotations, as well as by his own assertion that the truth of right reason is consistent, Henry concludes that Aristotle *must* have thought the same. Both the courageous citizen and the wise contemplative should sacrifice their lives for the community, even if they acquire no good for themselves in the process. When Henry returns to book IX

---

[46] Aristotle, *Ethics* III.9 1117^{b}9–15.

[47] Aristotle, *Ethics* III.9 1117^{b}7–9. Cf. Albertus Magnus, *Ethica* III.2.6, pp. 242–4; Henry of Ghent, *Quod.* I.20, pp. 168–9.

of the *Ethics*, therefore, he not only ignores the explicit reference to a greater good (*magis bonum*) but allows himself the liberty of making an improvement. By preferring one great, good action to many lesser ones, runs the text, those who die choose a great good for themselves. Perhaps, Henry suggests, Aristotle should have added 'because, even if this great good did not happen to them, they would still choose, according to right reason, to die in this fashion'.

Henry completes the quodlibet by tying up his remarks on the principle of inclusion. Having accepted the second of the proffered alternatives for Aristotle's view of contemplative happiness, he has to find a way of dismissing the first. The reason is clear. If it is in the contemplative's own interest to remain alive, then, according to the principle set down in *Quodlibet* IX.19, it would be legitimate for him to prefer his individual good only if it is not included within the common good. Two counter-propositions are therefore put forward. The contemplative individual, runs the first, is not obliged to sacrifice himself because, living, as he does, apart from the community and in the quasi-divine state described by Aristotle, his individual good is not included within the common good. The public good should be preferred to the private good only when the private good is included within it, and although it can still be preferred in an absolute sense, it should not be preferred from the point of view of the excluded private good.[48] Moreover, runs the second, the logical extension of this principle must be that the terminology of body and member, whole and part, simply cannot be applied to the contemplative individual because, unlike a contemplative, a limb does not possess its own intellect, motive force, nor a private good which is separate from the good of the whole.

Henry's response to these arguments is to repeat his reservations over Aristotle's view of contemplative happiness but with none of his earlier restraint. Aristotle, he writes, was correct on a number of matters concerning human action and, as such, he can certainly be considered to be in harmony with the Christian faith. Like other pagan philosophers, however, there are several key respects in which he was mistaken. The identification of the goal of human life as the life of virtue, as a purely temporal beatitude, provides a case in point. Henry cannot believe that Aristotle intended to suggest that the contemplative individual lives a life which is completely separate from the human community, since this would be a flat contradiction of natural law. The only other option, therefore, is that Aristotle was working on the assumption that contemplative happiness is not subject to the sinful state, a possibility which, from a Christian perspective, is unthinkable for anyone other than the saints in paradise. Henry accordingly returns to the disparity between fallen nature and redeeming grace which had proved so central to his own earlier comparison of Aristotle's community of goods with those of Plato and Augustine. In Henry's view, the human community is unable to demonstrate sufficient *caritas* to counteract the effects of original sin. Henry's own interpretation of human society, therefore, remains firmly grounded in Augustine's *remedium peccati*—wherever there is sin,

---

[48] Henry never deals with the second half of this argument.

there is a need for political authority.[49] Humans have a natural obligation to society
for their bad as well as their good actions, and it is in these terms that they have a
natural obligation to risk their lives on its behalf. The contemplative's positive individual good—the life of virtue—may not be 'included' in the public good but his
negative good—the avoidance of evil and sin—certainly is. This limited degree of
inclusion is sufficient, in Henry's eyes, for his original argument to stand.

In *Quodlibet* XII.13, as in *Quodlibet* IX.19, Henry goes to great lengths to retain the
precondition of inclusion, the principle that the common good should be preferred
to the individual good *only* if the individual good is in some sense included within it.
If the contemplative's private good is not included in the public good, even in a
negative sense, then Henry is quite prepared to concede that there is no situation in
which the contemplative would be obliged to sacrifice his life for the community.
Non-inclusion, however, can only mean that the contemplative is a saint in paradise,
since only the absence of sin can free the individual from his indebtedness to political authority, from his dependence on society as a *debitor rei publicae*. A life of contemplation can therefore never be completely separate from human society and, as a
result, every individual is, in some way, included within the political community.[50]

Having imposed such tight restrictions on the nature of the inclusion which characterizes the contemplative's membership of the political community, Henry turns
to the applicability of the imagery of body and limb, whole and part. His analysis of
the corporeal analogy in this context is as precise as it is guarded. To pick up the
suggestion made by the second counter-proposition and refuse any degree of 'self-
motivation' to the individual member would naturally have laid Henry's argument
open to the inference that the citizen is completely subordinate to the community
and to its head.[51] Henry is therefore careful to concede that each individual limb does
have its own intellect. At the same time, he also insists that these individual intellects
within the body ought to be united when judgement on a particular action needs to
be made according to right reason.[52] For Henry, however, the real significance of the
corporeal analogy is its capacity to be pressed into service as an illustration of his own
concept of positive and negative inclusion. Thus, on his reading, the private, positive
good of the individual limb might not be included in the public good of the whole
body but the limb itself is, albeit in a negative way (*quasi negativum*). Likewise, a private, positive good might not be included within the common good but it is still
dependent upon it (*dependet ab illo*). Were the contemplative to refuse to sacrifice
himself, then the sin which he would thereby incur would cause him to lose the private good which he was originally attempting to secure.

Armed with this principle, Henry sees off one final challenge to his account of
the limited participation of the contemplative in human society. Suppose that the

---

[49] Cf. Albertus Magnus, *Super Ethica* VIII.11, p. 635; Giles of Rome, *De Regimine Principum* I.i.4;
II.i.1–3; III.i.1–5.

[50] Cf. *Quod.* X.17, p. 282.

[51] Compare John of Naples, *Quaestiones Disputatae*, ed. D. Gravina (Naples, 1618), VIII, pp. 72–3.

[52] *Quod.* XII.13, p. 77.

contemplative is not part of the political community, is not comparable to the limb of a body, and is not under an obligation to sacrifice himself for the community. What if he ignores this freedom and goes ahead with the act of self-sacrifice? In this case, the contemplative would clearly lose every good, material as well as moral, and would gain nothing in return, not even the benefit of having avoided evil. Surely, therefore, such an individual ought not to die for the community, just as (as Henry himself had argued in his ninth quodlibet) no individual, righteous or unrighteous, ought to choose his own eternal damnation in order that everyone else may be saved. Henry's reply is emphatic: *sed non est ita*. The presupposition of non-inclusion on which such an argument would depend is fundamentally mistaken. In however small a way, the contemplative is still in need of something from the community and therefore always has a natural obligation towards it. Even if the contemplative is not a part of the community when it comes to performing the many political actions which are demanded by household, family, and friends, he is still a part of the community when it comes to the actions which are necessary for the conservation of the *salus rei publicae*. Whether this participation results in his own death or simply in the abandonment of his philosophical speculation in order to take part in government, the fact of his inclusion entails duty and obligation.

Throughout the course of *Quodlibet* XII.13, Henry is determined to maintain the precondition of the inclusion of the individual good within the common good. The connection with his argument in *Quodlibet* IX.19 is clear. The most significant parallel is provided by the notions of indirect inclusion and dependence. In Henry's ninth quodlibet, an individual secures a non-inclusive, common temporal good in preference to his individual temporal good, but, by means of this act of preference, he secures for himself his individual spiritual good. In Henry's twelfth quodlibet, the argument has the same circularity. The individual prefers to die because his good is included, and his own good is included because he prefers to die; the contemplative is included in the community because he is obliged to risk his life, and he is obliged to risk his life because he is included in the community.

Quodlibet XII.13 is at its weakest when it tackles the precise nature of the contemplative's participation in the community, a point which, to judge from the frequency with which the issue is raised, Henry himself may have realized. By the same token, this is also where *Quodlibet* XII.13 is at its most revealing. As an exposition of book IX of the *Ethics*, Henry's notion of 'negative' participation ultimately rests on two categories which are outside Aristotle's immediate frame of reference, namely natural law and the presence of sin. The case study of the contemplative certainly causes Henry to modify his earlier conception of the individual good, of 'good for oneself'. The move from positive good to negative inclusion and dependence is not simply a shift of focus caused by the move from an active member of the political community to the more solitary contemplative. In considering the latter, Henry applies negative inclusion to the political individual as well and, in so doing, presents his argument with difficulties which are never really resolved. The conclusion which he wants to avoid putting forward is that, by laying down his life, the contemplative actually acquires a good for himself, since this would be tantamount to arguing that an individual should prefer the lesser good of political virtue to the higher good of contemplation. By concluding, instead, that, by laying down his life, the contemplative simply succeeds in not committing an evil act, the burden of proof is thrown onto the contemplative's inclusion in the political sphere, a burden which Henry's argument struggles to sustain within Aristotle's own terms of reference. When the political individual chooses to sacrifice himself, he certainly avoids the evil of failing to lay down his life, but, by dint of his positive inclusion in the community, he must also acquire a good for himself in the form of political virtue. In order to find a definition of individual good which can serve as a common denominator for both the active and contemplative lives, therefore, Henry loses sight of the fact that, for the political individual, the acquisition of virtue and the avoidance of evil are inseparable.

Quodlibet XII.13 represents Henry's practical application of the theoretical principles laid down in *Quodlibet* IX.19. As a detailed analysis of the circumstances in which the common good should be preferred to the individual good, and as a painstaking exposition of self-sacrifice in book IX of the *Ethics*, these quodlibets represent two sides of the same argument. For all Henry's difficulties with the notion of indirect or negative inclusion, his underlying intention is clear—to maintain the presence of good for the individual in any action which secures the common good. If the question of self-sacrifice presents this principle of inclusion with a challenge which it is only partially successful in meeting, then this is, in itself, a very revealing perspective from which to assess Henry's political thought. His final conclusion—that self-sacrifice is, at root, a question of avoiding evil—strongly suggests that, in Henry's eyes, the fundamental characteristic of the political community is the presence of sin. Coupled with his blunt dismissal of Aristotle's conception of happiness, Henry's emphasis on the avoidance of evil represents a concerted attempt to juxtapose Aristotle's life of virtue with Augustine's *remedium peccati*.

Rather than represent a synthesis of 'Aristotelian' social morality and 'Christian' individualism, Henry's attitude to the common good of the political community represents a synthesis of Aristotelian self-love and an Augustinian *ordo caritatis*. Henry does not express a principle of love for the common good which goes beyond the categories of love of self, love of neighbour, and love of God. Natural love can certainly produce common benefits (*communes utilitates*) but the act of self-sacrifice is ultimately motivated by self-love, by an individual's concern for his own good. If Henry reveals a reluctance to appeal to the metaphysical principle of superiority which proved so attractive to Aquinas and Giles of Rome in other words, then this was due to his commitment to the more traditional terms of reference which had been established by Augustine's account of the operation of love and the effects of sin within the human community.

7

Henry of Ghent—Authority,
Obedience, and Resistance

Henry of Ghent's analysis of the relationship between the individual and the common good differs in at least one significant respect from the theories put forward by Albertus Magnus, Thomas Aquinas, and Giles of Rome. Rather than seek a metaphysical explanation for the principle of the superiority of the common good in human society, Henry spends most of his time demonstrating the importance of good for the individual. This difference in emphasis is indicative of a fundamental difference in approach. Self-love, inclusion, and dependence may not, in themselves, have been novel considerations to introduce into the debate. Nevertheless, by choosing to highlight these notions at the expense of any principle of love for a superior common good, Henry avoids the need to posit any correlation between goodness in the political community and goodness in the universe. Henry's emphasis on the presence of good for the individual should certainly still be seen as a contribution to the scholastic interpretation of Aristotle—stressing the importance of the 'greater good' for the self in book IX of the *Ethics* and minimizing the impact of the 'more perfect' common good in book I. However, it should also be seen as part of a wider debt to Augustine—defining the categories of the *ordo caritatis*, pointing up the shortcomings of a non-Christian conception of happiness, and realizing the limits of natural human perfectibility in a fallen world.

If Henry's abstract treatment of individual and community is short on references to the priority of the common good when it is compared to the theories of other scholastic theologians, then it also provides a contrast with the frequency with which a notion of the common good appears in his own discussion of more practical questions. Henry was thoroughly conversant, for example, with the idea that *utilitas* should define the exercise of authority on behalf of those subject to it—a prelate is instituted for the sake of *utilitas aliorum* and a temporal ruler for the sake of *communis utilitas*.[1] This is a general principle for which Henry provides a number of specific illustrations. In 1290, for example, he sets up *communis utilitas* as the criterion by which all demands for taxation should be judged—in order to be legitimate, they must secure the common benefit.[2] After the fall of Acre in 1291, *utilitas ecclesiae* is the criterion which he uses to justify the flight of a bishop from a city under siege—if the

---

[1] e.g. *Quod*. XII.28, p. 168, quoting Augustine, *De Civitate Dei*, ed. B. Dombart and A. Kalb (*CCSL* 48), XIX.19, p. 686.

[2] *Quod*. XIV.8 fo. 352r–v; see below, pp. 193–7.

community so threatened can still be ministered to, and if the bishop in question is saving himself for the greater benefit of the church, then flight is permissible provided that the benefit caused by the future exercise of his office will be greater than the harm caused by his bad example.[3]

A willingness to deploy the common good in practical rather than theoretical contexts is, in itself, a very suggestive conclusion to draw for Henry's moral and political philosophy, particularly if it is interpreted as a preference for the term *utilitas* rather than *bonum*, because *utilitas* is the benefit which results from the virtuous actions of individuals. However, it also points to the more concrete historical circumstances in which these ideas were actually put forward. Henry's interest in the practical applications of the common good was given a cutting edge in the 1280s by a further outbreak of controversy between secular masters and friars at the university of Paris. Unlike earlier phases of the dispute, this fresh conflict had been triggered by events well beyond the faculty of theology—in this instance, the privileges which had been granted to the friars by Pope Martin IV in December 1281 in *Ad fructus uberes*. The implications of this bull and, more importantly, of its interpretation by the friars themselves, aroused bitter hostility from significant elements within the French clergy. At stake, it was argued, was nothing less than the authority of bishops and clergy to minister to their flocks.[4] Henry himself drew livings from Bruges and Tournai, a background which made him a natural ally of this opposition, and his firm and vociferous support can be traced throughout his quodlibets.[5]

The ramifications of the controversy over *Ad fructus uberes* for Henry's use of the common good were considerable. Disputes between secular masters and mendicant friars had always involved discussion of the standard which should be used to compare the relative worth of the active and the contemplative lives. The issuing of *Ad fructus uberes*, however, also introduced questions of more immediate significance for the government of the church. First, it focused attention on the criteria which were necessary in order to legitimate a pope's exercise of his dispensing power. Second, it invited consideration of the precise point at which the obligation to obey an ecclesiastical superior became a justification to resist him. Henry's discussion of the

---

[3] *Quod.* XV.16 fo. 397v. Cf. *Quod.* XII.29, p. 238, where prelates are placed under a particular obligation to lay down their lives for others. For a discussion, see G. de Lagarde, 'La Philosophie sociale d'Henri de Gand et Godefroid de Fontaines', *AHDLMA* 14 (1943–5), 121–2; id., *La Naissance de l'esprit laïque au déclin du moyen âge*, 3rd edn. (5 vols.; Louvain, 1956–70), ii. 198.

[4] P. Gratien, 'Ordres mendiants et clergé séculier à la fin du XIIIe siècle', *Études Franciscaines*, 36 (1924), 499–518; A. G. Little, 'Measures taken by the Prelates of France against the Friars', *Studi e Testi*, 39 (1924), 49–66; P. Glorieux, 'Prélats français contre religieux mendiants: Autour de la bulle *Ad fructus uberes* 1281–90', *Revue d'Histoire de l'Église de France*, 11 (1925), 309–31, 471–95; G. Post, 'A Petition Relating to the Bull *Ad fructus uberes* and the Opposition of the French Secular Clergy in 1282', *Speculum*, 11 (1936), 231–7; K. Schleyer, *Anfänge des Gallicanismus im 13. Jahrhundert: Der Widerstand des französischen Klerus gegen die Privilegierung der Bettelorden* (Berlin, 1937); Y. M. J. Congar, 'Aspects ecclésiologiques de la querelle entre mendiants et séculiers dans la seconde moitié du XIIIe siècle et le début du XIVe', *AHDLMA* 28 (1961), 35–151; Henry of Ghent, *Quodlibet XII.31: Tractatus super Facto Praelatorum et Fratrum*, ed. L. Hödl and M. Haverals (*Opera Omnia* XVII), pp. v–cxvii.

[5] *Quod.* VII.22–7; *Quod.* X.1–4; *Quod.* XI.22–7. Cf. *Quod.* I.27–32.

relative merits of the active and contemplative lives, the exercise of papal dispensation, and the limits to obedience and resistance, all made extensive use of a notion of the common good. Moreover, his conclusions had repercussions which went much further than ecclesiology. Transferred to the most pressing temporal political question of the 1280s—the increasing levels of taxation which were being demanded by the kings of France—they established a notion of the common good which could be used to control the exercise of power by *all* government, temporal as well as ecclesiastical. Henry of Ghent may not have been as fervent as some other scholastic theologians in advocating the metaphysical significance of the common good but his application of the common good to particular ecclesiastical and political questions appears to have made him a much more radical scholastic political theorist.

Like Albertus and Aquinas, Henry of Ghent believes that the active and the contemplative lives can each be regarded as superior to the other depending on the criteria by which they are measured and that one such criterion is the benefit which they bring to other people. Unlike Albertus and Aquinas, however, and in a way which was, perhaps, only appropriate for a canon, archdeacon, and secular master, Henry uses this definition of the common good to defend an unqualified preference for the active life. He does so by distinguishing between two types of perfection—'acquisitive' and 'exercitative'—of which the first (*status perfectionis acquirendae*) is characteristic of the eremitical life and the second (*status perfectionis exercendae*) of pastoral care. Although these two conditions are not mutually exclusive, Henry concludes that the life of exercitative perfection (defined as mutual assistance, comfort, and leading by example) should be preferred to the solitary life of acquisitive perfection.[6]

According to Henry, perfection can be defined as the realization of something in its totality (*integritas rei consummata*) and, as such, it comprises two elements, wholeness and completion. This principle applies to material entities (a body is whole when it lacks none of its limbs, but it is whole in both a man and a boy; it is only fully realized or 'perfect' in a man) but also to immaterial or spiritual subjects. Thus, a doctor is perfect when he possesses the whole of medical knowledge such that no one else can know it better. Viewed in terms of acquisitive perfection, the doctor secures this complete knowledge in order to become a perfect doctor in himself (*in seipso*). To be in a condition of exercitative perfection, however, he must already be a perfect doctor practising this perfect knowledge upon others (*circa alios*). Acquisitive perfection, Henry concludes, has the purpose of increasing goodness in oneself, whereas exercitative perfection has the purpose of disseminating it to others. Henry supports this principle with a string of authorities—the apostle Paul, Augustine, Gregory the Great, Bernard of Clairvaux, and, finally, Aristotle. According to the *Ethics*, he writes, the virtue of justice is ordered towards another human being and should therefore be preferred to all the other moral virtues which are ordered towards

---

[6] *Quod.* II.14, pp. 82–95.

oneself; justice contains every virtue, or rather every perfect virtue, since virtue is perfect when it is directed, not towards oneself, but towards another person.[7]

In 1282, it was this distinction between two types of perfection which Henry used to determine whether it is 'more perfect' to renounce the material necessities of life than to possess them as personal property or as goods held in common. Individual goods and goods which are held in common, he argues, do not, in themselves, detract from either acquisitive or exercitative perfection, since, insofar as they are parts of Creation, they are all inherently good. Nevertheless, they can still detract from a human's spiritual good because of the effects of original sin on human love. The risk of this happening *does* depend on which type of perfection is being discussed. Exercitative perfection demands an individual who is already perfect (*iam perfectus*) and, for such a person, material goods held in common simply serve as the instruments of his virtuous actions on behalf of the church. It is quite a different matter for individuals whose actions are not ordered towards such a public ministry—goods held in common detract from acquisitive perfection in a way in which they do not detract from exercitative perfection.[8]

Henry spelled out the ecclesiological implications of this conclusion in 1288 when he connected the question of the superiority of the active life over the contemplative with the question of the superiority of the prelate over the religious.[9] Although the form of his argument amounts to a commentary on *Nisi cum pridem* (the text from canon law which was frequently at the centre of polemical exchanges between secular and mendicant masters),[10] its substance depends on a much wider analysis of the common good. Henry starts by accepting the standard distinction between normative and positive solutions to the question. If the contemplative and the active lives are compared according to their intrinsic goodness, he states, then the contemplative life is essentially better. Conversely, if they are compared according to the benefit which they bring to other people, then it is the active life which is preferable because it is beneficial to a greater number (*quia pluribus utilis est*). Henry's reasoning directly parallels his discussion of self-sacrifice in *Quodlibet* XII.13—although a prelate should strive to lead both a contemplative and an active life, he must be prepared to provide for the needs of the church because saintly individuals frequently have to exercise authority for the benefit of many (*pro utilitate multorum*).[11] However, even though Henry uses this notion of common benefit (*communis utilitas*) to elevate the position of the prelate, he characteristically avoids any reference to love for the

---

[7] *Quod.* VII.28, pp. 246–53. Cf. *Quod.* XI.27 fo. 231v. For the medical analogy, see Aristotle, *Metaphysics*, ed. G. Vuillemin-Diem (*Aristoteles Latinus* XXV.3.1–2), V.16 1021ᵇ14–17, p. 105; Averroes, *Aristotelis Metaphysicorum Libri XIV cum Averrois Cordubensis in eosdem commentariis* (editio Iuntina, 2nd edn., 11 vols.; Venice, 1562–74), viii fo. 130v. Cf. Aristotle, *Politics* III.11 1281ᵇ40–1282ᵃ4; Peter of Auvergne, *In Politicorum Continuatio*, ed. R. Busa, in *S. Thomae Aquinatis Opera Omnia*, vol. vii (Stuttgart–Bad Cannstatt, 1980), III.9.6, 414–15.

[8] *Quod.* VII.28, pp. 243–72; VII.29, pp. 278–309; VII.30, pp. 310–12. Cf. *Quod.* V.30 fo. 312v.

[9] *Quod.* XII.28, pp. 164–88; XII.29, pp. 188–249. Cf. *Quod.* XIII.14, pp. 140–85.

[10] For *Nisi cum pridem*, see *Decr. Greg. IX* I.9.10 (Friedberg, ii. 107–12). Cf. above p. 107 n. 23.

[11] *Quod.* XII.28, p. 184; Gregory the Great, *Moralia in Iob*, ed. M. Adriaen (*CCSL* 143), XII.52, p. 664.

common good. Indeed, when Henry compares the love which prelates and religious have for God, he confines himself to the argument that the prelate is superior to the religious because God is loved not just in Himself but also in one's neighbour.[12] Moreover, whereas Henry appears to regard common benefit (*communis utilitas*) and the good which is done to other people (*utilitas aliorum*) as interchangeable terms, his choice of *utilitas* is, in both cases, quite deliberate. Thus, even when the good towards which the more perfect position of prelate is ordered is defined in explicitly Aristotelian terms—as a final cause for more things (*potior finis*), as a good which is greater than the private good and, for that reason (*ideo*), more divine—this goal is still termed 'the common benefit'. Not only does Henry choose *communis utilitas* rather than *bonum commune* but he carefully glosses the comparative terminology of book I of the *Ethics* with a distinctly quantitative interpretation. The common benefit is more divine, he argues, because it is greater (*maius*) in the sense that it represents good which is done to more people (*quia pluribus*).[13]

If Henry is prepared to use the common good to support the superiority of prelates over religious, then he also demonstrates his continuing concern for the presence of good for the individual. In his first quodlibet (1276), Henry considers (appropriately enough for his first year as regent master) the relative merits of an individual continuing his studies or securing the salvation of souls. In the course of this discussion, he repeatedly argues that each individual should secure the greatest benefits for himself as well as for others.[14] In his twelfth quodlibet, he applies this conclusion to all those individuals who exercise authority within the church. According to Henry, two conditions must be met before the active life becomes better and more perfect for the prelate himself—the prelate must be compelled to accept his position by God or by his fellow-humans, and he must himself be superior in virtue. Both stipulations derive from Gregory the Great but the second carries the additional authority of Aristotle—the prelate must be already perfect (*iam perfectus*) because he is a public person capable of making other people perfect, and something is perfect when it can produce something similar to itself.[15]

Henry's insistence that the individual who leads the active life for the benefit of others is already perfect in virtue may well have been a response to the concerns which Aquinas had expressed on precisely this score.[16] It certainly reinforces his own stipulation that exercitative perfection requires an individual to be perfect in goodness *before* he becomes the source of goodness for others. However, it also supports his much broader commitment to the principle that the individual good must be included within the common good. In the context of the dispute over *Ad fructus*

---

[12] *Quod.* VII.28, pp. 244–6.

[13] *Quod.* XII.29, pp. 203–4. This is the nearest Henry comes to defining *divinius*; he later contrasts *publicum* and *privatum* as *maius* and *minus* (ibid. p. 238).

[14] *Quod.* I.35, pp. 195–202.

[15] Cf. *Quod.* VII.29, p. 278; Gregory the Great, *Homiliae in Hiezechihelem Prophetam*, ed. M. Adriaen (*CCSL* 142), I.2.4, pp. 170–1. Compare *Quod.* XII.29, pp. 227–8; Gregory the Great, *Regula Pastoralis* I.10–11 (*PL* 77, cols. 23–6).

[16] See above, pp. 107–9.

uberes, in other words, the personal perfection of prelates and the good which prelates secure for the church represent the practical application of Henry's theoretical analysis of good for an individual and the beneficial results which the virtuous actions of an individual will have on the rest of the community.

The controversy over *Ad fructus uberes* revived old disagreements between friars and secular clergy over the relationship between the active and contemplative lives. It also stimulated new debates on a series of more specific issues. The legitimacy of Pope Martin IV's actions in 1281, for example, were subjected to detailed scrutiny. If it was to be the case that individuals no longer had to repeat to their priests confessions which they had already made to a friar, it seemed only reasonable to ask whether the pope was thereby sanctioning a departure from the provisions laid down by the Fourth Lateran Council in *Omnis utriusque sexus*.[17] Henry of Ghent dealt with the general issue of dispensation well before the promulgation of *Ad fructus uberes* when he considered whether it was permissible for an individual to hold several benefices at once.[18] Dispensation from the letter of the law, he concluded, is permissible on two counts—evident necessity and common benefit. To prove the point, he cited a potent combination of canon law, Aristotle, and Bernard of Clairvaux. According to canon law, dispensation is justified by 'observed necessity and benefit' (Innocent III) or by 'evident necessity and benefit' (Honorius III).[19] According to book V of the *Ethics*, dispensation is an act of distributive justice and an exercise of equity. According to Bernard of Clairvaux, dispensation must be prompted by necessity and common benefit; if it is prompted by private benefit, then it is simply an act of crude dissipation.[20] Bernard himself had supported dispensation for pluralism if it met a great need in the church or if it secured a personal benefit. Henry repeated his own endorsement but pointed out that this 'personal benefit' must still be common to the church.[21]

By the time Henry was delivering his fifth quodlibet (Christmas 1280/Easter 1281), just prior to *Ad fructus uberes*, he clearly felt it opportune to issue a warning against the abuse of ecclesiastical power to alter, or dispense from, what is essential to the sacraments. Although Henry did not pick out any one sacrament in particular, the implications for confession were clear. The church may have the power to intervene freely in all positive law, Henry writes, but it cannot employ this power if the result will be contrary to divine or natural law.[22] In Christmas 1282, therefore, immediately after the promulgation of *Ad fructus uberes*, Henry showed little hesitation in

---

[17] For the text of *Ad fructus uberes*, see *CUP* no. 508 (i. 592–3) and, for *Omnis utriusque sexus*, see ed. N. P. Tanner, in *Decrees of the Ecumenical Councils* (2 vols.; London, 1990), i. 245.

[18] *Quod*. II.17, pp. 111–36; *Quod*. II.18, pp. 136–43.

[19] *Quod*. II.17, pp. 125–6; *Decr. Greg. IX* II.27.19 (Friedberg, ii. 403), III.5.33 (ibid., ii. 479).

[20] Bernard of Clairvaux, *De Consideratione ad Eugenium Papam*, ed. J. Leclercq and H. Rochais, *S. Bernardi Opera*, vol. iii (Rome, 1963), III.4, p. 445.

[21] Bernard of Clairvaux, *Epistolae*, ed. J. Leclercq and H. Rochais, *S. Bernardi Opera*, vol. viii (Rome, 1977), 271, p. 181. It was not clear from canon law whether private benefit was sufficient cause for dispensation to be made (J. Brys, *De dispensatione in iure canonico, praesertim apud decretistas et decretalistas usque ad medium saeculum decimum quartum*, Bruges, 1925, p. 258).

[22] *Quod*. V.36 fo. 319r–v. Cf. *Quod*. II.16, p. 102.

applying his earlier account of dispensation to the pope's recent action.[23] Once again, he appeals to a combination of Aristotle and Bernard of Clairvaux (although he is now careful to add two of the friars' own authorities, Bonaventure and Aquinas),[24] and, once again, the point which he emphasizes is that any privilege conceded by the pope should not favour the friars as such but the Christian people as a whole. If circumstances arise, he observes, when the well-being of the church (*salus ecclesiae*) depends on an individual confessing the same sins on two, or even more, occasions, then the act of confession must be reiterated. The power to receive confession has been granted to the friars in order to assist parish priests and to benefit the people who are making the confession (*ad utilitatem populi confitentis*). It has been granted for the good and advantage of others and not for the individual good and spiritual advantage of the friars themselves. In this respect, confession is like preaching. A pastor does not choose either of these ministries primarily for the sake of his own individual good or advantage, but undertakes them of necessity and for the good and advantage of others (*propter bonum et commodum aliorum*); only then will they rebound to his own good and the spiritual advantage. In Henry's opinion, therefore, *Ad fructus uberes* needs to be interpreted in such a way that it not only preserves the original stipulations of *Omnis utriusque sexus* but also greatly benefits the *res publica* and the *bonum commune*. It should guarantee the obedience and reverence which is owed to prelates and should ensure that the confession of all sins takes place irrespective of whether they have already been confessed to another individual. *Omnis utriusque sexus*, Henry argues, was instituted for the general and perpetual benefit of all people, and should not be infringed for private advantage. It may not belong to the category of law which should never be subjected to any alteration, and there may indeed be circumstances in which the pope can dispense from its provisions according to the needs of the moment.[25] However, Henry insists that what has been instituted for the common benefit ought not to be removed for private advantage. The implication of his next statement would not have been missed. It is not an easy matter, he observes, to produce public advantage by releasing individuals from the obligation to confess to their priests.[26]

The opposition of French bishops to *Ad fructus uberes* increased significantly in 1285 and 1286 after the firm lead given by Simon of Beaulieu, archbishop of Bourges, and after the return, empty-handed, of an embassy to Honorius IV. In December 1286, four archbishops and twenty-four bishops met in Paris to discuss the issue, and, in the same month, Henry used his tenth quodlibet to justify the measures which they took.[27] In April 1287, Honorius IV died (like Martin IV) without leaving a definitive interpretation of his own opinion on the matter. In February 1288, however, he was succeeded by Nicholas IV, a Franciscan friar who immediately set about

---

[23] *Quod.* VII.23, pp. 147–66; VII.24, pp. 167–232. Cf. *Quod.* XII.31, pp. 3–19, 46, 253, 258.

[24] *Quod.* VII.24, pp. 202–3, 231. Cf. *Quod.* XII.31, pp. 20–1.

[25] Cf. *Decretum* II.25.1.3 (Friedberg, i. 1007).   [26] *Quod.* VII.24, pp. 209–12, 218–20.

[27] *Quod.* X.1–4, pp. 3–55. Cf. Glorieux, 'Prélats français contre religieux mendiants', 471–8; Schleyer, *Anfänge des Gallicanismus*, 141–50; *Quodlibet XII.31*, ed. Hödl and Haverals, pp. lvii–lxix.

confirming that *Ad fructus uberes* did indeed exempt the mendicant orders from epis-copal jurisdiction. It was against this background, in December 1288, that Henry returned to the issue of dispensation. Originally delivered as a disputed question, Henry appears, on this occasion, to have reworked his arguments into a treatise which may even have been taken to the papal court by Simon of Beaulieu.[28]

Henry opens his treatise on *Ad fructus uberes* by repeating the distinction between two kinds of statute or privilege—one which directly contradicts divine or natural law and one which, in itself, does not contradict divine or natural law but which can have this effect in certain circumstances. The net effect of both types of statute is the same, namely the wholesale destruction of ecclesiastical order and the withdrawal of due reverence and obedience. It is the second type, however, with which Henry is principally concerned.[29] Henry clearly does not want to suggest (as Simon of Beaulieu did) that the pope would be directly contradicting a precept of divine law if he were to rule in favour of the friars and abolish the need for an individual to confess all his sins to a parish priest. What he does want to prove, however, is that this would be the indirect result given the particular circumstances of the church. Henry bases his argument on a distinction between the 'absolute' and the 'ordered' power of the pope. According to canon law, *potestas absoluta* was an extraordinary power which could be exercised either justly or unjustly, whereas *potestas ordinata* was an ordinary power which could be exercised only in accordance with justice.[30] Henry accepts that there can be no practical distinction between these powers when the authority exer-cising them is God. Because God cannot sin, He can do nothing by His absolute power which He does not do by His ordered power. For humankind, however, it is different. Because humans can sin, they are able to do something from their absolute power which they cannot do from their ordered power. Whilst absolute power is pos-sessed by both God and humans, therefore, only humans have the capacity to abuse it. According to Henry, Bernard of Clairvaux had been drawing precisely this dis-tinction when he argued that, in a particular instance, the pope is capable of acting from his plenitude of power even when he does not possess the additional power of

[28] *Quod.* XII.31 fos. 283r–289r; J. Marrone, 'The Absolute and Ordained Powers of the Pope: An Unedited Text of Henry of Ghent', *Mediaeval Studies*, 36 (1974), 7–27; R. Macken, 'Ein wichtiges Ined-itum zum Kampf über das Beichtprivileg der Bettelorden, der *Tractatus super facto praelatorum et fratrum* des Heinrich von Gent', *Franziskanische Studien*, 60 (1978), 306–7; *Quodlibet XII.31*, ed. Hödl and Haverals, pp. 3–268.

[29] Compare *Quod.* VII.24, pp. 167–232, where Henry had been careful to distance himself from this line of argument. Cf. Post, 'A Petition', p. 235: *ne ordo ecclesiasticus perturbetur.*

[30] Henry's use of this distinction in this context is not as clear as it might be. Cf. *Quod.* XIV.8 fo. 352v (see below, p. 196). Marrone ('The Absolute and Ordained Powers of the Pope') appears to regard *potes-tas absoluta* as a power which is essentially unjust. Cf. *Quod.* VI.10, pp. 87–127; Remigio dei Girolami, *Contra Falsos Ecclesie Professores*, ed. F. Tamburini (Rome, 1981), 37, pp. 78–9; L. Buisson, *Potestas und Caritas: Die päpstliche Gewalt in Spätmittelalter* (Cologne, 1958), 88–9; M. J. Wilks, *The Problem of Sover-eignty in the Later Middle Ages: The Papal Monarchy with Augustinus Triumphus and the Publicists* (Cam-bridge, 1963), 294–5, 319, 349. For the wider theological context, see E. Grant, 'The Condemnation of 1277: God's Absolute Power and Physical Thought in the Late Middle Ages', *Viator*, 10 (1979), 211–44; L. Moonan, *Divine Power: The Medieval Power Distinction up to its Adoption by Albert, Bonaventure and Aquinas* (Oxford, 1994).

justice.[31] As far as Henry is concerned, *Ad fructus uberes* provides a similar example. The pope can legitimately use his absolute power to grant such a privilege but this will have good or bad effects depending on the circumstances. In itself (*per se*), it may not harm the church, but, in certain circumstances (*per accidens*), it can. Such circumstances include a changing historical context in the sense that something which was suitable for the early church, when priests were few in number, may no longer be suitable for an age in which love has grown cold and iniquity is rampant (Matthew 24: 12).

On the strength of this analysis, Nicholas IV is asked by Henry to mull over a number of questions. If the pope can grant a privilege to the friars with an absolute power which is in accordance with justice (such that it would then be indistinguishable from an ordered power), but does so and finds that it is not in accordance with justice, should he not fear the application of the standard deposition texts from canon law?[32] If the particular abuse of papal plenitude of power to which Bernard of Clairvaux had been objecting was Eugenius III's grants of exemption to specific individuals, how much more strongly would Bernard now be objecting to the universal exemption from *Omnis utriusque sexus* which was being sought by all the friars? Henry underlines the two criteria which Bernard had insisted must be present in order for a grant of dispensation to be legitimate—necessity and benefit. He also repeats his own gloss on how this benefit should be defined—*utilitas* is not the personal advantage of the pope, nor of the person to whom the dispensation is granted, but the common benefit (*communis utilitas*). In granting the sort of exemption represented by *Ad fructus uberes*, Henry concludes, the pope should not be furthering the individual good of the friars but the public good of the whole Christian people. All that is left for Henry to do is to elaborate upon the threat of deposition. He does so in a very deliberate conditional clause. If, he suggests, it should turn out that the pope were to grant the privilege which the friars are pretending they already have, then the pope must be made the object of humble supplication from every bishop and prelate in order to persuade him to revoke it. Learned men (*viri litterati*) should then explain to the pope the consequences of any refusal to comply with these requests—a rapid descent into schism and disobedience which could only be avoided if the church were to find an alternative arrangement and quickly; in other words, a new pope. Far from being a delicate balancing act, Henry's argument leaves no doubt as to where his sympathies lie. The critical point which he wishes to communicate (and all the more forcefully if Simon of Beaulieu was actually circulating the text in Rome) is the very real threat that Nicholas IV could be deposed.

In the short term, Henry's stand met with spectacular failure. In November 1290, Benedict Gaetani, one of two cardinal legates sent to Paris to sort out the controversy,

---

[31] For a discussion of Bernard's views, see J. W. Gray, 'The Problem of Papal Power in the Ecclesiology of St. Bernard', *TRHS* 24 (1974), 1–17, and, for the way in which they were subsequently invoked by both advocates and opponents of papal *plenitudo postestatis*, J. Rivière, *Le Problème de l'église et de l'état au temps de Philippe le Bel* (Louvain–Paris, 1926), 405–23.

[32] Cf. *Decretum* I.40.6 (Friedberg, i. 146).

announced, in no uncertain terms, that the friars' interpretation of *Ad fructus uberes* would be upheld.[33] Henry immediately protested and the legate, sufficiently familiar with Henry's treatise to quote from it directly, promptly suspended him from teaching. Showing that he too could appeal to the *status universalis ecclesiae* and that he too could act in the name of obedience and what is universally beneficial, Benedict Gaetani then prohibited everyone else from further discussion of the question either in public or in private.[34] In the longer term, Henry's treatise had a more lasting significance. *Quodlibet* XII.31 contains his most pointed comments on the limits of obedience to a statute which does not further the *communis utilitas* and on the right to depose a ruler who refuses to revoke such a decree even after he has been corrected. The force of this argument owes much to Henry's reading of Bernard of Clairvaux and canon law as well as to his understanding of the *status ecclesiae* as a criterion which should govern every exercise of the pope's dispensing power. To this extent, Henry's justification of disobedience was not without precedent. Pope Innocent IV, no less, had already sanctioned such a possibility when the only alternative was violent disturbance.[35] Henry's reaction to *Ad fructus uberes*, however, also relied on broader developments within his own political thought.

Henry of Ghent's analysis of obedience and resistance, like that of Aquinas, originated in his examination of specifically religious communities. It was in this context, for example, in his first quodlibet (1276), that Henry justified resisting the decree of a superior when it is countermanded by the *ordo caritatis*.[36] Likewise, in his third quodlibet (Easter 1278), when he analysed the nature and purpose of all subjection to authority as part of a discussion on whether a religious rule in which complete obedience is sworn on all matters is more perfect than a rule in which it is sworn only for certain commands.[37] According to Henry, the subjection of one human being to another is justified insofar as the superior is able to rule the subject better than the subject is able to rule himself. The intended result of obedience, therefore, is for the subject to derive greater benefit, and be able to serve God better and more perfectly, than if he were left to his own devices. Subjection exists on no other account than God, and for no other reason than that it should be of benefit to the subject. Henry draws a loose parallel (*quodammodo*) with Aristotle's observation that it is beneficial to the slave to be ruled by his master. To argue otherwise, Henry exclaims, to suggest that an individual who is more capable of ruling himself correctly should subject himself to an individual who is less capable of doing so, is sheer stupidity (*hoc fatuitatis est*). Such a situation should simply never arise in a religious community since,

---

[33] Glorieux, 'Prélats français contre religieux mendiants', 491–4.

[34] H. Finke, *Aus den Tagen Bonifaz VIII: Funde und Forschungen* (Münster, 1902), III–VII.

[35] B. Tierney, 'Grosseteste and the Theory of Papal Sovereignty', *Journal of Ecclesiastical History*, 6 (1955), 14–15. However, it was also Innocent IV who insisted that a papal command must be obeyed even if it was unjust (Buisson, *Potestas und Caritas*, 262 n. 134).

[36] *Quod.* I.33, pp. 191–3. Cf. Bernard of Clairvaux, *De Praecepto et Dispensatione*, ed. J. Leclercq and H. Rochais, in *S. Bernardi Opera*, vol. iii (Rome, 1963), V–XII, pp. 261–74; ed. P. Glorieux, *Les Premières Polémiques thomistes I: Le Correctorium Corruptorii 'Quare'* (Paris, 1927), 264–7.

[37] *Quod.* III.20 fos. 127v–128r.

in Henry's opinion at least, it is a reasonable assumption that there will always be a more capable person (*peritior*) in authority within the church.

It was in his eighth quodlibet (Christmas 1284) that Henry began to confront the possibility that harmony between ruler and subject could sometimes break down. Once again, the question concerns a specifically religious community—if an individual is intending to perform a greater good, should he sacrifice it in order to perform a lesser good which has been commanded by his superior?[38] If obedience originates in love, and love prescribes that a greater good should always be preferred to a lesser good, then surely obedience cannot extend to a contradiction of the very principle by which it has been instituted? Henry opens his response by citing the standard scholastic justification for disobedience. If it is certain that a superior's command runs contrary to God, then it must be utterly rejected since a general vow of obedience can apply only to what is permissible, just, and honourable.[39] This is a justification, however, which cannot be employed if it is only *doubtful* whether the command in question is contrary to God. If the superior's command subsequently turns out to have been a good command, Henry explains, then there is every reason why the subject should have obeyed it in the first place. If the command subsequently turns out to have been iniquitous, then, because the subject has remained true to the good of obedience (*bonum obedientiae*), it is not the subject who has sinned but the superior. As a general rule, therefore, Henry suggests that the subject must assume that his superior has a reasonable cause for issuing a command and, in the case of competing goods, must rest content in the knowledge that the *bonum obedientiae* which he does secure will compensate for any greater good which he may have forfeited in the process. Where there is doubt, in short, obedience is the rule. Indeed, according to Henry, because obedience is better than all the other virtues,[40] virtuous actions which are performed as acts of disobedience can become vices as a result. Thus, when the subject has vowed to do what is good, permissible, and expedient, but subsequently decides, in good conscience and after reasonable deliberation, that breaking his oath will result in a greater good, it is still better and more fruitful for him to fulfil the terms of his vow because to break it would be to risk committing a mortal sin.

Henry concludes his argument by considering the apparent opposition of obedience and the *ordo caritatis* with which the quodlibet had started. For a subject to perform the lesser good, he insists, never runs counter to love, even though it may do (*forte*) for his superior. Although love prescribes that a greater good should, in absolute terms, be preferred to a lesser good, this principle operates only when an individual has both options open to him. Since a subject has only one option open to him (because he is bound by his oath of obedience), there is no contradiction in maintaining that love can also prescribe that greater preference should be given to a lesser good which is commanded by a superior at the expense of a greater good which is

---

[38] *Quod.* VIII.16 fo. 39r–v.   [39] *Decretum* II.11.3.92, 11.3.101 (Friedberg, i. 669, 671–2).
[40] Cf. pseudo-Augustine, *Sermo de Obedientia et Humilitate*, ed. D. G. Morin, in *S. Hieronymi Presbyteri Opera* II (*CCSL* 78), 552.

intended by the subject. In such circumstances, it is not only permissible but necessary for the subject to obey his superior because, even if he does not see it himself, he
must presume that his superior has commanded an action which is better for him. By
presupposing the good character of a superior, in other words, the subject must perform what he is commanded to do *as if* it were a greater good (*tamquam magis bonum*).

Given that Henry was delivering this quodlibet in 1284, three years after the issuing of *Ad fructus uberes*, it would appear that his immediate reaction to the controversy did not precipitate a radical review of his ideas on obedience and resistance. It
was only in 1288, when Nicholas IV's actions had finally removed the element of
doubt, that Henry was forced to reconsider his account of the good of obedience.
Even then, it is not a move which he makes lightly. It is the spectre of disobedience
which Henry conjures up as the inevitable result of a papal endorsement of the friars'
interpretation of *Ad fructus uberes*. In Henry's opinion, if the laity is allowed to choose
its confessors without reasonable cause, or without the consent of a priest or superior, then this will cause considerable harm both to individuals and to the *res publica*,
because the removal of obedience and reverence will ultimately affect, not just parish
priests and bishops, but also the king.[41] Nevertheless, by December 1288, Henry felt
obliged to put forward a position whereby the illegitimate exercise of dispensation,
the failure to secure common benefit for the church, can warrant disobedience to,
and ultimately deposition of, the pope.

If Henry's remarks on resistance in his treatise on *Ad fructus uberes* reflect more
general developments in his political thinking, then the consequences were not limited
to his views on the exercise of papal authority within the church. A deepening
awareness of the limits of obedience can also be traced in Henry's observations on the
relationship of ecclesiastical and temporal rulers to the property of their subjects. It
was generally recognized that, at a time of emergency or evident necessity (typically
the defence of the kingdom), a temporal ruler could impose extraordinary taxes on
private property.[42] New taxes were forbidden in Roman law, for example, unless they
were necessary for the common benefit.[43] Beaumanoir accordingly believed that the
French king was justified in demanding new taxes provided that they secured the
'commun pourfit' of his kingdom.[44] A similar restriction controlled the imposition of
new taxes in the church. The Third Lateran Council of 1179 allowed bishops to burden their subjects only in cases of necessity and only for a manifest and reasonable
cause and, even then, these demands had to be made in a spirit of love and for a

[41] *Quod*. X.4, p. 51.
[42] G. Post, *Studies in Medieval Legal Thought* (Princeton, 1964), esp. ch. 10; J. R. Strayer, 'Defense of
the Realm and Royal Power in France', in id., *Medieval Statecraft and the Perspectives of History* (Princeton, 1971), ch. 18; E. A. R. Brown, 'Taxation and Morality in the Thirteenth and Fourteenth Centuries:
Conscience and Political Power and the Kings of France', *French Historical Studies*, 8 (1973), 1–28, esp.
1–8; G. Spiegel, 'Defence of the Realm: The Evolution of a Capetian Propaganda Slogan', *Journal of
Medieval History*, 3 (1977), 115–33.
[43] *Codex Iustinianus*, ed. P. Krüger (Berlin, 1877), IV.62.1, p. 390.
[44] Philippe de Beaumanoir, *Coutumes de Beauvaisis*, ed. A. Salmon (2 vols.; Paris, 1899–1900), no. 1510,
ii. p. 261.

moderate amount of money.[45] The same criteria guided the decrees of the Fourth Lateran Council in 1215—whilst they expressly forbade the laity to impose taxation on the church, they conceded that such payment might be made when a bishop and his clergy perceived the need to be so great as to be incapable of being met by the laity on its own, an eventuality which enabled such a payment to be classified, not as taxation, but as aid for the common benefit.[46] It was this statute, however, which was then used by a series of thirteenth-century popes to justify the granting of clerical tenths to temporal powers who supported their 'political crusades'.[47] Not unnaturally, the right to tax on the grounds of 'common benefit' became an issue which tested both the patience and the obedience of the clergy. It is a concern which is all too evident in Henry of Ghent.

Henry first dealt with the subject of taxation in his sixth quodlibet (Christmas 1281/Easter 1282) when he was asked to consider whether the pope can grant to an individual the tenths which have been taken from the goods of laymen, and whether the pope can, if necessary, compel laymen to pay these exactions if they have been demanded for the sake of the *utilitas ecclesiae*.[48] Henry's initial response is to appeal to a model of divine government—just as Christ's kingship governs both the spiritual and the temporal spheres, so the pope's authority covers both ecclesiastical and temporal powers, ordering everything in Creation towards God. Henry then runs through the standard canon law texts for the exercise of papal plenitude of power—wherever there is a sin of commission, a sin of omission, a vacancy, or simply something difficult and ambiguous, the pope has the authority to intervene in the temporal sphere. However, although Henry concludes that the pope can judge a temporal ruler, even to the point of deposing him and setting up another ruler in his place,[49] he is far from being an apologist for unlimited papal power. Thus, when he quotes Aristotle's suggestion that the head of a household should commit his affairs to a steward in order to concentrate on the higher activities of the civic or philosophical life, Henry infers that, although the church may possess superior jurisdiction over temporal matters in theory, the exercise of this right in practice is not always beneficial. Indeed, according to Henry, the exercise of temporal jurisdiction by the church has, in the past, proved detrimental. Henry's final response, therefore, is

---

[45] *Decr. Greg. IX* III.39.6 (Friedberg, ii. 623). It was this decree which was subsequently cited in the glosses of Azo and Accursius (Brown, 'Taxation and Morality', 3–4).

[46] *Decr. Greg. IX* III.49.4, 7 (Friedberg, ii. 654–5); *Decrees of the Ecumenical Councils*, ed. Tanner, i. p. 255. Cf. the anonymous gloss on *Clericis laicos*, ed. R. Scholz, in *Die Publizistik zur Zeit Philipps des Schönen und Bonifaz' VIII* (Stuttgart, 1903), p. 484.

[47] N. Housley, *The Italian Crusades: The Papal–Angevin Alliance and the Crusades against Christian Lay Powers, 1254–1343* (Oxford, 1982), esp. ch. 6. For the French church in particular, see C. Fasolt, *Council and Hierarchy: The Political Thought of William Durant the Younger* (Cambridge, 1991), 56. For the original Saladin tithe of 1188, see J. W. Baldwin, *The Government of Philip Augustus* (Berkeley, 1986), 52–4; W. L. Warren, *Henry II* (London, 1973), 607–8. Cf. William of Tyre, *A History of the Deeds Done Beyond the Sea*, trans. E. A. Babcock and A. C. Krey (New York, 1943), II, p. 487.

[48] *Quod.* VI.23, pp. 210–22. Cf. Lagarde, 'La Philosophie sociale', 123–6; id., *La Naissance*, 200–1.

[49] *Decr. Greg. IX* IV.17.13 (Friedberg, ii. 714–16), II.1.13 (ibid., ii. 242–4), II.2.10 (ibid., ii. 250–1).

rather more measured than his initial reply might have suggested. If the church is threatened by such dire necessity that its well-being requires the provision of temporal goods, then it is sinful for anyone not to give this assistance. The pope can accordingly grant to an individual the power to receive and extract tenths if it is for the defence and maintenance of the church.[50] If the necessity is not imminent, however, then the pope should not seek such payments from the laity, or even from the clergy (although, in this case, the degree of necessity required is much smaller, since the clergy have fewer proprietorial rights over their goods).

Having recognized that the pope can justify the exaction (and allocation) of tenths on the grounds of necessity (*necessitas*), well-being (*salus*), and benefit (*utilitas*), Henry acknowledges that the temporal ruler can do the same. Thus, when he discusses a ruler's right to exercise his legal powers of prescription and usucaption, he argues that exception may be made from the letter of the law (in this case, from the requirements of just cause and good faith) if it furthers the goal of human law (*bonum et pax rei publicae*) or avoids its polar opposite (*detrimentum et disturbatio rei publicae*).[51] Henry does insist, however, that the benefit must be self-evident. It must be clear (*evidens*), even very clear (*evidentissima*), and it must be impossible to obtain by any other means. Temporal rulers, after all, do not own the goods of their subjects unless their subjects are slaves. Instead, they should be considered as guardians who receive an appropriate degree of maintenance in return for their rule. People, he points out, do not institute a ruler in order to subject themselves or their property to servitude. It is only if the need arises that every individual is under an obligation to make their contribution *in usum publicum* and it is only then that the temporal ruler can turn his subjects' property over to the *res publica* of which they form a part.[52]

By the time Henry was delivering his ninth quodlibet (Easter 1286), the issue of clerical taxation was causing considerable political concern. In September 1283, Pope Martin IV had granted Philip III of France a three-year tenth in order to finance the king's campaign against Aragon. In May 1284, the pope had extended both the duration of this tenth (from three to four years) and its scope (to include the diocese of Liège). In 1286, therefore, when Henry considered the obligation which was incumbent upon laity and clergy to pay exactions to cities or to temporal lords,[53] he was well aware of what was at stake. Henry had already argued that a temporal ruler could not lay hands on ecclesiastical goods even if his aim was to stop the church from badly dispensing the goods it had received from wills.[54] In 1286, therefore, he was careful to preface his remarks with the observation that the clergy are under no

[50] Cf. *Quod.* IX.26, p. 308: *necessitas facit commune quod erat proprium*; *Quod.* VII.29, p. 288.

[51] *Quod.* VIII.22 fos. 44r–45v. Cf. *Decr. Greg. IX* II.26.5 (Friedberg, ii. 383); Lagarde, 'La Philosophie sociale', 108; id., *La Naissance*, 188.

[52] *Quod.* VIII.22 fo. 45v. Cf. Lagarde, 'La Philosophie sociale', 111.

[53] *Quod.* IX.31, pp. 327–30. Cf. *Decretum* II.11.1.27–8 (Friedberg, i. 634), II.12.68 (ibid. i.709), II.15.1.40 (ibid., i.772–3); *Decr. Greg. IX* III.1.16 (ibid., ii.453–4); Lagarde, 'La Philosophie sociale', 126–7; id., *La Naissance*, 194–5.

[54] *Quod.* VI.28, pp. 253–5. The one exception is those goods which have originally been given by the king and over which he has retained a measure of *dominium*. Cf. Lagarde, 'La Philosophie sociale', 127–8.

obligation to pay exactions when they are required for the sake of a specifically temporal benefit (*communis utilitas laicorum*). Nevertheless, Henry clearly believes that,
when a temporal ruler is expending his resources on behalf of the church, the obligation to pay is as binding on the clergy as it is on the laity. Henry immediately adds
the reservation from the decrees of the Fourth Lateran Council that such payments
should be made at the request of bishops and not of the laity. Nevertheless, if the
bishop is unable to compel his clergy to pay, and if the necessity is so pressing that it
frees the individual from the normal restraints of law, then, in these circumstances,
temporal rulers may indeed lay their hands on ecclesiastical goods. Henry's definition of 'necessity' has a very wide frame of reference—it includes defence of the faith
but also defence of the kingdom or community. Fighting against the enemies of the
church is given an equally wide scope—it includes fighting against opponents of
the faith but also against opponents of justice, whether this justice is being exercised
by a particular king or a particular community. On this occasion, Henry does not
choose to specify that these emergency powers can be invoked only for *clear* necessity
or *clear* benefit. Four years later, however, these stipulations assumed paramount
importance when he was asked to consider whether a subject is obliged to obey
a superior's decrees even when it is not clear that they secure the *communis utilitas*.[55]

Henry's fourteenth quodlibet (Christmas 1290) brought into conflict the two
notions of obedience which had hitherto been kept separate in all his discussions of
ecclesiastical and political authority. On the one hand, there is the obedience which
is owed to any superior (*bonum obedientiae*), the good which can compensate for the
loss of whatever good might be gained from an act of disobedience. On the other
hand, there is the obedience which is conditional upon the superior securing the
good for which the act of subjection originally took place—the good of religious
observance or, in this case, the *communis utilitas*. It is with a more precise definition
of this common good, therefore, that Henry begins his response. According to
Henry, the goal of all superiors—rulers as well as prelates—ought to be to secure the
peace and well-being of the *res publica*. This should also be the goal of every one of the
superior's subjects insofar as (*inquantum*) they are parts of the community. Both ruler
and subject must pursue this goal because it constitutes the ruler's good and the good
of everyone in the community. Their individual goods and their every action must
accordingly be ordered towards it as circumstances require (*cum opus fuerit*).

The consequences of this elevation of the common good are far-reaching. Individuals who are bound to pursue a goal, Henry argues, are also bound to pursue those
things which are necessary in order to secure it. This is the function of the superior,
or ruler, when he arranges everything according to his 'architectonic' knowledge. It
is also the function of the subject when he obeys his superior's statutes. This obligation of obedience, moreover, remains binding even if it is not clear to these subjects
that a particular statute is, in fact, necessary to secure the common good. This is the

---

[55] *Quod.* XIV.8 fos. 352r–353r. Cf. Lagarde, 'La Philosophie sociale', 113–15; id., *La Naissance*, 192–3.

argument which Henry has already sketched out in his eighth quodlibet—when there is doubt, the goodness of the ruler must be taken on trust. On this occasion, however, he spells out just why this trust should exist. The ruler, he explains, is defined by his clear superiority in virtue over everyone else in the community. As a result, there is a sense (*quodammodo*) in which the good of the whole community resides in him. The good of the ruler is accordingly the good of each individual in the community, and it is from this good that each person ought to derive his own good. The ruler is beneficial to everyone in the community because he is the source of profit, lordship, and stewardship (*vel profectus vel dominatio vel procuratio*).[56] Subjects are, in turn, beneficial to the ruler but this does not produce the same sort of good as the good which a superior performs for his subjects nor the good which a free person performs for others. In fact, this second type of benefit borders on the servile (*paene servitus*). Henry does not explain this rather surprising term[57] but the underlying point remains. The obedience which subjects owe to a statute whose contribution to the *communis utilitas* they are unable to perceive must ultimately be founded on their trust in the wisdom and goodness of their ruler and (in their first and last appearance in this quodlibet) the ruler's counsellors.

Up to this point in the argument, Henry's conclusions have mirrored his earlier recommendation to members of a religious community to give the benefit of the doubt to any of their superior's commands which are unclear. However, Henry now sees fit to introduce a series of significant qualifications. Henry has previously argued that disobedience can be justified only when a command is evidently contrary either to God or to divine law or to natural law. He now adds 'or to the common good' to this list of exceptions. The precondition of *clear* evidence remains, but it is now deftly reversed. Obedience ceases to be obligatory when it can be established that a statute fails to further the public benefit and particularly when this can be proved to have been the case with a large number of similar statutes which have hitherto been obeyed. In such an eventuality, the ruler's subjects must follow the procedure with which Henry had already threatened a recalcitrant pope—supplication in order to obtain the revocation of the offending statute, or, having failed to secure such consent, action in order to secure the ruler's deposition. Henry does insist that bad statutes should be obeyed for as long as the superior is still tolerated in office. Even if the ruler refuses to revoke the offending statute, it is only when there is no hope of

---

[56] That such an argument is not always beneficial to the subjects is made clear when Henry considers the interdict imposed on a community for a crime which has been committed by its head (*Quod.* XIV.9 fo. 353r). Cf. Lagarde, 'La Philosophie sociale', 112.

[57] In *Quodlibet* III.20, Henry defines slavery as a subjection which is for the subject's own good. In *Quodlibet* VIII.22, however, he explicitly differentiates slavery from subjection to a temporal ruler, since slavery places an individual's property entirely at the disposal of a superior. It is this second definition of slavery which Henry now appears to have in mind—the slave is an instrument of his master. Cf. *Quod.* IX.6, p. 144. The shift from one definition to the other is mirrored by Aristotle's equivocation between common interest (*Politics* I.2 1252ᵃ34, I.6 1255ᵇ9–13) and instrumentality (*Politics* I.4 1253ᵇ23–1254ᵃ17). For a comprehensive discussion, see C. Flüeler, *Rezeption und Interpretation der Aristotelischen Politica im späten Mittelalter* (2 vols.; Amsterdam, 1992).

future correction that action should be taken. This remains as important a consideration for Henry's discussion of deposition as it was for Aquinas' discussion of private denunciation.[58] Obedience remains an obligation so long as the superior remains a superior—rather than tolerate a superior but disobey his statutes, subjects should first release themselves from their obligation to obey him by removing the offending superior from authority. Nevertheless, a ruler who does not further the common good can ultimately be deposed. Elsewhere, Henry was certainly capable of invoking the notion of a greater evil which might result from such an act of resistance.[59] He does not do so here.

Henry then begins to question his earlier presupposition that a ruler must be superior in wisdom and virtue by dint of his position. In the case of hereditary kingship, he points out, this depends on the further assumption that superiority of character can be transmitted by birth. Henry had already conceded, in his discussion of the perfect prelate (*iam perfectus*), that such people are, in reality, all too few in number in the church.[60] In his sermon for the feast day of St Catherine (1282), he extended the observation to cover temporal rulers as well.[61] Henry now makes the same point for hereditary rulers by appealing to book I of the *Politics*—it may be Nature's intention to achieve the transmission of good character but she is unable to realize it.[62] Scholastic commentators frequently used Aristotle's treatment of whether it is better to be ruled by a good man or by good laws as the basis for a discussion of the relative merits of elective and hereditary office.[63] For Henry of Ghent, it is an opportunity to cast doubt on the presumption of virtue in a superior. Once Henry recognizes that it might not be possible to trust a ruler's pre-eminence in virtue, once he accepts that a superior might not be *iam perfectus*, he immediately begins to question the extent of a subject's obligation of obedience to a bad ruler. According to Henry, the considerations which apply to a bad ruler are essentially the same as those which apply to a good ruler who issues a bad statute. For as long as a bad ruler is tolerated, he has the power to make statutes and he is owed the obedience of his subjects provided that his statutes are not evidently contrary to virtue. However, since it cannot be presumed that a bad ruler's statutes will, in fact, comprise actions of virtue, Henry considers it preferable (*potius*) to set about deposing him. Disobedience is certainly justified by clear evidence of a statute being bad but a bad ruler forfeits the benefit of the doubt as well. The assumption that his statutes will lack virtue is, in itself, sufficient for a process of deposition to be set in train. Henry's emphasis on tolerance

---

[58] See above, pp. 109–10.   [59] *Quod.* VII.23, p. 153; *Quod.* XIV.17 fo. 364r. Cf. above, p. 126.

[60] *Quod.* VII.30, p. 311.

[61] E. Hocedez, *Richard de Middleton, sa vie, ses oeuvres, sa doctrine* (Louvain–Paris, 1925), p. 516.

[62] Aristotle, *Politics* I.6 1255^{b}1–4. Cf. Henry of Ghent, *Quod.* IX.18, p. 291.

[63] For a general survey, see T. Renna, 'Aristotle and the French Monarchy 1260–1303', *Viator*, 9 (1978), 309–24. Cf. Giles of Rome, *De Regimine Principum* III.ii.20, III.ii.29 (see above, p. 139 n. 38); Peter of Auvergne, *Quaestiones super libros Politicos*, ed. Flüeler, in *Rezeption und Interpretation der Aristotelischen Politica*, III.22 (i. pp. 216–19); id., *In Continuatio Politicorum*, ed. R. Busa, in *S. Thomae Aquinatis Opera Omnia* (Stuttgart–Bad Cannstatt, 1980), III.15 (vii. pp. 420–1); James of Viterbo, *Quodlibet*, ed. E. Ypma (Würzburg, 1975), IV.30, pp. 107–10.

strikes a note of genuine caution, but no more so than in his treatise on *Ad fructus uberes*. In both instances, disobedience does not immediately follow the issuing of a bad statute—for as long as the ruler is in office, he must be obeyed as a superior; it is the failure to correct a bad statute once it has been identified which justifies his deposition. Caution is also evident in Henry's assumption that a good ruler must be superior in virtue because of his position. For a good ruler to be deposed, a statute must therefore be proved to be clearly contrary to the common good. For a bad ruler, however, the presupposition of virtue is not present and the threshold is correspondingly lower. As long as the bad ruler remains in authority, obedience is the rule, but, once the presupposition of virtue goes, so too does the benefit of the doubt.

Henry concludes his discussion by considering two possible justifications for disobeying a statute which does not clearly secure the *communis utilitas*. First, there is the claim that obedience is restricted to those demands which fulfil the specific terms of an oath or which are essential to the well-being of the community (*necessitas salutis*). Second, there is the suggestion that, if subjects were obliged to obey a statute which does not clearly secure the *communis utilitas*, then temporal rulers would be able to levy taxation from the laity in the same way that the pope levies tenths from the clergy. Henry's response is to argue that statutes which are of doubtful benefit to the common good still fall under a special oath of the community, and of the individuals within it, insofar as they continue to be parts of that community. Since subjects are free to move from one community to another at will,[64] their decision to remain physically present in a community obliges them to obey edicts which are issued for the good of that community; in fact, they are committing a grave error if they think otherwise. Obedience stems from tacit consent, or, to use Henry's term, it can be understood (*interpretative*).[65] Thus, if the ruler sees fit to levy tenths for the peace and well-being of the community, then the laity are indeed obliged to obey in the same way that the clergy are obliged to obey the pope. Nor is this obligation restricted to payment of a tenth. The laity must also sacrifice the half and even the whole of their property. In the last resort, they must even sacrifice their lives. This is a familiar catalogue. What is unusual here is the urgent warning which accompanies it. Although this is all true, Henry cautions, subjects should still be on their guard against their superiors. It must be quite clear, he writes, that a ruler's demand does fulfil its claim to be furthering the public or common benefit and not his own private good. Such a statute must be reasonable, he insists, it must have the authority of law and not command, and it must derive from the ruler's ordered and reasoned power rather than absolute power pure and simple. In this respect, he concludes, there is no difference between the relations of clergy and laity to their respective superiors, except in terms of the ease with which clergy can remove superiors who are unencumbered by hereditary right, and in terms of the greater freedom which the laity has in disposing of its goods.

---

[64] Cf. *Quod.* X.17, pp. 307–11, quoting Matthew 10: 13–14.

[65] For tacit consent, see Justinian, *Digest*, ed. T. Mommsen and P. Krüger, trans. A. Watson (4 vols.; Philadelphia, 1985), II.14.4, i. pp. 62–3. Cf. F. Oakley, 'Legitimation by Consent: The Question of the Medieval Roots', *Viator*, 14 (1983), 303–35.

Henry's discussion of obedience and the common good can be read on several different levels. The question itself is couched, as ever, in more general terms than the particular circumstances from which it originated in 1290. It is clearly prompted by the concern that a superior's demand for taxation should be obeyed *only* when there is clear benefit to the common good. In September 1288, Nicholas IV granted a three-year tenth to Philip IV in support of another 'crusade' against Aragon, and, in June 1289, it began to be collected. Thus, Henry's comment that the demands of a good ruler should be taken on trust *unless he has proved to be untrustworthy in making similar demands on many previous occasions* may well be a reference to the repeated exaction of tenths by the French king for his putative campaigns against Aragon. Although Philip IV remained concerned about raids on Languedoc until 1290, he effectively lost interest in mounting his own campaign after his father's humiliating failure of 1285. Indeed, in 1291, Nicholas IV was to refuse Philip IV's request for a renewal of these tenths on the grounds that the French king's officials were causing serious harm to churches in his kingdom.[66] Viewed in this light, Henry's insistence on *clear* benefit assumes a rather pointed significance. So too does the evaporation of Henry's earlier trust in the good character of the ruler and the inclusion of a stern warning for subjects to beware of the actions of their rulers in such circumstances. By withdrawing taxation from the category of statute whose benefit to the common good can support a measure of doubt, Henry may well have been following the prescriptions of canon and Roman law, but he was also giving voice to an opposition which had been gathering momentum ever since Urban IV's tenth of 1263–7.[67] Henry's reference to Philip IV is certainly explicit—the otherwise incidental comment that bad rulers should be deposed 'irrespective of the length of their lineage' is a reference to the much lauded pedigree of the Capetian line.

In December 1290, however, the university of Paris was contemplating more than just Philip IV's demands for taxation. It was also digesting Nicholas IV's decision to support the friars' interpretation of *Ad fructus uberes* and Benedict Gaetani's termination of all future discussion on the subject.[68] Viewed in this light, the very general terms in which Henry's fourteenth quodlibet is couched assume an even more calculated air. Henry is certainly capable of making principles which govern superiors in the temporal sphere interchangeable with principles which govern superiors in the spiritual sphere.[69] There is considerable evidence to suggest that he is doing exactly

---

[66] Cf. J. R. Strayer, 'The Crusade against Aragon', in id., *Medieval Statecraft and the Perspectives of History* (Princeton, 1971).

[67] Housley, *The Italian Crusades*, 197. According to Housley, however, 'there was no real ideological or material platform on which the clergy could oppose the decrees of the Apostolic See or its rigorous and extensive sanctions' (ibid. 196–7).

[68] G. Digard, *Philippe le Bel et le Saint-Siège de 1285 à 1304* (2 vols.; Paris, 1936), i. 256–7. There was also a financial aspect to the opposition to *Ad fructus uberes*—in 1289, the archbishops, bishops, and clergy of the French church were asked to pay one hundredth of their revenues towards the expenses of sending a delegation to Rome, a request which met with some degree of opposition. A provincial council of Bourges imposed this as a tax for five years *pro communi utilitate totius provinciae*. See A. G. Little, 'Measures Taken by the Prelates of France against the Friars', *Studi e Testi*, 39 (1924), 60.

[69] *Quod.* II.16, p. 103 (*princeps per quem intelligo praelatum ecclesiae*); *Quod.* XV.15 fo. 393r.

the same thing here. *Quodlibet* XIV.8 certainly accommodates many of the elements which have hitherto characterized Henry's discussion of the exercise of authority in specifically religious communities—the presence of doubt, the obligation of an oath, the assumption of a superior's good character, and the analogy with slavery. There is also at least one clear reference to the deposition of ecclesiastical superiors. Henry's use of the terminology 'rulers and prelates' (*principes vel praelati*), moreover, implies a sufficiently broad definition of 'superior' for the actions of the bishop of Rome to be included alongside those of the king of France. Likewise, the phrase *necessitas salutis* is sufficiently ambiguous to cover both a political ('well-being') and an ecclesiastical ('salvation') goal. So too the terms 'community' (where there is an explicit reference to béguines)[70] and 'consent' (a superior can be accepted through the choice of every person, through certain individuals acting on their behalf, through imposition by a higher authority, and not just through hereditary succession)—in each case, the terminology can be applied to the church as well as to the kingdom. The consequences of an ecclesiological reading of Henry's argument are certainly significant. *Quodlibet* XIV.8 would then read not only as a general commentary on *Ad fructus uberes* but as a specific commentary on Nicholas IV's prohibition on further discussion of the subject, a prohibition which Henry's ostensible concentration on obedience to a temporal ruler successfully circumvents.

The very fact that Henry was able to deliver two final quodlibets, in Christmas 1290 and Christmas 1291, has naturally left the efficacy of his suspension by Benedict Gaetani open to some speculation. Whether it was lifted or whether Henry simply continued to teach regardless,[71] it is clear that he was determined to continue his discussion of the limits of legitimate obedience. If the reference to 'superiors' in *Quodlibet* XIV.8 was indeed a veiled reference to the pope, then it was not long before Henry felt able to make this attack much more explicit. The question which he tackled in 1291 was nothing if not direct—is it permissible to discuss the power of prelates?[72] In response, Henry distinguishes between three possible motivations for engaging in such an activity. The first possibility, he suggests, is that someone may want to diminish the power of his ecclesiastical superiors and argue that they should be obeyed in fewer matters. Henry is emphatic in his condemnation of such a person—it is as impermissible to act with this motivation towards the power of ecclesiastical prelates (and, for that matter, towards the power of temporal rulers) as it would be to do this towards the power of God and of Christ. Since God has given

---

[70] This may well be more than just an oblique reference. Guillaume de Saint-Amour had already deftly defended himself by claiming that his criticisms of the mendicant orders had in fact been aimed at the béguines (E. Faral, 'Les Responsiones de Guillaume de Saint-Amour', *AHDLMA* 18, 1950–1, 380). For the latter, see E. W. McDonnell, *The Beguines and Beghards in Medieval Culture* (New Brunswick, 1954).

[71] R. Macken, 'Ein wichtiges Ineditum zum Kampf über das Beichtprivileg der Bettelorden, der Tractatus super facto praelatorum et fratrum des Heinrich von Gent', *Franziskanische Studien*, 60 (1978), 308–9.

[72] *Quod.* XV.15 fos. 393r–v. Cf. John of Paris, *De Potestate Regia et Papali*, ed. J. Leclercq (Paris, 1942), XXII, pp. 248–51.

power to prelates for the public benefit of the church, anyone who sets out to diminish it is effectively ranging himself against what has been ordained by God and is not showing any love for the public good.[73] A second possibility is that someone may be motivated in precisely the opposite direction, namely by the desire to increase the power of prelates. Henry is just as critical of this second type of individual as he is of the first (although he does concede that inflation is less of a sin than detraction). God has given power to prelates for the benefit of the church, he explains, but He has given it in particular amounts; to diminish *or* to increase it, therefore, does not result in the *utilitas ecclesiae*.

Henry is accordingly left with a third and final possibility. Someone, he suggests, may be motivated by the same intention which prompts discussion of the power of God and of Christ when it is necessary for teaching or for overcoming heretics. To discuss the power of prelates in this way, Henry insists, is not only permissible and very beneficial, but it is also very necessary. Good prelates, he pointedly suggests, should actually welcome such discussion and for one very good reason—it instructs both prelates and subjects in their duties. For their part, prelates will learn the extent of their power, what they can and cannot do, and they will thereby learn how to exercise their power legitimately and how to avoid abusing it. Their subjects, meanwhile, will learn the extent of their obligations, when they should and should not obey, and they will thereby learn how to obey their prelates legitimately, how to avoid unjustified rebellion (*indebita rebellio*), but also how to oppose their prelates when obedience would be wrong (*obedientia illicita*). Henry specifically states that he is not suggesting that *all* commands should be judged by subjects, nor that it cannot be beneficial for discussion of the power of prelates *not* to take place. What he does want to establish, however, is that all matters pertaining to the power of prelates should be tested and judged whenever there is a fear that something in their commands might be contrary to what has been laid down by God or be other than as truth would have it (*aliter quam veritas se haberet*). Individuals who find themselves in these circumstances, he suggests, should follow the biblical injunction to be as wise as serpents and as innocent as doves—wise in what they learn from such discussions and innocent in their willingness to obey. It is pure rashness, in Henry's view, to say that all commands of superiors should be obeyed, that no questions should be asked, and that prelates should be trusted in all matters. There is no sign here of the clerical *iam perfectus*. Indeed, Henry cannot resist suggesting that those prelates who do not actively seek such discussion thereby lay themselves open to the suspicion that they have something to hide. Although Henry immediately qualifies this remark to say that it is not always the case that the subject-matter on which they prohibit discussion is at variance with the truth, he does not need to spell it out. The fact that his example of a justified prohibition is Nicholas III's proscription of further debate on the Franciscan rule in 1279 stands in pointed contrast to the action of his namesake over the

---

[73] This appears to be the only occasion on which Henry speaks of a direct love for the common good.

privileges of the mendicant orders in 1288. Nicholas IV and his cardinal legates are the clear targets of Henry's parting shot.

Henry of Ghent's moral and political philosophy, like his metaphysics and epistemology, derives a particular quality from its mixture of different intellectual traditions. His treatment of the common good is no exception. In *Quodlibet* IV.20, Henry produces a concise summary of book I of the *Politics*—humans are political animals; the political community is instituted in order that humans might live well; political activity arises from the communion of individuals with one another since humans cannot be self-sufficient on their own. What Henry concentrates on in this summary, however, is the principle that the community is an integral whole and the citizens are its constituent parts, a view which he ascribes not just to Aristotle but also to the apostle Paul. It is in the nature of parts, he explains, to exist in a whole. Parts possess a well-being which is derived from their communion in a whole in the sense that they all derive (*deducere*)[74] their individual goods from the good of the whole. It is thus in the nature of humankind to live in political communities, since individuals derive the good life from their association with each other and from ordering their individual goods towards the good of the whole. The authority which Henry then cites is not Aristotle's *Politics* but Cicero's *De Officiis*:

since, as Plato has admirably expressed it, we are not born for ourselves alone but our country claims a share of our being and our friends a share; and since, as the Stoics hold, everything that the earth produces is created for man's use; and as men too are born for the sake of men, that they may be able mutually to help one another; in this direction we ought to follow Nature as our guide, to contribute to the general good (*communes utilitates in medium afferre*) by an interchange of acts of kindness, by giving and receiving, and thus by our skill, our industry and our talents, to cement human society more closely together, man to man.[75]

In his twelfth quodlibet, it is this quotation, together with three others from Cicero, with which Henry illustrates Aristotle's obligation to lay down one's life for one's country.[76] It also appears in his fourteenth quodlibet, together with another from the *De Officiis*, to illustrate the obligation of every citizen to support his community.[77] So too in his fifteenth quodlibet, once more to justify self-sacrifice, and once more with additional quotations from the first and fourth *Catiline* and from the (pseudo-Ciceronian) *Pridie quam in exsilium iret*. This time, however, it acts as a gloss on

---

[74] For this terminology, see Bonaventure, I *Sent.* 10.1.1 (see above, p. 67 n. 56). Cf. Giles of Rome, *De Regimine Principum* II.iii.6 (see above, p. 147).

[75] *Quod.* IV.20 fo. 197v; Cicero, *De Officiis*, ed. M. Winterbottom (Oxford, 1994), I.22, pp. 9–10; *Moralium Dogma Philosophorum*, ed. J. Holmberg (Uppsala, 1929), p. 27. Cf. Cicero, *Oratio pro Marcello* (Loeb, 1931), 25, p. 442.

[76] *Quod.* XII.13, p. 74, quoting pseudo-Cicero, *Pridie quam in exsilium iret* 8–9; *In Catilinam* I.27; *In Catilinam* IV.3. Cf. *Quod.* XIV.8 fo. 352r.

[77] *Quod.* XIV.13 fo. 357r–v, quoting *De Officiis* I.51, p. 21. In this instance, the community in question is Henry's student audience and the issue one which must have touched them directly: *utrum pupilli a tutoribus custodientibus bona sua possunt aliquid absque peccato recipere occasione bonorum illorum ultra sortem, salva sorte.*

Augustine's discussion of whether bishops and priests could flee their ministry in the face of a Vandal invasion.[78]

If Cicero provides a consistent point of reference for Henry's analysis of the relationship between individual and community, this provides a contrast with Henry's sporadic citation of Aristotle in the same context. There is a brief mention, in his sixth quodlibet, of Aristotle's analogies of the army and the harmony of music,[79] but, when Henry refers to the *duplex ordo* from the *Metaphysics*, he does not apply it to a specifically political community.[80] Likewise, when Henry emphasizes the superiority of the commander in whom the good of the army principally consists and towards whom everything else is ordered, his primary aim is to establish God as the principle of unity and goodness in the universe and not to recommend monarchy as the model of human government.[81] When Henry does discuss the human ruler, he does not quote book XII of the *Metaphysics* and, whilst he is prepared to identify the good of the prince with the good of the whole community, he is careful to insert a qualifying *quodammodo* and to stress the shared goal of the *bonum commune*.[82]

Henry's reluctance to cite Aristotle in those contexts where Albertus Magnus, Thomas Aquinas, and Giles of Rome had made such reference commonplace becomes particularly significant when Henry comes to define the precise nature of the goal of the human community.[83] Take the notion of 'living well' (*bene vivere*). This most fundamental of Aristotle's political tenets is not one which Henry readily chooses to employ. It does not appear, for example, in his discussion of the interconnection of the virtues,[84] or of the relation between justice and perfect virtue,[85] contexts from which it had been inseparable for Albertus, Aquinas, and Giles. Henry's approach to the life of virtue, in fact, appears to be consistent with his blunt dismissal of Aristotle's conception of the temporal goal of humankind.[86] The effects on Henry's use of the notion of the common good are marked. Henry rarely quotes the principle of superiority from book I of the *Ethics* and, when he does, it is not as a commonplace.[87] His interest in Aristotle's comparative terminology is likewise strictly limited. Henry does not examine *melius*, *perfectius*, or *divinius* in any detail, pausing only to underline the numerical superiority of the common good when he equates *divinius* with *maius* and justifies *melius* with a brief *quia pluribus utilis est*.[88] Rather than adopt an Aristotelian life of virtue, in fact, Henry prefers to define the goal of the

[78] *Quod.* XV.16 fo. 396r–v. Cf. ibid. fo. 394v, quoting *De Officiis* I.63, p. 26. For Augustine's argument, see *Ep.* 228 (*PL* 33, cols. 1013–19).

[79] *Quod.* VI.23, p. 213.   [80] *Summa* XXV.2 fo. 150r; XXIX.6 fo. 174v. Cf. *Quod.* V.17 fo. 282r.

[81] Cf. Lagarde, 'La Philosophie sociale', 110–11; id., *La Naissance*, 190–1.

[82] *Quod.* XIV.8 fo. 352r (above, p. 194).

[83] For Henry's knowledge of the *Ethics* and the *Politics*, see R. Macken, 'Les Sources d'Henri de Gand', *Revue Philosophique de Louvain*, 76 (1978), 11–14, 16–17. Henry had access to Averroes' middle commentary but, in general, he seems to have preferred the interpretations offered in Grosseteste's translation.

[84] *Quod.* V.17 fos. 282r–289r.   [85] *Quod.* VII.28, p. 253.

[86] See above, p. 175. See however, *Summa* XLIX.5 fo. 35v and *Quod.* V.17 fos. 282r–289r. Henry does describe the goal of human society as the conservation of the species but only to dismiss it (*Quod.* VI.13, pp. 148–9).

[87] *Quod.* XIV.8 fo. 352r.   [88] *Quod.* XII.28, p. 171. Cf. *Summa* LXII.1 fo. 187v.

human community by using a broad notion of 'peace and well-being' or 'peace and concord'.[89] Thus, *pax et concordia* is the objective of divine legislation in the Old and New Testaments;[90] *pax* or *quies* is the objective of human legislation in the civil community;[91] *bona quies* is the objective of good people,[92] good citizens,[93] and good rulers;[94] *pax civitatis vel patriae* is the goal of military bravery, *tranquillitas pacis* of bravery in general;[95] the *pax et quies* of the church is urged on Pope Nicholas IV.[96] Even when Aristotle's 'living well' is mentioned, therefore, it is swiftly associated with 'living peaceably' (*optime et pacatissime vivendum*).[97]

Henry's concentration on peace rather than virtue is significant on two counts. In the first instance, it echoes his preference for the term *communis utilitas* rather than *bonum commune* and supports the possibility that he saw the common good as the result, rather than as the goal, of individual acts of virtue. Henry is the only scholastic theologian in this period to have devoted an entire quodlibetic question to the relation of the individual to the common good. His conclusions reveal his own particular priorities. The common good should be preferred to the individual good only when it includes it; if it does not include it, either directly or indirectly, then the individual good should be preferred. Where Aristotle is an influential authority for Henry, therefore, and where he finds a plethora of supporting texts from Cicero, is in his analysis of the motivation behind individual acts of virtue and friendship in books VIII and IX of the *Ethics*. Even more important to this analysis, however, is what Henry adopts from Augustine's account of the operation of love. At the heart of Henry's understanding of the common good is an Augustinian account of the *ordo caritatis*.

In the second instance, Henry's concentration on peace rather than virtue associates his view of the human community with a particular type of political realism. Once again, this account has its roots in Augustine. Henry repeatedly points out the disjunction between an ideal community of grace and the sinful reality of human nature. Human beings may be integral parts of political communities but what ultimately defines their participation in the *res publica* is their need to be protected from the worst consequences of their own behaviour. Political authority is ultimately a *remedium peccati*. The most that can be expected of human society, therefore, is not an Aristotelian ideal but an Augustinian reality, not the achievement of activity in accordance with perfect virtue but the preservation of a limited degree of peace and harmony.

A concentration on the individual good and an awareness of the disparity between ideal and reality provide two good reasons why Henry should have been reluctant to draw a direct connection between the common good of the human community and participation in the operation of goodness in the universe. What is equally striking,

[89] *Quod.* XIV.8 fo. 352r; *Quod.* IV.20 fo. 198v. [90] *Summa* IX.1 ad 3 fo. 70v.
[91] *Summa* VII.10 fo. 60r. Cf. *Quod.* II.16, p. 105 (*pax humana*), *Quod.* VIII.22 fo. 44r (*pax et bonum rei publicae*, *publica pax*), *Quod.* X.3, p. 49 (*publica pax*).
[92] *Summa* XXV.2 fo. 150r. [93] *Summa* XXIX.6 fo. 166v. [94] *Quod.* V.17 fo. 282v.
[95] Ibid. [96] *Quod.* XII.31, p. 24. [97] *Quod.* IV.20 fo. 197v.

however, is that this did not prevent him from making extensive use of a particular definition of the common good as *communis utilitas* in his practical analysis of contemporary political issues. Henry's theoretical understanding of the common good may be notable for the absence of a metaphysical dimension—as participation in universal goodness, as the direct object of love, or as the goal of virtue—but this does not mean that he failed to use the common good in more practical political contexts. Henry of Ghent was a scholastic theologian who *could* separate politics from metaphysics. From his knowledge of Augustine, Cicero, Aristotle, Bernard of Clairvaux, and canon and Roman law, Henry explored the implications of establishing *communis utilitas* as the criterion which legitimates the actions of both spiritual and temporal powers. Henry's discussion of obedience and resistance in 1291 came at the end of a line of argument which he had been developing throughout the 1280s in the course of growing opposition to *Ad fructus uberes* and increasing hostility to papal and royal taxation. His conclusion is categoric. The common good is the legitimizing criterion for the exercise of *all* power in the human community, ecclesiastical as well as political, and, as a result, the obedience of subjects to their superiors is conditional upon this common good being *clearly* identified and discussed. Applied to the two most sensitive issues of the day—*Ad fructus uberes* and taxation—this culminated in a theory of conditional obedience in which Henry was clearly prepared to countenance not only resistance to, but deposition of, both pope and king.

8

Godfrey of Fontaines—Love, Virtue, and Justice

The career of Godfrey of Fontaines was shaped by some of the most significant figures in the Paris schools. He studied in the faculty of arts during the second regency of Thomas Aquinas (1269–72), almost certainly under the direction of Siger of Brabant, and then in the faculty of theology under Henry of Ghent and Servase (Gervase) of Mt St Elias. It is perhaps only natural, therefore, that, after his inception as regent master in 1285, Godfrey's own teaching should have reflected the impact of these very different influences.[1] Indeed, it is precisely this mixed pedigree which lies behind the relatively recent revival of interest in Godfrey's thought: 'sometimes styled a Thomist, sometimes an eclectic, he was an independent and critical thinker'.[2]

Godfrey of Fontaines's exposure to such a variety of intellectual influences had significant consequences for his philosophy and theology. Thus, although he was deeply influenced by the teaching of Aquinas, Godfrey was not averse to extending it, or even to departing from it, as and when he saw fit. For example, Godfrey refused to accept that the metaphysical distinction between essence and existence was a real difference (*secundum rem*) rather than just a logical difference (*secundum rationem*).[3] Godfrey's critique of certain Thomist positions, moreover, particularly in the terms

---

[1] *Quodlibets* I–XV, ed. M. de Wulf, A. Pelzer, J. Hoffmans, and O. Lottin (Les Philosophes Belges II–V, XIV; Louvain, 1904, 1914, 1924–31, 1932–5, 1937). For their chronology, see P. Glorieux, *La Littérature quodlibétique* (2 vols.; Paris, 1925, 1935), i. 149–68; J. F. Wippel, *The Metaphysical Thought of Godfrey of Fontaines: A Study in Late Thirteenth Century Philosophy* (Washington, DC, 1981), pp. xxiii–xxviii. For Godfrey's disputed questions, see Les Philosophes Belges XIV, pp. 259–61; *Quaestio Disputata* IV (O. Lottin, *Psychologie et morale aux XIIe et XIIIe siècles* (6 vols.; Louvain–Gembloux, 1942–60), iv. 581–8); XV (J. Koch, *Durandi de S. Porciano O. P. Tractatus de habitibus Quaestio Quarta* (Münster, 1930), 60–6); XVII (J. Grundel, *Die Lehre von dem Umstanden der menschlichen Handlung im Mittelalter* (Münster, 1963), 655–60); XIX (O. Lottin, 'Les Vertus morales acquises sont-elles de vraies vertus? La Réponse des théologiens de saint Thomas à Pierre Auriol', *RTAM* 21 (1954), 101–29, 114–22).

[2] J. F. Wippel, 'Godfrey of Fontaines', in *New Catholic Encyclopaedia*, vi. 578. Cf. M. de Wulf, *Un théologien-philosophe du XIIIe siècle: Étude sur la vie, les oeuvres et l'influence de Godefroid de Fontaines* (Brussels, 1906), 3–127; id., *Histoire de la philosophie médiévale*, 6th edn. (3 vols.; Louvain–Paris, 1934–47) ii. 293–6; R. J. Arway, 'A Half Century of Research on Godfrey of Fontaines', *New Scholasticism*, 36 (1962), 192–218; J. Lejeune, 'De Godefroid de Fontaines à la paix de Fexhe 1316', *Annuaire d'Histoire Liègoise*, VI.5 (1962), 1215–59.

[3] Wippel, *Metaphysical Thought*, ch. 2; id., 'The Relationship between Essence and Existence in Late Thirteenth Century Thought: Giles of Rome, Henry of Ghent, Godfrey of Fontaines and James of Viterbo', in P. Morewedge (ed.), *Philosophies of Existence: Ancient and Medieval* (New York, 1982), 131–64.

in which they were put forward by Giles of Rome, was often caused by his adherence to a stricter form of Aristotelianism drawn from the Greek commentaries translated by Grosseteste. It was this Aristotelianism, the legacy of his studies in the arts faculty, which left Godfrey firmly opposed to Bishop Tempier's condemnations of March 1277.[4] Such independence of mind was certainly characteristic of Godfrey's subsequent teaching as a secular master when he engaged in an open, and often pointed, dialogue with his fellow-theologians Henry of Ghent and James of Viterbo. Sparring with Henry of Ghent, in fact, appears to have prompted Godfrey to adopt some of his most distinctive doctrinal positions. Thus, it was Henry's 'neo-Augustinianism' which Godfrey sought to contradict in his own psychology and epistemology, when he stressed the passivity of sense in cognition, for example, or the superiority of the intellect over the will.[5]

A qualified affiliation to Aquinas, close reading of Aristotle, and direct engagement with other theologians are all characteristics which can be traced in Godfrey's moral and political philosophy.[6] They are given striking material testimony by Godfrey's personal handbook from the early 1270s and the list of works which he bequeathed to the Sorbonne on his death. From this evidence, it can be established, for example, that Godfrey possessed copies of all Aquinas' major works, including the first two books of the commentaries on the *Ethics* and the *Politics*, together with the *Ethics* and the *Politics* themselves and Cicero's *De Officiis*. He was also thoroughly conversant with nine of Henry of Ghent's *Quodlibets* (VII–XV) and Giles of Rome's *Apologia* (both of which texts are annotated with Godfrey's own corrections), as well as Giles's *De Regimine Principum*, Giles's commentaries on the first two books of the *Sentences*, and the first *Quodlibet* of James of Viterbo.[7] When Godfrey's own ethical and political ideas are placed in this intellectual context, each one of these elements—the guarded endorsement of Aquinas, the detailed exposition of Aristotle, and the direct engagement with Giles of Rome, Henry of Ghent, and James of Viterbo—can be seen to have influenced his particular understanding of the notion of the common good.

Aquinas' account of the analogical predication of goodness in Creation exercised a considerable attraction for Godfrey. Individual entities are good to the extent that

---

[4] *Quod.* VII.18, pp. 402–5; *Quod.* XII.5, p. 103. Cf. M. H. Laurent, 'Godefroid de Fontaines et la condamnation de 1277', *Revue Thomiste*, 13 (1930), 273–81; J. Hoffmans, 'La Table des divergences et innovations doctrinales de Godefroid de Fontaines', *Revue Néoscolastique de Philosophie*, 36 (1934), 412–36; G. de Lagarde, 'La Philosophie sociale d'Henri de Gand et Godefroid de Fontaines', *AHDLMA* 14 (1943–5), 74–5; id., *La Naissance de l'esprit laïque au déclin du moyen âge*, 3rd edn. (5 vols.; Louvain, 1956–70), ii. ch. 8, pp. 163–4; Wippel, *Metaphysical Thought*, 382. For Godfrey's interest in the condemnation of Giles of Rome, see *Apologia*, ed. R. Wielockx in *Aegidii Romani Opera Omnia*, vol. iii.1, chs. 1–2.

[5] F. van Steenberghen, *La Philosophie au XIIIe siècle*, 2nd edn. (Louvain, 1991), 443–4.

[6] e.g. C. Renardy, *Le Monde des maîtres universitaires du diocèse de Liège 1140–1350: Recherches sur sa composition et ses activités* (Paris, 1979), 360–1.

[7] P. Glorieux, 'Un recueil scolaire de Godefroid de Fontaines', *RTAM* 3 (1931), 37–53; J. J. Duin, 'La Bibliothèque philosophique de Godefroid de Fontaines', *Estudios Lulianos*, 3 (1959), 21–36, 137–60; *Aristoteles Latinus, Codices: Pars prior*, ed. G. Lacombe et al. (Rome, 1939), 575. Cf. *Apologia*, ed. Wielockx, 75 n. 3.

they participate in the principle of goodness which is common to the whole universe and which is expressed as a hierarchy of increasingly inclusive goods culminating in God. The influence of this schema can be detected, for example, in Godfrey's discussion of a separate good (*bonum extrinsecum*), the good on which all other goods depend and towards which they should all be ordered.[8] Godfrey's critical approach to Aquinas, however, meant that his debt to a Thomist hierarchy of goodness was also accompanied by a willingness to explore the problems which it had raised. Indeed, what makes Godfrey's analysis of this particular aspect of the common good so revealing is the way in which it can be read as an attempt to circumvent, or even solve, some of the difficulties which Aquinas' account had left outstanding. This is the case, for example, with the question of how terms which govern universal goodness can be translated into terms which govern the political community. Can this transfer take place without entirely incorporating the individual as a subordinate part within a more perfect whole? Godfrey's approach was to explore the possibilities provided by the connection between general justice and its constituent virtues in book V of the *Ethics*. If general justice is the same as its constituent virtues but also something different, might this explain how the common good can be the same as its component individual goods but also something different?

A similar picture emerges from Godfrey's debt to Aquinas' account of the *ordo caritatis*. According to Aquinas, greater love should be shown towards the good of the human community in the same way that greater love should be shown towards God. The supreme expression of this principle was, accordingly, to sacrifice one's life for the sake of a superior common good. This was an argument, however, which depended upon an identification of the common good of the community as the common good of happiness, as activity in accordance with perfect virtue. This identification was justified on the strength of Aristotle's account of the common good in book I of the *Ethics*. Yet, as Albertus Magnus had already recognized, this was not the only correlation which could be made in order to explain what should motivate an act of self-sacrifice. The good of the human community could also be identified as peace, concord, self-sufficiency, and material security. According to this definition of the common good, individuals who lay down their lives can be said to secure good primarily for themselves whilst the community simply benefits from the consequences of their virtuous action. This line of interpretation was also much easier to reconcile with the priority which Aristotle had given to love for the individual good in his own account of self-sacrifice in book IX of the *Ethics*.

When Godfrey adopted Aquinas' account of the operation of love for the common good, therefore, he associated himself with a particular explanation of how the superiority of the common good in book I of the *Ethics* could be related to the good of the individual in book IX. In doing so, however, he took up a position which had recently been challenged by Henry of Ghent. Henry's account of the operation of love was rather different from the account produced by Aquinas. It also resulted in a rather

---

[8] Lagarde, 'La Philosophie sociale', 103; id., *La Naissance*, 174.

different exposition of book IX of the *Ethics*. Self-sacrifice is motivated by self-love, by the individual's concern to secure the greater good of virtue for himself. Moreover, in Henry's opinion, the common good of the political community represented only what could be salvaged from his sombre assessment of the consequences of sinful human nature. Far from being the manifestation of metaphysical goodness or the object of greater love, this common good was simply the result of virtuous activity by those individuals whose self-love was directed towards God.

In accepting Aquinas' analysis of the place of the common good in a hierarchy of goodness and a hierarchy of love, therefore, Godfrey of Fontaines was presented with a series of questions. If he connected the good of the human community with the metaphysical good of the universe, then he had to demonstrate the continuing presence of good for the individual. If he championed Aquinas' identification of the good of the political community as the all-inclusive good of perfect virtue, then he had to find a means of maintaining the identity of the good of each individual human being. In both instances, Godfrey ran up against the challenge presented by Henry of Ghent's account of the *ordo caritatis*. For Godfrey, therefore, any abstract analysis of the relationship between the individual good and the common good in the human community had to start with an analysis of the connection between love for one's own good and love for the common good in book IX of the *Ethics*.

For Godfrey of Fontaines, the connection between the hierarchy of goodness and the hierarchy of love derives from the connection between the intellect and the will. Since the characteristic activity of the intellect is to apprehend being (or goodness) and the characteristic activity of the will is to love, any discussion of the relationship between the intellect and the will necessarily involves a discussion of the relationship between goodness and love. Like Aquinas, therefore, Godfrey describes the metaphysical nature of the common good in terms of an order or principle of goodness and the natural appetite of Creation towards it.[9] Like Henry of Ghent, however, he is equally concerned to demonstrate the presence of good for the individual. According to Godfrey, when an individual inclines towards a particular good within the *ratio boni*, the individual is willing his own well-being (*sibi bene esse*) in the sense that he is willing what is good in this particular instance for this particular individual.[10] Thus, although Godfrey can refer to universal goodness as *bonum in communi*,[11] he increasingly prefers the phrase *ratio boni et convenientis*.[12] The presence of this second term

---

[9] For individuation, see *Quod.* IV.2, *Quod.* VI.5, *Quod.* VII.5, *Quod.* X.2, and the discussion in Wippel, *Metaphysical Thought*, ch. 9, pp. 349–69; id., 'Godfrey of Fontaines, Peter of Auvergne and John Baconthorpe' in J. J. E. Garcia (ed.), *Individuation in Scholasticism: The Later Middle Ages and the Counter-Reformation 1150–1650* (Albany, NY, 1994), 222–8.

[10] *Quod.* X.14, p. 380. Cf. *Q. Ord.* III in 5, pp. 119–20; Albertus Magnus, *Ethica* I.2.6, p. 27.

[11] *Quod.* V.12, p. 55; *Q. Disp.* IV, p. 585. Cf. *Quod.* V.12, p. 57 (*bonum . . . in generali*); *Quod.* XV.1, pp. 2, 4–5 (*bonum in generali, bonum in universali*).

[12] e.g. *Quod.* V.12, p. 55; *Quod.* VI.7, pp. 148, 159, 167; *Quod.* VI.10, p. 215; *Quod.* VIII.2, pp. 21–2; *Quod.* VIII.16, pp. 154–5; *Quod.* XI.4, p. 23; *Quod.* XII.2, p. 86 (where the principle is ascribed to Anselm); *Q. Disp.* XV, pp. 61, 64; *Q. Disp.* XIX, p. 119. Cf. Albertus Magnus, *Ethica* VIII.3.4, p. 544; Henry of Ghent, *Quod.* XIII.9, pp. 56–64.

is an important addition. The human intellect might apprehend being (or goodness) but it cannot make it an object of the human will unless it appears suitable or congruent (*conveniens*). Being (or goodness) in an absolute sense is the object of the speculative intellect, but being (or goodness) which is congruent with the individual is the object of the practical intellect and the will.[13] This is the gloss which Godfrey accordingly gives to Aristotle's observation that everything seems to love what is (or appears to be) good for itself. Whether a particular good is honourable, pleasurable, or beneficial, the object of the will is always what is good *and* congruent.[14]

Godfrey's emphasis on the presence of good for the individual within the *ratio boni et convenientis*, however, does not imply that self-love should be the most important consideration within the *ordo caritatis*.[15] From the outset, Godfrey is determined to demonstrate that love for one's own good is far from being the sole or primary consideration in the exercise of an individual's will. Thus, in arguing (against Henry of Ghent) that the action of the intellect in cognition is superior to, and more perfect than, the action of the will in loving, Godfrey places particular emphasis on love as a power which unites its participants but also transforms them. In itself, this was a thoroughly conventional definition (and one which had been employed by Henry himself) but the use to which Godfrey puts it is striking. What Godfrey sets out to establish is that the transformative power of love derives from being ordered towards a goal which is additional to the goal secured by its operation. The will must be inferior to the intellect because the actions of the will, unlike those of the intellect, are sought on account of an additional goal and not for their own sake. In the case of an animal, therefore, its natural appetite or will is ordered towards its principal perfection, namely its continuation in existence, either in its own self or (through procreation) in its species. The love which an animal shows towards its offspring or its fellow-creatures is thus not the primary good of the animal or of the other animals towards which it inclines. Its primary good is, instead, the object of this inclination, the good which unites the two animals, the good in which they share and communicate. Its primary good is not love for the offspring nor the good of the offspring, but the good of the offspring when it is united with the good of the parent to effect the continuation of the individual in existence. Although Godfrey accepts that the primary perfection of humans is not their continuation in existence but the activity of their intellect, he applies exactly the same principle to the natural appetite of human beings. The human will is ordered towards a goal beyond that of the inclination itself.

---

[13] *Quod.* VI.10, pp. 201–2. Cf. O. Lottin, 'Le Libre arbitre chez Godefroid de Fontaines', 'Le Thomisme de Godefroid de Fontaines', *Revue Néoscolastique de Philosophie*, 40 (1937), 213–41, 554–73; id., *Psychologie et Morale*, i. 304–39; Wippel, *Metaphysical Thought*, 194–202.

[14] *Quod.* VI.10, pp. 191–2, 197. For Godfrey's familiarity with the distinction between a good of intrinsic moral worth and a good which is simply advantageous or beneficial, see *Quod.* I.13, pp. 33–4. Cf. Aristotle, *Ethics* III.4 1113ª31–4, VII.12 1152ᵇ26–31, VIII.2 1155ᵇ18–19.

[15] *Quod.* VI.10, pp. 182–218. Cf. P. Tihon, 'Le Sermon de Godefroid de Fontaines pour le deuxième dimanche après l'Epiphanie', *RTAM* 32 (1965), 50–1. For a general discussion, see B. Neumann, *Der Mensch und die himmlische Seligkeit nach der Lehre Gottfrieds von Fontaines* (Limburg, 1958), 32–9, as well as P. Tihon, *Foi et théologie selon Godefroid de Fontaines* (Bruges, 1966), 183 n. 3.

In this case, however, the additional goal can be identified as the principle of absolute and essential goodness (*ratio boni et finis simpliciter et per se*).

Godfrey's account of the transformative power of love and the inclination of the human will towards the principle of goodness has important consequences for his account of the love which humans have for one another when they are united in friendship. An individual, Godfrey argues, loves a friend on account of something other than the love which he has for himself and for his friend. Thus, although friendship involves the exercise of *amor benevolentiae* (the love by which the will inclines towards the good of another person), this inclination does not represent the primary good either for the person who is loved or for the person who is doing the loving. In Godfrey's view, the perfection of friendship lies, instead, in the good in which the two individuals are united, a good which he terms the greatest good (*maximum bonum*), the goal of being perfect according to the intellect. This goal constitutes the communication of friends in the primary object of their love, namely activity in virtue. Thus, the individual who is doing the loving wills himself to be perfect in virtue and to perform virtuous actions, but he also wills the same perfection for the individual whom he loves. It is therefore not enough to say, as Aristotle had done, that an individual loves a friend as 'another self'.[16] There must also be communication in knowledge and in virtuous action. Friendship between two individuals concerns more than just two individual goods. It may originate in self-love but its perfection requires transformation as well as union, 'communion' to produce something else. This communication is cooperation in the life of virtue.

According to Godfrey, the principle that the goal of love is not good for oneself but a shared or common good has its ultimate expression in the love which humans have for God. In making this connection, therefore, Godfrey is naturally drawn into a discussion of whether humans love God more than they love themselves. This was a frequently debated question in theology but it was given extra bite by the priority which Aristotle had apparently given to self-love in books VIII and IX of the *Ethics*.[17] The phrasing of the question with which Godfrey was faced in his tenth quodlibet (1294/5) puts the problem in a nutshell. If Aristotle is correct in maintaining that friendship originates in self-love, is it the case that humankind loves itself more than any other thing including, ultimately, God?[18] Godfrey's initial response to such a possibility is to appeal to the nature of goodness in general and to his own definition of the *ratio boni et convenientis*. Since the object of the will is what is good *and* what is congruent, and since God is the supreme and essential good *and* the common good on which the particular good of every being depends, every being must therefore be naturally inclined to love God as its goal and supreme good in the way that every part

---

[16] Aristotle, *Ethics* IX.4 1166ᵃ31–2. Cf. Henry of Ghent, *Quod.* X.12, pp. 274–85.

[17] e.g. Giles of Rome, *Quod.* IV.14. Cf. Lagarde, 'La Philosophie sociale', 96–8. Giles discusses the obligation of a part to sacrifice itself for the sake of its whole but only in the context of God and not of the political community. Cf. *Quod.* V.6; III *Sent.* 29.2.1.1, pp. 615–17.

[18] *Quod.* X.6, pp. 318–25. Cf. Lagarde, 'La Philosophie sociale', 101–3; id., *La Naissance*, 172–3; Neumann, *Der Mensch*, 32–4.

naturally loves the common good of the whole more than it loves its individual good. Godfrey then cites the illustrations which Aquinas used in exactly the same context—humankind has a greater natural love for God than it has for itself in the same way that the citizen lays down his life for the common good and the hand exposes itself to danger for the sake of the body.[19] Godfrey's initial conclusion is straightforward. God is the supreme, universal, and common good, both in virtue and in perfection; because God is every good and because this good contains humans and all Creation, it follows that humans have a greater natural love for God than they have for themselves.[20]

By appealing to the analogy of self-sacrifice in the political community, however, Godfrey recognizes that he has to explain how this conclusion can be harmonized with Aristotle's statement that the citizen lays down his life because he will thereby secure for himself the greatest good of virtue (*maximum bonum virtutis*). In his very first quodlibet (1285), Godfrey took this observation to mean that a virtuous individual can wish the greatest goods for himself and still lay down his life for his friends and community because he will thereby secure the greater good (*maius bonum*) of a perfect act of virtue and because the life which he would otherwise lead would not be as perfectly virtuous.[21] In 1294/5, Godfrey applies this principle to love for the common good in God and rephrases the original question accordingly—if an individual dies for this divine good, does he still love his own good more than anything else, more than the common good, more than God? Godfrey's response is to appeal to the fundamental principle that the individual good must be included within the common good. An individual, he argues, loves God *and* he loves himself and his own good. Since every human always naturally wills his own well-being (*sibi bene vel optime esse*), no one can love any good unless his own good, or well-being, is included within it.[22] In order to establish which of these two goods is the object of the greater love, Godfrey then develops the distinction between intrinsic and extrinsic goods which he found in Aquinas.[23] Since any action takes its form and perfection from its object, the individual must have a greater love for the divine good because, as the supreme good, it is the object of every individual good. Whilst the good of virtue is an intrinsic good which perfects the individual, it receives its own form and perfection from an extrinsic good, that is, the essential and primary object of love, namely God. It is this extrinsic object which perfects the individual because it acts as the means by which the individual will secure perfection. In this sense, the divine good *is* the individual's good.

Godfrey then turns to his own account of the principle that love is not an end in itself but a means towards an additional end. When something is loved on account of another good which will result, it is clearly not loved for its own sake. Love for God,

[19] Cf. Aquinas, *Quod.* I.4.3. Cf. *Ia* 60.5, *IaIIae* 109.3, *IIaIIae* 26.3, II *Sent.* 3.2.3, III *Sent.* 3.29.3, *De Div. Nom.* 4.9–10.

[20] *Quod.* X.6, pp. 318–19. Cf. *Quod.* X.1, p. 298.   [21] *Quod.* I.10, pp. 25–7.

[22] *Quod.* X.6, p. 320. Cf. *Quod.* VIII.5, p. 62, quoting Psalm 73: 28: *mihi adhaerere Deo bonum est.*

[23] e.g. Aquinas, *Ia* 103.2 (above, p. 87).

however, is different. An individual loves God in Himself, and for His own sake, because He is the supreme good and the supreme object of love. God is not loved in order that some other good—the individual's own good—will result. Although good for the individual arises as a result of this love being exercised, the individual will still love God irrespective of this consequence. In loving God more than he loves himself, the individual certainly loves himself more than if he were not loving God in this fashion and, as a result, he will secure a greater good for himself. Nevertheless, although this individual good is a necessary side effect, it is not the final cause of the individual loving God. The good of a part, after all, cannot be the good on whose account a common good is loved and preserved. This function is reserved for the perfect goodness of the common good, the good which is loved for its own sake and towards which the good of the part is ordered. It is on this basis that Godfrey modifies Aquinas' original terminology and concludes (with Giles of Rome) that, in loving God, the individual continues to will the greatest good for himself but only as an implicit consequence (*quasi ex consequenti et implicite*).

Having demonstrated that love for God includes love for the individual's own good, Godfrey returns to the specific issue of self-sacrifice. According to Godfrey, an individual who chooses to lose every intrinsic good in order to preserve an extrinsic good is clearly exhibiting greater love for the extrinsic good. The superiority of this love, however, does not abrogate the principle that this extrinsic good includes good for the individual. If I cannot will or love anything unless it includes my well-being and intrinsic good, then, in willing that my good, and even my existence, should be sacrificed in order to preserve an extrinsic good, I must thereby be acquiring an even greater intrinsic good and an even better form of existence, namely the state of being virtuous. To love the common good, in other words, even at the expense of one's individual good, is still an individual good inasmuch as it constitutes an act of virtue. However, even this 'greater good' of virtue is not loved by the individual as much as the extrinsic good from which it derives its goodness and which it has as its object. This is an important rider. If I will my own good to remain in existence at the expense of the divine good, I would not be willing my own greatest good because this act would be inordinate and sinful. To will God and to love the divine good is an intrinsic and virtuous good for the individual. However, the individual must still choose to will God and to love the divine good more than he wills himself willing God and more than he loves himself loving God.[24]

It is at this point in the argument that Godfrey draws an exact parallel between the common good in God and the common good of the political community. Self-sacrifice for the sake of the human community, he argues, obeys the same principles as self-sacrifice for the sake of God. However much the virtuous citizen loves himself and his own intrinsic good, he will still choose to die virtuously rather than let the common good perish. The soldier who flees in order to save his life does not, in fact, secure his own greatest good, despite his intention to do so, because he has scorned

---

[24] *Quod.* X.6, pp. 320–5.

the preservation of the community. When a virtuous citizen loves the good of the community and wills his own death on its behalf, it is true that he also loves himself loving the common good and dying in this way—Godfrey is prepared to concede this much to Aristotle's account of self-love. However, the individual must still love the common good more than he loves his individual good. If he does not, then there is, in Godfrey's view, an inherent contradiction. If the individual were to love himself more than he loves the community, he would clearly prefer to remain in his perfectly virtuous state whilst the common good perishes, rather than enable the common good to remain whilst his own perfection perishes. In doing so, however, the individual would be caught in an impossible dilemma. The perfection which the individual would be trying to maintain by avoiding the act of self-sacrifice is the very same perfection which involves a love for the common good and which includes the wish that the common good should be preserved at the expense of his own life. The preservation of the common good does not necessarily include the preservation of the individual because, without his existence, the common good can still continue. Conversely, without the existence of the common good, the individual would have no individual good to preserve. It is therefore possible for an individual to will the preservation of the common good by means of his death, but impossible for him to will his own preservation in the same action. He cannot will the preservation of the common good and his own death without wishing the preservation of the common good more than his own good. If he wills the common good more, then he must love it more.[25]

The consequences of drawing such an exact parallel between the demands of the divine good and the demands of the common good are worth spelling out. If an individual wills the preservation of his own good rather than of the divine good, he effectively ceases to will his own good. Why? Because, without the preservation of the divine good, there can be no individual good, since the individual good derives its goodness from God. The same conclusion, therefore, must also apply to the good of the political community. The common good of the political community is loved more than the individual good, more, even, than the individual good of loving the common good, because there would be no individual good without it. The individual good is included in the common good in that its goodness depends upon it and, for this reason, the individual good cannot be loved more than the common good. If it is, then it would not be an individual good. A part is included within the whole but cannot exist without it. Thus, for an individual to refuse to lay down his life for the common good in the hope that he will thereby secure his individual good would represent a contradiction in terms. According to Godfrey, therefore, the virtuous citizen who lays down his life for the community does choose the 'greatest good' for himself, since he acquires the good of virtue, that is, the goods which are congruent with his reason and intellect. Nevertheless, however much the virtuous individual loves himself and his intrinsic good, he will still choose to die virtuously rather than let the

[25] *Quod.* X.6, pp. 322–4.

common good perish. In Godfrey's view, this is why, when Aristotle had listed the goods which the virtuous individual is prepared to sacrifice for the common good, he did not include the good of the community. The individual, Godfrey concludes, must therefore love the common good more than he loves anything else.

Godfrey's analysis of self-sacrifice has clearly taken on board several of the arguments which were put forward by Henry of Ghent in his own discussion of book IX of the *Ethics*.[26] Both theologians are concerned to maintain an explicit principle of inclusion and to demonstrate that the individual secures good for himself as a consequence of preferring the common good. Godfrey differs from Henry, however, in refusing to envisage any situation in which an individual good is not included (or only indirectly included) within the common good. Henry of Ghent's more limited notion of the common good of the community made it much easier for him to conceive of a common good which did not include the individual good. By contrast, Godfrey of Fontaines keeps strictly to the principle of inclusion and to the imagery of part and whole—the common good is a good without which there would simply be no individual good. Indeed, his verdict on Henry's 'positive' and 'negative' goods, on the distinction between acquiring good and avoiding evil, is terse: *non videtur bene dictum*. According to Godfrey, an individual cannot perform a perfect action in order to avoid the evil of sin without thereby acquiring a great good of virtue (*magnum bonum virtutis*). If the individual incurs evil when he does not sacrifice himself as he ought, then he must correspondingly acquire virtue, and therefore a good, when he does. This is as true for the contemplative individual as it is for the individual who is involved in political life. Godfrey agrees with Henry that an act of political virtue is not essentially better or more perfect than an act of contemplation and that contemplation should therefore not be laid aside for political action except in particular circumstances (most notably when the common good cannot be preserved by any other means). However, this is as far as his agreement goes. According to Godfrey, not only is it generally better (*melius*) that the contemplative should lay down his life but the contemplative will also secure a greater good (*maius bonum*) for himself in the process. Once again, Godfrey follows the same line of reasoning which governs the divine good. The natural order requires each individual to love himself in such a way that he wishes the greatest goods (*optima bona*) for himself. By loving God more than himself, the individual does what is congruent with his own good in that it results in a greater good than if he primarily loved his individual good or if he did not love God more than himself. An individual ought not to perform any action, interior or exterior, unless he will thereby become an essentially better person (*melius simpliciter*). No one should choose any action which will make him worse, whatever the nature of the good he might be trying to preserve, even if that good is the good of the community. It is therefore wrong, for example, to fornicate for the good of the city just as it is wrong to do evil in order that good might result (Romans 3: 8).[27]

---

[26] See above, pp. 170–8.   [27] *Quod.* XII.2, p. 84.

Godfrey of Fontaines does not hide his frustration with those people who make Aristotle say that an individual ought to love himself and his own good more than anything else.[28] According to Godfrey, there is no difference between book IX of the *Ethics* and Matthew 19: 19 ('Love your neighbour as yourself').[29] It is on this basis that he draws the conclusion which had been so studiously avoided by Henry—an individual should have a greater love for a common good which is intermediate between God and the individual. Godfrey's irritation is still in evidence in his thirteenth quodlibet (1297/8) but, on this occasion, his target has shifted. Godfrey's second demonstration of how human love for God can be harmonized with the origin of friendship in self-love was delivered as a response to the arguments which had recently been put forward, not by Henry of Ghent, but by the new Augustinian master in theology, James of Viterbo.[30]

James of Viterbo proffered his own solution to whether humankind has a greater natural love for God at some stage between 1293 and 1296. He presented it as a choice between two clear alternatives—should the individual have a greater love for himself because he has a greater union with himself, or should he have a greater love for God because God is a greater good?[31] Although James's conclusion is rather tentative (*id quod probabilius . . . mihi videtur esse tenendum*), his discussion amounts to a thorough critique of the arguments put forward in Godfrey's tenth quodlibet.[32] James of Viterbo bases his argument on the traditional scholastic distinction between concupiscent love and benevolent love.[33] Reasoning creatures, he states, love God with both types of love. Thus, concupiscent love prompts an individual to will for himself (or for others) the supreme and perfect good that is God, whereas benevolent love (or, as James terms it, the love of friendship) prompts an individual simply to will God to be the supreme and perfect good that He is. This much was uncontroversial.

---

[28] Cf. B. Bazan, *Siger de Brabant, Ecrits de logique, de morale et de physique* (Louvain–Paris, 1974), pp. 103–5; Lagarde, *La Naissance*, ii. 46–7.

[29] *Quod.* X.6, p. 325. Cf. *The Greek Commentaries on the Nicomachean Ethics of Aristotle in the Latin Translation of Robert Grosseteste*, ed. H. P. F. Mercken (Corpus Latinum Commentariorum in Aristotelem Graecorum VI.1, 3; Leiden, 1973, 1991), ii. pp. 228–35; *Aristoteles over der vriendschap: Boeken VIII en IX van de Nicomachische Ethiek met de commentaren van Aspasius en Michaël in de Latijnse vertaling van Grosseteste*, ed. W. Stinissen (Brussels, 1963), pp. 114–19.

[30] A. d'Alès, 'Jacques de Viterbe, théologien de l'église', *Gregorianum*, 7 (1926), 339–53; D. Gutierrez, 'De vita et scriptis Beati Iacobi de Viterbio', *Analecta Augustiniana*, 16 (1937–8), 216–24, 282–305, 358–81; id., 'De doctrina theologica Beati Iacobi de Viterbio', ibid. 432–66, 523–52; E. Ypma, 'Recherches sur la carrière scolaire et la bibliothèque de Jacques de Viterbe', *Augustiniana*, 24 (1974), 247–82; id., 'Recherches sur la productivité littéraire de Jacques de Viterbe jusqu'à 1300', *Augustiniana*, 25 (1975), 223–82.

[31] James of Viterbo, *Quodlibet*, ed. E. Ypma (Würzburg, 1969), II.20, pp. 202–14. Cf. Neumann, *Der Mensch*, 34–6.

[32] That James's *quaestio* is a response to Godfrey's *Quod.* X.6 is suggested by several specific references—to the argument that the individual should love God more than himself because he thereby wills a good which is congruent and proper to himself (*sibi bonum conveniens et proprium ipsi*); to the endorsement of the distinction between strictly-defined and loosely-defined friendship (*ut quidam dicunt et bene*); and to the discussion of a virtuous citizen not preferring his own bodily survival to the destruction of the community. Cf. J. F. Wippel, 'The Dating of James of Viterbo's Quodlibet I and Godfrey of Fontaines' Quodlibet VIII', *Augustiniana*, 24 (1974), 348–86.

[33] See above, p. 59.

What James does next, however, is draw a sharp distinction between the operation of nature and the operation of grace. Concupiscent love, he argues, is exhibited towards God both as a natural love (that is, as a love for the universal good on which every good, including the individual's own good, depends for its existence) and as a supernatural love (that is, as a love for the good which brings the individual the blessing of heavenly beatitude). Benevolent love or friendship, on the other hand, is exhibited towards God only as a supernatural or gracious love. As a natural love, it can only move the individual towards himself in the same way that Aristotle had argued in book IX of the *Ethics*. In exercising the love of friendship, therefore, humans have a greater natural love for themselves than they do for God.

James bases his division of natural and supernatural love on Bernard of Clairvaux's fourfold classification—love of self on account of self, love of God on account of self, love of God on account of God, and love of God and self on account of God—of which the first two originate in nature and the second two in grace.[34] James uses the appearance of self-love as both a natural and a gracious love to illustrate the Thomist principle that grace does not overturn the order of nature but perfects it (*gratia non tollit naturam sed perficit*). Nevertheless, he insists that Bernard's classification demonstrates that it is only with the gracious love of friendship, with the supernatural love of *caritas*, that humans can love themselves on account of God. Natural love, by contrast, is always primarily motivated by love of self.[35] In exercising concupiscent love, therefore, the natural love which humans have for themselves may have God as its goal, as its final cause, but He is loved as a good which the individual will thereby secure for himself or for others. The same is true of benevolent love—in exercising the love of friendship, the natural love which humans have for God may have God as its motive cause, but He is loved for the sake of their own good in the same way that, according to Aristotle, friendship towards another person stems from friendship towards oneself.

The extent of James of Viterbo's disagreement with Godfrey becomes clearer still when he turns to summarize the arguments of those (unnamed) theologians who maintain that, in absolute terms (*simpliciter et absolute*), humans have a greater natural love for God than they have for themselves. James cites three propositions and shows how they are used to support such a conclusion. First, as a causal good, God brings everything into being and preserves it in existence; as such, God is closer to all individual things than they are to themselves. Second, as a final good, God is the goal of all things; as such, all things should be loved on His account. Third, as a total good, God contains the principle of all goodness; as such, every other good is related to God as a part is to its whole. James's response is to examine each one of these propositions in the light of the principle that greater love implies the presence of a greater unity. As a causal good, he concedes, God is indeed closer (*intimior*) to an

---

[34] Bernard of Clairvaux, *De Diligendo Deo*, ed. J. Leclercq and H. Rochais, in *S. Bernardi Opera*, vol. iii (Rome, 1963), VIII–X, pp. 138–44.
[35] Cf. James of Viterbo, *Quod.* III.21, p. 258: *amor sui ordinatus . . . principium et causa est omnium virtutum*.

individual entity than that entity is to itself because everything depends on God for its continuation in existence. However, judged in terms of union rather than preservation, an individual entity is closer to itself than it is to God and it is union which plays the most significant role in friendship or love. Likewise, whilst James concedes that, as a final good, God is indeed the greatest good, he also insists that humans do not always love what is better rather than what is closer (*coniunctior*). Since an individual has the greatest degree of unity with himself, this can only lead to one conclusion—humans have a greater natural love for themselves.

When James turns to the implications of discussing God as a total good, he carefully dismantles the appeal to the analogy of part and whole which was so central to Godfrey of Fontaines's notion of love for the common good. According to James, a part can be considered in two ways—insofar as it is included within the whole and insofar as it is separate from it. Viewed from the first perspective, the inclusion of the part within the whole implies that there is a sense in which the part is the same as the whole. Since there can be no relation between things which are not separate, the inclusion of the part must mean that love of self and love of the whole cannot be treated in terms of one being greater (or lesser) than the other. Viewed from this perspective, therefore, the part should be treated as being 'as one' with the whole, and, as such, the part will love itself and its whole equally and with the same affection. Viewed from the second perspective, however, there is a sense in which part and whole remain separate and, in this sense, the part will actually love itself more than it loves the whole. James therefore casts doubt on the applicability of the corporeal analogy on the grounds that it is not the natural inclination of the part which prompts it to expose itself to danger in order to preserve the body, but the natural inclination of the whole which exposes the part in order to preserve itself.[36] This is, after all, why a less worthy part, such as the hand, will be exposed for the sake of a more worthy part, such as the eye. The whole uses its parts in exactly the same way that God allows the presence of evil in the universe—for the sake of the good of the whole.

If James of Viterbo expresses doubts over the applicability of the corporeal analogy to the good in God, he has similar reservations over its connection with self-sacrifice in the political community. James bases his argument on an interpretation, once again, of book IX of the *Ethics*. In risking death for the preservation of the *res publica*, he states, the good citizen loves himself more than the community, since he loves his own good of virtue which results from aiming to secure the common good. The virtuous individual still loves the common good (*bonum commune*) but, by acting virtuously, he loves the good of virtue in himself more than he loves the good of well-being in the community (*bonum salutis communitati*). James therefore concludes with a rather different interpretation of self-sacrifice than the one put forward by Godfrey of Fontaines. The virtuous citizen who lays down his life for his community may well prefer that he should perish and the community be saved than that he should be

---

[36] Like Aquinas, however, James considers the citizen's self-sacrifice to be a case of reason imitating nature—only if the individual human were naturally a part of a city, he observes, would such an inclination be natural. Cf. Aquinas, *Ia* 60.5.

saved and the community perish, but this does not amount to loving the community more than himself. Even though his good of virtue would not exist without his love for the common good (*bonum commune*), the individual in question still has a greater love for his own action of virtue than he has for the well-being of the community (*salus communitatis*). This is clear from the fact that the individual will refuse to lose the good of virtue for the sake of saving the community. James of Viterbo, like Henry of Ghent (and Albertus Magnus), is clearly keen to distinguish a moral definition of the good of the community (*bonum commune*) from a material definition (*salus communitatis*). Thus, in James's opinion, the individual will have as much love for his own corporeal good as he does for the well-being of the community (the part loves itself and its whole equally and with the same affection) *unless* the act of sacrificing it will result in his own good of virtue. In this case, he will love the community more than he loves himself provided that they are being compared as corporeal goods. If they are being compared in terms of his own good of virtue, however, then the individual is still exhibiting an essentially greater love for himself. James concludes by reiterating the basic principle of natural love which he had found in the *Ethics*. He adds book II of the *Magna Moralia* for good measure. An individual, he states, should have the greatest love for himself by willing for himself the greatest goods (*optima bona*), namely the actions of virtue.

When Godfrey's analysis of love for the common good is read in the light of James's critique, it becomes clear why it was thought necessary to use his thirteenth quodlibet (1297/8) to return to the question for a second time. Godfrey tackles James head on, questioning his understanding both of the nature of love and of the principle of inclusion.[37] Thus, whilst Godfrey agrees with James that an individual does not love anything unless he is in some way 'as one' with it, he uses his own account of transformative love and the *ratio boni et convenientis* to insist that this unity occurs because love is a unitive power and because whatever is loved is loved according to the principle of congruence. When an individual thing is a natural part of some whole, therefore (in this case, when a human being is part of the supreme whole in God), each individual has a truer unity, or union, with regard to this whole than it does with regard to its own existence as an individual. As a part, an individual has a natural love for the common good of its whole because this whole is congruent with it and 'as one' with it. The union which is involved in friendship is of exactly this kind. Just as the good of the part is ordered towards the good of the whole, so the individual loves himself both as an individual unity and insofar as he benefits the good of the common unity which he comprises with his friend. It is this community, however, this common good, which constitutes the individual's primary good and the principal object of his will. A part loves the common good more than it loves its individual good inasmuch as it orders its individual good towards the common good.

---

[37] *Quod.* XIII.1, pp. 169–84. For the connection between James of Viterbo's third quodlibet and Godfrey's thirteenth quodlibet, compare e.g. James's *Quod.* III.12 with Godfrey's *Quod.* XIII.3, and James's *Quod.* III.1 in 1 with Godfrey's *Quod.* XIII.1.

Although the common good may include the greatest individual good, it is never ordered towards this individual good nor is this individual good the object of greater love. Godfrey, perhaps sensibly, does not attempt to make the corporeal analogy fit this conclusion. Instead, he focuses on the metaphor of self-sacrifice. An individual, he argues, does not risk death for his own good but for the common good. Although the greatest good of the part consists of ordering itself towards the common good, the individual does not love his own good more than the common good. It is the common good which is the essential and primary object of self-sacrifice, even though the virtuous individual also secures the greatest good for himself as a consequence (*suum bonum optimum consequitur*).

Godfrey of Fontaines, Henry of Ghent, and James of Viterbo were all agreed on drawing a distinction between concupiscence and benevolence, between loving for the sake of one's own good and loving for the sake of the good of the object loved. Where they differed was over whether natural love was exclusively directed towards the self and whether the common good was the goal or the result of an individual's virtuous actions. For Henry of Ghent, love should be directed towards God, self, and neighbour in descending order of priority. There was little room in this *ordo caritatis* for any notion of the common good other than as a beneficial consequence of individual virtue. For James of Viterbo, on the other hand, there could be love for a common good but this was only in the course of exhibiting a greater or equal love for oneself; a disinterested love for a common good could only be the effect, not of natural love, but of the gracious love of *caritas*. Godfrey of Fontaines, meanwhile, is determined to emphasize, against both Henry and James, that, even in a natural capacity, the primary motivation of an individual is not self-love, the natural love which he has for his individual good of virtue. To underline the point, Godfrey quotes Aquinas. Just because everything tends to love what is good for itself does not mean that it should love such good as an end; friendship may have its origin in love of self, as Aristotle had argued, but this does not necessarily represent its goal, its final cause.[38] This goal is, instead, (in the case of friendship) the cooperative life of virtue or (in the case of self-sacrifice) the common good of the community and the common good in God.

In examining the nature of self-love in book IX of the *Ethics*, Godfrey establishes clear limits to the priority which should be given to the individual good. Godfrey is able to argue that the individual good is always included in, and derived from, the common good in God because of his analysis of goodness in the universe as the *ratio boni et convenientis*. He has no hesitation in making the inclusion of the individual good within the good of the human community follow suit. Henry of Ghent and James of Viterbo may have prompted Godfrey to insist on a more explicit prescription of inclusion and on a more definite requirement of positive individual good than Aquinas had appeared to think necessary, but it is still a recognizably Thomist notion on which Godfrey relies—the common good is the natural object of the will and of

---

[38] Aquinas, III *Sent.* 29.1.3 in/ad 2, in/ad 3. Cf. *Q. Disp. de Virt.* II.4 in 2; *IIaIIae* 26.3 in 1.

love. Godfrey certainly shares Henry's emphasis on a principle of inclusion, on the presence of good for the individual. For Godfrey, however, this stems from the very different assumption that goodness in the political community follows the same principles of operation as goodness in the universe. Unlike Henry and unlike James (or, indeed, unlike Albertus Magnus), Godfrey does not concede that the common good of the human community can be defined as material security and well-being (*salus*). Like Aquinas, Godfrey consistently defines the common good of the human community as the life of virtue and, as a result, he is able to make it subject to exactly the same principles as the common good in God. By loving the common good as the good on which his own good depends for its existence, the individual loves the common good more than his individual good even though he knows that his individual good will result as a consequence of his virtuous action.

Godfrey's analysis of the relationship between the individual and the common good extends further than a discussion of the place of self-love within the *ordo caritatis*. In his account of friendship, for example, Godfrey points out the parallels which can also be drawn between the operation of love and and the operation of justice. Justice, he remarks, is pre-eminent amongst the virtues because all the other virtues concern only the intrinsic good of the individual who exercises them, whereas justice concerns the good of the individual towards whom it is exercised. Of all the various forms of friendship, therefore, the friendship which exists towards one's parents, towards the common good, and, above all, towards God, demonstrates the closest correspondence with the defining principle of justice.[39] Likewise, in his discussion of goodness in the universe, Godfrey distinguishes between a twofold good (*duplex bonum*). On the one hand, there is the private good, a good which is congruent with the individual and which Godfrey defines as personal perfection. On the other hand, there is the order of justice, a good which is congruent with the universe and which Godfrey defines as a *bonum . . . quoddam et maxime commune*. Goodness in the universe, he comments, does not exist only in the goodness of each individual but in the ordering of every individual towards the whole.[40]

Albertus Magnus and Thomas Aquinas had already demonstrated that the connection between the love of friendship and the exercise of justice could have an important bearing on the relationship between the individual and the common good in the human community. Godfrey of Fontaines picked up the same line of reasoning and applied it to the same contexts, one practical, the other theoretical. Thus, in the first instance, the connection between friendship and justice enables Godfrey to reconcile the apparently conflicting demands which are faced by an individual in a religious community when he is commanded by his superior to reveal a private sin which has been committed by his neighbour.[41] In his fourth quodlibet (1287), Godfrey's response to this dilemma is to argue that an individual is not obliged to obey his superior if obedience would run counter to *caritas* or to a precept such as the secrecy

---

[39] *Quod.* X.6, p. 321.   [40] *Quod.* VIII.10, pp. 100–1. Cf. *Q. Ord.* II, p. 111.
[41] Cf. above, pp. 109–10, 124, 162–3.

of the confessional. Since the love of *caritas* prescribes the correction of one's neighbour for his own good, a goal which might not be served by his delation to a superior, then there are clearly some instances in which disobedience is both permissible and justifiable. Nevertheless, if the sin in question harms individuals other than the perpetrator, then Godfrey is quite clear that the sinner must be denounced to his superior. However, although such action still aims to secure the correction of one's neighbour, its primary goal is the public good and, as such, this becomes a matter for justice rather than love.[42] Godfrey's position in 1287, therefore, is to follow Henry of Ghent and apply separate criteria to the individual and the common good—love secures the individual good, justice secures the common good. When Godfrey returns to the same question in 1296/7, however, he is careful to bring these two virtues within a single scale of reference.[43] Godfrey now betrays a certain unease with those *magni doctores* who express a preference for public delation without resolving the opposition of the requirements of *caritas* and justice. Godfrey's own solution accordingly follows that of Aquinas—the demands of individual and common good can be reconciled within an overriding order of love, a hierarchy which requires greater regard to be shown towards the common good than to the good of one person. If a neighbour's sin will harm other people unless they are forewarned, then *caritas* demands that this sin, even if it is hidden, should be revealed to those who are in a position to prevent such harm arising. Concern for the sinner should still be expressed but it is limited to trying as much as is legitimately possible to preserve his reputation (*fama*).[44]

In refusing to countenance the possibility of any opposition between the demands of *caritas* and the demands of justice, Godfrey is also drawn to consider the more theoretical question which the existence of such harmony raised. Like Albertus and Aquinas, Godfrey seeks to analyse the relationship between the individual good and the common good by expounding an otherwise elliptical statement from book V of the *Ethics*—justice is the same as all virtue but differs from it in essence; it is not a part of virtue but complete virtue.[45] It is, perhaps, a measure of the importance which Godfrey came to attach to Aristotle's connection between justice and virtue that he chose to devote much of his fourteenth quodlibet of 1298/9 to precisely this

[42] *Quod.* IV.20, pp. 294–7. Godfrey's first four quodlibets have been preserved in a *reportatio*; their precise wording has therefore to be treated with a certain caution and, for the third and fourth quodlibets, compared with another, shorter version of the text (*Brevis*). In this instance, for example, the role of the common good in *Quod.* IV.20 is made more explicit in the *Brevis* version (p. 351).

[43] *Quod.* XII.12, pp. 121–4.

[44] Cf. *Quod.* IX.14, pp. 258–60, where Godfrey discusses a son's obligation to his pagan father and to a Christian stranger. Godfrey concludes that the father's lack of faith does not abrogate the son's obligation because it is a purely personal matter and because it does not militate against the common good, a good which is otherwise better and more divine than the good represented by the father. If it did affect the common good, then Godfrey would presumably have restated the position which he adopted in response to whether Christ should have descended from the cross in order to comfort his grieving mother (*Quod.* VIII.13, p. 135). For the possible conflict between the commands of one's parents and the commands of one's *patria*, see Augustine, *Sermo* 62.5.8 (*PL* 38, cols. 414–23), col. 418.

[45] Aristotle, *Ethics* V.1 1129[b]25–33, 1130[a]8–13; see above, pp. 40–1, 117–18.

question.[46] Its importance to his wider understanding of the relationship between the individual good and the common good in the political community becomes clear as soon as he turns to the analogy of part and whole.

According to Godfrey, whatever constitutes a part also pertains to the whole, and, as a result, the good of the part is capable of being ordered towards the good of the whole. Since every human being forms a natural part of the political community, there is nothing so 'proper' to any individual which cannot be ordered towards the common good and the *res publica*. Thus, in addition to those virtuous dispositions which order individuals' actions towards themselves and towards other individuals qua individuals, there must also be a third disposition which orders these actions towards the community or towards other individuals qua members of that community. It is this disposition which Godfrey identifies as the virtue of justice. He then considers what makes justice unlike the other two dispositions in the sense of being a general rather than a particular virtue. Justice is general, he suggests, on two counts. In the first instance, rather than have a substance or subject-matter which is peculiar to itself, justice simply uses the actions of all the particular virtues. In the second instance, the goal of justice is a common goal because it comprises the good of the whole community, or of everyone in the community, and orders all the actions of the other virtues towards it. Godfrey is adamant that this common good is not common (or general) by abstraction from particular goods. It is, he argues, a single whole according to the principle of number, and common (or general) according to the many individual goods which it contains as integral parts. As illustrations of this type of whole, Godfrey offers city, province, kingdom, and world, each one of which represents a single object in itself but also something common (or general) in that it comprises every one of its constituent beings. In Godfrey's opinion, therefore, the goal of the general virtue of justice represents a specific sort of common good, a specific sort of 'community'—it is common by virtue and by aggregation because it is an integral whole which contains the good of every particular virtue.[47]

When Godfrey investigates the nature of this 'community', this generality 'by virtue and by aggregation', he differentiates four ways in which justice can be exercised in any given action. The first category of justice is the correct disposition of an individual towards the act itself. In this sense, justice is general only by predication—it is identical in essence with every particular virtue in the way that a genus is identical in essence with each one of its species. The second category of justice is the disposition of an individual's actions towards another person. In this sense, too, justice is general by predication. It differs from the first category, however, because

---

[46] *Quod.* XIV.1, pp. 303–17. Cf. *Quod.* XIV.3, pp. 340–1; Lagarde, 'La Philosophie sociale', 103; id., *La Naissance*, 174; Neumann, *Der Mensch*, 37. For the form in which *Quod.* XIV was originally delivered, see A. Pelzer, *Les Philosophes Belges* XIV, 223; P. Glorieux, 'Notations brèves sur Godefroid de Fontaines', *RTAM* 11 (1939), 170–1.

[47] Godfrey compares this goal to happiness (*felicitas*) since this too is a common good (*quoddam bonum commune*) which comprises the good of all the virtues (cf. Aristotle, *Ethics* I.7 1098ª16–18; *Politics* VII.8 1328ª37–8, VII.13 1332ª7–9). However, he does not explain how it then differs from the goal of justice.

this predication is not univocal but analogous and equivocal. The third category of justice, meanwhile, is the disposition of an individual's actions towards another person, not in the sense of any other person but in the sense of one individual in particular. This form of justice (which Godfrey identifies with Aristotle's distributive and retributive justice) is unlike the first two categories in that it is a single virtue in its essence (*secundum essentiam*). Its unity is thus the unity of a species rather than a genus and, since it is a particular virtue in its own right just like courage or temperance, it cannot be general to the other virtues. It is therefore left to the fourth and final category of justice to provide Godfrey with a definition which covers the disposition of an individual's actions with regard to everything which can be ordered towards the common good. Justice in this sense is, like the third category, a single virtue *secundum essentiam* in that it possesses a form and a species according to which it is essentially different from all the other virtues. However, it is also general to these other virtues, not (like the first and second categories) by predication, but by power and virtue (*efficacia et virtute*) and by aggregation and inclusion (*generalitate cuiusdam aggregationis et continentiae*). 'Power and virtue', Godfrey explains, means acting as a universal cause. This type of justice is therefore a general virtue in terms of the effects which it contains and the actions which it orders. 'Aggregation and inclusion', on the other hand, means being an integral whole. The object of this type of justice comprises the community of humans and the community of their goods, a community in which all virtues and all humans are gathered together and contained. Justice in this fourth sense is thus a virtue which is both general and particular—general in that it uses and comprises all the other virtues, particular in that it has its own distinct goal and principal object, namely a common good towards which the actions of all its constituent virtues can be ordered.

It is with his fourth definition of justice that Godfrey explains Aristotle's statement in book V of the *Ethics* that justice is the same as all virtue but differs from it in essence. On Godfrey's reading, this 'general' or 'legal' justice has no other subject-matter than the subject-matter and the actions of the other virtues. It is the same as every particular virtue, therefore, because there are certain actions in any virtue which can be ordered towards the formal or final object of justice, namely the common good. It is this goal, however, which also gives this justice its 'formal and specific essence', which makes general justice 'essentially' distinct from every particular virtue. General justice is therefore more than just a matter of 'ordering', of being every virtue according to a directive power. It is also a matter of containing every virtue in a real and substantial way. This type of justice is a general virtue by power *and* by aggregation. An action of general justice, in other words, comprises the action of any particular virtue when it is ordered towards the common good as its principal object and goal. General justice is thus a single virtue in terms of its essence and species, but it is all virtues, or all virtue, in terms of its substance or subject-matter (*una virtus secundum essentiam et speciem . . . omnes virtutes sive omnis virtus materialiter*).

Godfrey's analysis of the connection between justice and virtue in book V of the *Ethics* provides a more complete exposition of Aristotle's text than anything which was offered by either Albertus Magnus or Aquinas.[48] This is due, in part, to Godfrey's recognition that the connection between virtue and general justice is central to the relationship between the individual and the common good. It is also due to the precision of his terminology. Thus, whereas Godfrey himself has previously been content to use the term 'inclusion' (*includere*), the language of his fourteenth quodlibet becomes much more exact. Just as general justice is described as the same as, but also different from, particular virtue, and the common good is described as the same as, but also different from, the individual good, so Godfrey refers to them as 'comprising' (*comprehendere*) as well as 'containing' (*continere*) the virtues and goods which they include (*includere*). Godfrey is equally careful in his use of the term 'ordered'. As soon as the analogy of part and whole is used in the context of the operation of justice within the political community, Godfrey (like Albertus and Aquinas) feels obliged to point out that the good of the part is not 'necessarily ordered' towards the good of the whole (*referendum*) but 'capable of being ordered' (*referibile*). When the good of the individual is ordered towards the common good in God, Godfrey does use gerundive forms (*ordinandum, ordinanda et referenda*), but when the good of the whole is the good of the human community, the individual good is 'in some way capable of being ordered' towards the common good (*aliquo modo referibile*).[49] Thus, whereas Godfrey starts the quodlibet by suggesting that 'all actions' of particular virtues are ordered towards the common good (*ad ipsum omnes actus aliarum virtutum referuntur*), he soon limits this scope to 'certain actions' of all virtues (*quaedam referibilia*), or simply to 'actions' of all virtues. By the end of the quodlibet, he is conceding that, although justice comprises all those virtuous actions which can be ordered in some way towards the good of the community, there are still certain actions which cannot be made common because of their essential nature.

Having established what makes general justice identical with individual virtues, Godfrey turns to the question of what makes them different. In particular, he examines whether the distinction between an action of a particular virtue and an action of this virtue when it is ordered towards the goal of legal justice is a real and essential difference (*secundum rem et essentiam*) or simply a logical or conceptual difference in the goal by which it is defined (*secundum rationem*). Godfrey clearly wants to avoid concluding that it is only a difference *secundum rationem* because, were this to be the case, it would then be indistinguishable from the difference which exists when an action of a particular virtue is ordered towards another particular virtue. To draw this conclusion would leave no distinction between an act of particular justice and an act of general justice. Godfrey accordingly spends some time spelling out how a difference in essence is more than just a difference of ends. The position which he is attempting to modify was originally propounded by Aquinas but, once again, the immediate object of Godfrey's attention appears to be James of Viterbo. According

---

[48] Cf. *Eustratii et Michaelis et Anonyma in Ethica Nicomachea Commentaria*, ed. G. Heylbut (Commentaria in Aristotelem Graeca XX; Berlin, 1892), pp. 209, 211. Cf. *Aristotelis Opera cum Averrois Commentaria* (editio Iuntina, 2nd edn., 11 vols.; Venice, 1560–2), iii fo. 65r–v.

[49] Cf. *Quod.* XIII.1, p. 179.

to James, all human actions are ordered towards the *bonum humanum* as parts are ordered towards a whole. It is this ordering towards a single goal which provides the principle of unity for the moral virtues under the direction of prudence (in the intellect) and general justice (in the will). Aristotle's observation that general justice is, in a sense, all virtue, is therefore understood by James to mean all virtue according to its subject-matter (*materia*). General or legal justice is thus the moral virtue which takes those actions which concern another human being insofar as he belongs to the community and orders them towards the common good. It is therefore a general virtue, not through predication nor through its object, but through its substance or subject-matter (the matter of every virtue) and through causation (ordering the actions of these virtues towards the goal of the common good).[50]

Godfrey's discussion of the relationship between essence and existence formed an important part of his metaphysical thought. Within a philosophical context, his insistence on the real identity of essence and existence represented an attack on the position of Aquinas, or, more precisely, on the Thomist position put forward by Giles of Rome. In Godfrey's opinion, if there are different accidents in a single entity, then there will also be different existences which are differentiated by these different accidents. A single object, therefore, can possess one substantial existence (*esse subsistentiae*, *esse simpliciter*) and several accidental existences (*esse existentiae*, *esse secundum quid*) according to the different combinations of accidents which this subject can take on.[51] Within the context of moral philosophy, Godfrey's insistence on the real identity of essence and existence provides him with a framework for his own account of the difference between general justice and its constituent virtues.

According to Godfrey, there are as many accidental existences as there are different forms (that is, as there are different combinations of accidents for a given object). As a result, since existence is the same as essence, a formal difference can also be expressed as a difference in essence, where essence is understood to mean accidental existence (*esse existentiae*). Godfrey understands Aristotle's definition of justice in book V of the *Ethics* in the light of this conclusion. General justice is different from particular virtue in the sense that, although there is no formal difference in goodness between the good of one individual and the good of many individuals, there is still a formal (in the sense of existential) difference between them, because individual goods are ordered towards one another such that the good of the whole community results. In order to justify the attribution of this formal difference, Godfrey quotes Aquinas' commentary on book I of the *Politics*—the formal difference between the common good and the individual good is a difference in species. However, Godfrey insists that this formal difference is also a difference in essence (*secundum formam et essentiam*).[52] This is because 'being ordered towards something' qualifies as a relation and, as such, it should be classified among the ten categories. Being ordered towards something is thus a really existing accident, just like the other individual properties

---

[50] James of Viterbo, *Quod.* II.17, pp. 177–9; *Quod.* III.21, pp. 253–4. Cf. *Quod.* IV.28, p. 102.
[51] Wippel, *Metaphysical Thought*, ch. 5.   [52] *Quod.* XIV.3, p. 346.

which are described by the nine accidental categories. According to Godfrey, there-fore, the addition of an accident to an entity represents a change in that entity's essence where essence is defined as its accidental existence.

Godfrey's analysis of the difference between general justice and virtue is depend-ent upon this account of the relationship between essence and existence. The action of a particular virtue, he argues, and the action of a particular virtue when it is ordered towards the goal of general justice are one and the same action *secundum rem et substantiam* but they are different not just *secundum rationem* but also *realiter*. This 'real' difference derives from the fact that each action is comprised (*comprehendere*) by a separate decision-making process. Godfrey cites the example of the same person when he is at home and when he is at the theatre. Defined in terms of his essence across time (that is, essence in the sense of substantial existence), the individual is one and the same individual *secundum rem* and different only *secundum rationem*. Defined in terms of his essence in the house (that is, essence in the sense of accidental exist-ence) and his essence in the theatre, he is two 'really' different things.[53] Thus, the difference between an individual's actions when they are ordered towards a particu-lar good and an individual's actions when they are ordered towards the common good is a distinction *secundum rationem*. However, in terms of the whole (*totum*) which is composed of (*quod est*) the individual and his actions when they are ordered towards a particular good, and the whole which is composed of the individual and his actions when they are ordered towards the common good, there is also a real and essential difference, namely a difference in the genus of moral decision. If a particular virtue is considered not only in the sense of being ordered towards a common goal but also in the sense of being a whole which is composed of its action and its goal, then it differs from a single, particular virtue absolutely and essentially and not just *secundum rationem*. Thus, the whole which is constituted by the man in the theatre is really different from the same man considered in himself. This difference might be in accidental rather than substantial reality but it is a real difference nevertheless.

This is not an easy argument to grasp.[54] Godfrey is arguing that the same object can have two different combinations of accidents which ultimately define this object as it is in reality. When the individual man is at home, he has the accidental property of location, of being at home, whereas, when the same man is in the theatre, he has the accidental property of being at the theatre and not at home. Thus, the same object can have one real accidental characteristic (location) according to which it will differ from one state to another. The person is still the same in both places but he is also 'really' different in the sense of having a different accidental property in each place.

---

[53] *Quod.* XIV.1, p. 310.

[54] Take, for example, an apple when it is unripe and when it is ripe; although it is the same apple when it is green and when it is red, it is also really different. Since an individual apple exists as a combination of accidents, any change in its accidents implies a change in existence. Thus, if essence and existence are the same entity (as e.g. the existence of Socrates and the essence of Socrates are the same in that they consti-tute the same individual), and if individuals exist only in accidents, then any change in the accidents of an individual (Socrates going bald) implies a change in existence even though the essence of that individual (Socrates' humanity) remains the same across time.

This conclusion is then applied to the relationship between individual virtues and general justice, although in the case of the latter the real accidental characteristic is the quality of being ordered towards the common good. Returning to Aristotle's statement that virtue is the same as legal justice but different in essence (*esse*), therefore, Godfrey sets his own interpretation side by side with that of James of Viterbo. According to James's (Thomist) definition, identity in substance should be understood as identity in matter, and difference in *esse* as difference in the order of ends (*secundum rationem*). According to the second definition (Godfrey's own), the action of one particular virtue when it is ordered towards its end, and the same action when it is considered as a whole which comprises both the action and the common goal, are identical in substance and subject, but different in form, species and essence (that is, essence in the sense of accidental existence): *unum et idem secundum substantiam vel materiam et subiectum, differens tamen secundum esse formale et specificum.*[55]

If the first question raised in Godfrey's fourteenth quodlibet is exclusively concerned with the connection between general justice and its component virtues, then the second question raises the wider issue of the relation between the virtue of general justice and the virtues of friendship and love.[56] This is, in many respects, a natural progression since, on the strength of Godfrey's response to the first question, friendship and love would appear to be rival candidates for the description of 'general virtue' which Godfrey has just applied to justice.[57] It is also a question which, once again, drew Godfrey into a debate with James of Viterbo. In James's view, the virtue of friendship (*amicitia*) should be regarded as interchangeable with general or legal justice, since both of them are virtues which direct an individual's actions towards another individual. Both friendship and justice can therefore be termed the 'form' of the moral virtues which are directed by prudence. They can be differentiated from one another, however, by distinguishing between their ends. Thus, the goal of legal justice is the common good, whereas the goal of friendship is the honourable good (*bonum honestum*) or, more precisely, the supreme and greatest good, namely blessedness (*beatitudo*) or happiness (*felicitas*). James does not explore the implications of drawing such a clear distinction between the common good and beatitude or happiness. What he does do is argue that there is more justification for making friendship the 'form' of the moral virtues than there is for legal justice. In his opinion, this is why Aristotle's *Ethics* had treated friendship at such length *after* it had dealt with the other virtues, including justice. It is also why Aristotle's *amicitia* can serve as a parallel for Christian *caritas*. Just as acquired friendship is the form of all the moral virtues, so infused friendship is the form of all the virtues which are infused by grace. An individual, he concludes, will love himself and his fellow-humans with the general virtue of *amicitia* insofar as his friendship is ordered towards the good of natural beatitude but he will love himself and his fellow-humans

---

[55] *Quod.* XIV.3, pp. 349–50.

[56] *Quod.* XIV.2, pp. 320–38. Cf. Neumann, *Der Mensch*, 38. For *amicitia* and *caritas*, see *Quod.* XIV.5, pp. 373–432, and compare Henry of Ghent, *Quod.* X.12, pp. 274–85.

[57] For prudence, see *Quod.* XIV.3, p. 353; *Q. Ord.* III, pp. 119–37. Cf. Neumann, *Der Mensch*, 90.

with the general virtue of *caritas* insofar as his friendship is ordered towards the good of supernatural beatitude.[58]

Godfrey of Fontaines disagrees with James of Viterbo's claim that friendship is a general virtue on the grounds that the object of *amicitia* is necessarily limited to the good of one person, or of a few, and does not extend, like legal justice, to the common good of the multitude or community.[59] In Godfrey's view, friendship can be called 'general' only in terms of its material object (because the good which an individual wishes for his friend includes all possible virtues) and not in terms of its essence or nature. Strictly speaking, therefore, the various forms of friendship which Aristotle describes in the *Ethics* do not, in his opinion, include any which constitute a general virtue. If an individual has the good of the whole community as his object (that is, the good of his friend insofar as it pertains to the common good), then his action pertains to the general virtue of justice. Thus, to love one's neighbour with reference to the common good (*sub ratione boni communis*) is to perform an act, not of *amicitia*, but of legal justice.[60]

The love which an individual demonstrates in friendship, however, is not the same as the love which an individual demonstrates in relation to his ultimate goal, namely the common good in God. Thus, if Godfrey is prepared to dismiss James of Viterbo's account of friendship as a general virtue, his account of *caritas* is an altogether different matter. Godfrey has already observed, in his thirteenth quodlibet, that *caritas* is similar to legal justice because it has the common good as its object and because it orders the actions of all particular virtues towards it. The common good towards which *caritas* is ordered is God, the most common and universal good of all. Goodness in God is, like the good of the community, common, not by abstraction or predication, but by virtue and perfection in the sense that God contains all goods within Himself as the principle from which they all derive and the goal towards which they are ordered in return. The one difference between goodness in God and goodness in the community is that, unlike the common good of the community, the common good in God is an aggregate of many goods which retain their real difference from one another.[61] In his fourteenth quodlibet, Godfrey explores the parallels between *caritas* and justice a little further—*caritas* is one virtue *secundum essentiam* but it is also a 'general' virtue because it orders the actions of all virtues towards the divine good.[62] God is again described as a common good, the supreme good, the good of all good, the good which contains the good of each individual part of Creation in a more perfect way than creatures do themselves.[63]

Whilst Godfrey is prepared to argue accordingly that *caritas* is a general virtue which is comparable to legal justice, he is also careful to establish just where the two

---

[58] James of Viterbo, *Quod.* III.21, pp. 254–8.

[59] *Quod.* XIV.2, p. 328. Cf. Giles of Rome, *Quod.* IV.18 fo. 56r. Compare *Quod.* I.10, pp. 25–7, where Godfrey argues that the love of friendship can be directed towards one's country (*patria*) or the common good (*bonum commune*).

[60] *Quod.* XIV.2, pp. 325–6. Cf. *Quod.* XIV.3, p. 348.   [61] *Quod.* XIII.1, p. 179.

[62] *Quod.* XIV.1, p. 308.   [63] *Quod.* XIV.2, pp. 327–30. Cf. Neumann, *Der Mensch*, 90–1.

virtues differ.[64] Legal justice has no other subject-matter than the actions of the particular virtues which it orders towards the common good. *Caritas* displays the same characteristic but it also possesses activities which pertain only to itself, namely loving God and willing His good for its own sake. In loving God, an individual loves not only a common good but also a specific individual. In loving God with *caritas*, therefore, an individual must exercise both a general virtue and a particular form of friendship which is found only in the truth of faith. Legal justice, meanwhile, is concerned with the common good in this life and governs those activities which are appropriate to natural human capacities. As a result, even if legal justice is pre-eminent among the virtues, even if it can be defined by book V of the *Ethics* as perfect or complete virtue, then this is only within philosophical terms of reference. *Caritas*, in contrast, applies to the common good in God and it must therefore be more perfect and more noble than legal justice because its object is God Himself. The more common a good is, Godfrey explains, the more divine and more worthy it is, yet God is not just 'more' common or 'more' divine, but the good which is common for all things and which is the very principle of divinity.[65]

In disagreeing with James of Viterbo's classification of friendship as a general virtue, Godfrey makes it quite clear that none of the forms of friendship described by Aristotle can be placed in this category because they are all directed towards particular individuals rather than towards a common good. On this reckoning, in order to qualify as a general virtue, love has to be directed towards a common good. What makes generality possible for the form of friendship denoted by *caritas*, therefore, is the fact that the particular individual towards whom *caritas* is directed, namely God, is also the metaphysical common good of all Creation. This raises the further question, however, of what role *caritas* plays in love for the common good, not in God, but of the human community, either as an object in itself or when it is personified in another individual.[66] If the act of self-sacrifice, for example, is motivated by love for the common good, should this be classified as an act of *caritas* or as an act of legal justice? According to Godfrey, when *caritas* acts as a general virtue in relation to a particular virtue, it demonstrates the same defining principle which is exhibited when legal justice acts as a general virtue in relation to a particular virtue. What happens when the virtue which *caritas* is acting upon is itself the general virtue of legal justice? According to Godfrey, *caritas* is a general virtue primarily in terms of its causality, that is, because it orders individual virtues towards the ultimate goal of human life. It

    [64] Cf. Cicero, *De Officiis*, ed. M. Winterbottom (Oxford, 1994), I.20, p. 9.
    [65] Godfrey does not develop the point but he does suggest that this difference in subject-matter might be due to the fact that the object of legal justice—the common good of the community—is loved, not for its own sake, but for the sake of the person who is doing the loving, that is, not with the love of friendship but with the love of concupiscence. Although this remains no more than a suggestion (*potest esse*), it is certainly a surprising one, since it is hard to reconcile with Godfrey's account of a natural love for the common good in *Quodlibet* X.6.
    [66] Cf. *Q. Ord.* I, p. 89, where Godfrey argues that whatever good an individual does to another individual constitutes the good of the whole and the good of the individual performing it inasmuch as everyone communicates in one common good.

is general in its form (that is, in the way in which general justice is the aggregate 'community' of individual virtues) only in a secondary sense. Indeed, in this sense, Godfrey is prepared to argue that *caritas* is identical to general justice in virtue (*virtualiter*) inasmuch as it has the same power of causality and the same practical effect.[67] Self-sacrifice, in other words, can be seen either as an act of *caritas* or as an act of legal justice. The only difference appears to be whether the common good for the sake of which this act is performed is ultimately ordered towards the common good in God. Self-sacrifice is therefore an act of *caritas* when it is performed by a Christian and an act of legal justice when it is performed by a virtuous pagan.

Godfrey's discussion of the relationship which exists between *caritas* and legal justice when they are exercised towards the same common good clearly presupposes a particular view of the relationship between theological and moral virtue. Godfrey's wider interest in this question is well known.[68] Indeed, the relationship between moral and theological virtue is a recurrent theme in his *Disputed Questions*, where a distinction is repeatedly drawn between the natural and the supernatural goals of humankind, between the dual happiness (*duplex felicitas*) of a human and a heavenly community (*civilitas*), and between the virtues which direct humans towards these ends, namely acquired virtue and the virtue which is infused through *caritas*.[69] In *Quaestio Disputata* XIX, Godfrey embarks upon a detailed discussion of the connection which exists between these two goals and their respective virtues when he considers the question of whether an individual can possess acquired virtue without possessing theological virtue.[70]

In their own discussions of the relation between acquired and infused virtue, Henry of Ghent and James of Viterbo both argued that moral virtue needs to be perfected by *caritas*—Henry on the basis of Augustine's *Contra Iulianum*,[71] James on the basis of Aquinas' principle that grace does not abolish nature but perfects it.[72] Godfrey of Fontaines provides an altogether more complex account than either of his

---

[67] *Quod.* XIV.1, p. 309; *Quod.* XIV.2, pp. 330–1; *Quod.* XIV.3, p. 349. Cf. *Q. Disp.* V (Lottin, *Psychologie et morale*, iv. pp. 591–7).

[68] O. Lottin, 'Les Vertus morales acquises sont-elles de vraies vertus? La Réponse des théologiens de saint Thomas à Pierre Auriol', *RTAM* 21 (1954), 101–29. For Godfrey of Fontaines, see ibid. 122. Cf. Lottin, *Psychologie et morale*, iv. 494–510, 575–99.

[69] *Q. Disp.* I (Neumann, *Der Mensch*, 152–66) p. 156; *Q. Disp.* V (Lottin, *Psychologie et morale*, iv. pp. 593–4); *Q. Disp.* XI (Lottin, *Psychologie et morale*, iii. pp. 497–502); *Q. Disp.* XV (Koch, *Durandi de S. Porciano*, pp. 60–6); *Q. Disp.* XVII (Grundel, *Die Lehre von dem Umstanden*, pp. 656–7). Their chronology remains in doubt. Lottin (*Psychologie et morale*, iii. 502 n. 1; iv. 598 n. 1) has placed questions which concern the virtues to between 1285 and 1290; Wippel (*Metaphysical Thought of Godfrey of Fontaines*, xxxi–xxxii) believes that some of the others should be placed in the 1290s. See also id., 'Godfrey of Fontaines: Disputed Questions 9, 10, 12', *Franciscan Studies*, 33 (1973), 351–72. Cf. Gérard d'Abbeville, *Quodlibet* IV (P. Glorieux, 'Pour une édition de Gérard d'Abbeville', *RTAM* 9, 1937, 79–80).

[70] *Q. Disp.* XIX (Lottin, 'Les Vertus morales acquises', pp. 113–22).

[71] Henry of Ghent, *Quod.* V.17 fos. 286v–287r; *Quod.* XIII.10, pp. 69–78. Cf. Augustine, *Ep.*, 167.8, ed. J. Schmid, in *SS Eusebii Hieronymi et Aurelii Augustini Epistulae Mutuae* (Bonn, 1930), pp. 113–24; *De Moribus Ecclesiae* (*PL* 32, cols. 1309–44), XV, col. 1322; *Contra Iulianum* (*PL* 44, cols. 641–874), IV.3.19–21, cols. 747–9.

[72] James of Viterbo, *Quod.* II.20, pp. 203, 209–11; *Quod.* III.1, p. 20; *Quod.* III.20, p. 251.

colleagues. At the heart of his analysis is a distinction between three ways in which virtues can be connected to one another—essence, accidence, and disposition. Godfrey divides connection in essence into three further categories. The first is represented by the connection of moral virtue with prudence. The second is represented by the connection of a particular virtue with general justice. The third is represented by the connection of one particular virtue with another particular virtue in order to form a perfect whole. To illustrate the second category of connection in essence, of particular virtue with general justice, Godfrey summarizes his account of the dependence of the individual good on the good of the whole community. In the natural ordering of a particular virtue towards general justice, he states, a particular virtue derives its perfection and well-being (*suum bene esse*) as a consequence (*consequitur*) of general justice. To illustrate the third category of connection in essence, of one particular virtue with another, Godfrey discusses the composition of the world and of knowledge. In order for the world to be perfect, it requires the presence of all its principal parts; in order for an individual to be perfectly knowledgeable, he must be a whole comprising all the different parts of knowledge. In both illustrations, not only do the parts require each other in order to constitute a perfect whole but they also require each other in order to secure their own perfection. They depend for their well-being, therefore, upon the whole but also upon each other. Godfrey does not make the parallel explicit but this third category of connection in essence is very close to the *duplex ordo* from book XII of Aristotle's *Metaphysics*—the ordering of parts towards each other and towards a common goal. What Godfrey does do is analyse the difference between this third connection (of one particular virtue with another) and the second (of one particular virtue with general justice). The difference arises, he argues, because the second connection relates a part, or parts, to an absolute unity, whereas the third connection relates a part, or parts, to a unity only of order. Godfrey justifies this distinction by repeating the definition of general justice which he gave in his fourteenth quodlibet (the constituent virtues of justice are ordered towards a single goal but justice is itself a single virtue in its own right) as well as his disagreement with Aquinas (the common good of the community is more than simply the ordering of individual parts towards a common goal). What makes general justice an illustration of the second connection rather than the third is its essential unity, a unity which is not present in the world or in the knowledgeable individual.

Godfrey's discussion of his second category of essential connection, of particular virtue with general justice, raises some intriguing questions. In differentiating a community which derives its unity by virtue of being a single entity from a community which derives its unity by virtue of being ordered towards a single goal, Godfrey draws a distinction between the 'community' which is constituted by all the virtues and the 'community' which is constituted by the world. Such a separation is hard to reconcile with his fourteenth quodlibet, where the world is used as a prime example of the type of community represented by general justice. If Godfrey is presenting these two different 'communities' as two different models for the common good of the human community, then this is a significant departure. The definition of the good of the human community as the perfect good of all virtue has hitherto consistently underpinned his use of the analogy of part and whole, the principle of inclusion, and the connection with goodness in God. It is this definition which has enabled him to argue that the human will is inherently drawn to love the common good more than the individual good which arises as a consequence of that love. It is on this basis, too, that Godfrey has treated 'common good' and 'good of the community' as interchangeable terms.[73] If he is now accepting that the city, the kingdom, and the world all constitute a different type of community from the community which is denoted by general justice and the virtues, then this marks a rare acceptance that the common good of the political community could be defined in any other sense than as the common good of virtue.

Godfrey's second category of connection in essence produces a rather less problematic, but equally revealing, conclusion when it is applied to the main question under discussion, namely whether moral virtue can exist without theological virtue. In the first category of essential connection, of moral virtue with prudence, Godfrey stipulates that two requirements must be fulfilled in order for any act to be classified as virtuous—it must be good and it must be congruent with an individual's goal or nature. Thus, the good which is congruent with an individual's nature insofar as he is human (*secundum quod homo*) is to act according to right reason, an activity which is possible without the additional operation of grace. Prudence, in other words, can operate without *caritas*. In the second category of essential connection, of particular virtue with general justice, Godfrey first specifies what he means by a particular virtue securing its own well-being (*suum bene esse*). When a virtue which orders an individual towards a particular good depends, in its turn, on a second virtue by which it is itself ordered towards a common good, this dependence does not affect the essential goodness of the virtue. What it does affect is its well-being (*bene esse*) in the sense of achieving completion or perfection. It is in this sense, Godfrey suggests, that every acquired moral virtue does depend on the additional action of *caritas*. Any act which is not ordered towards the good which is the object of *caritas* falls short of securing its perfection. Nevertheless, even though it is not complete, an act which lacks *caritas* can still be regarded as, in essence, both good and virtuous. Once again, this is a conclusion which provides Godfrey with a particular perspective on the nature of the common good.

According to Godfrey, the relationship which exists between a particular virtue and general justice corresponds to the relationship which exists between acquired moral virtue and *caritas*. Both relationships, however, can also be expressed in terms of the individual good and the common good. Thus, just as a particular virtue concerns the individual good whilst general justice concerns the common good, so acquired virtue concerns the good of an individual insofar as he is human whilst *caritas* concerns the perfect common good in God. Moreover, just as every individual good should be ordered towards the good of the community, so the good of all Creation

[73] e.g. *Quod.* X.6, pp. 321–2; *Quod.* XIV.1, p. 311 (*communicatio politica vel bonum commune*), p. 315 (*bonum commune vel communitatis*).

should be ordered towards the divine good. In both instances, a particular good is made more perfect. In both instances, an individual is culpable when he fails to act as he should, either by not ordering an action of a particular virtue towards the common good of the community or by not ordering it towards the common good in God. In the case of the latter, however, the action itself remains essentially good—Godfrey does not deny this to the virtuous pagan. The fault lies in not ordering this virtue towards its required goal, a connection which would then make it perfect.

Godfrey's discussion of the relationship between moral and theological virtue in terms of his third category of connection in essence, of parts or virtues with one another, was either not delivered or it has simply not survived. Godfrey's discussion of his second general type of connection (accidental connection) met a similar fate. Only Godfrey's account of his third general type (connection in disposition) is preserved in the text, and it is with this that his analysis concludes. Defined in terms of their respective dispositions, Godfrey suggests, the moral and theological virtues exhibit a mutual dependence.[74] The absence of an account of accidental connection is, to say the least, frustrating. In his description of the second category of connection in essence, Godfrey raises the possibility that a virtuous action can be essentially good without being perfect. This strongly suggests that he was going to argue that the perfection which is brought about by *caritas* can be regarded as accidental rather than essential to moral goodness. Such a possibility is certainly strengthened by the later remarks of John of Paris and Durand of St Pourçain.[75] If true, then Godfrey's argument would mark a significant and influential modification of Aquinas' argument that moral virtue is necessarily perfected by grace.

In his theoretical analysis of the common good, Godfrey of Fontaines tackles the arguments of Thomas Aquinas, Henry of Ghent, and James of Viterbo with considerable subtlety. The sophistication of this analysis stems, in part, from the way in which Godfrey scrutinizes the terms in which the relationship between the individual and the common good is discussed. Thus, the principle of goodness in the universe is not only good (*bonum in communi*) but congruent (*ratio boni et convenientis*); inclusion is covered by the terms *continere* and *comprehendere* rather than just *includere*; dependence is described as consequential (*ex consequenti*); intrinsic good (*bonum*) is distinguished from perfection (*bene esse*); a part is not ordered towards a whole (*referendum*) but capable of being ordered towards a whole (*referibile*); a whole is common to its parts in terms of their shared substance (*secundum essentiam*) as well as in terms of sharing a single goal (*secundum rationem*). Such precision in terminology enables Godfrey, above all else, to produce an exhaustive exposition of how justice can be both the same as all virtue but also different.

---

[74] *Q. Disp.* XIX, pp. 121–2. Cf. *Q. Disp.* IV (Lottin, *Psychologie et morale*, iv. p. 587).
[75] For Durand and Pierre de la Palu, see Lottin, *Les Vertus morales*, 125–8. For John of Paris, see below, pp. 288–90. Cf. Aquinas, *IaIIae* 65.2; *IIaIIae* 23.7, discussed by Lottin, 'Les Vertues morales acquises', 101–3. See also id., 'Les Vertus morales acquises sont-elles de vraies vertus? La Réponse des théologiens de Pierre Abélard à saint Thomas d'Aquin', *RTAM* 20 (1953), 36–8.

The implications of Aristotle's definition of justice in book V of the *Ethics* for Godfrey's understanding of the common good should not be underestimated. In the first instance, it provides him with an explanation of how the common good could be the same as the individual good but also different. The good of the human community is activity in accordance with complete or perfect virtue; complete or perfect virtue is the same as justice; the relationship between the common good and the individual good is therefore the same as the relationship between general justice and its constituent virtues. In the second instance, it precipitates a discussion of the relationship between general justice and *caritas*, between the virtue which secures the common good of the human community and the virtue which secures the common good in God, between moral and theological virtue.

If the sophistication of Godfrey's analysis of the common good rests on the detail in which he is prepared to discuss the connections between general justice and virtue and between general justice and *caritas*, it also depends on the care with which he describes the operation of the *ordo caritatis*. Thomas Aquinas, Henry of Ghent, James of Viterbo, and Godfrey of Fontaines are all agreed that love is the critical element in the relationship between the individual and the common good. When Godfrey appeals to the principle of the superiority of the common good, therefore, it is almost invariably in terms of love,[76] and, when he quotes book I of the *Ethics*, he does so with the original protasis—'although it is worthy of love to secure good for the individual' (*si amabile est bonum quod est bonum uni soli, melius et divinius est quod est bonum genti et civitatibus*).[77] Where Godfrey begs to differ from both Henry and James is over the exact role which should be ascribed to self-love, to love for the individual's own good. Thus, in discussing friendship and self-sacrifice in book IX of the *Ethics*, Godfrey deploys a notion of transformative love as a means of moving beyond the twin categories of self-love and the good of another individual. By its very nature, he concludes, love gives rise to a common good, because it is communion in this good, in the life of virtue, which unites two individuals. If there is accordingly less opposition between self-love and the common good in Godfrey than there is in Henry or James, then it is due to his endorsement of the account of the *ordo caritatis* which he found in Aquinas and Giles of Rome. Unlike James of Viterbo, Godfrey was prepared to credit a purely natural love with something more than just an orientation towards the self.

Godfrey's insistence that the relationship between the individual and the common good is characterized by love for the superior common good does not mean that Godfrey ignores the presence of good for the individual. Indeed, what makes Godfrey's account similar to Henry of Ghent's is the point which both of them are trying to emphasize—the principle of inclusion, the presupposition that good for the individual is included within the common good, the argument that the individual wills not just the good in common but the good which is congruent with what is good for himself. In many ways, therefore, Godfrey's third *Quaestio Ordinaria* provides a suitable

---

[76] *Quod.* X.6, *passim*; *Quod.* XII.12, p. 122; *Quod.* XIV.2, p. 330.   [77] *Quod.* XIV.1, p. 305.

summary of his 'theory' of the common good.[78] Discussing the *bonum humanum* as the goal of prudence and of the moral virtues, Godfrey maintains that this good is one and the same (*unum et idem*) in the individual, the household, and the city. In order for an individual to be essentially good, he explains, to be good in absolute terms (*bonus simpliciter etiam secundum seipsum*), he must exercise prudence towards his fellow-humans. Otherwise, the individual will not be securing the good of friendship and the good of legal justice. Godfrey, like Albertus Magnus, takes book VI of the *Ethics* as his text: 'It is for this reason that we think that Pericles and men like him have prudence because they can see what is good for themselves and what is good for other men.'[79] Individuals are wrong to think that they ought to seek only their own good and not the good of others,[80] since to do so is to act out of an inordinate love for themselves. An individual should certainly seek his own good but he should also seek the good of the household and the city of which he is a part. This is a principle of right reason. According to 1 Corinthians 13: 5 ('love is not self-seeking'), it is also a requirement of *caritas*. Love for the individual good is included in love for the common good, as a passage from the same epistle makes clear. Paul may well have said that he was seeking what would lead to the salvation of many and not what was beneficial to himself (1 Corinthians 10: 33). Godfrey of Fontaines, however, maintains that, by acting in this way, the apostle's own greater good of perfection was, in fact, included: *licet tamen in hoc etiam suum maius bonum perfectionis includatur.*

[78] *Q. Ord.* III, pp. 133–4.
[79] Aristotle, *Ethics* VI.5 1140^b7–10. Cf. Albertus Magnus, *Super Ethica* VI.11, p. 470; *Ethica* VI.1.10, p. 418 (above, p. 46).
[80] Cf. Aristotle, *Ethics* VI.8 1142^a7–10.

9
Godfrey of Fontaines—Authority, Obedience, and Resistance

The exchanges of opinion which took place between Godfrey of Fontaines, Henry of Ghent, and James of Viterbo in the 1280s and 1290s suggest that the scholastic notion of the common good could accommodate a significant measure of disagreement. Of the three theologians, it was Godfrey who chose to follow Aquinas in drawing a close connection between metaphysical goodness in the universe and the political good of the human community. As a result, although he made a point of emphasizing that the common good includes the presence of good for the individual, it was Godfrey who displayed the fewest reservations over subordinating the individual to the political community as a part within a perfect whole. It would be a natural temptation to conclude, on this basis, that, of the three theologians, it should have been Godfrey who had the most to say about the overriding importance of the common good in concrete political contexts. Examples of its practical application are certainly widespread throughout his work. However, Henry of Ghent demonstrated that it was quite possible for a scholastic theologian to place the common good at the heart of his political analysis at the same time as having a very weak notion of any metaphysical 'good in common' and a very limited definition of the goods which are actually secured by the human community. It remains an open question, therefore, whether Godfrey's discussion of the practical consequences of the common good in human society was *necessarily* connected to his analysis of goodness in God and in the universe.

Godfrey's interest in the political application of a notion of the common good emerged from the same contemporary contexts which so stimulated Henry of Ghent. Godfrey was a canon at Liège and (like Henry) at Tournai, and some historians have accordingly inferred a shared sense of Flemish urban 'corporatism'.[1] Much more pertinent, perhaps, was the fact that, as a secular master, Godfrey was, like Henry, an interested party to the controversy over *Ad fructus uberes*. The debates over the legitimacy of the pope's dispensing power and over the relative merits of secular clergy and religious orders which this controversy spawned turned 'benefit to

---

[1] C. Renardy, *Le Monde des maîtres universitaires du diocèse de Liège: Repertoire biographique 1140–1350* (Paris, 1981), 258; G. de Lagarde, 'La Philosophie sociale d'Henri de Gand et Godefroid de Fontaines', *AHDLMA* 14 (1943–5), 73–142; id., *La Naissance de l'esprit laïque au déclin du moyen âge*, 3rd edn. (5 vols.; Louvain, 1956–70), ii, ch. 8. In Lagarde's view, this sense is stronger in Godfrey than Henry and leads him to interpret the common good as a formal and 'constitutional' expression of the community (*La Naissance*, 212).

others', 'common benefit', and 'common good' into critical categories of ecclesio-logical analysis.[2] Like Henry, moreover, Godfrey was also influenced by widespread concern over the criteria which were being used to justify increasingly heavy levels of taxation. Henry's death in 1293 meant that he did not have to experience the exac-tions which were imposed as a result of Philip IV's wars in Aquitaine and Flanders nor the loyalties which were divided as a result of the king's disputes with Boniface VIII. Godfrey of Fontaines was not so fortunate. The gravity of political events in the late 1290s brought to a head issues which, as a member of the university in Paris, Godfrey could not avoid confronting.

Any discussion of the legitimacy of the pope's right to dispense from existing le-gislation necessarily involved discussion of the nature of papal power within the church. Any discussion of the legitimacy of taxation, meanwhile, necessarily involved a discussion of the nature of lordship (*dominium*) within the political com-munity. Since taxation in the 1280s and 1290s was ecclesiastical as well as lay, lord-ship was understood, in this instance, to cover the spiritual as well as the temporal power, the relationship of the pope to the material goods of the church as well as the relationship of the king to the material goods of his subjects. Moreover, since there was an intrinsic connection between lordship defined as ownership of property and lordship defined as exercise of jurisdiction, any analysis of the particular issue of taxation necessarily had wider implications for the exercise of all authority within human society. In many ways, therefore, the use to which Godfrey put the common good in his discussion of practical political issues went to the heart of scholastic polit-ical thought. Godfrey of Fontaines, like Henry of Ghent, understood the common good of the human community to be the criterion which could determine both obedience and resistance.

Godfrey of Fontaines was thoroughly conversant with many of the same authorities which Henry of Ghent had used in order to justify giving a central role to the com-mon good in the political community. He was familiar, for example, with Isidore's stipulation that the goal of the legislator should be the common benefit and not pri-vate advantage,[3] with the insistence in Roman law that the evidence of this benefit must be clear,[4] with the use of the common good as a justification for waging war,[5] and with the observation of 1 Corinthians 12: 7 that the gifts of the Holy Spirit have been bestowed for the benefit of others (a text which Godfrey applied to his own public duty of teaching the truth in theology *ad utilitatem aliorum*).[6] Godfrey's use of the common good in such contexts also stemmed from a familiarity with canon law. Together with the necessity which knows no law (*magna et evidens necessitas*),[7] 'com-mon benefit' (*communis utilitas*) and 'benefit to the church' (*utilitas ecclesiae*) gave

---

[2] Y. M. J. Congar, 'Aspects ecclésiologiques de la querelle entre mendiants et séculiers dans la seconde moitié du XIIIe siècle et le début du XIVe', *AHDLMA* 28 (1961), 35–151.

[3] *Quod.* I.6, p. 17.   [4] *Quod.* VI.18, p. 263. Cf. *Quod.* XI.14, p. 65.

[5] *Quod.* XIII.17, p. 299.   [6] *Quod.* VIII.7, p. 78; *Quod.* XII.6, p. 106. Cf. *Quod.* XII.5, p. 103.

[7] *Quod.* XI.11, pp. 54, 56.

Godfrey the criteria on which he was able to judge a series of specific questions on ecclesiastical matters. Godfrey cites these notions, for example, as grounds for tolerating some abuses (such as pluralism and absenteeism)[8] whilst condemning others (such as beneficing an individual who is ignorant of the local language).[9] Likewise, in the case of moneylending, Godfrey advises temporal and ecclesiastical rulers that they must always encourage good and destroy evil by referring their actions to the common good (*prout ordinantur ad bonum commune*). Godfrey defends the suggestion that rulers might therefore have to desist from expelling usurers rather than risk the greater evil which expulsion would cause to their communities on the Augustinian grounds that certain evils are permissible in a well-ordered city.[10] However, he adds his own gloss that these evils are ordered towards the good of the community. Just as God permits the presence of evil in the universe, Godfrey argues, so human law cannot prohibit every evil lest such proscription remove many benefits in its train. Nevertheless, the balance is a fine one, and Godfrey accepts that, if the presence of usurers remains an evil even in the light of what is good for communities (*bonum communitatum*), then they should be expelled without compunction. This is the case, in Godfrey's view, with all moneylenders of foreign birth. Indigenous offenders, by contrast, are not numerous, do not demand excessive rates of interest, and, as a result, may still provide many good services to the community.[11]

Godfrey is certainly aware that there are some contexts in which the common good has to be invoked with caution. In discussing, for example, whether the victim of false witnesses should pay to be absolved from an unjust sentence of excommunication,[12] Godfrey considers the suggestion that it would be better for the wronged man to remain excommunicate because submission to an unjust conviction would encourage wicked men to abuse the law. The individual, this argument goes, will thereby demonstrate his love, not for some temporal good of his own, but for the

---

[8] *Quod.* IV.11, pp. 264–72; *Quod.* XI.10, pp. 51–3. Cf. *Decrees of the Ecumenical Councils*, ed. N. P. Tanner (2 vols.; London, 1990), i. p. 249; *Decr. Greg. IX* III.4.1–17 (Friedberg, ii. 460–4); K. Pennington, 'The Canonists and Pluralism in the Thirteenth Century', *Speculum* 51 (1976), 35–48. In 1274, the Council of Lyons had insisted on the need to secure papal dispensation for pluralism and non-residence, the abuses most commonly associated with clergy in royal service. In 1298, Boniface VIII granted a dispensation for study at university (*Sexti Decretales* I.6.34; Friedberg, ii. 964–5).

[9] *Quod.* XI.13, p. 63. Cf. *Quod.* XV.13, p. 64; G. Barraclough, *Papal Provisions* (Oxford, 1935).

[10] Augustine, *De Ordine*, ed. W. M. Green (*CCSL* 29), II.4.12, p. 114. Cf. *Quod.* VI.18, p. 263, quoting Augustine, *De Libero Arbitrio*, ed. W. M. Green (ibid.), I.5.13, pp. 218–19.

[11] *Quod.* XII.9, pp. 114–17. Cf. *Quod.* X.19, pp. 398–405; *Quod.* XIII.15, pp. 286–95. In 1288, Charles II of Sicily expelled Jews from Anjou and Maine; in 1290, Edward I of England expelled Jews from all his territories, including Gascony; in 1291–2, Italian moneylenders were obliged to pay a large sum in order to remain in business in France; in 1292, the inhabitants of Poitou and the French part of Saintonge paid a hearth tax in order to finance the expulsion of the Jews from their lands. In 1306, Jews were to have their goods seized and be expelled from France altogether. Cf. Aquinas, *Q. Disp. de Malo* XIII.4; Henry of Ghent, *Quod.* VIII.22 fo. 45r. For canon law, see *Decr. Greg. IX* V.19.1–19 (Friedberg, ii. 811–16), *Sexti Decretales* V.5.1–2 (ibid. 1081–2). For the suggestion that there is a specifically Flemish context to Godfrey's views, see Lagarde, 'La Philosophie sociale', 106–7; id., *La Naissance*, 187–8; J. Lejeune, 'De Godefroid de Fontaines à la paix de Fexhe 1316', *Annuaire d'Histoire Liègoise*, VI.5 (1962), 1239.

[12] *Quod.* XII.15, pp. 129–32. Cf. *Decretum* II.11.3.46 (Friedberg, i. 656–8); Henry of Ghent, *Quod.* II.16, pp. 101–10.

common good which would otherwise be harmed by abuse of the law. Godfrey refutes this suggestion by turning it on its head. It is the refusal to pay, he argues, which would cause greater harm to the common good because a sentence of excommunication ought to be considered just and should not be brought into general contempt. To weaken or remove the stigma of excommunication would result in many evils for the *res publica* because the efficacy of ecclesiastical discipline would be severely impaired. Indeed, holding excommunication in contempt would cause the individual in question much greater injury in terms of sin than the material inconvenience which would be incurred by spending money to secure absolution. It is thus the individual who pays to absolve himself from an unjust excommunication, and not the individual who remains defiant in his protestation of innocence, who performs the greater good towards the *res publica* and towards himself.

Perhaps the most topical of Godfrey's practical applications of the common good concerns the fate of Philip III's body after the king's death in October 1285. Within a few months of Philip IV's decision to bury his father's heart at the Dominican church in Paris rather than at St Denis, Godfrey was arguing that necessity and public benefit are sufficiently 'just and necessary reasons' to override an individual's last will and testament and to bury part of his body other than where the deceased has designated.[13] Philip IV subsequently made several attempts to transfer the remains of his grandfather, Louis IX, to the Sainte Chapelle and, in 1297, he ordered his own heart to be buried next to his father's whilst the remainder of his body was to remain in St Denis. In 1292/3, Godfrey clearly thought it opportune to specify the precise nature of the benefit which could justify dividing a body into separate parts and interring them in different places.[14] Any departure from what is normally appropriate and in accordance with reason, he argues, must be justified by a particular necessity or 'benefit' but this benefit must be the common spiritual benefit of the universal church or of many Christians. The example which Godfrey cites is that of the dismemberment of saints, individuals who are comparable to kings in that they have a peculiarly 'public' nature (*quasi personae publicae*). The dispersal of saints' relics, in Godfrey's view, redounds to the glory of God by stimulating the veneration of saints, the increase of divine worship, and the devotion of the faithful. Such common spiritual benefit, Godfrey concludes, can therefore justify the custom of dismemberment even if the saints themselves did not originally choose to have their bodies divided in this way. By contrast, the temporal benefit which may be derived by those people in whose church a part of a body may subsequently reside is insufficient justification for such a division to be made. According to Godfrey, a spiritual good is always superior

---

[13] *Quod*. I.11, pp. 29–30. Cf. *Codex Iustinianus*, ed. P. Krüger (Berlin, 1954), III.44.1, p. 149: *iusta et necessaria causa*.

[14] *Quod*. VIII.9, pp. 86–98. Cf. *Decretum* II.13.2.4, 6–7 (Friedberg, i. 722–3); *Decr. Greg. IX* III.28.1–14 (ibid., ii. 548–54); *Sexti Decretales* III.12.1–5 (ibid., ii. 1045–8). No mention is made of necessity or public benefit in this canon law. Cf. Henry of Ghent, *Quod*. IX.12, pp. 225–40; E. A. R. Brown, 'Death and the Human Body in the Later Middle Ages, the Legislation of Boniface VIII on the Division of the Corpse', *Viator*, 12 (1981), 221–70, esp. 235–46; id., 'Philippe le Bel and the Remains of St. Louis', *Gazette des Beaux Arts*, 95 (1980), 175–82.

to a common material benefit even if this spiritual good pertains only to a single individual. Suppose, he writes, that money donated for pious purposes can result either in great benefit to the *res publica* and the church or in the individual benefit of the donor (by taking up a crusading vow, for example, and securing the remission of all his sins). Sometimes, Godfrey observes, it is better for an individual to perform a noble action of great virtue which has great merit in terms of its heavenly reward than to perform something which results simply in considerable material advantage (*magnum commodum*).

Moneylending, excommunication, and relics provide the most concrete of the situations in which Godfrey seeks to apply a notion of the common good. However, as well as deploying the common good in these singular instances, Godfrey also uses it to resolve more general issues with much wider implications for his political thought. This is particularly true of his contribution to the debate over *Ad fructus uberes*. Controversy over the privileges granted to the friars in 1281 served to highlight several long-standing points of conflict between the secular clergy and the mendicant orders at the schools of Paris, including the relative merits of the active and the contemplative lives within the church. It comes as no surprise, therefore, to find Godfrey being asked, in 1288, whether being a prelate or a parish priest is more perfect than being a member of a religious order.[15] Nor is it a surprise to find Aquinas on the list of those authorities whom Godfrey chooses to take to task for their misguided opinions. It is a mistake (*non videtur bene dictum*), Godfrey states, to claim that particular actions of priests may be more perfect than particular actions of religious but that, when all their actions are considered together, the aim of completely and perfectly securing one's own salvation is a greater goal than performing individual actions for the salvation of others whilst imperfectly securing one's own.[16] Rather than align himself with Aquinas, Godfrey opens his analysis of the relative merits of the active and the contemplative lives with the distinction which Henry of Ghent made central to his discussion of the issue earlier in the same year. Indeed, Godfrey expresses his approval (*bene dicitur*) of those theologians who maintain that the position of being a prelate involves exercitative, not acquisitive, perfection, and that it therefore requires its incumbent to be already perfect. With his own characteristic emphasis on *caritas*, Godfrey takes love as the particular (*praecipue*) hallmark of this personal perfection, and identifies its chief manifestation as the willingness to devote and even sacrifice one's life for the benefit of one's neighbours (*ad utilitatem proximorum*).[17] Godfrey's conclusion is very similar to Henry's. Bishops and parish priests occupy a more perfect position than members of religious orders because they are

---

[15] *Quod.* V.16, pp. 71–86. Cf. Lagarde, 'La Philosophie sociale', 132.

[16] See above, p. 108. For Godfrey's possession of works by Gérard d'Abbeville, see, P. Glorieux, 'Un Recueil scolaire de Godefroid de Fontaines', *RTAM* 3 (1931), 39. Cf. id., 'Les Polémiques *contra Geraldinos*, les pièces du dossier', *RTAM* 9 (1937), 61–2.

[17] Cf. *CUP* no. 539 (ii. pp. 8–10), a report, possibly by Godfrey himself, of the Paris assembly of December 1286, including a summary of the sermon on *caritas* which was delivered by Simon of Beaulieu, archbishop of Bourges.

required to be already perfect (*iam perfecti*) and because their actions (teaching, guiding, correcting, and administering the sacraments) are ordered towards the perfection of others. Indeed, Godfrey actually quotes (*ut aliqui dicunt*) Henry's argument that, if an observance is superior because it is ordered towards a more perfect end, and if the common good is greater than the private good because it is more divine, then the observance which secures the salvation of souls has a superior and more perfect status than the one which pursues contemplation alone.[18]

Godfrey draws the same conclusion when he clarifies a second source of secular–mendicant disagreement. Under what circumstances does entry into a religious order represent a transfer to a stricter and 'more perfect' life? A priest, Godfrey argues, should not leave his post unless it would be better and healthier (*salubrius et melius*) both for himself and for his flock. Such a move is permissible in canon law only when a priest is aware either of some personal disability or of some danger to his parish or when he is certain that it could be better governed by someone else.[19] Otherwise, if a priest realizes that he would probably be better able to govern his parish himself or that he would be more beneficial to the common good by doing so, any desire on his part to relinquish his office cannot be prompted by God. This is because the Holy Spirit always leads humans to what is better, and the common good is both better and more divine.

The connection which Godfrey establishes between the exercise of pastoral authority and the goal of the common good also extends to the role of property.[20] Material goods, he states, are instrumental to perfection and to the general benefit which is served by fruitful preaching and salvific instruction. As a result, Godfrey argues on behalf of prelates and priests as Aquinas had argued on behalf of friars—they should receive the necessities of life in return for the work they do for the benefit of their subjects.[21] A perfect prelate possesses temporal goods, not by choice nor for his own benefit, but by necessity and for the common benefit of others. Although Godfrey concedes (like Henry of Ghent) that the general effect of material goods on particular individuals will always be determined by the love which these individuals show towards them, he points out that the prelate's concern for material goods derives from *caritas*, a love which is not self-seeking (1 Corinthians 13: 5). Material goods are instrumental to the prelate's exercise of social virtues in a community in a way which is impossible in the solitary life of the religious, since the virtues of the contemplative individual order him towards God and not towards his fellow human beings. Being a prelate, therefore, does not mean acquiring perfection but exercising acquired perfection towards one's neighbours and on account of God.

Godfrey's overall solution to the question of the relative merits of the active and the contemplative lives, therefore, is to argue that the contemplative is essentially

---

[18] See above, p. 183.

[19] *Decretum* II.19.1.1, 19.2.1–2, 19.3.1–3 (Friedberg, i. 839–41); *Decr. Greg. IX* I.9.1–15 (ibid., ii. 102–15).

[20] *Quod.* VIII.11, pp. 102–25.

[21] *Quod.* XII.19, p. 152; *Quod.* XII.20, p. 158, 164. Cf. *Quod.* XIII.10, p. 261.

better than the active (*melius simpliciter*) but that the active can still be better than the contemplative within certain terms of reference and in certain circumstances (*secundum quid et in casu*). The prime example of such circumstances is when the active life serves the needs of other people.[22] In putting forward this conclusion, however, Godfrey also decides to raise the further question of the relationship which exists between the common good of the church and the individual good of the prelate. A priest, he argues, should choose his position, not because it is something intrinsically better and more perfect for himself, but because it is something intrinsically more necessary and more beneficial to others. Nevertheless, even though contemplation is better in itself, the priesthood can still be termed better for the individual in the sense that it is more meritorious. According to Philippians 1: 23–4, after all, no less a person than the apostle Paul longed to depart to be with Christ, something which was 'better by far', but considered it 'more necessary' for his flock that he should remain.[23] Godfrey justifies this juxtaposition of what is better and meritorious for the priest with what is necessary and beneficial for the Christian flock by appealing to book XIX of *De Civitate Dei*. According to Augustine, he states, the love of truth seeks the life of contemplation but the necessity of love undertakes righteous involvement in affairs.[24] When the prelate sacrifices his contemplation for the benefit of other people, Godfrey concludes, it is this necessity (*necessitas caritatis*) which makes his action meritorious. The position of prelate should therefore be sought, not for its own sake, but in certain circumstances and on account of the necessity of the people (*in casu et propter necessitatem populi*). In Godfrey's opinion, the same consideration should also govern material goods. Such goods should be sought, not for their own sake, but on account of the necessity or benefit of the people (*propter necessitatem sive utilitatem populi*). Although the possession of material goods might harm the prelate in the sense that he will be taken away from his perfect contemplation, he will gain compensation for this loss in the form of the public benefit (*per utilitatem publicam recompensatur*).[25] In taking up his pastoral ministry for the sake of God and the *necessitas populi*, therefore, the prelate acts from a powerful and perfect love. Even if his actions will inevitably detract from his contemplative perfection, his life will nevertheless be more fruitful and more meritorious on account of its corresponding benefit to the community (*propter recompensationem utilitatis communis*).[26]

Having drawn up this balance-sheet for the individual good of the prelate and the common good of the church, Godfrey then tackles the question which was raised by

---

[22] *Quod.* XI.6, pp. 32–7. Cf. James of Viterbo, *Quod.* II.24, pp. 235–6.

[23] *Quod.* V.16, p. 84. Cf. *Quod.* VI.10, pp. 195–6; *Nisi cum pridem* (Friedberg, ii. 107–12), col. 110; see above, pp. 107, 182.

[24] *Quod.* XI.6, p. 34; *Quod.* V.16, p. 84; Augustine, *De Civitate Dei*, ed. B. Dombart and A. Kalb (*CCSL* 48), XIX.19, p. 687; *Decretum* II.8.1.11 (Friedberg, i. 593–4). Cf. Henry of Ghent, *Quodlibet* XII.28 (see above, p. 182).

[25] Cf. Albertus Magnus, IV *Sent.* 38.18, p. 419 (see above, p. 66).

[26] *Quod.* VIII.11, pp. 102–25. Cf. *Nisi cum pridem* (Friedberg, ii. 107–12), col. 111. In February 1295, Boniface VIII granted his papal nuncios in France the power to commute vows into other pious works.

Henry of Ghent in exactly this context. To what extent is the individual good of the prelate 'included' within the common good of the church? According to Godfrey, the position of prelate requires an incumbent who is perfect in understanding and in love, who is always prepared to sacrifice his life for the well-being of his subjects, and who is generally superior in every virtue. Godfrey accordingly quotes Gregory the Great's account of personal perfection in support of Aristotle's statement that the individual in authority must be 'like a god'.[27] What Godfrey is particularly keen to emphasize, however, is that the active life which is adopted by a contemplative individual when he becomes a prelate is beneficial not only to the people whom he comes to serve but also to himself. According to Godfrey, book IX of the *Ethics* demonstrates that one hour of perfect contemplation by a prelate is better than a life of continuous contemplation of less intensity by a member of a religious order. Repeating his attack on Henry of Ghent's notion of a 'negative' good, therefore, Godfrey concludes that the life of pastoral activity is better for the prelate himself because it is more meritorious to avoid a sin *and* because he secures a greater good (*maius bonum*) for himself.[28] An individual, Godfrey explains, is obliged to assume a position of authority when there is no other means of meeting the needs of a group of people. Inasmuch as he is a part of the community, inasmuch as his good ought to be (*debet*) included in the good of the community, and inasmuch as it is a greater good (*maius bonum*) for the community to be preserved, such a person must submit to an interruption of his individual good of contemplation if the only alternative is to let the community perish. It is, in fact, sinful for an individual to refuse such a position of authority in order to remain in a state of perfect contemplation, just as it is sinful for an individual to refuse to eat in order to avoid interrupting his contemplation with an action. The contemplative who assumes a position of authority in the church loses his individual good of contemplation but he gains another in return, namely greater merit. Indeed, Godfrey professes himself amazed at how 'intelligent men' can take book IX of the *Ethics* to mean that the actions of a virtuous individual have no connection with merit and that the individual who lays down his life acquires no good of his own. For Godfrey, the individual good of the prelate must be included within the common good of the church.[29]

Godfrey's contribution to the controversy over *Ad fructus uberes* was not limited to his discussion of the relative merits of the active and the contemplative lives. In Christmas 1286, the year after his inception as master, Godfrey was asked to discuss, first, whether an individual should reiterate to his own priest a confession he has already made to a friar; second, whether a friar can pronounce absolution in matters which are legally and customarily reserved to bishops; third, whether a prelate can condemn an opinion as erroneous or heretical; and finally, whether a doctor of

---

[27] *Quod.* XI.6, p. 33, quoting Gregory the Great, *Regula Pastoralis* II.3, II.5 (*PL* 77, cols. 28–30, 32–4); Aristotle, *Politics* III.13 1284ª3–17.

[28] *Quod.* XI.6, pp. 34–5, quoting Gregory the Great, *Regula Pastoralis* I.5 (*PL* 77, col. 18), *Moralia in Job*, ed. M. Adriaen (*CCSL* 143), VII.14.17, p. 345.

[29] *Quod.* XI.6, pp. 35–7.

theology can pronounce on matters which pertain to the pope alone.[30] All four issues sprang directly from the December meeting of the bishops and the university of Paris and, like Henry of Ghent, Godfrey was immediately called upon to make his own position clear.[31] According to Guillaume de Macon, Godfrey promptly responded by joining Henry, Servase (Gervase) of Mt St Elias, and Nicholas du Pressoir, in coming down in favour of the bishops.[32]

In 1287, Godfrey was asked to consider whether a master in theology should refuse to discuss a question which is necessary for salvation but which is a matter of legal contention. Godfrey makes no bones about taking the general reference to a 'contentious and scandalous' matter as a reference to *Ad fructus uberes*.[33] Having established the precise meaning of scandal ('an opportunity for sin'), Godfrey argues that, if the truth in question is beneficial and fruitful (*fructuosa*), and particularly if it concerns the salvation of souls, then it ought to be taught openly. His next question accordingly goes to the very heart of *Ad fructus uberes*. Does the licence to preach and to hear confession have to be confirmed by the local bishop and clergy?[34] Godfrey's immediate response (at least in the *reportatio* in which it has survived) is limited to a terse discussion of individual texts from canon law. Analysis of the more general principles at stake comes later in the same quodlibet when he tackles the topic which Henry of Ghent had seen as equally central to the dispute—the legitimate exercise of the pope's dispensing power.

In discussing whether something which is intrinsically bad can in some circumstances become good, Godfrey concentrates on the question of pluralism, the example on which Bernard of Clairvaux had pinned his influential discussion of papal dispensation in *De Consideratione*.[35] Godfrey starts his own analysis by distinguishing between three different categories of action. The first category comprises actions which are intrinsically good according to natural law. These actions are those which are prescribed by the Ten Commandments, the first four of which order humankind towards the ultimate common good of God whilst the remainder order humankind towards itself in the observance of justice. In neither case, Godfrey concludes, can the original law be changed except by divine authority. Whilst Godfrey's third category of action comprises actions which are intrinsically indifferent, he devotes most of his attention to his second category, that is, to those actions which are intrinsically good insofar as they derive from natural law. These are the actions which are prescribed by *iura communia*, positive human laws which vary according to time and circumstance, but which generally further the common good for which they have been instituted. Since these laws are beneficial in most cases but not in all, exception

---

[30] *Quod.* III.7–10. It is perhaps significant that no *Brevis* version of these questions has survived.

[31] P. Glorieux, 'Prélats français contre religieux mendiants: Autour de la bulle *Ad fructus uberes* 1281–90', *Revue d'Histoire de l'Église de France*, 11 (1925), 309–31, 471–95, 471–5.

[32] Letter of Guillaume de Macon, bishop of Amiens, to Pierre Barbette, archbishop of Rheims, 1287 (*CUP* no. 543, ii. 13–17), p. 13. Cf. R. Hissette, 'Une Question quodlibétique de Servais du Mont-Saint-Eloi sur le pouvoir papal de l'évêque', *RTAM* 49 (1982), 234–42; Giles of Rome, *Quod.* II.28 fo. 27v.

[33] *Quod.* IV.13, pp. 274–7. Cf. *Brevis*, pp. 340–1.

[34] *Quod.* IV.14–15, pp. 277–9. Cf. *Brevis*, pp. 341–3. [35] *Quod.* IV.11, pp. 264–72.

can be made in their execution by human authority. However, Godfrey insists on imposing two restrictions on their suspension—the power to make such a dispensation belongs only to a legitimate authority, and it must always be exercised in accordance with reason and the common good. Laws, he explains, are, by definition, instituted for the sake of the common good and any act of dispensation must always respect this goal; otherwise it is not valid. Like Henry of Ghent in 1277 (and, in more polemical fashion, in 1288), Godfrey justifies this account of dispensation with a particular reading of Bernard of Clairvaux's *De Consideratione* and his letter to count Theobald. According to Bernard, he states, dispensation is permissible only because of the benefit it brings to the common good of the church; otherwise it is an act of crude dissipation.[36] In the case of pluralism, Godfrey concludes, dispensation is permissible only on account of the pressing necessity or benefit of the church.

Despite Pope Nicholas IV's attempt to silence public debate on *Ad fructus uberes*, the controversy over its implications continued to simmer until at least the promulgation of *Super cathedram* in 1300. In 1294/5, therefore, Godfrey was not slow to pick up on the implications of being asked what happens when the pope has granted a dispensation which does not secure the common benefit of the church. Henry of Ghent had already demonstrated how an oblique and general question could be used as a means of circumventing Nicholas IV's prohibition on further discussion of the specific details of Martin IV's bull. Thus, although the precise scenario is different (whether, without the approval of his superior, a monk can request a licence from the pope to confess to someone other than his own abbot), the terms of the question are so close both to the central issue of the controversy (whether an individual can confess to a friar without the approval of his own priest or bishop) and to the principles which were claimed to be at stake (the hierarchy of ecclesiastical authority and the good order of the church) that it is a reasonable inference that the parallels with *Ad fructus uberes* were not only intended but drawn.[37]

Godfrey opens his argument by echoing the criticism which had been most famously expressed by the episcopal opponents of Pope Gregory VII—no pope should treat his bishops as if they were bailiffs on his estates. According to Godfrey, the pope's relations with his bishops are not the same as those of a king with his *baillis*, since prelates receive their authority from Christ and the pope calls them 'brothers'.[38] In his view, the pope can therefore remove individuals from the authority of their immediate superiors and dispense them from their vows of obedience only if there is a reasonable cause. A monk, he concludes, should not seek a licence to confess which runs counter to the command of his superior, or if he has, and the pope has granted it, then he must not make use of it. Why? Because to do so would harm the

---

[36] Bernard of Clairvaux, *De Consideratione ad Eugenium Papam* III.4, *Ep.* 271 (above, pp. 184, 186–7). Cf. *Decretum* II.21.1.1–6 (Friedberg, i. 852–4); *Decr. Greg. IX* I.6.54 (ibid., ii. 93).

[37] *Quod.* X.17, pp. 391–4.

[38] *Quod.* X.17, p. 392. Cf. *Quod.* V.16, p. 73; Lagarde, 'La Philosophie sociale', 136–7. For Godfrey's view of episcopal authority within the church, based on Luke 10: 1 and *Decretum* I.21.2 (Friedberg, i. 69–70), see *Quod.* XI.7, pp. 38–40. Cf. Lagarde, *art. cit.*, 135–6.

common good and the good order of the church in that subjects would no longer respect their superiors and many evils, including 'scandal', would result. The implications for *Ad fructus uberes* are clear. Like Henry of Ghent, Godfrey judges the pope's dispensing power by the simple test of whether or not it secures the common good. Not to use a papal dispensation when it is in one's favour, however, is a different matter from actively resisting it when it is to one's disadvantage. As a general principle, and as a commentary on *Ad fructus uberes*, Godfrey's argument occupies a strikingly moderate position, closer, indeed, to the self-imposed restraint urged by some friars than to the uncompromising threats issued by Henry of Ghent. Whilst Godfrey is prepared to join Henry in his appeal to the common good as the standard by which the pope's action should be judged, and even to raise the spectre of disorder and disrespect for authority as the consequences of failing to meet such a standard, he is not prepared to use this argument to justify active disobedience.

The moderation of Godfrey's account of papal dispensation was reinforced in his eleventh quodlibet (1295/6) when he considered whether the obligation to obey an immediate superior is greater than the obligation to obey a higher, but more remote, authority.[39] As far as the relationship between members of religious orders and their bishops is concerned, Godfrey distinguishes between two kinds of obedience—voluntary obedience and obedience according to the law (*ius commune*). Oaths to obey superiors which are sworn by members of religious orders are placed in the first category. Such obedience is voluntary and concerns those matters which carry no obligation in 'common law' (that is, in Roman, canon, or customary law). In these matters, Godfrey concludes, the religious has a greater obligation to obey his immediate superior than a higher authority such as his bishop. However, on all other matters, namely those which derive from common law (*ius commune*) or divine command, the religious has a greater obligation to obey his bishop than his immediate superior. If a conflict arises between them, if, for example, a superior commands obedience in something covered by a voluntary oath whilst a bishop commands obedience in something covered by common law, and if both commands cannot simultaneously be obeyed, then Godfrey insists that the individual has a greater obligation to obey his bishop. According to Godfrey, those matters enjoined by voluntary obedience must not contravene common law and the common good, nor must they prejudice the obedience which is owed to a bishop according to that law. Once again, the consequences for *Ad fructus uberes* are clear. The obligation which is owed to the common laws of the church is greater than the obligation which is owed to the particular oaths of religious orders.

In the case of religious orders, Godfrey establishes two principles—common law and the common good—which can override particular and voluntary oaths of obedience. Only where matters do not come within the scope of *ius commune* and *bonum commune* are members of religious orders placed under a greater obligation to their immediate superior than to their bishop. Godfrey then transfers this principle from

---

[39] *Quod.* XI.9, pp. 49–51.

the obedience which is owed to bishops to the obedience which is owed to the pope. In *any* oath sworn by a Christian, he argues, reservation must be made for the authority of the pope. An individual, he explains, has a greater obligation to a superior power than he does to an inferior power when the inferior is wholly (*totaliter*) subordinate to, and dependent upon, the superior in all matters (*in omnibus*). In the church, therefore, every ecclesiastical power which is ordered towards the well-being and good of the whole community is in some way (*aliquo modo*) dependent upon the pope by virtue of the pope's plenitude of power. As a result, whatever the nature of the particular obligations which Christians take upon themselves, be they oaths of obedience to other individuals or the performance of certain actions or offices, there is always an understanding that the power of the pope is excepted. Because the pope is owed a greater obedience in all matters, Godfrey concludes, he can override any existing obligation to an inferior power. Thus, the pope is able to dispense from all vows, however solemn, and especially in cases of necessity or of clear benefit to the community (*necessitas vel evidens utilitas rei publicae*).

Godfrey's emphasis on the obedience owed to papal authority in 1295/6 is revealing on several counts. The controversy over *Ad fructus uberes* raised the question of the pope's ability to dispense from the statutes of the Fourth Lateran Council and the episcopate's ability to disobey a grant of dispensation which did not evidently secure the common good. A correlation between the obligation of obedience and the attainment of the common good is clearly drawn by Godfrey when he subordinates members of religious orders to their bishops. Like Henry of Ghent, Godfrey uses the principle that obedience is conditional upon the common good as a means of controlling the independence of the religious orders. He accordingly appeals to the corporeal imagery of the *corpus mysticum* and to Augustine's statement that a part must not be discordant with its whole. The oaths which are undertaken by members of religious orders, he concludes, are not in accordance with reason if they prejudice the common laws of the church, since the common laws of the church are ordered towards a more common good (*quae ad bonum magis commune ordinantur*).[40] Godfrey's reaction is much more measured, however, when it comes to the possibility of using the common good as a means of qualifying the obedience which is owed to the pope. Whilst he does recognize the possibility that the pope can make a dispensation which does not meet the stipulations laid down by Bernard of Clairvaux, he does not push the point home. Thus, in contrast to Henry of Ghent (who treats illegitimate papal dispensation as a warrant for reproof, resistance, and ultimately deposition), Godfrey is only prepared to counsel self-restraint on the part of those who have benefited from such a grant. In 1295/6, therefore, the appearance of the common good in Godfrey's ecclesiology supports, rather than restricts, the exercise of authority by the pope. On the one hand, Godfrey appears keen to modify the dependence of all ecclesiastical authorities on the pope by introducing the term 'in some way' (*aliquo modo*). The details are left unspecified but it is clear from his refusal to admit any

---

[40] *Quod.* XIII.12, p. 272.

correspondence between the relationship between pope and bishops and the relationship between king and *baillis* that this qualification must carry some weight. On the other hand, he is equally insistent that the power of the pope is present 'in all matters' (*in omnibus*). On this occasion, Godfrey sees no need to insist on the sort of qualification which he had inserted into his earlier discussion of papal dispensation and which he chooses to repeat later in his eleventh quodlibet—dispensation is permissible only when it benefits the common good of the church; otherwise it is an act of crude dissipation.[41] Indeed, on this occasion, Godfrey does not even restrict papal intervention to those matters which exclusively concern the common good—the pope can dispense from all oaths 'especially' (*praecipue*) when it will benefit the common good.

Godfrey's ecclesiology was defined by a number of critical events in the 1280s and early 1290s of which the most important was the controversy over *Ad fructus uberes*. Thus, in considering whether the obligation to obey an immediate superior is greater than the obligation to obey a higher, but more remote, authority, Godfrey is primarily concerned with the obedience which is owed by members of religious orders to their bishops. By the mid-1290s, however, Godfrey was also engaged in an issue with even wider political repercussions—taxation of the church by temporal rulers. In 1296, Boniface VIII specifically commanded all members of the clergy not to pay any exactions which were demanded by their temporal rulers without the prior consent of the pope. This bull, *Clericis laicos*, explicitly addressed prelates, secular clergy, members of religious orders, and members of universities, insisting that they all accept the pope's ruling by virtue of their obedience and on pain of excommunication.[42] In 1295/6, therefore, Godfrey's discussion of obedience to lesser and higher authorities may also reflect the very real possibility of a conflict between the obedience which is owed by a Christian to his king and the obedience which he owes to the pope. Read as a commentary on *Clericis laicos*,[43] Godfrey's use of the common good to elevate the power of the pope is all the more striking. According to Godfrey, the obligation to obey the pope is incumbent upon all Christians. The pope therefore has the power to dispense individuals from any oath to an intermediate authority if it is a case of necessity or clear benefit to the *res publica*.

When Philip IV started to wage war in Aquitaine and Flanders, the relations of pope and king to temporal goods became a matter of acute political and material concern to the French clergy. Between September 1294 and February 1295, a series of

---

[41] *Quod.* XI.14, pp. 64–8.

[42] *Les Registres de Boniface VIII*, ed. G. Digard, M. Faucon, A. Thomas, and R. Fawtier (4 vols.; Bibliothèque des Écoles Françaises d'Athènes et de Rome, 1907–39), no. 1567 (vol. i, cols. 584–5). Cf. J. Marrone and C. Zuckerman, 'Cardinal Simon of Beaulieu and Relations between Philip the Fair and Boniface VIII', *Traditio*, 31 (1975), 195–222; C. Zuckerman, 'The Ending of French Interference in the Papal Financial System in 1297: A Neglected Episode', *Viator*, 11 (1980), 261–88.

[43] Godfrey's eleventh quodlibet is generally dated to between 1295 and 1296. *Quod.* XI.10, pp. 51–3, reads very much as if it is a commentary on Boniface VIII's condemnation of absenteeism in *Traxit hactenus* (March 1296). *Clericis laicos* was issued in February 1296 and published in France in April. There is a strong possibility, therefore, that Godfrey delivered his eleventh quodlibet later the same year.

provincial councils granted a two-year tenth to Philip IV, a tax which was collected in 1295 and 1296. In 1296, Philip requested another.[44] In February 1296, Boniface VIII issued *Clericis laicos* in an attempt to prevent the kings of both France and England from taxing any church property without papal consent.[45] In September 1296, he issued *Ineffabilis amor*, stating that papal permission was necessary for any exactions taken from the clergy for the defence of the kingdom (*pro defensione ac necessitatibus regni*).[46] In February 1297, however, in the immediate aftermath of England's alliance with Flanders, Boniface VIII softened his line towards the French king in *Romana mater*, declaring that his previous utterances did not prevent the clergy themselves from consenting to make contributions or to pay tenths in moments of extreme need (*in articulo necessitatis*).[47] Later the same month, in *Coram illo fatemur*, Boniface conceded the principle that, in an emergency so immediate as to preclude consultation with the pope, the clergy could be taxed freely and of their own accord *before* papal consent was given.[48] In March 1297, a double tenth was granted by a council at Paris. In July, Boniface repeated his concessions in *Etsi de statu*, withdrew the provisions of *Clericis laicos* from France, and agreed that Philip IV did not need to consult if there was clear danger to his kingdom (*evidens periculum*) and if it was a case of clear common necessity (*casus communis et evidentis necessitatis*).[49] The king of France now had the right to judge whether or not there was an urgent necessity. In 1298 and 1299, a double tenth was promptly granted by councils at Paris and Lyons on the orders of the king.

Godfrey first dealt with the issue of taxation in his seventh quodlibet (1290–2) in the course of commenting upon a very specific case. A lord imposes an unjust tax on a community subject to him and, in order to avoid a greater evil for themselves and for their community, the rulers of that community promise to pay this lord a lump sum. In order to raise this sum, the rulers of the community institute a just method of collection, for example, by imposing a certain amount on each individual according to an assessment of the goods in his possession. Suppose that one of the citizens,

[44] J. H. Denton, 'Philip the Fair and the Ecclesiastical Assemblies of 1294–1295', *Transactions of the American Philosophical Society*, 81 (1991). For opposition to this taxation, see e.g. *Livre de Guillaume le Maire*, ed. C. Port (Paris, 1877), 322–31.

[45] For a general discussion of *Clericis laicos*, see G. Digard, *Philippe le Bel et le Saint-Siège de 1285 à 1304* (2 vols.; Paris, 1936), 263–310, and, for its impact on the politics of the English church, J. H. Denton, *Robert Winchelsey and the Crown: A Study in the Defence of Ecclesiastical Liberty* (Cambridge, 1980), 90–126. Edward I had secured from the clergy a notorious moiety in September 1294, and a tenth in November 1295, but was rebuffed in January and August 1297, a reverse which prompted the king to order the seizure of all the temporalities of those who had withheld their consent. For the crisis of 1297–8, see M. Prestwich (ed.), *Documents Illustrating the Crisis of 1297–8 in England* (London, 1980). *Clericis laicos* was itself revoked by Pope Clement V in February 1306.

[46] *Registres*, no. 1653 (I, cols. 614–20). Cf. Digard, *Philippe le Bel*, i. 273–86.

[47] *Registres*, no. 2312 (I, col. 908). Cf. ibid., no. 2308 (I, cols. 905–6); Digard, *Philippe le Bel*, i. 286–97.

[48] *Registres*, no. 2333 (I, cols. 918–20). Cf. ibid., no. 1933 (I, cols. 738–9); Digard, *Philippe le Bel*, i. 304–10.

[49] *Registres*, no. 2354 (I, cols. 941–3). Boniface VIII subsequently revoked all his concessions to Philip IV with *Salvator mundi* in December 1301 (ibid., no. 4422).

promising to pay the whole sum of money to the lord, either at once or in instalments, receives this sum from the rulers of the community as a farm or fixed payment which is to be collected in the prescribed manner. Suppose, then, that other individuals within the same community, considering the original taxation to be unjust and for that reason not to be paid except under compulsion, withhold payment of the sums for which they have been assessed. The question which Godfrey was now invited to consider is whether those individuals who withhold their payments ought to make restitution to the citizen who was due to receive the collected sum as a farm. Is an individual who withholds something which is not lawfully owed to another person nevertheless under an obligation to pay up when what he is withholding has been demanded for the good of the community (*pro bono communitatis*)?[50]

Godfrey opens his response by outlining the criteria which usually make taxation legitimate. According to Godfrey, there is a sense in which all the members of a community constitute a single body. This body must be sustained in times of hardship by means of individual members making contributions in accordance with the principles of justice. When a ruler has reasonable cause to exact taxation for the benefit of the *res publica* or community, therefore, every member of the community ought willingly to pay what is imposed upon him and, if anyone withholds such payment, he ought to make restitution. Turning to the precise scenario under discussion, Godfrey concedes that it is wrong for the lord to receive the money which has been exacted from the community, since it has been exacted without justice. Nevertheless, although the lord has extorted this money tyrannically and by threats of violence, each individual in the community is still obliged to pay what he owes to the citizen who holds the farm. The rulers of the community have chosen payment as the lesser of two evils and thus, insofar as the taxation has been imposed by them rather than by the lord, it has been imposed justly. Payment may have been made from fear of a greater evil rather than from love or in accordance with law, but, in aiming to avoid the greater evil, each individual is expressing his obligation to legal or general justice, a virtue which orders the actions of all particular virtues towards the good of the community. Each individual, each part, is obliged to make a proportionate contribution to the preservation of the common good, just as each individual is also obliged to relinquish his external goods for the preservation of his own well-being.

Godfrey's line of argument follows the pattern set by Albertus Magnus (an individual ought to give material goods to a tyrant rather than allow himself to be killed) and Aristotle (an individual should throw his goods into the sea rather than risk sinking with them on board).[51] In Godfrey's view, general principle and actual practice do not contradict each other in the specific scenario described because it frequently

---

[50] *Quod.* VII.14, pp. 395–6. It was to be a feature of Philip's taxation in the 1290s that communities paid a lump sum in order to make their own assessment instead of submitting to outside assessment on individual members (Strayer, *Reign of Philip the Fair*, 106; id., 'Consent to Taxation', 17–19, 25–31, 45–54). Godfrey's emphasis on an unjust tax may be a reference to the tenths levied between 1284 and 1291 for the sake of a campaign against Aragon which never materialized (above, p. 197).

[51] Albertus Magnus, *Super Ethica* III.1, p. 142 (above, p. 69); Aristotle, *Ethics* III.1 1110ᵃ8–11.

happens that what is unjustly received by one individual can be justly exacted from another. He therefore gives the additional, and very pertinent, example of a king who is fighting for the benefit of the *res publica* against enemies who are waging an unjust war. If the king is captured and cannot be freed except by the payment of a certain sum by the community, then the rulers of that community may justly impose a levy on its members. Everyone in the community is obliged to pay his portion even though the enemy who ultimately receives that money will do so unjustly and should, by right, repay it.[52] Payment of an unjust tax, it would seem, is preferable to disobedience in both negative and positive terms. Surrender of a material good is a better course of action if the alternative is a greater evil (namely the death of the individual taxed or the damage which would otherwise occur to the common good) or if the result is a greater good (namely benefit to the *res publica*).

Godfrey's initial analysis of taxation in 1290–2 represents a combination of his own theoretical model of legal or general justice with a practical notion of *utilitas publica* taken from Roman law. There are also clear similarities with the position which Henry of Ghent outlined in his own discussion in 1290.[53] By 1295/6, however, Godfrey had another foil for his arguments in the faculty of theology—James of Viterbo. The profits of usury became an important political and financial issue in the 1290s as a result of Philip IV's exactions from Jews, Lombards, and Florentines. In 1293/4, James of Viterbo was asked accordingly to consider whether the pope could absolve a usurer from the obligation of making restitution for his exactions.[54] The question was critical because, according to canon law, the profits of usury, like the profits of theft, could be treated as contributions towards a just war or crusade only if they could not be returned to the people from whom they had been taken.[55] In response, James is clearly at pains to argue that the pope is indeed able to grant absolution from restitution. In the course of his discussion, however, he also chooses to outline the more general principles which should govern the relation of temporal and ecclesiastical powers to the material goods which are under their control.

According to James of Viterbo's reading of Augustine and canon law, temporal and ecclesiastical powers are not lords (*domini*) but stewards, protectors, and distributors (*procuratores et tutores et dispensatores*).[56] According to his reading of 1 Corinthians 4, moreover, stewardship requires good faith. As far as James is concerned, the presence of good faith means that those in authority in the church are obliged to

---

[52] In June 1284 Charles of Salerno, son of Charles of Anjou and heir to the throne of Sicily, was captured by the Aragonese; in January 1285 his father died and Charles became king. The protracted negotiations which preceded his release in October 1288 included demands for substantial amounts of money (E. Léonard, *Les Angevins de Naples*, Paris, 1954, 156–71). Edward I's fifteenth of 1290 was intended to meet the expenses both of his stay in Gascony and of his efforts as arbiter in the dispute. For the course of these negotiations, see Digard, *Philippe le Bel et le Saint-Siège*, i. 34–7, 43–4, 63–4, 76–9, 100–101.

[53] See above, pp. 193–7.

[54] James of Viterbo, *Quodlibet*, ed. E. Ypma (Würzburg, 1967), I.17, pp. 207–15.

[55] J. A. Brundage, *Medieval Canon Law and the Crusader* (Madison, 1969), 186.

[56] Eschmann, 'Thomistic Glossary', 126. Cf. Cicero, *De Re Publica*, ed. J. E. G. Zetzel (Cambridge, 1995), II.29.51, p. 81: *tutor et procurator rei publicae*; Aquinas, *De Reg. Iudaeorum* VI (*procurator utilitatis communis*).

dispense temporal goods for a reasonable cause and according to the demands of love (criteria which are fulfilled, for example, when these goods are distributed for the benefit of the church, the relief of the poor, or other 'pious uses'). Temporal rulers too are accordingly obliged to demand or receive temporal goods from their subjects only for a reasonable cause. In the case of the profits of usury, therefore, any absolution from the obligation to make restitution can only be permitted if it is for a reasonable or legitimate cause. Thus, in the case of goods which have originally been exacted from the laity rather than the clergy, the pope should require temporal rulers to waive the obligation to make restitution only if it is beneficial to the church by, say, providing it with defence or assistance. If a temporal ruler refuses, then the pope can grant the dispensation himself through his own superior jurisdiction. Once again, however, this is an appropriate course of action only if it secures an appreciable benefit for the church (*propter magnam utilitatem ecclesiae*).

James of Viterbo repeats his insistence on the presence of a reasonable cause and of benefit to the common good when he discusses prescription, that is, the legal transfer of property to the possessor after the elapse of a specified period of time. According to James, a ruler is not a lord (*dominus*) but a protector and defender who can receive goods from his subjects only for certain reasons and for the sake of the common good. Because the ruler is a guardian, steward, and distributor, he can legitimately remove property from one person and give it to someone else only when there is a reasonable cause.[57] James's insistence on these criteria also extends to the payment of taxation to a temporal ruler by the church. Like Henry of Ghent, James is very careful to establish the grounds on which a king can legitimately demand such payment. James points out, for example, that those parts of canon law which do envisage payments by the church to a temporal power do not represent payment made to a superior in recognition of his lordship (*dominium*) but payment made for the sake of peace. Payment is justified, therefore, because, according to other parts of canon law, the church is under a particular obligation to protect the *pax et quies* of the human community.[58] James makes the same point in response to being asked whether a general custom may excuse a sinful action. The custom in question is described in abstract terms, namely one which is invoked for the sake of a substantial common good such as the peace of the *res publica*. However, the significance of the phrasing would not have been lost on an audience faced with Philip IV's demand to help defend his kingdom in defiance of *Clericis laicos*.[59] James's position is uncompromising. However long-standing and however general the custom may be, however great the good which would result from it being allowed to continue, such considerations have no force against divine or natural law. Custom can only be invoked as an argument against specifically human law and even then it must be a reasonable custom. Thus, whilst there are occasions on which custom and the common good of peace may justify waiving the temporal penalty which would otherwise

[57] James of Viterbo, *Quod*. II.21, pp. 215–23.
[58] James of Viterbo, *Quod*. I.17, p. 213. Cf. below p. 270 n. 26.
[59] For the dating of James's third quodlibet, see above, p. 217.

be exacted for a particular sin, this is never the case for those sins which run counter to divine or natural law.[60] As examples of such sins, James gives adultery and pillage (*rapina*). Adultery was a common enough debating point in deciding whether a common good can justify committing an individual evil.[61] Pillage, however, was a different matter because *rapina* was the term generally applied to taxation which was unjustly exacted and which could only be expurgated by restitution.[62]

Like James of Viterbo, Godfrey of Fontaines was only too familiar with the way in which necessity and common benefit were being used by the king of France in order to justify his demands for taxation in the 1290s. 'Necessity', 'defence of the kingdom', and 'benefit to the *res publica*' were all principles cited by Philip IV,[63] as well as by the authors of *Antequam essent clerici* and the *Disputatio inter clericum et militem*.[64] In 1295, the king exacted a general subsidy of one hundredth on the lands, goods, and revenues of all his subjects; in 1296, he renewed it at the higher rate of one fiftieth. This second levy was greeted with much more opposition than the first, including in Godfrey's native Flanders where it was treated as an unwarranted extension of royal authority. In 1290, Henry of Ghent had warned his audience of the capacity of temporal rulers to abuse their right to appeal to the common benefit of the community and had insisted that the evidence of such benefit should be clear. Henry, however, had failed to give any details as to how such evidence was to be assessed. In 1295/6, therefore, when Godfrey of Fontaines was asked whether a ruler can impose a tax simply by *claiming* that it will benefit the *res publica*, he made the burden of proof a central consideration. Is it the case that a ruler can impose a tax without manifest cause so long as it seems to him to be expedient, or should a ruler who rules over free subjects rely on the consent and knowledge of the leading and wisest members of the community?[65]

In order to guarantee that taxation is actually justified by the common good, Godfrey turns to the guidelines for the exercise of political authority which had been set down in book III of the *Politics*. According to Aristotle, a ruler ought to be the best

---

[60] James of Viterbo, *Quod*. III.19, pp. 243–7.   [61] See above, pp. 68–71.

[62] Brown, 'Taxation and Morality', 2. Cf. *Decr. Greg. IX* II.24.18 (Friedberg, ii. 365–6); A. Grunzweig, 'Les Incidences internationales des mutations monétaires de Philippe le Bel', *Le Moyen Age*, 59 (1953), 117–72.

[63] J. R. Strayer, 'Defense of the Realm and Royal Power in France', in id., *Medieval Statecraft and the Perspectives of History* (Princeton, 1971), ch. 18; id., 'Consent to Taxation under Philip the Fair', in J. R. Strayer and C. H. Taylor, *Studies in Early French Taxation* (Cambridge, Mass., 1939), 8 n. 9; C. Fasolt, *Council and Hierarchy: The Political Thought of William Durant the Younger* (Cambridge, 1991), 105: *ex causa publice utilitatis et defensionis regni sui*; E. A. R. Brown, 'Taxation and Morality in the Thirteenth and Fourteenth Centuries: Conscience and Political Power and the Kings of France', *French Historical Studies*, 8 (1973), 1–28, esp. 1–8. For a discussion of the same issues under Edward I, see G. L. Harriss, *King, Parliament and Public Finance in Medieval England to 1369* (Oxford, 1975). Cf. Prestwich, *Documents Illustrating the Crisis of 1297–8*, 134.

[64] P. Dupuy, *Histoire du différend d'entre le Pape Boniface VIII et Philippes le Bel Roy de France, Actes et Preuves* (Paris, 1655), pp. 21–3; ed. N. N. Erickson, 'A Dispute between a Priest and a Knight', *Proceedings of the American Philosophical Society*, 111 (1967), pp. 299–300. Cf. T. Renna, 'Kingship in the *Disputatio inter clericum et militem*', *Speculum*, 48 (1973), 675–93.

[65] *Quod*. XI.17, pp. 76–8.

man in a community, pre-eminent in his practical wisdom and almost like a god with respect to his fellow human beings. Like Henry of Ghent, Godfrey echoes Aristotle's reservations over the likelihood of hereditary succession ever producing such a perfect individual, although, unlike Henry, Godfrey spells out that election must therefore be a better means of achieving the same end. The section from book III of the *Politics* in which Godfrey is primarily interested, however, is Aristotle's discussion of whether the community should be ruled by a good man or by good laws.[66] Aristotle himself had argued that, since even the best ruler cannot be immune from human passions, the best man ought to rule in accordance with correctly established laws. According to Aristotle, whoever institutes the rule of the intellect by means of laws established according to right reason effectively institutes the rule of God and of just laws, whereas whoever makes a human being rule risks empowering a wild beast. Godfrey takes his lead from this line of reasoning. Even when it is generally agreed that a particular ruler is the best man, he argues, those matters which are capable of being determined by law should still be judged by the law. Godfrey then reinforces this principle with Aristotle's stipulation that the government of a good ruler ought to be ordered primarily, not towards his individual good, but towards the good of the whole community. When a ruler rules over a free people, therefore, he does not possess his right to rule (*ius principandi*) except by virtue of the whole community. According to Godfrey, this precondition can be expressed in a variety of ways—by election, institution, or consent—but the consequences are the same in each case. Since a ruler has no other goal than the common good and the common benefit, he should not impose anything on the community which is burdensome or harmful to its members unless it fulfils one of three conditions. Either such an imposition meets with the consent of all his subjects, or it is derived from a law instituted by wise people in accordance with reason and prudence, or it is derived from an extra-legal source such as the considered opinion of the ruler and his counsellors.

In theoretical terms, the connection between taxation and consent could be interpreted very widely in the late thirteenth century. Consent could come either from all those upon whom an extraordinary tax was going to be levied, or from a majority of their number, or from the wiser part (*sanior pars*).[67] Thus, whilst Godfrey is certainly familiar with the Roman law maxim 'what touches all must be approved by all' (*quod omnes tangit ab omnibus comprobetur*),[68] he is careful to keep his options open when it comes to defining exactly how this approval can be registered. Godfrey accordingly

---

[66] Aristotle, *Politics* III.15–17 1286ᵃ7–1288ᵃ29. Lejeune ('De Godefroid de Fontaines à la paix de Fexhe', 1226) draws a parallel with Pierre Dubois who appears, like Godfrey, to have been a pupil of Siger of Brabant, and who cites his opinion that it is far better for a community to be ruled by correct laws than by good men (*De Recuperatione Terre Sanctae*, ed. C. V. Langlois, Paris, 1891, 121–2). James of Viterbo deals with the same question (*Quod.* IV.30, pp. 107–110) but makes no reference to the common good. Cf. T. Renna, 'Aristotle and the French Monarchy, 1260–1303', *Viator*, 9 (1978), 309–24; see above, pp. 139 n. 48, 195 n. 63.

[67] G. Post, *Studies in Medieval Legal Thought: Public Law and the State 1100–1322* (Princeton, 1964), 168–80.

[68] *Quod.* III.9, p. 217.

gives several definitions of the way in which a ruler can be said to rule 'by virtue of the whole community' and several definitions of the way in which a burdensome demand can be imposed on that community. Godfrey devotes most of his attention, however, to one option in particular, namely the suggestion that a burdensome demand can be placed upon a community when it results from the considered opinion of the ruler and his counsellors. In practical terms, Godfrey's concentration on this scenario is hardly surprising. What was at stake in the dispute over clerical taxation in 1296 and 1297 was not so much the claim of Philip IV to defend his kingdom as the question of just *who* should judge when the need was so great as to require extraordinary taxation to be levied. Thus, the king himself took particular care to point out that his 1296 fiftieth was demanded on the advice of his prelates and barons,[69] whilst, for his part, the pope made the consent of the clergy central to *Coram illo fatemur.*[70] Unlike Henry of Ghent, therefore, who mentioned counsellors only in passing, Godfrey of Fontaines makes their identity central to his discussion.

According to Godfrey, counsellors must be in a better position than other people to decide what is better and more beneficial. They should therefore not be members of the ruler's household, nor his close associates, because these people will inevitably find it difficult to contradict their master's wishes. Counsellors should instead be prudent, just, and faithful men, as well as natives of the ruler's territory upon whom the burden of the proposed taxation will directly fall. If they do not fulfil these requirements, then Godfrey is prepared to issue a stark warning. If the ruler limits his consultation to his own private council and if he is unwilling to let other people know of the cause or necessity on account of which his tax is being imposed, then he is effectively giving subjects the right to disobey his command (*de iure non tenentur obedire*). Godfrey does introduce two practical qualifications. Subjects can legitimately resist only 'if they are able to do so' (*si possent*) and, even then, they should wait until such a time as the matter has been sufficiently discussed by prudent men. Of these restrictions, the second is self-explanatory but the first is left without any elaboration.[71] What *is* made clear is the consequence of subjects failing to act as they should. If no resistance is offered to such royal conduct, then the kingdom will gradually turn into a tyranny and free subjects will become slaves. Godfrey therefore closes with an even more pointed observation, expressing the fear lest, as he speaks

---

[69] Strayer, 'Consent to Taxation', 48–51. Cf. id., 'Philip the Fair: A "Constitutional" King', *American Historical Review*, 62 (1956), 18–32; Housley, *Italian Crusades*, 220.

[70] See above, p. 248. It is a striking feature of Archbishop Winchelsea's opposition to Edward I, an opposition which was founded on principles of consent and the community of the realm and which was articulated by a secular master previously conversant with the theological ideas of both Thomas Aquinas and Henry of Ghent, that there is little or no use of scholastic political theory as opposed to canon law (Denton, *Robert Winchelsey and the Crown*, 13). Winchelsea does appeal to such broad notions as common defence, urgent necessity, common good, public good, and the *utilitas rei publicae*, but his most important authority remains *Coram illo fatemur*. The principle of consent seems to have played a much larger role in the opposition of the clergy in England than in France; it was extended to the laity in the *Remonstrances* and the *De Tallagio Non Concedendo* of 1297 (Prestwich, *Documents*, nos. 98 and 151, pp. 115–17, 154).

[71] Cf. Aquinas, II *Sent.* 42.2.2 (above, p. 126); Peter of Auvergne, *In Politicorum Continuatio*, ed. R. Busa, in *S. Thomae Aquinatis Opera Omnia*, vol. vii (Stuttgart–Bad Cannstatt, 1980), V.1.5, p. 434.

(*hodie*), the cowardice of many and the unfaithfulness of others has produced the worst possible result. Spurning the counsel of their free subjects, he writes, almost all rulers are attempting to rule as tyrants, ordering everything towards their private honour or advantage and to the detriment of their subjects. A just ruler, he states, can hardly be found.

Godfrey's concern with the role of consent has been taken as a hallmark of his political thought, a reflection of his association with Liège and even of its struggles against its prince-bishop.[72] It is clear from his eleventh quodlibet, however, that, as far as Godfrey of Fontaines was concerned, consent was not an absolute or universal ideal but simply one of several means by which extraordinary taxation could be legitimized. It is also a means which could be paralleled both in earlier writers (such as Peter the Chanter and Raymond of Pennafort) and in contemporary practice.[73] Godfrey does not espouse the principle *quod omnes tangit* except as a means of ensuring that subjects voluntarily recognize their obligation of obedience, a goal which this principle shares with two other alternatives, namely good legislation and the counsel of wise men. Indeed, Godfrey is far less interested in recommending universal consent than he is in calling for the counsel of a group of prudent men independent of the circle immediately surrounding Philip IV.[74] What remains far more important to Godfrey's discussion of taxation is the principle with which Aristotle had distinguished good from bad forms of government, rule over free men from rule over slaves. Consent, good legislation, and counsel were all means to this one end. If an imposition secures the common good, subjects will voluntarily recognize their obligation of obedience however this imposition has originated. The common good, not consent, remains the ultimate measure of legitimacy for those in authority over others.

Godfrey's eleventh quodlibet of 1295/6 establishes a categoric test for taxation. If a ruler imposes a tax for the benefit of the *res publica*, then his subjects must willingly choose to pay, whether their consent is expressed directly or whether it is mediated through wise and prudent counsellors. If, on the other hand, the burden which a ruler places on the community is not alleviated by the required benefit, and if the ruler does not himself excel in wisdom, faithfulness, and love for the common good, then his subjects are released from their obligation of obedience. Even though it may be customary for the ruler to claim that a particular burden is being imposed for the necessity of the *res publica* and for the benefit of all his subjects, he cannot lawfully impose such a tax if this is not, in fact, the case. To argue otherwise, to believe that it is sufficient for the ruler simply to say that it is being imposed for the common good

---

[72] Lagarde, 'La Philosophie sociale', 118–21; id., *La Naissance*, 195–7; Lejeune, 'De Godefroid de Fontaines à la paix de Fexhe', 1243–6, 1248–9; C. Renardy, *Le Monde des maîtres universitaires du diocèse de Liège 1140–1350: Recherches sur sa composition et ses activités* (Paris, 1979), 361–2.

[73] Brown, 'Taxation and Morality', 4, 11. Cf. Beaumanoir, *Coutumes de Beauvaisis*, ed. A. Salmon (2 vols.; Paris, 1899–1900), ii. p. 264: 'par resnable cause et pour le commun pourfit et par grant conseil'; W. Stubbs, *Select Charters and other Illustrations of Constitutional History*, 9th edn., rev. H. W. C. Davis (Oxford, 1921), p. 491: 'fors ke par commun assent de tout le roiaume, e a commun profist de mesmes le roiaume'.

[74] For similar appeals, see Strayer, 'Consent to Taxation', 50. Cf. ibid., 60, 65–6, 92.

and that he has made his decision with good counsel, is to condone the behaviour of tyrants.[75] In 1295/6, concern over unjust taxation appears to have made Godfrey apply the common good as a measure of legitimacy for the exercise of power by a temporal ruler much more rigorously than in 1290–2 when he had been prepared to advise the victims of tyranny to lose their material goods rather than their lives. The widespread bitterness which accompanied the opposition to Philip IV's financial expedients in the 1290s must have had a considerable bearing on this shift in emphasis. If Godfrey's eleventh quodlibet was delivered in the immediate aftermath of *Clericis laicos*, then Boniface VIII's action may well have given Godfrey the lead he required. Only now did Godfrey finally follow Henry of Ghent and argue that resistance is justified whenever a ruler's command does not secure the common good.

If the events of 1295/6 sharpened Godfrey's belief that the common good should be established as the measure of legitimacy for the exercise of authority by the temporal power, this does not mean that his attitude to the exercise of authority within the church was entirely unaffected. Godfrey's immediate response to *Clericis laicos* appears to have been to underline the obligation of all Christians to obey the pope, irrespective of any vows of obedience which they may have taken to more immediate superiors, and especially if it was a case of necessity or clear benefit to the *res publica*.[76] In 1295/6, therefore, when Godfrey of Fontaines came to discuss the pope's role in the payment of tenths, his conclusion was similar to the position put forward by James of Viterbo. The church or the pope has the power to order Christians to pay tenths, or for that matter any other proportion of their temporal goods, insofar as this action will further the good of the Christian people (*bonum populi christiani*).[77] However, in 1295/6, Godfrey, like James, also judged it advisable to accompany this statement with a significant disclaimer. This conclusion, he adds, does not mean that the pope possesses jurisdiction and lordship (*ius et dominium*) over all the temporal goods of all the inhabitants of the earth and that he can therefore do with them whatever he pleases. Godfrey recognizes that this is what some people seem to think (*sicut aliqui videntur sentire*) but he, for one, begs to differ. Godfrey argues against giving the pope so much power on quite practical grounds. Not only would the pope then be able generally to reallocate the goods and personnel of the church, appointing and removing bishops at will, but he would also be able to divide and unite kingdoms, appointing and removing temporal rulers without even having to appeal to the principle *ratione peccati*. To credit the pope with such a capability, Godfrey ventures to suggest, will simply not meet with the approval of temporal rulers.[78] With this

---

[75] A similar conclusion was reached by Peter of Auvergne in Christmas 1298 when he discussed the legitimacy and duration of emergency taxation. See E. A. R. Brown, '*Cessante causa* and the Taxes of the Last Capetians: The Political Applications of a Philosophical Maxim', *Studia Gratiana*, 15 (1972), 567–87, esp. 585–7. Cf. Richard of Middleton, *Quodlibet*, II.30, in E. Hocedez (ed.), *Richard de Middleton, sa vie, ses oeuvres, sa doctrine* (Louvain–Paris, 1925), p. 417.

[76] See above, pp. 245–7.   [77] *Quod*. XI.12, p. 60. Cf. Lagarde, 'La Philosophie sociale', 122–3.

[78] Philip IV's opposition to *Clericis laicos* was based on the claim that Boniface VIII was attempting to assert his jurisdiction over all the temporal goods of the king. See e.g. *Antequam essent clerici* (Dupuy, *Histoire du différend, Actes et Preuves*, 21–3). Cf. Dupuy, *op. cit.*, 44, 60, 67.

observation, Godfrey is otherwise content to accept the principle that God has given the pope a plenitude of power in spiritual matters and in those things which are ordered towards the well-being (or salvation) of the people (*in his quae ad salutem populi ordinantur*). With this observation, indeed, Godfrey is content to accept that the pope also has power (*potestas*) over the temporal goods of individuals when they are necessary for securing this goal.

If Godfrey judged it necessary to qualify his otherwise firm endorsement of papal plenitude of power in 1295/6, a similar reservation is evident again in 1296/7. On this occasion, he uses the same legal distinctions as James of Viterbo to argue that the pope is a public person, a prelate who is, in a sense (*quodam modo*), the general distributor of all ecclesiastical goods for the benefit of the *res publica*, and who, in a sense (*aliquo modo*), possesses jurisdiction and lordship (*ius et dominium*) over these goods by virtue of his office.[79] In 1297/8, Godfrey explains what he means by 'in a sense'. According to Godfrey, when ownership (*proprietas*) of the material goods of the church is defined as lordship (*ius et dominium*), it does not belong to one single person but to the whole community. In the church of Paris, therefore, the bishop is only the distributor of its goods whilst, in the church as a whole, the pope is only the principal and general distributor, the steward (*procurator*) of its temporal possessions.[80]

Godfrey's insistence that the pope exercises stewardship over the material goods of the church provides one further restriction to his justification of plenitude of power. In 1296/7, he adds another. According to Godfrey, the common good is the essential and primary goal of the political prudence which is intrinsic to every ruler, ecclesiastical as well as temporal. Appealing to a combination of Aristotle (book I of the *Ethics*), Augustine (book XIX of *De Civitate Dei*), and the apostle Paul (2 Corinthians 10: 8, 13: 10, and Romans 13: 1), Godfrey insists that securing the common good is a principle which should guide all the actions of a prelate (*illud est faciendum quod magis expedit ad bonum commune*).[81] Godfrey then applies this litmus test to the specific question of whether the pope can remove from his subjects what is within their competence by law. A superior authority, he concludes, should not remove from a subordinate authority anything which is within the latter's competence by law (*de iure*) unless a situation arises where such an action will benefit the community. Thus, if the pope sees that it is the custom of the canons of a particular church to be unruly in their elections or to elect inferior candidates, and that this behaviour is disadvantageous to the *res publica*, then it is neither bad nor illegal for him temporarily to remove their powers of election in order to correct the canons and bring benefit to the church. Such an action would be justified because it is performed on account of the common good.[82] Appealing to a string of texts from

---

[79] *Quod.* XII.19, p. 147. Cf. *Quod.* III.12, p. 224 (*Brevis*, p. 320); *Quod.* XIII.7, pp. 232–3.

[80] *Quod.* XIII.5, pp. 222–9. Cf. Lagarde, 'La Philosophie sociale', 137–8; id., *La Naissance*, 209.

[81] *Quod.* XII.3, pp. 93–5. Cf. Lagarde, 'La Philosophie sociale', 107; id., *La Naissance*, 205, 208.

[82] The issue of papal provisions to benefices was a repeated bone of contention between Philip IV and Boniface VIII. Godfrey, however, may have a more specific case in mind, namely the disputed election at Cambrai, where Boniface nominated one of his notaries only to find that the archbishop of Rheims had

Gratian,[83] Godfrey gives this statement a universal application. Every time the pope restrains or suspends the customary activities of his subordinates, he is obliged to ensure that these activities make a greater contribution to the honour of God and the benefit of the church.[84]

It is in the midst of this account that Godfrey does what he has studiously avoided in all his previous discussions of papal power.[85] Instead of using the notion of the common good simply to justify papal intervention he now also uses it to measure its abuse and, more importantly, to justify resistance to it. Like James of Viterbo, who insisted that the pope should always be presumed to be acting with a reasonable cause unless it is particularly clear (*valde manifeste*) that the opposite is true, Godfrey is careful to stipulate that it must be evident that such an abuse has taken place. Unlike James, however, Godfrey now elaborates on what the consequences of finding such proof would be. If a superior authority has acted, not to the benefit, but to the detriment of a community, then this action should not be accepted, or rather the prelate responsible should not be tolerated in office unless he corrects his error. This is precisely the conclusion which had been drawn by Henry of Ghent in 1288 and which Godfrey had applied to an abuse of temporal power in 1295/6. It is only in 1296/7 that Godfrey applies it to an abuse of papal power within the church. Good government, he explains, and particularly ecclesiastical government, ought not to be tyrannical. Rulers in the church ought to conduct themselves according to the best form of government, that is, the constitution in which a ruler does not attempt to secure his own good but the good of his subjects. Subjects are free people, not slaves, and free people possess the power to oppose their ruler should he wish to act like a tyrant towards them. Godfrey's very next question in the quodlibet accordingly deals with voluntary and involuntary removal from office, the deposition of a pope as well as his resignation.

Godfrey had already discussed the general question of episcopal resignation in 1288.[86] By 1296/7, however, it had assumed a very different perspective as a result of the unprecedented abdication of Pope Celestine V in 1293. The legitimacy of this act, and, by extension, the legitimacy of the pontificate of his successor, rapidly became a bitter bone of contention at Rome in the struggle of the Colonna faction against Boniface VIII. This conflict came to a head in May and June 1297 when the Colonna cardinals declared Celestine's abdication to be illegal and called on a General Council to put an end to the tyranny of the pope. Boniface VIII's actions, they claimed, had caused great scandal, and his abuse of papal plenitude of power at whim (*pro libito*) was wreaking destruction within the church.[87] In such circumstances, whether the

---

confirmed a French candidate. In February 1297, the pope removed the diocese of Cambrai from the jurisdiction of the archbishop and chapter of Rheims and placed it under immediate papal control (*Registres*, no. 1672, col. 631). In June 1297, however, he restored the archbishop's right to confirm bishops and abbots (*Registres*, no. 1868, col. 707). For the pope's earlier difficulties with the canons of Rheims, see e.g. *Registres*, no. 1082, cols. 381–2.

[83] *Decretum* I.99.5 (Friedberg, i. 351); II.11.1.39 (ibid., i. 638); II.25.2.8 (ibid., i. 1014).
[84] Cf. *Quod.* XIII.7, pp. 233–4.   [85] Cf. *Quod.* I.17, p. 40.   [86] See above, p. 240.
[87] *Die Denkschriften der Colonna gegen Bonifaz VIII und der Cardinäle gegen die Colonna*, ed. H. Denifle (Freiburg, 1885–93), v. pp. 519–24. For the role of councils in the dispute between Philip the Fair

bishopric of Rome was subject to the same considerations as the office of an ordinary bishop or priest naturally became a particularly sensitive question.[88] Godfrey's twelfth quodlibet (1296/7) marks his own contribution to this debate.[89]

Godfrey's approach to the Colonna appeal, like his approach to *Ad fructus uberes* in 1287, was to provide a detailed scrutiny of the relevant texts from canon law, in this case *Nisi cum pridem* and the stipulations covering the voluntary and involuntary removal of an individual from ecclesiastical office. Once again, however, the principles which underpin his discussion of papal resignation and deposition are based on a much broader understanding of the role of the common good in the human community. According to Godfrey, a prelate holds authority in the church not for his own sake but for the sake of the benefit which he brings to others. Although a prelate will secure his own spiritual benefit by ruling well, there is a sense (*aliquo modo*) in which, by placing himself under this obligation towards his subjects, he has also transferred power over himself to the church whom he has 'married'. In order to be released from his obligation, therefore, a prelate has to obtain the consent of these people or of the superior prelate who acted on their behalf when investing him with his office. Godfrey cites the standard legal arguments—a prelate cannot be released from his pastoral obligations unless he is prevented from the due performance of his office by some impediment either on his own part or on the part of his subjects or else by some other 'reasonable cause'.[90] Consent, however, is a less important consideration for Godfrey than his own, characteristic concern with the benefit which the prelate should bring to himself and to others. In the circumstances envisaged by canon law, he concludes, the prelate is obliged to resign as much for his own well-being as for the well-being of his people (*tam propter salutem populi quam propter salutem propriam*). Indeed, Godfrey ends up by questioning whether the consent of the prelate's superior or of his subjects needs to be secured at all. Rather than insist on the legal requirement of consent, Godfrey emphasizes the need to secure the good of the prelate and the good of the church. Thus, in Godfrey's view, even if consent is not forthcoming, a prelate can, and should, resign. No voluntary oath can prejudice the obligation which an individual has to his own spiritual well-being. According to the canonists, this obligation stems from the Holy Spirit.[91] According to Godfrey, it stems from the *ordo caritatis*. If lawyers need to dress up this principle in the guise

and Boniface VIII, see H.-X. Arquillière, 'L'Appel au concile sous Philippe le Bel et la genèse des théories conciliaires', *Revue des Questions Historiques*, 89 (1911), 23–55; H. F. Dondaine, 'Documents pour servir à l'histoire de la province de France: L'Appel au concile (1303)', *Archivum Fratrum Praedicatorum*, 22 (1952), 381–439; R. Kay, 'Ad nostram praesentiam evocamus: Boniface VIII and the Roman Convocation of 1302', *Proceedings of the Third International Congress of Medieval Canon Law* (Rome, 1971), 165–89.

[88] Pierre Jean Olivi, '*Petri Iohannis Olivi De Renuntiatione Papae Coelestini V Quaestio et Epistola*', ed. P. L. Oliger, *Archivum Franciscanum Historicum*, 11 (1918), 340–73; Giles of Rome, *De Renuntiatione Papae*, ed. J. R. Eastman (Lewiston, NY, 1992). Cf. J. Leclercq, 'La Renonciation de Célestin V et l'opinion théologique en France du vivant de Boniface VIII' *Revue d'Histoire de l'Église de France*, 25 (1939), 183–92; J. R. Eastman, *Papal Abdication in Later Medieval Thought* (Lewiston, NY, 1990); id., 'Giles of Rome and his Use of St. Augustine in Defense of Papal Abdication', *Augustiniana*, 38 (1988), 129–39.

[89] *Quod.* XII.4, pp. 96–9. Cf. Lagarde, 'La Philosophie sociale', 134.

[90] *Decr. Greg. IX* I.9.10 (Friedberg, ii.107–12).   [91] *Decretum* II.19.2.2 (Friedberg, i. 839–40).

of a superior's consent, then they should consider the 'superior prelate' to be none other than God (*summus praelatus deus*).

By considering the good of the prelate as well as the good of his flock, Godfrey is able to concentrate his discussion on the plea of personal deficiency which Celestine V had entered as the basis of his own resignation from the papal office. By insisting that consideration of the individual and the common good can, if necessary, override the need to secure consent, Godfrey also establishes a principle which is applicable to involuntary as well as voluntary removal from office. According to canon law, deposition requires the consent, not of a superior, but of a Council.[92] According to Godfrey, deposition is determined by whatever secures the individual good of the prelate and the common good of the church. In the case of voluntary resignation, Godfrey concludes, just as the pope is elected, not by a superior, but by the college of cardinals acting on behalf of the whole church, so this college possesses the authority to approve the resignation of the pope. They represent the universal church and are obliged to consider its good (*bonum universalis ecclesiae*). However, if they do not fulfil this obligation and if they withhold their consent, then Godfrey is again insistent that a pope who is of no benefit whatsoever (*omnino inutilis*) can, and should, resign. In styling himself the *servus servorum Dei*, the pope must consider himself a servant who is obliged to secure the good of the servants of God (*bonum servorum Dei*).

Godfrey's discussion of papal authority in 1296/7 marks a significant shift in his attitude to the exercise of authority within the church. Like Henry of Ghent in 1290 and 1291, Godfrey uses a notion of the common good to provide a theoretical justification, first, for opposing tyrannical conduct by a pope, and, second, for insisting on the resignation, or even deposition, of the offending individual. Unlike Henry of Ghent, Godfrey appears reluctant to come to such a conclusion. His lament on the abuse of authority by the temporal power in 1295/6, for example, is much more vociferous than his acknowledgement of the possibility of an abuse of plenitude of power by the pope in 1296/7. Indeed, if Godfrey is prepared to countenance the deposition of a pope in 1297/8 on the grounds of an illegitimate intervention in an episcopal election, then it is not long before he reverts to a much more moderate line of argument. Thus, in his thirteenth quodlibet (1297/8), Godfrey concedes that the church has a right (*ius*) to those material goods which are necessary to maintain ministers responsible for the government and salvation of the faithful. Without these goods, Godfrey argues, neither the order of the church nor the common good secured by good governance would be able to exist.[93] Godfrey's moderation is even more apparent in the same quodlibet when he gives his own solution to the scenario which had so troubled James of Viterbo in 1293/4, that is, a time of imminent danger to the Christian faith when it is necessary to seek the assistance of men who possess goods which should, by right, be restored to their owners, namely goods which have been acquired through pillage (*rapina*), usury, or other unjust means.[94] Is the pope

---

[92] *Decretum* I.21.7 (Friedberg, i. 71).   [93] *Quod.* XIII.8, p. 247.

[94] *Quod.* XIII.5, pp. 222–9. Cf. Lagarde, 'La Philosophie sociale', 137–8; id., *La Naissance*, 209.

able to dispense these men from the obligation to make restitution if they will use these goods to meet the common need of the church (*communis necessitas ecclesiae*)?

In 1297/8, the question of restoring pillaged goods would have struck a particularly significant chord. For all the concessions made in *Etsi de statu*, in July 1297 Boniface warned Philip IV that anything which was exacted above and beyond what was required for the common defence of the kingdom would endanger the souls of those who received it and would have to be restored to those from whom it had been levied.[95] Indeed, Philip IV had to wait until 1305 before Clement V conceded to him all the goods which he had taken from the church in defiance of Boniface VIII and absolved him from the obligation to make restitution. In 1297/8, therefore, faced with both the dire warning in *Etsi de statu* and the exaction of a double tenth, restitution of unjustly acquired goods was a particularly live issue. Godfrey's solution was to draw a distinction between the different types of goods which are unjustly possessed. If they are ecclesiastical or clerical goods, he argues, then the pope is within his rights to grant a dispensation for any reasonable cause, although the goods in question must be used for the good or the benefit of the church. However, if the property in question belongs to the laity, then, although the pope can still grant a dispensation, this can only be in a case of clear necessity. If it is anything less, then Godfrey is adamant that the pope does not have the same rights over the goods of the laity as he does over the goods of the church. With this qualification, however, Godfrey's general principle is clear. The pope can compel the laity to contribute a portion of their temporal goods in order to assist the church in its hour of need. All individuals, he explains, laity as well as clergy, are obliged to risk their lives and property in order to preserve the good of the community and, above all, if this good is the spiritual good of the Christian faith. In the case of illicitly acquired goods, the same principle applies. If the good of the community would be endangered unless the individuals in question defend it, and if they cannot defend it unless they remain in possession of their unjustly acquired goods, then they must be allowed to keep these goods. The pope can also grant such a dispensation if the beneficiaries would otherwise be heretics or opponents of the church, that is, people who might wish to use their restored goods to attack the church. Such a dispensation, Godfrey argues, is nothing other than a declaration of a basic principle of natural law—material goods become common at a time of necessity. This principle, he points out, was designed, in the first instance, to keep people alive, but it is even more applicable if it defends the common good. Indeed, whoever refuses to share their own goods in such circumstances is guilty of a serious sin. After the events of 1296–7, Godfrey's argument bears every sign of attempting to find a compromise between Philip IV and Boniface VIII.

Establishing a direct connection between Godfrey of Fontaines's theoretical analysis of the common good and his discussion of its practical applications is a difficult task.

---

[95] *Registres*, no. 2354, cols. 941–3.

There are occasions on which the connection is made explicit, for example, when Godfrey appeals to his definition of legal or general justice in the course of discussing papal dispensation, or when he cites the principle that the individual good must be included within the common good in the course of describing the merits of the office of prelate. In both of these cases, Godfrey is drawing on his extensive theoretical analysis of the common good—in the first instance, on his exposition of book V of the *Ethics* in terms of the distinction between essence and existence, and, in the second instance, on his exposition of book IX of the *Ethics* in the light of Aquinas' account of the *ordo caritatis*. Otherwise, Godfrey draws on different sources of inspiration, from canon and Roman law (for the notions of necessity and benefit) and from book III of the *Politics* (for the distinction between good and bad forms of government and for its discussion of the relationship between good laws and a good ruler).

Godfrey of Fontaines, like Henry of Ghent, places the common good at the heart of his practical analysis of the human community as a response to a series of bitter contemporary controversies. The dispute over *Ad fructus uberes* caused him to re-examine the relative merits of the active and the contemplative lives and the pope's exercise of the power of dispensation. The burden of papal and royal taxation, mean-while, caused him to reassess the pope's relation to material goods in the church and the king's relation to the temporal property of his subjects. Compared to Henry, Godfrey was much more hesitant in presenting the common good as a criterion which should control the exercise of authority by the pope. Until 1295/6 at least, Godfrey was content to use the common good as a justification for the exercise of papal plenitude of power and not as a limitation on the obligation of obedience to an illegitimate papal grant of dispensation. Only in 1296/7 did Godfrey explicitly acknowledge the possibility of a pope abusing this plenitude of power and being forced to resign from his office. Even then, it was prompted by undue interference in episcopal elections rather than by any claim to exercise lordship over temporal goods. Godfrey's reaction to the dispute over *Clericis laicos*, indeed, reveals a studied mod-eration—insisting that the pope is only a steward of the goods of the church but acknowledging his right to control the temporal goods of all Christians when it is a matter of the *salus christiani populi*.

Godfrey shows much less hesitation in following Henry of Ghent's discussion of the exercise of power by the temporal ruler. Philip IV's campaigns in Aquitaine and Flanders, and the taxation which they precipitated, not only focused Godfrey's attention on the use and abuse of concepts such as common benefit, necessity, and defence of the kingdom, but resulted in a passionate insistence on the need for good counsel and a radical demonstration of the consequences of its absence. Like Henry, Godfrey argues that any extraordinary demand for taxation must be justified by clear evidence of benefit and necessity. Unlike Henry, Godfrey sets out just how this evidence is to be judged—by the counsel of wise, just, and prudent individuals who are not the close associates of the king. Thus, if Godfrey ends up making the common good just as radical a concept in his own political philosophy as it had been in Henry of Ghent's, then this is more a feature of his attitude towards the exercise of authority by the temporal ruler than it is of his approach to the power of the pope. Taken together, however, Henry of Ghent and Godfrey of Fontaines came to exercise a profound influence on subsequent scholastic political thinking. The next time conflict arose between Philip IV and Boniface VIII there would be a substantial body of political thought in which the consequences of establishing the common good as the goal of all authority, temporal as well as spiritual, were exploited to the full.

10

The Life of Virtue—Giles of Rome, James of Viterbo, and John of Paris

Relations between Philip IV and Boniface VIII broke down on two occasions—in 1296, when the pope prohibited all taxation of the church which did not have his prior consent, and, more seriously, in 1301, when the king arrested the bishop of Pamiers on charges of treason. Philip IV's actions were guided, in each case, by counsellors who were trained in the study of law.[1] Whilst it may be argued, therefore, that the political ideas of theologians, as opposed to jurists, had little direct influence on the conduct of events,[2] this does not mean that theological opinion was not regarded as an essential source of legitimation by both the pope and the king. In 1296–7, for example, university masters were cited in *Clericis laicos*, alongside prelates, secular clergy, and members of religious orders, and threatened with excommunication if they failed to comply with the pope's injunctions. Not unnaturally, this precipitated a spate of discussion in Paris over the legitimacy of the king's exactions for his campaigns in Flanders and Aquitaine. In 1301, masters in theology were summoned by *Ausculta fili*, again alongside archbishops, bishops, and abbots, in order to discuss Philip IV's government of his kingdom at a papal council to be held in Rome the following year. The king's response was to invite the university to sanction the legitimacy of his own proceedings against the pope in Paris at a series of general 'councils' in 1302 and 1303.

In practical terms, Parisian masters clearly found themselves, like the rest of the French clergy, in a deeply uncomfortable position, caught between their duty to obey the pope and their need to find some sort of accommodation with the king. The events of 1296–7 and 1301–3 had a correspondingly profound impact on the political and ecclesiological ideas which they put forward during these years. In theoretical terms, scholastic theologians were being forced to choose between competing claims to lordship (*dominium*). The first dispute focused attention on the connection of *dominium* with ownership of property and, as a result, scholastic discussion concentrated on the respective relations of pope and king to the material goods of the church and the laity. The second dispute extended this idea to cover jurisdiction as well. The broadening of the terms in which the second dispute was analysed mirrored the escalation of the means by which it was conducted. It also moved scholastic discussion

---

[1] R. Scholz, *Die Publizistik zur Zeit Philipps des Schönen und Bonifaz' VIII* (Stuttgart, 1903), 353–443; J. Favier, 'Les Légistes et le gouvernement de Philippe le Bel', *Journal des Savants*, 1969, 92–108; F. Pegues, *The Lawyers of the Last Capetians* (Princeton, 1962), 124–37.

[2] J. R. Strayer, *The Reign of Philip the Fair* (Princeton, 1980), p. xiii.

beyond the immediate academic confines of quodlibetic and disputed questions. Three theologians in particular, Giles of Rome, James of Viterbo, and John of Paris, were drawn into making a more public statement of their views.

Giles of Rome had left Paris to become, in 1291, Prior General of the Augustinian Order and, in 1295, Archbishop of Bourges. In 1302, he humbly delivered to Boniface VIII 'a compilation of some remarks on ecclesiastical power', a thumping endorsement of the superiority of the pope's jurisdiction which he entitled *De Ecclesiastica Potestate*.[3] Giles was immediately joined by James of Viterbo, his successor as Augustinian master in theology who had himself subsequently left Paris in 1300 in order to direct the *studium generale* at Naples. He too dedicated to the pope a defence of plenitude of power, *De Regimine Christiano*, and in September and December 1302 he was made, successively, Archbishop of Benevento and Naples.[4] However, whilst Boniface could take comfort from the support of these prominent theologians, one of them a leading French bishop, the same could not be said of the rejoinder, *De Potestate Regia et Papali*, which was immediately produced by their erstwhile Dominican colleague, John of Paris.[5] Given that Giles of Rome and James of Viterbo completed their treatises in Italy before September 1302, it is tempting to posit a formal connection with the general council which Boniface VIII had summoned to Rome for November of that year in order to discuss the conduct of the French king. By the same token, if *De Ecclesiastica Potestate* and *De Regimine Principum* were precipitated by the imminence of this papal council, then *De Potestate Regia et Papali* may have owed its inception to Philip IV's Paris councils of 1302 and 1303, perhaps even the Louvre assembly of June 1303 which included members of the university and which delivered an endorsement of the king's position to which John of Paris himself subscribed.[6]

[3] Aegidius Romanus, *De Ecclesiastica Potestate*, ed. R. Scholz (Weimar, 1929); trans. R. W. Dyson (Woodbridge, 1986). For its composition between February and August 1302, see Scholz, *ed. cit.*, p. xi.
[4] James of Viterbo, *De Regimine Christiano*, ed. H.-X. Arquillière, *Le Plus Ancien Traité de l'Église: Jacques de Viterbe* (Paris, 1926); trans. R. Dyson (Woodbridge, 1995). The precise relationship of *De Regimine Christiano* to *De Ecclesiastica Potestate* is far from clear. For its composition in Naples at some time between December 1301 and September 1302, see Scholz, *Die Publizistik*, 132; Arquillière, *Le Plus Ancien Traité de l'Église*, 16; D. Gutierrez, '*De vita et scriptis Beati Iacobi de Viterbio*', *Analecta Augustiniana*, 16 (1937–8), 296; E. Ypma, 'Recherches sur la carrière scolaire et la bibliothèque de Jacques de Viterbe', *Augustiniana*, 24 (1974), 260.
[5] ed. J. Leclercq, *Jean de Paris et l'ecclésiologie du XIIIe siècle* (Paris, 1942), 173–260; ed. F. Bleienstein, *Johannes Quidort von Paris: Über königliche und päpstliche Gewalt* (Stuttgart, 1969), 69–211; trans. J. Watt (Toronto, 1971); trans. A. P. Monahan (New York, 1974). For its composition, see Scholz, *Die Publizistik*, 296–8 (April 1302–March 1303); Leclercq, *op. cit.*, 10–14 (November 1302–May 1303); Bleienstein, *op. cit.*, 13–14 (January–June 1302). Watt (*op. cit.*, 28) argues from the absence of any reference to *Unam sanctam* that it must pre-date November 1302; in view of the problems surrounding the circulation of *Unam sanctam*, this hardly seems conclusive. Compare P. Saenger, 'John of Paris, Principal Author of the *Quaestio de Potestate Papae* [*Rex Pacificus*]', *Speculum* 56 (1981), 51 n. 51, who places it as late as June–October 1303. For an altogether different reading, and dating, of the text, see the ingenious arguments of J. Coleman, 'The Dominican Political Theory of John of Paris in its Context', in D. Wood (ed.), *The Church and Sovereignty c.590–1918: Essays in Honour of Michael Wilks* (Oxford, 1991), 187–223.
[6] W. Courtenay, 'Between Pope and King: The Parisian Letters of Adhesion of 1303', *Speculum*, 71 (1996), 577–605. Cf. T. N. Bisson, 'The General Assemblies of Philip the Fair: Their Character Reconsidered', *Studia Gratiana*, 15 (1972), 539–64. For Philip IV's subsequent attempt to secure the support of

When controversy erupted between Philip IV and Boniface VIII over their respective rights of jurisdiction, it was clear to Giles of Rome, James of Viterbo, and John of Paris that, in order to determine the responsibilities of the spiritual and the temporal power, they would have to provide a more precise definition of the goal of the political community. As scholastic theologians, they could draw on two broad concepts. On the one hand, there was the common good of peace and material security (*communis utilitas*); on the other, there was the common good of happiness and the life of virtue (*bonum commune*). Applied to the relationship between the spiritual and the temporal power, this left Giles of Rome, James of Viterbo, and John of Paris with a clear choice. If they limited their definition of the common good to the goal of peace and security, as Augustine had done, then this would mean that the jurisdiction of the temporal power would be restricted to corporeal goods. As a result, any judgement which involved more than purely material considerations would have to be placed firmly within the jurisdiction of the church. Choosing Augustine's material definition certainly had the advantage of simplicity. By providing such a clear separation of temporal and spiritual goods, it would cut the Gordian knot of overlapping jurisdictions. However, this would also be at the cost of ignoring a central tenet of the *Ethics* and the *Politics*. If they accordingly extended their definition of the common good in order to include the life of virtue, then this would clearly give the temporal power authority over more than just corporeal goods. Choosing Aristotle's moral definition, however, posed its own set of questions. Is the goal of the political community attainable merely through natural virtue or does it require the presence of Christian faith? Are the cardinal virtues self-sufficient or do they need to be perfected by the theological virtues? Is the life of moral virtue the sole responsibility of the king or does it require the supervision of the church? Adopting the life of virtue as the goal of temporal authority, in other words, placed the relationship between nature and grace, moral and theological virtue, at the centre of political controversy.

Giles of Rome tackled the relationship between the spiritual and the temporal power in some detail in his commentary on the *Sentences*. However, since nearly forty years separate the first redaction of this text in the early 1270s from its final (and only extant) version after 1309, it is unclear whether Giles's discussion should be read as a near-contemporary gloss on *De Regimine Principum* or as a later postscript to *De Ecclesiastica Potestate*.[7] His analysis certainly recycles several Aristotelian principles which are familiar from *De Regimine Principum* and his commentary on the *Rhetorica*—society originates in the social and political nature of humankind; the rule of a single individual is a reflection of the divine order in the universe; all forms of government divide into three good forms and three bad.[8] However, when Giles

Paris theologians for his actions against the Templars, see *Le Dossier de l'affaire des Templiers*, ed. G. Lizerand (Paris, 1923), 62–71.

[7] Cf. R. Kuiters, 'De Ecclesiastica Potestate sive De Summi Pontificis Potestate secundum Aegidium Romanum', *Analecta Augustiniana*, 20 (1946), 146–214.

[8] In *II Librum Sententiarum* (Venice, 1581), 44.1.2, p. 681; 44.1.3, p. 685.

comes to define the goal of good government in his commentary on the *Sentences*, his argument is much closer to his later hierocratic polemic than it is to his earlier *speculum principis*. This shift is very suggestive.

Giles of Rome opens with a straightforward summary of Aristotle—the natural sociability of humans stems from their inability, on their own, to lead a self-sufficient life or to live in a good manner (*bono modo per se vivere*). Of these two characteristically Aristotelian principles, however, Giles is far more concerned with self-sufficiency than he is with the life of virtue. Thus, the city is described as 'perfect', not because of the completeness of its moral function, but because it is the only type of natural community which can use trade to provide everything that humans need for the duration of a lifetime. When Giles defines the goal of human life, he refers, not to the life of virtue, but to the attainment of God. Insofar as Aristotle is cited in this context, it is for the *duplex ordo* from book XII of the *Metaphysics*—the good of order is the greatest good after the good of the army commander and, as such, it consists of all human authorities being ordered towards a single ruler, namely God.[9]

Giles's interest in Aristotle's account of order, moreover, is closely tied to Augustine's analysis of God's providential government of political authority in human society. Whether a particular human ruler is good or bad, Giles argues, does not affect the divine origin of the order in which it participates since, according to Augustine, temporal goods and temporal evils befall good and wicked people alike as they are squeezed in the olive press of the world.[10] The presence of an evil ruler does not contravene the principle that good will always result from authority because an evil ruler still benefits the elect. Once again, Giles cites Augustine—all good things (with the exception of the virtues) can be rightly or wrongly used.[11] Authority is thus a good in itself even if it can be wrongly acquired and wrongly used. All lordship (*dominium*), Giles concludes, and all authority (*principatus*), is good inasmuch as it represents a principle of order derived from God. Authority which is abused simply derives from God in a different way. This does not mean that all evil rulers are owed obedience. According to Giles, obedience should not be shown to any command which runs counter to God or to natural law, even if it were to originate from the pope. Even a just authority can be disobeyed when it commands a sinful action (in which case death or martyrdom is preferable to obedience) or when it insists on something which is not in accordance with custom (such as new tolls or taxes).[12] Equally, however, an unjust authority is not owed obedience until it brings such benefit to its subjects that they voluntarily consent to its power and thereby make it just. As an example of this sort of benefit, Giles suggests peace (*pax*) and he illustrates it with Augustine's discussion of the legitimacy of the pagan Roman Empire.

---

[9] II *Sent.* 44.1.2, pp. 681–2. Cf. I *Sent.* 2.1.3–4, pp. 81, 84; III *Sent.* 2.3.1, pp. 261–2; 9.1.2, p. 408.

[10] Augustine, *Sermo*, XIX.6 (*PL* 38, cols. 132–7), col. 137; *De Civitate Dei*, ed. B. Dombart and A. Kalb (*CCSL* 47), I.8, pp. 7–8.

[11] Augustine, *Retractiones*, ed. A. Mutzenbecher (*CCSL* 57) I.9, pp. 26–7.

[12] Giles refrains from further comment on taxation by claiming that this is a subject for the jurist, not the theologian.

Although Christians had been liberated with regard to their spiritual goods, Giles points out that they were still subject to the authority of an infidel ruler with regard to their bodily goods. He then extends this distinction to cover all *dominium* and not just that of the non-Christian ruler. All authority, Giles concludes, and primarily the authority of lay rulers, is instituted for the sake of temporal or corporeal goods.[13]

For Giles's commentary on the *Sentences* to emphasize providential order rather than good government, and to view political authority in terms of material self-sufficiency rather than virtue, presents a marked contrast with *De Regimine Principum*, a work which repeatedly defines the common good secured by temporal authority as the life of virtue. It is noticeable, moreover, that when Giles does give a specific illustration of good government, he takes it from Augustine rather than from Aristotle, identifying the good use of political authority as the provision of the temporal good of peace. Dividing human authority into temporal and corporeal, on the one hand, and ecclesiastical and spiritual, on the other, is a long way from treating the spiritual life of virtue as the defining goal of good kingship.[14]

If a contrast with *De Regimine Principum* is evident from Giles's commentary on the *Sentences*, then it is even more marked in *De Ecclesiastica Potestate*. Not only does Giles go out of his way to state that participation in the political community is not a necessary precondition to attaining the ultimate goal of eternal beatitude,[15] but, when he defines the function of the temporal ruler, he limits it to meeting external and material needs. The role of the ruler is to ensure justice, he writes, but this is not in order to make his subjects virtuous but simply to restrain them from injuring one another's person and property.[16] According to Giles, this 'material' justice is primarily designed to facilitate the role of the church in society. Earthly rulers prepare individuals for ecclesiastical rulers; they ensure that justice is observed in temporal affairs in order that peace and tranquillity may be secured in spiritual affairs; they impose a bridle on the laity in order that the spiritual power may rule more freely.[17] As a result, justice is a subordinate element of the overriding lordship which is possessed by the ecclesiastical power. According to Giles, an earthly power can judge what is just or unjust only inasmuch as it acts in virtue of the spiritual power. If justice concerns a spiritual matter (that is, anything which concerns the perfection of the soul and not the body), then it is the spiritual power which must act as judge.[18]

The transformation which Giles's attitude towards the common good undergoes between the composition of *De Regimine Principum* and *De Ecclesiastica Potestate* is very revealing. By restricting the goal of temporal authority to the provision of material goods, Giles is able to produce a simple, straightforward justification of the

---

[13] II *Sent.* 44.2.1, p. 688; 44.2.2, pp. 690–1; 44.2.3, p. 692.

[14] Giles does concede that the temporal power can concern itself with spiritual goods *per redundantiam vel ex consequenti* (II *Sent.* 42.2.2, p. 691) but no further explanation is offered.

[15] *De Ecclesiastica Potestate* [henceforth *DEP*], ed. Scholz, II.vi.13, p. 65.

[16] *DEP* II.vi.19, p. 68. Cf. II.xiii.7, p. 113. The one mention of the inculcation of virtue as the goal of the temporal power is at I.ix.7, p. 33.

[17] *DEP* II.vi.21, p. 68. For the analogy, see Aristotle, *Ethics* I.1 1094^{a}10–12.

[18] *DEP* II.x.14, p. 92.

comprehensive scope of ecclesiastical jurisdiction—the church can exercise its power whenever the spiritual good of virtue is concerned. The corresponding devaluation of temporal jurisdiction from moral to material concerns does not necessarily contradict the earlier argument of *De Regimine Principum*. Defining the goal of political authority as the common good of virtue may well have been intended as a means of *implying* that the king will therefore be supervised and judged by the church. This was, after all, the corollary which had been drawn in *De Regno ad Regem Cypri*— virtue is a good of the soul and the good of the soul is necessarily the responsibility of the spiritual power. Thus, *De Regno* limited the temporal power to the provision of material goods and introduced the life of virtue only *after* establishing a supervisory role for the church. Faced with this conclusion, *De Regimine Principum* defined the goal of the temporal ruler as the life of virtue but avoided any discussion of the relationship between a good Christian king and the authority of the church which this definition might entail. The fact that Giles did not draw this corollary in so many words may simply indicate that he thought such a conclusion prudent to avoid in the late 1270s.[19] Nevertheless, by conceding in principle that the life of moral virtue could fall within the jurisdiction of the temporal power without explicitly stressing the supervision of the church, *De Regimine Principum* did demonstrate how an Aristotelian definition of the political community might be used to justify the independent jurisdiction of the temporal power on moral issues. By accepting that, in the life of virtue, the temporal power had its own spiritual function, *De Regimine Principum* effectively threatened exactly the papalist line which Giles found himself trying to endorse in 1302. In *De Regimine Principum*, in other words, Giles of Rome found he had fashioned a double-edged sword. In *De Ecclesiastica Potestate*, and in his commentary on the *Sentences*, he set about removing this ambivalence altogether.

Although *De Ecclesiastica Potestate* carefully restricts the goal of temporal authority to material concerns, Giles does not pass up the opportunity presented by retaining a more general notion of the common good as a justification for the pope's exercise of *plenitudo potestatis*. Central to Giles's argument is the contention that the church has *dominium* over everything temporal but that the exercise of such 'superior and primary' jurisdiction is not always immediate and executive. As a result, he argues that the church will concern itself with spiritual affairs and directly intervene in temporal matters only in special cases, such as when a corporeal good results from a spiritual good.[20] Much of *De Ecclesiastica Potestate* is accordingly designed as an extended commentary on the 'casual' exercise of *plenitudo potestatis* for what canon law termed 'certain causes' and 'special circumstances'.[21] When Giles sets out these

---

[19] See above, pp. 150–5.

[20] *DEP* III.iv.6, p. 163. Cf. III.iv.12, p. 166; II *Sent.* 44.2.2, pp. 690–1. Compare *Quaestio in utramque partem*, ed. M. Goldast, in *Monarchia Sancti Romani Imperii* (3 vols.; Hanover, 1612–14), ii. pp. 99, 101, 105. For Giles's relation to this work, see R. Kuiters, 'Aegidius Romanus and the Authorship of *In utramque partem* and *De Ecclesiastica Potestate*', *Augustiniana*, 8 (1958), 267–80; J. Watt, 'The *Quaestio in utramque partem* Reconsidered', *Studia Gratiana*, 13 (1967), 411–54.

[21] *DEP* III.iv.7–8, pp. 163–4.

causes and circumstances, therefore, he relies on the standard legal criteria—the involvement of a spiritual good or of sin (*ratione peccati*); the crimes of oath-breaking, usury, and heresy; the transfer of dowries and inheritances; and (the most elastic band of all) the presence of difficulty or ambiguity.[22] Giles also includes one further category—benefit to the church and the public good.[23] Whilst a notion of *utilitas ecclesiae* had a long pedigree amongst canonists, its conjunction with the common good was a combination recently favoured by Henry of Ghent and Godfrey of Fontaines. It is no less important to Giles of Rome. In his view, the *bonum publicum* justifies ecclesiastical jurisdiction over all spiritual goods whilst the *bonum commune* justifies the occasional institution of temporal power, not just through, but by the spiritual power.[24] Like Henry of Ghent, Giles accepts that the church should not show too much concern for temporal affairs lest it be distracted from its true spiritual function. Nevertheless, when the common good is at stake, Giles insists that such *solicitudo* is perfectly legitimate, his only proviso being that the resulting action should be appropriate to the nature of the church.[25] The church, he writes, has frequently and justly wielded its spiritual sword against usurpers and those in illegitimate possession of property. Intervention is therefore particularly necessary and justifiable wherever the public peace and the public good are being disturbed.[26]

The principle that the spiritual power could intervene in temporal affairs on grounds of public benefit rather than in the presence of sin was exactly the point at issue in December 1301 when Boniface VIII summoned the French archbishops (including Bourges), bishops, abbots, and masters of theology to discuss Philip IV's maladministration of his kingdom. According to *Ausculta fili*, the pope could judge all matters which concerned the *utilitas publica*.[27] It was this contention which the king's counsellors promptly presented as an unprecedented claim to exercise lordship in temporal as well as spiritual matters. Boniface VIII protested, in his turn, that this was a gross misrepresentation and agreed that such a doctrine would indeed be 'fatuous'. His cardinals, moreover, insisted that ecclesiastical intervention in temporal affairs was still restricted to matters involving sin (*ratione peccati*).[28] Nevertheless, by

---

[22] *DEP* II.xiv.14, p. 134; III.v.1–19, pp. 168–75; III.vi.9, 11–12, pp. 177–9. Cf. *Decr. Greg. IX* IV.17.13 (Friedberg, ii. 714–16).

[23] *DEP* III.vii.8, p. 182.   [24] *DEP* III.iv.1, p. 161; II.v.16, p. 59. Cf. II.vi.2, p. 61; III.iv.5, p. 163.

[25] *DEP* II.v.17–18, pp. 59–60. For the significance of this final qualification, see II.xiv.16, p. 135. Cf. II.xiv.14, p. 134, where the common good can require papal abstention rather than intervention.

[26] *DEP* II.x.13, p. 91. Cf. III.vi.9, p. 177. For Innocent III's claim that the church had a particular responsibility to intervene for the sake of peace, see *Novit* (*Decr. Greg. IX* II.1.13; Friedberg, ii. 242–4), col. 244.

[27] *Les Registres de Boniface VIII*, ed. G. Digard, M. Faucon, A. Thomas, and R. Fawtier (4 vols.; Bibliothèque des Écoles Françaises d'Athènes et de Rome, 1907–39) no. 4424 (III, cols. 328–35): *bonum regni, publica utilitas, salus et utilitas publica, utilitas publica*. In June 1298 Boniface VIII had referred to the *pax et concordia* between the English and French kings, expressing his desire not to jeopardize *communis utilitas tanti boni* (ibid., no. 2811; II, cols. 255–6); in 1301 he described the contents of his letters to Philip IV as *ea quae publicam utilitatem, libertatem ecclesiae et etiam tuum tuique regni respiciunt bonum statum* (ibid., no. 4440; III, col. 348). Cf. the anonymous gloss on *Clericis laicos* (Scholz, *Die Publizistik*, 479).

[28] P. Dupuy, *Histoire du différend d'entre le Pape Boniface VIII et Philippes le Bel, roy de France, Actes et preuves* (Paris, 1655), 63–6, 74–9. For *Sciat tua maxima fatuitas*, see ibid. 44.

November 1302, a provocatively similar claim was being articulated in *Unam sanctam*—the pope not only possessed the right to judge the temporal power whenever its government 'strayed' (*si deviat*), but he could also require the subjection of the temporal power in everything which was necessary to the 'well-being' or 'salvation' (*salus*—the term was cleverly ambiguous) of the faithful.[29] When Giles of Rome argued that the spiritual power could intervene for the sake of the common good, therefore, he was clarifying the most contentious issue in the second dispute between Philip IV and Boniface VIII. *De Ecclesiastica Potestate* leaves his own position in no doubt. Just as superior virtues supply the defects of inferior virtues by directing them towards the public good, so the superior spiritual power in human government acts as adviser and judge wherever an inferior temporal power is either deficient, goes astray, or does not attain the public good. Whereas 'deficiency' and 'error' both involve blame (*culpa*), this does not apply to 'failure to attain the public good', since this can occur through impotence, unavoidable ignorance, and many other mitigating circumstances. Giles is adamant, therefore, that, even without any culpability on the part of an inferior power, it can still be admonished by a superior power if this action will benefit the common good and the *res publica*. Deficiency, abuse, or subsequent benefit to the common good—it is a comprehensive definition of papal *plenitudo potestatis*.[30]

The contrast between *De Ecclesiastica Potestate* and *De Regimine Principum* can certainly be exaggerated.[31] A polemical treatise which was dedicated to the pope by an archbishop of Bourges and which comprised a public statement of papal *plenitudo potestatis* based on Augustine was always going to be different from an educational *speculum principis* which was dedicated to the king of France by a Paris theologian and which comprised a rhetorical examination of natural principles of government laid down by Aristotle. Nevertheless, even when allowances are made for these differences in purpose, genre, and historical circumstance, the contrast between the two texts remains revealing. Thus, whereas in *De Regimine Principum*, the king's *dominium* is justified by his pursuit of the common good, in *De Ecclesiastica Potestate*, it rests on two principles taken directly from Augustine. According to *De Civitate Dei*, there is no true justice except in the *res publica* whose founder and ruler is Christ, and, when this true justice is absent, kingdoms are nothing but large-scale bands of robbers.[32] There is no just lordship, Giles concludes, over humans or over property, unless it

---

[29] *Unam sanctam* (Friedberg, ii. 1245–6). Cf. Kuiters, 'De Ecclesiastica Potestate', 204–10; D. E. Luscombe, 'The *lex divinitatis* in the Bull *Unam sanctam* of Pope Boniface VIII', in C. N. L. Brooke, D. E. Luscombe, G. H. Martin, and D. Owen (eds.), *Church and Government in the Middle Ages* (Cambridge, 1976), 205–21.

[30] *DEP* II.x.6, p. 88. Cf. III.v.1–19, pp. 168–75.

[31] Cf. Arquillière (ed.), *Le Plus Ancien Traité de l'Église*, 66; Lagarde, *La Naissance*, ii. 130; Scholz, *Die Publizistik*, 40–1, 118–19. Compare Kuiters, 'De Ecclesiastica Potestate', 160–3; J. Rivière, *Le Problème de l'église et de l'état au temps de Philippe le Bel* (Louvain–Paris, 1926), 225–7. Cf. W. D. McCready, 'Papal *plenitudo potestatis* and the Source of Temporal Authority in Later Medieval Papal Hierocratic Theory', *Speculum*, 48 (1973), 654–74, where the two texts are said to operate on 'two conceptual levels'.

[32] Augustine, *De Civitate Dei*, II.21, p. 55; IV.4, p. 101. Cf. *DEP* I.v.5, p. 15; II.vii.9, p. 73; III.i.19, p. 149; III.ii.12, pp. 153–4; III.x.8, p. 198; III.xi.5–6, p. 201.

has been instituted under, and through, the church.[33] Non-Christian and, by extension, tyrannical governments may exist, but only as a concession of divine providence and not by its direct command.[34] Government in *De Ecclesiastica Potestate*, in other words, is legitimated, not by whether it secures the common good, but by whether it is in accordance with the true justice of God, a requirement which is established through the approval of His church and His vicar.[35] By removing the common good from his definition of what legitimizes a temporal power, Giles succeeds in making the dependence of the temporal power on the spiritual power all the more explicit. Where he does retain the common good, it serves as a justification for the pope's exercise of *plenitudo potestatis* on behalf of the spiritual, moral, and material good of the community.

Public controversy over the relationship between the spiritual and the temporal powers seems to have convinced Giles of Rome that the cause of papal supremacy would be best served by limiting the goal of temporal authority to the material goods of peace and tranquillity and by making the life of virtue the exclusive responsibility of the spiritual power. Such a neat separation certainly had the advantage of clarity. It did not find favour, however, with his fellow Augustinian, James of Viterbo. Indeed, writing from the *studium generale* at Naples, James of Viterbo was prepared to put a rather different construction on the respective responsibilities of the two powers.

James of Viterbo was given the opportunity of tackling the relationship between the spiritual and temporal powers some eight years before the composition of *De Regimine Christiano* in his very first quodlibet at Paris (1293/4).[36] In defending the claim that the pope possesses temporal as well as spiritual power, James relies heavily on the corollaries which could be drawn between the hierarchy of these powers and the hierarchy of their ends. According to James, the spiritual power is superior to the temporal power in terms of its dignity (a truth, he points out, which is universally acknowledged) but it is also superior in terms of its causality. The temporal power must therefore depend on the spiritual power in the same way that the body is ruled by the soul because the temporal power is more concerned with the government of the bodily life and the spiritual power is more concerned with the life of the soul. Quoting extensively from Hugh of St Victor, James deduces that spiritual authority has the power both to institute and to judge the temporal (*et instituere et iudicare*), since the power which is concerned with the primary and ultimate goal must be able to command those powers which are concerned only with secondary goals. The spiritual power is accordingly superior to the temporal power because the supernatural goal of the spiritual power is a more important final cause than any other goal, including that of the temporal power. This hierarchy of causality, moreover,

---

[33] *DEP* II.vii.2, pp. 70–1. Cf. II.vii.12, pp. 74–5; *Unam sanctam* (Friedberg, ii. 1245–6).

[34] *DEP* II.v.2, pp. 54–5. Cf. II.ix.4–5, p. 83; II.x.1, p. 86; II.xi.1–11, pp. 96–100; III.ii.3, pp. 149–50; III.iv.12, p. 166.

[35] *DEP* III.ii.14, p. 154.

[36] James of Viterbo, *Quodlibet*, I.17, ed. E. Ypma (Würzburg, 1968), pp. 207–15.

entails a hierarchy of dependence on the grounds that whatever is present in an effect has a superior and prior existence in what has caused it. As a result, the spiritual power has superior and prior possession of all temporal jurisdiction in the sense that the pope possesses both spiritual and temporal powers immediately from God, whereas the temporal ruler possesses his temporal power only through the mediation of the pope.

The practical political consequences of James's understanding of hierarchy are considerable. Not only can the spiritual power establish laws to which temporal rulers must tailor the exercise of their jurisdiction but it must also ratify any laws which temporal rulers derive from elsewhere, from sources other than the pope. James thinks it only reasonable that, since there is one church, one faithful people, and one mystical body of Christ, there should also be one head on which all the limbs of this *corpus mysticum* depend for their temporal as well as their spiritual existence. Every power, he argues, spiritual as well as temporal, depends on Christ and His vicar on earth, in whom both spiritual and temporal power reside. As a result, just as royal power is instituted, ordained, sanctified, and blessed through Christ, so royal power is sanctified through the blessing of the church and is 'formed' through its institution by the sacerdotal power. James appeals, once again, to Hugh of St Victor but also to the text from Augustine which was to prove so important to Giles of Rome in *De Ecclesiastica Potestate*. A *res publica* cannot be governed without justice, he observes, and true justice is not present in a *res publica* whose ruler is anyone other than Christ. James, like Giles, is prepared to accept that the pope's temporal power should not always be exercised directly, on the grounds that the spiritual power should be free from the impediments of temporal concerns. However, James, like Giles, also takes great care to list those cases which *are* deemed appropriate in canon law—whenever something temporal has been granted to the church through the devotion of temporal rulers, whenever something is difficult or ambiguous, whenever sin is present (*ratione delicti*), whenever a temporal judge is found wanting (*defectus iudicis*), and whenever there is a vacancy.[37]

Quodlibet I.17 was written well before Philip IV's second dispute with Boniface VIII but it anticipates several important positions outlined in *De Regimine Christiano*—the superiority of the spiritual power in causality as well as dignity, the occasional or 'casual' intervention of the spiritual power in temporal matters, and the transmission of the royal as well as the sacerdotal power of Christ. *Quodlibet* I.17 also marks James's first attempt to locate an Aristotelian life of virtue within a hierarchy of ends which is directed towards God. According to James, the common good of the human community consists primarily of a life lived according to virtue because happiness, which is the perfect and final goal of all humans, consists of the activity of virtue. It is therefore the goal of the temporal power as much as the spiritual power to secure this *bonum multitudinis*. When James turns to the relationship between the temporal and the spiritual power, however, he distinguishes between the different

---

[37] *Quod.* I.17, pp. 210–12. Cf. *Decr. Greg.* IX IV.17.13 (Friedberg, ii. 714–16).

ways (*differenter*) in which they secure happiness and the life of virtue. The temporal
power, he states, aims at what can be achieved through natural or acquired virtue,
together with those things which are instrumental to this good (*illa quae ad hoc bonum
adminiculantur*). The spiritual power, on the other hand, aims at the supernatural
good of eternal beatitude. Nevertheless, having established that the temporal power
and the spiritual power are therefore distinct (*distinctae*), James does not elaborate on
the relationship which exists between natural virtue and eternal beatitude within this
bonum multitudinis.[38] It is only in *De Regimine Christiano* that he considers it necessary
to set this connection out in detail.

De Regimine Christiano opens with an endorsement of the natural origin of the
human community and the natural division of human society into household, city,
and kingdom. For all its Aristotelian resonances, however, the authority actually
cited is Augustine.[39] Indeed, it is only after James has quoted additional definitions of
civitas from Augustine, Isidore, and Gregory the Great that he explicitly appeals to
book I of the *Politics*.[40] Likewise, when James discusses the relative perfection of each
community as parts within an increasingly inclusive whole, the argument is
Aristotle's (the more perfect the community is, the greater the good towards which it
is ordered since the more common a good is, the greater it is) but the authority
Augustine's.[41] Moreover, if James begins his treatise with the natural origins of
human society, then it is only to prove a still more fundamental premiss, namely that
the church, although not itself a 'natural' community, can still be considered as a
household, as a city, and, above all, as a kingdom, because it provides what is
sufficient for the spiritual life.[42]

Although James accepts that Augustine's two cities or kingdoms, the *regnum dei*
and *regnum terrenum*, are only separable on the Day of Judgement, he carefully enu-
merates the characteristics which the *regnum ecclesiae* should still possess whilst it is
present on this earth as the church militant. It must be orthodox (that is, 'properly
glorious')[43] and, following the Nicene creed (and, for that matter, foreshadowing
Unam sanctam), one, catholic, holy, and apostolic.[44] Each one of these characteristics
is then patiently expounded. The glory of the church is divided into ten categories,
the third of which is *ordo* (which James defines as directing different elements
towards the benefit of the whole), the fourth harmony (*concordia*), the seventh abundance (*beatitudo . . . est status omnium bonorum aggregatione perfectus*),[45] and the ninth
peace and security (*pax et quies*). The unity of the church, meanwhile, is divided into

[38] *Quod.* I.17, pp. 210, 213.
[39] *De Regimine Christiano* [henceforth *DRC*] I.i, p. 89. James admits that this tripartite division is only
implied (*insinuat*) by *De Civitate Dei*, XIX.7, p. 671.
[40] *DRC* I.i, p. 91. Cf. II.iii, pp. 176–7; II.x, p. 295. For James's knowledge of the *Ethics*, the *Magna
Moralia*, and Eustratius, see Ypma, 'Recherches sur la carrière', 280–1.
[41] *DRC* I.i, pp. 91–3; Augustine, *De Civitate Dei*, XIX.16, p. 683. Cf. *DRC* II.v, pp. 204–5.
[42] *DRC* I.i, p. 89, 93–5.   [43] *DRC* I.ii, pp. 100–105. Cf. II.iv, p. 191.
[44] *DRC* I.iii, pp. 106–21; I.iv, pp. 122–8; I.v, pp. 129–37; I.vi, pp. 138–44. Cf. *Unam sanctam ecclesiam
catholicam et ipsam apostolicam* (Friedberg, ii. 1245–6), col. 1245.
[45] Boethius, *Philosophiae Consolatio*, ed. L. Bieler (*CCSL* 94), III.2, p. 38. Cf. above, pp. 37 n. 33,
159 n. 12.

five categories (*unitas totalitatis, unitas conformitatis, unitas attributionis, unitas secundum perfectionem, unitas secundum ordinem*) and differentiated from two more (*unitas suppositi et personae, unitas naturae speciei*). James then demonstrates the connection which exists between these various characteristics and their consequences for the ecclesiastical 'kingdom'. Unity, he writes, is the cause of peace because peace is the effect of love (*caritas*) and the defining function of love is to unite. Peace, meanwhile, is the tranquillity of order (a definition for which James is again dependent on Augustine) in that the peace of the human community is the ordered agreement of citizens in what should be commanded and obeyed.[46]

James's analysis of the ecclesiastical community in terms of order, harmony, peace, unity, and love is, in itself, a dexterous application of 'political' characteristics to the nature of the church. It is only in the second part of his treatise, however, that the implications of classifying the church as a kingdom become fully apparent. By introducing this identification, James is able to make two significant moves. In the first instance, he expands upon his earlier association of the universal kingship of Christ with the rule of His vicar on earth. In *Quodlibet* I.17, the pope possesses a royal priesthood (*regale sacerdotium*) in that, as *vicarius Christi*, he has inherited the royal as well as the sacerdotal power of Christ.[47] In *De Regimine Christiano*, Christ's governing power has become threefold—sacerdotal, royal, and miraculous—but the consequences for the power of the pope are the same. As a result of the diffusive nature of God's goodness and in order to benefit humankind, Christ has transmitted to His vicars not just the first of these powers but the second as well.[48] It is only a short etymological step, after all, from *rector* to *rex*, and, as the *rex iustitiae* and *rex pacis*, Christ is the ruler of the eternal and heavenly kingdom but also of the temporal and earthly.[49] It is this royal power, therefore, to which James devotes the remainder of his treatise as the basis for an extended exposition of papal *plenitudo potestatis*. In the second instance, when James turns to the relationship between the pope and the temporal ruler, a broad definition of 'kingdom' and 'royal' enables him to move beyond the traditional polarity of 'spiritual' and 'temporal' power. In its place, he introduces a more refined tripartite classification—earthly royal power, spiritual royal power, and sacerdotal spiritual power. It is this middle term, spiritual royal power, which enables James to elevate the office of pope at the same time as incorporating an Aristotelian definition of the common good as the life of virtue.

There are two types of royal power, James writes, one of which is termed earthly, temporal, or secular, whilst the other is termed spiritual and heavenly. Earthly royal

---

[46] *DRC* I.iii, p. 120; Augustine, *De Civitate Dei* XIX.13, p. 679.

[47] *Quod.* I.17, pp. 210–11. Cf. Aquinas, IV *Sent.* 20.1.4c: *dicendum quod papa habet plenitudinem pontificalis potestatis quasi rex in regno*.

[48] *DRC* II.ii, pp. 163–9. Cf. II.v, p. 202.

[49] *DRC* I.vi, p. 140; II.i, pp. 161–2. James repeatedly resorts to etymological arguments and in particular to *regnum a regibus est dictum* (I.i, p. 90) and *rex a regendo dicitur* (II.iii, pp. 148–9; II.iii, p. 181, 184; II.iv, p. 187). Cf. Augustine, *De Civitate Dei* V.12, p. 143; Isidore, *Etymologiae*, ed. W. M. Lindsay (Oxford, 1911), IX.3. For James's knowledge of Isidore, see Ypma, 'Recherches sur la carrière', 281. Cf. *DRC* I.i, p. 95; I.i, p. 118; II.v, pp. 206–7; *Quod.* II.24, pp. 232–6.

power derives from nature, is of human institution, and is exercised in accordance with natural law. Spiritual royal power, meanwhile, derives from grace, is of divine institution, and accords with supernatural law. Whether it is held by a bishop or by a pope, spiritual royal power entitles its possessor to claim the status of king, more so, even, than the earthly royal power which is held by a temporal ruler. Although bishops are not called kings in practice (and, James adds, for very good reasons), the underlying principle of their authority remains the same. Royal and sacerdotal power are not mutually exclusive terms. It is his royal nature which gives a bishop the power of jurisdiction and his sacerdotal nature which gives him the power of orders.[50] It is on this basis that James returns to his opening analysis of the political community and proceeds to apply to prelates many of the conventional attributes of kings—judgement, providing and distributing external and material goods, establishing the unity and peace which preserve a community in existence. However, whereas at the start of *De Regimine Christiano* James limits the good towards which human society is ordered to mutual assistance and a self-sufficient life (*sufficientia vitae huius*), he now invokes the inculcation of virtue. Like *De Regno ad Regem Cypri*, in other words, James delays introducing the life of virtue as a defining function of earthly kingship until after royal power has been associated with the authority of the church. The intention of the king, the judge, and the legislator, he now writes, must be to make individuals live according to virtue, to make them good and virtuous.[51]

Once James has introduced virtue into his discussion of spiritual royal power, he has no hesitation in incorporating explicitly Aristotelian material into his theory of papal monarchy. In his quodlibets, James has already argued that law orders any action of virtue towards the common good on the basis of Aristotle's insistence that justice is all virtue.[52] In *De Regimine Christiano*, he applies the same principle to the law of the church by means of the biblical example of Solomon. Insofar as prelates direct their teaching towards purifying the minds of their subjects, he states, they act as a sacerdotal power. Insofar as they direct the exterior actions of their flock, however, they act as a royal power.[53] Likewise, when James comes to justify the premiss that the church should have one head, he uses an Aristotelian form of the argument that the best form of government is a monarchy and that it is intrinsic to kingship for one individual to aim at the common good of the multitude. Unity, James states, is intrinsic to the principle of goodness, and the unity and peace of a multitude are more easily secured through the unity of its ruler. Likewise, when James explains why the pope's power should be universal, he does so on an Aristotelian formulation of the principle that any multitude should have a single, ruling power which aims at the common good. Such power, James states, is 'more divine' because its greater commonality has a greater similitude with the primary good in which the principle of all goodness is contained.[54]

---

[50] *DRC* II.iii, pp. 176–86. Cf. II.x, pp. 288–9, 295.   [51] *DRC* II.iv, pp. 189–91.
[52] *Quod.* III.21, p. 254; IV.28, p. 102.   [53] *DRC* II.iv, p. 195.
[54] *DRC* II.v, pp. 208–11.

Drawing such a close connection between the nature of papal power and the nature of kingship naturally brings James face to face with the question of what scope this has left for attributing any specific function to earthly royal power. In defining the power of earthly kings, James cites Aristotle alongside Isidore, Augustine, Cyprian, Hugh of St Victor, Richard of St Victor, and the Old Testament. In doing so, he extends the definition of the goal of the temporal ruler with which *De Regimine Christiano* opens (the life of material self-sufficiency, unity, and peace) in order to include the life of virtue.[55] Society may be natural, James suggests, but it cannot continue in existence if there is no one to take care of the common good of the community. This is the function of the king. Temporal rulers must therefore act, not as tyrants seeking their own good or glory, but as kings aiming at the common good of the multitude. It is when they are ruling for the benefit of those subject to them that the individual good of these rulers will result. It is thus the ruler's primary duty to provide material goods, to direct the ignorant, to restrain and punish the wicked, to defend the innocent, to counter selfish love, and to preserve society.[56] In specifying the nature of the common good which is secured by earthly kingship, James repeats the definition which he used in his first quodlibet—the *bonum multitudinis* constitutes the good life, the virtuous life, and those goods which are instrumental to it (*quae ad ipsam adminiculantur*).[57] On this occasion, however, he does not duck the question of just where this leaves the relationship between the earthly royal power and the spiritual royal power. Indeed, in many ways, his discussion of this relationship provides the pivotal section of the entire treatise.

James opens his analysis with a clear statement of precisely the conclusion which Giles of Rome so resolutely refused to explore in *De Regimine Principum* and so firmly rejected in *De Ecclesiastica Potestate*. The term 'spiritual', James argues, is susceptible to two interpretations—whatever pertains to the rational part of the soul, and whatever pertains to the soul, not in natural terms, but in terms of grace. If the first definition is adopted, then James cannot agree (*hoc dictum habet dubium*) with those writers, such as Giles, who would simply classify ecclesiastical power as spiritual and temporal power as corporeal, the former concerning itself with the soul, the latter with the body.[58] According to James, the goal of the temporal power is, instead, to direct its subjects towards a life of virtue, a life which primarily concerns the soul. If the temporal power also provides external goods for the life of the body, then this is only because the actions of the soul cannot take place in this life without them. The primary objective of the temporal power is thus the life of virtue, and, since it is concerned with the actions of the soul, it must also be a spiritual power. This, for James, is the logical corollary of accepting Aristotle's definition of *bene vivere*.

Having conceded that the temporal power can concern itself with more than just

---

[55] *DRC* II.viii, pp. 258–67.   [56] *DRC* II.x, pp. 302–3. Cf. II.ii, p. 166; II.iii, p. 184.
[57] *DRC* II.viii, p. 259.
[58] *DRC* II.vi, pp. 223–4. Cf. Giles of Rome, *DEP* I.vii.1–15, pp. 22–7; *Quaestio in utramque partem*, ed. Goldast (1613), pp. 99, 103. James accepts this distinction only when it is being applied to the punishments which are appropriate to each power (*DRC* II.vi, pp. 227–8).

material goods, however, James promptly concludes that the ecclesiastical power can be defined as 'spiritual' and the secular power as 'temporal' only if a different definition of spiritual is adopted, that is, if a definition is used which restricts 'spiritual' to the effect on the soul of the operation of grace. In this sense, he argues, the spiritual power concerns itself with the grace which transforms human nature into the image of God, whereas the temporal power concerns itself with human nature insofar as it is human. Even in this second sense of spiritual, James makes it quite clear that the 'earthly' purpose of the temporal power should not be restricted to exterior or material goods.[59] Nevertheless, once he gets hold of this second definition of spiritual, he never looks back to the first. By acknowledging that the goal of the temporal ruler is the life of virtue, the life of humankind's rational nature, James successfully distances himself from an exclusively 'material' account of the political community. Having done so, however, he proceeds to use the operation of grace as a means of establishing the complete subordination of the temporal ruler to the superior jurisdiction of the church.

In *Quodlibet* I.17, James used the hierarchy of ends to argue that the spiritual power is the cause of the earthly royal power because the temporal goal of natural happiness is ordered towards the spiritual goal of eternal beatitude. In *De Regimine Christiano*, he refines this argument by further dividing causality into its various types—material, efficient, formal, and final. Once again, James is keen to distance himself from what he regards as overly simplistic distinctions. Viewed in material terms, for example, the superiority of the spiritual power is not represented as a straightforward opposition of the contemplative life to the active, of supernatural perfection to natural perfection, of wisdom to prudence.[60] Likewise, rather than maintain that the spiritual power is simply superior in dignity to the temporal power, James carefully runs through the different permutations made possible by his distinction between sacerdotal spiritual power, spiritual royal power, and earthly royal power. Thus, spiritual royal power is, in absolute terms, superior in dignity to sacerdotal spiritual power but, in certain circumstances, the reverse may be true. Spiritual royal power, on the other hand, is, in absolute terms, superior in dignity to earthly royal power.[61] Sacerdotal spiritual power, meanwhile, is essentially superior in dignity to earthly royal power although, in certain circumstances, the reverse may be true (when the earthly royal power is acting as an instrument of the spiritual royal power, for example, or when the sacerdotal spiritual power is using temporal goods for which it is dependent on an earthly royal ruler).[62]

When James tackles the superiority of the spiritual power as a final cause, he again distances himself from what he describes as a simplistic argument, in this case, that the temporal power only possesses justice if it has been 'instituted' by the spiritual power.[63] In its place, James puts forward a *via media*. In order to be legitimate, he

---

[59] *DRC* II.vi, pp. 224–5.   [60] *DRC* II.vi, p. 227.   [61] *DRC* II.vii, p. 230.
[62] *DRC* II.iv, pp. 199–200.
[63] Cf. Giles of Rome, *DEP* II.vii.2, pp. 70–1; *Unam sanctam*, col. 1246.

argues, spiritual royal power requires the power of orders as well as the power of jurisdiction, a correct relationship to God as well as the exercise of judgement over others. Earthly royal power, on the other hand, requires only the power of jurisdiction. In order to be perfect, therefore, earthly royal power may require the Christian faith but in order to be legitimate it does not. Temporal power owes its existence in an incipient and material sense to the natural inclination of humans to live in society and, as such, it derives directly from God just like any other work of nature. However, temporal power owes its existence in a perfect and formal sense to the spiritual power. James uses the analogy of light informing a colour. His model is recognizably Thomist—grace does not remove nature but perfects it and gives it form; spiritual power does not exclude temporal power but perfects it and gives it form.[64] James applies this principle to every type of human government.[65] Since all human communities are natural communities, the legitimacy of infidel governments should not be denied; it should simply be considered unformed and imperfect on the grounds that temporal powers are only fully formed and perfect if they are approved and ratified by the spiritual power of the church.

According to James, this is the gloss which should be applied to Hugh of St Victor's use of *instituere*. It is also the interpretation which he places on Augustine's discussion of Cicero's definition of the *res publica* as 'an association of a multitude united by a common sense of right and by a community of interest'.[66] Rather than follow the interpretation of Giles of Rome (that only the church can fulfil the terms of this definition, since only the church possesses true justice, true benefit, and true community), James cites another text from Augustine, or rather from the pseudo-Augustinian *Sentences* of Prosper of Aquitaine quoted by Aquinas—where the knowledge of eternal and immutable truth is not present, virtue is false, even in the best moral life (*in optimis moribus*).[67] Without the Christian faith, James comments, no power is entirely true, but this only means that it is not perfect, not that it is entirely illegitimate. It remains true and legitimate in a certain sense (*aliqualiter*). In order to be entirely true and perfect it requires the presence of faith and the ratification of the spiritual power.[68] Strictly speaking, therefore, a kingdom where justice is in some way lacking (*defectus iustitiae*) is indeed, in Augustine's phrase, a band of robbers, but, in James's view, it can still be called just within certain terms of reference (*secundum aliquid*).[69] Good use and submission to God may be the two criteria on which political power is judged legitimate according to divine law, but this does not remove the legitimacy which it possesses according to human law.[70]

---

[64] *DRC* II.vii, pp. 230–3. Cf. II.iii, pp. 176–7; II.x, p. 297.

[65] James also applies this principle to the institution of prelates to authority within the church, a process which 'perfects' their initial institution by election (II.vii, p. 243), and to the 'natural' priesthood of the Old Testament which was perfected by the divinely instituted priesthood of the New (II.iii, pp. 175–6). It also underpins his treatment of the Donation of Constantine (II.v, pp. 221–2; II.viii, pp. 255–6).

[66] *DRC* I.iv, p. 128. Cf. *Quod.* I.17, pp. 209–11.

[67] Prosper of Aquitaine, *Sententia* 106 (*PL* 51, col. 441). Cf. Aquinas, *IaIIae* 23.7, 65.2.

[68] *DRC* II.vii, pp. 232–3.   [69] *DRC* II.x, pp. 305–6.   [70] *DRC* II.vii, pp. 241–2.

Having devoted a substantial part of *De Regimine Christiano* to accommodating the two basic tenets of an Aristotelian political community—natural origin and the life of virtue—James then incorporates them both into a thoroughly hierocratic reading of the hierarchy of ends. According to James, the spiritual power is superior to the temporal power because the goal of the temporal power (natural happiness) is ordered towards the goal of the spiritual power (supernatural happiness).[71] Christian society, he argues, is not founded on two principles, nor is it ruled by two heads, since this would represent exactly the sort of dualism which Boniface VIII repeatedly branded as Manichean.[72] The unity of Christian society derives, instead, from a hierarchy in which whatever is superior in dignity and nobility thereby has the right to institute, judge, and command anything which is inferior to it.

The claim that the spiritual power could 'institute' the temporal power was usually justified with a direct appeal to Hugh of St Victor, but it ultimately derived from Jeremiah 1: 10 ('See today I appoint you over nations and kingdoms to uproot and tear down, to destroy and overthrow, to build and to plant'). This was a favourite text of both Gregory VII and Boniface VIII. It was also the passage on which Matthew of Acquasparta, the Cardinal-Bishop of Porto, chose to expound in his meeting with French ambassadors in June 1302.[73] For James of Viterbo, the power to institute derives from the hierarchy of ends. Superiority in dignity necessarily means that the spiritual power is entitled to judge, correct, direct, and command the temporal power, to punish it with temporal as well as spiritual penalties, and, if the crime is a sin of sufficient severity, to secure its overthrow. If the spiritual power can confer power to rule over the faithful, then it must also be able to take it away because the spiritual power 'includes' the temporal power in the sense that the temporal power pre-exists within it. It is on this basis that James constructs the comprehensive statement of papal plenitude of power with which he concludes the whole treatise. The temporal power, he states, is subject to the spiritual power, it obeys it, is instituted by it, is judged by it, is ordered towards it as a goal, is included in it, and is preserved in it.

Drawing from the same legal sources as *Quodlibet* I.17, James's definition of papal *plenitudo potestatis* mirrors the definition provided by Giles of Rome. Temporal power pre-exists in the spiritual power in the form of a primary and supreme authority but not in the form of a general and immediate execution. As a result, the superior temporal jurisdiction which the spiritual power possesses must not be exercised regularly but only in certain cases.[74] James lists the conditions—spiritual matters, dowries, inheritances, crimes which are spiritual evils, crimes which break the peace, oaths, judicial appeals (particularly in those cases where it is customary to appeal to

---

[71] *DRC* II.vii, pp. 231, 236. Cf. Giles of Rome, *DEP* I.iv.3, pp. 12–13; II.iv.4, p. 49; II.iv.14, p. 52; II.vi.1–24, pp. 60–70; II.xiii.29–43, pp. 122–8; III.i.13, p. 146.

[72] *Ausculta fili*, cols. 328–9; *Unam sanctam*, cols. 1245–6.

[73] G. Digard, *Philippe le Bel et le Saint-Siège de 1285 à 1304* (2 vols.; Paris, 1936), ii. 107–8. Cf. *Ausculta fili*, col. 329; *Unam sanctam*, col. 1246. For Giles of Rome's discussion of the same text, see C. Luna, 'Un nuovo documento del conflitto fra Bonifacio VIII e Filippo il Bello: Il discorso *De potentia domini pape* di Egidio Romano', *Documenti e studi sulla tradizione filosofica medievale*, III.1 (1992), 221.

[74] *DRC* II.vii, pp. 234–7; II.viii, pp. 248–57.

Rome), temporal gifts to the church, and anything which is difficult or ambiguous. Casual intervention is justified wherever there is any deficiency in temporal lordship—vacancy, negligence, malice, failure to secure justice, failure to show proper obedience to the spiritual power, and, finally, failure to act for the common good (*propter commune bonum*).[75] As an adjunct to *plenitudo potestatis*, the common good can cover a multitude of sins but, on James's reading, sin is only part of its definition. James, like Giles, bases his understanding of the common good in this context on a notion of *utilitas ecclesiae*. He also appeals to his own earlier definition of the function of kingship. The spiritual power, he writes, is the principal authority in human society and the temporal power provides the means to secure its end. Since the temporal power acts as its assistant (*accessorium*), the spiritual power can make demands of the temporal power for the sake of the defence of the church. The spiritual power can, for example, require the temporal power to contribute money and property for the common benefit of the church. This is no less a right, James observes, than the one enjoyed by the temporal power when it makes exactions for the good condition of the *res publica* or for other reasons which are sanctioned by custom.

Although the subjection of the temporal power to the spiritual power applies to the whole church, it is primarily expressed in the plenitude of spiritual power which belongs to the pope. Thus, greater obedience should be shown in temporal affairs to a temporal ruler than to a bishop when they concern the political good (*bonum civile*), but, if there is any conflict between the command of the secular ruler and the command of the pope, then it is the pope who should be obeyed.[76] The spiritual power is therefore able to exercise its superior temporal jurisdiction wherever it benefits the 'well-being' or 'salvation' (*salus*) of the faithful.[77] Like the author of *Unam sanctam*, James chooses this final term very carefully. Its remit includes, for example, the correction of tyranny on the grounds that tyranny destroys the *salus* of both ruler and subject.[78] Fear of being judged by the superior power of the church, James argues, is an effective restraint on tyrannical behaviour and one which is ultimately sanctioned by a God who wishes the church to secure the *salus fidelium*. It is for the common good of all humankind, after all, that both the spiritual and the temporal power were originally instituted by God.[79]

Although James of Viterbo echoed the justification of papal intervention in temporal affairs which was given by Giles of Rome, he showed himself to be a much more adventurous propagandist than his Augustinian confrère. By making jurisdiction the defining criterion of royal power, James was able to bestow the status of king on both pope and bishops. By distinguishing between earthly royal power and spiritual royal power, he was able to apply all the ideology of kingship to the exercise of authority within the church. Unlike Giles, therefore, James did not restrict temporal authority to purely material goods. As a result, by insisting that the life of virtue is the function

[75] *DRC* II.viii, pp. 254–5.   [76] *DRC* II.vii, p. 238; II.vii, pp. 240–1.
[77] *DRC* II.ix, pp. 269–77. Cf. *Unam sanctam*, col. 1246 (above p. 271).
[78] *DRC* II.vii, pp. 243–4. Cf. II.iii, p. 184; II.viii, p. 258.
[79] *DRC* II.x, p. 280. Cf. II.ii, pp. 167, 172.

of the temporal as well as the spiritual power, James staked a much more effective claim on Aristotle for the papalist cause.

That James of Viterbo was able to take the most characteristic tenet of Aristotelian political thought and appropriate it as an argument for the superiority of papal power owes much to his Thomist reading of the perfection of nature by grace. It has long been recognized that a distinctive feature of *De Regimine Christiano* stems from its reworking of certain Thomist precepts within an Augustinian framework.[80] This approach is the direct result of the problem which James was trying to solve. By accepting the Thomist model of nature and grace, James was able to subordinate the temporal power to the spiritual *without* denying that the goal of political authority is the life of moral virtue. Unlike Giles of Rome in *De Ecclesiastica Potestate*, James is prepared to concede that the king is a ruler with a spiritual function. Incorporated into a Thomist model of perfection, however, this does not affect his ultimate conclusion that the relation of the temporal power to the the the church is governed by a strict hierarchy of ends. The immediate goal of the temporal power (*finis proximus*) may be different from the immediate goal of the spiritual power (natural happiness as opposed to supernatural beatitude), but the ultimate goal (*finis ultimus*) is the same. The virtuous life of the multitude should be correctly ordered towards heavenly beatitude and the power of temporal rulers should therefore be ordered towards the goal of the spiritual power.[81] James of Viterbo's hierocracy may ultimately have proved to be no less emphatic than Giles of Rome's but this cannot disguise the differing means by which each Augustinian sought to produce the same result.

If James of Viterbo should be credited with using Aquinas to turn the *Politics* and the *Ethics* into pillars of papalist supremacy, then his hierocratic interpretation of Aristotle came under immediate attack from within the faculty of theology at Paris and from a member of Aquinas' own order. John of Paris has generally been seen as a moderate, a Dominican theologian whose claim to be charting a *via media* between the claims of the spiritual and the temporal powers should be taken at face value.[82] *De Potestate Regia et Papali* certainly includes trenchant criticism of many of the standard hierocratic arguments which were used by both James of Viterbo and Giles of Rome—the allegory of the two swords and the sun and the moon; the authority of Hugh of St Victor and Bernard of Clairvaux; the nature of superiority in dignity, causality, and time; and the implications of *Novit* and the Donation of Constantine.[83]

---

[80] e.g. Arquillière (ed.), *Le Plus Ancien Traité de l'Église*, 7–81, where James's use of Aristotle and Aquinas is presented as a restraining influence on the 'theocratic logic' of Augustine.

[81] *DRC* II.viii, pp. 257, 260. In arguing that the life of virtue is an essential function of the political community only insofar as it is directed by the church towards eternal beatitude, *De Regimine Christiano* would also have received strong support from *De Regno ad Regem Cypri*, a text which was being circulated between 1300 and 1305 as part of Ptolemy of Lucca's *De Regimine Principum*, ed. R. M. Spiazzi, in *Divi Thomae Aquinatis Opuscula Philosophica* (Rome, 1954), 257–358. Cf. above, p. 132 n. 13.

[82] Rivière, *Le Problème de l'église et de l'état*, 281–300; Scholz, *Die Publizistik*, 275–333; Leclercq, *Jean de Paris et l'ecclésiologie*, 162–4; Watt, *On Royal and Papal Power*, 56–7, 62–3; *CHMPT*, 405–10; T. Renna, 'Aristotle and the French Monarchy', *Viator*, 9 (1978), 319–24.

[83] Watt (*On Royal and Papal Power*, 42–3) has cast doubt on John's familiarity with the treatises of Giles of Rome and James of Viterbo. However, as Watt recognizes, not only is it characteristic for John not to

On the other hand, whilst recognizing the existence of separate spheres for temporal and ecclesiastical jurisdiction, *De Potestate Regia et Papali* never makes this separation absolute. If John of Paris allows the king a role in the deposition of the pope, then he also allows the pope a role in the deposition of the king. In this respect, *De Potestate Regia et Papali* leaves a central claim of papal *plenitudo potestatis* unchallenged—the king of France can still be subjected to the sacerdotal authority of the pope *incidenter et casualiter*.[84]

For all this studied moderation, however, John of Paris has also been seen as a radical, a theologian whose analysis of property right effectively anticipated John Locke and whose 'constitutional' ecclesiology represented 'the most consistent and complete formulation of conciliar doctrine before the outbreak of the Great Schism'.[85] Placed in the context of thirteenth-century scholastic political thought, what is so striking about the radicalism of John's views on property and ecclesiology is their immediate source of inspiration. In presupposing that the relation of the pope to the universal church is equivalent to that of a bishop to his chapter, John may have been applying the corporatism of canon law with greater rigour than the canonists themselves had ever done. That he should have done so, however, was due less to the application of 'une logique intransigeante'[86] than to the influence of Godfrey of Fontaines.

The intellectual debt which John of Paris owed to Godfrey of Fontaines is evident as early as his commentary on the *Sentences* (1292–6).[87] It is, if anything, even more marked in *De Potestate Regia et Papali*, where John's application, first, of canon law to papal authority and, second, of Roman law to property right, can both be paralleled in Godfrey's quodlibets.[88] When John discusses the power which temporal and ecclesiastical authorities exercise over the material goods of individuals, for example, he repeats Godfrey's differentiation between the power of the pope and the power of the king. Since ecclesiastical property belongs to communities and not to individuals, only the community (the local church in the case of the bishop, the universal church in the case of the pope) has *dominium* over it. Like Godfrey, John concludes that bishop and pope simply administer the goods of the church as stewards for the

cite his sources by name but John specifically states that he is responding to arguments which he has heard as well as read (*audire vel colligi*). Cf. Leclercq, *Jean de Paris et l'ecclésiologie*, 31.

[84] *De Potestate Regia et Papali* [henceforth *DPRP*], ed. Leclercq, XIII, p. 214. Cf. *Quaestio in utramque partem*, pp. 99–100.

[85] J. Coleman, 'Medieval Discussions of Property: *ratio* and *dominium* according to John of Paris and Marsilius of Padua', *History of Political Thought*, 4 (1983), 209–28; id., '*Dominium* in Thirteenth and Fourteenth Century Political Thought and its Seventeenth Century Heirs: John of Paris and Locke', *Political Studies*, 33 (1985), 73–100; id., 'Property and Poverty', in *CHMPT*, 638–40; B. Tierney, *Foundations of the Conciliar Theory* (Cambridge, 1955), 157–78. Cf. F. Oakley, 'Natural Law, the *corpus mysticum* and Consent in Conciliar Thought from John of Paris to Matthias Ugonis', *Speculum*, 56 (1981), 786–810.

[86] Leclercq, *Jean de Paris et l'ecclésiologie*, 9. Cf. ibid., 148–9.

[87] *Jean de Paris [Quidort]: Commentaire sur les Sentences*, ed. J. P. Muller (2 vols.; Rome, 1961, 1964), a work which draws heavily on Godfrey of Fontaines, *Quodlibets* II, V–X.

[88] Cf. Leclercq, *Jean de Paris et l'ecclésiologie*, 34, who considers Godfrey's influence to be second only to that of Aquinas.

benefit of the whole. Lay property, in contrast, belongs not to the community but to its constituent individuals. They alone have *dominium*, not the pope or the king. Once again, John follows Godfrey's lead. When the king intervenes to restore the civil peace which has been disturbed by disagreements over possession, he does so, not as a lord, but as an arbiter, and he exercises the power, not of ownership, but of jurisdiction.[89]

Individual property rights of the laity, moreover, are not, in John's view, inviolable. There are certain conditions, notably the defence or the necessity of the *res publica*, which make it both essential and desirable that these rights should be overridden. This is the standard legal argument familiar from Godfrey. When the kingdom is in danger, the king possesses extraordinary powers, including taxation, in order to secure its defence. John follows Godfrey in drawing a parallel with the powers which the pope can exercise in a case of spiritual necessity. At a time when faith and morals are in dire need, a pagan invasion for example, the goods of the faithful (even the chalices used in churches)[90] will become common property. As a result, the pope can demand a tenth, or any other amount, from all Christians. Like Godfrey, however, John also insists that, beyond such a dire necessity, the pope has no right to the goods of laymen.[91] A spiritual common good which falls short of necessity cannot oblige an individual to submit to the pope's demands on his property. Instead, the pope must content himself with offering indulgences in order to attract the assistance he requires. As a limitation on papal power, this argument is significant, despite John's rather tentative 'in my opinion' (*ut puto*), since it stands in marked contrast to the degree of power which John is prepared to concede to the king. Like Godfrey, John gives a much greater power over the property of the laity to the king than he does to the pope. He does so by conceding that it is not only acute necessity but also general benefit which can justify such emergency action on the part of a temporal ruler. It is thus only for the king's rights that John uses the pairing 'necessity *and* benefit' (*necessitas vel utilitas*). A ruler, he argues, is established by the people not only because of the disturbance to the peace which is caused by property disputes but also because individuals do not share their goods as the necessity and benefit of their country demands. The ruler is the judge of what is just and unjust, he explains, the avenger of injuries, but he is also the authority who reckons the just proportion of goods which should be received from individuals for the common necessity and common benefit.[92]

John's concern to establish the respective rights of the spiritual and the temporal power to the material goods of the Christian people needs to be seen as part of the

---

[89] *DPRP* VI–VII, pp. 185–90. Cf. Godfrey of Fontaines, *Quodlibet* XIII.5 (above, p. 257).

[90] The reference is to Boniface VIII's bull (September 1296) *Ineffabilis amor* (Dupuy, *Histoire du différend..., Actes et Preuves*, p. 18).

[91] *DPRP* VII, pp. 189–90. Compare John's justification of the king's right to prevent the transit of bishops (XX, p. 239), an issue which was prompted by Philip IV's refusal to allow French bishops to attend the papal council of November 1302.

[92] *DPRP* VII, p. 189. Cf. *DPRP* XVII, p. 225.

vigorous debate over papal tenths and royal taxation which had been so characteristic of scholastic political discussion throughout the 1290s. The disparity which
emerges between ecclesiastical and royal rights, however, is revealing of John's own
priorities in Paris in 1302–3. According to *De Potestate Regia et Papali*, the temporal
power, unlike the spiritual power, can appeal beyond dire necessity, beyond the need
to suspend all property right in an emergency. In John's opinion, the temporal power
can also appeal to the common good. It is this common good which accounts for the
initial institution of kingship, for the consensual and conventual origins of the political community, and the goal towards which society is ordered. When John defines a
kingdom as the government of a multitude perfectly ordered towards the common
good by one person, he suggests that this common good is best secured by a single
ruler because a king serves to direct the interests of individuals, the property of individuals, towards the common good. John takes his argument word for word from
De Regno ad Regem Cypri. What is individual and what is common are not identical—
people differ in the former and are united in the latter. In addition to the principle
which moves each individual towards his own good, therefore, there must be something which moves the individual towards the common good of many. This is the
function of the king.[93]

In contrast to the role which the common good occupies in his account of the
king's relationship to property within the political community, when John turns to
the pope's authority within the church, he uses the common good, not as a justification for the exercise of power, but as a limitation. Like Godfrey of Fontaines, John
bases this argument not only on the principles which govern all ecclesiastical prelates
in canon law but also on the paradigm provided by the Aristotelian tyrant. A ruler
who furthers his own private interest rather than the common good, he states, breaks
the trust which has been placed in him. Initially, such a ruler should be admonished
(even Henry of Ghent had urged supplication as a first resort) but, if this has no
effect, then abbots, bishops, *and* popes can all be deposed once it becomes apparent
that they have dissipated the goods of their communities.[94] As was the case for both
Henry of Ghent and Godfrey of Fontaines, the evidence for such impropriety must
be clear but, with this qualification, John states that the pope should be judged for
any abuse of his power. John thereby makes the pope accountable to the common
good of the whole church. He also makes this good comprise material as well as
spiritual concerns. The pope can thus be deposed for heresy or for a notorious crime
but also for his mismanagement of ecclesiastical property.[95] As illustrations, John
offers a pope who confers prebends for his own private good rather than for the common necessity of the church and a pope who exhibits such moral failings as fornication, drunkenness, and other wicked acts.[96] Viewed in the context of the accusations
which had been levelled against Boniface VIII by the Colonna cardinals in 1296–7,
and the charges which were then methodically assembled by Guillaume de Nogaret

---

[93] *DPRP* I, pp. 176–7; *De Regno ad Regem Cypri* I.1. Cf. *DPRP* XII, p. 208.
[94] *DPRP* VI, p. 188.   [95] *DPRP* XIII, p. 215.   [96] *DPRP* XXII, p. 249.

for the Louvre assembly of 1303, this was far from being a list of hypothetical technicalities.[97]

There is a similarly sharp edge to *De Potestate Regia et Papali* when John uses the common good to justify papal resignation. Once again, John's argument echoes that of Godfrey of Fontaines. The pope, he argues, is elected for no other purpose than to benefit the common good of the church. If, after his election, he finds himself (or is found to be) totally inept and useless (*inutilis*), or if he develops a disability such as madness, then he must seek release from his office either by means of the people or the college of cardinals acting on their behalf. Even if their consent is not forthcoming, however, the pope must still resign, since what has been instituted by love must not run counter to love by failing to benefit the church or the individual's own soul.[98] Consent is not infallible. Any oath that is sworn to the contrary (that is, to the effect that a pope must always remain in office) is utterly illegitimate, since it can militate against the common good. Using the same analogy of the prelate who is wedded to his church, John, like Godfrey, compares the common good served by resignation to the good secured by marriage. The spiritual bond is stronger than the carnal in the same way that the common good is greater than the particular good. Dissolution of the carnal bond can only secure a particular good. Dissolution of the spiritual bond, however, can secure a common good, and the individual good of the prelate must not be placed above the common good of the church.[99]

The contrast which is exhibited by John's deployment of the common good in the temporal and the ecclesiastical spheres, justifying the authority of the king in the former but limiting the authority of the pope in the latter, should not obscure the parallelism which otherwise governs the temporal and the spiritual powers in *De Potestate Regia et Papali*. If John of Paris uses the common good to justify both the resignation of Celestine V and the possible resignation or deposition of Boniface VIII, then, like Henry of Ghent and Godfrey of Fontaines, he also accepts the possibility that this notion can also justify resistance to a king. His argument is noticeably brief but, at least in theory, he does admit that a king can be deposed. If the king becomes a heretic, or if he transgresses a broad category of 'ecclesiastical crime', then the pope can excommunicate him, absolve his subjects from their oaths of obedience and thus, albeit indirectly, secure his overthrow. The result is the same if the king 'sins' in temporal matters, although, in this case, the barons and peers of the kingdom should be the first to correct him, adopting, in effect, the same role as the cardinals of the church in the deposition of a pope.[100] By emphasizing that the common good is

---

[97] For the accusations set before the assembly of June 1303, see Dupuy, *Histoire du différend . . . , Actes et Preuves*, 102–6.

[98] *DPRP* XXIV, p. 254. Cf. Godfrey of Fontaines, *Quodlibet* XII.4 (above, pp. 258–60); Giles of Rome, *De Renuntiatione Papae*, ed. J. R. Eastman (Lewiston, NY, 1992); J. Leclercq, 'La Renonciation de Célestin V et l'opinion théologique en France du vivant de Boniface VIII', *Revue d'Histoire de l'Église de France*, 25 (1939), 190–1; J. R. Eastman, *Papal Abdication in Later Medieval Thought* (Lewiston, NY, 1990).

[99] *DPRP* XXV, pp. 256–9.

[100] *DPRP* XIII, p. 214. For the parallelism between temporal and ecclesiastical government, see J. M. Blythe, *Ideal Government and the Mixed Constitution in the Middle Ages* (Princeton, 1992), ch. 8. Contrast

the legitimating criterion for the exercise of both temporal and spiritual government, John of Paris not only made the pope accountable to the benefit of the church but also the king accountable to the common good of the kingdom. Given that the course of the second dispute between Philip IV and Boniface VIII was driven, on one side, by the king's hostility to any notion that the pope should judge his conduct in temporal matters and, on the other, by the pope's insistence that *Ausculta fili* entailed competence to judge the king's government of his kingdom, this was an important concession to make.

James of Viterbo and Giles of Rome used a notion of the common good to support a comprehensive definition of papal *plenitudo potestatis*, a power which included 'casual' intervention to secure the deposition of a king. John of Paris is prepared to accept the force of this argument. However, he also uses the same notion of the common good to justify the indirect intervention of the king to secure the deposition of a pope. Thus, whilst James of Viterbo and Giles of Rome deployed the common good as a justification for the pope's intervention in temporal affairs, John of Paris turns the argument around to demonstrate that the common good could serve equally well as a justification for the king's intervention in spiritual affairs. John's description of the casual and incidental jurisdiction which can be exercised by the king for the sake of the common good, whatever it may owe to a juristic concept of *necessitas regni*, reads as a secularized plenitude of power.[101] Sin, deficiency, abuse, and a subsequent benefit to the common good—John's criteria for the deposition of a pope are identical to those of James of Viterbo and Giles of Rome for the deposition of a king. It was a neat reversal.

In establishing the principle that the common good is the goal of all good government, spiritual as well as temporal, John of Paris was maintaining a line of argument which had already been expounded by Henry of Ghent and Godfrey of Fontaines. It is when John turns to Aristotle's definition of the common good as the life of virtue that the real originality of his treatise emerges. In his initial definition of the political community, John lists food, clothing, defence, and speech as the primary motives for the original establishment of human society. Soon afterwards, the function of the political community appears in more typical Aristotelian guise as *bene vivere* and *bene vivendum in communi*.[102] For John of Paris, temporal power is ordered not only towards the common good but also towards the common good of a life of virtue. John is therefore happy to echo James of Viterbo's reservations over making too simplistic an equation between, on the one hand, the temporal power and the body and, on the other, the spiritual power and the soul. Indeed, John makes it quite explicit that virtue is a good of the soul.[103] In doing so, he does not deny that there is a further purpose to human society, a supernatural as well as a natural end, the goal of eternal

---

T. J. Renna, 'The *populus* in John of Paris' Theory of Monarchy', *Tijdschrift voor Rechtgeschiedenis*, 42 (1974), 243–68.

[101] Cf. *MGH Constitutiones* II, no. 156, p. 192; R. Fawtier, *The Capetian Kings of France* (London, 1960), 193.

[102] *DPRP* II, p. 178; III, p. 180.   [103] *DPRP* XVII, p. 225.

beatitude towards which the life of virtue must be ordered. In fact, he quotes directly from *De Regno ad Regem Cypri* to this effect—if eternal beatitude could be secured by human virtue, then the responsibility to direct people towards it would lie with a human king; however, since this goal is attainable only by divine virtue, such responsibility must rest with the divine kingship of Christ.[104] John is therefore content to accept the basic premiss of a hierarchy of ends, namely that the Christian priesthood is superior to kingship because it is ordered towards a higher end. Nevertheless, where he begs to differ, and to differ fundamentally, is the extent to which this superiority in dignity *necessarily* entails a superiority in causality. Unlike James of Viterbo, John of Paris does not assume an automatic correlation between the two. A hierarchy of dignity is *not* the same as a hierarchy of authority.[105]

De Potestate Regia et Papali assembles a catalogue of arguments in support of hierocratic papalism. Number 23 summarizes the linear hierarchy of ends which was put forward by James of Viterbo and Giles of Rome—the supernatural end is greater than, and superior to, any other end, including the natural end of the life of virtue; the spiritual power of the church is accordingly superior to the temporal power in dignity *and* causality; the spiritual ruler can therefore command how the temporal ruler should act. Number 27, meanwhile, summarizes the argument which Giles of Rome extrapolated from Augustine—the earthly community cannot fulfil its proper function, the life of virtue, without being ordered towards Christ and therefore towards His vicar on earth.[106] John of Paris's response to these two arguments, so central to the papalist case, reveals how difficult he found it to divest an Aristotelian life of virtue from a hierocratic interpretation. John's first move is to point out that, when an inferior discipline is subject to a superior in one respect, it does not follow that the same subjection applies in all respects. Thus, a doctor may command an apothecary when he requires something for the health of a patient but he does not always issue him with specific directions; he may inform him and judge the correctness of his medicine, but he does not institute him in his post or remove him from it. The latter is the function of the ruler to whom both doctor and apothecary are subject. Pope and king, therefore, are subject to the supreme power of God, but the king is subject to the pope only in spiritual matters. John of Paris then takes this argument one step further. The hierarchy of ends is applicable to two disciplines, one superior, the other inferior, only when the inferior discipline is a means to an end and in no sense an end in itself. According to John, however, this is not the case with the political community. Aristotle had maintained that friendship, knowledge, and the power of sight are all goods in their own right. John suggests that the life of virtue should be placed in the same category—it is a good in its own right and not only when it is ordered towards something else. The life of virtue is certainly capable of being

---

[104] *DPRP* II, p. 178.

[105] Cf. C. Fasolt, *Council and Hierarchy: The Political Thought of William Durant the Younger* (Cambridge, 1991), 167.

[106] *DPRP* XI, p. 204. Cf. Giles of Rome, *DEP* I.ii.1–7, pp. 6–9, I.v.1–12, pp. 13–17, I.ix.1–10, pp. 31–4; James of Viterbo, *Quod.* I.17, pp. 210–11, *DRC* II.vii, p. 235.

ordered towards eternal beatitude (*ordinabilis*) but this must not be allowed to obscure the fact that the life of virtue is good and desirable in itself (*secundum se*).[107] It is only a short step to John's blunt reply to Giles of Rome's interpretation of Augustine's *De Civitate Dei*. Perfect justice *can* exist in a political community, even a pagan community, which is not subject to Christ or to His vicar; moral virtues *can* be acquired perfectly without their theological counterparts.

Whether this conclusion makes its author a faithful disciple of Aquinas, pushing Thomist principles to their logical conclusion, or whether it represents a significant point of departure,[108] John's account of perfect moral virtue is one of the most striking statements in *De Potestate Regia et Papali*. Its importance should not be underestimated. Hierocratic treatises such as *De Regno ad Regem Cypri* and *De Regimine Christiano* successfully subordinated the Aristotelian political community to the authority of the church by demonstrating that its defining characteristic—the life of virtue—is a good of the soul and that, as such, its attainment is ultimately the responsibility of the spiritual power. John of Paris realized that, if Aristotle's life of virtue was to be cited as the goal of the temporal ruler without thereby subjecting the king to the church, then moral virtue would have to be released from its necessary connection with grace.

As with his other 'radical' positions on ecclesiological corporatism and individual property, it would appear that John is using an argument which he found in Godfrey of Fontaines, turning a theoretical discussion of accidental perfection in moral theology to an overtly political purpose. His first approach is to claim the authority of Augustine, even if he admits that it is only an inference (*ut innuit*), and to appeal to the same text cited by James of Viterbo, namely the pseudo-Augustinian *Sentences* of Prosper of Aquitaine.[109] John thereby concedes that the moral virtues can still acquire a certain perfection from the theological virtues. Nevertheless, he insists that this represents only an 'accidental' perfection (*quadam accidentali perfectione*).[110] His original statement therefore still stands—moral virtues can be acquired perfectly without their theological counterparts. John then tries to put as favourable construction as he can on the statement of Augustine which was so frequently quoted by Giles of Rome. There *can* be true and perfect justice where Christ is not the ruler, namely when the kingdom is ordered towards the life of acquired moral virtue. What *De Civitate Dei* really means, John suggests, is not that true justice *cannot* exist without Christ but that it *did* not exist amongst people who believed they were serving justice by serving demons and idols. John tries one final approach. Augustine's comments on true justice can also be taken as referring to the specifically Christian *res publica*, a

---

[107] *DPRP* XVII, pp. 226–7; XIX, p. 234. Cf. Aristotle, *Ethics* VIII.1 1155^{a}28–9, X.3 1174^{a}4–6.

[108] Leclercq, *Jean de Paris et l'ecclésiologie*, 149; M. F. Griesbach, 'John of Paris as a Representative of Thomistic Political Philosophy', in C. J. O'Neil (ed.), *An Etienne Gilson Tribute* (Milwaukee, 1959), 33–50. Cf. L. E. Boyle, 'The *De Regno* and the Two Powers', in J. R. O'Donnell (ed.), *Essays in Honour of Anton Charles Pegis* (Toronto, 1974), 243–7.

[109] Prosper of Aquitaine, *Sententia* 7 (*PL* 51, col. 428). Cf. *Sententiae* 144, 160, 177, 259, 289, 292, 304 (cols. 447–73).

[110] Cf. Godfrey of Fontaines, *Quaestio Disputata* XIX (above, pp. 229–32).

community which cannot be ruled correctly except by the pope. However, John carefully points out that the pope is the vicar of Christ only in spiritual affairs and is therefore owed obedience only in spiritual matters.[111]

The distinction which John of Paris draws between the unitary and universal character of spiritual and papal authority and the natural pluralism of political and kingly societies is one element in his rejection of the comprehensive claims of papal *plenitudo potestatis*. A second is his assertion that both the spiritual and the temporal power derive immediately from God and are therefore not subordinate to one another in any hierarchy. The third, and the most radical, is his separation of moral virtue from theological virtue in his definition of the common good which should be secured by the temporal power. The accidental perfection which Christian faith can still bring to the political community is certainly an important qualification. Once again, John wants to separate the temporal from the spiritual but not to make this separation absolute, just as he wants to leave an incidental right of reciprocal inter-vention in both the ecclesiastical and the temporal spheres. Nevertheless, even though nature *may* be perfected by grace, moral virtue *may* be perfected by theo-logical virtue, and justice *may* be perfected by *caritas*, in each case the action of the latter is not *necessary* for the perfection of the former. The consequences for the rela-tionship between the spiritual power and the temporal power are clear. The tem-poral power is not only legitimate without the ratification of the spiritual power but it can also be perfect. The temporal power can concern itself with more than material goods, with moral goods, without necessarily placing itself under the supervision of the church.

Set in the context of the scholastic understanding of the notion of the common good, the contribution of scholastic theologians to the political polemic of Philip IV and Boniface VIII rests on two fundamental tenets and their consequences for the rela-tionship between the temporal and the spiritual power. First, there is the principle that the purpose of authority in human society is to secure the common good, together with its corollary, that this is what distinguishes good forms of government from bad, the practice of kingship from the practice of tyranny. Second, there is the definition of this common good as happiness, as activity in accordance with perfect virtue. In 1302, both propositions were successfully incorporated into the armoury of papalist arguments assembled by Giles of Rome and James of Viterbo. In both cases, their appropriation was immediately challenged by John of Paris.

Like Giles of Rome and James of Viterbo, John of Paris is firmly committed to the notion that the goal of all good government should be the common good. Like Giles and James, John also accepts that this principle can be associated with the canonists' concept of *utilitas ecclesiae* in order to provide a comprehensive justification for the exercise of papal plenitude of power in temporal affairs. However, by pointing out that the common good is the legitimating criterion of all good government, spiritual

---

[111] *DPRP* XVIII, p. 229.

as well as temporal, John also turns this notion back against the pope. John of Paris, like Henry of Ghent and Godfrey of Fontaines, recognizes that the same principle can cut both ways. The common good can also be used to justify a theory of disobedience, resistance, and ultimately papal deposition.

When John of Paris tackled the question of the precise definition which should be given to this common good, he was faced with two arguments. For all his discussion of virtue in *De Regimine Principum*, twenty years later Giles of Rome deliberately restricts the goal of the temporal ruler to the provision of material goods. Rather than rely on Aristotle's *Ethics* and *Politics*, therefore, Giles bases his case in *De Ecclesiastica Potestate* on Augustine's *De Civitate Dei*. True justice cannot exist in any political community which is not subject to Christ and to His vicar on earth; the most that temporal authority can achieve on its own is a degree of peace and material security. As a result, the task of claiming Aristotle's life of virtue for the papalist cause was left to James of Viterbo. Thus, whilst John of Paris tackles Giles as a commentator on Augustine, he tackles James as a commentator on Aristotle and Aquinas.

By arguing that the temporal power is concerned with more than just material goods, that the common good of the political community is a life lived according to moral virtue, John of Paris agrees with James of Viterbo as well as with *De Regno ad Regem Cypri*. Once again, however, he agrees only up to a point. Both *De Regimine Christiano* and *De Regno* used the presence of virtue as a means of subordinating the temporal ruler to the authority of the church. Moral virtue should be subordinated to theological virtue just as the goal of temporal happiness should be ordered towards the goal of eternal beatitude. Like James, John accepts that virtue is a good of the soul. Unlike James, John believes that the rational part of the soul which pertains to nature can be separated from the part of the soul which pertains to grace. Rather than conclude that grace necessarily perfects nature, therefore, John of Paris insists that such perfection is only accidental. The government of a temporal kingdom, he concludes, is only incidentally connected to the church, the jurisdiction of the temporal power only accidentally subordinate to the jurisdiction of the spiritual power. John thereby severs the connection between a hierarchy of ends and a hierarchy of power. Eternal beatitude may constitute a higher goal than temporal happiness, the spiritual power may be superior in dignity to the temporal power, but this does not mean that the spiritual power possesses a superior authority. In the absence of papal ratification, temporal authority can not only be legitimate but it can also attain the life of perfect moral virtue.

The polemical literature which was generated by the disputes between Philip IV and Boniface VIII is, in more than one sense, a well-mined field. Viewed from the perspective of the history of political thought, the treatises of Giles of Rome, James of Viterbo, and John of Paris are often presented as central to the emergence of 'the idea of the secular state', as the result of an argument which was simply waiting to happen once Aristotle's location of the origin of the political community in nature came into contact with Augustine's account of its providential institution as a remedy for sin. It is on this basis, for example, that an 'Augustinian' Giles of Rome is

contrasted with an 'Aristotelian' John of Paris, or, indeed, the 'Augustinian' con-
servatism of Giles's *De Ecclesiastica Potestate* with the 'Aristotelian' radicalism of
De Regimine Principum. Placed in the context of debates within the faculty of theology, however, the polarization of 'Augustinian' and 'Aristotelian' as a clash between
hierocratic and secularizing intellectual traditions needs to be substantially refined.
Henry of Ghent and Godfrey of Fontaines had already demonstrated that, as the goal
of all good government, the common good could be used to provide a measure which
must guide the exercise of authority by popes as well as kings. This was a line of argument which opponents of either the pope or the king could push to a radical conclusion, limiting the ruler's power to legislate and the subject's obligation to obey in
both the spiritual and the temporal spheres. In itself, there was nothing specifically
'Aristotelian' about such a thesis. A correlation between obedience and the common
good could certainly be justified with Aristotelian texts but it derived its authority,
and its appeal, from its capacity to be deduced from similar principles in Augustine,
Gregory the Great, Bernard of Clairvaux, and Roman and canon law. Where a distinction between Aristotle and Augustine *did* make a difference to the relationship
between the spiritual and the temporal power was in specifying the exact nature of
the common good which should be secured by all good government. If the treatises
of Giles of Rome, James of Viterbo, and John of Paris demonstrate anything, it is that
the *casus belli* of scholastic political polemic in 1302 and 1303 was, not the natural
origin of the political community, but the end towards which it was ordered.

Remigio dei Girolami—The Order of Love

The historical significance which is usually ascribed to Remigio dei Girolami derives from two aspects of his life and work. Remigio attended the faculty of arts in Paris in the late 1260s and joined the Dominican convent of Saint Jacques during the second regency of Thomas Aquinas. His subsequent activities as a Dominican friar in Florence are therefore frequently cited as an example of how academic scholasticism could serve wider pastoral concerns in society. As lector at Santa Maria Novella from c.1273 to 1319, not only did Remigio prepare a corpus of written material for the Dominican *studium*, but, by his preaching and teaching, he also mediated the learning of the Paris schools to a much wider audience amongst his fellow-citizens.[1] Remigio is thus a prime candidate for providing the 'disputazioni de li filosofanti' which Dante describes attending in the 'scuole de li religiosi'.[2] Remigio has attracted attention, however, for more than just his propagation of scholastic philosophy and theology. As the author of *De Bono Communi* and *De Bono Pacis*,[3] he is also frequently cited as the proponent of an 'extreme corporationalism', a political theorist who used Aristotle's account of the perfect human association in order to subordinate the individual to a 'dangerous idealisation' of the commune.[4]

---

[1] C. T. Davis, 'Remigio de' Girolami O.P. Lector of S. Maria Novella in Florence', in *Le Scuole degli Ordini Mendicanti* (Convegni del Centro di Studi sulla Spiritualità Medievale 17.1986, Todi, 1978), 283–304; E. Panella, *Per lo studio di Fra Remigio dei Girolami* (*Memorie Domenicane* 10.1979), esp. appendix II 'Contributi alla Biografia Remigiana', 183–241; appendix III, 'Le Opere di fra Remigio dei Girolami', 243–83. Cf. D. R. Lesnick, *Preaching in Medieval Florence: The Social World of Franciscan and Dominican Spirituality* (Athens, Ga., 1989), 96–118; D. L. D'Avray, *Death and the Prince: Memorial Preaching before 1350* (Oxford, 1994), 79–85, 142–7.

[2] Dante, *Convivio*, ed. E. G. Parodi and F. Pellegrini, in *Le Opere di Dante*, 2nd edn. (Florence, 1960), II.12, p. 185. Cf. M. Grabmann, 'Remigio de' Girolami, der Schüler des Heiligen Thomas und Lehrer Dantes', in id., *Mittelalterliches Geistesleben* I (Munich, 1926), 361–9; E. Gilson, 'Les Philosophantes', *AHDLMA* 19 (1952), 135–40; C. T. Davis, 'Remigio de' Girolami and Dante: A Comparison of their Conceptions of Peace', *Studi Danteschi*, 36 (1959), 123–36; id., *Dante and the Idea of Rome* (Oxford, 1957), 80–6.

[3] ed. M. C. de Matteis, *La 'teologia politica communale' di Remigio de' Girolami* (Bologna, 1977), pp. 3–51, 55–71. Cf. L. Minio-Paluello, 'Remigio Girolami's *De bono communi*: Florence at the Time of Dante's Banishment and the Philosopher's Answer to the Crisis', *Italian Studies*, 11 (1956), 56–71.

[4] C. T. Davis, 'An Early Florentine Political Theorist: Fra Remigio de' Girolami', *Proceedings of the American Philosophical Society*, 104 (1960), 669–70. Cf. R. Egenter, 'Gemeinnutz vor Eigennutz: Die soziale Leitidee im *Tractatus de bono communi* des Fr. Remigius von Florenz', *Scholastik*, 9 (1934), 79–92; G. de Lagarde, *La Naissance de l'esprit laïque au déclin du moyen âge*, 3rd edn. (5 vols.; Louvain, 1956–70), ii. 316; E. H. Kantorowicz, *The King's Two Bodies* (Princeton, 1957), 478–80; J. K. Hyde, 'Contemporary Views on Faction and Civil Strife in Thirteenth and Fourteenth Century Italy', in L. Martines (ed.), *Violence and Disorder in Italian Cities 1200–1500* (Berkeley, 1972), 302–3; Matteis, *La 'teologia politica communale'*, pp. cxxx–cxxxi; P. Hibst, *Utilitas Publica—Gemeiner Nutz—Gemeinwohl* (Frankfurt, 1991), 189–93.

Remigio's transmission of Parisian scholasticism and his reflections on the city-state of Florence present their own particular problems of interpretation. Establishing an appropriate intellectual context for Remigio's political thought, for example, is made difficult by the absence of watertight dates for his attendance at the schools in Paris. Remigio had certainly completed the arts course when he entered the Dominican order in *c.* 1267. What is not clear is precisely when he returned from Florence for the one or two years during which he read the *Sentences*. Thus, the traditional *terminus ante quem* of 1281 has recently been replaced with a much later date of between 1297 and 1299.[5] A period of study at Paris in the late 1290s would have a substantial bearing both upon the exclusively Thomist nature of Remigio's intellectual pedigree and upon the bitterness with which he subsequently recorded his own experience of the schools in *Contra Falsos Ecclesiae Professores*.[6] It naturally invites the question of with whom, and with whose writings, Remigio may have come into contact during this period. Godfrey of Fontaines? James of Viterbo? John of Paris? At least one distinctive proposition which John of Paris subsequently put forward in *De Potestate Regia et Papali* (the denial of Christ's temporal lordship) is singled out by Remigio for some hostile criticism in *Contra Falsos Ecclesiae Professores*.[7] Direct contact with his fellow Dominican between 1297 and 1299 would certainly make sense of the lengthy excursus on the relationship between the temporal and the spiritual power which Remigio inserts into *Contra Falsos Ecclesiae Professores*. If chapters 1–4 and 38–99 of this work represent Remigio's response to the lamentable state of affairs which he had encountered in the faculty of arts during his first period in the schools, then the later insertion of chapters 5–37 may constitute, not so much an addition made for the sake of completeness, but a refutation of the latest example of erroneous teaching which he had found distracting Parisian masters, this time in the faculty of theology.

Remigio's acquaintance with a later generation of Parisian theologians than Thomas Aquinas is not the only issue which is raised by chapters 5–37 of *Contra Falsos Ecclesiae Professores*. The sheer range of the arguments which it assembles on the subject of the relationship between the spiritual and the temporal power also prompts the question of the purpose which such an exhaustive compilation was designed to serve. In particular, it opens up the possibility that *Contra Falsos* was intended to provide, not so much a systematic analysis, as an arrangement of material for subsequent, and selective, employment by other Dominican preachers at Santa Maria Novella.[8] This 'encyclopaedic' quality to Remigio's text poses, in its

---

[5] Davis, 'Remigio de' Girolami O.P. Lector', 286; Panella, *Per lo studio*, 193–8.

[6] *Contra Falsos Ecclesie Professores*, ed. F. Tamburini (Rome, 1981). Cf. Panella, *Per lo studio*, 107–51. For its composition, see Tamburini, *ed. cit.*, pp. xxxii–xxxix; Panella, *Per lo studio*, 68–78.

[7] *Contra Falsos Ecclesie Professores* [henceforth *Contra Falsos*] 27, p. 62. Cf. John of Paris, *De Potestate Regia et Papali*, ed. J. Leclercq (Paris, 1942), VIII, pp. 191–2.

[8] Although Remigio's systematic revision of his writings at some stage before 1314 makes their precise chronological relationship difficult to assess, his cross-references suggest that he mined his own sermons and *Contra Falsos* for *De Bono Communi*, and then quarried *De Bono Communi* for *De Bono Pacis*. See Davis, 'Remigio de' Girolami O.P. Lector', 288–98.

turn, a wider methodological question for Remigio's other treatises as well. One of the most striking features of *De Bono Pacis*, after all, is the methodical arrangement of the various categories (scriptural, patristic, philosophical, and legal) into which all its authorities are sorted.[9] *De Bono Communi*, meanwhile, actually concludes by inviting the assiduous reader to rearrange the preceding arguments in order to provide a better demonstration of the truth.[10]

The encyclopaedic nature of Remigio's writing is an important aspect of the distinctive character of his political thinking. Remigio was, first and foremost, a preacher, not a speculative theologian,[11] and, as a preacher, he had a keen awareness of the range of techniques which were available to the public speaker. Thus, he devotes a whole section of *Contra Falsos* to an exposition of why, when, to whom and, above all, how an individual should preach. As a result, Remigio knew that there were some occasions on which he should keep silent, namely when his audience was unable, unwilling, or unworthy to receive his words.[12] The influence of this rhetorical training on the form of Remigio's 'political thought' should not be overlooked. Take, for example, his repeated claim that it is 'beyond doubt' (*indubitanter, procul dubio, certe*) that the common good should be preferred to the individual good.[13] Should this be taken as evidence of an uncompromising 'corporatism' or simply of an attempt at persuasive rhetoric? Much the same question might be asked of Remigio's notorious claim that, if someone is not a citizen, then he is not a human being (*si non est civis, non est homo*).[14] Taken on its own, or read in conjunction with Dante's account of Charles Martel, this statement can be read as the disquieting expression of a northern Italian communitarian ethos.[15] Placed in its intellectual and rhetorical context, however, it can be read as a punchy reformulation of the Aristotelian commonplaces which it immediately precedes—humankind is, by nature, a political animal; if an individual does not live in a political community, then he is either a god or a beast.

As a preacher, Remigio was trained to deliver what was appropriate (*aptum*) to his immediate audience. In Remigio's case, this means that his political ideas were formed against a background of public controversy in which familial feuding, class conflict, party violence, and competition for office were increasingly regarded as evils endemic to civic life.[16] The generic term 'treatise', therefore, should not disguise the specific circumstances in which Remigio developed his theoretical reflections on the political community. His *Tractatus de Iustitia*, for example, appears to have

---

[9] *De Bono Pacis* [henceforth *DBP*], p. 55. For medieval treatments of this theme, see K. Arnold, '*De bono pacis*: Friedensvorstellungen in Mittelalter und Renaissance', in J. Petersohn (ed.), *Uberlieferung, Frömmigkeit, Bildung als Leitthemen der Geschichtsforschung* (Wiesbaden, 1987), 133–54.

[10] *De Bono Communi* [henceforth *DBC*], p. 50.

[11] G. Salvadori and V. Federici, 'I Sermoni d'occasione, le sequenze e i ritmi di Remigio Girolami Fiorentino', in *Scritti Vari di Filologia a Ernesto Monaco* (Rome, 1901), 476–500; E. Panella, 'Il Repertorio dello Schneyer e i sermonari di Remigio dei Girolami', *Memorie Domenicane*, 11 (1980), 632–50.

[12] *Contra Falsos* 39, pp. 84–7. Cf. ibid. 4, p. 9.

[13] *DBC* pp. 3, 15, 17, 38. Cf. *Contra Falsos* 6, p. 19.   [14] *DBC* p. 18.

[15] Dante, *Paradiso* VIII 115–17. Cf. Kantorowicz, *The King's Two Bodies*, 479 n. 78.

[16] Hyde, 'Contemporary Views on Faction and Civil Strife', 273–307.

originated as a sermon in which Remigio reflects on the nature of punishment, particularly in relation to considerations of social status and the overriding need to secure the common good. This treatise has accordingly been located in the period 1293–5 when Florence was governed by the Ordinances of Justice.[17] *De Bono Pacis* is a treatise which is likewise concerned with one particular issue, namely whether those legal penalties which are due for personal injury or for the expropriation of property can be waived for the sake of establishing peace.[18] This was a burning question in Florence in the discussions which surrounded the papal peace initiative of 1304.[19] In both instances, moreover, Remigio was responding to events in which he was personally involved. As a member of the Girolamo family, he had a brother, Salvi del Chiaro, who was one of the first Priors to govern the city in 1282, and three nephews (Chiaro, Mompuccio, and Girolamo) all of whom held this office in the 1290s (Mompuccio as a signatory to the Ordinances of Justice). In 1294 and 1295, therefore, when Remigio delivered four sermons in the presence of the Priors and instructed them to place the common good above considerations of self-interest or social status, this was more than a matter of political theorizing.[20] Likewise, in 1302–3, when Remigio composed *De Bono Communi* in order to urge his fellow-citizens to demonstrate their love for the common good, this was more than just the recycling of a scholastic commonplace. It was Remigio's direct response to the expulsion of the 'White' Guelf faction. The most famous of these exiles may have been Dante but they included Remigio's nephew, Girolamo, who was in office in November 1301 and who was subsequently convicted of murder in his absence.[21]

The difficulties which are presented by Remigio's highly personal combination of systematic analysis, encyclopaedic research, exhortatory preaching, and political controversy, together with the uncertainty surrounding the date of his second period of study in Paris, make an examination of his political thought a peculiarly problematic task. By the same token, *De Bono Communi* and *De Bono Pacis* provide a particularly important perspective from which to consider some of the most significant issues in scholastic political and ethical thought. Remigio's practical application of scholastic ideas to the politics of an Italian city-state, for example, raises the question of the relationship between theoretical ideal and historical reality, between political theory and political practice. Remigio's political writings can accordingly provide some indication of the wider impact of the scholastic reception of Aristotle's *Ethics* and *Politics* in the late thirteenth and early fourteenth centuries. Remigio's political writings can also serve as an index to the scholastic understanding of the relationship between the individual and the common good. His modern characterization as an extreme corporatist, as a writer who subordinated everybody and everything to the

---

[17] O. Capitani, 'L'Incompiuto Tractatus de Iustitia de Fra' Remigio de' Girolami', *Bulletino dell'Istituto Storico Italiano per il Medio Evo e Archivio Muratoriano*, 72 (1960), 91–134.

[18] *DBP* p. 55.   [19] Davis, 'Remigio de' Girolami and Dante', 108–9 (below, pp. 318–19).

[20] *Sermones*, 24–5, 27–8, ed. Salvadori and Federici, pp. 481–4.

[21] Davis, 'Remigio de' Girolami and Dante', 108; Panella, *Per lo studio*, 206–33. For the fortunes of the Girolami, see Lesnick, *Preaching in Medieval Florence*, 215–16.

good of the city-state, owes much to the perceived influence of an Aristotelian conception of political society. Remigio is thus a prime subject for assessing the impact of Aristotelian ideas not only on the subordination of the good of each citizen to the good of the political community but also on the subjection of the spiritual power of the church to the political power of temporal authority.

If only to judge from the titles of his two main political treatises, a notion of the common good is clearly critical to Remigio's understanding of human society. It is a concept, however, which is consistently glossed with one particular meaning. Remigio's references to the common good as a metaphysical principle of goodness (*bonum in communi*), for example, are noticeably sparse and, when he does discuss the good which all things seek (*bonum quod omnia appetunt*), it is for its connection with the hierarchical order of love (*ordo caritatis*). All things, he states, have a natural love for the good in common. According to Remigio, because universal goodness (*bonum sumptum in communi*) is more congruent with a common good than with a particular good, it necessarily follows (*certe sequitur*) that the common good should be loved in preference to any particular good.[22] Remigio draws the same connection when he discusses the nature of the common good as the conservation of the species. The preservation of the individual, he states, is an intrinsic effect of a love which is directed towards the species. However, this effect is produced more by the whole of which the individual forms a part than it is by the part itself.[23] In order to explain this, Remigio draws an analogy with fire, something, he observes, with which love has a great similitude.[24] A flame may naturally move upwards in order to preserve itself, but it actively generates fire, not on its own account, but for the sake of the good of what is generated (the conservation of its form) and for the sake of the common good (the conservation of its species). Thus, the extent to which the flame itself is preserved in a fire is ultimately governed by the preservation of the whole.[25]

A concern to demonstrate that the relationship between the individual good and the common good is governed by a principle of love is immediately apparent from the opening words of *De Bono Communi*. People of his own era, Remigio writes, and, above all, his fellow-countrymen, were witnessing the fulfilment of Paul's prophetic last days, 'terrible times' in which 'people will be lovers of themselves, greedy, boastful, proud, abusive, disobedient to their parents, ungrateful, unholy, without love, unforgiving, slanderous, without self-control, brutal, not lovers of the good, treacherous, rash, conceited, lovers of pleasure rather than lovers of God' (2 Timothy 3: 1–4). The root cause of this parlous state was, in Remigio's eyes, an excessive and inordinate love of self which was leading individuals to neglect the goods which they had in common (*bona communia*). Remigio himself was in no doubt (*indubitanter*) that, according to the *ordo caritatis*, the common good should, instead, be preferred to the particular good, the good of the multitude to the good of one single person. This is the antidote which he prescribes for the incessant destruction which was

---

[22] *DBC* p. 15.   [23] *DBC* p. 34. Cf. ibid. p. 48.   [24] *DBC* p. 21.   [25] *DBC* p. 37.

being wrought at the inspiration of the devil.[26] It is thus the hierarchy of the *ordo caritatis* (love of God, love of what is in common, and love of self) which provides Remigio with the thesis which dominates his entire treatise. Individuals should love the common good in preference to their particular good because not to do so would be to violate an order which is both natural and divine.[27] *De Bono Communi* is therefore as much a treatise on the operation of love as it is on the nature of the common good in the political community. For Remigio, the two subjects are inseparable.

The list of Christian authorities which Remigio quotes in support of the superiority of the common good is, in the main, a round-up of the usual texts from the apostle Paul, Augustine, and 'Boethius'.[28] Mindful, perhaps, of his predicatory brief, Remigio also adds an illustration from the Old Testament. According to 2 Maccabees 15: 12, he writes, the high priest Onias was a 'good and kind man, of modest bearing and gentle manner, one who spoke fittingly and had been trained from childhood in the virtues'. According to Remigio, he was also a perfect man (*vir perfectus*). As a result, when Onias informed Seleucus, king of Asia, of the wickedness of Simon, captain of the temple of Jerusalem, Remigio suggests that the high-priest was acting, not as the accuser of his fellow-citizen, but as the guardian of the common benefit of the whole multitude.[29] This episode, which is also cited both in *Contra Falsos* and in *De Bono Pacis*,[30] provides Remigio with his paradigm for an individual who is compelled to act on behalf of the common good of the multitude by the *ordo caritatis*.[31]

When Remigio moves from Christian to pagan authorities, he underlines the importance of love for the common good by quoting, in full, the comparative terminology from book I of the *Ethics*.[32] Although Remigio adds book IX of the *Ethics*, a string of quotations from Cicero (including all those cited by Henry of Ghent),[33] and an illustration of the natural love for the common good which is shown by bees,[34] it is Aristotle's association of *amabile* with *divinius* with which he is most impressed. Indeed, when Remigio argues that the more an individual participates in divinity, the more that individual will love what is in common, he actually congratulates Aristotle for making this connection (*bene coniunxit*) and proceeds to place book I of the *Ethics* alongside Augustine's *Regula*.[35] He subsequently repeats both the praise and the summary. Greater love is the prerequisite for the superiority of the common good

---

[26]   *DBC* p. 3.   [27]   *DBC* pp. 21, 37, 42.

[28]   1 Corinthians 13: 5; Augustine, *Praeceptum*, ed. G. Lawless, in *Augustine of Hippo and his Monastic Rule* (Oxford, 1987), 94; Seneca, *Ad Lucilium Epistulae Morales*, ed. L. D. Reynolds (Oxford, 1965), I.6, p. 10 (cf. Boethius, *Philosophiae Consolatio* III.10; above, pp. 67 n. 56, 147 n. 94. Cf. *DBP* pp. 56–7.)

[29]   *DBC* p. 3; 2 Maccabees 4: 4–6. Cf. *Biblia Latina cum Glossa Ordinaria* (4 vols.; Turnholt, 1992), iii. p. 594.

[30]   *Contra Falsos* 45, p. 116; *DBP* p. 56.

[31]   *DBC* p. 4. Cf. *Sermo* 25, p. 482. According to Remigio, it is the same compulsion (*compellente caritate*) which forced Caiaphas (also a high priest but this time an evil man) to utter the prophetic words in John 11: 49–50: 'it is better for you that one man should die for the people than that the whole nation perish' (*DBC* p. 4; cf. *DBP* p. 56).

[32]   *DBC* pp. 4–5.   [33]   *DBC* p. 5. Cf. *DBP* p. 56; above, p. 200.

[34]   Ambrose, *Exameron*, ed. C. Schenkl (*CSEL* 32.1), V.21, pp. 189–93. Cf. Thomas of Chantimpré, *Bonum universale de apibus*, ed. G. Colvenerius (Douai, 1627), 64.

[35]   *DBC* pp. 19–20.

because to love is the same as to will the good.[36] It is hardly surprising, therefore, to find that *praeamare* is the verb with which Remigio consistently prefers to express the principle of the superiority of the common good.[37]

In arguing that the common good is the manifestation of a correctly ordered love, Remigio was following a path already set by Thomas Aquinas, Giles of Rome, and Godfrey of Fontaines. His discussion accordingly takes a familiar line, running through the different categories of love (natural, rational, and divine), connecting *caritas* with the exercise of virtue,[38] identifying it as a unitive and transformative power (*vis unitiva*),[39] and separating concupiscent love (*amor concupiscentiae*) from the benevolent love of friendship (*amor amicitiae*).[40] In the process, however, Remigio also finds himself forced to clarify his own position on the subject which had so divided Giles of Rome and Godfrey of Fontaines from Henry of Ghent and James of Viterbo. Does an individual have a greater natural love for his own good than for any other good, including the common good and, ultimately, God? As a result, whilst the first part of *De Bono Communi* sets out to demonstrate that the common good has a pre-eminent claim on an individual's love, the second part of the treatise lists an array of counter-propositions which are designed to prove that individuals have, in fact, a greater natural love for themselves and for their own good.[41] Such is the scope of these counter-propositions that they provide, in effect, a convenient index of the central issues which were raised by the scholastic notion of the common good (Fig. 11.1). In responding to each of these counter-propositions, Remigio thereby sets himself the task of tackling most of the issues which had divided scholastic theologians in their understanding of this concept. What is the motivation behind the individual who lays down his life for the community in book IX of the *Ethics*? What are the consequences of making self-love the root of all natural love, including the love of friendship in book VIII of the *Ethics*? What should be understood by the absence of the common good from Augustine's *ordo caritatis*? Does a part love itself more than it loves its whole? Does an individual love the common good primarily because he thereby secures his own individual good? Do humans love God because they thereby secure salvation? Is it possible for an individual, through his natural love (*amor*), to love God and the common good more than he loves himself, or does this require the operation of gracious love (*caritas*)? Can an individual commit a sin for the sake of the common good? Should an individual will his own damnation if he thereby secures the salvation of all humankind?

Remigio's refutation of the claim that greater love should be shown towards the self and the individual good depends, in at least fifteen of these nineteen counter-propositions, on an analysis of the *ordo caritatis* in terms of the analogy of part and whole. As a result, much of Remigio's argument follows a well-worn path. As an

---

[36] *DBC* pp. 41, 43.

[37] *DBC* pp. 15–16, 25, 27, 29–32, 37, 42–4, 49. Cf. *praeferre* (*DBC* pp. 3, 9, 15, 41; *DBP* p. 55); *praeponere* (*DBC* pp. 11, 21); *proferre* (*DBC* p. 10).

[38] *DBC* pp. 26–7.   [39] *DBC* pp. 30–1.

[40] *DBC* p. 49.   [41] *DBC* pp. 36–47.

[i]   Human beings have a greater natural love for themselves than for anything else.

[ii]   All parts of Creation, according to their nature, seek their own advantage (*commodum*)
          and therefore have a greater love for it; only God is an exception to this rule.

[iii]   All human beings, according to their nature, love themselves more than they love what
          they have in common (*suum commune*).

[iv]   All things have a natural love for their own good; the more personal a good is, therefore,
          the more it will be loved.

[v]   The individual who lays down his life for the good of the community does so on
          account of his own greatest good, the good of virtue.

[vi]   The greatest good is the good which has the greatest unity, through predication or
          attribution to one and the same subject; the greatest good of the part is therefore the
          good of that part; since the greatest good is worthy of the greatest love, the part will
          have the greatest love for its own good.

[vii]   Something may be a greater good in its own right but, however great it is, it should not
          be the object of greater natural love unless it is a greater good for the subject loving it.

[viii]   Although an individual must love God above all other things, God is still loved on
          account of the individual's own good.

[ix]   If there is no good in someone gaining the whole world if he thereby forfeits his soul
          [Matthew 16: 26; Mark 8: 36; Luke 9: 25], then the good of one individual soul should
          be preferred to the good of the whole world.

[x]   An individual must prefer himself to remain sinless whilst the community sins than
          that he should sin whilst the community remains sinless.

[xi]   An individual must prefer that the community, even the whole world, should be
          damned than that he should be damned and not the community.

[xii]   According to Augustine, there are four objects of love, namely God, self, neighbour,
          and the body; 'community' (*commune*) fits into this classification only under the head-
          ing of neighbour; one's neighbour should be loved only *after* oneself; so too, therefore,
          should 'community'.

[xiii]   Love can only be shown to creatures with a reasoning capacity, but 'what is in common'
          (*commune*) does not possess this characteristic.

[xiv]   An individual is loved more than a community since what is in common is not loved
          directly except through its parts; what is congruent with a whole through one of its
          parts has a greater congruence with the part through which it is congruent.

[xv]   A son has a greater natural love for his mother than he has for his country (*patria*).

[xvi]   According to law, God must be loved first, parents second, and country third; an indi-
          vidual should therefore love himself more than his country.

[xvii]   In asking God 'if it is possible, may this cup be taken from me; yet not as I will but as
          you will' [Matthew 26: 39], Christ reveals that his sinless, natural will was to love
          himself more than the whole of humankind.

[xviii]   According to the *ordo caritatis*, and as is clearly the case with heavenly beatitude
          [proposition xi], an individual should love the *caritas* which exists in himself more than
          the *caritas* which exists in the rest of the world.

[xix]   Humans are not able to strive after eternal beatitude with a natural love; nor are they
          able to strive after it in any other common entity than heaven.

FIG. 11.1. Remigio dei Girolami, *De Bono Communi*, pp. 36–47.

aesthetic judgement, for example, he cites the standard text from Augustine's *Confessions*—the beauty of a part derives from its congruence with its whole.[42] Ever the preacher, however, Remigio also appends a series of illustrations of his own—the beauty of the nose is relative to the face, that of the face to the body, the piazza to the city, and the cloister or dormitory to the monastery.[43] Without such congruence, Remigio concludes, a part cannot possess any beauty of its own.[44] This is one sense in which the beauty of the part can be said to 'depend' on the beauty of the whole. Another sense is provided by the way in which something which is ugly in itself can become beautiful when it is incorporated as a part within a whole. Augustine himself had demonstrated the way in which evil is providentially ordered within the universe.[45] Remigio picks up Augustine's illustration of the presence of black and grey in a painting,[46] but, once again, he adds rather more vivid illustrations of his own—stables and privvies in a palace, emunctories and pudenda in the human body.[47] An individual, Remigio concludes, should have a greater natural love for the community than for himself because it is natural for more love to be shown towards something which is more beautiful. In spelling out the political consequences of Augustine's aesthetic, Remigio uses the distinction which had been employed by Aquinas. The beauty of a community is greater than the beauty of an individual citizen, he argues, in the sense that the beauty of the whole is greater than the beauty of the part 'extensively' (since it contains more things of beauty) and 'intensively' (since the beauty of the part depends on the beauty of the whole).[48] There are therefore two reasons why the citizen has a greater natural love for the city than for himself. First, the city possesses a greater abundance of intellectual, moral, and theological virtue than one citizen (since a city contains a greater number of virtuous individuals). Second, the individual citizen can become more virtuous by existing in a community than he can by living in isolation.[49]

A second standard analogy to which Remigio appeals is the corporeal metaphor and the natural instinct of the hand to defend the head. The life of the whole body, he states, depends on the head, heart, and stomach, and, as a result, all the other parts and limbs will make sacrifices in order to preserve these three in existence.[50] As a justification for laying down one's life for the political community, this analogy had a long pedigree. What is noticeable about Remigio's treatment of it is the depth to which he explores the precise meaning of the 'dependence' of the parts of the body upon the whole. He starts by appealing to the principle which Albertus Magnus had drawn from book VII of Aristotle's *Physics*—a whole has more being than one of its parts because the whole exists in actuality, whereas the part, as such, exists only in potential.[51] What actual existence the part does possess, therefore, depends on the

---

[42] *DBC* p. 15; *Contra Falsos* 2, p. 4; Augustine, *Confessions*, ed. J. J. O'Donnell (Oxford, 1992), III.8, p. 29.
[43] *DBC* pp. 15–16.   [44] *DBC* p. 27.
[45] Augustine, *Enchiridion*, ed. E. Evans (*CCSL* 46), III.10–11, IV.12–13, pp. 53–5.
[46] Augustine, *De Civitate Dei*, ed. B. Dombart and A. Kalb (*CCSL* 47–8), XI.23, p. 342.
[47] *DBC* pp. 15–16.   [48] *DBC* p. 27. Cf. above, p. 96.   [49] *DBC* pp. 25–6.   [50] *DBC* p. 7.
[51] *DBC* p. 17; Aristotle, *Physics* VII.5 250ª19–25 (above, p. 38). For this distinction, see *DBC* p. 30, quoting Aristotle, *Physics* I.8 191ª23–ᵇ27 (an actual being is an *ens simpliciter* whereas a potential being is

existence of the whole since a part which exists outside of a whole is not a part. Aristotle's example in the *Politics* had been that of a hand which is separated from a body—it is a hand only equivocally or homonymously in the same way that a painted or sculpted hand 'is' a hand.[52] Remigio concludes that, because a part depends on the whole for its actual existence, the same principle must also apply to all the other qualities of the part. Thus, a part's goodness (*bonum*), beauty, pleasure, and benefit (*utilitas*) all depend, in their turn, on the goodness, beauty, pleasure, and benefit of the whole.[53] It is this account of dependence which Remigio uses as the basis for his refutation of counter-proposition [ii]. The part, he states, secures more advantage (*commodum*) from the whole than it does from itself.[54]

Remigio regards dependence as a principle which is inherent in every part of Creation. Everything depends on something else for its preservation and for its own good. This ontological dependence accordingly defines his exposition of Aristotle's comparative terminology from book I of the *Ethics*. The whole, he argues, is 'better' than the part (*melius*) in the sense that the entire goodness of the part is dependent on the whole.[55] The same argument applies to *maius*. The good of the whole is 'greater' than the good of the part in the sense that the part depends for its existence, and for every good which presupposes this existence, on the existence and the good of the whole. In Remigio's view, this is also the sense of Aristotle's observation that the whole necessarily has 'greater priority' than the part (*prius*) and the city 'greater priority' than the household and every individual human.[56] It is on this basis that Remigio refutes counter-propositions [vi] and [vii]. Since a part is only called a part with respect to its whole, he states, it has the greatest natural affinity, and the greatest natural love, for the good of the whole because its existence is completely (*totaliter*) dependent upon it. Although the good of the whole is not as personal to the individual part as the good of that part is to itself (Remigio does concede this point to counter-proposition [iv]), the part clearly has a greater natural love for the whole since the whole is the very principle and cause of its existence.[57] One effect of love, after all, is to preserve the subject who is doing the loving, and the part is certainly (*certum est*) preserved through its connection with the whole more than it is preserved through itself.[58]

In Remigio's exposition of the corporeal analogy, moreover, the dependence of the individual good of the part on the common good of the whole is closely associated with the principle that the individual good of the part is included in the common good of the whole. 'What is in common', Remigio states, is a greater good (*magis bonum*) than what is particular because the particular is included in what is in common.[59] This principle of inclusion gives Remigio his initial answer to counter-proposition [v]. There is no doubt (*absque dubio*), he writes, that the good of the part is included in the good of the whole. Like Godfrey of Fontaines, however, Remigio

---

only an *ens secundum quid*). Remigio's own example is an egg—essentially it is an egg, but, within certain terms of reference, it is an animal.

[52] *DBC* p. 17; Aristotle, *Politics* I.2 1253ª20–22.   [53] *DBC* pp. 27, 29.   [54] *DBC* p. 37.
[55] *DBC* p. 47.   [56] *DBP* p. 61. Cf. *DBC* p. 17.   [57] *DBC* p. 39.
[58] *DBC* p. 34.   [59] *DBC* p. 15.

is also careful to point out that, although the individual is included within the common good, this does not mean that the good of the part is the *primary* goal of the part. According to Remigio, the good of the whole is a greater good in itself (*maius bonum simpliciter*) as well as a greater good for the part (*maius bonum ipsi*).[60] Thus, when a good citizen lays down his life, he does not do so in order to secure his individual good of virtue as his primary goal (*principalis finis*). This individual good of virtue acts, instead, as the formal, not the final, cause of his action. Remigio illustrates this argument by means of two further analogies. Heat, he states, is the formal cause of the action of fire when it warms, just as gravity is the formal cause of the action of a stone when it falls. Thus, fire warms on account of heat, the stone falls on account of gravity and, in the same way, the individual dies on account of the good of virtue. In each case, 'on account of' (*propter*) represents the inclusion of an individual good only in the sense of a formal cause or a secondary goal and not in the sense of a final cause or an ultimate goal.[61] The same principle also governs the operation of *amor amicitiae* and *amor concupiscentiae*. The natural love which a part has for its whole should be termed the love of friendship (willing the good of the object loved) rather than the love of concupiscence (willing the good of the subject loving). The good of the object loved certainly includes the good of the subject loving. A part can therefore be said to love its whole 'on account of' (*propter*) its own individual good. However, this does not entail the part ordering the good of the whole towards its own individual good. On the contrary, the individual good of the part is ordered towards the good of the whole.[62]

By consistently emphasizing that the individual good is not the primary goal of virtuous action even though the individual good is included within the common good, Remigio sides with Aquinas, Giles of Rome, and Godfrey of Fontaines against Henry of Ghent and James of Viterbo. The most intriguing aspect of Remigio's contribution to this debate occurs when he considers whether the indisputable conclusion (*certum est*) that the good of an individual soul should be preferred to every worldly good would continue to hold true if 'gaining the whole world' were to be glossed as a spiritual good. Remigio's response to counter-propositions [ix], [x], and [xi] is unequivocal. If an individual were to 'gain' the world in a spiritual sense (as a preacher 'gains' people for Christ by bringing them to repentance) but forfeit his soul in the process (through preaching hypocritically), he would not, in fact, be expressing true love for the whole world. The love of the part for the whole must include the love of the part for itself, and the good of the whole must include the good of the part. The hypocritical preacher cannot love the human community, therefore, because the act of sinning does evil to his soul and, as such, is an expression of hatred towards himself.[63] Similarly, when Exodus 23: 2 reads 'do not follow the crowd in doing wrong', this does not mean (as counter-proposition [x] would have it) that the individual, by preferring that the community should sin, is willing his own good rather

---

[60] *DBC* p. 38. Cf. Henry of Ghent, *Quodlibet* XII.13 (above, pp. 172–3).
[61] *DBC* pp. 38, 40 (*finis sub fine*).   [62] *DBC* p. 49.   [63] *DBC* pp. 40–1.

than the good of the community. Remigio lays down three objections to such an inference being drawn. First, in avoiding his own sin, the individual is placing above his love of the community, not his love of self, but his love of God (and, according to the *ordo caritatis*, the individual must love God above all other things). Second, just as love of the whole includes love of the part, so the sin of the whole includes the sin of the part. Just as the individual should love the good of the community more than he loves his own good, therefore, so he should want to prevent the community sinning more than he wants to avoid sinning himself.[64] The evil of the whole is a greater evil for the part than the evil of the part because the part is thereby deprived of a greater good. The evil of the whole deprives the part of its actual good and the cause of its actual goodness, whereas the evil of the part deprives the part only of its potential good and what has been caused by it.[65] Third, according to both Aristotle and Augustine, something which is evil by nature, such as sin, cannot become good through being ordered towards a good end. No love can justify the commission of sin on its account.[66] Remigio does not offer any reflection, in this context, on the question of whether adultery could be committed, or prostitution tolerated, if they secure the common good, nor on the consistency of his statement with his comments on the beautification of an inherently ugly part.[67] What he does do is raise the question of the ultimate evil for the human community, namely universal damnation.

Counter-proposition [xi] suggests that an individual is obliged to will that his community be condemned to hell if it is a choice between this and his own damnation. Remigio's response has been variously interpreted as a straightforward rebuttal of this claim, as an example of half-playful rhetorical hyperbole, but also as a sinister elevation of the claims of the political community over the individual.[68] In fact, Remigio's response bears close comparison with the position which had already been put forward on exactly this issue by Henry of Ghent.[69] Remigio, like Henry, bases his argument on Augustine's distinction between penalty and fault, between the suffering which occurs through experiencing evil (*poena*) and the suffering which occurs through performing evil (*culpa*). Since performing evil is sinful and, as such, causes offence to God, evil done (*malum culpae*) should not be willed on any account. Evil suffered (*malum poenae*), on the other hand, causes harm only to the individual who is experiencing it. According to Remigio, therefore, the original proposition needs to be rephrased in the form of the question 'can the individual will the community to experience evil rather than experience it himself?'. By definition, the evil which is suffered in the course of damnation presupposes evil done as well as evil suffered and, as such, presupposes an offence being caused to God. Since humankind ought

---

[64] *DBC* p. 42.   [65] *DBC* p. 34.

[66] *DBC* p. 42; Aristotle, *Ethics* II.6 1107ª14–17; Augustine, *De Civitate Dei* XIV.11, pp. 431–2. Cf. *Tractatus de Iustitia*, p. 127.

[67] Cf. *DBP* p. 57.

[68] Davis, 'An Early Florentine Political Theorist', 670; Kantorowicz, *The King's Two Bodies*, 479–80; Hyde, 'Contemporary Views on Faction and Civil Strife', 303.

[69] Henry of Ghent, *Quodlibet* IX.19 (above, p. 167).

to love God more than the whole world, an individual should rejoice that the punishment of hell has been justly inflicted, irrespective of the degree of community which it affects. However, if it were possible for such punishment to be suffered without guilt, without evil being performed, then the individual, by virtue of the *ordo caritatis* and insofar as he is part of the community, would be obliged to prefer to suffer this punishment himself whilst the community remains immune, rather than let the community incur the punishment whilst he remains immune.[70] The assumption behind this suggestion is clear. In such a scenario, the individual would incur punishment without guilt and therefore without sin; he would act in virtue of the *ordo caritatis*, a principle which requires the individual to show greater love for the common good but which cannot sanction the performance of an evil action on its behalf. Remigio does not proceed to offer any further clarification of the distinction between sinless eternal punishment and sinful eternal damnation. Elucidation can be derived, however, from three scriptural texts discussed earlier in the treatise, texts with which Remigio was evidently sufficiently intrigued to analyse them in considerable depth.

In Exodus 32: 31, after the Israelites fashioned the idolatrous golden calf, Moses sought atonement for this terrible sin by beseeching God either to forgive his people or, if not, to blot his own name out from the Book of Life. In Romans 9: 1–4, the apostle Paul spoke of his sorrow and anguish over the Jewish people and affirmed 'I could wish that I myself were cursed and cut off from Christ for the sake of my brothers'. In Hebrews 13: 12, the sacrifice of Christ is described as a sin-offering suffered in order to sanctify humankind. Remigio takes these three texts and examines them one by one. First, he points out that, when Moses made his request to be blotted out from the Book of Life, he had already inflicted the punishment of death on three thousand Israelites. In doing so, Remigio argues, Moses had already acted in accordance with the *ordo caritatis* in that he had demonstrated a love which placed God above the multitude and the majority of the multitude above a minority of three thousand. According to Remigio, Moses' request can therefore be interpreted in different ways. If it was not spoken from reason (since Moses should not have willed his own damnation for the sake of the community), then it was inspired either by emotion (*de impetu animi*) or by the knowledge that what he was requesting was impossible. For Remigio, it was as if Moses were saying to God 'since it is impossible for you to delete me from the Book of Life, I pray that it can only happen that you forgive them'. Remigio supports this interpretation by appealing to Augustine's argument (as reported by Petrus Comestor) that the dialectical equivalence of 'either delete me or forgive them' should be glossed as 'if you do not delete me, then forgive them'.[71] Once the antecedent clause has been made redundant (either because of its injustice should it be fulfilled, or because of the knowledge that it would never be fulfilled), the second clause stands on it own.[72]

[70] *DBC* pp. 42–3.
[71] Petrus Comestor, *Historia Scholastica* (*PL* 198, cols. 1054–1722), cols. 1190–1.
[72] *DBC* pp. 11–12.

Remigio applies exactly the same line of argument to the wish expressed by the apostle Paul. Like Moses, Paul had already demonstrated love in accordance with the *ordo caritatis*, this time by not seeking his own benefit but the salvation of the multitude (1 Corinthians 10: 33) and by being prepared to lay down his life for his fellow-humans (2 Corinthians 12: 15). Like Moses, therefore, Paul's desire to be cursed by God was accompanied by the knowledge that this would be impossible to fulfil. On Remigio's reading, it was for this reason that Paul did not say 'I wish' (*opto*) but 'I could wish' (*optabam*) in that the apostle knew that such an upright and sinless individual as himself could not be separated from Christ. What was nevertheless secured by expressing even a hypothetical wish was a demonstration of his love for the Jews.[73]

Both Moses and Paul were offering to suffer a putative punishment, a penalty whose impossibility of being fulfilled derived from their own state of virtue. This unfulfilled condition is accordingly reflected in Remigio's own use of the subjunctive when generalizing the principle which he elicits from both texts. If the individual were able to incur punishment without guilt, Remigio writes, he would be under an obligation (*si posset . . . deberet*).[74] It is only when Remigio turns, finally, to the person of Christ that he finds an example of an individual who lacked sin or guilt himself yet *did* incur the greatest punishment on behalf of the whole human community. Remigio himself does not discuss whether Christ's action should be understood as a paradigmatic act of self-sacrifice for all human beings or an act which only Christ could perform. He simply quotes Matthew 20: 28 ('the son of Man did not come to be served but to serve and to give his life as a ransom for many').[75] Nevertheless, it is clear from his discussion of Moses and Paul that an individual should will the community to secure salvation at the expense of his own damnation only if his damnation did not involve any evil done on his own part. This condition is impossible for anyone other than Christ. In all other cases, therefore, Remigio is in agreement with Henry of Ghent. An individual must prefer his own salvation even at the expense of the damnation of the whole community.

Remigio's analysis of self-sacrifice provides a characteristically biblical gloss on what had become the *locus classicus* for all scholastic discussion of whether an individual has a greater love for his own good than he has for the good of the community. Underpinning Remigio's analysis is a trenchant restatement of the principles which had typified the broadly 'Thomist' line of interpretation put forward by Godfrey of Fontaines (the individual should show greater love for the common good because the individual is a part within a whole, because the good of the part depends for its existence on the good of the whole, and because the good of the individual is included within the good of the whole). *De Bono Communi*, however, does more than simply transmit a digest of scholastic opinion on the *ordo caritatis*. It also makes a point of dealing with the specific issue which had so divided Godfrey of Fontaines from James of Viterbo in 1297/8, namely the principle that greater love is dependent upon the presence of greater union or unity. According to James, an individual should show

---

[73] *DBC* pp. 12–13.   [74] *DBC* p. 42.   [75] *DBC* p. 13.

greater natural love for his own good because he is closer (*coniunctior*) to himself than to anything else. According to Godfrey, an individual shows a greater love for the common good because he has a greater unity with the whole of which he forms a part.[76]

When Remigio examines the connection between love and knowledge (nothing can be loved except what is known), he argues that the part has a greater natural love for the whole than it has for itself because it has a greater natural knowledge of the whole than it has of itself. The whole, he concludes, has a greater priority (*prius*) to the part, and something which has a greater priority must be the object of greater knowledge. It is, for example, easier (*facilius*) for the human mind to know a whole by considering it as a whole than by considering it in terms of its distinct parts. By the same token, the whole can also be known with greater certainty (*certius*). Remigio reaches, once again, for a more concrete illustration and finds it in a pile of coins and a group of people. An individual knows that there is a pile of coins with greater certainty than he knows the particular coins which constitute the pile; he knows the number of people gathered together with greater certainty than he knows the individuals themselves.[77]

By insisting that greater love is dependent on greater or more certain knowledge, Remigio is faced with the task of harmonizing this principle with the *ordo caritatis*. Given that an individual would appear to have a greater knowledge of his neighbour than he has of God, and a knowledge of Creation which is prior to his knowledge of the Creator, should he therefore have a greater love for his neighbour and Creation than he has for God? Even Godfrey of Fontaines, after all, had conceded that a part was 'nearer' to itself than it was to its whole. Remigio's solution to this objection is to argue that greater knowledge is not, in itself, a sufficient cause of greater natural love. Whilst it may go some way towards producing this effect, it also requires three further conditions to be met. The object of greater knowledge must be a greater good in itself; it must have both similitude (*similitudo*) and greater conjunction (*coniunctio*) with the subject doing the loving. It is in exploring the second and third of these conditions that Remigio offers his own contribution to the debate between Godfrey of Fontaines and James of Viterbo.

Remigio bases his argument on the nature of being or existence. Every part of Creation is necessarily a being in the sense that it has existence. Since every created being has a natural love for itself, for its own existence, it also has a natural love for everything in which it finds itself and its own existence, that is, for everything with which it shares these characteristics, with which it has a similitude (*similitudo*). This love will therefore be all the greater for something in which it finds more likeness, which is closer (*vicinior*), and which is a more potent cause (*potius*) of its own existence and preservation. A part must therefore have a greater love for its whole because something which has actual existence, such as a whole, is greater (*maior*) than something, such as a part, which has only potential existence. However close the part is to itself, it is still closer to the whole. Its closeness to itself (*vicinitas*) depends on its

---

[76] See above, pp. 214–18.   [77] *DBC* pp. 22–4.

closeness to the whole, just as its existence as a being (without which there would be no closeness in the first place) depends on the existence of the whole. On this reckoning, Remigio concludes that the citizen has a greater love for the community than for himself because the similitude of a part to its whole is greater than the similitude of the part to itself.[78] It is on this basis that Remigio also draws a connection with the nature of love as a *vis unitiva*. Love is a power (*virtus*) which joins the subject doing the loving to the object which is loved. This union, he explains, is such that the two individuals (the subject loving and the object loved) can be said to be 'in' one another, just as the part is 'in' the whole and the whole is 'in' the part. However, whereas the whole is 'in' itself inasmuch as one part of it is in another part, the part is 'in' itself inasmuch as it is in the whole. Remigio uses the example of a jug of wine, where one part, the wine, is in another part, the jug. The union (*unio*) of the part to the whole is thus greater (*maior*) than the union of the part to itself. Remigio gives two reasons. First, the union of the part to itself is a union of something which only exists in potential, whereas the union of the part to the whole is a union of something which exists in actuality. Second, the union of the part to itself is caused by the union of the part to its whole. The individual citizen, Remigio concludes, has a greater natural love for his community than he has for himself.[79]

Remigio follows Godfrey of Fontaines in presupposing that every individual, insofar as he is a human being, will have a greater natural love for something with which he has a greater tie of unity or conjunction. Remigio explains what this means by invoking his favoured analogy for love. Just as fire warms what is close to it (*propinqua*), so an individual will love himself more than he loves a neighbour, a relative more than he loves a stranger, a son more than a brother, and so on. The conjunction of an individual part with its whole, however, is still greater than the conjunction of this part with itself and, as a result, the part should show a correspondingly greater degree of love to the whole than it does to itself. In order to prove that an individual part has a greater unity with its whole than it does with itself, Remigio returns to his acount of dependence and appeals to a general metaphysical principle of causality. Whatever is the origin and cause of something else must be more potent (*potius*, that is, acting as a cause of more things) than the something else to which it gives rise. This is particularly the case if it not only causes something to come into existence but also preserves it in being.[80] Thus, the conjunction which a part has with itself is caused by the conjunction which the part has with the whole; it is also preserved by its conjunction with the whole in the sense that a part which exists outside of a whole is not a part. The existence of the part, in other words, depends on the existence of the whole. Conjunction presupposes existence just like goodness, beauty, pleasure, benefit, advantage, and every other quality in Creation. Something which does not exist, a part without its whole, cannot be conjoined at all, either with itself or with anything else. The conjunction of the part with its whole, Remigio concludes, is greater than (*maior*) the conjunction of the part to itself.[81]

---

[78] *DBC* p. 30.   [79] *DBC* pp. 31–2.   [80] *DBC* pp. 47–9.   [81] *DBC* pp. 21–2.

Conjunction is clearly a notion which plays a central role in Remigio's understanding of the unity which individuals have within themselves and the unity which they have by virtue of being parts of some whole. It is on this basis, for example, that he refutes counter-proposition [i]. The whole, he writes, has a greater conjunction with the part than the part has with itself. The whole is the very principle and cause of the part's existence since the part itself exists only in potential. The conjunction of the whole with the part is therefore actual, whereas the conjunction of the part with itself is only potential.[82] This is also the notion to which Remigio returns, and at even greater length, towards the end of *De Bono Communi*. In logical terms, he states, any one thing can be defined in two ways. Either something can be described as a subsisting subject or supposit (*res suppositalis*, *suppositum*) or it can be described as an agent, as an initiator of action (*res virtualis*, *agens*). When defined as a subject, something has a greater conjunction with itself qua subject than it has when it is defined as an agent. When it is defined as an agent, it has a greater conjunction with itself qua agent than it has with itself qua subject, since its activity (that is, its power of existence and preservation) does not derive from itself but from what has influenced or caused its activity. Remigio refines his earlier argument in the light of this new distinction. The whole has a greater conjunction with the part than the part has with itself provided that the part is being considered as an agent. If the part is being considered as a subject, the reverse is true. However, the conjunction of the whole with the part qua agent is more potent (*potius*) than the conjunction of the part with itself qua subject. As a result, in absolute terms (*simpliciter*), the whole has a greater conjunction with the part than the part has with itself. It is only within certain terms of reference (*secundum quid*) that the part has a greater conjunction with itself than with the whole.[83]

Remigio's analysis of the *ordo caritatis*, together with his detailed investigation of the terms 'congruence', 'dependence', 'inclusion', 'similitude', and 'conjunction', is critical to his explanation of how the relationship between the individual and the community can be understood as a relationship between a part and its whole. That a citizen should show a greater love for the common good is the fundamental principle behind the litany of exempla (classical, biblical, historical, and contemporary) which Remigio assembles in order to demonstrate the obligation of every citizen to sacrifice property, limbs, family, and even life itself, for the good of the community.[84] This is an argument, however, which has been labelled questionable, even dangerous, in its implications for the subordination of the 'rational autonomy' of the individual to the interests of the political community. Remigio, it is suggested, 'often does not take account of the fact that there is an essential difference between a part which has no existence outside an organic whole and an individual who has a very real existence outside the associative unity of the state'.[85] Remigio's characterization as a political

[82] *DBC* p. 36.   [83] *DBC* pp. 48–9.   [84] *DBC* pp. 8–14.
[85] Davis, 'An Early Florentine Political Theorist', 670 (summarizing Egenter, 'Gemeinnutz vor Eigennutz', 79–84). Cf. id., 'Remigio de' Girolami and Dante', 115–16.

theorist who subordinates the individual to a dangerous idealization of the Florentine commune rests on two claims—first, that Remigio rarely acknowledges the difference between the individual and the citizen and, second, that he identifies the
'whole' community (*commune sive totum*) exclusively with 'the state'. Both assumptions stand in need of some clarification.

Remigio not only refers to a distinction between the individual and the citizen,
between the part qua individual and the part qua part of some whole, but he does so
throughout *De Bono Communi*. The common good includes the particular good, he
states, 'inasmuch as it is particular' (*in quantum huiusmodi*); the part exists only in
potential 'insofar as it is a part' (*ut pars*); the part has a greater knowledge of the whole
than of itself 'inasmuch as it is a part' (*in quantum pars*); the existence of the part is
completely dependent on the whole 'inasmuch as it is a part' (*in quantum huiusmodi*);
the whole is the very principle and cause of the existence of the part 'inasmuch as it is
a part' (*in quantum huiusmodi*); the existence of the part depends on the whole 'inasmuch as it is a part' (*in quantum huiusmodi*).[86] In each case, Remigio uses *in quantum* as
a qualifying term. Such qualification is instrumental, for example, to his solution to
counter-proposition [xviii] when he suggests that the loving individual can be considered in two ways, either as some sort of whole or as a part of some multitude
(*ut quoddam totum vel sicut pars multitudinis*). It also underpins his solution to counter-
proposition [xix] when he argues that the individual can be considered as an individual in his own right and as a part of a community (*in quantum est quoddam individuum
in se . . . in quantum ipse est pars communis*).[87] It is equally central to his refutation of
counter-propositions [xv] and [xvi]. A son, he states, inasmuch as he is an individual
and a whole in his own right (*in quantum est quoddam individuum et quoddam totum per
se subsistens*), has a greater natural love for his parents than for his country, since, when
he is considered in these terms, his parents have a greater union ('conjunction') with
him. When he is considered as a part of his country, however, a son should have a
greater love for his country than for his parents. Any human being, in fact, inasmuch
as he is considered, not as part of his country, but as a whole in his own right (*ut quoddam totum per se subsistens et non ut pars patriae*), should love his parents more than his
neighbours (the category under which country would then be classified), since,
within these terms of reference, parents represent the greater point of conjunction.[88]

Remigio's repeated use of the qualification *in quantum est pars*, his insistence on
drawing a distinction between the individual qua individual and the individual qua
part of a community, provides an important check on the characterization of his
political thought as 'corporatist'. For the purposes of remedying the immediate
political situation in Florence, Remigio may well have been primarily interested in
establishing the obligations which he thought were incumbent upon individuals
inasmuch as they were parts of the community, but this does not mean that he denied
or even failed to acknowledge that these individuals had qualities, and activities,
which existed outside of their definition qua parts.

---

    [86] *DBC* pp. 15, 17, 22, 27, 39, 45.   [87] *DBC* pp. 45–7.   [88] *DBC* pp. 44–5.

At the same time, Remigio's account is not without its ambiguities. A particularly problematic passage, for example, occurs in the course of his refutation of counter-proposition [vi]. The part, Remigio writes, can be considered in two ways, inasmuch as it is a part (*in quantum est pars*) and inasmuch as it is something with some sort of existence (*in quantum est res quaedam aliquod esse habens*). Remigio then argues that the good which is natural to the part inasmuch as it is a part (namely the good of the whole) is more potent and more natural (*potius et naturalius*) than the good which is natural to it inasmuch as it is something with some sort of existence.[89] This conclusion has been interpreted to mean that Remigio believed that the common good of a political community is intrinsically superior to *any* private sphere of activity by the individual.[90] However, the immediate context of Remigio's discussion is not an analysis of the political community but an analysis of goodness in the universe, the goodness which is interchangeable with existence (*bonum convertitur cum ente*) and with truth (*bonum convertitur cum veritate*). Defined in these terms, it would appear that this common good, the good of this whole (namely goodness in general), causes and preserves every part of Creation in a way which is superior to the good of each particular thing (*res quaedam*), since the latter depends for its existence and goodness on the presence of existence and goodness in the universe. Remigio's definition of the superiority of the good of the whole as 'more natural' (*naturalius*) is certainly an unusual comparative term to apply to the common good in this context. The use of 'more potent' (*potius*) is more readily explicable—the good of the whole has a greater capacity to cause something to come into being and to preserve it in its existence. This is the metaphysical argument already familiar from both Thomas Aquinas and Godfrey of Fontaines. Aquinas and Godfrey had used the 'corporatist' terminology of part and whole as a means of analysing the metaphysical nature of goodness in the universe and the dependence of every individual thing in Creation. They had both been prepared to apply this imagery to the form which this metaphysical goodness then took in the human community, namely as the happiness of activity in accordance with perfect virtue. However, this did not mean that they were incapable of qualifying such dependence and inclusion as and when the context required it. Remigio is no exception. In this case, therefore, Remigio is careful to concede that some form of existence still pertains to the part qua individual. As such, his argument bears comparison with the distinction between subject and agent to which Remigio chooses to devote the last section of his treatise. In absolute terms (*simpliciter*), he writes, the whole has a greater conjunction with the part qua agent than the part has with itself qua agent because the whole acts as a cause of more things. By participating in moral goodness, in other words, by living in a community, the individual human can become more virtuous by acting virtuously towards a greater number of people.[91] However, within certain terms of reference (*secundum quid*), most notably when the part is considered as a subsisting subject (*suppositum*) rather than in terms

---

[89] *DBC* p. 39.   [90] Cf. Davis, 'Remigio de' Girolami and Dante', 116.
[91] See below, pp. 327–8.

of its essence as a moral agent (*essentia*), the part has a greater conjunction with itself than with its whole.[92]

Remigio was not only acutely aware of the different senses in which 'the individual' can be understood but he also recognized that the analogy of part and whole can apply to the entire range of 'wholes' of which an individual human can form a 'part', including, in this instance, the principle of goodness in the universe. He therefore uses *commune, communitas*, and *civitas* as terms which can describe all the various 'communities' of which every individual is a member, be it the city, the province, the church, the kingdom, the human species, the world, Creation (*cum ens sit communissimum*), and even God.[93] In Remigio's eyes, 'what is in common' and 'whole' are explicitly interchangeable terms (*commune sive totum*).[94] Like Godfrey of Fontaines, Remigio accordingly treats 'common good' (*bonum commune*), 'good of the community' (*bonum communitatis*), and 'good of the city' (*bonum civitatis*) as equivalent phrases. Like Augustine, therefore, Remigio uses the term 'city' to describe the church militant (*civitas ecclesiastica*) and the church triumphant (*civitas Dei*).[95] Remigio's phrase 'the good of the Commune' (*bonum communis*) should be regarded as one more manifestation of the same principle.[96] Indeed, there are several occasions when 'Commune' would clearly be a misleading translation of the term *commune*—when the Roman legate Fabricius is described as *amator sui communis*, for example, or when the natural gregariousness of humankind is described as an inclination to form a city or some other *commune*, or when an individual's joy at the just sentence of damnation is described as an appropriate reaction whatever the size of *commune* (be it the political community or the whole of humankind) which suffers this punishment.[97]

The breadth of Remigio's understanding of the term *commune* is best illustrated, perhaps, when he turns to the three categories in Augustine's *ordo caritatis*, namely love of God, love of self, and love of neighbour. According to Remigio, 'what is in common' can be fitted into this classification when *commune* is understood to apply to the categories of 'God' and 'self' and not just (as counter-proposition [xii] would have it) to the category of neighbour.[98] Remigio agrees that, when the individual is considered as an individual in his own right, 'what is in common' will come under Augustine's heading of 'one's neighbour'. Viewed in these terms, *commune* represents a good which should *not* be loved more than oneself. When the individual is

---

[92] *DBC* p. 49. Cf. Aristotle, *Metaphysics* V.8 1017ᵇ23–26. For Aquinas' interpretation of this passage, see *Ia* 29.2, where he distinguishes between two senses of substance. On the one hand, there is the essence (*essentia*) or 'whatness' of a thing (*quidditas*) which is encapsulated by its definition. On the other, there is the subject (*subiectum*) or the underlying thing (*suppositum*) which subsists in the category of substance. For Godfrey of Fontaines's account, see above, pp. 224–5.

[93] *DBC* pp. 5, 30, 37, 43.   [94] *DBC* p. 23.   [95] *DBC* pp. 45–6.

[96] e.g. *Sermo* 25, p. 482. Cf. N. Rubinstein, 'Political Ideas in Sienese Art: The Frescoes by Ambrogio Lorenzetti and Taddeo di Bartolo in the Palazzo Pubblico', *Journal of the Warburg and Courtauld Institutes*, 21 (1958), 185; Q. Skinner, *Foundations of Modern Political Thought* (2 vols.; Cambridge, 1978), i. 52–9, 74. According to Skinner, Remigio introduced 'in a novel and dramatic style' a 'deliberate ambiguity' into the scholastic notion of the common good by equating *bonum commune* with *bonum communis*.

[97] *DBC* pp. 8, 29, 42.   [98] *DBC* p. 43.

considered as part of a whole, however, Remigio insists that 'what is in common' will then come under the heading of 'self'. Viewed in these terms, *commune* represents a good which *should* be loved more than one's neighbour.[99] The term *commune* can therefore cover both self and neighbour when they are considered as parts of a whole (*in quantum partes eius*). It can also refer to God when He is considered as the common good and the whole good of all things (*commune et totale bonum omnium*). God is a *totale bonum* because, like the whole, He expresses the fundamental rationale for something to be the object of greater love. Everything has a greater natural love for God because He is the cause of every being and goodness, just as parts have a greater love for the whole because the whole is the cause of their own being and goodness.[100] In this sense, the common good should be loved more than the individual good because the common good has a greater likeness (*assimilatio*) to God. Thus, God is sought *communiter* by all parts of Creation; God contains all created things *communiter*; God is present in all created things *communiter*; and God is the cause of all created things *communiter* in the sense that He brings them all into being and preserves them all in existence. This is why Remigio approves of Aristotle's connection between greater divinity and greater love for what is in common (*communitas*). The more something participates in the nature of God, he states, the more love it will have for what is in common (*communitas*).[101] The common good is thus loved second only to God (*post Deum*).[102] Like Thomas Aquinas and Godfrey of Fontaines before him, Remigio accordingly modifies Augustine's hierarchy of the *ordo caritatis* by adding a fourth term, so that it would now read God, common good, self, and neighbour.

Having explained how the common good can be inserted into Augustine's hierarchy of love, Remigio proceeds to demonstrate the various forms which the term *bonum commune* can take for any given human being. The common good can be defined, for example, as the whole which is constituted by all rational creatures, a whole which has greater likeness (*assimilatio*) to God than any of its parts have on their own. Any one of these parts (which, by definition, must include the individual human being, neighbour as well as self) should therefore have a greater natural love for God and, after God, for the whole of reasoning Creation, than it does for any other part or for itself.[103] The common good can also be defined in less comprehensive terms. This is the case, for example, when it takes the form of the universal church. According to the *ordo caritatis*, Remigio writes, any individual will have a greater love first for God, second for the city of God (militant and triumphant), third for himself, and fourth for a fellow-citizen considered in his own right (that is, rather

---

[99] *DBC* pp. 46–7.
[100] *DBC* p. 43, reading *a partibus* for *apertibus*. Cf. James of Viterbo, *Quodlibet* II.20 (above, pp. 215–16).
[101] *DBC* pp. 18–20.   [102] *DBC* p. 43.
[103] *DBC* p. 44, reading *a parte qualibet* for *aperte quamlibet*. Remigio stops short of discussing the relative superiority of the similitude of Creation to the Creator and the similitude of the individual human to God. He opts instead (*DBC* pp. 49–50) for the safer observation that the similitude (*similitudo*) which an individual has to God is greater than the similitude which an individual has to his neighbour. The individual's similitude to God is imitation (*imitatio*), whereas the individual's similitude to his neighbour is participation in something shared. The individual should therefore love God more than his neighbour.

than as the common good personified or as part of the common good).[104] The common good can, finally, take the form of the political community. Preaching a sermon on the death of Corteccione dei Bustichi, for example, Remigio praises the love which the deceased had shown towards (in descending order) God, his community, and his neighbour.[105]

Provided the principle is maintained that more love should be shown towards something which is more common, Remigio's use of the common good clearly covers the complete range of communities of which a human being can form a part. It is on this basis that Remigio concludes that the good of the universal church should be loved more than the good of a kingdom, the good of a kingdom more than the good of a province, the good of a province more than the good of a city and, last of all, the good of a city more than the good of a citizen.[106] This is the light in which Remigio's specifically political deployment of the relationship between part and whole should be viewed. Remigio may have concentrated on the love which Florentines should show to their own city, the particular *commune* of which they were parts, but the underlying principle that greater love should be shown for the common good is, in his view, a principle which should determine their relation to any of the other communities, any of the other 'communes', of which they could be members. Remigio's use of the common good in the context of obedience serves as one final case in point. An individual, he argues, should be prepared to suffer for the sake of the common good. However, the individual is not justified in committing a sin or incurring damnation for the sake of the common good because the love which the individual should have for God will always constitute a superior requirement.[107] The individual should therefore be obedient to the demands of the good of his community but this obligation is always subject to certain reservations. A part should show greater obedience to the whole than to its own will, and a citizen should therefore show greater obedience to the command of his community than to his own will. This does not extend, however, to a command which runs counter to the demands of the good of a even more superior 'community'. Every human being, Remigio writes, has a greater natural love for the good of what is superior to him, namely the good of his community (*sui communis*). The community, after all, is superior in the sense that it possesses greater jurisdiction, it is wiser in the sense that it has clearer perception, and it is better in the sense that it wills what is better with greater affection. However, if a particular community acts contrary to God, then the individual has greater supernatural love for what pertains to God than for what pertains to his community.[108] This is the touchstone of all obedience. When compliance with a command will run counter to *caritas*, Remigio concludes that an individual should disobey without fearing excommunication or any human command.[109] As long as it is a *clear* case of contradiction (the reservation is as important to Remigio as it had been to Henry of Ghent and Godfrey of Fontaines), the superior common good in God has

---

[104] *DBC* p. 46.   [105] *Sermo* 72, p. 500.   [106] *DBC* p. 5.   [107] *DBC* pp. 16, 41.
[108] *DBC* pp. 33–5.   [109] *DBP* p. 66. Cf. *Contra Falsos* 37, pp. 78–9.

greater claims on an individual's obedience than the lesser good of the ecclesiastical community or the lesser good of the political community.

Remigio dei Girolami's theoretical analysis of the relationship between the individual and the common good possesses its own distinctive qualities, most notably its detailed scriptural exegesis of self-sacrifice (Moses, Paul, and Christ) and its vivid illustrations (fire, gravity, piazzas, privvies, eggs, jugs of wine, and piles of coins) of a series of philosophical principles. Remigio thereby succeeds in making his own contribution to the most important of the questions which had been discussed by a generation of scholastic theologians in Paris. By locating the common good firmly within the *ordo caritatis*, Remigio aligns himself with both Thomas Aquinas (the individual should show greater love for the common good than for his own good) and Godfrey of Fontaines (the individual good is included within the common good but this is not the primary goal or final cause of an individual's action). By examining, and in such detail, the precise nature of congruence, dependence, inclusion, similitude, and conjunction, Remigio presents an exhaustive analysis of the degree to which the relationship between the individual and the common good is governed by the relationship between a part and its whole. In doing so, he associates himself with Godfrey of Fontaines (the individual part loves the whole more than itself because it has more unity with the whole than it does with itself) and against James of Viterbo (the individual part loves itself more than the whole because it has greater unity with itself).

Set in this broad intellectual context, it would clearly be doing a grave disservice to Remigio's thought to concentrate exclusively on his application of the corporeal imagery of part and whole to the politics of the city-state. Even in purely theoretical terms, this would be to overlook two significant aspects of his argument. First, there is the range of other 'wholes' in which Remigio sees every individual human being forming a 'part'. Second, there is the series of qualifications to such participation which Remigio repeatedly inserts into his account, most notably the individual considered insofar as he is a part (*inquantum est pars*) and the individual considered as a subsisting subject rather than as a moral agent. Remigio dei Girolami was not a Florentine patriot seeking a rationalization for an all-inclusive, 'corporatist' political philosophy. He was a moralist and a preacher seeking to expound a fundamental principle of love which should guide the actions of every Christian individual. To appeal to the responsibility of the individual Christian to love 'what is in common' in obedience to the *ordo caritatis* is not the same as being forced by factionalism and self-ishness to express a political corporatism which left the individual no 'proper' function of his own beyond his obligation to the political community. A human being should love the common good more than the individual good in whatever form this 'community' might take within the *ordo caritatis*, be it God, Creation, church, kingdom, province, or household, and not just the city-state.

Remigio dei Girolami—Peace and Order

Remigio dei Girolami was interested in more than just an intellectual defence of the principle that greater love should be shown towards the common good as the good on which the individual good depends for its existence. He was also intent on explaining just how this principle could, and should, be translated into the actual conduct of the community he was addressing. Remigio's handling of the scholastic notion of the common good accordingly provides a revealing example of the complexity of the connection between the theoretical analysis of goodness by a scholastic theologian and its practical application to political society. On occasion, Remigio offers his own actions as a model for such a transfer.[1] In requiring that the Priors should consider the common good to be their own good, for example, and that they should demonstrate a greater love for it in accordance with Augustine's *Rule*, Remigio points out that one such manifestation would be a contribution towards the cost of a building which Remigio had just begun for the needs of the Dominican Order and the good of the political community (*nostrum et etiam communis bonum et necessitatem*) and to which he had himself contributed by raising funds from the sale of Dominican books.[2] Likewise, in expressing his own unwillingness to go to Paris to read the *Sentences*, he suggests that it would be offset were it to be subordinated to the good of the Dominican Order.[3] The real force of Remigio's practical application of his analysis of the common good, however, was reserved for Florentine politics.

Remigio's understanding of the relationship between the individual and the common good was conditioned by a particularly turbulent decade in the history of Florence. From 1293 to 1295, political life was dominated by the anti-magnate movement of the *popolani* under Giano della Bella, a conflict which culminated in the proscription of certain noble families from holding public office. After 1295, politics were dominated by bitter familial feuding between the Cerchi and the Donati, the 'White' and 'Black' Guelfs. In May 1300, Boniface VIII appointed Cardinal Matthew of Acquasparta as legate to Florence, a move which he made explicitly in the interests of peace but which only resulted in a series of excommunications. In

---

[1] It is worth pointing out, in this context, the possible personal relevance of giving such prominence to 2 Maccabees 4: 4–6 (above, p. 298). Onias was a priest in authority over a city, whose actions in seeking outside assistance from a king in order to put an end to internal political disruption are explicitly distinguished from betrayal.

[2] *Sermo* 28 (G. Salvadori and V. Federici, 'I Sermoni d'occasione, le sequenze e i ritmi di Remigio Girolami Fiorentino', *Scritti Vari di Filologia a Ernesto Monaco*; Rome, 1901), p. 484. Cf. *Contra Falsos Ecclesie Professores* 63, ed. F. Tamburini (Rome, 1981), p. 189.

[3] *Sermo* 35, pp. 486–7.

1301, Boniface VIII invited into Italy Philip IV's brother, Charles of Valois, in order to restore Tuscany to 'peace and a good state', a move which merely resulted in the expulsion of the Whites and the division of the victorious Donati into further partisan factions. In March 1304, Benedict XI sent Cardinal Nicholas of Prato on another mission to establish 'peace' within Florence but, within three months, the legate was issuing an interdict against the city.[4]

These events form a critical backdrop to Remigio's political writings. *De Bono Communi*, for example, was composed in 1302, in the immediate aftermath of the intervention of Charles of Valois, *De Bono Pacis* in 1304, after (or possibly during) the embassy of Nicholas of Prato. Remigio's 'theory' of the common good was inextricably bound up with its application to this political reality. The connection is often tangible. If faction was the dominant feature of Florentine politics in this period, then faction was the particular vice against which Remigio ranged his account of the priority of love for the common good. This was his theme in 1294–5, for example, when he delivered a sermon in the presence of the Priors setting out the duties which should guide their tenure of office. Expounding Judges 19: 30 ('Form an opinion and decide in common what should be done'), Remigio argues that 'in common' should be understood in the sense of advancing the interests of the community (*ad communis promotionem*). Priors should therefore decide what to do, not for the sake of the good of one particular person or household, nor of one particular group of people, but for the sake of the common good (*pro communi bono*), the good of the political community (*pro bono communis*).[5] In 1302, Remigio's message was the same. Dissension, discord, and disordered love were destroying the unity and harmony which were necessary to preserve not just Florence but any city in existence.[6]

As a lesson on showing love for the common good, Remigio's exhortation fell on deaf ears. Indeed, Remigio's pastoral and familial involvement in Florentine politics appears to have left him all too aware of the disparity between his own ideal of moral goodness and the sinful reality of the behaviour of his fellow citizens. The consequences for his approach to the notion of the common good were profound. Of his two political treatises, *De Bono Communi* was a general appeal to fulfil the demands of the *ordo caritatis* within human society, whereas *De Bono Pacis* was a precise demonstration of how this principle could be put into practice within a bitterly divided community. This shift in emphasis suggests more than just a difference in approach between the theoretical and the practical. For Remigio to discuss the common good

---

[4] Dino Compagni, *Chronicle of Florence*, trans. D. E. Bornstein (Philadelphia, 1986), III.1, 4–7, pp. 63, 66–70. More generally, see G. Holmes, *Florence, Rome and the Origins of the Renaissance* (Oxford, 1986), ch. 7. Cf. M. B. Becker, 'A Study in Political Failure: The Florentine Magnates 1280–1343', *Mediaeval Studies*, 27 (1965), 246–308; J. M. Najemy, *Corporatism and Consensus in Florentine Electoral Politics 1280–1400* (Chapel Hill, 1982), chs. 1–2.

[5] *Sermo* 25, p. 482. Cf. C. T. Davis, 'An Early Florentine Political Theorist: Fra Remigio de' Girolami', *Proceedings of the American Philosophical Society*, 104 (1960), 666–7; J. K. Hyde, 'Contemporary Views on Faction and Civil Strife in Thirteenth and Fourteenth Century Italy', in L. Martines (ed.), *Violence and Disorder in Italian Cities 1200–1500* (Berkeley, 1972), 282.

[6] *De Bono Communi*, ed. M. C. de Matteis, in *La 'teologia politica communale' di Remigio de' Girolami* (Bologna, 1977), pp. 3, 18, 28–9; *De Bono Pacis* (ibid.) p. 62.

in two different ways in two separate treatises also raises the issue of how he understood the connection between their two eponymous 'goods'.

Set in the context of late thirteenth- and early fourteenth-century Florentine politics, Remigio's translation of the all-embracing common good of *De Bono Communi* into the mutual benefit of peace of *De Bono Pacis* was, in many ways, a perfectly natural move to make. As a preacher at Santa Maria Novella, Remigio was addressing a community whose 'peace' was the explicit pretext for both the intervention of Charles of Valois in 1301 and the mediation of Remigio's fellow Dominican, Nicholas of Prato, in 1304. As a scholastic theologian, however, Remigio would also have been familiar with the significance of moving from a definition of the common good in terms of love and moral goodness to a definition of the good of the political community in terms of peace and material security. Set in the context of late thirteenth- and early fourteenth-century political thought, in other words, Remigio's two treatises involve more than just Remigio's view of the relationship between the moral ideal of the Christian community and the political reality of early fourteenth-century Florence. *De Bono Communi* and *De Bono Pacis* also raise the question of Remigio's understanding of the relationship between an Aristotelian ideal of happiness, of activity in accordance with perfect virtue, and an Augustinian reality of a *remedium peccati*, of containing the effects of original sin. In both cases, bitter experience appears to have taught Remigio that the primary good which could be secured by the exercise of political authority in human society was peace. This conclusion, however, raises one further question. If the goal of authority in the political community is simply to secure the material benefit of peace, how is this connected to the moral goodness which is still to be secured by individuals in the ecclesiastical community and in the community of heaven? In the immediate aftermath of the disputes between Philip IV of France and Pope Boniface VIII, this was far from being a purely theoretical question. Remigio's account of the earthly goal of humankind may have been produced by his recognition of the imperfect connection between moral ideal and practical reality, but it also conditioned his analysis of the relationship between the temporal and the spiritual power.

De Bono Pacis is the result of Remigio's investigation of the practical political consequences which should follow from the demonstration of greater love for the common good. The core of this treatise is therefore an impassioned appeal for every citizen to sacrifice their individual good in order to achieve the good of the community, to give up their property in the interests of securing peace. This is Remigio's response to a very specific question. Does the establishment of peace provide sufficient justification for overlooking the injuries and damages which have been inflicted and suffered by hostile cities and, if so, can this be done without the consent of all the individuals within each community and even against the will of some of those people who have suffered loss?[7] Such precise phrasing immediately ties Remigio's discussion to the

---

[7] *DBP* p. 55.

negotiations which surrounded the papal peace initiative between March and June 1304, when the cardinal legate, Nicholas of Prato, brought into the city a group of leading 'White' exiles whose property had been confiscated in 1302.[8]

Given that his nephew, Girolamo, was among those who had suffered confiscation, Remigio's own views on the matter are judiciously even-handed. According to *De Bono Pacis*, the common good of peace should take precedence over injury to private property. In Remigio's opinion, however, any remission of the legal penalties which would normally apply to the perpetrators of such injury should not be extended to those cases where the plundered property is still in the possession of the spoliator, where the injured party is known, and especially where this individual is in need. Thus, if the remission of legal penalties is to be extended to cover all injuries, including these exceptional cases, then Remigio insists that the needy injured party must be compensated from public revenues.[9] With this important proviso, Remigio's argument is unequivocal. The consent or will of the aggrieved parties themselves should provide no serious obstacle to such a settlement. Even though it amounts to the removal of an individual's property, strictly speaking it should not even be considered as an injurious or unjust action, nor even as a case of inflicting on a blameless individual the experience of suffering evil (*malum poenae*). Many benefits, Remigio points out, can be conferred on people who are unwilling to receive them. The deprivation of an individual's property for the sake of peace is a case in point because the attainment of peace, as the good of the community, is a greater good for that particular person than if his property were not taken away in this manner. Remigio accordingly takes the opportunity to summarize the theoretical argument already outlined in *De Bono Communi*. The good of the whole is a greater good for the part than its own individual good inasmuch as it is a part of that whole (*in quantum pars est*). The existence of the part, inasmuch as it is a part, depends on the existence of the whole and, as a result, every good which follows from this existence is also dependent on the good of the whole. Personal property can therefore legitimately be removed for the sake of the good of peace even if this takes place against the will of those who have previously been in possession of it.[10]

Remigio makes it clear from the start of his treatise that the property under discussion belongs to the church as well as to the laity. As a supplement to those authorities already listed in *De Bono Communi*, therefore, Remigio appends a catalogue of canon law texts which deal with precisely this eventuality. Starting from the premiss that peace is the goal towards which war is ordered, for example, an argument which is based on Aristotle, Augustine, and Gratian,[11] Remigio maintains that the church is not immune from the general obligation to contribute property for the defence of the community or for the establishment of peace.[12] Peace, he states, is the good of the church, and an ecclesiastical good should be preferred to a temporal good. Thus,

---

[8] Compagni, *Chronicle* III.7, pp. 69–70.   [9] *DBP* p. 71.

[10] *DBP* p. 63.   [11] *DBP* pp. 57, 59.

[12] *DBP* p. 57. Cf. *Decretum* II.23.8.22 (Friedberg, i. 961); *Decr. Greg. IX* III.49.2 (Friedberg, ii. 654); *Decr. Greg. IX* V.36.8 (Friedberg, ii. 879).

whilst canon law may prohibit the laity from actually controlling what belongs to the church, it makes an exception when the common benefit is at stake. This is what guided the ruling on taxation given by the Fourth Lateran Council. Bishops and clergy may regard the need or benefit (*necessitas vel utilitas*) to be so great that they decide, under no external pressure, that churches should provide assistance (*subsidia*) in order to secure the common good (*communes utilitates vel necessitates*) when the laity is unable to do so.[13] Moreover, if churches are already bound by the obligation incumbent upon all property-holders to contribute towards the building and repair of bridges, then it is even more appropriate for ecclesiastical goods to be given to the laity for the sake of peace.[14] In Remigio's view, it does not lower the status of the church to make such a contribution. On the contrary, it emphasizes its elevated position, since no other good can equal the common good of peace for which such a sacrifice is made.[15]

Remigio's discussion of canon law served a pressing purpose. In May 1304, Benedict XI modified the terms of *Clericis laicos*, softening Boniface VIII's insistence that clergy who contributed goods to the laity without express papal approval, and laymen who received these goods, should be declared excommunicate. According to Benedict XI, such a penalty would henceforth apply only to those who make such demands and to those who assist and encourage these exactions. It would not apply to those who give their goods freely nor to those who receive what has been donated in this way.[16] *Clericis laicos* had been at the heart of the first dispute between Philip IV and Boniface VIII. It continued to colour the king's relationship to the material property of the church in both France and England.[17] *De Bono Pacis* reveals that it also had a particular relevance for Florence. It is thus to the terms of Benedict XI's exception that Remigio appeals. Excommunication, he argues, is incurred only when goods have been given to the laity under duress. It should not be incurred by clergy who have consented to pay of their own accord, nor by laymen who have agreed to accept the goods of the church as gifts freely offered. According to Remigio, therefore, whilst it may be a requirement of both canon law and the *ordo caritatis* that the church (that is, the pope together with his cardinals) should always be consulted, the outcome of such consultation should be a formality given the particular obligation of the church to secure the common good of peace.[18] As a result, the pope's decision should normally be obeyed without question (*sine dubio*). However, Remigio points out that there may be occasions on which this will not be the case. Remigio is careful to insist that it must be known for certain that obeying the pope's decision would run counter to the demands of *caritas*. Nevertheless, with this caveat, he states that, on these occasions, individual

---

[13] *DBP* p. 65; *Decr. Greg. IX* III.49.4 (Friedberg, ii. 654); ed. N. P. Tanner, *Decrees of the Ecumenical Councils* (2 vols.; London, 1990), i. 255 (above, p. 191).

[14] *DBP* p. 65. Cf. *DBP* pp. 69–70.   [15] *DBP* p. 66.

[16] *DBP* p. 66; *Extravagantes Communes* III.13 (Friedberg, ii. 1287–8). Cf. *Clericis laicos*, in *Les Registres de Boniface VIII*, ed. G. Digard, M. Faucon, A. Thomas, and R. Fawtier (4 vols.; Rome, 1884–1939) no. 1567, cols. 584–5.

[17] See above, pp. 247–8.   [18] *Decr. Greg. IX* II.1.13 (Friedberg, ii. 242–4), col. 244 (above, p. 270).

Christians should fear neither human command nor spiritual excommunication but simply disobey their ecclesiastical superiors. The obedience of the individual Christian to those in authority in the church is always conditional upon the latter being in harmony with Christ. When they are not, then God should be obeyed rather than man.[19] The preservation of peace constitutes just such an eventuality. If it is a case of material sacrifice for the common good of peace, then there should be no possibility of an individual refusing to contribute ecclesiastical goods to the laity even if this does mean disobeying those in authority in the church. No action should in any way contravene *caritas*, and the effect of *caritas* is peace.[20] God and divine law, Remigio concludes, place the good of peace above every other temporal good.[21]

Viewed as Remigio's response to a specific series of political events, the argument put forward in *De Bono Pacis* fulfils two immediate aims. In the first instance, it is designed to urge his fellow-citizens to set aside their legitimate grievances in the interests of securing the greater good of the whole community. In the second instance, it represents a call to his fellow-clergy to disobey all those ecclesiastical authorities who were forbidding the cession of material goods for the sake of peace.[22] Remigio's response to the issue of property disputes, in other words, is to underline the need for individual Florentines, clergy as well as laity, to sacrifice their temporal goods in the interests of peace. As a practical, political exhortation, the argument of *De Bono Pacis* has a clear theoretical foundation in *De Bono Communi*. Viewed as political theory, however, it has been seen in a more sinister light, as a sanction for the use of force to expropriate personal property for the 'good of the state', as a call to neglect or even harm the individual good and the claims of justice in order to secure the 'interest of the state'.[23]

It is certainly true that, in suggesting that the good of one particular individual could be 'neglected' for the sake of peace in the community, Remigio introduces a rather surprising modification to his analysis of the corporeal analogy. When a doctor secures the common good of the body, Remigio writes, he preserves the good of any limb *as far as he is able*. Likewise, when a ruler preserves the good of the body politic (*corpus populi*), he ought to preserve unharmed the good of any citizen *as far as he is able*.[24] The reservation which is implicit in the phrase *quantum potest* certainly strikes a different note to the principle which had been such a prominent feature of *De Bono Communi*, namely that the individual good must be included within the common good. Different but not necessarily contradictory. It was a scholastic commonplace that a diseased limb could, if necessary, be amputated for the sake of the health of the whole body.[25] *De Bono Communi*, moreover, maintains, not that an

---

[19] *DBP* p. 60.   [20] *DBP* p. 66.   [21] *DBP* p. 65.   [22] *DBP* p. 60.

[23] Davis, 'An Early Florentine Political Theorist', 670; id., 'Remigio de' Girolami and Dante: A Comparison of their Conceptions of Peace', *Studi Danteschi*, 36 (1959), 115, 118.

[24] *DBP* p. 71. For the analogy between ruler and doctor, see e.g. Seneca, *De Ira*, in *Dialogorum Libri Duodecim*, ed. L. D. Reynolds (Oxford, 1977), I.6.1–4, pp. 45–6; Aquinas, *Summa contra Gentiles* III.146; John of Paris, *De Potestate Regia et Papali*, ed. J. Leclercq XVII (Paris, 1942), p. 227.

[25] *DBC* p. 35; above, pp. 111–12.

individual should avoid suffering evil (*malum poenae*), but that an individual should not commit evil (*malum culpae*). Evil can still be tolerated for the sake of a greater good, the common good.[26] *De Bono Pacis*, meanwhile, makes it clear that, strictly speaking, the compulsory sacrifice of material goods does not constitute an innocent individual suffering evil. It is, instead, an expression of the *ordo caritatis*, since peace is the effect of love. Every individual is therefore obliged to sacrifice his material goods for the sake of love, just as the hand should not keep food for itself but must give it to the whole body.[27] As an appeal for self-sacrifice, Remigio's exhortation may have been made 'somewhat unrealistically'.[28] As a counsel of perfection, it was nothing less than an appeal to an individual's overriding Christian obligation to obey the *ordo caritatis*, the divine law, and the will of God.

Viewed as political theory, the importance of Remigio's exposition of the *ordo caritatis* extends further than the immediate question of sacrificing material property for the sake of peace. A connection between love and peace is fundamental to Remigio's understanding of the very nature of 'community' and he detects its presence in everything which he considered to be a community, not just the city-state but also the household, the church, heaven, and even God. When the good of the church is defined as a 'pacific union', for example, Remigio describes how it consists of the good of the faithful in the same way that the good of the body consists of the peace of its members, and the good of the household consists of the peace of its parts.[29] Defining the good of the political community as peace, however, is not the conclusion which might reasonably have been expected to come from a Dominican theologian so familiar with the writings of both Aristotle and Aquinas. Indeed, one of the most striking features of Remigio's political thought, in *De Bono Communi* as well as in *De Bono Pacis*, is a reluctance to identify the common good of the political community as anything *other* than the good of peace. In *De Bono Communi*, the common good of the multitude is 'indisputably' (*nimirum*) peace, just as bodily health is 'without doubt' (*certe*) the common good of the whole body.[30] In *De Bono Pacis*, peace is the good of the community; it is the highest good and goal of the multitude, just as health is the highest good of the body.[31] Thus, whilst Remigio is happy to quote Aristotle's statement that humankind is, by nature, a sociable and political animal, he insists that the good towards which such association is ordered is peace. According to Remigio, the common good of peace (*bonum commune et pacis*) cannot be equalled by any other good.[32] Peace is a divine good (*pax est bonum Dei et ad Deum pertinens*).[33] Peace is the goal which all things seek.[34] Peace is the proper object of the will because peace is the

---

[26] *DBC* p. 16. Cf. *DBP* p. 57, where Remigio's one appeal to civil rather than canon law concerns the toleration of prostitution and usury for the sake of the common good, an argument which he had chosen not to discuss in any detail in *De Bono Communi*.

[27] *DBC* p. 35.   [28] Davis, 'Remigio de' Girolami and Dante', 118.   [29] *DBP* p. 64.

[30] *DBC* pp. 3–4.   [31] *DBP* pp. 55–6, 61. Cf. *DBP* p. 67.   [32] *DBP* pp. 62, 66.   [33] *DBP* p. 55.

[34] *DBP* p. 66, quoting Augustine, *De Civitate Dei*, ed. B. Dombart and A. Kalb (*CCSL* 47–8), XIX.12, p. 675; pseudo-Dionysius, *De Divinis Nominibus*, ed. P. Chevallier, *Dionysiaca: Recueil donnant l'ensemble des traductions latines des ouvrages attribués au Denys de l'Aréopage* (2 vols.; Bruges, 1937, 1950) XI.1, i. 495–8.

effect of love, and love is the characteristic activity of the will.[35] The absence of the Aristotelian life of virtue could not be more marked.[36]

When Remigio identifies the good of the political community as peace, moreover, he adds one further element to his definition. In a sermon on Job 25: 2 ('Power and awe belong to Him who establishes harmony in the heights'), Remigio maintains that the highest good of the city is the union or conjunction of people's hearts and wills when they are directed towards the same objective.[37] Remigio calls this union 'harmony' (*concordia*). Just as peace is the goal of all rulers, he concludes, so unanimity, that is, the harmony of a common will, should be the goal of the Priors.[38] In *De Bono Pacis*, it is this harmony of wills which is specified alongside peace in the opening words of the treatise: *quaeritur utrum pro bono pacis et concordie* . . .[39] It is this harmony which also enables Remigio to attribute peace to the nature of God. When the Trinity is understood in terms of its component elements, he argues, unity can be ascribed to the Father, equality to the Son, and the harmony of unity and equality to the Holy Spirit. Since peace is the effect of love, this harmony of the Holy Spirit can be described as the highest love (*summa caritas*).[40]

Remigio's definition of the common good as peace has a clear source of inspiration. The firm association of love with peace and harmony (*pax et concordia*) was a formula with which he was familiar, not from Aristotle, but from Augustine. Remigio is quick to acknowledge the debt, extending the standard appeal to 1 Corinthians 13 and Augustine's *Rule* in order to include book XIX of *De Civitate Dei*: 'the good of peace is so great that even in earthly and mortal concerns nothing is heard with greater pleasure, nothing is coveted with greater desire, and finally nothing better can be found'.[41] In identifying peace as the good of the political community, therefore, Remigio defines it as the peace which is produced by harmonious order, or ordered agreement, concerning what is to be commanded and what is to be obeyed (*imperandi ordinata atque obediendi concordia civium*).[42] This is, once again, a quotation from Augustine.[43] It occurs in book XIX of *De Civitate Dei* in a passage from which Remigio quotes the first and last phrases as a continuous sentence:

---

[35] *DBP* p. 66.

[36] Cf. Davis, 'Remigio de' Girolami and Dante', 110. Davis admits that Remigio is departing from Aristotelian terminology when he defines common welfare as peace, but argues that the 'positive conception' of peace as something which involves justice and love is 'obviously very similar' to acting in accordance with virtue. For Remigio's fusion of Aristotelian and Augustinian principles, see Matteis, *La 'teologia politica communale'*, pp. cxxiv–cxxvii.

[37] *Sermo* 27, p. 482.

[38] *Sermo* 25, p. 482; *Sermo* 19, p. 480. Cf. *Contra Falsos* 18, p. 42.   [39] *DBP* p. 55.

[40] *DBP* p. 58; Augustine, *De Doctrina Christiana*, ed. R. P. H. Green (Oxford, 1995), I.5, p. 16; *De Trinitate*, ed. W. J. Mountain (*CCSL* 50), VII.3.6, p. 254. Cf. *DBP* p. 66, where the peace of humankind is defined as the Son of God (Ephesians 2: 14).

[41] *DBP* p. 57; Augustine, *De Civitate Dei* XIX.11, p. 675. Cf. D. R. Lesnick, *Preaching in Medieval Florence: The Social World of Franciscan and Dominican Spirituality* (Athens, Ga., 1989), 104–5.

[42] *DBP* pp. 62–3.

[43] *DBP* p. 60. For the importance of Augustine to Remigio's argument, see Matteis, *La 'teologia politica communale'*, pp. cxlv–cxlvi.

The peace of the body is the ordered proportioning of its parts, the peace of the irrational soul is the ordered repose of its appetites, the peace of the rational soul is the ordered agreement of knowledge and action, the peace of body and soul is the ordered life and well-being of something living, the peace between mortal human and God is ordered obedience in faith under the eternal law, the peace of humans is ordered agreement, the peace of the household is the ordered agreement in command and obedience of those who live together, the peace of the city is the ordered agreement of citizens concerning what is to be commanded and what is to be obeyed, the peace of the heavenly city is the supremely ordered and harmonized fellowship in the enjoyment of God and in the enjoyment of each other in God. The peace of all things is the tranquillity of order and order is the arrangement of equal and unequal things which gives to each its due position.[44]

Three features of Augustine's exposition of *pax et concordia* appear to have struck a particular chord with Remigio. His immediate response to this passage is to pick out the phrase 'tranquillity of order' (*tranquillitas ordinis*) as a term which describes the good of the whole world. In support of this observation, he cites Aristotle's analogy of the army from book XII of the *Metaphysics*—all things are ordered towards one another as well as towards their ultimate goal.[45] More oblique, but no less important, is the connection which Remigio then makes between the order which gives each thing its due position and the justice which gives each person their due.[46] Peace and justice are concepts which Remigio regards as closely related. This is, in itself, a thoroughly conventional association but Remigio draws particular attention to the *causal* relation of one to the other. Thus, in *De Bono Communi*, the common good of the multitude is acquired and preserved by means of justice, a process which Remigio illustrates with Isaiah 32: 17: 'the fruit [*opus*] of justice is peace'.[47] He uses the same biblical text in two sermons to the Priors of Florence. If they want to rule in peace, he argues, then, according to Isaiah, justice must be done. Only justice and virtue can restore harmony to the city since, without justice, no city can be ruled well.[48]

It is the third element in Remigio's understanding of book XIX of *De Civitate Dei* which is, perhaps, the most intriguing. According to Aquinas, good could be defined in two senses. Either something is truly and essentially good (*vere et simpliciter bonum*) or it has a certain resemblance to good (*bonum secundum quamdam similitudinem*).[49] Like Albertus Magnus and James of Viterbo, therefore, Remigio acknowledges that human communities can exhibit a 'bad' as well as a 'good' form of peace. Peace, he writes, can be understood in a proper and true sense (*proprie et vere*) or it can be understood metaphorically (*metaphorice*). In its true sense, peace and order will always be part and parcel of moral goodness in the same way that 'there is no peace for the wicked' (Isaiah 57: 21). In its metaphorical sense, however, peace does not imply the presence of moral goodness. Remigio picks up Aquinas' reference

---

[44] Augustine, *De Civitate Dei* XIX.13, pp. 678–9.
[45] *DBP* p. 60; Aristotle, *Metaphysics* XII.10 1075ª11–15.
[46] For Remigio's use of this principle, see Davis, 'An Early Florentine Political Theorist', 668.
[47] *DBC* p. 4.   [48] *Sermo* 24, p. 481; 27, p. 483. Cf. *DBC* p. 9.   [49] Aquinas, *IIaIIae* 45.1, 47.13.

to Aristotle's claim that there can be such a thing as a 'perfect' thief, and adds his own illustration from the Bible—according to Wisdom 14: 22, those who are ignorant of God can still use peace to describe the numerous evils by which their lives are characterized.[50] Remigio's immediate purpose in drawing a distinction between these two senses of peace is to defend himself against the argument that peace cannot be the highest good for the community, since God expressly took it away from the people of Israel (Jeremiah 16: 5). God, Remigio responds, removes peace according to the dual action of divine providence. Either good peace is removed from humans causally, that is, as a means of punishing people for their wickedness, or it is removed permissively, that is, by simply allowing sinful people to fall into an evil peace (*mala pax*).[51] In more general terms, Remigio's distinction between these two senses of peace establishes a firm connection with his discussion of the notion of utility or benefit.

In Augustine's terminology, *utilitas* describes the temporal peace which is 'used' by members of both the City of God and the Earthly City. Although each community makes use of this peace from radically different motives (love of God and love of self respectively), it still marks a certain conjunction of wills towards a benefit which is shared for the duration of this temporal life (*communis utilitas*).[52] In Aristotle's terminology, *utilitas* describes the second of the three categories of goodness which can be the object of love, namely honour, benefit, and pleasure.[53] Aristotle's tripartite division is one to which Remigio turns on several occasions. In arguing that the Priors should exhibit a harmony of wills, for example, he glosses the object of their love, the common good, as the 'benefit, pleasure, and honour' of the community.[54] In *De Bono Communi*, 'honour, pleasure, and benefit' are cited as three of the four reasons why individuals have a natural love for other humans. Individuals love one another, according to Remigio, either because of the virtue which exists in the individual loved, or because of the pleasure which is derived from beautiful goods, or because of the temporal benefit which results (*temporalis utilitas*), or, finally, because of the similitude (*similitudo*) of the individuals concerned.[55] In expounding the third of these alternatives, Remigio suggests that the temporal benefit which individuals derive from their natural love for one another is indicative of human imperfection, because something which is loved for its benefit (*utilitas*) is loved for the sake of the good which it brings to the individual loving. According to Aristotle, a love which is founded on benefit is characteristic of the love which is exhibited by old people. According to Remigio, this can therefore serve as an indictment of his own era. Everybody, he laments, now seems to love one another out of self-interest. Christians love Saracens and Jews in the hope that they will be rewarded by them, whilst Saracens and Jews love Christians for the same reason. Cities, meanwhile, love one another only for the sake of mutual assistance in war and other beneficial acts which each of them will perform.[56]

---

[50] *DBP* p. 59; Aristotle, *Metaphysics* V.16 1021ᵇ17–19.   [51] *DBP* p. 59. Cf. *Sermo* 27, p. 482.
[52] See above, pp. 19–21.   [53] Aristotle, *Ethics* VIII.2 1155ᵇ17–21.
[54] *Sermo* 25, p. 482.   [55] *DBC* pp. 24–30.   [56] *DBC* pp. 28–9.

Remigio's discussion of benefit rather than honour, of mutual advantage rather than moral worth, is a striking feature of *De Bono Communi*. Remigio still makes a point of arguing that, even on the level of benefit rather than moral worth, the citizen should love the community more than he loves himself, because the benefit of a part depends on the benefit of its whole.[57] The part, he explains, shows greater consideration for its whole than for itself because the whole is the source of greater honour, greater pleasure, and greater benefit. An individual should work more for the sake of the community than for his own sake because the community is the source of greater reward, greater glory, and greater peace (*quies*).[58] Remigio sees proof of this in the natural origins of human society when individuals gathered together to form a community for the sake of their own benefit (*utilitas propria*). The human community originated, therefore, as a means of supplying the material deficiencies of life which could not be made up by any one person living on their own. One individual provided what another was lacking, be it shoes, housing, clothes, agriculture, weapons, or anything else which human life required. With the destruction of a community, such benefits will inevitably disappear. An individual citizen will not be able to be of benefit either to himself or to another citizen; he will only be a source of harm. This is the fate which Remigio holds out for Florence. Gone are the days when her reputation attracted foreigners eager to deposit their money in the hope of securing temporal benefits (*utilitates temporales*) and their own financial gain.[59]

To conclude that Remigio considers that the common good achieved by the political community is the material benefit of peace, a benefit which can be 'used' by both good and wicked individuals alike, does not mean that *whenever* he employs the term *utilitas* it denotes an exclusively material benefit. In *De Bono Pacis*, after all, 'benefit' and 'common benefit' are employed because they are the terms which are used by the texts which form the core of Remigio's discussion, namely canon law. Nevertheless, the fact that Remigio associates *utilitas* so closely with peace suggests that the equation of peace with temporal benefit is of some importance to his political thinking. If *utilitas* does carry a more morally neutral connotation than *bonum*, then the implications for Remigio's understanding of the common good of the political community are considerable. They are best illustrated by Remigio's reaction to that most Aristotelian of connections, between the common good of the political community and activity in accordance with perfect virtue.

Although Remigio refuses to adopt Aristotle's definition of the goal of the political community as the life of virtue, this does not mean that he believes that virtue is not necessary for life within the political community. Far from it. Remigio is well aware of Augustine's definition of virtue as an order of love (*ordo amoris*),[60] and it is on this basis that he argues that no political action can be performed well or virtuously in the absence of correctly ordered love. Unanimity amongst the Priors, therefore, derives from correctly ordered love, just as the multitude of believers in the

---

[57] *DBC* p. 29.   [58] *DBC* p. 35.   [59] *DBC* pp. 28–9.
[60] Augustine, *De Civitate Dei* XV.22, p. 488.

early church were of one heart as well as one mind (Acts 4: 32).[61] Since the love which is directed towards the common good is also defined as correctly ordered love, this too must be classified as an act of virtue.[62] Remigio's view of the relationship between virtue and the common good, however, is not straightforward. In his discussion of book IX of the *Ethics*, for example, Remigio observes that the highest good of the citizen is the good of virtue, but he then associates it with good for the individual rather than with the common good. The good of virtue, he argues, may be the formal cause of an individual's action but it is, in turn, included within a higher good, the primary goal of this action, namely the common good.[63] Remigio does not specify, in this context, how this common good differs from the good of virtue. He does raise the issue, however, when he discusses the love which one human being has for another. According to Aristotle, he states, the love of true friendship is exhibited, not for the sake of any benefit secured by the individual doing the loving, but for the sake of the virtue which is possessed by the individual being loved.[64] On the assumption that the individual should therefore exhibit more love for someone (or something) which possesses a greater degree of virtue, Remigio concludes that the citizen should have a greater natural love for the city than for himself. Remigio gives two reasons. Not only does the city possess a greater quantity of virtue than one citizen but it also enables the participant in the community to become, in human terms, more virtuous than if he were to live a life of solitude.[65] It is this last observation which prompts Remigio to discuss the relationship between virtue and the common good.

In an eloquent statement of the advantages of living in association with one's fellow human beings, Remigio opens with the model of education which had proved so attractive to both Albertus Magnus and Godfrey of Fontaines. Individuals on their own, Remigio states, can acquire wisdom through discovery (*inventio*), but, in a political community, they can also acquire it through instruction (*disciplina*). The individual can profit from common practice with other students (*exercitium*), or, if he is a teacher himself, from his own instruction of others. Because one person possesses what another person lacks, living in a community provides mutual assistance and cooperation in everything which is necessary for the gaining of wisdom—intellectual ability, memory, books, and funding. Whilst Remigio can therefore accept the force of Aristotle's statement that the solitary individual is more self-sufficient or suited (*magis aptus*) to the contemplation of wisdom, he parries it by quoting Aristotle's additional observation that humans have a greater capacity (*potentiores*) to think and to act when they are in the company of friends.[66]

If this conclusion holds true for intellectual virtue, then, in Remigio's view, it applies to moral and theological virtue as well. By living in a community, individuals can also become more morally and theologically virtuous. This occurs in two ways. In the first instance, individuals can be stimulated to virtue and good deeds by means

---

[61] *Sermo* 28, pp. 483–4.   [62] *DBC* p. 8.   [63] *DBC* p. 38.
[64] Aristotle, *Ethics* VIII.3 1156b7–17.   [65] *DBC* p. 25.
[66] *DBC* p. 26; Aristotle, *Ethics* VIII.1 1155a15–16, X.7 1177a32–b1.

of the example of those people who are more virtuous than themselves. In the second instance, individuals can increase their moral and theological virtue by putting these virtues into practice, in the same way that people will become more correct, more generous, just, prudent, and also more loving, if they exercise these virtues towards others rather than towards themselves. Remigio quotes book X of the *Ethics* ('the just person needs people towards whom, and with whom, he can act justly, and the temperate person, brave person and each of the others is in the same position') and pairs it with Luke 12: 33 ('no one lights a lamp and puts it in a place where it will be hidden. Instead he puts it on a stand so that those who come in may see the light'). Intellectual, moral, and also theological virtue, Remigio writes, are not only all present in human society but all of them are better practised in common than in isolation. The conjunction 'and also' or 'and even' (*et etiam*) may represent an acknowledgement that the addition of theological virtue to this list will be the source of some surprise to his audience.[67] Remigio himself, however, is quite clear about the justification for its inclusion. Love (*caritas*) is a gracious gift of God but it is also a disposition to be exercised towards one's fellow-humans. Although *caritas* is infused directly by God and imparted through his grace, it is still a disposition which is developed through an individual's own actions and which is better achieved in a multitude than in one person. According to Matthew 18: 20, after all, 'where two or three come together [*congregati sunt*] in my name, there am I with them'.[68]

In Remigio's account, virtue, peace, and harmony are all consequences of correctly ordered love within the human community, they are all the result of individuals living as Christians in an earthly society. Of the three, however, only peace and harmony are included in Remigio's definition of the exercise of *authority* in the political community. To argue that the moral, intellectual, and theological virtues should be exhibited by individuals within the political community is clearly not the same as arguing that the authority of the temporal power is directly responsible for the moral, intellectual, and theological virtue of its subjects. For Remigio, the common good secured by the political community is always the goal of peace. When virtue does enter the equation, it is introduced as a function of the association of individuals with their fellow human beings and not as a defining goal of political authority. This point needs to be underlined and not just because of the light which it can shed on Remigio's conception of the relationship between a Christian ideal and a Florentine political reality, or between an Aristotelian ideal and an Augustinian reality. It also provides a critical perspective from which to judge Remigio's analysis of the relationship between the temporal power and the spiritual power. Giles of Rome, for

---

[67] Throughout his discussion of the advantages of life in a community (*DBC* p. 25), Remigio is careful to insert the qualification 'in human terms' (*humaniter loquendo*). Without any inconsistency, therefore, he can also adopt the suggestion of book X of the *Ethics* and book I of the *Politics* that the contemplative individual should be considered, not in human terms, but divine. Defined in these terms, the superiority of the solitary life does not express the preference of love for the individual over love for the community but the preference of love of God over love of any created thing (*DBC* p. 47).

[68] *DBC* pp. 26–7.

example, would have concurred that the goal of the political community is peace. For Giles, this was a means of demonstrating that the authority of the temporal ruler facilitated, was instrumental to, and acted as a bridle for, the exercise of authority by the Christian church. For Remigio to identify the goal of the political community as peace rather than virtue, in other words, raises the question of whether he too should be read in the same light.[69]

Insofar as the relationship between the temporal and the spiritual power is discussed at all in *De Bono Communi*, Remigio's argument gives little away. His certainty (*indubitanter sequitur*) that every citizen should place the common good of the city above his own good is extended to the obligation which is incumbent upon every Christian to prefer the common good of the whole church. Rather than compare these two obligations, however, they are treated in parallel and the connection between them restricted to a simple 'and' (*et*).[70] Similarly, the list of communities to which Remigio describes human beings belonging (God, Creation, church, kingdom, city-state, province, and household) is designed primarily to highlight the ubiquitous operation of the *ordo caritatis* rather than the relative value of these communities in comparison to one another. Thus, when Remigio divides the human community between the temporal and the ecclesiastical power in the course of his discussion of obedience, these authorities are again treated in parallel. If the human community acts contrary to God, Remigio states, the individual will prefer what pertains to God (*quod Dei est*) to what pertains to his immediate community. In doing so, the individual will fear neither the temporal nor the spiritual power, neither human command nor ecclesiastical excommunication.[71] Only once does Remigio explicitly compare the temporal and spiritual powers in *De Bono Communi*, namely when the hierarchy of common goods—city, province, and kingdom—is made to culminate in the *bonum universalis ecclesiae*. The good of the universal church, Remigio concludes, is greater than the good of one kingdom.[72] The precise meaning of *maius*, however, is neither explained nor explored.

Remigio is rather more forthcoming on the subject of the relationship between the temporal and the spiritual power in *De Bono Pacis*, when he examines the peace of the political community from the perspective of its analogical relationship to the health of the human body. The peace which is universally sought, he states, is of two kinds—the peace of this life (*pax viae*) and the peace of heaven (*pax patriae*). Although the peace of heaven is, in absolute terms, the ultimate and perfect goal of humankind, the peace of this life is still a goal in its own right.[73] For the moment, Remigio does not explore the connection between these two types of peace beyond

---

[69] To conclude, for example, that 'for Remigio the old Augustinian idea of the state as a restraint on evil is still important but is overshadowed by the more positive and optimistic Aristotelian conception of the state as an opportunity for virtue' begs the question of what the precise implications of 'opportunity' are for the relationship between the temporal and the spiritual power (Davis, 'An Early Florentine Political Theorist', 669, 676).

[70] *DBC* p. 15. Cf. ibid. p. 16: *civis vel christianus . . . civitas vel ecclesia.*

[71] *DBP* pp. 33, 66.   [72] *DBC* p. 5.   [73] *DBP* p. 66.

observing that any goal is preferable to those things which contribute towards it and that all other goods should therefore be set aside for the sake of the good of peace. In supporting this contention, however, Remigio puts forward a revealing counter-argument based on the analogy of health. Although the goal of both the doctor and the art of medicine is the health of the human body, both the doctor and the art of medicine are, in absolute terms, superior (and therefore preferable) to health, the end towards which they are ordered. Thus, the doctor possesses reason and is a sub-stance, whereas the health of the body is lacking in reason and is an accident. The art of medicine, meanwhile, is a perfection of the soul, whereas the health of the body is a perfection of the body.

Remigio's response to this argument is to arrange the four causes (final, efficient, formal, and material) into their own hierarchy of dignity. A final cause ranks first because a final goal moves an efficient cause. An efficient cause, in turn, moves matter to receive form, whereupon a formal cause, having been introduced by the effi-cient cause, perfects the matter into which it has been introduced. A material cause, lastly, is simply potential being. Two basic combinations exist between these four types of cause—a mutual ordering of formal and material cause, and a mutual order-ing of final and efficient cause. It is on these combinations which Remigio concen-trates. A formal cause, he argues, is the formal cause of matter, and a material cause is the material cause of form. A formal cause is therefore, in absolute terms, more worthy than matter (*simpliciter nobilior*) because it actualizes and perfects matter. However, within certain terms of reference (*secundum quid*), the reverse is true, because matter maintains form. The same reciprocity is present in the relative values of a final cause and an efficient cause. The final goal causes the efficient cause in absolute terms, that is, in a primary sense (inasmuch as an efficient cause will effect nothing in actuality unless it is first moved by a goal). However, the efficient cause causes the final goal within certain terms of reference, that is, in a secondary sense (although it only moves by virtue of the goal which has first moved it, in the course of moving it still leads towards the final goal).[74]

Remigio's hierarchical arrangement of the four causes bears close scrutiny. One of the most notable features of Remigio's discussion of the hierarchy of ends in *De Bono Pacis* is the care with which he points out that just because something is intrinsically superior in a given hierarchy does not stop it being inferior or less worthy within cer-tain terms of reference.[75] To acknowledge that a strict hierarchy of ends is suscep-tible to modification, to suggest that there are certain circumstances in which a higher good can be ordered towards a lesser goal, is a significant concession to make in a dis-cussion of the relationship between the temporal and the spiritual powers. One of the most important arguments put forward by supporters of hierocratic papalism was the principle of the hierarchy of ends. The goal of the spiritual power is eternal beatitude, whereas the goal of the temporal power is earthly beatitude; since eternal beatitude is superior to earthly beatitude, the spiritual power must be superior to the

---

[74] *DBP* pp. 67–8. Cf. Aquinas, *Ia* 5.5.   [75] *DBP* p. 70.

temporal power; the church therefore has the right both to institute and to judge the temporal ruler.[76] This was the basis of the strict equation between superiority in dignity and superiority in causality which was drawn, for example, by Giles of Rome. By modifying such a corollary, Remigio puts himself somewhere between the radicalism of his fellow Dominican, John of Paris, and the moderation of James of Viterbo. According to John of Paris, the spiritual power is intrinsically more worthy (*dignior*) than the temporal power but this superiority in dignity within a hierarchy of ends does not necessarily translate into a superiority of command or jurisdiction.[77] According to James of Viterbo, superiority in dignity does translate into superiority of jurisdiction but, although this means that the spiritual royal power of the church is essentially superior in dignity to the earthly royal power of a temporal ruler, this does not preclude the reverse being true in certain circumstances.[78] Whilst James of Viterbo does not give any specific examples of what these circumstances might be, it is exactly this sort of exception which Remigio seems determined to explore in *De Bono Pacis*. According to Remigio, the good of the church is greater than the good of a kingdom (*maius*) but this hierarchy of superior and inferior ends does not preclude an intrinsically more worthy good (*nobilior*) being ordered towards an intrinsically less worthy goal in certain circumstances and within certain terms of reference.

Remigio's immediate concern in this particular line of argument, and throughout *De Bono Pacis*, is to prove that individual goods should be sacrificed for the sake of the good of peace even if this means that goods which are in themselves more worthy (namely the property of the church) will be ordered towards an intrinsically less worthy goal (namely the good of the temporal community). In Remigio's eyes, it would be wrong to conclude that, because peace is the goal of the body politic towards which the human community is ordered, it must be intrinsically more worthy than those things, be they people or goods, which are ordered towards it. On the contrary, Remigio claims that it is possible to argue that, in absolute terms, what is ordered towards the goal of peace may in fact be more worthy than the goal itself. In arguing that the good of the church is intrinsically more worthy than the good of the political community, therefore, Remigio regarded the good of the political community as an intrinsically less worthy goal towards which the church can nevertheless, in certain circumstances, be ordered.

This is an argument which can be extrapolated further. If this is true of the goods which are ordered towards the good of peace, then is it also true of the individual human subject (*subiectum*) whose good is ordered towards the good of the community? What makes Remigio's modification of the hierarchy of ends in *De Bono Pacis* so significant for his broader understanding of the common good is the connection which exists with the conclusion of *De Bono Communi* that, for any given action within the political community, the formal cause should be the good of virtue and the final cause the common good.[79] If the individual human being is the material cause of

---

[76] e.g. *Unam sanctam* (Friedberg, ii. 1245–6).   [77] See above, p. 288.
[78] See above, p. 278.   [79] See above, p. 303.

such an action, and if peace is its efficient cause, then it is a reasonable inference that peace will effect nothing unless it is first moved by the common good but that, once moved, peace will cause the common good by leading towards it. Remigio himself does not make this connection explicit. However, he does set out the implications of his discussion of causality for the analogy with which he has previously associated the peace of the political community, namely the health of the human body. According to book II of Aristotle's *De Anima* (and Themistius' commentary on it), there is a goal which is (*finis quod*) and a goal towards which (*finis cui*).[80] For Remigio, there is therefore no contradiction in maintaining that something which is sought as a goal can still be less worthy (*minus nobilis*) than what is ordered towards this goal. Themistius had used the example of health and happiness and Remigio follows suit. Complete perfection of body and soul, he suggests, is certainly (*certe*) a goal which is, in absolute terms, less worthy than the body and the soul themselves. Any substance is essentially more worthy than its accidents in that the latter do not comprise its ultimate goal; the ultimate goal of a substance is the subject (*subiectum*) for which this goal is sought. Thus, health is not the goal of a doctor, nor of the art of medicine, except insofar as both the doctor and the art of medicine are ordered towards the perfection of an individual human being. A soul is not perfected by medicine, nor a body perfected by health, except insofar as both soul and body belong to a human being. An individual human being is, in fact, essentially more worthy than every accidental perfection which that individual may acquire.[81]

Relations between the temporal power and the spiritual power are tangential to the main concern of *De Bono Communi* and are given a very specific form in *De Bono Pacis*. *Contra Falsos Ecclesiae Professores*, by contrast, includes a lengthy discussion of every aspect of the relationship between the authority of the church and the authority of temporal rulers.[82] The ecclesiology put forward in *Contra Falsos*, however, has caused considerable unease amongst modern commentators, largely on the grounds that Remigio appears to be giving with one hand what he has taken away with the other, championing the authority of the temporal power in *De Bono Communi* and *De Bono Pacis* only to subordinate it entirely to the spiritual power in *Contra Falsos*. This has been attributed, in turn, to the encyclopaedic approach of *Contra Falsos*, to a straightforward inconsistency between the treatises, and to Remigio's own shortcomings as a systematic political thinker.[83]

Remigio spends the majority of chapters 5–37 of *Contra Falsos* arguing that the spiritual power may be superior to the temporal power but that this does not entitle it to the exercise of primary and direct jurisdiction in those temporal matters where

---

[80] Aristotle, *De Anima* II.4 415ᵃ28–b1, 6–7, 20 (above, pp. 30, 81 n. 13); *Themistius: Commentaire sur le traité de l'âme d'Aristote*, ed. G. Verbeke (Corpus Latinum Commentariorum in Aristotelem Graecorum I; Louvain–Paris, 1956), 116–17.

[81] *DBP* p. 69.

[82] *Contra Falsos Ecclesiae Professores*, ed. F. Tamburini (Rome, 1981), 14–80; E. Panella, *Per lo studio di Fra Remigio dei Girolami, Memorie Domenicane*, 10 (1979), 107–51.

[83] Davis, 'An Early Florentine Political Theorist', 672–7; id., preface to Tamburini, *ed. cit.*, pp. xi–xx. Cf. Panella, *Per lo studio*, 43–78.

such jurisdiction belongs primarily and directly to the temporal power and only mediately and indirectly to the church.[84] This distinction between direct and indirect, primary and mediated, accordingly lies at the heart of Remigio's exposition of the analogies of the two swords and of the sun and the moon.[85] It enables him, for example, to join John of Paris in criticizing the Donation of Constantine, and to support the separation of the pope's relation to the patrimony of St Peter from his relation to the rest of the world.[86] It also leads Remigio to refute two important arguments in the hierocratic arsenal, namely that a superior power can extend itself directly and primarily to everything which is inferior to it, and that, if the temporal power originates in the spiritual, then the latter retains what it originally bestows.[87]

A distinction between the direct and indirect exercise of temporal power does not, in itself, indicate the adoption of either a radical or a moderate position. Both Giles of Rome and James of Viterbo were capable of expressing strong reservations over the *persistent* intervention of the spiritual power in the temporal sphere. Indeed, when Remigio turns to the criteria which can justify the occasional exercise of such intervention, with or without the suspension of existing channels of justice (*praeiudicium iuris*), the scope which he envisages is nothing if not comprehensive. The pope can intervene in temporal jurisdiction whenever something spiritual is involved, whenever sin is present (*ratione delicti*), or whenever the primary judicial authority is found wanting (*defectus iudicis principalis*).[88] Remigio's exposition of this final criterion comprises a comprehensive list of possibilities—the death of a ruler; the withdrawal or delay of justice; the presence of ambiguity or difficulty; those countries or cases in which it is already customary to have recourse to the pope; those cases for which the principle of intervention has been granted by papal privilege; the involvement of a connected ecclesiastical matter such as marriage and the dowry; and those instances in which a temporal judge is simply suspect.[89] In this respect, Remigio ends up with a list of legal criteria which almost exactly mirrors the description of papal *plenitudo potestatis* which had been produced by Giles of Rome and James of Viterbo.[90] Remigio may have used a theory of indirect power to keep the spiritual and the temporal power separate (*distinctae*), as authorities which differ in species,[91] but he was equally insistent that, at root, the temporal power still originates in and depends upon the spiritual power (*oritur et dependet*).[92] Indeed, his notion of casual intervention leaves him, characteristically, in no doubt (*sine dubio*) that the rule of the church is greater than any other rule not just in extent and dignity but also in authority.[93]

In allowing the superiority of the spiritual over the temporal power to comprise authority as well as dignity, it is clear that, despite their similarities, Remigio's

---

[84] *Contra Falsos* 26, p. 59.   [85] *Contra Falsos* 28, pp. 67–8; 30, p. 70.
[86] *Contra Falsos* 25–6, pp. 56–9. Cf. John of Paris, *De Potestate Regia et Papali* XXI, pp. 243–7.
[87] *Contra Falsos* 27, pp. 60–1.
[88] *Contra Falsos* 19, p. 47; 21, p. 52; 29, p. 68; 32, p. 71; 33, p. 72; 37, p. 76.
[89] *Contra Falsos* 37, pp. 74–6.   [90] See above, pp. 269–71, 280–1.   [91] *Contra Falsos* 26, p. 59.
[92] *Contra Falsos* 35, p. 72. Remigio generally prefers to use *dependere* (*Contra Falsos* 27, p. 67; 28, p. 68; 35, p. 72; 36, p. 73) rather than any variant on Hugh of St Victor's *instituere*.
[93] *Contra Falsos* 6, pp. 19–20.

ecclesiology is based on quite different foundations to those established by John of
Paris. Remigio was certainly prepared to concede that a hierarchy of dignity did not
preclude a superior power being ordered towards an inferior end but he was equally
careful to insist that such an eventuality did not amount to an inferior power actually
having authority over a superior. Even though he accepts that ecclesiastical goods
can be given to the temporal power in certain circumstances, he remains adamant
that the consent of the church should always be freely given (*sponte*) and that it
should always be sought as if from a superior (*tamquam superior*). Whilst individual
Christians are free to disobey the authority of pope, cardinals, and bishops, there is
no question (or at least not one which Remigio is prepared to countenance) of the
temporal power commanding or compelling their Christian subjects to fulfil this
higher obligation to the demands of *caritas*. This would appear to remain the function of the preacher alone. Those ecclesiastical goods which are to be sacrificed by the
clergy in *De Bono Pacis*, therefore, are donated freely and in accordance with *caritas*.
Insofar as a superior authority is involved, it is a command of the *ordo caritatis* and not
a command of the temporal power. In fact, Remigio saves some choice language in
Contra Falsos for those writers, such as John of Paris, who glossed John 18: 36 ('My
kingdom is not of this world') to mean that Christ did not possess lordship over temporal goods. Those who argue this, he writes, are oblivious of moderation, insane in
their presumption, and frenzied in their worldliness. Christ did possess universal
lordship. What he did not do was transmit the primary and direct exercise of its jurisdiction to His vicar on earth because the pope might thereby have been distracted by
such involvement from the primary goal of the church, namely securing spiritual
good.[94] It is only on these grounds that Remigio joins John of Paris in condemning
the Donation of Constantine. In doing so, he does not wish to deny that, in certain
circumstances, the pope can, and should, exercise the direct jurisdiction of a superior
power over temporal goods.

   Within *Contra Falsos* itself, the consistency of Remigio's justification of an indirect papal authority which occasionally exercises direct temporal jurisdiction is clear
enough.[95] Its perceived inconsistency with *De Bono Communi* and *De Bono Pacis*
depends in large measure on two further assumptions—first, that the gift of ecclesiastical goods in order to secure peace should be interpreted as the subordination of
an inferior good to a superior end and, second, that the goal of political authority
should be defined in the all-inclusive terms of the life of virtue. It is on this basis, for
example, that Remigio has been presented as a theorist who had the courage to follow
John of Paris for the politics of the city-state but who baulked at applying the same
logic to a kingdom or the empire.[96] Both assumptions, however, are open to question.
A different, and rather more coherent, picture begins to emerge as soon as the gift of
ecclesiastical goods in order to secure peace is interpreted as the extraordinary subordination of a superior good to an inferior end within certain terms of reference, and

---

[94] *Contra Falsos* 27, pp. 62–5. Cf. John of Paris, *De Potestate Regia et Papali* VIII, p. 191.
[95] Panella, *Per lo studio*, 55–6.   [96] Davis, 'An Early Florentine Political Theorist', 676.

as soon as Remigio's definition of the goal of political authority is understood to be, not the life of virtue, but the material and corporeal peace which then facilitates the life of virtue.

One of Remigio's working assumptions in *Contra Falsos* is that spiritual and ecclesiastical authority can be equated with the soul, whilst temporal and political authority can be equated with the body.[97] This was an analogy which had been vigorously endorsed by Giles of Rome and studiously avoided by James of Viterbo. Just as the soul is superior to the body in its dignity and in its power of ruling, so the authority of the pope is superior to the authority of every temporal ruler. Remigio is happy to accept this argument on the grounds that any end is superior to what contributes towards it and a primary goal is superior to what facilitates it (*accessorium*).[98] There is nothing here, however, which is necessarily inconsistent with the position put forward in *De Bono Communi* (the good of the whole church is greater than the good of kingdom) or *De Bono Pacis* (a superior good may be ordered towards an inferior goal in certain circumstances, *secundum quid*, but it is still intrinsically superior, *simpliciter*). Likewise, when Remigio defines the goal of temporal power in *Contra Falsos*, he maintains the restricted definition already established in *De Bono Communi* and *De Bono Pacis*. Whereas the authority of the pope is ordered primarily towards the worship of God, the authority of temporal rulers is ordered primarily towards the goal of making humans live peaceably with one another (*pacifice vivere*). This definition produces a clear hierarchy of dignity. The power of greater dignity is the power which is ordered towards the goal of greater dignity.[99] However, Remigio then draws the conclusion which is only implicit in *De Bono Communi* and *De Bono Pacis*. Temporal power and ecclesiastical power, he argues, must be ordered towards one another. Since the authority of the pope is concerned with heavenly things and the soul, whereas the authority of temporal rulers is concerned with earthly things and the body, the latter should be ordered towards the former as it would be towards something superior (*excellentior*). Remigio is, again, happy to accept this argument on the grounds that it represents a hierarchy, although this time the hierarchy is defined in terms of formal and efficient causes rather than final goals. As a formal cause, the ordering of earthly body towards heavenly soul applies to the relation of all Christians towards the pope; as a primary, efficient cause, it extends to all humans in the relation of the whole universe towards Christ.[100] Remigio's discussion of hierarchy in *Contra Falsos* does not extend to the reciprocal combinations of final, formal, and efficient causes which he uses in *De Bono Pacis*. Once again, however, neither does it preclude the possibility that, in certain circumstances, most notably for the sake of establishing peace, an exception can be made and a more worthy good can be ordered towards a less worthy goal.

As long as Remigio envisages the relationship between the spiritual and the temporal power as a relationship between the soul and the body, his argument remains

---

[97] *Contra Falsos* 18, pp. 40–2, 44; 26, p. 57; 37, p. 74.   [98] *Contra Falsos* 18, pp. 41, 46.
[99] *Contra Falsos* 18, pp. 42, 46.   [100] *Contra Falsos* 18, pp. 43–4, 47.

close to that of Giles of Rome. The defining goal of political authority is the provision
of a material and corporeal peace which is instrumental to the activity of the church
towards which it is ordered. Where Remigio's argument becomes more problematic
is when he has to discuss the presence of virtue in the political community, an issue
which, as James of Viterbo and John of Paris both realized, a simple division between
soul and body necessarily left open to dispute. The fact that the question of virtue
arises on only one occasion in *Contra Falsos* is therefore, in itself, significant. It occurs
in the course of a list of arguments which Remigio assembles to support the contention that the authority of the pope exceeds (*excedat*) every authority in the world.
Whereas the rule of temporal rulers rests upon (*innititur*) the political and human
virtues, it reads, the rule of pope rests primarily on the theological virtues; the root
and form of these theological virtues is *caritas*; just as the theological virtues are
superior to the political and human virtues, therefore, so the authority of the pope is
superior to the authority of temporal rulers.[101] When Remigio comes to discuss this
argument, the position which he outlines is very similar to that of James of Viterbo.
Not only does he quote the same text from the pseudo-Augustinian *Sentences* by
Prosper of Aquitaine ('where the knowledge of eternal and unchangeable truth is
absent, virtue is false, even in the best moral life'), but he follows James's exposition
closely.[102] Augustine uses the term 'false', Remigio argues, in a relative sense
(*respective*). Virtue is false, therefore, when it is compared to eternal beatitude, just as
silver is said to be base relative to gold. However, virtue is also false in the sense of
being imperfect when it lacks the form of *caritas*, just as a silver coin is said to be a
false coin if it is not stamped.[103] Remigio does not deny that the term 'virtue' can be
applied to the best moral life of an unbeliever, nor does he regard it as equivocal or
analogical in the way he defined a bad 'peace' (or, for that matter, an infidel
'church').[104] For Remigio, as for James of Viterbo, such virtue is simply imperfect
and unformed when it is without the theological virtue of *caritas*. Unlike James, however, Remigio does not pursue the consequences for temporal authority. As far as
Remigio is concerned, the significance of this discussion is limited to its own terms of
reference. Just as the political virtues are directly concerned with human actions and
are caused by them in a way that the theological virtues are not, so the temporal
power is directly concerned with temporal matters.[105] When Remigio does bring up
the question of virtue in the political community, in other words, the last thing he
does is make the sort of polemical connection between virtue and political authority

---

[101] *Contra Falsos* 18, p. 41.

[102] *Contra Falsos* 27, p. 61; Prosper of Aquitaine, *Sententia* 106 (*PL* 51, col. 441); Aquinas, *IaIIae*
65.2, *IIaIIae* 23.7; James of Viterbo, *De Regimine Christiano*, ed. H.-X. Arquillière (Paris, 1926), II.7,
pp. 232–3 (above, p. 279).

[103] *Contra Falsos* 27, pp. 61–2.

[104] *DBP* p. 59; *Contra Falsos* 37, p. 79. Cf. *Tractatus de Iustitia* (O. Capitani, 'L'Incompiuto Tractatus de
Iustitia de Fra' Remigio de' Girolami', *Bulletino dell'Istituto Storico Italiano per il Medio Evo e Archivio
Muratoriano*, 72, 1960), p. 126, where Remigio argues that virtue should be loved for its own sake even if
it should subsequently be ordered towards the higher end of eternal beatitude and the supreme good.

[105] *Contra Falsos* 27, p. 62.

which was made (with such differing results) by James of Viterbo and John of Paris. Whilst Remigio acknowledges the presence of virtue amongst individuals within the political community, he does not make it a defining criterion of the exercise of political authority.[106] When Remigio does quote the text from the pseudo-Augustinian *Sentences* which had provoked such controversy between James of Viterbo and John of Paris, he restricts it to a firmly apolitical context.[107]

The cogency of Remigio's discussion of the relationship between the temporal and the spiritual power becomes much clearer when it is placed within the terms of reference set by Giles of Rome, James of Viterbo, and John of Paris. Like Giles of Rome, Remigio gives temporal authority the function of securing a material good of peace which then facilitates the effective operation of the spiritual power. Unlike Giles, however, Remigio does not deny the legitimacy of a temporal power which has not been ratified by the church. Like James of Viterbo, Remigio considers moral virtue to be imperfect without the 'form' of the theological virtue of *caritas*. Unlike James, he does not apply this relationship between moral and theological virtue to the relationship between temporal and spiritual authority. Like John of Paris, Remigio maintains that the temporal power and the spiritual power should be regarded as separate, as distinct powers with their own specific responsibilities. Unlike John, he does not argue that the hierarchy of superior and inferior ends is therefore only a hierarchy of dignity and not a hierarchy of authority and jurisdiction.

A period of study in Paris towards the end of the 1290s may well have made Remigio familiar with the terms of the first dispute—over ecclesiastical property—between Philip IV and Boniface VIII. It may also have brought him into direct contact with James of Viterbo and John of Paris themselves. The composition of his own texts after 1302–4, and their later revision before 1314, certainly leaves scope for his subsequent acquaintance with the texts of *De Ecclesiastica Potestate*, *De Regimine Christiano*, and *De Potestate Regia et Papali*. Remigio himself was present at the papal court at Perugia in 1297 and, more significantly, in 1302, when the second dispute between Philip IV and Boniface VIII was in full spate.[108] Engagement with the arguments of Giles of Rome, James of Viterbo, and John of Paris, therefore, should not be taken simply as the product of learned pedagogy. Remigio's treatment of the ecclesiological ramifications of the common good of peace demonstrates a consistent, if complex, line of thought throughout each of his political treatises. In *De Bono Pacis* and *Contra Falsos*, the relationship between the spiritual power and the temporal power is expressed in terms of the intrinsic superiority of the church within a hierarchy of ends, dignity, and authority. In *De Bono Pacis*, however, Remigio also explicitly envisages certain circumstances in which the superior power of the church can be ordered towards the inferior power of a temporal ruler. Political events in Florence during the spring and early summer of 1304, in other words, appear to have

---

[106] Cf. *Contra Falsos* 18, p. 41; 30, p. 70.   [107] *Contra Falsos* 44, p. 112.
[108] Panella, *Per lo studio*, 215–16. Remigio was also familiar with Ptolemy of Lucca who was prior of Santa Maria Novella in 1301–2.

represented one such exceptional scenario. In this instance, at least, a hierarchy of superior and inferior ends does not preclude a superior good being ordered towards an inferior goal *secundum quid*. Otherwise, Remigio's original argument still stands— in absolute terms (*simpliciter*), the inferior power of a temporal ruler should be ordered towards the superior goal of the church.

Remigio's differentiation between, on the one hand, peace and harmony and, on the other, love and virtue, raises a number of critical questions for an understanding of the role of the common good in his political theology—what is the connection between ideal and reality, the difference between Aristotle and Augustine, and the relationship between the spiritual and the temporal power? If *caritas*, *pax*, *concordia*, and *utilitas* are the terms which subsequently emerge as central to his analysis, then this strongly suggests that Remigio's traditional characterization as an extreme exponent both of a communitarian ethos and of a 'robust Aristotelian optimism' needs to be revised. Whilst Remigio may have written at length on the obligations which were incumbent upon his fellow-citizens in Florence, this must be seen in the context of the wider obligation which is incumbent upon every individual Christian to obey the *ordo caritatis* in whatever 'community' they found themselves, whatever the 'whole' of which they formed a 'part', be it God, Creation, church, kingdom, city-state, province, or household. Likewise, whilst Remigio's treatises may have used a great deal of Aristotelian material, the fact that this was accompanied by biblical and patristic citation is indicative of more than just a desire to produce an encyclopaedic *florilegium* for use in sermons. When Remigio defines the goal of the political com-munity, his choice of 'living peaceably' (*pacifice vivere*) rather than 'living well' (*bene vivere*) is significant. Remigio's biblical and patristic authorities reflect a profoundly Augustinian conception of the reality of sinful human society.

   Throughout *De Bono Communi* and *De Bono Pacis*, Remigio understands the common good of the political community to be the temporal benefit of peace, the effect of correctly ordered love. The common good of the political community is defined accordingly as an Augustinian 'peace and harmony', not as an Aristotelian 'life of virtue'. Virtue is certainly present in the political community but only insofar as individual humans are enabled by peace and harmony to live in accordance with the *ordo caritatis*. Virtue may be the defining feature of correctly ordered love within the human community, it may be what political authority 'rests upon', but it is not the defining criterion of the exercise of political authority. Remigio's political thought should therefore be seen primarily as a discussion of peace, harmony, order, and temporal benefit in human society, the health of the body politic and not the hap-piness of its soul. *De Bono Communi* and *De Bono Pacis*, in other words, should be seen primarily as an exposition, not of Aristotle's *Ethics* and *Politics*, but of August-ine's *De Civitate Dei*.

Conclusion

The history of late thirteenth- and early fourteenth-century scholastic political thought is frequently construed along the lines of two important twentieth-century interpretations. The first of these explanatory frameworks is generally traceable, in one form or another, to the influence of Walter Ullmann. The rediscovery of Aristotle's *Ethics* and *Politics*, it is argued, had an inevitably corrosive influence on medieval hierocracy once the rediscovery of the principle that humankind is political by nature rather than by sin prompted the conceptual transformation of the subject into the citizen and the emergence of a 'secular' theory of 'the state'.[1] The second of these interpretations is usually associated with the work of Georges de Lagarde. The dissolution of a hitherto dominant ecclesiastical corporatism, it is argued, was hastened by a novel concentration on individual consent and individual rights which was inspired by the refusal of nominalist epistemology and metaphysics to accept anything 'real' outside of the individual.[2]

The attribution of either of these twentieth-century paradigms to scholastic political and ethical thought, either as 'secular' naturalism or as 'secular' individualism, needs to be reassessed in the light of the scholastic understanding of the common good. The first interpretation, for example, invites an analysis of what the scholastic notion of the common good reveals about the secularizing potential of the reintroduction of Aristotle's *Ethics* and *Politics*. Did the reception of these texts constitute the inherently revolutionary force which it is sometimes claimed to be? The second interpretation, meanwhile, invites an analysis of what the scholastic notion of the relationship between the individual and the common good reveals about the inclusivity of medieval corporatism. Did the idea of 'the individual' have to wait for nominalism in order to be freed from a complete and absolute subordination to the political and ecclesiastical hierarchies? In suggesting alternative solutions to these issues, moreover, two further questions arise. Once it is established that scholastic theologians were able to distinguish between what is morally good and what is advantageous, this naturally invites a consideration of the consequences for scholastic political thought of being able to choose between two different definitions of the common good, between *bonum commune* and *communis utilitas*. Likewise, once it

---

[1] e.g. *The Cambridge History of Medieval Political Thought*, 360: 'The chief innovation of late medieval political thought was the development of the idea of the secular state as a product of man's political nature. This concept was acquired through the rediscovery of Aristotle's *Politics* and *Ethics*. Aristotle provided a ready-made theory of politics and the state as existing within a purely natural and this-worldly dimension.'

[2] G. de Lagarde, *La Naissance de l'esprit laïque au déclin du moyen âge*, 3rd edn (5 vols.; Louvain, 1956–70), vols. iii–v.

becomes clear that scholastic theologians discussed the notion of the common good as both a metaphysical theory and a political idea, this naturally raises the question of the connection which exists between them. What is the correlation, for example, between conceiving of the common good as the principle of goodness in the universe in which individual rational beings must participate in order to be good and conceiving of the common good as the good which is secured by political authority in the human community and to which individual citizens must direct all their actions?

The scholastic understanding of the notion of the common good, therefore, can be analysed in terms of four elements—the reception of Aristotle, the relationship between the individual and the common good, the distinction between *bonum commune* and *communis utilitas*, and the connection between metaphysical theory and political thought. Taken together, these four issues provide the basis, first, for a reassessment of the role of Aristotle in scholastic discussions of the relationship between the spiritual and the temporal powers and, second, for a re-evaluation of the 'secularizing' influences on medieval scholastic political thought.

The Reception of Aristotle

Although the translation of Aristotle's *Ethics* and *Politics* prompted an influx of new ideas into late thirteenth- and early fourteenth-century scholastic political thinking, this should not be allowed to disguise the degree to which it also served to formalize existing concepts. The common good provides a case in point. Henry of Ghent, Godfrey of Fontaines, and Giles of Rome all readily accepted the principle which they found in book III of the *Politics* that the common good is the legitimating criterion for all government in human communities which distinguishes good forms from bad. As a justification for the exercise of ordinary power and (when tied to the notion of equity which Henry, Godfrey, and Giles found in book V of the *Ethics*) extraordinary power, this definition of the common good fitted neatly into an existing tradition of thought. In this instance, the use of an Aristotelian common good served to consolidate the ideas of *status ecclesiae, salus ecclesiae,* and *utilitas ecclesiae* which had already been developed by theologians such as Bernard of Clairvaux and canonists such as Hostiensis in their discussions of papal *plenitudo potestatis*. It also served to consolidate the ideas of *defensio regni, salus rei publicae,* and *necessitas vel communis utilitas* with which Roman lawyers had supported temporal appeals for new or emergency taxation by temporal rulers. In terms of political theory, therefore, the use of this notion of the common good demonstrates the ease with which Aristotle's *Ethics* and *Politics* were capable of being associated with existing authorities and the readiness with which they could be applied to the power of both the pope and the king.

The correspondence which this notion of the common good reveals between the principles which could be applied to the temporal and the spiritual powers was, in itself, no innovation. Once again, it reflected the continuation of a much older tradition, in this case the presupposition that the ruler is a minister of God who is therefore subject to the precepts enjoined on any individual who is charged with pastoral care of the Christian community. The quasi-divine ruler of book III of the *Politics*, therefore, an individual whose function requires the possession of complete or perfect virtue, could be dovetailed into Gregory the Great's ideal of the clerical *iam perfectus*. It was also a two-way process. James of Viterbo not only showed the extent to which the church could, in turn, assume the characteristics of a kingdom but also demonstrated just how comprehensive a definition of papal *plenitudo potestatis* could be produced when the common good was used to justify the extraordinary jurisdiction of the pope. In terms of political practice, therefore, the use of this notion of the common good demonstrates how scholastic theologians deployed a particular concept as a reaction to specific political events—primarily the controversy over the promulgation of *Ad fructus uberes* but also the granting of clerical tenths, the resignation of Celestine V, the dispute over *Clericis laicos*, and the demands for taxation by Philip IV of France. These were the events which prompted Henry of Ghent and Godfrey of Fontaines to examine existing legal texts on dispensation, on disobedience, and on the need for proof that there was *clear* benefit to the common good, and use them as the basis for a systematic and comprehensive account of legitimate government and legitimate resistance. Thus, John of Paris was treading a familiar path when he constructed his ecclesiology on a combination of Aristotle with Gratian, on a mixture of the *Ethics* and the *Politics* with canon law texts on papal stewardship, deposition, and the limits to *plenitudo potestatis*.

Where, then, does this syncretism leave the identity of any specifically 'Aristotelian' notion of the common good, a notion of the common good which was based exclusively on Aristotle himself? When Albertus Magnus first read book I of the *Ethics*, he clearly assumed that the good of the community was superior to the good of the individual in a quantitative sense (*maius*) and he explained its greater divinity (*divinius*) in terms of the continuation in existence of the species. As soon as he read the *Politics*, however, Albertus realized that this aggregate model needed to be replaced by one which could accommodate a difference in kind, a difference *secundum speciem*. Albertus' second commentary on the *Ethics* accordingly presented the common good as a shared goal relative to which individuals could be proportionally closer or further away. When Thomas Aquinas came to comment on the *Ethics*, his analysis of the common good owed a considerable debt to this gloss. Aquinas adopted Albertus' illustration of victory in the army, for example, and used the *duplex ordo* from book XII of the *Metaphysics* in order to make it a principle for all communities, up to and including the whole of Creation. Every community, Aquinas argued, demonstrates a twofold organization in which individuals are arranged in relation to an intrinsic and an extrinsic common good—they are ordered towards each other and then towards their ruler and the good of the whole. Aquinas also picked up on Albertus' notion of analogy or proportion in order to demonstrate that it is impossible for individuals to be good unless they are correctly directed or ordered towards the common good, participating in the good of the whole as the good on which their own partial goods depend for their existence. As a result, Aquinas established a hierarchy of ends or goals according to which an individual good must be ordered towards the common good within which it is included.

Aquinas' treatment of the common good, however, is not necessarily characterized by the sort of synthetic harmony with which 'Thomist' political and ethical philosophy is frequently credited. Some conflicts, notably between obedience and resistance, were left without a more satisfactory resolution than the disparity between political theory and political practice. Other conflicts, between *caritas* and justice for example, or between *otium* and *negotium*, were incapable of reconciliation short of the perfection of heaven and the person of Christ. Only in the latter could a resolution be found between the demands of love and the demands of justice, or between the needs of an active life and the purity of a contemplative life. This type of conflict represented a dialectic which was inherent in all moral theology influenced by Augustine. Viewed from the perspective of the common good, perhaps the most significant of these discordances (and one which had been highlighted, again, by Albertus Magnus) originated from within the text of the *Ethics* itself. On the scholastic reading of Aristotle, there was a fundamental difference in emphasis, even a discrepancy, between two definitions of the common good of the human community. In book I, the common good appears as happiness, as the life of virtue; in book IX, it appears as peace, as material security and well-being. Defined as moral goodness (*bonum commune*), the common good was superior to and inclusive of the individual good; defined as benefit to the community (*communis utilitas*), the common good was the product of individual acts of virtue.

By clarifying the various meanings of the common good—as the goal of all good government, as the continuation in existence of the species, as the good in common, as the goal of justice, as the object of love, and as the life of virtue—Albertus Magnus and Thomas Aquinas laid the foundations for all subsequent scholastic discussions of the term. It was therefore the next generation of scholars who provided the most detailed and penetrating discussion of the various problems which these different meanings raised for the role of the common good as the goal of the human community. Often it was a closer reading of Aristotle and his Greek commentators which led these theologians to push positions further than either Albertus or Aquinas had been willing or able to do. Godfrey of Fontaines' account of the relationship between general justice and the virtues is a good example. On the scholastic reading of Aristotle, there was an ambiguity in the definition of general justice provided by book V of the *Ethics*—on the one hand, justice is 'righteousness', that is, perfect and complete virtue; on the other, it is a virtue in its own right. In emphasizing the parallel which exists between the relationship of justice to its constituent virtues and the relationship of the common good to its constituent individual goods, Godfrey provided a detailed analysis of how an individual virtue derives its well-being (*bene esse*) as a consequence of being directed towards general justice. Justice, Godfrey concludes, has the same subject-matter as all the virtues; it is 'general' by aggregation and inclusion (*generalitate cuiusdam aggregationis et continentiae*) and by power and virtue (*efficacia et virtute*) in the sense that it represents the collective presence of all the virtues.

Justice is different from all the virtues, however, not just by being ordered towards a different end (*secundum rationem*) but by actually being different in the sense of having a different accidental existence; it is therefore different in essence as well as species and form (*secundum rem et essentiam*). According to Aquinas, general justice is the same as all virtue in its substance or subject-matter (*idem subiecto*) and in its essence (*idem in essentiam*) but different in its species and in its end or goal (*differens ratione*). The common good is made to follow suit—the common good is the same as the individual good but it is different in species and in its goal (*secundum rationem*). According to Godfrey, they are different in essence as well as end (*unum et idem secundum substantiam vel materiam et subiectum, differens tamen secundum esse formale et specificum*).

Henry of Ghent, meanwhile, picked up on the absence of the common good from the three categories which underpinned Augustine's analysis of *caritas*—love of self, love of neighbour, and love of God—and sought to harmonize Augustine's account of this *ordo caritatis* with Aristotle's analysis of self-love and friendship in books VIII and IX of the *Ethics*. Like Albertus and Aquinas, Henry saw that a fundamental difficulty lay at the heart of self-sacrifice. Does a person lay down their life for a friend and for a community in order to secure their own greater good, the good of virtue, or in order to secure the common good of the friend and of the community? In his own analysis of the relationship between the common good and the individual good, Henry accordingly considered every possible permutation of spiritual and corporeal good, where 'common' and 'individual' were within the same genus and where they were not. For Henry, the common good should be preferred to the individual good only when the common good includes the individual good; without this precondition, it is the individual good which takes precedence. Godfrey of Fontaines echoed this insistence. Indeed, in Godfrey's hands, this principle of inclusion was turned into a sophisticated instrument which could distinguish between good (*bonum*), well-being (*bene esse*), and perfection (*optime esse*). Godfrey also developed Aquinas' observation that the individual secures his own good as a consequence of securing the common good by echoing Giles of Rome's distinction between direct consequence (*ex consequenti*) and accidental consequence (*ex consequenti et quasi per accidens*). According to Godfrey, an intrinsic good (namely an individual's perfection in virtue) must be subordinate to an extrinsic good (the good from which this intrinsic good derives its form and perfection). The love which is due to each good must follow the same order—the individual primarily and principally (*primo et principaliter*) loves the common good which exists in God, as the good from which his own individual good will result as a consequence (*quasi ex consequenti et implicite*). The individual does not love the common good in order to secure his own good, but, by loving the common good, his own good will result. To refuse to lay down one's life for the common good in the hope that one might thereby secure one's individual good would therefore represent a contradiction in terms—the good of a part depends upon the good of the whole and it cannot exist without it. Godfrey thereby makes his own connection between Augustine's account of the *ordo caritatis* and Aquinas' account of the *ratio boni* as a metaphysical order of goodness in the universe. According to Godfrey, this *ratio boni* not only represents good in absolute terms but is also good which is congruent with the good of the individual. Goodness in general includes what is good for the individual; it is the *ratio boni et convenientis*.

The Common Good and the Individual

Where does this account of the reception of Aristotle leave the scholastic understanding of the relationship between the common good and the individual? Should the common good be relativized, reduced to meaning different things in different contexts, or is it possible to salvage a more consistent approach to the comparative values of individual and community? If the individual was going to be 'suppressed' anywhere in scholastic political and ethical thought, then the most likely place to find it is in the concept of hierarchy, where too strict a mediation of ends, too precise a correlation between 'structure' and 'dynamic', could leave an individual good necessarily incorporated into a superior common good in order to attain its ultimate goal.[3] It is clear from Thomas Aquinas, however, that, whenever there was such a conflict between the hierarchical structure of the created universe and its Christocentric and anthropocentric dynamic, then the primacy of the 'individual' could always be preserved by means of a bypass (*praetermissio ordinis*). Aquinas understood the superiority of the common good as a principle which applied only when common good and individual good were within the same genus, and, even when they were, he carefully qualified this principle with the distinction between something which is true 'in absolute terms' (*simpliciter, secundum se*) and something which is true 'within certain terms of reference and in certain circumstances' (*secundum quid et in casu*).

Hierarchy in the universe, in fact, appears to have been far less important to the scholastic understanding of a 'superior' common good than the ontological participation of each individual in goodness and in being. It was this metaphysical principle, rather than hierarchy as such, which led to the application of the inclusive imagery of whole and part to the political community by Aquinas, Godfrey of Fontaines, and Remigio dei Girolami. Here too, however, the translation of abstract metaphysics to the concrete reality of a human community was tempered by an acknowledgement that, in a political context, the common good could take on much less inclusive forms. Remigio dei Girolami may have constructed an all-inclusive ideal of goodness upon which, in theory, each individual good depends for its very existence, but he could rapidly switch to a material good of peace and security to which, in practice, every individual citizen should direct their actions. Albertus Magnus, Thomas Aquinas, Henry of Ghent, and Godfrey of Fontaines likewise all sought to give greater precision to the word 'good' by distinguishing comparison in terms of greater worth (*dignius, nobilius, honorabilius*) from comparison in terms of greater benefit (*utilius, fructuosius*). This was the distinction which could be used to

---

[3] See above pp. 4–6.

harmonize the perfect political community of book I of the *Ethics* with the supreme act of self-sacrifice in book IX, and the life of contemplation in book X of the *Ethics* with the life of action in the *Politics*. It was this distinction, therefore, which enabled the principle of the superiority of the common good to be maintained at the same time as the greater intrinsic good of the individual.

The language with which 'corporatist' political thinking is generally associated, the metaphorical imagery of whole and part and body and limb, could be applied with varying degrees of precision. James of Viterbo, for example, made much of the fact that limbs do not possess independent motivation and therefore do not provide a strict parallel with individual members of the community. All scholastic theologians, moreover, were capable of specifying which of the various logical categories of 'whole' they were invoking. Albertus saw the common good as a potential or virtual whole, Aquinas and Henry of Ghent saw the political community as an integral whole, whilst Godfrey of Fontaines managed to combine the two, the integral whole of the political community with the virtual whole of general justice. More modern references to the 'organic' whole of medieval society need to be re-examined in this light. An integral whole depends for its existence on all its integral parts being arranged together and, when one integral part is removed, the whole is automatically destroyed. The word *totus* could be applied to an integral whole collectively or divisively, to all its parts together (a group of individuals hauling a ship) or to all its parts on their own (soldiers fighting in a battle). Aquinas was fully aware that analogies of men hauling a ship and of the army securing victory implied that a 'community' could achieve an end which was impossible for an individual on their own and which was indivisible into individual quantities according to Zeno's paradox of falling millet. However, it is noticeable that, when the context was the political community, Aquinas qualified both analogies in order to suggest that the individual has an independent action which is not the action of the whole. Likewise, Aquinas was fully aware that the definition of justice as all virtue implied a comprehensiveness which could not be inferred from the definition of justice as a virtue which is limited to external actions performed towards another individual. This is most noticeable in the case of suicide when Aquinas used the idea of the mystical body of Christ (*corpus mysticum*) to argue that whatever an individual does to himself is done to the whole community. Nevertheless, when it came to discussing the operation of human justice within the political community, Aquinas, Godfrey of Fontaines, and Giles of Rome all qualified the inclusive nature of the goal of justice as the common good of virtue. General justice, they argued, can direct every virtue but not every *action* of every virtue. Aquinas, Godfrey, and Giles, therefore, were all careful to use 'capable of being directed' (*ordinabile, referibile*) rather than 'must be directed' (*ordinandum, referendum*). Only divine law orders every action of every virtue and it is only for the common good which exists in God that Aquinas and Godfrey use the gerundive forms. Even Remigio dei Girolami, the theologian whose political writings are often held to represent the extremes of corporatist language, was careful to refer to the individual 'insofar as he is a part' (*inquantum est pars*) and 'insofar as he is a citizen' (*inquantum est civis*), as well as to distinguish between the various senses in which 'the individual' can be defined—as a subsisting subject (*suppositum*), as a moral entity (*res virtualis*), and as a moral agent (*res agens*).

This is not to say that there were not differences in emphasis between one scholastic theologian and another. A statement such as 'the common good includes the individual good', for instance, could be reached by a variety of routes. Giles of Rome, for example, chooses to take up Aquinas' insistence that the good of a community is dependent on all its members being virtuous in order to underline the principle that the common good is the good of all the members of the community. It is Giles, therefore, who points out that Aristotle's definition of democracy as a multitude aiming to secure its own selfish good does not preclude even this perverse form of government securing some sort of common good (*quasi bonum commune*) on the grounds that this selfish good involves the good of a considerable number of individuals. Henry of Ghent's reading of Augustine, meanwhile, makes him give greater weight to the origins of love in love of self. For Henry, love for the common good must, by definition, mean that the individual good is included. James of Viterbo goes further still and argues that the part, when it is considered within a whole, loves itself and the whole with an equal affection but that, when it is considered as something separate, the part has a greater love for its individual good. Godfrey of Fontaines, in contrast, relies on Aquinas' model of the *ordo caritatis* and of the participation of the human will in the *ratio boni*. Godfrey's common good is automatically congruent with the individual good in that the individual good depends upon the common good for its existence.

An insistence on the inclusion of the individual good within the common good could clearly be reached from different starting points. Either this conclusion derived from the assumption that the individual always wills *sub ratione boni et convenientis* or it followed from the assumption that self-love is at the heart of the *ordo caritatis*. This divergence carried certain consequences in its train. The closer the connection which was made with the metaphysical good in the universe (*bonum in communi*), then the more corporatist the terminology which was applied to the human community and the more moral the identity which was given to the goal of political authority. The looser the connection, then the more individualist the terminology applied and the more material the identity given. It is in this context that perhaps the most revealing difference in emphasis occurs amongst scholastic theologians in their discussions of the notion of the common good. It is provided, once again, by the relationship between general justice and its component virtues and it is exemplified by Godfrey of Fontaines. Godfrey's modification of Aquinas' account of justice in book V of the *Ethics* prompted him to draw a distinction between two types of community. On the one hand, there is the community which is indicated when referring to the common good and, on the other, there is the community which is indicated when referring to the world or the universe. To explain what he means by the community of the world, Godfrey uses Aristotle's model of the *duplex ordo*—the ordering of individuals towards each other and the ordering of individuals towards a common goal. The world, he concludes, is a whole which is comprised of individual parts and, insofar as these parts have a unity, it is a unity of order. The community of the common good, meanwhile, has more than just a unity of order. The common good is composed of individual goods which derive their unity from being ordered towards a common goal. However, they also derive their unity from the essential unity of their object—individual goods are ordered not just towards a common goal but also towards something which, like general justice, is 'one' in its own right. The fact that Godfrey chooses to connect the notion of the common good with justice rather than the universe, with virtue rather than with Creation, has important repercussions for his understanding of the nature of the community which is represented by human political association. A choice between these two types of good, between a unity of goodness and a unity of order, derives from a conceptual distinction between *bonum* and *utilitas*.

Bonum commune and communis utilitas

When Leonardo Bruni translated the *Ethics* into Latin in 1417, he delivered a scathing verdict on his thirteenth-century predecessors. In giving such eloquent expression to the philologist's contempt for medieval scholasticism, Bruni singled out for particular ridicule the 'absurd' decision to render *to kalon* by nothing more precise than *bonum*.[4] However, to conclude, on this basis, that scholastic political philosophy was incapable of drawing a distinction between *bonum*, *honestum*, and *utile* would be seriously mistaken. The distinction between what is good (*bonum*), what is advantageous (*utile*), and what is pleasurable (*delectabile*), a distinction which had been so central to Aristotle's discussion of the natural appetite of the human will and the various forms of human friendship, *did* survive in Grosseteste's translation. This is, perhaps, hardly surprising given that the distinction between what is right or morally virtuous (*ius*, *honestum*) and what is useful or advantageous (*utile*, *commodum*) had also been central to Cicero's discussion of the conduct of the virtuous individual in the *res publica*. Indeed, from Albertus Magnus on the subject of lying and adultery to Henry of Ghent and Remigio dei Girolami on the subject of universal damnation, it was a combination of Aristotle with Cicero, of book III of the *Politics* with book III of *De Officiis*, which invigorated the debate over the relationship between *ius* and *utile*, between individual moral worth and collective political advantage, between the virtue of the good man and the virtue of the good citizen. Jean Buridan's commentary on the *Politics*, therefore, can serve as a late but instructive example. Written in the faculty of arts at Paris some time between 1320 and 1358, it opens with a detailed discussion of whether the common good should be preferred to the private and particular good. Not only did Buridan immediately distinguish between moral worth (*honestum*) and benefit (*utile*), between that which is sought for its own sake (*appetibile propter se ipsum*) and that which is sought in order that good may result (*appetibile ut inde bonum sequeretur*), but he did so in the course of examining whether an evil act

---

[4] *Leonardo Bruni Aretino: Humanistisch-philosophische Schriften mit einer Chronologie seiner Werke und Briefe*, ed. H. Baron (Leipzig, 1928), 79.

can be performed for the sake of some greater good.[5] Whatever Renaissance human-
ists might have thought, scholastic political philosophy had both an opportunity and
a motive for distinguishing between different types of goodness. Scholastic theologians were not only capable of drawing a distinction between moral goodness and
advantage, but they recognized the significance of this distinction for the relationship of the individual to the political community.

Metaphysics and Politics

If the distinction between *bonum* and *utilitas*, between goodness and benefit, was such
an important element in scholastic political and ethical thinking, then the consequences for the scholastic understanding of the notion of the common good were
profound. For a modern historian to grasp the relationship between scholastic political thought and scholastic metaphysics is difficult at the best of times, but the task is
made even more problematic once it is recognized that there was more than one set
of metaphysical principles on which scholastic theologians could draw. It is significant, therefore, that the scholastic notion of the common good offered, not one, but
two possible models for the good of the political community—the principle of goodness (*ratio boni*) and the good of order (*bonum ordinis*)—each of which presents different possibilities for the status of the individual human being within the human
community. The complexity of the scholastic understanding of the common good,
therefore, derives, in part, from its capacity to draw from either of these models.
According to the principle of goodness, an individual must participate in the universal good (*bonum in communi*) in order to be good. In this schema, an individual's good
cannot exist without the common good, individuals can will what is good for themselves only by willing the common good, and the good of the part is dependent on the
good of the whole. According to the good of order, on the other hand, an individual
participates in the community in a *duplex ordo*, of individuals ordered towards each
other and of individuals ordered towards a common goal. In this schema, the universe as a whole provides a more perfect similitude of divine goodness than any one
of its parts but some of these parts, namely the 'principal' parts, constitute, as individuals, a more perfect image of God.

Which of these two models is used to represent the human community, the *ratio
boni* or the *duplex ordo*, has far-reaching consequences for the role of the individual in
scholastic political and ethical thought. In the first instance, it determines more precisely the definition which is given to the goal of the political community. An individual's participation in the *ratio boni*, for example, is denoted by the definition of the
common good as the life of virtue, whereas an individual's participation in the good
of order is denoted simply by the definition of the common good as peace. Defined as
a principle of moral goodness, the common good expresses the same ambivalence as

---

[5] Jean Buridan, *Quaestiones in Octo Libros Politicorum Aristotelis*, ed. W. Turner (Oxford, 1640), I.1,
pp. 1–3. Cf. id., *Quaestiones in Decem Libros Ethicorum Aristotelis* (Paris, 1513), II.11 fos. 32v–33v; VIII.4
fos. 165r–166v.

general justice and its constituent virtues. Just as justice is the same as every particular virtue but also something distinct, so the common good of the political community is identical to the individual good but also something different. Viewed in these terms, the ease with which scholastic theologians could maintain that the common good is both the same as the individual good and superior to it becomes readily explicable. Defined as the good of order, on the other hand, the common good represents the existence of peace and harmony within the political community. Viewed in these terms, it is clear how scholastic theologians could consider the common good to represent the product of virtuous activity by individuals, the arena within which individuals could perform their virtuous actions.

To demonstrate that scholastic theologians were capable of drawing a distinction between *bonum* and *utilitas*, and to maintain that they used it to draw a distinction between *bonum commune* and *communis utilitas*, is, in itself, an important conclusion to draw. This conceptual precision provides, however, only half the picture. That scholastic theologians were able to use this distinction to differentiate the *ratio boni* from the *duplex ordo*, the principle of goodness from the good of order, and to choose between these two types of community as models for human political association, still leaves one important question unanswered. What exactly was the connection which scholastic theologians made *between* these two types of good, what was the relation between virtue and order, between happiness and peace, between the presence of goodness in the universe and the organization of a human community? The *duplex ordo*, after all, comprises two types of good—an intrinsic common good of order between individuals (peace and harmony) and an extrinsic common good for which this order is instrumental (the life of moral virtue and eternal beatitude)—but implies that the attainment of either good cannot be achieved without the other. When Aquinas discusses the goal of God's providential government of the world, for example, he specifically asks whether the common good is simply the intrinsic good of order and peace or whether this *pacificus ordo* has to be ordered, in its turn, towards an extrinsic and transcendent good in God.[6] The questions which this connection then raised for the human community were significant. Did peace *have* to be directed towards the life of virtue and eternal beatitude? Could *utilitas* apply *only* to the advantage which accompanies an act of moral virtue or an act of Christian *caritas*? Did *ordo* and *utilitas* therefore bear the same restricted meaning as they had done for Augustine when he had distinguished between *uti* and *frui*? The answer to these questions rested on far-reaching assumptions in moral theology. Their particular relevance for the scholastic understanding of the common good is indicated as soon as the notion of *communis utilitas* is considered in the light of what happens to the notions of 'peace' and 'virtue' in the course of the late thirteenth and early fourteenth centuries.

According to Augustine, both peace and virtue required a correct relationship to exist towards God; they *had* to be used as a means of securing the ultimate goal, the

---

[6] Aquinas, *Ia* 103.2 in/ad 3.

'enjoyment' of God. Otherwise (at least according to Prosper of Aquitaine), they represented false peace and false virtue.[7] This distinction was recapitulated by both
Albertus Magnus and Remigio dei Girolami. It was also picked up by Buridan. True
peace, Buridan argues, is the product of a union of wills which is governed by reason
and directed towards the required goal of virtue (*honestum*). In a looser sense, however, peace can also be produced by a union of wills which may or may not be governed by reason but which is simply directed towards what is advantageous (*utile*).[8]
Buridan certainly makes a point of insisting, as both Albertus Magnus and Remigio
dei Girolami had done, that, strictly speaking, the use of 'peace' to describe something which is based simply on what is advantageous is an improper use of the term.
Nevertheless, all three writers are prepared to concede that this sort of case is an
imperfect rather than a false manifestation of peace. Their concession suggests that
Augustine's original strictures were not being observed by scholastic theologians and
that the term peace was being applied to the political community with a considerable
degree of latitude.

In the case of virtue, the replacement of Augustinian 'falsehood' by scholastic
'imperfection' provides, if anything, an even more striking shift from an absolute to
a relative scale of measurement. According to Augustine, the virtue of the pagan
Romans was false virtue because it was performed for the sake of glory rather than
God; at their best, therefore, the actions of the pagan Romans could only be
described oxymoronically as 'shining vices' (*splendida vitia*). For scholastic theologians, however, the sharpness of this judgement was substantially modified by
Aquinas' exposition of the principle that grace does not abolish nature but perfects it
(*gratia non tollit naturam sed perficit*). Both James of Viterbo and Remigio dei Girolami, for example, were able to insist that Augustine's view of non-Christian virtue
could thereby be re-evaluated in a much more moderate light. According to James,
'false' can certainly be understood in an absolute sense but it can also be considered
in relative terms, as a notion which is subject to greater or lesser degrees of perfection. As a result, Augustinian virtue appears to have been exposed to the same sort of
modification as Augustinian peace. Rather than represent the absolute alternatives of
Augustine's own *uti* and *frui*, or indeed of the Stoic conception of virtue and vice, the
scholastic understanding of virtue and peace placed them both on Aristotle's sliding
scale of degrees of goodness. Temporal peace is not illegitimate if it fails to be
directed towards eternal beatitude, it is simply imperfect; moral virtue is not illegitimate in the absence of grace and *caritas*, it is simply incomplete. The consequences
for the scholastic understanding of the relationship between *bonum* and *utilitas* are
clear. Peace and order do not have to be directed towards the attainment of moral
goodness or eternal beatitude in order to be accepted as legitimate goals for the
political community.

---

[7] Augustine, *De Civitate Dei*, ed. B. Dombart and A. Kalb (*CCSL* 47–8), XIV.1, 4, pp. 414, 418;
Prosper of Aquitaine, *Sententia* 106 (*PL* 51, col. 441).
[8] Buridan, *Quaestiones in Octo Libros Politicorum Aristotelis* IV.17, p. 222.

The Relationship between the Spiritual and the Temporal Powers

If the relationship between *bonum* and *utilitas*, between moral goodness and the order of peace, invited a particular view on the relationship between heavenly beatitude and earthly goods, then this had unavoidable consequences for the scholastic under-standing of the relationship between the spiritual and the temporal powers. Discus-sion of the impact of Aristotle's *Ethics* and *Politics* on medieval political thought has tended to focus attention on the effect of their translation on the way in which temporal political authority was subordinated to the jurisdiction of the church. In particular, it has been argued that Aristotle's *Politics* was a text which lent itself to the justification of the autonomy of temporal rulers from the authority of the pope. According to this school of thought, after the reintroduction of the *Politics* in the 1260s it was only a matter of time before Aristotle was used to produce a 'secular' theory of the state.

Rather than serving as some sort of 'secularizing' influence, however, Aristotle's *Ethics* and *Politics* appear to have been quickly and smoothly incorporated into the battery of authorities which could be deployed in support of the superiority of papal jurisdiction. In the first instance, the notion that life in the political community ori-ginated in nature rather than as a providential remedy for sin was safely accommo-dated into papalist writings on the grounds that grace does not abolish nature but perfects it. In the second instance, the notion that the function of life in the political community is not just to live but to live well, not just to secure material self-sufficiency but to live the life of virtue, was safely incorporated within a hierocratic thesis on the grounds that virtue is a good of the soul and therefore the responsibility of the spiritual power. The final argument was set in place as soon as an Aristotelian teleology was applied to the hierarchical order of goods in the universe. If the goal of political community is an earthly common good, then this goal must, in turn, be ordered towards the heavenly common good of eternal beatitude as a means towards an end. The suggestion that Aristotle's political philosophy inevitably lent itself to a justification of the independence of temporal authority from the jurisdiction of the church, and the claim that it was only a matter of time before the *Politics* and the *Ethics* were used to produce a theory of the secular state, would therefore seem to fall some way short of the mark. This is made particularly clear by the notion of the com-mon good. The function of the temporal ruler is to secure the common good; the common good of the political community is the life of moral virtue; the life of moral virtue is a good of the soul; the good of the soul is the responsibility of the spiritual power; supervision of the goal of the political community must therefore be the ultim-ate responsibility of the church. This was the line of argument which dictated the editorial arrangement of *De Regno ad Regem Cypri*, which produced a prudent silence from Giles of Rome in *De Regimine Principum*, and which was given its most persua-sive formulation by James of Viterbo in *De Regimine Christiano*. Indeed, with the composition of *De Regimine Christiano*, the hierocratic assimilation of Aristotle's *Ethics* and *Politics* appears to have been complete.

Discussion of the connection between the spiritual and the temporal powers by scholastic theologians can be approached from several different angles. An instructive perspective from which to analyse these debates is the classification of the common good into its three component elements—an intrinsic good of order, an extrinsic good of virtue, and an extrinsic good of eternal beatitude. Defined in these terms, for example, the relationship between the spiritual and the temporal powers turns on the precision of the connection which scholastic theologians drew between each of these three types of common good. Thomas Aquinas and James of Viterbo, for example, can be seen to have taken great care in connecting responsibility for the intrinsic common good with responsibility for the extrinsic common good. The temporal ruler secures the goal of peace and order independently; he then secures the life of virtue under the supervision of the church, since this is a goal which will subsequently lead to the ultimate end of eternal beatitude. Giles of Rome, meanwhile, presented two separate and very different arguments. The 'Aristotelian' *De Regimine Principum* entrusts the temporal ruler with both the life of peace and the life of virtue, with *communis utilitas* and *bonum commune*, but it does not proceed to specify how these goods will then be connected to eternal beatitude. The 'Augustinian' *De Ecclesiastica Potestate*, meanwhile, restricts the responsibility of the temporal ruler to *communis utilitas*, to the provision of material conditions in which individuals are to be guided by the ecclesiastical power towards their extrinsic common good of eternal beatitude, but it does not proceed to specify the role of the life of virtue.[9]

Although Henry of Ghent and Godfrey of Fontaines did not use the common good to analyse the exact relation of the temporal to the ecclesiastical power, their discussions of the relationship of each of these powers to individuals within their respective communities can still be credited with exercising a considerable influence on those of their colleagues who did. In the course of his discussion, in fact, Henry of Ghent seems, as a secular master, to be more representative of an 'Augustinian' tradition than either Giles of Rome or James of Viterbo, members of the Augustinian Order. According to Henry, the political community originated as a corrective to sin (*remedium peccati*). As a result, he is far more interested in the limited goals of *pax*, *quies*, *concordia*, and *salus* than he is in any Aristotelian ideal of *bene vivere*. Henry is therefore far more concerned to underline Augustine's realistic assessment of what can practically be achieved in a sinful human community than he is to echo Aristotle's idealization of the common good of virtue. Godfrey of Fontaines, by contrast, constructs an explicitly Aristotelian community. Recognizably Thomist in its inspiration, it is the product of a much closer reading of the *Ethics* and of a much closer

---

[9] For the tripartite distinction between external goods, goods of the body, and goods of the soul, see Aristotle, *Ethics* I.8 1098^b12; Albertus Magnus, *Super Ethica*, I.9, p. 45; *Pol. Lib. Oct.* VII.1, p. 621; Henry of Ghent, *Quodlibet* VII.24 fo. 427v. In *De Regimine Principum* III.ii.34, Giles maintains that three goods derive from the political community—virtue, *salus*, and *pax et tranquillitas*. For the tripartite distinction between virtues, health, and powers of the soul, see Augustine, *De Libero Arbitrio*, ed. W. M. Green (*CCSL* 29), II.19.50, p. 85; Albertus Magnus, *Super Ethica*, I.9, p. 45; Giles of Rome, *De Regimine Principum* I.i.3. Cf. Aquinas, *IaIIae* 72.4, where a *triplex ordo* is put forward—actions towards one's fellow humans, actions of human reason, and actions in accordance with divine law.

integration of political society with the universal order of goodness. The subsequent significance of Godfrey's argument lay in its examination of the relationship between the two extrinsic common goods, between the life of virtue and eternal beatitude, between moral virtue and grace. It was this discussion which enabled John of Paris to make such a radical break from both Aquinas and James of Viterbo. According to John of Paris, the temporal power could be perfected by the ecclesiastical power but this was an accidental, not an essential, completion of its role.

John of Paris's *De Potestate Regia et Papali* demonstrates just how difficult it was to argue that temporal authority could be independent from the jurisdiction of the church at the same time as accepting Aristotle's account of virtue as the defining goal of the political community. John's response to James of Viterbo appears to have involved a particular reading of Godfrey of Fontaines. In seeking to distinguish general justice from *caritas* (each being a general virtue aimed at securing a common good, that is, the human community and God respectively), Godfrey argued that the relation of moral virtue to theological virtue could be considered in different ways according to the different kinds of perfection which could be brought by the action of grace. For Godfrey, the relation between moral and theological virtue remained first and foremost a question of moral theology. For John of Paris, however, it had significant political implications. For John, the interest of this question lay in what could be done with the notion of accidental perfection. If it could be argued that it was possible for individuals to live the life of perfect moral virtue without *necessarily* possessing the theological virtues, then it could be maintained that it was possible for the political community to achieve the Aristotelian life of virtue without *necessarily* being subject to the church. According to *De Potestate Regia et Papali*, therefore, the temporal power did not have to be subordinated to the spiritual power in order to secure the goal of virtue because moral virtue did not have to be guided by grace in order to be perfect. Such subordination and such guidance *could* take place but this was an expression of an accidental, rather than essential, perfection. This was a conclusion which fitted well with the qualified dualism which was expressed elsewhere in John's treatise, when an 'incidental' power of intervention is conceded to both the church and the king and when the spiritual and temporal functions of human society are separated but without this separation being made absolute. It is a conclusion which, interestingly enough, also makes sense of the qualified dualism which has otherwise proved such a troublesome feature of Dante's *Monarchia*. According to Dante, humankind has a twofold goal. This *duplex finis*, however, can still admit some (*quodammodo*) subordination of the earthly to the heavenly beatitude in the form of filial respect and paternal grace. Dante attacks the papalist interpretation of the dependence of the moon upon the sun as an analogy for the dependence of the temporal power upon the spiritual power. He still accepts, however, that the influence of the sun can enable the moon to function 'more virtuously' (*virtuosius*).[10]

[10] Dante, *Monarchia*, ed. P. Shaw (Cambridge, 1995), III.xvi.17–18, p. 148; III.iv.17–20, pp. 110–12. Cf. E. Gilson, *Dante and Philosophy* (New York, 1963), ch. 3; M. Reeves, 'Marsiglio of Padua and Dante Alighieri', in B. Smalley (ed.), *Trends in Medieval Political Thought* (Oxford, 1965), 91–2.

De Potestate Regia et Papali reveals that if Aristotle's *Ethics* and *Politics* were going to be used as a way of resolving the relationship between the spiritual and temporal powers in favour of the temporal power, then either some means would have to be found of overcoming the obstacles presented by classifying virtue as a good of the soul or an entirely different route would have to be taken. John of Paris sought a solution in the accidental perfection of virtue by grace. It was this notion which enabled him to argue that the political community could achieve its goal of perfect moral virtue without necessarily being subject to the church. This was an argument, however, which does not appear to have found favour with subsequent political writers. A different, and ultimately more influential, method of using Aristotle to support the superiority of the temporal power was the approach which was taken by Marsilius of Padua.

What Marsilius of Padua did, in contrast to John of Paris, was to change the Aristotelian definition of the goal of the political community altogether, avoiding the life of virtue and emphasizing instead the life of material sufficiency, the life of peace and material security. This was not, in itself, either a radical or an inherently 'secularizing' move. Giles of Rome, after all, had put forward exactly this premiss in *De Ecclesiastica Potestate*. In Giles's case, it enabled him to demonstrate that the spiritual power should control the direction of all material goods as the soul controls the body. If Marsilius was aiming to remove any justification for ecclesiastical intervention in temporal affairs by limiting the goal of the political community to peace and material security, therefore, then he had to prevent *utilitas* from being glossed as a good which *must* be directed towards a higher good in God. In many respects, this transformation was a much easier task to perform for *utilitas* than it was for virtue. Once *utilitas* in the political community could be classified simply as a material or corporeal benefit, as a good which, like property or wealth, should ideally be directed towards a higher goal but did not have to be in order to be classified as a good, then *utilitas* could be separated from the constraints of an Augustinian reading of *uti*. Indeed, once *utilitas* could be glossed in this more neutral sense, once it no longer implied something being used as a means towards the end of fulfilment in God, it became possible to re-evaluate Augustine and Cicero and apply their discussions of *utilitas* in a way which had been impossible before.

Aristotle, the Common Good, and 'Secularization'

Historians have, perhaps, reached a little too quickly for 'original', 'radical', 'modern', and 'revolutionary' as terms with which to describe Marsilius of Padua and the *Defensor Pacis*.[11] What is less readily acknowledged is the simplicity of Marsilius'

---

[11] Marsilius of Padua, *Defensor Pacis*, ed. C. W. Prévité-Orton (Cambridge, 1928). Cf. A. Gewirth, *Marsilius of Padua: The Defender of the Peace* (2 vols.; New York, 1951), vol. i, *Marsilius of Padua and Medieval Political Philosophy*; J. Quillet, *La Philosophie politique de Marsile de Padoue* (Paris, 1970); C. J. Nederman, *Community and Consent: The Secular Political Theory of Marsiglio of Padua's Defensor Pacis* (Lanham, Md., 1995).

work, its lack of speculative depth. Marsilius was a maverick grazing on the margins of scholastic discourse. The *Defensor Pacis* is not a sophisticated academic treatise. It is a work of polemic which is directed specifically against papal *plenitudo potestatis*. Its much vaunted idea of 'popular sovereignty', for example, was primarily designed to deny the most basic presupposition of hierocratic apologists, namely the vicariate of Christ, rather than to provide a definition of political legitimacy in exclusively this-worldly, 'secular' terms. Marsilius was not original in the sense of establishing a radically new theoretical framework. It was thus a principle common to both Marsilius and papal theorists that peace requires a unity of jurisdiction. What Marsilius did, quite simply, was to turn a papalist argument on its head. Rather than establish any 'dualist' principle of coordinate spiritual and temporal powers, he returned to traditional monism, agreeing that a multiplicity of jurisdictions would destroy society but insisting that ultimate jurisdiction must belong, not to the pope, but to the human legislator, to the whole body of citizens or its representative.

The characterization of *Defensor Pacis* as a 'secularizing' text, as a work which explores the full implications of Aristotle's political ideas for the relationship between the spiritual and the temporal powers, needs to be treated with a similar degree of caution. The reasons for this emerge as soon as the work is set within the context of the scholastic notion of the common good. Marsilius' reading of the *Politics* led him to explore the natural origin of all human associations, from the household to the political community, and their progression towards the self-sufficient, complete, and 'perfect' community which secures all those things which are necessary for the good life. However, although Marsilius adopted an Aristotelian account of humankind's political nature, there was nothing inherently secularizing in such a move. What is far more important is what he did not transfer from Aristotle. Marsilius was certainly aware of the moral goal which could be attributed to human society on the strength of Aristotle's work. However, what is so striking about the *Defensor Pacis* when it is read in the context of previous scholastic expositions of the common good is its reluctance to identify the goal of the political community as the life of virtue. In part, this was due to the fact that the 'Aristotelianism' of the *Defensor Pacis* is drawn from the *Politics* rather than the *Ethics*. The object of enquiry in the *Defensor Pacis* is therefore the efficient cause of political life, its preconditions, and not its final cause, its goal. However, that this was not simply a matter of emphasis, of concentrating on 'living' and of taking 'living well' for granted, is clear from Marsilius' treatment of *communis utilitas*.

Whatever the view taken on whether Marsilius' ostensibly Aristotelian ideas originate with Cicero and Augustine,[12] his limitation of the goal of the political

---

[12] Gewirth, *Marsilius of Padua and Medieval Political Philosophy*, esp. 78–97; J. V. Scott, 'Influence or Manipulation? The Role of Augustinianism in the Defensor Pacis of Marsiglio of Padua', *Augustinian Studies*, 9 (1978), 59–79. Cf. D. G. Mulcahy, 'The Hands of Augustine but the Voice of Marsilius', *Augustiniana*, 21 (1971), 457–66; id., 'Marsilius of Padua's Use of St. Augustine', *Revue des Etudes Augustiniennes*, 18 (1972), 180–90; C. Condren, 'On Interpreting Marsilius' Use of St. Augustine', *Augustiniana*, 25 (1975), 217–22.

community to *communis utilitas* is fundamental to his attack on papalist claims to supreme jurisdiction in temporal affairs. According to Marsilius, the community can be defined as a multitude which is ordered towards a single principle in that its aim and purpose is to secure peace and tranquillity (*pax et tranquillitas*). Defined as the avoidance of strife, the peace which Marsilius defends is the necessary precondition of existence for the whole social body. Human society is inherently prone to strife because humankind is a naturally quarrelsome animal.[13] As a result, Marsilius' primary concern is to establish that only the exercise of coercive authority can secure the concord necessary for the fulfilment of humankind's physical needs. It is thus the goal of the political community to prevent further evils rather than act as a means towards a higher end. Where the common good appears in his argument, therefore, it is as an Augustinian *communis utilitas*, as an intrinsic common good of peace and order. Marsilius accordingly quotes in support of this argument, not Aristotle, but the passage from Cicero which was cited so frequently by Henry of Ghent.[14]

Marsilius' idea that the law has as its object the common benefit can be construed as an acknowledgement of an objective moral standard which makes law more than just a matter of command and coercion.[15] Marsilius certainly cites justice, equity, prudence, and benevolence as qualities which are desirable in the legislator. It is also his opinion that the capacity to coerce is insufficient to make a law perfect or complete. Nevertheless, coercion remains the only *necessary* element in Marsilius' definition of what makes a law legitimate. Marsilius appears determined to avoid defining the legitimacy of law in terms of its object or goal. Thus, even when the common good is acknowledged as a goal of legislation, it is ultimately subordinated to the exercise of common consent. This stipulation underpins the second stage of Marsilius' attack on papalist claims to supreme jurisdiction in temporal affairs. Not only does the *Defensor Pacis* limit the goal of political authority to material rather than moral concerns but it locates the source of legitimacy for political authority in the consent of the whole political community. This is where a secularizing tendency in Marsilius' political thinking *can* be attributed to the influence of Aristotle's *Politics*. Aristotle was important to Marsilius not because of what he had to say about the origin of political society in nature, nor because he had identified the goal of political society as moral virtue. Marsilius was interested in Aristotle because of what he had said about the connection between *communis utilitas* and consent.

It is difficult to avoid the impression that, in Marsilius' eyes, *communis utilitas* amounts to a practical effect rather than a prescriptive moral standard. Marsilius was able to use book III of the *Politics* to establish the importance of the consent of the political community to legislation and to credit the community as a whole with the capacity to judge what is to its own advantage. According to Marsilius, the efficient cause of the political community is peace, security, and the life of material

---

[13] *Defensor Pacis* I.4.4, p. 13; Augustine, *De Civitate Dei* XII.28, p. 384 (*nihil enim est quam hoc genus tam discordiosum vitio, tam sociale natura*).

[14] *Defensor Pacis* I.1.4, p. 4; Cicero, *De Officiis*, ed. M. Winterbottom (Oxford, 1994), I.22, pp. 9–10.

[15] Quillet, *La Philosophie politique de Marsile de Padoue*, ch. 10.

sufficiency. While this does not preclude the possibility that its final cause might be the life of virtue or eternal beatitude, the point for Marsilius is that such a final cause does not necessarily determine the means by which the efficient cause of peace can be secured. These means are provided by the consent of the political community. Consent, moreover, is understood, not as the active exercise of deliberative reason by every member of the political community, but as the recognition of what will be to their advantage. This was an argument which Marsilius extrapolated from Aristotle's suggestion that the whole community is a better judge of what is in its own interest than a smaller number of wise or prudent individuals. The whole community, he argues, is almost always a better judge of what is in its own interest. Thus, despite the fact that the common interest, the common good of the community, is the goal of the community, if the community consents to something which is not to its advantage, which does not secure the *communis utilitas*, then it is still legitimate as law by virtue of the fact that it has been willed by the whole community.[16] Marsilius uses this argument as a means of pointing out that it is not the common good which legitimates a particular law. Although the community retains the capacity to direct its legislative will towards a universal norm of justice, or even towards the ultimate goal of eternal beatitude, this does not *have* to be the case in order for law in that community to be legitimate.

The argument of the *Defensor Pacis* has often been seen running into difficulties when Marsilius concedes that a connection can still exist between the political community and the Christian faith, notably when it is a matter of heresy and excommunication.[17] In the first part of his treatise, Marsilius outlines a theoretical model of legitimacy for the political community based on entirely rational and philosophical grounds. As such, the one reference to religion treats it quite dispassionately as something which can be useful to the intrinsic good of the political community. For Marsilius, fear of eternal punishment enables citizens to observe those measures which are necessary for civil *pax et tranquillitas*. In the second part of his treatise, Marsilius considers the reality of political life in the *regnum Italicum*, namely a community of citizens which also happens to be a community of Christians. In this particular instance, therefore, the lawful sovereign, the body of citizens, is the same as the body of the faithful. Because of this accidental equation it is inevitable, given the consensual basis for law, that the same human legislator will find itself dealing with both political and Christian activity. Once again, all Marsilius has done is turn a traditional argument on its head—society is the church and the church is society. It is this numerical identity of citizen and Christian which makes the lawful sovereign in the Christian political community the sole authority in the government of the church. Political life itself is concerned only with exterior ('transient'), not interior ('immanent'), action. The interior spiritual life of each Christian is a matter not for precept but for counsel, not for the legislator but for the individual's own conscience.

---

[16] *Defensor Pacis* I.12.6, p. 52. Cf. Gewirth, *Marsilius of Padua and Medieval Political Philosophy*, 58.

[17] *Defensor Pacis* II.6.12–13, pp. 168–73; II.21.8, pp. 334–5. Cf. Gewirth, *Marsilius of Padua and Medieval Political Philosophy*, 155–66; Quillet, *La Philosophie politique de Marsile de Padoue*, 142–51.

Nevertheless, exterior action still includes the temporal consequences of spiritual acts and it is this principle which lies behind Marsilius' treatment of excommunication, heresy, and violations of divine law. Although the determination of articles of faith is necessary to preserve the unity of the Christian faith, Marsilius does not condone their enforcement. More precisely, he states that the authority to coerce their observance belongs to the human legislator only if it is permissible (*si liceat hoc fieri*), that is, if it is justified by external repercussions, if it affects the peace and tranquillity of the community, and if it is subject to consent.[18]

Marsilius of Padua's repeated insistence on the incompatibility of faith and coercion depends upon a particular conception of Christianity. His aim was to provide a definition of divine law which would limit ecclesiastical authority to the power of orders rather than the power of jurisdiction, and a definition of human law which would place it entirely within the competence of the temporal sphere. By avoiding natural law in the traditional sense of a higher norm, by defining human law as something which simply secures peace, order, stability, and common benefit, by restricting the sanctions of divine 'law' to the next life, and by consequently denying the legitimacy of ecclesiastical jurisdiction itself, Marsilius sought to remove, one by one, all the grounds on which the church had traditionally justified its intervention in the government of the political community.

When Marsilius adopted the Franciscan paradigm of poverty and humility in the early church, and when he made the distinction between ownership and use so universal in its application that the church was disendowed of all those temporal goods not needed for worship, maintenance, and acts of charity, the argument was complete. Combined with a theory of legitimate jurisdiction which was based on consent, this ideal of the Christian church reformed in accordance with evangelical practice may, indeed, amount to a 'secular' theory of politics. In practice, however, the numerical identity of citizens and Christians militated against the absolute separation of the human from the divine. The similarity here with the arguments put forward by John of Paris is worth noting. According to John of Paris, moral virtue is perfect without theological virtue but it can still receive an accidental perfection from the infusion of grace; the temporal power is ordinarily free from the jurisdiction of the spiritual power but it can still be subject to the incidental power of the pope. According to Marsilius of Padua, the temporal legislator necessarily concerns itself with self-sufficiency, material security, peace, and tranquillity but, because of its numerical identity with the *communitas fidelium*, it can also concern itself with matters touching eternal beatitude should it be justifiable and should it consent to do so. John of Paris and Marsilius of Padua, in other words, represent two different solutions to the same question—how to separate the temporal from the spiritual power without making that separation absolute, how to treat the temporal goods of virtue, peace, and *utilitas* without making them *necessarily* dependent on being directed towards eternal beatitude.

---

[18] *Defensor Pacis* II.5.7, p. 154.

If scholastic political thought appears to offer the twin goals of peace and virtue as alternative elements within a notion of the common good, then this is an important perspective from which to approach William of Ockham, the theologian who has been identified, along with Marsilius, as the instigator of 'the birth of the lay spirit'. In many respects, Ockham's ideas present the difficulties posed by the relation of scholastic metaphysics to scholastic political thought in their most acute form. Not only are Ockham's philosophical works chronologically separated from his political works but there is a lack of political comment in his speculative works and a paucity of nominalist passages in his political works. Where the relations between Ockham's theology, philosophy, and politics have been examined, they have yielded the conclusion that their author simply worked at different, and separate, levels of abstraction and polemic.[19] Like Marsilius' treatise, moreover, Ockham's political writing is primarily destructive in its intent, whether it takes the form of a refutation of John XXII's bulls on property and poverty or an attack on the regular exercise of temporal jurisdiction by the spiritual power. As a result, Ockham's political writings do not readily provide a 'theory' of the temporal political community. Ockham does not rely, for example, on any Aristotelian account of the needs and fulfilment of human nature, nor on a detailed and systematic analysis of popular sovereignty. Ockham's approach to political thought is, instead, characteristically Franciscan, thoroughly scriptural and patristic in its sources. Thus, his attempt to establish the independence of the Empire, and of the temporal power in general, draws primarily on biblical texts which acknowledge the legitimacy of dominion and jurisdiction amongst non-believers. Where the function of the temporal power is discussed in non-biblical terms, it is based on a recognizably Augustinian 'minimalism'. Temporal authority is simply instrumental to social existence; it is not an embodiment of higher values; its primary function is to exercise coercion as a means of preventing or punishing injustice.

Ockham's lack of interest in the philosophical foundations of political theory makes his use of the common good and his account of its relationship to the individual good particularly problematic. However, even if it is, in both senses of the word, unrealistic to look for a precise correlation between nominalism and an inability to treat the community in any other terms than those of aggregate composition and individual autonomy, this does not mean that a notion of the common good is unimportant to Ockham's political argument. Henry of Ghent, after all, had already demonstrated that it was quite possible to combine a distinct lack of interest in the metaphysical nature of the common good in the universe with a powerful sense of the practical application of the common good in the political community. William of Ockham does something very similar.

<hr/>

[19] A. S. McGrade, *The Political Thought of William of Ockham: Personal and Institutional Principles* (Cambridge, 1974). Cf. J. B. Morrall, 'Some Notes on a Recent Interpretation of William of Ockham's Political Philosophy', *Franciscan Studies*, 9 (1949), 335–49. For an account of Ockham's individualism which is favourable to Lagarde, see L. Vereecke, 'Individu et communauté selon Guillaume d'Ockham', *Studia Moralia*, 3 (1965), 150–77, and, for an opposing view, A. S. McGrade, 'Ockham and the Birth of Individual Rights', in B. Tierney and P. Linehan (eds.), *Authority and Power: Studies on Medieval Law and Government Presented to Walter Ullmann* (Cambridge, 1980), 149–65.

The guiding principle of Ockham's political argument is a profound sense that human affairs will always be subject to a series of highly contingent factors. According to Ockham, there are three modes of natural law—absolute and universal norms, principles of natural equity which can be modified by human law in accordance with reason, and particular responses to non-rational circumstances such as the effects of sinful human behaviour. It is to the third of these categories that politics is ascribed. Ockham's theory of consent is a prime example of such contingency. In Ockham's view, it would seem that consent is, in itself, insufficient for political legitimacy, since he regards different forms of government to be appropriate for different political communities in different circumstances. A profound sense of contingency also governs Ockham's account of freedom. His commitment to individual liberty can be traced to its origins in a voluntarist theory of ethics and to a Franciscan reading of the New Testament as *lex evangelica lex libertatis*, as the law which gives freedom (James 1: 25). In political terms, however, this commitment does not produce the chaotic and anarchic individualism of which it has sometimes been accused. Ockham typically only gives political freedom a minimal and negative definition (liberty is what is opposed to the slavery of absolute papal jurisdiction). He also subjects it to a number of significant qualifications, the most important of which is a notion of the common good. According to Ockham, the temporal freedom of individuals within the political community is always circumscribed by the requirements of the intrinsic common good. Thus, the legitimate rights of individuals can always give way to considerations of necessity, equity, and *communis utilitas*.[20] It remains the responsibility of 'good and wise men' to judge when the criteria of public need or evident benefit are present. Once again, however, it is a noticeably limited notion of *communis utilitas* which Ockham invokes. Ockham understands the common good, not as the life of virtue, but as the social necessity of peace and tranquillity (*pax et tranquillitas*). The individual is subordinated only to those external obligations which have been imposed by spiritual and temporal authority in order to enable humans to live together in peace and tranquillity.

Like Marsilius of Padua, William of Ockham relies for his political theory primarily on a Franciscan exposition of the New Testament—'My kingdom is not of this world' (John 18: 36). Ockham's advocacy of an apostolic ideal in the dispute over property and poverty within the Franciscan order prompted him to restrict the material goods of the church to what was needed for preaching and administering the sacraments. As far as the spiritual power was concerned, this ideal necessarily entailed a restricted definition of what constituted the legitimate exercise of coercive commands. As a pastoral ministry, Ockham argued, the church will exercise such a power only when it is vitally necessary for the good of the church or for the salvation

---

[20] C. Bayley, 'Pivotal Concepts in the Political Philosophy of Ockham', *Journal of the History of Ideas*, 10 (1949), 199–218. Cf. M. Grignaschi, 'L'Interprétation de la 'Politique' d'Aristote dans le 'Dialogue' de Guillaume d'Ockham', in *Liber Memorialis Georges de Lagarde* (Études présentées à la Commission Internationale pour l'histoire des assemblées d'états 38, Louvain–Paris, 1970), 59–72; Morrall, 'Some Notes on a Recent Interpretation', 354.

of its members. In terms of theory, this was a thoroughly orthodox principle. Giles of Rome and James of Viterbo had both argued that papal *plenitudo potestatis* could justify casual intervention in temporal affairs only when it was exercised to give clear benefit to the common good and that, otherwise, the church should confine itself to fulfilling its spiritual functions. It is Ockham's practical application of this theory which is different. Ockham may have concluded that the spiritual power has a theoretical claim to intervene in the actions of the temporal power but he promptly subjected this to a detailed series of substantial limitations. Like John of Paris, for example, Ockham insists that the principal responsibility for the correction and deposition of rulers rests with the political community. Ockham's primary concern was not to establish a speculative 'monism' or 'dualism' but to widen the actual distance between the temporal and spiritual governments by limiting the practical scope of their respective jurisdictions. This pragmatic 'separatism' was achieved, on the one hand, by removing the moral dimension from his definition of the goal of the political community, and on the other, by replacing the legalistic emphasis of ecclesiastical government with an ideal of pastoral ministry based on Acts and on Bernard of Clairvaux's *De Consideratione*. It is in the context of this argument that the replacement of the moral goal of politics with the more realistic definition of *communis utilitas* assumes a critical importance. By treating the promotion of virtue as a nonessential function of temporal government, Ockham followed Marsilius in separating the necessary function of temporal rulers from the activity and supervision of the Christian church. He retains the intrinsic common good of peace and the extrinsic common good of beatitude but removes altogether the extrinsic common good of the life of virtue. If Ockham is to be described as a herald of 'secularization', therefore, this should not be because of any radical theory of individualism or consent but because he believed, like Marsilius, in an apostolic ideal of ecclesiastical reform and because he advocated, like Godfrey of Fontaines and John of Paris, a practical political programme which could countenance the deposition of a heretical pope, the right of the temporal ruler to tax the clergy, and the exercise of 'casual' ecclesiastical intervention for the common benefit of human society.

It is too often taken for granted that late medieval political theory witnessed the development of an idea of the 'secular state' as the product of humankind's political nature, a concept not of secularization but of secularism, a secular humanism which was rapidly acquired through the rediscovery of Aristotle's *Ethics* and *Politics*. The 'reception of Aristotle' in the late thirteenth century reveals, on the contrary, the flexibility with which the natural origins of the political community and the common good of the life of virtue could be applied to political and ethical thought. By the early fourteenth century, both of these tenets had been securely accommodated within a firmly papalist argument. Likewise, it is too often taken for granted that late medieval political theory witnessed the liberation of the individual from complete subordination to hierocratic corporatism. The relationship between the common good and the individual good reveals, on the contrary, how the distinction between *bonum* and *utilitas* enabled scholastic theologians to continue in their strong sense of the value of the individual human being and to retain their insistence on the importance of the individual good as, and when, it was felt to be under threat.

Debates within medieval scholastic philosophy and theology have been increasingly seen, not as the inevitable opposition of monolithic schools of thought, but as particular disagreements in specific areas over different combinations of the same authorities. For example, rather than treat the vitality of late thirteenth- and early fourteenth-century scholasticism as the product of a conflict between Aristotelian and Augustinian metaphysics, or between Aristotelian and Augustinian epistemology, it is often far more accurate to treat it as the product of a conflict between different types of Aristotelianism.[21] Debates within scholastic political thought now need to be treated in the same light. Viewed from this perspective, the question which Aristotle generated for the scholastic understanding of the common good was very similar to the question posed by Augustine—not 'what is the natural origin of society' but 'what is the relation of the common good of the life of virtue to the intrinsic common benefit of peace and the extrinsic common good in God?' This is the question which exercised scholastic theologians in the late thirteenth and early fourteenth centuries.

For John of Paris, once moral virtue was capable of being made independent from theological virtue, Aristotle's 'life of virtue' could indeed be used to justify the autonomy of the temporal power from ecclesiastical jurisdiction. For Marsilius of Padua and William of Ockham, however, any 'secularizing' definition of political authority came, not from endorsing the moral end of the political community but from leaving it out altogether, not from emphasizing the ideal of *bonum commune* but from recognizing the reality of *communis utilitas*. This was the result, therefore, not of any desire to champion Aristotle, but of the choice of a minimalist tradition of political argument which was rooted in Augustine and in the Bible.[22] For Marsilius and for Ockham, the beneficiary of such a shift was intended to be the church as much as the temporal power, the pope as much as Ludwig of Bavaria. If the early fourteenth century is to be credited with giving birth to 'l'esprit laïque', therefore, then such a development would seem to have been precipitated, not by a positive alternative of 'secular' power, but by criticism and reform of the church from within, not by the use of Aristotle's political philosophy as a radical alternative framework, but by the integration of certain aspects of the *Ethics* and the *Politics* with existing patristic and biblical authorities. Viewed in this light, the truly radical texts in scholastic political thought were provided, not by Aristotle, but by Augustine and the Bible.

---

[21] e.g. F. van Steenberghen, *La Philosophie au XIIIe siècle*, 2nd edn. (Louvain, 1991).

[22] G. Leff, 'The Apostolic Ideal in Later Medieval Ecclesiology', *Journal of Theological Studies*, 18 (1967), 58–82.

BIBLIOGRAPHY

I. PRIMARY SOURCES

ABELARD, *Theologia Christiana*, ed. E. M. Buytaert (*CCCM* 12; Turnholt: Brepols, 1969).

—— *Dialogus inter Philosophum, Iudaeum et Christianum*, ed. R. Thomas (Stuttgart–Bad Cannstatt: Frommann–Holzboog, 1970).

AEGIDIUS ROMANUS—see Giles of Rome

ALAN OF LILLE, *De Fide Catholica* (*PL* 210, cols. 305–430).

ALBERTUS MAGNUS, *Opera Omnia*, ed. A. Borgnet (38 vols.; Paris: Vivès, 1890–9).

    Ethicorum Libri Decem, vol. vii (1891).

    Politicorum Libri Octo, vol. viii (1891).

    De Anima Libri Tres, vol. v (1890).

    Enarrationes in Evangelium secundum Lucam, vol. xxiii (1895).

    Commentarii in IV Sententiarum, vols. xxv–xxx (1893–4).

—— *Opera Omnia*, ed. B. Geyer, W. Kübel, et al. (50 vols.; Münster: Aschendorff, 1951–).

    Super Ethica commentum et quaestiones, ed. W. Kübel, vol. xiv.1–2 (1968, 1987).

    Metaphysica, ed. B. Geyer, vol. xvi.1–2 (1960, 1964).

    Physica, ed. P. Hossfeld, vol. iv.1–2 (1987, 1993).

    Super Dionysium De Caelesti Hierarchia, ed. P. Simon and W. Kübel, vol. xxxvi.1 (1993).

    Tractatus de Natura Boni, ed. E. Filthaut, vol. xxv.1 (1974).

    De Bono, ed. H. Kühle, C. Feckes, B. Geyer, and W. Kübel, vol. xxviii (1951).

AMBROSE, *De Officiis*, ed. M. Testard (2 vols.; Paris: Les Belles Lettres, 1984, 1992).

—— *Exameron*, ed. C. Schenkl (*CSEL* 32.1; Vienna, 1896).

[anon.], Gloss on *Clericis laicos* (R. Scholz, *Die Publizistik zur Zeit Philipps des Schönen und Bonifaz' VIII* (Stuttgart, 1903), 471–84).

[anon.], Account of the Legatine Council in Paris, December 1290 (H. Finke, *Aus den Tagen Bonifaz VIII: Funde und Forschungen* (Vorreformationsgeschichtliche Forschungen II; (Münster, 1902), pp. iii–vii).

Antequam essent clerici (P. Dupuy, *Histoire du différend d'entre le Pape Boniface VIII et Philippes le Bel, roy de France. Actes et Preuves* (Paris, 1655), 21–3).

AQUINAS—see Thomas Aquinas

ARISTOTLE, *Nicomachean Ethics*, ed. L. Bywater (Oxford Classical Texts; Oxford: Clarendon Press, 1894).

—— *Ethica Nicomachea, Praefatio*, ed. R. A. Gauthier (*Aristoteles Latinus* XXVI.1; Leiden–Brussels: E. J. Brill–Desclée de Brouwer, 1974).

—— *Ethica Nicomachea, Recensio pura*, ed. R.-A. Gauthier (*Aristoteles Latinus* XXVI.3; Brussels–Leiden: Desclée de Brouwer–E. J. Brill, 1972).

—— *Ethica Nicomachea, Recensio recognita*, ed. R.-A. Gauthier (*Aristoteles Latinus* XXVI.4; Brussels–Leiden: Desclée de Brouwer–E. J. Brill, 1973).

—— *Ethica nova*, ed. R.-A. Gauthier (*Aristoteles Latinus* XXVI.2; Brussels–Leiden: Desclée de Brouwer–E. J. Brill, 1972).

ARISTOTLE, *Metaphysica*, ed. G. Vuillemin-Diem (*Aristoteles Latinus* XXV.3.1–2; Leiden: E. J. Brill, 1995).

—— *Politica*, ed. W. D. Ross (Oxford Classical Texts; Oxford: Clarendon Press, 1957).

—— *Aristotelis Politicorum Libri Octo cum vetusta translatione Gulielmi de Moerbeka*, ed. F. Susemihl (Leipzig: Teubner, 1872).

—— *Politica I–II, Translatio prior imperfecta*, ed. P. Michaud-Quantin (*Aristoteles Latinus* XXIX.1; Bruges: Desclée de Brouwer, 1961).

—— *Rhetorica*, ed. W. D. Ross (Oxford Classical Texts; Oxford: Clarendon Press, 1959).

—— *Rhetorica, Translatio Anonyma sive Vetus et Guillelmi de Moerbeka*, ed. B. Schneider (*Aristoteles Latinus* XXXI.1–2; Leiden: E. J. Brill, 1978).

[*Auctoritates Aristotelis*] *Les Auctoritates Aristotelis: Un florilège médiéval, étude historique et édition critique*, ed. J. Hamesse (Philosophes Médiévaux XVII; Louvain–Paris: Publications Universitaires–B. Nauwelaerts, 1974).

ASSER, *De Rebus Gestis Aelfredi*, ed. W. H. Stevenson, rev. D. Whitelock (Oxford: Clarendon Press, 1959).

AUGUSTINE, *Confessionum Libri XIII*, ed. J. J. O'Donnell (Oxford: Clarendon Press, 1992).

—— *Contra Faustum*, ed. J. Zycha (*CSEL* 25; Vienna: Tempsky, 1891).

—— *Contra Iulianum* (*PL* 44, cols. 641–874).

—— *Contra Mendacium*, ed. J. Zycha (*CSEL* 41; Vienna: Tempsky, 1900).

—— *De Civitate Dei*, ed. B. Dombart and A. Kalb (*CCSL* 47–8; Turnholt: Brepols, 1955).

—— *De Diversis Quaestionibus LXXXIII*, ed. A. Mutzenbecher (*CCSL* 44; Turnholt: Brepols, 1975).

—— *De Doctrina Christiana*, ed. R. P. H. Green (Oxford Early Christian Texts; Oxford: Clarendon Press, 1995).

—— *De Genesi contra Manichaeos* (*PL* 34, cols. 173–220).

—— *De Genesi ad Litteram*, ed. J. Zycha (*CSEL* 28.1; Vienna, 1894).

—— *De Libero Arbitrio*, ed. W. M. Green (*CCSL* 29; Turnholt: Brepols, 1970).

—— *De Mendacio*, ed. J. Zycha (*CSEL* 41; Vienna: Tempsky, 1900).

—— *De Moribus Ecclesiae* (*PL* 32, cols. 1309–44).

—— *De Musica* (*PL* 32).

—— *De Ordine*, ed. W. M. Green (*CCSL* 29; Turnholt: Brepols, 1970).

—— *De Trinitate*, ed. W. J. Mountain (*CCSL* 50; Turnholt: Brepols, 1968).

—— *Enchiridion*, ed. E. Evans (*CCSL* 46; Turnholt: Brepols, 1969).

—— *Epistulae*, ed. A. Goldbacher (*CSEL* 34–5, 44; Vienna: Tempsky, 1895, 1904).

—— *Epistula* 67 (ed. J. Schmid, *SS Eusebii Hieronymi et Aurelii Augustini Epistulae Mutuae* (Florilegium Patristicum 22; Bonn, 1930), 113–24).

—— *In Ioannis Evangelium Tractatus* (*CCSL* 36; Turnholt: Brepols, 1954).

—— *Praeceptum* (ed. G. Lawless, *Augustine of Hippo and his Monastic Rule* (Oxford: Clarendon Press, 1987), 80–102).

—— *Retractionum Libri II*, ed. A. Mutzenbecher (*CCSL* 57; Turnholt: Brepols, 1984).

—— *Sermones* (*PL* 38).

AVERROES, *Aristotelis Opera cum Averrois Commentariis* (editio Iuntina, 2nd edn., 11 vols.; Venice, 1562–74).

  vol. iii. *Aristotelis Stagiritae libri moralem totam philosophiam complectentes cum Averrois Cordubensis in Moralia Nicomachia Expositione . . . et in Platonis libros de Republica Paraphrasi.*

vol. viii. *Aristotelis Metaphysicorum Libri XIV cum Averrois Cordubensis in eosdem Commentariis et Epitome.*

AVICENNA, *Avicenna Latinus: Liber De Anima seu sextus de naturalibus I–II–III*, ed. S. van Riet (Leiden: E. Peeters–E. J. Brill, 1972).

BASIL OF CAESAREA, *Homiliae* (*PG* 31).

BEAUMANOIR, PHILIPPE DE, *Coutumes de Beauvaisis*, ed. A. Salmon (2 vols.; Collection de textes pour servir à l'étude et à l'enseignement de l'histoire, fasc.14, 30; Paris, 1899–1900).

BERNARD OF CLAIRVAUX, *De Consideratione ad Eugenium Papam* (ed. J. Leclercq and H. Rochais, *S. Bernardi Opera*, vol. iii (Rome: *Editiones Cistercienses*, 1963), 393–493).

   De Diligendo Deo (ibid. 119–54).

   De Praecepto et Dispensatione (ibid. 253–94).

—— *Epistolae* (*S. Bernardi Opera*, vols. vii–viii (Rome, 1974, 1977)).

Biblia Latina cum Glossa Ordinaria (Strassburg, 1480–1; facsimile edn., 4 vols.; Turnholt: Brepols, 1992).

Biblia Sacra iuxta Vulgatam Versionem, ed. B. Fischer and R. Weber (2 vols.; Stuttgart: Würtemburgische Bibelanstalt, 1969).

BOETHIUS, *De Musica* (*PL* 63, cols. 1167–1300).

—— *Liber de divisione* (*PL* 64, cols. 875–92).

—— *Liber de unitate et uno* (*PL* 63, cols. 1075–8).

—— *Philosophiae Consolatio*, ed. L. Bieler (*CCSL* 94; Turnholt: Brepols, 1984).

BONAVENTURE, *Commentarius in quattuor libros Sententiarum Petri Lombardi*, vols. i–iv (*Opera Omnia*, ed. Collegium S. Bonaventurae; 10 vols.; Quaracchi, 1882–1902).

[Boniface VIII], *Les Registres de Boniface VIII*, ed. G. Digard, M. Faucon, A. Thomas, and R. Fawtier (4 vols.; Bibliothèque des Écoles Françaises d'Athènes et de Rome, 1884–1939).

BRUNI, LEONARDO, *Humanistisch-philosophische Schriften mit einer chronologie seiner Werke und Briefe*, ed. H. Baron (Leipzig: Teubner, 1928).

BURIDAN, JEAN, *Quaestiones in Octo Libros Politicorum Aristotelis*, ed. W. Turner (Oxford, 1640).

—— *Quaestiones in Decem Libros Ethicorum Aristotelis* (Paris, 1513).

Chartularium Universitatis Parisiensis, vols. i–ii, ed. H. Denifle and E. Chatelain (4 vols.; Paris: Delalain, 1889–97).

CICERO, *De Officiis*, ed. M. Winterbottom (Oxford Classical Texts; Oxford: Clarendon Press, 1994).

—— *De Inventione* (Loeb Classical Library, 1949).

—— *De Finibus* (Loeb Classical Library, 1931).

—— *De Republica*, ed. J. E. G. Zetzel (Cambridge Greek and Latin Classics; Cambridge: Cambridge University Press, 1995).

—— *De Amicitia* (Loeb Classical Library, 1923).

—— *In Catilinam* I–IV (Loeb Classical Library, 1977).

—— *Oratio Pro Marcello* (Loeb Classical Library, 1931).

[COLONNA], *Die Denkschriften der Colonna gegen Bonifaz VIII und der Cardinäle gegen die Colonna*, ed. H. Denifle (Archiv für Literatur- und Kirchengeschichte des Mittelalters; Freiburg im Breisgau, 1885–93, v. 493–529).

Corpus Iuris Canonici, ed. E. Friedberg (2 vols.; Leipzig: Tauchnitz, 1879–81).

[*Correctorium Corruptorii*], ed. P. Glorieux, *Les Premières Polémiques thomistes I: Le Correctorium Corruptorii 'Quare'* (Bibliothèque Thomiste 9; Paris: Kain, 1927).

DANTE ALIGHIERI, *Convivio*, ed. E. G. Parodi and F. Pellegrini (*Le Opere di Dante*, 2nd edn.; Florence: Società Dantesca Italiana, 1960).

—— *Monarchia*, ed. and trans. P. Shaw (Cambridge Medieval Classics, 4; Cambridge: Cambridge University Press, 1995).

Decrees of the Ecumenical Councils, ed. N. P. Tanner (2 vols.; London: Sheed and Ward, 1990).

Disputatio inter Clericum et Militem (ed. N. N. Erickson, 'A Dispute between a Priest and a Knight', *Proceedings of the American Philosophical Society*, 111 (1967), 288–309).

DUPUY, P., *Histoire du différend d'entre le Pape Boniface VIII et Philippes le Bel, roy de France. Actes et Preuves* (Paris, 1655).

EINHARD, *Vita Karoli Magni Imperatoris*, ed. L. Halphen, 5th edn. (Paris: Les Belles Lettres, 1981).

EUSTRATIUS—see [Grosseteste]

Eustratii et Michaelis et Anonyma in Ethica Nicomachea Commentaria, ed. G. Heylbut (Commentaria in Aristotelem Graeca, XX; Berlin, 1892).

FREDEGAR, *Chronicle*, ed. J. M. Wallace-Hadrill (London: Nelson, 1960).

GÉRARD D'ABBEVILLE, *Quodlibet* XIV.1 (*S. Thomae Aquinatis Opera Omnia*, vol. xli, pp. B.56–62).

GERVAIS DE MONT SAINT ELOI—see Servais de Mont Saint Eloi

GILES OF ROME, *Opera Omnia*, ed. F. Del Punta and G. Fioravanti (Unione Accademica Nazionale, Corpus Philosophorum Medii Aevi, Testi e Studi; Florence: Olschki, 1985–).
   Apologia, ed. R. Wielockx (vol. III.1, 1985).
   Repertorio dei Sermoni, ed. C. Luna (vol. I.6, 1990).

—— *De Differentia Rhetoricae, Ethicae et Politicae* (ed. G. Bruni, 'The *De Differentia Rhetoricae, Ethicae et Politicae* of Aegidius Romanus', *New Scholasticism*, 6 (1932), 1–18, 5–12).

—— *De Ecclesiastica Potestate*, ed. R. Scholz (Weimar: H. Böhlaus Nachfolger, 1929).

—— *De Regimine Principum* (Venice, 1502).

—— *De Renuntiatione Papae*, ed. J. R. Eastman (Texts and Studies in Religion, 52; Lewiston, NY: Mellon Press, 1992).

—— *In II Librum Sententiarum* (Venice, 1581).

—— *Quodlibeta* (Venice, 1504).

—— *Super Libros Rhetoricorum* (Venice, 1542).

—— *Li Livres du gouvernement des rois: A XIIIth Century French Version of Egidio Colonna's Treatise De Regimine Principum*, ed. S. P. Molenaer (New York: Macmillan, 1899).

GODFREY OF FONTAINES, *Quodlibet* I–IV, ed. M. de Wulf and A. Pelzer (Les Philosophes Belges, II; Louvain, 1904).

—— *Quodlibets* V–VII, ed. M. de Wulf and J. Hoffmans (Les Philosophes Belges, III; Louvain, 1914).

—— *Quodlibets* VIII–X, ed. J. Hoffmans (Les Philosophes Belges, IV; Louvain, 1924–31).

—— *Quodlibets* XI–XIV, ed. J. Hoffmans (Les Philosophes Belges, V; Louvain, 1932–5).

—— *Quodlibet* XV and three *Quaestiones Ordinariae* (Les Philosophes Belges, XIV; Louvain, 1937).

—— *Quaestiones Disputatae* I, VII–VIII, XIII and XV (B. Neumann, *Der Mensch und die himmlische Seligkeit nach der Lehre Gottfrieds von Fontaines* (Limburg: Lahn, 1958), 152–66).

—— *Quaestiones Disputatae* IV–V (O. Lottin, *Psychologie et morale aux XIIe et XIIIe siècles* (6 vols.; Louvain–Gembloux: Abbaye du Mont César–J. Duculot, 1942–60), iv. 581–8, 591–7).

—— *Quaestiones Disputatae* IX, X and XII (J. F. Wippel, 'Godfrey of Fontaines: Disputed Questions 9, 10 and 12', *Franciscan Studies*, 33 (1973), 351–72).

—— *Quaestio Disputata* XI (O. Lottin, *Psychologie et morale aux XIIe et XIIIe siècles* (6 vols.; Louvain–Gembloux: Abbaye du Mont César–J. Duculot, 1942–60), iii. 497–502).

—— *Quaestio Disputata* XV (J. Koch, *Durandi de S. Porciano O.P. Tractatus de habitibus Quaestio Quarta* (Opuscula et Textus, Series Scolastica, fasc. 8; Münster: Aschendorff, 1930), 60–6).

—— *Quaestio Disputata* XVII (J. Grundel, *Die Lehre von dem Umstanden der menschlichen Handlung im Mittelalter* (Beiträge zur Geschichte der Philosophie und Theologie des Mittelalters, 39.5; Münster, 1963), 655–60).

—— *Quaestio Disputata* XIX (O. Lottin, 'Les Vertus morales acquises sont-elles de vraies vertus? La Réponse des théologiens de saint Thomas à Pierre Auriol', *RTAM* 21 (1954), 101–29, 114–22).

—— *Sermon* (P. Tihon, 'Le Sermon de Godefroid de Fontaines pour le deuxième dimanche après l'Epiphanie', *RTAM* 32 (1965), 43–53, 50–1).

GREGORY THE GREAT, *Homiliae in Evangelia* (*PL* 76, cols. 1075–1312).

—— *Homiliae in Hiezechihelem Prophetam*, ed. M. Adriaen (*CCSL* 142; Turnholt: Brepols, 1971).

—— *Moralia in Iob*, ed. M. Adriaen (*CCSL* 143; Turnholt: Brepols, 1979).

—— *Regulae Pastoralis Liber* (*PL* 77, cols. 13–128).

[GROSSETESTE], *The Greek Commentaries on the Nicomachean Ethics of Aristotle in the Latin Translation of Robert Grosseteste, Bishop of Lincoln*, ed. H. P. F. Mercken (Corpus Latinum Commentariorum in Aristotelem Graecorum VI.1, 3; Leiden: E. J. Brill, 1973, 1991).

—— *Aristoteles over der vriendschap: Boeken VIII en IX van de Nicomachische Ethiek met de commentaren van Aspasius en Michaël in de Latijnse vertaling van Grosseteste*, ed. W. Stinissen (Verhandelingen van de Koninklijke Vlaamse Academie voor Wetenschappen, Letteren en Schone Kunsten van België, Klasse der Letteren jg. 26, nr. 45; Brussels, 1963).

GUILLAUME LE MAIRE, *Livre de Guillaume le Maire*, ed. C. Port (Collection de documents inédits sur l'histoire de France; Mélanges historiques, choix de documents; 5 vols.; Paris, 1873–86), ii. 203–537.

HELINAND OF FROIDMONT, *Flores* (*PL* 212, cols. 721–46).

HENRY OF GHENT, *Opera Omnia*, ed. R. Macken et al. (Leuven–Leiden: University Press–E. J. Brill, 1979–).

    Quodlibet I, ed. R. Macken (vol. 5, 1979).

    Quodlibet II, ed. R. Wielockx (vol. 6, 1983).

    Quodlibet VI, ed. G. A. Wilson (vol. 10, 1987).

    Quodlibet VII, ed. G. A. Wilson (vol. 11, 1991).

    Quodlibet IX, ed. R. Macken (vol. 13, 1983).

    Quodlibet X, ed. R. Macken (vol. 14, 1981).

    Quodlibet XII, ed. J. Decorte (vol. 16, 1987).

    Quodlibet XII.31: Tractatus super Facto Praelatorum et Fratrum, ed. L. Hödl and M. Haverals (vol. 17, 1989).

    Quodlibet XIII, ed. J. Decorte (vol. 18, 1985).

—— *Quodlibeta aurea*, ed. V. Zuccolius (2 vols.; Venice, 1613).

—— *Quodlibeta* (Oxford, Merton College MS 107).

—— *Summa Quaestionum Ordinariarum* (2 vols.; Paris, 1520).

HENRY OF GHENT, *Sermon for the Feast Day of St. Catherine* (E. Hocedez, *Richard de Middleton, sa vie, ses oeuvres, sa doctrine* (Spicilegium Sacrum Lovaniense, Etudes et Documents, VII; Louvain–Paris, 1925), 509–17).

HERMANNUS ALEMANNUS—see *Summa Alexandrinorum*

ISIDORE OF SEVILLE, *Etymologiarum sive Originum libri XX*, ed. W. M. Lindsay (2 vols.; Oxford Classical Texts; Oxford: Clarendon Press, 1911).

JAMES OF VITERBO, *De Regimine Christiano*, ed. H.-X. Arquillière, *Le Plus Ancien Traité de l'Église: Jacques de Viterbe, De Regimine Christiano* (Paris: G. Beauchesne, 1926).

—— *Quodlibet* I, ed. E. Ypma, *Jacobi de Viterbio OESA Disputatio Prima de Quolibet* (Cassiciacum supplementband 1; Würzburg: Augustinus–Verlag, 1968).

—— *Quodlibet* II, ed. E. Ypma, *Jacobi de Viterbio OESA Disputatio Secunda de Quolibet* (Cassiciacum supplementband 2;Würzburg: Augustinus–Verlag, 1969).

—— *Quodlibet* III, ed. E. Ypma, *Jacobi de Viterbio OESA Disputatio Tertia de Quolibet* (Cassiciacum supplementband 3; Würzburg: Augustinus–Verlag, 1973).

—— *Quodlibet* IV, ed. E. Ypma, *Jacobi de Viterbio OESA Disputatio Quarta de Quolibet* (Cassiciacum supplementband 5; Würzburg: Augustinus–Verlag, 1975).

JOHN THE DAMASCENE, *De Fide Orthodoxa* (*PG* 94).

JOHN OF NAPLES, *Quaestiones Disputatae*, ed. D. Gravina (Naples, 1618).

JOHN OF PARIS, *De Potestate Regia et Papali*

—— ed. J. Leclercq, *Jean de Paris et l'ecclésiologie du XIIIe siècle* (L'Église et l'État au Moyen Âge, 5; Paris: J. Vrin, 1942), 173–260.

—— ed. F. Bleienstein, *Johannes Quidort von Paris: Über königliche und päpstliche Gewalt* (Frankfurter Studien zur Wissenschaft von der Politik; Stuttgart: E. Klett, 1969).

—— *Commentarium in Libros Sententiarum*, ed. J. P. Muller, *Jean de Paris (Quidort): Commentaire sur les Sentences* (2 vols.; Studia Anselmiana, 47, 52; Rome, 1961, 1964).

JOHN OF SALISBURY, *Policraticus*, ed. C. C. J. Webb (2 vols.; Oxford, 1909).

JUSTINIAN, *Codex*, ed. P. Krüger (Berlin: Weidmann, 1877).

—— *Digest*, ed. T. Mommsen and P. Krüger, trans. A. Watson (4 vols.; Philadelphia: University of Pennsylvania Press, 1985).

LATINI, BRUNETTO, *Li livres dou tresor*, ed. F. Carmody (Publications in Modern Philology, 22; Berkeley: University of California, 1948).

LUPUS OF FERRIÈRES, *Epistolae*, ed. P. K. Marshall (Leipzig: Teubner, 1984).

MARSILIUS OF PADUA, *Defensor Pacis*, ed. C. W. Prévité-Orton (Cambridge: Cambridge University Press, 1928).

MATTHEW PARIS, *Chronica Maiora*, ed. H. R. Luard (7 vols.; Rolls Series; London, 1872–83).

MICHAEL OF EPHESUS—see [Grosseteste]

Moralium Dogma Philosophorum, ed. J. Holmberg, *Das Moralium Dogma Philosophorum des Guillaume de Conches, lateinisch, altfranzösisch und mittelniederfränkisch* (Arbeten utgivna med understöd av Vilhelm Ekmans Universitetsfond, 37; Uppsala, 1929).

NITHARD, *Historiarum Libri IV*, ed. P. Lauer (Paris: Les Belles Lettres, 1926).

OCKHAM—see William of Ockham

ORDERIC VITALIS, *Historia Ecclesiastica*, ed. M. Chibnall (6 vols.; Oxford: Clarendon Press, 1969–80).

PASCHASIUS RADBERTUS, *De Vita Walae seu Epitaphium Arsenii* (*PL* 120, cols. 1559–1650).

PETER OF AUVERGNE, *Quaestiones super libros Politicos* (ed. C. Flüeler, *Rezeption und Interpret-*

ation der Aristotelischen Politica im späten Mittelalter (2 vols.; Amsterdam: Grüner, 1992), i. 169–227).

—— *In Politicorum Continuatio*, ed. R. Busa, in *S. Thomae Aquinatis Opera Omnia* (Stuttgart–Bad Cannstatt: Frommann-Holzboog, 1980), vol. vii. *Aliorum Medii Aevi Auctorum Scripta*, 412–80.

PETRUS COMESTOR, *Historia Scholastica* (*PL* 198, cols. 1054–1722).

PETER LOMBARD, *Sententiae in IV Libris Distinctae* (Quaracchi, 1916; 3rd edn., 2 vols.; Spicilegium Bonaventurianum, IV–V; Rome, 1971–81).

PIERRE DUBOIS, *De Recuperatione Terre Sancte*, ed. C. V. Langlois (Collection de textes pour servir à l'étude et à l'enseignement de l'histoire, fasc. 9; Paris, 1891).

PIERRE JEAN OLIVI, *Petri Iohannis Olivi De Renuntiatione Papae Coelestini V Quaestio et Epistola*, ed. P. L. Oliger, *Archivum Franciscanum Historicum*, 11 (1918), 309–73.

[Propositions condemned in 1277], *Siger de Brabant et l'averroïsme latin au XIIIe siècle*, ed. P. Mandonnet (Les Philosophes Belges, VII; Louvain, 1908), 175–91.

PROSPER OF AQUITAINE, *Sententiae* (*PL* 51, cols. 427–96).

—— *Expositio super Psalmis* (*PL* 51, cols. 277–426).

PSEUDO-AUGUSTINE, *Sermo de Obedientia et Humilitate* (ed. D. G. Morin, *S. Hieronymi Presbyteri Opera* II (*CCSL* 78; Turnholt: Brepols, 1958), 552–5).

PSEUDO-CICERO, *Pridie quam in exsilium iret*, ed. J. C. Orelli (*M. Tulli Ciceronis Opera quae supersunt Omnia* (8 vols.; Turin, 1833–61), ii.2. 1412–20).

—— *Rhetorica ad Herennium* (Loeb Classical Library, 1954).

PSEUDO-DIONYSIUS, *S. Thomae Aquinatis in Librum B. Dionysii De Divinis Nominibus Expositio*, ed. C. Pera et al. (Turin–Rome: Marietti, 1950).

—— *De Caelestis Hierarchia*, ed. G. Heil, trans. M. de Gandillac (Sources Chrétiennes, 58; Paris, 1978).

—— *Dionysiaca: Recueil donnant l'ensemble des traductions latines des ouvrages attribués au Denys de l'Aréopage*, ed. P. Chevallier (2 vols.; Bruges: Desclée de Brouwer, 1937, 1950).

PTOLEMY OF LUCCA, *De Regimine Principum* (ed. R. M. Spiazzi, *Divi Thomae Aquinatis Opuscula Philosophica* (Turin–Rome: Marietti, 1954), 257–358).

Quaestio in utramque partem (ed. M. Goldast, *Monarchia S. Romani Imperii, sive Tractatus de Iurisdictione Imperiali seu Regia, et Pontificia seu Sacerdotali* (3 vols.; Hanover–Frankfurt, 1612–14), ii. 96–107).

REMIGIO DEI GIROLAMI, *De Bono Communi* (ed. M. C. de Matteis, *La 'teologia politica communale' di Remigio de' Girolami* (Bologna: Patron, 1977), 3–51).

—— *De Bono Pacis* (ibid. 55–71).

—— *Contra Falsos Ecclesie Professores*, ed. F. Tamburini (Utrumque Ius, Collectio Pontificiae Universitatis Lateranensis, 6; Rome, 1981).

—— *Sermones* (G. Salvadori and V. Federici, 'I sermoni d'occasione, le sequenze e i ritmi di Remigio Girolami fiorentino', *Scritti Vari di Filologia a Ernesto Monaco* (Rome, 1901), 455–508).

—— *Tractatus de Iustitia* (O. Capitani, 'L'incompiuto Tractatus de Iustitia di Fra' Remigio de' Girolami', *Bulletino dell'Istituto Storico Italiano per il Medio Evo e Archivio Muratoriano*, 72 (1960), 91–134).

RICHARD OF MIDDLETON, *Quodlibet* II.30 (E. Hocedez, *Richard de Middleton, sa vie, ses oeuvres, sa doctrine* (Spicilegium Sacrum Lovaniense, Etudes et Documents, VII; Louvain–Paris, 1925), 417).

RICHARD OF ST VICTOR, *De Trinitate*, ed. J. Ribaillier (Textes Philosophiques du Moyen Âge, VI; Paris: J. Vrin, 1958).

ROBERT GROSSETESTE—see Grosseteste

ROGER OF WENDOVER, *Flores Historiarum* (Rerum Britannicarum Medii Aevi Scriptores; London, 1890).

RUFINUS, *De Bono Pacis* (*PL* 150, cols. 1593–1638).

SEDULIUS SCOTTUS, *Liber de Rectoribus Christianis*, ed. S. Hellmann (Quellen und Untersuchungen zur lateinische Philologie des Mittelalters, I.1; Munich, 1906).

SENECA, *De Ira* (ed. L. D. Reynolds, *Dialogorum Libri Duodecim* (Oxford Classical Texts; Oxford: Clarendon Press, 1977)).

—— *Ad Lucilium Epistulae Morales*, ed. L. D. Reynolds (2 vols.; Oxford Classical Texts; Oxford: Clarendon Press, 1965).

SERVAIS DE MONT SAINT ELOI, *Quodlibet* (R. Hissette, 'Une Question quodlibétique de Servais du Mont-Saint-Eloi sur le pouvoir papal de l'évêque', *RTAM* 49 (1982), 234–42).

[SIGER DE BRABANT], B. Bazan, *Siger de Brabant: Écrits de logique, de morale et de physique* (Philosophes médiévaux, XIV; Louvain–Paris: Publications Universitaires—B. Nauwelaerts, 1974).

STUBBS, W., *Select Charters and Other Illustrations of Constitutional History*, 9th edn., rev. H. W. C. Davis (Oxford: Clarendon Press, 1921).

Summa Alexandrinorum L'Etica Nicomachea nella tradizione latina medievale, ed. C. Marchesi (Messina: A. Trimarchi, 1904), appendix, pp. xli–lxxxvi.

[Templars], *Le Dossier de l'affaire des Templiers*, ed. and trans. G. Lizerand (Paris: H. Champion, 1923).

[Themistius], ed. G. Verbeke, *Themistius: Commentaire sur le traité de l'âme d'Aristotle* (Corpus Latinum Commentariorum in Aristotelem Graecorum, I; Louvain–Paris: Publications Universitaires–B. Nauwelaerts, 1956).

THOMAS AQUINAS, *Opera Omnia* (Leonine edition, Rome, 1882–).
    Compendium Theologiae (vol. xlii, 1979).
    Contra Impugnantes Dei (vol. xli, 1970).
    De Perfectione Spiritualis Vitae (vol. xli, 1970).
    De Regimine Iudaeorum ad Ducissam Brabantiae (vol. xlii, 1979).
    De Regno ad Regem Cypri (vol. xlii, 1979).
    De Substantiis Separatis (vol. xl, 1967–8).
    Expositio super Iob (vol. xxvi, 1965).
    In Libros De Caelo et Mundo (vol. iii, 1886).
    Quaestio Disputata de Malo (vol. xxiii, 1982).
    Quaestio Disputata de Veritate (vol. xxii, 1970–6).
    Sententia Libri Ethicorum (vol. xlvii, 1969).
    Sententia Libri Politicorum (vol. xlviii, 1971).
    Summa Theologica (vols. iv–xii, 1888–1906).
    Summa contra Gentiles (vols. xiii–xv, 1918–30).
    Tabula Libri Ethicorum (vol. xlviii, 1971).

—— *Opera Omnia*, ed. R. Busa (Stuttgart–Bad Cannstatt: Frommann-Holzboog, 1980).
    De Duobus Praeceptis Caritatis (vol. 6).
    Expositio in Librum Boethii De Hebdomadibus (vol. 4).
    Expositio super Romanos (vol. 5).

Expositio super I ad Corinthianos (vols. 5–6).

Expositio super II ad Corinthianos (vol. 6).

Expositio super ad Philippenses (vol. 6).

Expositio super ad Timothaeum (vol. 6).

Expositio super ad Hebraeos (vol. 6).

Principium Biblicum (vol. 3).

Quaestio Disputata de Potentia (vol. 3).

Quaestio Disputata de Virtutibus (vol. 3).

Quaestiones Quodlibetales I–XI (vol. 3).

Responsio ad Lectorem Venetum de Articulis XXX (vol. 3).

Responsio ad Lectorem Venetum de Articulis XXXVI (vol. 3).

Sententia super Metaphysica (vol. 4).

Super Ioannem (vol. 6).

Super Librum De Causis (vol. 4).

Super Librum Dionysii De Divinis Nominibus (vol. 4).

Super IV Libros Sententiarum (vol. 1).

THOMAS OF CHANTIMPRÉ, *Bonum universale de apibus*, ed. G. Colvenerius (Douai: B. Belleri, 1627).

WILLIAM OF OCKHAM, *Octo Quaestiones de Potestate Papae* (ed. H. S. Offler, *Guillelmi de Ockham Opera Politica* (4 vols.; Manchester: Manchester University Press, 1940–97), i. 15–217).

II. PRIMARY SOURCES IN TRANSLATION

ARISTOTLE, *The Complete Works of Aristotle: The Revised Oxford Translation*, ed. J. Barnes (2 vols.; Princeton: Princeton University Press, 1984).

—— *Nicomachean Ethics*

 —— trans. H. Rackham (Loeb, 1947).

 —— trans. D. Ross, rev. J. L. Ackrill and J. O. Urmson (The World's Classics; Oxford: Oxford University Press, 1980).

 —— trans. T. Irwin (Indianapolis: Hackett, 1985).

—— *Politics*, trans. T. A. Sinclair, rev. T. J. Saunders (Harmondsworth: Penguin Classics, 1981).

—— *On Rhetoric*, trans. G. A. Kennedy (Oxford: Oxford University Press, 1991).

—— *Physics*, trans. P. H. Wicksteed and F. M. Cornford (2 vols.; Loeb, 1934).

—— *De Anima*, trans. W. S. Hett (Loeb, 1957).

—— *Metaphysics*, trans. H. Tredennick (2 vols.; Loeb, 1933–5).

—— *Magna Moralia*, trans. G. C. Armstrong (Loeb, 1935).

AUGUSTINE, *City of God*, trans. H. Bettenson (Harmondsworth: Penguin Classics, 1972).

CICERO, *De Officiis*, trans. W. Miller (Loeb, 1913).

—— *De Amicitia*, trans. W. A. Falconer (Loeb, 1923).

—— *In Catilinam I–IV*, trans. C. MacDonald (Loeb, 1977).

—— *Pro Marcello*, trans. N. H. Watts (Loeb, 1931).

—— *De Inventione*, trans. H. M. Hubbell (Loeb, 1949).

COMPAGNI, DINO, *Chronicle of Florence*, trans. D. E. Bornstein (Philadelphia: University of Pennsylvania Press, 1986).

DANTE, *The Divine Comedy*, trans. C. S. Singleton (Princeton: Princeton University Press, 1970).

DIONYSIUS—see pseudo-Dionysius

GILES OF ROME, *On Ecclesiastical Power*, trans. R. W. Dyson (Woodbridge: Boydell Press, 1986).

JAMES OF VITERBO, *On Christian Government*, trans. R. W. Dyson (Woodbridge: Boydell Press, 1995).

JOHN OF PARIS, *On Royal and Papal Power*
—— trans. A. Monahan (Records of Civilisation, Sources and Studies, 90; New York: Columbia University Press, 1974).
—— trans. J. Watt (Toronto: PIMS, 1971).

MARSILIUS OF PADUA, *The Defender of the Peace*, ii, trans. A. Gewirth (2 vols.; Records of Civilisation, Sources and Studies, 46; New York: Columbia University Press, 1951).

MOSES MAIMONIDES, *Guide of the Perplexed*, trans. S. Pines (Chicago: University of Chicago Press, 1963).

PLATO, *Republic*, trans. R. Waterfield (Oxford: Oxford University Press, 1993).

[Propositions condemned in 1277], trans. E. L. Fortin and P. D. O'Neill, in ed. R. Lerner and M. Mahdi, *Medieval Political Philosophy: A Sourcebook* (Toronto: Macmillan, 1963), 337–54.

PSEUDO-CICERO, *Rhetorica ad Herennium*, trans. H. Caplan (Loeb Classical Library, 1954).

PSEUDO-DIONYSIUS, *The Complete Works*, trans. C. Luibheid (The Classics of Western Spirituality; New York: Paulist Press, 1987).

THOMAS AQUINAS, *On Kingship to the King of Cyprus*, trans. G. B. Phelan, rev. I. Th. Eschmann (Toronto: PIMS, 1949).

—— *Selected Political Writings*, ed. A. P. d'Entrèves, trans. J. G. Dawson (Oxford: Blackwell, 1959).

—— *Summa Theologiae*, trans. T. Gilby et al. (61 vols.; Blackfriars edition; London: Eyre and Spottiswoode, 1964–80).

WILLIAM OF TYRE, *A History of the Deeds Done Beyond the Sea*, trans. E. A. Babcock and A. C. Krey (Records of Civilisation, Sources and Studies, 35; New York: Columbia University Press, 1943).

III. SECONDARY SOURCES

ACKRILL, J. L., 'Aristotle and *Eudaimonia*', *Proceedings of the British Academy*, 60 (1974), 339–59.

ALÈS, A. D', 'Jacques de Viterbe, théologien de l'église', *Gregorianum*, 7 (1926), 339–53.

ARNOLD, K., '*De bono pacis*: Friedensvorstellungen in Mittelalter und Renaissance', in J. Petersohn (ed.), *Uberlieferung, Frömmigkeit, Bildung als Leitthemen der Geschichtsforschung: Vorträge beim wissenschaftlichen Kolloquium aus Anlass des achtzigsten Geburtstags von Otto Meyer* (Wiesbaden: Reichert, 1987), 133–54.

ARQUILLIÈRE, H.-X., 'L'Appel au concile sous Philippe le Bel et la genèse des théories conciliaires', *Revue des Questions Historiques*, 89 (1911), 23–55.

—— *L'Augustinisme politique—essai sur la formation des théories politiques du moyen âge*, 2nd edn. (L'Église et l'État un Moyen Age, 2; Paris: J. Vrin, 1955).

ARWAY, R. J., 'A Half Century of Research on Godfrey of Fontaines', *New Scholasticism*, 36 (1962), 192–218.

AUBERT, J. M., *Le Droit romain dans l'oeuvre de saint Thomas* (Bibliothèque Thomiste, 30; Paris: J. Vrin, 1955).

BALDWIN, J. W., *The Government of Philip Augustus: Foundations of French Royal Power in the Middle Ages* (Berkeley: University of California Press, 1986).

BARRACLOUGH, G., *Papal Provisions: Aspects of Church History Constitutional, Legal and Administrative in the Later Middle Ages* (Oxford: Basil Blackwell, 1935).

BAYLEY, C., 'Pivotal Concepts in the Political Philosophy of Ockham', *Journal of the History of Ideas*, 10 (1949), 199–218.

BAYNES, N. H., *The Political Ideas of St. Augustine's De Civitate Dei* (London: Historical Association Pamphlet, 1936).

BAZAN, B. C., 'La *quaestio disputata*', in *Les Genres littéraires dans les sources théologiques et philosophiques médiévales* (Actes du Colloque International de Louvain-la-Neuve 1981; Louvain, 1982), 31–49.

BECKER, M. B., 'A Study in Political Failure: The Florentine Magnates 1280–1343', *Mediaeval Studies*, 27 (1965), 246–308.

BEER, S. H., 'The Rule of the Wise and the Holy: Hierarchy in the Thomistic System', *Political Theory*, 14 (1986), 391–422.

BERGES, W., *Die Fürstenspiegel des hohen und späten Mittelalters* (Leipzig: K. W. Hiersemann, 1938).

BISSON, T. N., 'The General Assemblies of Philip the Fair: Their Character Reconsidered', *Studia Gratiana*, 15 (1972), 539–64.

BLACK, A., 'The Individual and Society', in *CHMPT*, 588–606.

—— 'Society and the Individual from the Middle Ages to Rousseau: Philosophy, Jurisprudence and Constitutional Theory', *History of Political Thought*, 1 (1980), 145–66.

—— *Political Thought in Europe 1250–1450* (Cambridge: Cambridge University Press, 1992).

BLANCHETTE, O., *The Perfection of the Universe according to Aquinas: A Teleological Cosmology* (University Park: Pennsylvania State University Press, 1992).

BLYTHE, J. M., 'The Mixed Constitution and the Distinction between Regal and Political Power in the Work of Thomas Aquinas', *Journal of the History of Ideas*, 47 (1986), 547–65.

—— *Ideal Government and the Mixed Constitution in the Middle Ages* (Princeton: Princeton University Press, 1992).

BOASE, T. S. R., *Boniface VIII* (London: Constable, 1933).

BONNER, G., '*Quid imperatori cum ecclesia*? St Augustine on History and Society', *Augustinian Studies*, 2 (1971), 231–51.

BOSSIER, F., 'Méthode de traduction et problèmes de chronologie', in J. Brams and W. Vanhamel (eds.), *Guillaume de Moerbeke: Recueils d'études à l'occasion du 700e anniversaire de sa mort (1286)* (Leuven: Leuven University Press, 1989), 257–94.

BOUGEROL, J. G., 'Saint Bonaventure et le Pseudo-Denys l'Aréopagite', Actes du Colloque Saint Bonaventure, *Etudes Franciscaines*, 18 (1968), 33–123.

BOYLE, L. E., 'The *De Regno* and the Two Powers', in J. R. O'Donnell (ed.), *Essays in Honour of Anton Charles Pegis* (Toronto: PIMS, 1974), 237–47.

BROWN, E. A. R., '*Cessante causa* and the Taxes of the Last Capetians: The Political Applications of a Philosophical Maxim', *Studia Gratiana*, 15 (1972), 567–87.

—— 'Taxation and Morality in the Thirteenth and Fourteenth Centuries: Conscience and Political Power and the Kings of France', *French Historical Studies*, 8 (1973), 1–28.

—— 'Philippe le Bel and the Remains of St. Louis', *Gazette des Beaux Arts*, 95 (1980), 175–82.

—— 'Death and the Human Body in the Later Middle Ages: The Legislation of Boniface VIII on the Division of the Corpse', *Viator*, 12 (1981), 221–70.

BROWN, M., '*An sit authenticum opusculum S. Thomae De Regimine Principum*', *Angelicum*, 3 (1926), 300–3.

BRUNDAGE, J. A., *Medieval Canon Law and the Crusader* (Madison: University of Wisconsin Press, 1969).

BRYS, J., *De dispensatione in iure canonico, praesertim apud decretistas et decretalistas usque ad medium saeculum decimum quartum* (Universitas Catholica Lovaniensis, Dissertationes Series II, t.14; Bruges, 1925).

BUISSON, L., *Potestas und Caritas: Die päpstliche Gewalt in Spätmittelalter* (Forschungen zur kirchlichen Rechtsgeschichte und zum Kirchenrecht, 2; Cologne: Böhlau Verlag, 1958).

BURNS, J. H. (ed.), *The Cambridge History of Medieval Political Thought c.350–c.1450* (Cambridge: Cambridge University Press, 1988).

BUSA, R., *Index Thomisticus* (Stuttgart–Bad Cannstatt: Frommann–Holzboog, 1974–80).

CALLUS, D. A., 'The Date of Grosseteste's Translations and Commentaries on the Pseudo-Dionysius and the *Nicomachean Ethics*', *RTAM* 14 (1947), 186–210.

CANNING, J. P., 'The Corporation in the Political Thought of the Italian Jurists of the Thirteenth and Fourteenth Centuries', *History of Political Thought*, 1 (1980), 9–32.

—— 'Ideas of the State of Thirteenth and Fourteenth Century Commentators on the Roman Law', *TRHS* 33 (1983), 1–27.

—— 'Introduction: Politics, Institutions and Ideas', *CHMPT*, 341–66.

CARLYLE, R. W., and CARLYLE, A. J., *A History of Medieval Political Theory in the West* (6 vols.; Edinburgh: W. Blackwood, 1903–36).

CARON, P. G., 'Aequitas et interpretatio dans la doctrine canonique aux XIIIe et XIVe siècles', in *Proceedings of the Third International Congress of Medieval Canon Law* (Biblioteca Apostolica Vaticana, 1971), 131–41.

—— '*Aequitas*' *romana*, '*misericordia*' *patristica ed* '*epicheia*' *aristotelica nella dottrina dell'* '*aequitas*' *canonica* (Milan: A. Giuffrè, 1977).

CATTO, J. I., 'Ideas and Experience in the Political Thought of Aquinas', *Past and Present*, 71 (1976), 3–21.

CELANO, A. J., 'The *finis hominis* in the Thirteenth Century Commentaries on Aristotle's *Nicomachean Ethics*', *AHDLMA* 53 (1986), 23–53.

—— 'Boethius of Dacia, On the Highest Good', *Traditio*, 43 (1987), 199–214.

—— 'The Concept of Worldly Beatitude in the Writings of Thomas Aquinas', *Journal of the History of Philosophy*, 25 (1987), 215–26.

CHENU, M.-D., *Nature, Man and Society in the Twelfth Century: Essays on New Theological Perspectives in the Latin West*, trans. J. Taylor and L. K. Little (Chicago: University of Chicago Press, 1960).

—— *Toward Understanding St. Thomas*, trans. A.-M. Landry and D. Hughes (Chicago: Henry Regnery, 1964).

CHODOROW, S., *Christian Political Theory and Church Politics in the Mid-Twelfth Century: The Ecclesiology of Gratian's Decretum* (Berkeley: University of California Press, 1972).

CHROUST, A. H., 'The Corporate Idea and the Body Politic in the Middle Ages', *Review of Politics*, 9 (1947), 423–52.

COLEMAN, J., 'Medieval Discussions of Property: *ratio* and *dominium* according to John of Paris and Marsilius of Padua', *History of Political Thought*, 4 (1983), 209–28.

—— '*Dominium* in Thirteenth and Fourteenth Century Political Thought and its Seventeenth Century Heirs: John of Paris and Locke', *Political Studies*, 33 (1985), 73–100.

—— 'Property and Poverty', in *CHMPT*, 607–48.

—— 'The Dominican Political Theory of John of Paris in its Context', in D. Wood (ed.), *The Church and Sovereignty c.590–1918: Essays in Honour of Michael Wilks* (Studies in Church History, Subsidia 9; Oxford: Blackwell, 1991), 187–223.

COLISH, M., *The Stoic Tradition from Antiquity to the Early Middle Ages*, 2nd edn. (2 vols.; Leiden: E. J. Brill, 1990).

CONDREN, C., 'On Interpreting Marsilius' Use of St Augustine', *Augustiniana*, 35 (1975), 217–22.

CONGAR, Y. M. J., 'Maître Rufin et son *De Bono Pacis*', *Revue des Sciences Philosophiques et Theologiques*, 41 (1957), 428–44.

—— 'Aspects ecclésiologiques de la querelle entre mendiants et séculiers dans la seconde moitié du XIIIe siècle et le début du XIVe', *AHDLMA* 28 (1961), 35–151.

—— '*Status ecclesiae*', *Studia Gratiana*, 15 (1972), 3–31.

COURTENAY, W., *Capacity and Volition: A History of the Distinction of Absolute and Ordained Power* (Bergamo, 1990).

—— 'Between Pope and King: The Parisian Letters of Adhesion of 1303', *Speculum*, 71 (1996), 577–605.

CROFTS, R. A., 'The Common Good in the Political Theory of Thomas Aquinas', *The Thomist*, 37 (1973), 155–73.

DAVIS, C. T., *Dante and the Idea of Rome* (Oxford: Clarendon Press, 1957).

—— 'Remigio de' Girolami and Dante: A Comparison of their Conceptions of Peace', *Studi Danteschi*, 36 (1959), 107–36.

—— 'An Early Florentine Political Theorist: Fra Remigio de' Girolami', *Proceedings of the American Philosophical Society*, 104 (1960), 662–76.

—— 'Remigio de' Girolami O.P. Lector of S. Maria Novella in Florence', in *Le Scuole degli Ordini Mendicanti* (Convegni del Centro di Studi sulla Spiritualità Medievale, 17.1986; Todi, 1978), 283–304.

D'AVRAY, D. L., *Death and the Prince: Memorial Preaching before 1350* (Oxford: Clarendon Press, 1994).

DAWSON, J. D., 'William of Saint-Amour and the Apostolic Tradition', *Medieval Studies*, 40 (1978), 223–38.

DEANE, H. A., *The Political and Social Ideas of St. Augustine* (New York: Columbia University Press, 1963).

DEL PUNTA, F., DONATI, S., and LUNA, C., 'Egidio Romano', in *Dizionario Biografico degli Italiani* (Rome: Istituto Enciclopedia Italiana, 1960–), xlii. 319–41.

DENTON, J. H., *Robert Winchelsey and the Crown 1294–1313: A Study in the Defence of Ecclesiastical Liberty* (Cambridge Studies in Medieval Life and Thought, Third series 14; Cambridge: Cambridge University Press, 1980).

—— 'Philip the Fair and the Ecclesiastical Assemblies of 1294–1295', *Transactions of the American Philosophical Society*, 81, pt. 1 (1991), 1–82.

DIGARD, G., *Philippe le Bel et le Saint-Siège de 1285 à 1304* (2 vols.; Paris: Sirey, 1936).

DONATI, S., *Studi per una cronologia delle opere di Egidio Romano: Le Opere prima del 1285. I commenti aristotelici*, in *Documenti e studi sulla tradizione filosofica medievale*, I.1 (1990), 1–111; I.2 (1991), 1–74.

DONDAINE, H. F., 'Documents pour servir à l'histoire de la province de France: L'Appel au concile (1303)', *Archivum Fratrum Praedicatorum*, 22 (1952), 381–439.

DONDAINE, H. F., *Le Corpus Dionysien de l'université de Paris au XIIIe siècle* (Rome: Edizioni di Storia e Letteratura, 1953).

DOUIE, D. L., *The Conflict between the Seculars and the Mendicants at the University of Paris in the Thirteenth Century* (Aquinas Papers, 23; London: Blackfriars, 1954).

DUFEIL, M. M., *Guillaume de Saint-Amour et la polémique universitaire parisienne 1250–1259* (Paris: Picard, 1972).

—— 'Gulielmus de Sancto Amore: Opera Omnia 1252–1270', *Miscellanea Mediaevalia*, 10 (1976), 213–19.

—— 'Ierarchia: Un concept dans la polémique universitaire parisienne du XIIIe siècle', *Miscellanea Mediaevalia*, 12 (1980), 56–83.

DUIN, J. J., 'La Bibliothèque philosophique de Godefroid de Fontaines', *Estudios Lulianos*, 3 (1959), 21–36, 137–60.

DUNBABIN, J. H., 'The Two Commentaries of Albertus Magnus on the *Nicomachean Ethics*', *RTAM* 30 (1963), 232–50.

—— 'Ethical Problems as Discussed by Masters of Arts and Theologians in Thirteenth Century Universities', D.Phil. thesis (Oxford, 1965).

—— 'Aristotle in the Schools', in B. Smalley (ed.), *Trends in Medieval Political Thought* (Oxford: Basil Blackwell, 1965), 65–85.

—— 'Robert Grosseteste as Translator, Transmitter and Commentator on the *Nicomachean Ethics*', *Traditio*, 28 (1972), 460–72.

—— 'The Reception and Interpretation of Aristotle's *Politics*', *CHLMP*, 723–37.

—— 'Government', *CHMPT*, 477–519.

EASTMAN, J. R., 'Giles of Rome and his Use of St Augustine in Defense of Papal Abdication', *Augustiniana*, 38 (1988), 129–39.

—— *Papal Abdication in Later Medieval Thought* (Texts and Studies in Religion, 42; Lewiston, NY: Edwin Mellen Press, 1990).

EGENTER, R., 'Gemeinnutz vor Eigennutz: Die soziale Leitidee im Tractatus de bono communi des Fr. Remigius von Florenz', *Scholastik*, 9 (1934), 79–92.

EICHINGER, J., 'Individuum und Gemeinschaft bei Ägidius Romanus', *Divus Thomas*, 13 (1935), 160–6.

ENTRÈVES, A. P., D', *The Medieval Contribution to Political Thought: Thomas Aquinas, Marsilius of Padua, Richard Hooker* (Oxford: Clarendon Press, 1939).

ESCHMANN, I. TH., 'A Thomistic Glossary on the Principle of the Pre-eminence of a Common Good', *Mediaeval Studies*, 5 (1943), 123–65.

—— '*Bonum commune melius est quam bonum unius*: Eine Studie über den Wertvorrang des Personalen bei Thomas von Aquin', *Mediaeval Studies*, 6 (1944), 62–120.

—— 'Studies on the Notion of Society in St Thomas Aquinas I: St Thomas and the Decretal of Innocent IV *Romanae ecclesiae*', *Mediaeval Studies*, 8 (1946), 1–42.

—— 'Studies on the Notion of Society in St Thomas Aquinas II: Thomistic Social Philosophy and the Theology of Original Sin', *Mediaeval Studies*, 9 (1947), 19–55.

—— 'A Catalogue of St. Thomas's Works: Bibliographical Notes', in E. Gilson (ed.), *The Christian Philosophy of St. Thomas Aquinas*, trans. L. K. Shook (London: Victor Gollancz, 1957), 381–439.

—— 'St. Thomas Aquinas on the Two Powers', *Mediaeval Studies*, 20 (1958), 177–205.

EVANS, G. R. (ed.), *A Concordance to the Works of St. Anselm* (4 vols.; Millwood, NY: Kraus International, 1984).

FARAL, E., 'Les *Responsiones* de Guillaume de Saint-Amour', *AHDLMA* 18 (1950–1), 337–94.

FASOLT, C., *Council and Hierarchy: The Political Thought of William Durant the Younger* (Cambridge Studies in Medieval Life and Thought, Fourth Series; Cambridge: Cambridge University Press, 1991).

FAVIER, J., 'Les Légistes et le gouvernement de Philippe le Bel', *Journal des Savants*, 1969, 92–108.

FAWTIER, R., *The Capetian Kings of France: Monarchy and Nation 987–1328* (London: Macmillan, 1960).

FEEHAN, T., 'Augustine on Lying and Deception', *Augustinian Studies*, 19 (1988), 131–9.

—— 'Augustine's Moral Evaluation of Lying', *Augustinian Studies*, 21 (1990), 67–81.

—— 'Augustine's Own Examples of Lying', *Augustinian Studies*, 22 (1991), 165–90.

FITZGERALD, L. P., 'St. Thomas Aquinas and the Two Powers', *Angelicum*, 36 (1979), 515–56.

FLÜELER, C., 'Die Rezeption der Politica des Aristoteles an der Pariser Artistenfakultät im 13. und 14. Jahrhundert', in J. Miethke and A. Bühler (eds.), *Das Publikum Politischer Theorie im 14. Jahrhundert* (Munich, 1992), 127–38.

—— *Rezeption und Interpretation der Aristotelischen Politica im späten Mittelalter* (2 vols.; Amsterdam: Grüner, 1992).

FUCHS, H., *Augustin und der antike Friedensgedanke: Untersuchungen zum neunzehnten Buch der Civitas Dei* (Neue Philologische Untersuchungen, III; Berlin: Weidmannsche Buchhandlung, 1926).

FURLEY, D. J., and NEHAMAS, A. (eds.), *Aristotle's Rhetoric: Philosophical Essays* (Princeton: Princeton University Press, 1994).

GARCIA, J. J. E., *Introduction to the Problem of Individuation in the Early Middle Ages*, 2nd edn. (Munich: Philosophia Verlag, 1988).

—— (ed.), *Individuation in Scholasticism: The Later Middle Ages and the Counter-Reformation 1150–1650* (Albany: State University of New York Press, 1994).

GAUDEMET, J., '*Utilitas publica*', *Revue Historique de Droit Français et Étranger*, 29 (1951), 465–99.

GAUTHIER, R.-A., 'Trois commentaires "Averroïstes" sur l'Éthique à Nicomaque', *AHDLMA* 22–3 (1947–8), 187–337.

—— 'La Date du commentaire de Saint Thomas sur l'Éthique à Nicomaque', *RTAM* 18 (1951), 66–105.

—— *Ethica Nicomachea, Praefatio* (*Aristoteles Latinus* XXVI.1; Brussels–Leiden: Desclée de Brouwer–E. J. Brill, 1974).

—— 'Le Cours sur l'*Ethica nova* d'un maître ès arts de Paris 1235–40', *AHDLMA* 42 (1975), 71–141.

—— and JOLIF, J. Y. (eds.), *L'Éthique à Nicomaque*, 2nd edn. (3 vols.; Louvain–Paris: Publications Universitaires, 1958–9).

GENICOT, L., 'Le *De Regno*: Spéculation ou réalisme?', in G. Verbeke and D. Verhelst (eds.), *Aquinas and the Problems of his Time* (Mediaevalia Lovaniensia, series 1, studia 5; Louvain: Leuven University Press, 1976).

—— (ed.), *Typologie des sources du moyen âge occidental* (Turnholt: Brepols, 1972–), fasc. 44–5 (1985), 'Les Questions disputées et les questions quodlibétiques dans les facultés de théologie, de droit et de médecine', parts i–ii.

Les Genres littéraires dans les sources théologiques et philosophiques médiévales (Actes du Colloque International de Louvain-la-Neuve 1981; Louvain, 1982).

GEWIRTH, A., *Marsilius of Padua: The Defender of the Peace*, vol. i. *Marsilius of Padua and*

Medieval Political Philosophy (2 vols.; Records of Civilisation, Sources and Studies, 46; New York: Columbia University Press, 1951).

GEWIRTH, A., 'Philosophy and Political Thought in the Fourteenth Century', in F. L. Utley (ed.), *The Forward Movement of the Fourteenth Century* (Columbus: Ohio State University Press, 1961), 125–64.

GIERKE, O. VON, *Political Theories of the Middle Age*, trans. F. W. Maitland (Cambridge: Cambridge University Press, 1900).

GILBY, T., *Principality and Polity: Aquinas and the Rise of State Theory in the West* (London: Longmans, 1958).

GILSON, E., *L'Esprit de la philosophie médiévale* (Paris: J. Vrin, 1932).

—— 'Les Philosophantes', *AHDLMA* 19 (1952), 135–40.

—— *A History of Christian Philosophy in the Middle Ages* (London: Sheed and Ward, 1955).

—— *The Christian Philosophy of St. Thomas Aquinas*, trans. L. K. Shook (London: Victor Gollancz, 1957).

—— *Dante and Philosophy*, trans. D. Moore (New York, 1963).

GLORIEUX, P., 'Prélats français contre religieux mendiants: Autour de la bulle *Ad fructus uberes* 1281–90', *Revue d'Histoire de l'Église de France*, 11 (1925), 309–31, 471–95.

—— *La Littérature quodlibétique* (2 vols.; Bibliothèque Thomiste 5, 21; Paris: J. Vrin, 1925, 1935).

—— 'Un Recueil scolaire de Godefroid de Fontaines', *RTAM* 3 (1931), 37–53.

—— 'Les Polémiques *contra Geraldinos*, les pièces du dossier', *RTAM* 6 (1934), 5–41.

—— '*Contra Geraldinos*, l'enchaînement des polémiques', *RTAM* 7 (1935), 129–55.

—— 'Pour une édition de Gérard d'Abbeville', *RTAM* 9 (1937), 56–84.

—— 'Notations brèves sur Godefroid de Fontaines', *RTAM* 11 (1939), 168–73.

—— 'Le Conflit de 1252–7 à la lumière du Mémoire de Guillaume de Saint-Amour', *RTAM* 24 (1957), 364–72.

—— 'Les Premiers écrits de Gilles de Rome', *RTAM* 41 (1974), 204–8.

GÓMEZ CAFFARENA, J., 'Cronología de la "Suma" de Enrique de Gante por relación a sus "Quodlibetos"', *Gregorianum*, 38 (1957), 116–33.

GRABMANN, M., *Mittelalterliches Geistesleben I–III* (Munich: M. Hueber, 1926–56).

—— *Studien über den Einfluss der aristotelischen Philosophie auf die mittelalterlichen Theorien über das Verhältnis von Kirche und Staat* (Sitzungsberichte der Bayerischen Akademie der Wissenschaften, Philosophisch-historische Abteilung Jg.1934, Heft 2; Munich, 1934).

—— 'Eine für Examinazwecke abgefasste Quaestionensammlung der Pariser Artisten-fakultät aus der ersten Hälfte des 13. Jahrhunderts', *Revue Néoscolastique de Philosophie*, 36 (1934), 211–26; reprinted in id., *Mittelalterliches Geistesleben II* (Munich, 1936), 183–99.

—— 'Das Studium der Aristotelischen Ethik an der Artistenfakultät der Universität Paris in der Ersten Hälfte des 13. Jahrhunderts', *Philosophisches Jahrbuch der Görres-Gesellschaft*, 55 (1940), 339–54; reprinted in id., *Mittelalterliches Geistesleben III* (Munich, 1956), 128–41.

GRANT, E., 'The Condemnation of 1277: God's Absolute Power and Physical Thought in the Late Middle Ages', *Viator*, 10 (1979), 211–44.

GRATIEN, P., 'Ordres mendiants et clergé séculier à la fin du XIIIe siècle', *Études Franciscaines*, 36 (1924), 499–518.

GRAY, J. W., 'The Problem of Papal Power in the Ecclesiology of St Bernard', *TRHS* 24 (1974), 1–17.

GRIESBACH, M. F., 'John of Paris as a Representative of Thomistic Political Philosophy', in C. J. O'Neil (ed.), *An Étienne Gilson Tribute* (Milwaukee: Marquette University Press, 1959), 33–50.

GRIGNASCHI, M., 'L'Interprétation de la "Politique" d'Aristote dans le "Dialogue" de Guillaume d'Ockham', in *Liber Memorialis Georges de Lagarde* (Études présentées à la Commission Internationale pour l'histoire des assemblées d'états, 38; Louvain–Paris: Nauwelaerts, 1970), 59–72.

GRUNZWEIG, A., 'Les Incidences internationales des mutations monétaires de Philippe le Bel', *Le Moyen Âge*, 59 (1953), 117–72.

GUTIERREZ, D., '*De vita et scriptis Beati Iacobi de Viterbio*', *Analecta Augustiniana*, 16 (1937–8), 216–24, 282–305, 358–81.

—— '*De doctrina theologica Beati Iacobi de Viterbio*', *Analecta Augustiniana*, 16 (1937–8), 432–66, 523–52.

—— *The Augustinians in the Middle Ages 1256–1356* (History of the Order of St Augustine, i; Villanova, 1984).

HACKETT, J., 'State of the Church: A Concept of the Medieval Canonists', *The Jurist*, 1963, 259–90.

HAGGARTY, W. P., 'Augustine, the Mixed Life and Classical Political Philosophy: Reflections on *compositio* in Book XIX of the City of God', *Augustinian Studies*, 23 (1992), 149–63.

HARDIE, W. F. R., *Aristotle's Ethical Theory*, 2nd edn. (Oxford: Clarendon Press, 1980).

HARDING, A., 'The Reflection of Thirteenth Century Legal Growth in St Thomas's Writings', in G. Verbeke and D. Verhelst (eds.), *Aquinas and the Problems of his Time* (Mediaevalia Lovaniensia, series 1, studia 5; Louvain: Leuven University Press, 1976), 18–37.

HAREN, M., *Medieval Thought: The Western Intellectual Tradition from Antiquity to the Thirteenth Century*, 2nd edn. (London: Macmillan, 1992).

HARRISON THOMSON, S., 'The "Notule" of Grosseteste on the *Nicomachean Ethics*', *Proceedings of the British Academy*, 19 (1933), 195–218.

HARRISS, G. L., *King, Parliament and Public Finance in Medieval England to 1369* (Oxford: Clarendon Press, 1975).

HENNINGER, M. G., *Relations: Medieval Theories 1250–1325* (Oxford: Clarendon Press, 1989).

HIBST, P., *Utilitas Publica—Gemeiner Nutz—Gemeinwohl* (Europäische Hochschulschriften; Frankfurt: P. Lang, 1991).

HILLGARTH, J. N., 'L'Influence de la Cité de Dieu de saint Augustin au haut moyen âge', *Sacris Erudiri*, 28 (1985), 5–34.

HISSETTE, R., *Enquête sur les 219 articles condamnés à Paris le 7 mars 1277* (Philosophes Médiévaux, 22; Louvain–Paris: Publications Universitaires, 1977).

—— 'Etienne Tempier et ses condamnations', *RTAM* 47 (1980), 231–70.

HOCEDEZ, E., 'Gilles de Rome et Henri de Gand sur la distinction réelle 1276–1287', *Gregorianum*, 8 (1927), 358–84.

—— 'La Condamnation de Gilles de Rome', *RTAM* 4 (1932), 34–58.

HOEFLICH, M. H., 'The Concept of *utilitas populi* in Early Ecclesiastical Law and Government', *Zeitschrift der Savigny-Stiftung für Rechtsgeschichte, Kanonistische Abteilung*, 67 (1981), 36–74.

HOFFMANS, J., 'La Table des divergences et innovations doctrinales de Godefroid de Fontaines', *Revue Néoscolastique de Philosophie*, 36 (1934), 412–36.

HOLMES, G., *Florence, Rome and the Origins of the Renaissance* (Oxford: Clarendon Press, 1986).

HONSELL, T., 'Gemeinwohl und öffentliches Interesse im klassischen römischen Recht', *Zeitschrift der Savigny-Stiftung für Rechtsgeschichte, Romanistische Abteilung*, 95 (1978), 93–137.

HOUSLEY, N., *The Italian Crusades: The Papal–Angevin Alliance and the Crusades against Christian Lay Powers, 1254–1343* (Oxford: Clarendon Press, 1982).

HUET, F., *Recherches historiques et critiques sur la vie, les ouvrages et la doctrine de Henri de Gand* (Ghent, 1838).

HYDE, J. K., 'Contemporary Views on Faction and Civil Strife in Thirteenth and Fourteenth Century Italy', in L. Martines (ed.), *Violence and Disorder in Italian Cities 1200–1500* (Berkeley: University of California Press, 1972), 273–307.

IRWIN, T. H., *Aristotle's First Principles* (Oxford: Clarendon Press, 1988).

JOSSUA, J.-P., 'L'Axiome "bonum diffusivum sui" chez S. Thomas d'Aquin', *Revue des Sciences Religieuses*, 40 (1966), 127–53.

KANTOROWICZ, E. H., '*Pro patria mori* in Medieval Political Thought', *American Historical Review*, 56 (1951), 472–92.

—— *The King's Two Bodies: A Study in Medieval Political Theology* (Princeton: Princeton University Press, 1957).

KAY, R., 'Ad nostram praesentiam evocamus: Boniface VIII and the Roman Convocation of 1302', in *Proceedings of the Third International Congress of Medieval Canon Law* (Biblioteca Apostolica Vaticana, 1971), 165–89.

KAYSER, J. R., and LETTIERI, R. J., 'Aquinas' *regimen bene commixtum* and the Medieval Critique of Classical Republicanism', *The Thomist*, 46 (1982), 195–220.

KNUDSEN, C., 'Intentions and Impositions', in *CHLMP*, 479–95.

KOROLEC, J. B., 'Jean Buridan et Jean de Jandun et la relation entre la rhétorique et la dialectique', *Miscellanea Mediaevalia*, 13 (1981), 622–7.

KRETZMANN, N., 'Syncategoremata, Sophismata, Exponibilia', *CHLMP*, 211–45.

—— KENNY, A., and PINBORG, J. (eds.), *The Cambridge History of Later Medieval Philosophy: From the Rediscovery of Aristotle to the Disintegration of Scholasticism 1100–1600* (Cambridge: Cambridge University Press, 1982).

KUITERS, R., 'De Ecclesiastica Potestate sive De Summi Pontificis Potestate secundum Aegidium Romanum', *Analecta Augustiniana*, 20 (1946), 146–214.

—— 'Aegidius Romanus and the Authorship of *In utramque partem* and *De ecclesiastica potestate*', *Augustiniana*, 8 (1958), 267–80.

LACOMBE, G. (ed.), *Aristoteles Latinus, Codices: Pars prior* (Corpus Philosophorum Medii Aevi, Union Académique Internationale, Libreria dello Stato, Rome, 1939).

LADNER, G. B., 'The Concepts of *ecclesia* and *christianitas* and their Relation to the Idea of Papal *plenitudo potestatis* from Gregory VII to Boniface VIII', in *Sacerdozio e Regno da Gregorio VII a Bonifacio VIII* (Miscellanea Historiae Pontificiae, 18; Rome, 1954), 49–77.

LAGARDE, G. DE, 'Individualisme et corporatisme au moyen âge', in *L'Organisation corporative du moyen âge à la fin de l'ancien régime* (Études présentées à la Commission Internationale pour l'histoire des assemblées d'états II; Louvain, 1937), 1–60.

—— 'La Philosophie sociale d'Henri de Gand et Godefroid de Fontaines', *AHDLMA* 14 (1943–5), 73–142.

—— *La Naissance de l'esprit laïque au déclin du moyen âge*, 3rd edn. (5 vols.; Louvain: E. Nauwelaerts, 1956–70).

LAMBERT, M. D., *Franciscan Poverty: The Doctrine of the Absolute Poverty of Christ and the Apostles in the Franciscan Order 1210–1323* (London: SPCK, 1961).

LAMBERTINI, R., 'Philosophus videtur tangere tres rationes. Egidio Romano lettore ed interprete della *Politica* nel terzo libro del *De regimine principum*', in *Documenti e studi sulla tradizione filosofica medievale*, I.1 (1990), 277–325.

—— 'Il filosofo, il principe e la virtù. Note sulla ricezione e l'uso dell' Etica Nicomachea nel *De regimine principum* di Egidio Romano', in *Documenti e Studi sulla Tradizione Filosofica Medievale*, II.1 (1991), 239–79.

—— 'Tra etica e politica: La prudentia del principe nel *De regimine principum* di Egidio Romano', in *Documenti e studi sulla tradizione filosofica medievale*, III.1 (1992), 77–144.

—— 'Individuelle und politische Klugheit in den mittelalterlichen Ethikkommentaren (von Albert bis Buridan)', *Miscellanea Mediaevalia*, 24 (1996), 464–78.

LAURENT, M. H., 'Godefroid de Fontaines et la condamnation de 1277', *Revue Thomiste*, 13 (1930), 273–81.

LAVÈRE, G. J., 'The Problem of the Common Good in St Augustine's *civitas terrena*', *Augustinian Studies*, 14 (1983), 1–10.

LECLERCQ, J., 'La Renonciation de Célestin V et l'opinion théologique en France du vivant de Boniface VIII', *Revue d'Histoire de l'Eglise de France*, 25 (1939), 183–92.

—— *Jean de Paris et l'ecclésiologie du XIIIe siècle* (L'Église et l'État au Moyen Âge, 5; Paris: J. Vrin, 1942).

LEFF, G., 'The Apostolic Ideal in Later Medieval Ecclesiology', *Journal of Theological Studies*, 18 (1967), 58–82.

—— *Heresy in the Later Middle Ages: The Relation of Heterodoxy to Dissent c.1250–1450* (2 vols.; Manchester: Manchester University Press, 1967).

LEJEUNE, J., 'De Godefroid de Fontaines à la paix de Fexhe 1316', *Annuaire d'Histoire Liègoise*, VI.5 (1962), 1215–59.

LÉONARD, E. G., *Les Angevins de Naples* (Paris: Presses Universitaires de France, 1954).

LESNICK, D. R., *Preaching in Medieval Florence: The Social World of Franciscan and Dominican Spirituality* (Athens: University of Georgia Press, 1989).

LEWIS, E., 'Organic Tendencies in Medieval Political Thought', *American Political Science Review*, 32 (1938), 849–76.

—— 'Natural Law and Expediency in Medieval Political Theory', *Ethics*, 50 (1940), 144–63.

—— *Medieval Political Ideas* (2 vols.; London: Routledge and Kegan Paul, 1954).

LEWRY, P. O., 'Rhetoric at Paris and Oxford in the Mid-Thirteenth Century', *Rhetorica*, 1 (1983), 45–63.

LIBERA, A. DE, *Albert le Grand et la philosophie* (Paris: J. Vrin, 1990).

LITTLE, A. G., 'Measures taken by the Prelates of France against the Friars', *Studi e Testi*, 39 (1924), 49–66.

—— and PELSTER, F., *Oxford Theology and Theologians 1282–1302* (Oxford Historical Society, 96; Oxford: Oxford University Press, 1934).

LOTTIN, O., 'Le Libre arbitre chez Godefroid de Fontaines', *Revue Néoscolastique de Philosophie*, 40 (1937), 213–41.

—— 'Le Thomisme de Godefroid de Fontaines', *Revue Néoscolastique de Philosophie*, 40 (1937), 554–73.

—— *Psychologie et morale aux XIIe et XIIIe siècles* (6 vols.; Louvain–Gembloux: Abbaye du Mont César–J. Duculot, 1942–60).

Lottin, O., 'Les Vertus morales acquises sont-elles de vraies vertus? La Réponse des théologiens de Pierre Abelard à St Thomas d'Aquin', *RTAM* 20 (1953), 13–39.

—— 'Les Vertus morales acquises sont-elles de vraies vertus? La Réponse des théologiens de saint Thomas à Pierre Auriol', *RTAM* 21 (1954), 101–29.

LUNA, C., 'Un nuovo documento del conflitto fra Bonifacio VIII e Filippo il Bello: Il discorso "De potentia domini pape" di Egidio Romano', *Documenti e studi sulla tradizione filosofica medievale*, III.1 (1992), 167–243.

LUSCOMBE, D. E., 'The *Lex Divinitatis* in the Bull *Unam sanctam* of Pope Boniface VIII', in C. N. L. Brooke, D. E. Luscombe, G. H. Martin, and D. Owen (eds.), *Church and Government in the Middle Ages: Essays Presented to C. R. Cheney on his 70th Birthday* (Cambridge: Cambridge University Press, 1976), 205–21.

—— 'Thomas Aquinas and Conceptions of Hierarchy in the Thirteenth Century', *Miscellanea Mediaevalia*, 19 (1988), 261–77.

—— 'Wyclif and Hierarchy', in *Studies in Church History* (Subsidia 5; Oxford: Blackwell, 1987), 233–44.

MCCREADY, W. D., 'Papal *plenitudo potestatis* and the Source of Temporal Authority in Late Medieval Hierocratic Theory', *Speculum*, 48 (1973), 654–74.

—— 'Papalists and Anti-Papalists: Aspects of the Church–State Controversy in the Later Middle Ages', *Viator*, 6 (1975), 241–73.

MCDONNELL, E. W., *The Beguines and Beghards in Medieval Culture* (New Brunswick, NJ: Rutgers University Press, 1954).

MCEVOY, J., *The Philosophy of Robert Grosseteste* (Oxford: Clarendon Press, 1982).

MCGRADE, A. S., *The Political Thought of William of Ockham: Personal and Institutional Principles* (Cambridge Studies in Medieval Life and Thought, Third Series, 7; Cambridge: Cambridge University Press, 1974).

—— 'Ockham and the Birth of Individual Rights', in B. Tierney and P. Linehan (eds.), *Authority and Power: Studies on Medieval Law and Government Presented to Walter Ullmann on his Seventieth Birthday* (Cambridge: Cambridge University Press, 1980), 149–65.

—— 'Rights, Natural Rights and the Philosophy of Law', *CHLMP*, 738–56.

MCKEON, R., 'Rhetoric in the Middle Ages', in R. S. Crane (ed.), *Critics and Criticism: Ancient and Modern* (Chicago: University of Chicago Press, 1952), 260–96.

MACKEN, R., 'La Théorie de l'illumination divine dans la philosophie d'Henri de Gand', *RTAM* 39 (1972), 82–112.

—— 'Les Corrections d'Henri de Gand à ses quodlibets', *RTAM* 40 (1973), 5–51.

—— 'La Volonté humaine, faculté plus élévée que l'intelligence selon Henri de Gand', *RTAM* 42 (1975), 5–51.

—— 'Ein wichtiges Ineditum zum Kampf über das Beichtprivileg der Bettelorden, der *Tractatus super facto praelatorum et fratrum* des Heinrich von Gent', *Franziskanische Studien*, 60 (1978), 301–10.

—— 'Les Sources d'Henri de Gand', *Revue Philosophique de Louvain*, 76 (1978), 5–28.

MANDONNET, P., 'La Carrière scolaire de Gilles de Rome, 1276–1291', *Revue des Sciences Philosophiques et Théologiques*, 4 (1910), 480–99.

MANSION, A., 'Autour de la date du commentaire de Saint Thomas sur l'Éthique à Nicomaque', *Revue Philosophique de Louvain*, 50 (1952), 460–71.

MARENBON, J., *Later Medieval Philosophy 1130–1350: An Introduction* (London: Routledge and Kegan Paul, 1987).

MARIANI, U., *Chiesa e stato nei teologi agostiniani del secolo XIV* (Uomine e Dottrine, 5; Rome: Edizioni di storia e letteratura, 1957).

Maritain, J., *The Person and the Common Good* (London: Geoffrey Bles, 1948).

MARKUS, R. A., 'Two Conceptions of Political Authority: Augustine's *De Civitate Dei* XIX.14–15 and Some Thirteenth Century Interpretations', *Journal of Theological Studies*, 16 (1965), 68–100.

—— *Saeculum: History and Society in the Theology of St. Augustine* (Cambridge: Cambridge University Press, 1970).

—— 'The Latin Fathers', in *CHMPT*, 92–122.

MARRONE, J., 'The Absolute and Ordained Powers of the Pope: An Unedited Text of Henry of Ghent', *Mediaeval Studies*, 36 (1974), 7–27.

—— and ZUCKERMAN, C., 'Cardinal Simon of Beaulieu and Relations between Philip the Fair and Boniface VIII', *Traditio*, 31 (1975), 195–222.

MARRONE, S. P., *Truth and Scientific Knowledge in the Thought of Henry of Ghent* (Speculum Anniversary Monographs, 11; Cambridge, Mass.: Medieval Academy of America, 1985).

MARROU, H., 'Civitas Dei, civitas terrena—num tertium quid?', *Texte und Untersuchungen zur Geschichte der Altchristliche Literatur*, 64 (1957), Studia Patristica II, 342–50.

MARTIN, C., 'The Commentaries on the Politics of Aristotle in the Late Thirteenth and Fourteenth Centuries, with Reference to the Thought and Political Life of the Time', D.Phil. thesis (Oxford, 1949).

—— 'Some Medieval Commentaries on Aristotle's Politics', *History*, 36 (1951), 29–54.

MAURER, A., 'Henry of Ghent and the Unity of Man', *Mediaeval Studies*, 10 (1948), 1–20.

MERCKEN, H. P. F., 'The Greek Commentators on Aristotle's Ethics', in R. Sorabji (ed.), *Aristotle Transformed* (London: Duckworth, 1990), 407–43.

MICHAUD-QUANTIN, P., *Universitas: Expressions du mouvement communautaire dans le moyen âge latin* (L'Église et l'État au Moyen Âge, 13; Paris: J. Vrin, 1970).

MICHEL, S., *La Notion thomiste du bien commun: Quelques-unes de ses applications juridiques* (Paris: J. Vrin, 1932).

MIETHKE, J., 'Geschichtsprozess und zeitgenössisches Bewusstsein: Die Theorie des monarchischen Papats im hohen und späteren Mittelalter', *Historische Zeitschrift*, 226 (1978), 564–99.

—— 'Zur Bedeutung der Ekklesiologie für die politische Theorie im späteren Mittelaltern', *Miscellanea Mediaevalia*, 12 (1980), 369–88.

—— 'Die Rolle der Bettelorden im Umbruch der politischen Theorie an der Wende zum 14. Jahrhundert', in K. Elm (ed.), *Stellung und Wirksamkeit der Bettelorden in der städtischen Gesellschaft* (Berlin: Duncker und Humblot, 1981), 119–53.

—— 'Die Traktate "De potestate papae": Ein Typus politiktheoretischer Literatur im späten Mittelalter', in *Les Genres littéraires dans les sources théologiques et philosophiques médiévales* (Actes du Colloque International de Louvain-la-Neuve 1981; Louvain, 1982), 193–211.

MINIO-PALUELLO, L., 'Remigio Girolami's *De bono communi*: Florence at the Time of Dante's Banishment and the Philosopher's Answer to the Crisis', *Italian Studies*, 11 (1956), 56–71.

MODDE, A., 'Le Bien commun dans la philosophie de saint Thomas', *Revue Philosophique de Louvain*, 47 (1949), 221–47.

MOONAN, L., *Divine Power: The Medieval Power Distinction up to its Adoption by Albert, Bonaventure and Aquinas* (Oxford: Clarendon Press, 1994).

MORRALL, J. B., 'Some Notes on a Recent Interpretation of William of Ockham's Political Philosophy', *Franciscan Studies*, 9 (1949), 335–69.

—— *Political Thought in Medieval Times*, 3rd edn. (London: Hutchinson, 1971).

MULCAHY, D. G., 'The Hands of Augustine but the Voice of Marsilius', *Augustiniana*, 21 (1971), 457–66.

—— 'Marsilius of Padua's Use of St Augustine', *Revue des Etudes Augustiniennes*, 18 (1972), 180–90.

MULGAN, R. G., *Aristotle's Political Theory* (Oxford: Clarendon Press, 1977).

MURPHY, J. J., 'Aristotle's Rhetoric in the Middle Ages', *Quarterly Journal of Speech*, 52 (1966), 109–15.

—— 'The Scholastic Condemnation of Rhetoric in the Commentary of Giles of Rome on the Rhetoric of Aristotle', in *Arts Libéraux et Philosophie au Moyen Age* (Actes du Quatrième Congrès International de Philosophie Médiévale; Montreal–Paris, 1969), 833–41.

NAJEMY, J. M., *Corporatism and Consensus in Florentine Electoral Politics 1280–1400* (Chapel Hill: University of North Carolina Press, 1982).

NASH, P. W., 'Giles of Rome: Auditor and Critic of St Thomas', *Modern Schoolman*, 28 (1950), 1–20.

—— 'Giles of Rome', in *New Catholic Encyclopedia* (McGraw-Hill, 1967), vi. 484–5.

NEDERMANN, C. J., 'Nature, Sin and the Origins of Society: The Ciceronian Tradition in Medieval Political Thought', *Journal of the History of Ideas*, 49 (1988), 3–26.

—— *Community and Consent: The Secular Political Theory of Marsiglio of Padua's Defensor Pacis* (Lanham, Md.: Rowman and Littlefield, 1995).

NEUMANN, B., *Der Mensch und die himmlische Seligkeit nach der Lehre Gottfrieds von Fontaines* (Limburg: Lahn, 1958).

O'CONNOR, W. R., 'The uti/frui Distinction in Augustine's Ethics', *Augustinian Studies*, 14 (1983), 45–62.

O'DONNELL, J. R., 'The Commentary of Giles of Rome on the Rhetoric of Aristotle', in T. A. Sandquist and M. R. Powicke (eds.), *Essays in Medieval History presented to Bertie Wilkinson* (Toronto: University of Toronto Press, 1969), 139–56.

O'DONOVAN, O., *The Problem of Self-Love in Augustine* (New Haven: Yale University Press, 1980).

—— '*Usus* and *fruitio* in Augustine *De Doctrina Christiana* I', *Journal of Theological Studies*, 33 (1982), 361–97.

—— 'Augustine's City of God XIX and Western Political Thought', *Dionysius*, 11 (1987), 89–110.

O'RAHILLY, A., 'Notes on St Thomas IV: *De Regimine Principum*', *Irish Ecclesiastical Record*, 31 (1928), 396–410.

—— 'Notes on St Thomas V: Tholomeo of Lucca, the Continuator of the *De Regimine Principum*', *Irish Ecclesiastical Record*, 31 (1928), 606–14.

O'ROURKE, F., *Pseudo-Dionysius and the Metaphysics of Aquinas* (Leiden: E. J. Brill, 1992).

OAKLEY, F., 'Celestial Hierarchies Revisited: Walter Ullmann's Vision of Medieval Politics', *Past and Present*, 60 (1973), 3–48.

—— 'Natural Law, the *corpus mysticum* and Consent in Conciliar Thought from John of Paris to Mathias Ugonis', *Speculum*, 56 (1981), 786–810.

—— 'Legitimation by Consent: The Question of the Medieval Roots', *Viator*, 14 (1983), 303–35.

OLSEN, G., 'The Idea of the *Ecclesia Primitiva* in the Writings of the Twelfth Century Canonists', *Traditio*, 25 (1969), 61–86.

PAGE, C., 'The Truth about Lies in Plato's Republic', *Ancient Philosophy*, 11 (1991), 1–33.

PANELLA, E., *Per lo studio di Fra Remigio dei Girolami, Memorie Domenicane*, 10 (1979).

—— 'Il Repertorio dello Schneyer e i sermonari di Remigio dei Girolami', *Memorie Domenicane*, 11 (1980), 632–50.

PAULUS, J., *Henri de Gand: Essai sur les tendances de sa métaphysique* (Paris: J. Vrin, 1938).

—— 'Les Disputes d'Henri de Gand et de Gilles de Rome sur la distinction de l'essence et de l'existence', *AHDLMA* 13 (1940–2), 323–58.

PEGUES, F., *The Lawyers of the Last Capetians* (Princeton: Princeton University Press, 1962).

PELZER, A., 'Les Versions latines des ouvrages de morale conservés sous le nom d'Aristote en usage au XIIIe siècle', *Revue Néoscolastique de Philosophie*, 23 (1921), 316–41, 378–400.

—— 'Le Cours inédit d'Albert le Grand sur la Morale à Nicomaque, recueilli et rédigé par S. Thomas d'Aquin', *Revue Néoscolastique de Philosophie*, 24 (1922), 333–61, 479–520.

PENNINGTON, K., 'The Canonists and Pluralism in the Thirteenth Century', *Speculum*, 51 (1976), 35–48.

—— *Pope and Bishops: The Papal Monarchy in the Twelfth and Thirteenth Centuries* (Philadelphia: University of Pennsylvania Press, 1984).

—— *The Prince and the Law 1200–1600: Sovereignty and Rights in the Western Legal Tradition* (Berkeley: University of California Press, 1993).

PETERS, E., *The Shadow King: Rex Inutilis in Medieval Law and Literature 751–1327* (New Haven: Yale University Press, 1970).

POST, G., 'A Petition Relating to the Bull *Ad fructus uberes* and the Opposition of the French Secular Clergy in 1282', *Speculum*, 11 (1936), 231–7.

—— *Studies in Medieval Legal Thought: Public Law and the State, 1100–1322* (Princeton: Princeton University Press, 1964).

—— 'Philosophy and Citizenship in the Thirteenth Century: Laicisation, the Two Laws and Aristotle', in W. C. Jordan, B. McNab, and T. F. Ruiz (eds.), *Order and Innovation in the Middle Ages: Essays in Honor of J. R. Strayer* (Princeton: Princeton University Press, 1976), 401–8.

POWICKE, F. M., 'Reflections on the Medieval State', *TRHS* 19 (1936), 1–18.

PRESTWICH, M. (ed.), *Documents Illustrating the Crisis of 1297–8 in England* (Royal Historical Society, Camden Fourth Series, 24; London, 1980).

QUILLET, J., *La Philosophie politique de Marsile de Padoue* (L'Église et l'État au Moyen Âge, 14; Paris: J. Vrin, 1970).

—— 'Nouvelles études marsiliennes', *History of Political Thought*, 1 (1980), 391–410.

REEVES, M., 'Marsiglio of Padua and Dante Alighieri', in B. Smalley (ed.), *Trends in Medieval Political Thought* (Oxford: Basil Blackwell, 1965), 86–104.

RENARDY, C., *Le Monde des maîtres universitaires du diocèse de Liège 1140–1350: Recherches sur sa composition et ses activités* (Bibliothèque de la Faculté de Philosophie et Lettres de l'Université de Liège, fasc. 227; Paris: Société d'Édition 'Les Belles Lettres', 1979).

—— *Les Maîtres universitaires dans le diocèse de Liège: Répertoire biographique 1140–1350* (Bibliothèque de la Faculté de Philosophie et Lettres de l'Université de Liège, fasc. 232; Paris: Société d'Édition 'Les Belles Lettres', 1981).

RENNA, T. J., 'Kingship in the *Disputatio inter clericum et militem*', *Speculum*, 48 (1973), 675–93.

RENNA, T. J., 'The *populus* in John of Paris' Theory of Monarchy', *Tijdschrift voor Recht-geschiedenis*, 42 (1974), 243–68.

—— 'Aristotle and the French Monarchy, 1260–1303', *Viator*, 9 (1978), 309–24.

REUTER, T., and SILAGI, G. (eds.), *Wortkonkordanz zum Decretum Gratiani* (Monumenta Germaniae Historica, Hilfsmittel 10.1–5; Munich, 1990).

REYNOLDS, S., *Kingdoms and Communities in Western Europe 900–1300* (Oxford: Clarendon Press, 1984).

RIVIÈRE, J., *Le Problème de l'église et de l'état au temps de Philippe le Bel* (Spicilegium Sacrum Lovaniense, Etudes et Documents, VIII; Louvain–Paris, 1926).

ROBERT, S., 'Rhetoric and Dialectic according to the First Latin Commentary on the Rhetoric of Aristotle', *New Scholasticism*, 31 (1957), 484–98.

ROENSCH, F. J., *Early Thomistic School* (Dubuque: Priory Press, 1964).

RORTY, A. O. (ed.), *Essays on Aristotle's Ethics* (Berkeley: University of California Press, 1980).

RUBINSTEIN, N., 'Political Ideas in Sienese Art, the Frescoes by Ambrogio Lorenzetti and Taddeo di Bartolo in the Palazzo Pubblico', *Journal of the Warburg and Courtauld Institutes*, 21 (1958), 179–207.

RUSSELL, F. H., *The Just War in the Middle Ages* (Cambridge Studies in Medieval Life and Thought, Third Series, 8; Cambridge: Cambridge University Press, 1975).

SAENGER, P., 'John of Paris, Principal Author of the *Quaestio de Potestate Papae* [*Rex Pacificus*]', *Speculum*, 56 (1981), 41–55.

SCHLEYER, K., *Anfänge des Gallicanismus im 13. Jahrhundert: Der Widerstand des französischen Klerus gegen die Privilegierung der Bettelorden* (Historische Studien Heft 314; Berlin: E. Ebering, 1937).

SCHOLZ, R., *Die Publizistik zur Zeit Philipps des Schönen und Bonifaz' VIII: Ein Beitrag zur Geschichte der politischen Anschauungen des Mittelalters* (Kirchenrechtliche Abhandlungen Heft 6–8; Stuttgart: F. Enke, 1903).

SCOTT, J. V., 'Influence or Manipulation? The Role of Augustinianism in the Defensor Pacis of Marsiglio of Padua', *Augustinian Studies*, 9 (1978), 59–79.

SKINNER, Q., *Foundations of Modern Political Thought* (2 vols.; Cambridge: Cambridge University Press, 1978).

—— 'Ambrogio Lorenzetti, the Artist as Political Philosopher', *Proceedings of the British Academy*, 72 (1986), 1–56.

—— 'Machiavelli's *Discorsi* and the Pre-Humanist Origins of Republican Political Ideas', in G. Bock, Q. Skinner, and M. Viroli (eds.), *Machiavelli and Republicanism* (Ideas in Context; Cambridge: Cambridge University Press, 1990).

SMALLEY, B., *English Friars and Antiquity in the Early Fourteenth Century* (Oxford: Blackwell, 1960).

SPIEGEL, G., 'Defence of the Realm: The Evolution of a Capetian Propaganda Slogan', *Journal of Medieval History*, 3 (1977), 115–33.

STAICO, U., 'Retorica e politica in Egidio Romano', in *Documenti e studi sulla tradizione filosofica medievale*, III.1 (1992), 1–75.

STEENBERGHEN, F. VAN, *La Philosophie au XIIIe siècle*, 2nd edn. (Philosophes Médiévaux, XXVIII; Louvain: Peeters, 1991).

—— *Maître Siger de Brabant* (Philosophes Médiévaux, 21; Louvain–Paris: Publications Universitaires, 1977).

STEWART, J. A., *Notes on the Nicomachean Ethics of Aristotle* (Oxford: Clarendon Press, 1892).

STRAYER, J. R., 'Consent to Taxation under Philip the Fair', in J. R. Strayer and C. H. Taylor, *Studies in Early French Taxation* (Harvard Historical Monographs, XII; Cambridge, Mass.: Harvard University Press, 1939), 3–105.

—— 'Philip the Fair: A "Constitutional" King', *American Historical Review*, 62 (1956), 18–32.

—— 'The Crusade against Aragon', in id., *Medieval Statecraft and the Perspectives of History* (Princeton: Princeton University Press, 1971), ch. 9.

—— 'Defense of the Realm and Royal Power in France', in id., *Medieval Statecraft and the Perspectives of History* (Princeton: Princeton University Press, 1971), ch. 18.

—— 'The Laicization of French and English Society in the Thirteenth Century', in id., *Medieval Statecraft and the Perspectives of History* (Princeton: Princeton University Press, 1971), ch. 16.

—— 'The Costs and Profits of War: The Anglo-French Conflict of 1294–1303', in H. A. Miskimin, D. Herlihy, and A. L. Udovitch (eds.), *The Medieval City* (New Haven: Yale University Press, 1977), 269–91.

—— *The Reign of Philip the Fair* (Princeton: Princeton University Press, 1980).

STRUVE, T., *Die Entwicklung der organologischen Staatsauffassung im Mittelalter* (Stuttgart: Hiersemann, 1978).

—— 'Die Bedeutung der aristotelischen Politik für die natürliche Begründung der staatlichen Gemeinschaft', in J. Miethke and A. Bühler, *Das Publikum Politischer Theorie im 14. Jahrhundert* (Munich: Oldenbourg, 1992), 153–71.

SWANSON, J., *John of Wales: A Study of the Works and Ideas of a Thirteenth Century Friar* (Cambridge Studies in Medieval Life and Thought, Fourth Series 10; Cambridge: Cambridge University Press, 1989).

SYNAN, E. A., 'Albertus Magnus and the Sciences', in J. A. Weisheipl (ed.), *Albertus Magnus and the Sciences: Commemorative Essays 1980* (Toronto: PIMS, 1980), 1–12.

TIERNEY, B., *Foundations of the Conciliar Theory: The Contribution of the Medieval Canonists from Gratian to the Great Schism* (Cambridge Studies in Medieval Life and Thought, New Series 4; Cambridge: Cambridge University Press, 1955).

—— 'Grosseteste and the Theory of Papal Sovereignty', *Journal of Ecclesiastical History*, 6 (1955), 1–17.

—— *Medieval Poor Law: A Sketch of Canonical Theory and its Application in England* (Berkeley: University of California Press, 1959).

—— *Religion, Law and the Growth of Constitutional Thought* (Cambridge: Cambridge University Press, 1982).

—— 'Tuck on Rights: Some Medieval Problems', *History of Political Thought*, 4 (1983), 429–40.

—— 'Origins of Natural Rights Language: Texts and Contexts 1150–1250', *History of Political Thought*, 10 (1989), 615–46.

—— and LINEHAN, P. (eds.), *Authority and Power: Studies on Medieval Law and Government Presented to Walter Ullmann on his Seventieth Birthday* (Cambridge: Cambridge University Press, 1980).

TIHON, P., *Foi et théologie selon Godefroid de Fontaines* (Bruges: Desclée de Brouwer, 1966).

TUCK, R., *Natural Rights Theories: Their Origin and Development* (Cambridge: Cambridge University Press, 1979).

TUGWELL, S., *Albert and Thomas: Selected Writings* (The Classics of Western Spirituality; New York: Paulist Press, 1988).

TUMMERS, P. M. J. E., 'The Commentary of Albert on Euclid's Elements of Geometry', in J. A. Weisheipl (ed.), *Albertus Magnus and the Sciences: Commemorative Essays 1980* (Toronto: PIMS, 1980), 479–99.

ULLMANN, W., review of T. Gilby, *Principality and Polity*, *EHR* 73 (1958), 706–7.

—— *Principles of Government and Politics in the Middle Ages* (London: Methuen, 1961).

—— *The Individual and Society in the Middle Ages* (London: Methuen, 1967).

—— *The Carolingian Renaissance and the Idea of Kingship* (London: Methuen, 1969).

—— *The Growth of Papal Government in the Middle Ages*, 3rd edn. (London: Methuen, 1970).

—— *A History of Political Thought: The Middle Ages*, 3rd edn. (Harmondsworth: Penguin, 1975).

—— 'Boniface VIII and his Contemporary Scholarship', *Journal of Theological Studies*, 27 (1976), 58–87.

URMSON, J. O., *Aristotle's Ethics* (Oxford: Blackwell, 1988).

VALE, M. G. A., *The Angevin Legacy and the Hundred Years War 1250–1340* (Oxford: Blackwell, 1990).

VANSTEENKISTE, C., 'Das erste Buch der Nikomachischen Ethik bei Albertus Magnus', in G. Meyer and A. Zimmerman (eds.), *Albertus Magnus, Doctor Universalis 1280–1980* (Mainz: Grünewald, 1980), 373–84.

VAUX, R. DE, 'La Première entrée d'Averroes chez les latins', *Revue des Sciences Philosophiques et Théologiques*, 22 (1937), 193–245.

VERBEKE, G., 'La Date du commentaire de S. Thomas sur l'Éthique à Nicomaque', *Revue Philosophique de Louvain*, 47 (1949), 203–20.

—— *The Presence of Stoicism in Medieval Thought* (Washington, DC: Catholic University of America Press, 1983).

VEREECKE, L., 'Individu et communauté selon Guillaume d'Ockham', *Studia Moralia*, 3 (1965), 150–77.

VERPAALEN, A. P., *Der Begriff des Gemeinwohls bei Thomas von Aquin: Ein Beitrag zum Problem des Personalismus* (Sammlung Politeia Bd. VI; Heidelberg: F. H. Kerle Verlag, 1954).

VIROLI, M., *From Politics to Reason of State: The Acquisition and Transformation of the Language of Politics 1250–1600* (Ideas in Context; Cambridge: Cambridge University Press, 1992).

VOOGHT, P. DE, 'La Méthode théologique d'apres Henri de Gand et Gérard de Bologne', *RTAM* 23 (1956), 61–87.

WALLACE-HADRILL, J. M., *The Long-Haired Kings* (London: Methuen, 1962).

WARREN, W. L., *Henry II* (London: Methuen, 1973).

WATT, J. A., *The Theory of Papal Monarchy in the Thirteenth Century: The Contribution of the Canonists* (London: Burns and Oates, 1965).

—— 'The *Quaestio in utramque partem* Reconsidered', *Studia Gratiana*, 13 (1967), 411–54.

WEISHEIPL, J. A., *Friar Thomas d'Aquino: His Life, Thought and Work* (Oxford: Basil Blackwell, 1975; 2nd edn. Washington, DC, 1983).

—— 'The Life and Works of St Albert the Great', in id. (ed.), *Albertus Magnus and the Sciences: Commemorative Essays 1980* (Toronto: PIMS, 1980), 13–51.

—— *Thomas d'Aquino and Albert his Teacher* (Toronto: PIMS, 1980).

WEITHMAN, P. J., 'Augustine and Aquinas on Original Sin and the Function of Political Authority', *Journal of the History of Philosophy*, 30 (1992), 353–76.

WIELAND, G., 'The Reception and Interpretation of Aristotle's *Ethics*', in *CHLMP*, 657–72.

—— 'Happiness: The Perfection of Man', in *CHLMP*, 673–86.

—— *Ethica—Scientia practica: Die Anfänge der philosophischen Ethik im 13. Jahrhundert* (Beiträge zur Geschichte der Philosophie und Theologie des Mittelalters, Neue Folge, 21; Münster: Aschendorff, 1981).

WIELOCKX, R., 'La Censure de Gilles de Rome', *Bulletin de Philosophie Médiévale*, 22 (1980), 87–8.

WILKS, M. J., *The Problem of Sovereignty in the Later Middle Ages: The Papal Monarchy with Augustinus Triumphus and the Publicists* (Cambridge Studies in Medieval Life and Thought, Second Series 9; Cambridge: Cambridge University Press, 1963).

WILLIAMS, R., 'Politics and the Soul: A Reading of the City of God', *Milltown Studies*, 19–20 (1987), 55–72.

WIPPEL, J. F., 'Godfrey of Fontaines and the Real Distinction between Essence and Existence', *Traditio*, 20 (1964), 385–410.

—— 'Godfrey of Fontaines', *New Catholic Encyclopedia* (McGraw-Hill, 1967), vi. 577–8.

—— 'The Dating of James of Vierbo's Quodlibet I and Godfrey of Fontaines' Quodlibet VIII', *Augustiniana*, 24 (1974), 348–86.

—— 'The Condemnations of 1270 and 1277 at Paris', *Journal of Medieval and Renaissance Studies*, 7 (1977), 169–201.

—— *The Metaphysical Thought of Godfrey of Fontaines: A Study in Late Thirteenth Century Philosophy* (Washington, DC: Catholic University of America Press, 1981).

—— 'The Quodlibetic Question as a Distinctive Literary Genre', in *Les Genres littéraires dans les sources théologiques et philosophiques médiévales* (Actes du Colloque International de Louvain-la-Neuve 1981; Louvain, 1982), 67–84.

—— 'The Relationship between Essence and Existence in Late Thirteenth Century Thought: Giles of Rome, Henry of Ghent, Godfrey of Fontaines and James of Viterbo', in P. Morewedge (ed.), *Philosophies of Existence: Ancient and Medieval* (New York: Fordham University Press, 1982), 131–64.

—— *Metaphysical Themes in Thomas Aquinas* (Washington, DC: Catholic University of America Press, 1984).

—— 'Thomas Aquinas and Participation', in J. F. Wippel (ed.), *Studies in Medieval Philosophy* (Washington, DC: Catholic University of America Press, 1987), 117–58.

—— 'Metaphysics', in N. Kretzmann and E. Stump (eds.), *The Cambridge Companion to Aquinas* (Cambridge: Cambridge University Press, 1993), 85–127.

WOOD, C. T., *Philip the Fair and Boniface VIII* (New York–London: Holt, Rinehart and Winston, 1967).

WULF, M. DE, *Un Théologien-philosophe du XIIIe siècle: Étude sur la vie, les oeuvres et l'influence de Godefroid de Fontaines* (Mémoires de l'Academie Royale de Belgique, Classe des Lettres et des Sciences Morales et Politiques et Classe des Beaux Arts I.2; Brussels: Hayez, 1906).

—— 'L'Individu et le groupe dans la scolastique du XIIIe siècle', *Revue Néoscolastique de Philosophie*, 22 (1920), 341–57.

—— *Philosophy and Civilisation in the Middle Ages* (Princeton: Princeton University Press, 1922).

WULF, M. DE, *Histoire de la philosophie médiévale*, 6th edn. (3 vols.; Louvain–Paris, 1934–47).

YPMA, E., 'Recherches sur la carrière scolaire et la bibliothèque de Jacques de Viterbe', *Augustiniana*, 24 (1974), 247–82.

—— 'Recherches sur la productivité littéraire de Jacques de Viterbe jusqu'à 1300', *Augustiniana*, 25 (1975), 223–82.

ZUCKERMAN, C., 'The Relationship of Theories of Universals to Theories of Church Government in the Middle Ages: A Critique of Previous Views', *Journal of the History of Ideas*, 36 (1975), 579–94.

—— 'The Ending of French Interference in the Papal Financial System in 1297: A Neglected Episode', *Viator*, 11 (1980), 261–88.

INDEX OF CITATIONS

GENERAL INDEX

absenteeism 237, 247 n.
accusation 110
Achilles 143, 144
active life:
  compared with contemplative life 7, 66–8,
    106–8, 180–1, 181–4, 239–40, 240–1, 242,
    342
Adam 14, 100
Ad fructus uberes 7, 180, 184, 185, 186, 187, 188,
  190, 196, 197, 198, 203, 235, 239, 242, 243,
  244, 245, 246, 247, 259
admonition 162, 285
adultery 68–9, 70, 71, 140, 252, 304
Albertus Magnus 8, 76, 77–8, 79–80, 85, 86, 87,
  103, 105, 109, 111, 112, 114, 115, 118,
  119–21, 122, 126, 135–6, 139, 143, 159–60,
  162, 165, 172, 179, 181, 201, 206, 217, 219,
  223, 234, 249, 301, 324, 327
Ambrose 16, 298
amor benevolentiae 59, 161, 163, 209, 214–15, 218,
  228 n., 299, 303
amor concupiscentiae 59, 214–15, 218, 228 n., 299,
  303
amputation 110, 111, 122, 163, 321
analogy 12, 13–14, 27, 31, 34, 35, 36, 40, 43,
  79–80
  see also goodness; metaphors
angels 88–9, 90, 95, 96, 98, 103
Antequam essent clerici 252, 256 n., 270 n.
apostolic church 7, 164, 187, 358, 360–1, 362
Aquinas 8, 13, 14, 18–19, 130, 132, 139, 143,
  146, 150, 158, 159, 161–2, 165, 171, 172,
  178, 179, 181, 183, 185, 188, 195, 201, 204,
  205, 206, 207, 210, 211, 215, 218, 219, 220,
  223, 224, 229, 230, 235, 239, 240, 279, 282,
  289, 291, 293, 299, 301, 303, 311, 313, 315,
  324
  authorship of *De Regno ad Regem Cypri* 132,
    155 n.
archangels 88, 90
Aristotle 2, 3, 4, 6, 8, 16, 22, 23, 26–7, 52–3,
  73–5, 100–1, 127–8, 130–3, 155, 157–8, 178,
  179, 200–3, 205, 206–7, 233, 262, 266,
  290–7, 296–7, 338, 339, 340–4, 347–8,
  351–4, 354–8, 361–2
  on contemplation 327
  on equity 65
  on friendship 49, 50, 59
  on the good man and the good citizen 42

on rule by the good man or by good laws
  139 n., 195, 253
on goodness 23, 26–7
on happiness 26, 27, 36–7, 42, 49
on justice 40, 117
on property 163
on prudence 42, 117
on self-sacrifice 49, 51, 170–1, 172
on virtue 6, 33, 47
translation of *Ethics* 27–8
translation of *Politics* 33
translation of *Rhetorica* 131
De Anima 30, 81 n., 94 n., 332
Magna Moralia 217, 274 n.
Metaphysics 11–12, 35, 37, 41, 93 n., 94 n., 97,
  100, 103, 109, 116, 127, 182 n., 201, 230,
  267, 312 n., 324, 325
Physics 11–12, 37–38, 41, 88 n., 301
Rhetorica 131–2, 133, 137–8, 140–1, 142–3,
  143–4, 155
Topica 66
Asser 15
association, see *communicatio*
Auctoritates Aristotelis 28 n., 120 n., 160 n.
Augustine 16, 19, 69, 71 n., 74, 97 n., 123, 125,
  157, 159, 160, 163, 164, 168, 175, 178, 179,
  181, 201, 202, 203, 220 n., 229, 237, 246,
  250, 266, 267, 277, 279, 282, 288, 289, 291,
  292, 298, 300, 301, 304, 305, 312, 319, 338,
  354, 355, 362
  definition of *res publica* 19–21, 126, 279
  distinction between *uti* and *frui* 21, 22,
    349–50
  doctrine of the two cities 20, 21, 164, 274, 325
  Confessions 32 n., 93 n., 301
  De Civitate Dei 15, 19, 21, 23, 24, 32 n., 54 n.,
    67 n., 75, 93 n., 120 n., 126 n., 179, 241,
    257, 267 n., 271, 273, 274, 275, 289–90,
    291, 301 n., 304 n., 322, 323–4, 326, 338,
    350, 356 n.
  De Doctrina Christiana 21, 22, 104 n., 160 n.,
    323 n.
  De Libero Arbitrio 123 n., 170, 237 n., 352 n.
  De Trinitate 145 n., 160 n., 172, 323 n.
  Regula 15 n., 73, 298, 316, 323
Ausculta fili 264, 270, 280 n., 287
Averroes 5, 28, 40 n., 51 n., 86, 118 n., 131, 157,
  182 n., 201 n., 223 n.
Avicenna 8, 10 n., 30